Crucible

A DOMINION EASTER OFFERING.

MISS CANADA.—"THANK YOU, SIR GEORGE! I'VE BEEN WAITING FOR HIM SUCH A LONG TIME! BUT DON'T YOU THINK AFTER ALL, HE MAY PROVE RATHER TROUBLESOME?"

National Library of Canada Cataloguing in Publication

Russell, Frances, 1941 –
The Canadian crucible : Manitoba's role in Canada's great divide /
Frances Russell. — 1ˢᵗ ed.

Includes bibliographical references and index
ISBN 1-896150-28-4

Bilingualism—Political aspects—Manitoba—History.
2. Language policy—Manitoba—History.
3. Bilingualism—Canada—History.
4. Language policy—Canada—History. I. Title

FC3370.B55R88 2003-09-23   971.27'03   C2003-905083-1

To Nicole,

The
Canadian
Crucible

Manitoba's Role
in Canada's Great Divide

By Frances Russell

Prologue by Jacqueline Blay
Epilogue by Roger Turenne

*In Tribute to a great
Canadian and Manitoban—
Georges Forest.*

Frances Russell

Heartland Associates, Inc.
Winnipeg, Canada

Printed in Manitoba, Canada

Credits

Editor
Barbara Huck

Editorial assistance
Karen McElrea

Index
Adrian Mather

Cover design & layout
Dawn Huck

Prepress
Avenue 4, Winnipeg, Canada

Printing
Printcrafters, Winnipeg, Canada

Cover image
From an editorial cartoon by "Cayouche",
first published in *La Liberté*.

Back cover image
Mallette / *Winnipeg Free Press*

Created with the generous support of the
Manitoba Arts Council/Conseil des Arts du Manitoba

Table of Contents

Acknowledgements

Touching actual history is both thrilling and sobering. Just how thrilling and sobering came home to me one day in mid-July 2003. I was at le Centre du Patrimoine (the St. Boniface Historical Society), gingerly using the archivist's white gloves to turn the large and incredibly fragile pages of a leather-bound volume of *Le Manitoba*, Manitoba's first French language newspaper.

What leapt out at me wasn't the date, but the black ink bordering every column – nineteenth century journalism's expression of deep mourning. The masthead read November 19, 1885, the weekly newspaper's first opportunity to report on the hanging of Louis Riel in Regina three days earlier on November 16, 1885.

I have, of course, seen and read many accounts of that event. But nothing compared to that front page. Those black borders seemed to project a far deeper, wider and poignant mourning – for an idea of a country.

I know the thesis of this book will be controversial. But it is based on history, history that, as Cornelius Jaenen, Jacqueline Blay and Roger Turenne say, was hidden, submerged, silenced, for the better part of a century. I therefore ask readers to put aside the history of Manitoba and Canada as most of us learned it at school and to approach this book with open minds. You will, I hope, see Louis Riel, Manitoba, and Canada itself through new eyes.

I, too, was completely ignorant of this new history until my final year at university when Cornelius Jaenen was my professor at United College, now the University of Winnipeg. He changed my concept of Canada. His teachings were reinforced when, as a political journalist for the *Winnipeg Tribune* in the 1970s I encountered a young Franco-Manitoban historian,

Robert Painchaud. It was he who opened my eyes to how events in Manitoba frustrated the dreams of Sir George-Étienne Cartier, Canada's first deputy prime minister, Adams Archibald, Manitoba's first lieutenant-governor and by extension, Prime Minister Sir John A. Macdonald himself, for a bilingual-bicultural Western Canada.

My first and deepest debt of gratitude is, therefore, to these two historians. One, Robert Painchaud, died tragically in an airplane crash in Newfoundland in June, 1978 while serving as a member of the Historic Sites and Monuments Board of Canada. The other, Cornelius Jaenen, graciously consented not just to read my manuscript but also write the book's kind and moving Foreword.

Of equal importance are the contributions of three other individuals. Historian Gerald Friesen not only pointed me to most of my source materials, but, in an act of extreme generosity and forebearance, read my manuscript not once, but twice, the second time while he was trying to enjoy a holiday with his grandchildren. Manitoba author and journalist Jacqueline Blay provided invaluable assistance in no less than three vital areas. She either translated herself, or verified the translation of, the French language newspapers and documents used in the text. She gave me all her own research materials from her masters thesis and subsequent book on Manitoba's 1983-84 French language crisis in this province, an event we covered as journalists and one that changed our lives. Finally, she wrote the powerful and perceptive Prologue. Roger Turenne, Manitoba's first director of French language services, gave me hours of his time, his masters thesis on the political behaviour of the Franco-Manitoban community, his personal memos and an Epilogue that provides an important optimistic antidote to the sometimes pessimistic observations of the conclusion.

There is always a danger in writing acknowledgements because of the inevitable appearance of a hierarchy when there are many people whose contributions were equally vital. Political scientist Raymond Hébert allowed me to quote liberally from the first chapter of his forthcoming book on the Manitoba language crisis of 1983-84. He also provided valuable corrections and insights to my text. His colleague at le Collège Universitaire de Saint-Boniface, Luc Côté, helped me navigate the Manitoba Schools Question. Provincial Judge Richard Chartier, chair of the 1998 provincial commission on the status of French language government services in Manitoba, took time from a very busy life for a lengthy interview. And Rénauld Rémillard, director of l'Institut Joseph Dubuc, stepped in at a moment's notice to fill in an important blank in the text.

The staffs of the Legislative Library, the University of Manitoba Elizabeth Dafoe Library, le Centre du Patrimoine and the St. Boniface Public Library were unstinting in their assistance. Special thanks goes to Jacinthe Duval of le Centre du Patrimoine and Bev Bosiak, deputy clerk of the Legislative Assembly of Manitoba.

As with my book on Lake Winnipeg, *Winnipeg Free Press* editor Nicholas Hirst and Lynn Crothers and Anita Magnus of the newspaper's library gave me carte blanche to its achives. This book would not have been possible without this trust and generosity. *La Liberté* editorial cartoonist Réal Bérard (Cayouche) and *Winnipeg Free Press* editorial cartoonist Dale Cummings kindly agreed to allow their work to be reproduced in the text. Charles and Cynthia Hou offered their extensive collection of editorial cartoons to us, for which I am grateful, and Miguel Vielfaure translated several of Cayouche's cartoons, allowing their full meaning to be understood.

A special tribute goes to editor Karen McElrea who performed what I consider a miracle. She made a welter of scrambled chapter notes conform to the top standards in the trade – a feat that leaves me forever deeply in her debt. And Adrian Mather has produced a first-class index.

Along with Heartland Associates, I also wish to thank the following publishers, who have agreed to allow excepts to be published in the text: HarperCollins for *Riel: A Life of Revolution*, by Maggie Siggins; McClelland & Stewart for *Gabrielle Roy: A Life,* by François Ricard and *George-Étienne Cartier: a biography,* by Alastair Sweeny; the University of Toronto Press for *The Canadian Prairies: A History,* by Gerald Friesen, as well as *The French-Canadian View of Confederation: 1860-1900,* by Arthur Silver, *Priests and Politicians: Manitoba schools and the election of 1896,* by Paul Crunican, and *Manitoba: A History,* by W. L. Morton. Frits Pannekoek kindly gave me permission to quote form his *Snug Little Flock: The Social Origins of the Riel Resistance of 1869-70.*

I wish to again express my appreciation to my publisher, Heartland Associates, to Barbara Huck, my editor, Peter St. John, her partner, and Dawn Huck, the book's designer. They are a joy to work with, always supportive and alive with creative and innovative ideas, not to mention moral support. Once again, they believed in me. My gratitude is profound.

A final homage goes to my husband, Ken Murdoch, who once more lived through the ups and downs of sharing a life with someone struggling to climb new and daunting metaphorical mountains.

The Canadian Crucible

Foreword

THERE ARE MANY FORGOTTEN LOYALTIES and pioneering ventures of the past that have left their mark on the history of a region, but few have remained in more neglect or misunderstanding than the role of franco-phones in the history of Manitoba. This superb work recalls historical facts and the tragic tale of the struggle of a minority to regain a portion of its rightful place in provincial and national affairs.

When I read the manuscript I found the account so compelling that I could not set it down but had to continue reading to the very end. It does not recount pleasant events, but there is a sense that eventually some justice was brought to bear, without at the same time diminishing the rights or role of other ethno-cultural communities. The struggle of a minority to reassert its legitimate rights is emotionally and intellectually challenging for all who are engaged in the preservation of sacred compacts, or are observers of the social scene.

I am not a disinterested observer; I served as a member of the provincial Advisory Committee on Bilingualism and Biculturalism formed by Premier Duff Roblin, as well as a Manitoba delegate to the Etats Généraux du Canada français. I also taught in Manitoba for almost two decades at every level from the one-room rural elementary school through to private boys' school, high school and university. The francophone struggle for language rights in a multicutural setting was never far removed from my preoccupations. I was aware of the deliberate silence in the curriculum and textbooks concerning the foundational francophone and Métis heritage of the province. The consequent assumption by newcomers was that Manitoba was conceived as, and always had been, an anglophone province. What happened, of course, was that demographic changes – notably the arrival of Ontarians, Mennonites and Icelanders – led to attitudinal changes favouring assimilative unilingualism. This led in turn to institutional changes in local government, the bicameral legislature, and the dual confessional school system toward anglo-conformity. Finally, this led to the ultra vires constitutional amendment to impose unilingualism.

This study by Frances Russell, to my mind, is not only a significant historical work in its own right but also an appropriate publication in a distinguished journalistic career. I have observed her progress as a thoughtful student at United College and later as a perceptive journalist in Winnipeg. This book reflects both the methodological concerns of the historian and the social consciousness of the observer and critic of one's own society.

Cornelius J. Jaenen
Professor Emeritus
L'Université d'Ottawa

MALLETTÉ / *WINNIPEG FREE PRESS*

The Canadian Crucible

Prologue

Do YOU REMEMBER WHEN?

How often have we asked this question, as a parent, as a friend? As individuals we ask it often. Unfortunately, however, that is not the case for governments or politicians. If it was, the history recounted in this book would have been different. Perhaps it would never have happened at all.

We ask ourselves these questions because we know the answers and we hope that by remembering, we will not repeat our mistakes. Politicians are elected to avoid repeating painful and divisive history, history associated with intolerance and ignorance. If, during the last century, politicians in Manitoba had not only asked "do you remember when?", but also, "do you remember why?", it would have meant that they knew their history and francophones would have been able to thrive as a community, as Manitobans and as Canadians.

When the habitants, voyageurs and coureurs de bois began building the Province of Manitoba, they were the majority. They saw French and English as equal partners in a nation-building process. As years went by, the English minority became the majority and the French majority became the minority. Difficult times ensued. The majority started chipping away at language rights under the guise of saving money. The real objective, however, was to assimilate Franco-Manitobans into the growing anglophone majority at the end of the nineteenth century.

An aura of déjà vu hung over these events in Manitoba, which is not surprising perhaps, for history does seem to repeat itself. Two hundred years earlier, when Europeans first began to settle in what is now Canada, they were led by the Acadians and the French settlers of Nouvelle France. Over time they developed a distinct society, not only settling, building and legislating, but, guided by Native peoples – the original inhabitants of North America, – venturing across the continent all the way to the Rockies. Despite this, the French in North America were not only threatened but, in the instance of the Acadians, deported and told that they could not come back to their country. Their villages were burned, some people were driven into the sea; others died or went into exile. When a community is dealt such a blow, it reacts by drawing inward and seeking to maintain a strong bond with core values like language and religion. The community's collective memory becomes a protection against external threats. "Je me souviens" (I will remember) was lived and practiced by Acadians well before the people of Québec adopted it. It was a constant reminder of the importance and value of their history.

The collective memory of Canadians fills many history books and chronicles the recurring tensions between the nation's two founding Euro-Canadian linguistic groups. Quite often, this involves all-too-familiar stories of francophones losing their school system or their language rights. But in the last thirty years, the dynamic has shifted to stories of legal challenges in the highest courts of the land where those rights are finally being restored.

Canadian history from Nouvelle France to modern times prompts one to wonder, like Lord Durham, why these two nations continuously warred in the bosom of a single state. He found "a struggle not of principles, but of races". Despite his many misjudged and misinformed opinions about French habitants and his aristocratic opinions about the English settlers, Lord Durham was not far from the truth. French and English were often at odds in Canada and the discord was often racially based. It seems that Canada's "founding races" brought, in the holds of their ships, the hostility of their two Hundred Years Wars, preferring to cling to their ancient animosities rather than seek the shared vision and mutual respect needed to start afresh and create a new nation.

The discord and discontent stemmed in part from different lifestyles. The French tended to be an agrarian, church-oriented society while the English were more inclined to business and to allegiance to the values of Great Britain. The languages, religions, customs, and legal systems of Canada's two founding peoples were different and therein lay the first barriers to a harmonious colonial life. Each group was often not ready to accept the other's traditions and governance principles.

Power relationships being what they are, one group always tries to dominate the other. The fact that the "mother countries" often changed colonial policies out of greed, expedience or lack of vision, created confusion as well as opportunities for conquest and surrender. The history of the Acadian people should have sent chills through colonial offices in both France and England. But in 1755, mass displacement as a method of conquest was not considered a cause for alarm and disapproval. The Acadian tragedy was barely noticed by the world.

The two 1837 rebellions in Lower and Upper Canada were a wake-up call for political leaders of the time. The rebellions prompted England to send an investigator with a mandate to suggest solutions and make recommendations to remedy such a dire state of affairs. It was the first instance of what has become a very Canadian instrument for solving problems – a royal commission. In 1838, Lord Durham, the aristocrat, did not mention in his report the fate suffered by the Acadians, their remarkable endurance during the intervening eighty-three years as they wandered the world or settled in the Louisiana swamps. In his report, Lord Durham indicated that since French settlers were a "backward people" and because French and English were incompatible, the French should be assimilated into the majority. A planned and orderly assimilation would, in turn, lead to a strong (read British) Canada, able to speak to its southern neighbour with one voice and language. Of course, Lord Durham did not succeed, but his message of forced assimilation was not lost on either side. The French renewed their vigilance and mistrust increased. The English felt that assimilation was an appropriate course of action, if not immediately, then certainly down the road. "Responsible government", as recommended by Lord Durham was instituted but turned out to be less than a workable solution to the Canadian problem. In fact, it accentuated two very different ways of life.

Two men, brought together by history and politics, set out to fulfill the dream of a bilingual and bicultural Canada. John A. Macdonald and George-Étienne Cartier understood that by having Upper and Lower Canada divided and in a constant state of discord, both risked becoming the prey of their southern neighbour. In 1865, reason prevailed. Negotiations were held and speeches were made, resulting in promises of respect and understanding.

From the discussions between the Fathers of Confederation was born the Imperial Act, which promised to protect the "other minority". Cartier did not believe that a majority would impose its will on a minority. And John A. Macdonald believed that the French language was one of the fundamental principles of Confederation. Their naiveté would be proven wrong and Manitoba became the case in point. Had they been right in their vision and tolerance, Canada would have been a very different country. The failure of subsequent leaders to act on this original premise almost destroyed this first vision of linguistic and cultural duality.

Once the Canadian Confederation was founded, the new provinces moved in the same direction of nation building, but remained quite different from each other. Language, religion, school systems and laws had little in common but each province was comfortable in its separateness. Each side of the linguistic divide devoted itself to building its respective province.

Enter Louis Riel and the Red River colonists, who wanted to join the newly minted Canadian Confederation. On the Prairies, in the shadow of the Saint-Boniface Cathedral and around The Forks, the two linguistic groups had been living side-by-side for decades, sometimes at odds, but mostly at peace. Francophones were the majority and their leader Louis Riel, a Métis, negotiated the creation of Manitoba. Riel was a new kind of leader, a native of a colony west of Montréal and Toronto. Educated and bilingual, he could be seen to embody this new Canada in his personal duality. His Métis heritage stood out in a political landscape composed entirely of semi-aristocratic and white-collared politicians from Eastern Canada. His natural wisdom, his remarkable maturity and his political flair enabled him to ensure that Manitoba was a model of tolerance, bilingualism and foresight. But this dream was not to be completely fulfilled.

Power as exercised by a majority over a minority is exactly what it appears to be – bullying. Franco-Manitobans, faced with three major onslaughts on their rights, reacted like any other minority, that is, strategically and using all political and legal weapons at their disposal. Unfortunately, instead of challenging the 1890 abolition of their constitutional language rights, they chose to challenge the assault on their schools. One wonders if that decision was based on a deep ultramontanism, which advocated the supremacy of the Church over the state. We will never know exactly why, because the decision was not couched in those terms. However, the outcome remains. Franco-Manitobans lost all their constitutional rights – to their schools as well as to their language. This book details their odyssey.

In 1982, Pierre Elliott Trudeau gave Canada a constitutional Charter of Rights and Freedoms. He faced fierce opposition from a majority of provincial premiers and a strong stream of political opinion in the country warning that "unelected and unaccountable" judges and courts would replace democratically-elected and accountable legislatures and parliaments. However, Canadian history is a stern reminder that sometimes, democratically elected officials lose sight of fundamental values, especially where minority rights are concerned. And minorities have benefited from the Charter. Judges do not need to keep an eye on the ballot box or the polls and can root their decisions in history, precedents and jurisprudence.

In Manitoba's case, they restored what politicians had abolished in 1890 and 1916. The courts also threw the book at the province in the 1980s, because politicians had continued to ignore political decency and mistreat the only founding minority, even after the flouted constitutional law had been reaffirmed.

This book details a story of mistrust, anxiety and loss, but also a tale of resilience and ultimately, survival and restoration, against daunting odds. The purpose of this book, aptly titled *The Canadian Crucible*, is to try to understand why Cartier's dream of Manitoba as the "template" for the westward expansion of the nation failed to materialize. Frances Russell brings many answers, supported by solid and intelligent research, sagacious analysis and deep insight into the psyche of this province.

We must never forget what happened – or why – so it does not happen again and again. The story of French language rights in Manitoba is a story that needed to be told, because, as Frances Russell says: "the beast of linguistic and ethnic hostility and bigotry only sleeps, it never dies."

Jacqueline Blay M.A.
Author of *L'Article 23 – Les péripéties législatives et juridiques du fait français au Manitoba (1870–1986)*

Introduction

M
ANITOBANS TAKE PRIDE in calling their province the "keystone" of Confederation's pan-continental arch. But Manitoba's centrality, its location as the bridge between east and west, has not been an altogether happy experience, either for it or for Canada. Manitoba is Canada's canary in the mine. It touches and strums each of Canada's most sensitive nerves. All our historical and political flashpoints collide and contest in Manitoba: language, religion, ethnicity, class, ideology, nation, province.

Of these, language was – and still is – the most profound and incendiary. This book attempts to place the history of Manitoba's linguistic struggle within the wider context of its fundamental impact on the course of Canadian history.

Manitoba was where the Old Canada died. Manitoba was also where the New Canada was born. Preston Manning, the driving force behind the creation of the western-based Reform Party and its successor, the Canadian Alliance, is the originator of the phrase "Old Canada and New Canada", finally giving a name to the evident sociological and ideological differences between "Eastern" (including Central) Canada and "Western" Canada. New Canada is much more in the image of the United States and therefore at polar opposites from the Old Canada. It echoes the American motto of *E Pluribus Unum*, out of many one, whereas the Old Canada, despite its growing multi-cultural character, has retained its two founding European cultures of French and English. The New Canada is more individualistic and libertarian; the Old Canada, more communitarian and classically conservative, imbued with the *noblesse oblige* traditions of activist government and social responsibility.[1]

Above all, the New Canada believes in one nation, one culture and one language as opposed to the Old Canada of two nations, two cultures and two languages. And it regards Canada as a nation of individual citizens and provinces, while the Old Canada sees the primal national structure as two organic linguistic and cultural societies – hence the oft-repeated phrase "deux nations", a phrase always guaranteed to prompt a viscerally angry reaction in New Canada.

Old and New Canada is our second national duality and every bit as real as the duality of language, of French and English. It is a duality of values and social and political cultures, of rural and urban, and predominantly but not exclusively, of east and west. From its vantage point, Manitoba becomes not Confederation's keystone but Confederation's faultline.

What happened in Manitoba to carve this invisible and immensely debilitating divide that created west or New Canada and east or Old Canada? As the first province to join Confederation after the original four in 1867, Manitoba was to be the template for the creation of new provinces in the former lands of the Hudson's Bay Company, lands purchased by the new nation to realize Prime Minister Sir John A. Macdonald's grand project to build a transcontinental nation in the northern half of North America and frustrate American dreams of Manifest Destiny. In 1870, when Manitoba entered Confederation, its population stood at 12,500, of whom about 6,500, or fifty-two per cent, were French-speaking.[2] However, the climactic events of 1869-70 – the rise of Louis Riel, the creation of the provisional government, the subsequent negotiation and passage of the Manitoba Act making Manitoba bilingual and bicultural, the execution of Thomas Scott and the ensuing fury fomented in Ontario by the ultra-imperialist and virulently Protestant and Orange Canadian Party – cemented elite and street opinion in French Canada that Québec and not Canada was the French Canadian homeland. Accordingly, efforts to extend the French language and culture to the Canadian West would not only be doomed to certain failure but would bleed away Québec's all-important political strength within Confederation to defend the French fact in North America.

So it was that the Manitoba Census of 1886 found that Manitoba's British-origin population had increased more than eleven times, from about 6,500 in 1870 to about 76,000. In the process, it achieved dominance over the 11,000-strong French-speaking population, a population that had not even doubled since Confederation and had collapsed from fifty-two per cent

SATURDAY NIGHT MAGAZINE / *GREAT CANADIAN POLITICAL CARTOONS: 1915–1945*

to just ten per cent of the provincial total. Of the 109,000 Manitobans numbered in that Census, fully sixty-eight per cent were of British (English, Irish and Scottish) origin.[3] Thus, within a meagre sixteen years, Manitoba went from a province that, at its birth, was largely French-speaking and Roman Catholic, to an English-speaking and Protestant-dominated society. Franco-Manitobans were now a tiny threatened minority in Confederation's keystone province.*

During this same twenty-year period from 1870 to 1890, history tells us that a mass exodus similar to Ontario's was also occurring in Québec. While the lure of good cheap farmland beckoned young Ontarians west to Manitoba and beyond, the chance for steady work enticed about 400,000 French Canadians to the mill and factory towns of New England. [4] It is true

---

* Actual figures on Québécois immigration to Manitoba are unavailable due to what historian W.L. Morton calls "the imperfect statistics of the time". The all-important 1891 Census did not inquire as to either the ethnic origin or maternal language of Canadians. However, it – like its predecessors in 1881 and 1886 – did ask for place of birth. In 1881 – the first census to include Manitoba – 4,085 Manitobans reported their birthplace as Québec; in 1886,

that the migration of French Canadians to New England was part of the nineteenth century's socio-economic shift from the farm to the town, from the agricultural to the industrial economy. But it is also undeniable that had only a fraction, say, a quarter, of those 400,000 emigrating French Canadians chosen Manitoba or the North West Territories rather than New England, the provinces of Manitoba, Saskatchewan, Alberta and even perhaps British Columbia would be very different today and Manning's Old Canada and New Canada might never have happened.

Compounding the understandable reluctance of French Canadians to come west was a fatal error by those French Canadians already in Manitoba. When, at the stroke of its legislative pen in 1890, Manitoba's Anglo-Protestant Ontario majority illegally and unconstitutionally wiped out the official French Roman Catholic minority's rights to its language and confessional schools, the Franco-Manitoban community, urged on by its church, chose to stand and fight, not for its language, but for its schools. At that time, the choice seemed obvious. A battle for schools would gain the tiny minority important allies from the many Catholics among the burgeoning throngs of new immigrants. Of even greater importance, it would bring on board co-religionists within the all-powerful anglophone elite. However, the school victory gained from these strategic alliances, such as it was, was swept away within less than thirty years. Worse, those alliances and that pyrrhic victory dealt a further devastating body blow to Manitoba francophones. It turned them into just another ethnic minority. In contrast, as testified by two defining Supreme Court judgements almost a century later, had Franco-Manitobans chosen to fight for their language, their victory would have been more certain, but-tressed as that cause was by the identical language guarantees governing Québec and Canada itself – the guarantees of Section 133 of the British North America Act, the core of the Canadian compact of 1867. The continued

---

5,976 did so; and in 1891, 7,555, for a net increase of 3,470. In his *Manitoba: A History*, W.L. Morton says that "well over 2,000 French Canadians came to Manitoba from the United States between 1874 and 1887", based on the reports of the Department of Agriculture in the Sessional Papers, 1874 to 1881. Yet another figure is provided in *The Honourable Joseph Dubuc, K.S.M.G.*, a 1981 biographical pamphlet produced by the Manitoba Department of Cultural Affairs and Historic Resources. Dubuc was co-founder of La Société de Colonisation organized to recruit French Canadian settlers from the United States and Québec. The article gives a figure of 15,000 French Canadians arriving between 1875 and 1880, but checks with Karen Nicholson of the Provincial Historian's Office and comparisons with other sources indicate both the number of settlers and the 1890 date to be in error.

visibility of the French language within Manitoba would have bolstered Franco-Manitobans' ability to regain their schools and kept alive the great confederal pact in this province and, by presence and example, probably in Alberta and Saskatchewan as well. Both these provinces and the North West Territories from which they were created in 1905 were originally bilingual and bicultural. Even better, the maintenance of Manitoba's official bilingualism would have prevented the historical revisionism of English Canada that, through successive generations of federal immigration officials and authors of Canadian school texts, hid Manitoba's founding story from millions of new Canadians and wiped it from the national consciousness. The fallacy that Canada was an "English" country outside federal institutions and the province of Québec, was allowed to stand unchallenged for almost a century, the century that formed Western Canada. This revisionist triumph was to prove immensely useful to future cadres of unscrupulous politicians anxious to instill in all Canadians of non-English, non-French background the belief that any restoration of rights to French Canadians would turn them into "third class" citizens.

Once again, there would not have been an Old Canada and a New Canada, at least, not as we understand those terms today.

1

The Sowing of the Seed

He has opened Pandora's Box

THE HEAT AND HUMIDITY HUNG HEAVY inside Manitoba's magnificent
limestone Legislative Building that Friday morning, May 20, 1983. Just as
the bells began ringing to summon members, Georges Forest walked into
the cluttered, steamy *Winnipeg Free Press* gallery office on the second floor. He
asked permission to listen to the proceedings over the three speakers spotted
about the big, high-ceilinged room looking out over the north-east grounds.

Forest was anxious and intent. A passionate Canadian of Métis
descent, he loved to tell the story of how his grandmother had hidden
Louis Riel in her closet on one of his flights to safety across the American
border. He delighted in appearing at Le Festival de Voyageur as Jean-Baptiste
Lagimodière, the maternal grandfather of the legendary Métis hero, now
recognized by many historians as le Père du Manitoba and the first western
Father of Confederation. Four years earlier, Forest's appeal of a unilingual
English parking ticket had gone all the way to the Supreme Court of Canada
and ended what Franco-Manitobans called "90 years of injustice". The high
court had ruled that Manitoba's 1890 legislation, which outlawed French and

made English the only official language of the province, violated its constitution and was illegal.

Forest was worried. He suspected the Progressive Conservative Party Opposition, led by one of Manitoba's most controversial politicians, former premier Sterling Lyon, was about to stir up trouble, big trouble, for the province's tiny francophone community. The Tory leader was to speak on the New Democratic Party government's proposed constitutional amendment. It had been drafted to head off a new legal challenge to the province's body of 4,500 unilingual English laws. Following Forest's ground-breaking path, the constitutional challenge had been launched by law student Roger Bilodeau over another English-only traffic ticket, this time for speeding. Bilodeau argued it was illegal because Manitoba's unilingual English Highway Traffic Act also was illegal. Four years after Forest's successful ruling, it still had not been passed, printed and published in French, as required by Section 23 of the province's constitution. Bilodeau's case was thus a dagger pointed at the very heart of Manitoba's legal structure. Although Bilodeau had failed in the Manitoba Court of Appeal, the decision was split. The case was now headed to the far more sympathetic Supreme Court of Canada.

A year earlier, seizing the chance both to redress a grievous historic wrong and escape major legal and administrative difficulties, the NDP government of Howard Pawley had begun a dialogue with Bilodeau, the federal government and La Société franco-manitobaine. Negotiated behind closed doors, the proposed amendment to the province's constitution, the Manitoba Act of 1870, declared Manitoba officially bilingual. It also exchanged the provision of limited but expanding French language provincial government services in communities where numbers warranted for a less onerous regimen of statute translation. For its part, Ottawa agreed to provide financial assistance for the task of translating 450 "core" laws. Under Canadian law, amendments to a province's constitution must be passed by the provincial legislature and the federal parliament.

Forest's worst fears were quickly confirmed the moment the former premier rose to speak. One of the most skilled parliamentarians in Manitoba history, Lyon was a superb orator, but often tarred his brilliance with a rigid political ideology and a penchant for ad hominem attack. "Socialists" of all stripes and "the mid-Atlantic Gallic mind" of Pierre Elliott Trudeau were targets he singled out for special venom. "Socialists," he frequently said, viewed the world "through the wrong end of a sewer pipe"; therefore, none of their ideas or policies could ever merit consideration. "The dogs bark; but the caravan moves on," he'd often add.

This speech was to be the first of several vintage Lyon performances during the language imbroglio, replete with withering sarcasm, haughty contempt and barely-concealed plays on prejudice. The amendment was unnecessary, he thundered. No court, most especially, not the Supreme Court of Canada, was in the business of creating legal chaos. Then he waved Manitoba's bloody shirt. The amendment would "bilingualize" Manitoba in the way that the federal Liberals under Pierre Trudeau had "bilingualized" Canada. "Very dangerous" judge-made law would replace the will of the people as expressed through their elected representatives in the legislature.

RÉAL BÉRARD (CAYOUCHE) / LA LIBERTÉ

**Can it be true that the king of the jungle is rewriting history
as the king of the rednecks too?**

I foresee grave problems, such as arise in the United States
where court-ordered busing has caused grave social disorder
in that country. This kind of court-ordered bilingualism,
Sir, is in violation of our whole tradition of parliamentary
supremacy in this country and I can regrettably foresee
social divisiveness ... [1]

Lyon's oratory set loose the politically-explosive spectre of linguistic
fear and loathing; of the French language being forced down Manitobans'
throats by constitutional "dictats" won by emboldened "linguistic zealots".
The legislature hushed. MLAs, particularly on the government side, sat mute
and aghast.

Manitoba, Lyon concluded, should not cave in to federal "blackmail"
and minority "tyranny". It should let the Bilodeau case proceed to the Supreme
Court. "Courtesy", not entrenchment, was sufficient to respond to the needs
of Manitoba's official language minority.

Forest slumped back in his chair as the former premier's blatant pitch
to prejudice gathered steam. "He has opened Pandora's Box," he said finally.
Then he walked out.

The prophecy was portentous. Within days, Manitoba's social peace
was shattered. The spectacle of a province tearing itself to pieces in an all-out
linguistic war riveted a nation and twice reverberated through the halls of
parliament. The spectre of linguistic fear and loathing continued its dance
for nearly a year before it ruptured the legislature and finally was consumed
by its own fire.

Georges Forest's Pandora's Box metaphor precisely describes the
menacing forces Lyon and others unleashed in Manitoba in 1983 for frankly
partisan ends. The late United States historian, Richard Hofstadter of Columbia
University, coined the phrase "the paranoid style in American politics" in an
essay written about forty years ago. It describes the political tactic of casting
one's enemies as pawns in a vast conspiracy being manipulated by sinister
and powerful forces. Hofstadter says that while the clinical paranoid believes
the conspiracy is directed at him personally, the political paranoid sees the
conspiracy "directed against a nation, a culture, a way of life." The Manitoba
Conservatives and their political allies bundled together "French Power",
Prime Minister Pierre Elliott Trudeau, the federal Liberals and Manitoba's
New Democratic government as conspirators, whose aim was to rob Manitoba

and all Western Canada of their cherished British traditions and symbols – the English language and parliamentary supremacy. Thanks to Canada's constitution and rule of law, this latest in a long line of English Canadian attempts to extinguish the French aspect of the Manitoban and Canadian collectivity was unable to succeed. But it inflicted deep and lasting wounds on Manitoba's national image and Canada's psyche.

Language, race, culture, blood, religion, class, ethnicity. Evocative and powerful, these are more than descriptive terms; they are the anvils upon which history is forged. Down through the ages, in combinations and sometimes alone, they have formed and shaped the course of civilization. The core of every individual and society, they root most human conflict, including war between and sometimes within nations.

University of Manitoba historian D.N. Sprague calls them "status issues". They play in the incendiary arena of group and individual self-image and esteem and power inter-relationships. In the hands of unscrupulous politicians, they become tools of tyranny. Because status politics stimulates the raw nerve of rivalry based on race, colour, religion, language or class, it can unleash almost limitless antagonisms. Inevitably, the victims of status politics are minorities.

LE CANARD / MONTREAL / *GREAT CANADIAN POLITICAL CARTOONS: 1820–1914*

Sir John: (standing on the Metis and the French flag) Let's go, gentlemen. You have come to the end of my territory. You are going to have to jump into the Pacific or work with the rest of the settlers. Make your choice.

The blunt instrument of majoritarian rule is the favoured weapon of those who seek to bludgeon the forces of difference in pluralistic democratic societies. It has a ring of legitimacy, because democracy is popularly described as government of, by and for the people. But when majorities use the ballot to decide minority rights, as British Columbia did in 2002 over the issue of Aboriginal land claims, democracy can become vigilantism. The rule of law, a necessary corollary to the rule of the majority if civilization is to be preserved, can then be torn asunder, as it was when lynch mobs roamed the southern United States terrorizing black Americans.

For a country like Canada, which prides itself on not having a single national narrative to which all citizens are expected to subscribe, status politics is perilous. [2] But Canadian history is pockmarked with status politics and Manitoba has been the battleground for many of the most brutal wars over one of our most enduring status issues, language. Historian Gerald Friesen says language is fundamental because it goes to the heart of culture and communication in society. It is therefore basic to a citizen's sense of self and empowerment. In its momentous ruling in the 1985 reference on the Manitoba language issue, the Supreme Court of Canada also spoke of the centrality of language. The importance of language rights is "grounded in the essential role that language plays in human existence, development and dignity," the justices wrote in their unanimous judgement. "It is through language that we are able to form concepts; to structure and order the world around us. Language bridges the gap between isolation and community, allowing humans to delineate the rights and duties they hold in respect of one another and thus to live in society…" [3]

Because of Manitoba's unique history, language quickly became and remained the overarching symbol for a package of status issues, those of race, blood, culture, religion and class. This may explain the singular potency and viciousness that any debate over language summons from the Manitoba psyche.

As both the first province and the first western province to join Confederation after the original four of 1867, Manitoba drew heavily from three sources for its societal framework. The first two, hierarchical mid-nineteenth century white Anglo-Saxon Protestant Ontario and melting pot America, combined to forge a melting pot, but a melting pot with a difference. The top element remained impervious to the heat. Like Ontario itself, Manitoba was, at least from 1875 to 1969, John Porter's vertical mosaic, with the British "charter" class at the top. A charter class defines the culture and language of the entire community. This hierarchical melting pot was Manitoba's defining provincial characteristic and it functioned as an engine of intolerance.

But unlike Ontario and to a greater extent than other western provinces, Manitoba also had a century-old history drawn from the wellspring of the other half of the Canadian reality, French Canada. By 1890, the forces of Ontario WASP hierarchy and American individualistic equality were strong enough to frame the new province's society, but never strong enough to eradicate the communitarian ideals of French Canada. They had been planted one hundred and fifty years earlier by the adventurers and the voyageurs of the fur trade. And they were nourished by generations of French Catholic clergy from Québec, Québec immigrants and Western Canada's own nationality, the Métis, the offspring of Aboriginal women and those early Québec adventurers and voyageurs.

Manitoba could be seen as a petrie dish for a very interesting sociological explanation of how the "New World" of the Americas was defined by its various conquerors – Spanish, Portuguese, French and English. Known as the "Hartzian fragment" theory of history, it was first set out by social historian Louis Hartz in his scholarly book, *The Founding of New Societies*. Put simply, when older societies spin off substantial chunks of their citizenry to establish colonial outposts of their empires, these new societies tend to freeze-frame around the cultures and values of the mother country at that precise moment in time. No matter how many new arrivals come to these new societies, the original culture/value construct can only be modified but never eradicated. In large part, that is because the ongoing waves of new immigrants come precisely because they are attracted to that construct and want to help perpetuate and even extend it. At the same time, because of its separation and often relative isolation, the "fragment" society doesn't face the on-going new challenges still present in the old. Its ideology thus becomes dominant and uncontested and usually less flexible and adaptable than its parent.

The United States is a classic example of Hartzian theory. To this day its national character is marked by the motivating beliefs of its two founders: the social conservatism and religiosity of the seventeenth-century Puritans and the assertive individualism and libertarianism of eighteenth-century Enlightenment philosophers. The theories of John Locke and Jean-Jacques Rousseau animated the Thirteen Colonies' British merchant class, whose leading citizens penned the Declaration of Independence in 1776, fought the Revolutionary War to throw off England's yoke and wrote the American Constitution of 1783.

So too with Manitoba. University of Manitoba historian J. Edgar Rea argues that the huge influx of Ontarians into Manitoba immediately after 1870 replicates Hartz's thesis. Rea writes that "From the clash of the early pioneers with the Métis, the most persistent social theme of the Prairies has been the struggle for cultural dominance. It has been more than merely a sub-plot to the central Canadian conundrum of French and English because it has internally been more heterogeneous." [4]

While Ontario and Québec were geographically linked, each had a life of its own and, as Rea puts it, "there was a right and wrong side of the town and everyone knew to which he belonged." But the social structure of the Prairies was more complex and subtle "and in times of stress, more abrasively discriminatory ... Ontario attitudes towards the Canadian cultural dilemma appear in the Manitoba fragment. Free from the restraints and traditions of Ontario, the fragment can go much further in giving effect to its assumptions." In other words, linguistic and religious intolerance got free rein, especially after the wave of immigration from Ontario swamped Manitoba's initial francophone majority and "Manitoba was reborn in the image of Ontario".[5]

However the Hartzian fragment theory also breathed lasting life into the collectivist, French and Catholic side of the Manitoba character. And like the English and Protestant Ontarians, it, too, had constitutional law on its side. The British North America Acts of 1867 and 1871 and the Manitoba Act of 1870 conferred constitutional status on the French as well as the English language and on confessional Roman Catholic schools. Still, the influence of Protestant Ontario was sufficiently potent and durable to repeal and then deny the province's founding law for almost a century. Manitoba's Ontario "fragment" subsumed all the incoming ethnicities, languages and cultures into the dominant WASP order and, whenever necessary, called upon them to band together as one to fight any encroachment of the "alien" francophone reality.

Unlike any other province in the new dominion, therefore, Manitoba carried within its bosom the two great and diametrically opposed strains of Canadian nationalism: the English ideal of a society of individuals governed by a majoritarian political system and the French Canadian ideal of a society of two founding collectivities governed by a constitutional code of rights and responsibilities. Both were totemic, self-defining, in a word, tribal. As York University historian Ramsay Cook wrote in his review of Mordecai Richler's controversial book, *Oh Canada! Oh Quebec! Requiem for a Divided Country*, published in 1992, tribal or totemic nationalism "establishes a we/they relationship that understandably makes minorities uneasy. The choice between exclusion and assimilation replaces an acceptance of diversity as a social value." [6]

French was the first European language to be spoken on the southern plains of what is now Canada. Indeed, it predates English by almost 100 years because of the very different nature of the fur trade as practiced by those two great empires. The French were engaged personally from the outset. Directed by Aboriginal guides, their coureurs de bois and voyageurs began plying the water highways of the vast land west from Lake Superior in the early part of the eighteenth century. Meanwhile the English, who had had a royal charter to the lands draining into Hudson Bay since 1670, chose the sedentary life, staying in their forts by the frozen bay and expecting their Aboriginal trading partners to harvest the continent's fur bounty and bring it to them. French Canadians and Métis began trading near the confluence of the Red and Assiniboine Rivers in the 1730s, more than a half-century before English-speaking traders moved into the area and eighty years before the first group of Selkirk settlers arrived in Fort Garry by York boat in 1812.

If the French language was the European tongue of choice in the southern West, English was the European language of the Hudson Bay tidewater. English acquired an official status of sorts with the Imperial Act of 1731 which stipulated not only that justice would be enforced according to the laws of England as set out in the Hudson's Bay Company Charter of 1670, but that justice all across the company's vast empire would be meted out in English only.

Still, it wasn't until 1812 and the establishment of a colony at the confluence of the Red and Assiniboine rivers by Thomas Douglas, fifth Earl of Selkirk, that English – and Gaelic – became customary tongues in the lands destined to become Manitoba. The Red River Colony, named Assiniboia, encompassed 116,000 square miles (300,000 square kilometres) of land purchased at the nominal sum of ten shillings by the earl from the Hudson's Bay Company. It extended eighty kilometres in all directions from the river forks and was governed by an appointed governor and council.

The Council of Assiniboia, created in 1822, had only seven English members and initially operated solely in that language. When the Hudson's Bay Company resumed its governmental, as well as commercial, monopoly in 1835, that began to change. First, representatives of the small French Canadian community and finally, the majority Métis population, were appointed and the body, by then expanded to fifteen, was forced by necessity to function in French too.

Dualism and bilingualism were, therefore, the Manitoba reality for more than a half-century before the province's founding and it is important to remember that Manitoba became bilingual when English was introduced, not the other way around. French clearly predated it.

> Since the early 1600s there had been some *Métissage*, or intermarriage, between the French and Native peoples among whom they travelled and lived. By the eighteenth century sizeable communities of mixed bloods – later called Métis – were to be found along the shores of Lake Superior. As the French fur trade and military expeditions moved into the Prairie West in the 1730s, some Métis settled in the valleys of the Red and Assiniboine rivers. Although the French withdrew their military garrisons from this region in 1755, the fur trade continued after the cession of Canada to Britain. [7]

As the French fur trade spread farther west, reaching the Athabasca region, more and more Métis settled at Red River. The Roman Catholic Church established permanent missions at Red River in 1818 with the arrival of Monseigneur (later to be Bishop) Joseph Norbert Provencher and Reverend S. Dumoulin, followed by les Soeurs Grises de Montréal in the 1840s. Provencher founded the new mission church of St. Boniface while the Grey Nuns, also known as the Sisters of Charity, began the first convent school. Intermarriage also occurred around the HBC posts and forts in the north.

The Selkirk settlers, who arrived beginning in 1812, were poor Scottish crofters evicted from their lands by Britain's brutal agricultural land removals or "clearances". Predominantly Presbyterian, they had been promised their "kirk" by their benefactor, the earl, who, as a member of the British aristocracy, was an Anglican. For more than thirty years, the Scottish crofters had to make do with the Church Missionary Society of the Anglican

Church, which set up shop at Red River in 1820 under the auspices of the Rev. John West. To soothe the settlers' anti-establishmentarian sensibilities, the Anglican services were "low church". Finally, in 1851, the Presbyterian Church in the person of the Reverend John Black came to minister to the people of Red River.

Thus, by the second decade of the nineteenth century, "four elements had converged to create a dualistic community at Red River," according to University of Ottawa historian Cornelius Jaenen. "There were Europeans of British and French origin, and there were mixed-blood peoples who were also perceived as being Anglophone and Protestant or Francophone and Catholic." [8]

Two contrasting societies, each bound by the powerful forces of language, religion, culture, blood and race, set down their roots in the rich alluvial soil of the lands around the river forks. The families of the English and French parishes alike established their long, rectangular farming plots with their "in" and "out" fields along the sinuous courses of the Red, the Assiniboine and the Sale (now La Salle) Rivers – the early highways of trade and commerce. Jaenen says Manitoba's pre-Confederation bilingualism arose from the demographic reality of biculturalism. "The English had been first at Hudson Bay, the French first at Red River. Both came together at the beginning of the nineteenth century at The Forks and soon the anglophone and francophone communities became almost equal in number, with the French-speaking population being slightly more numerous." [9]

In 1848, the French parishes petitioned to name delegates from the francophone communities to the Council of Assiniboia, the colony's government. The appeal for dual representation was agreed upon and sent to the HBC's governing committee. It requested "the infusion into the Council of Assiniboia of a certain proportion of Canadian and half-breed members." [10] However, in his three-part series for *The Beaver* entitled, "The Métis and Canadien Councillors of Assiniboia", Lionel Dorge notes that the French-speaking element, which always constituted more than half the population, never held even a third of the seats. Initially, both the French, who called themselves Canadiens or Canayens, and the Métis were used in "lesser positions, as if to … serve a novitiate", primarily as magistrates. [11] Gradually, the virulent bigotry and prejudice of the likes of noted francophobe Judge Adam Thom, one of the chief authors of the Durham Report that recommended the total assimilation of Canada's French-speaking population, faded and the

Hudson's Bay Company endeavoured to provide some semblance of representative government. States Dorge: "Of the ... Métis or Canadiens appointed to the Council of Assiniboia between 1835 and 1870, three stand out – l'abbé Louis-François Laflèche, François Bruneau and Bishop Alexandre Taché. They were men of vision, if not statesmen; practical men, if not politicians." [12]

The first French-speaking councillors were Bishop Norbert Provencher and fur trader Cuthbert Grant, appointed in 1837 and 1839 respectively. In 1850, Laflèche was appointed on the recommendation of Governor George Simpson. That same year, Simpson wrote to the governor and committee in London proposing the appointment of "two or three of the more respectable of the Canadian Halfbreeds". Altogether, the council had had fourteen Métis and Canadien members by the time it went out of existence in 1870. As the colony matured, the non-British councillors moved from their novice status to an equal footing with their English-speaking compatriots. According to Dorge, after provincehood, several went on to active careers in municipal and provincial affairs. "For them the Council of Assiniboia had been an excellent training school." [13]

In 1849, the French parishes won the right to have the law administered in their tongue by French-speaking magistrates. On May 31st of that year, the Council of Assiniboia recognized French as a language of judicial proceedings by the following order. "The conducting of all judicial business through the medium of a judge who would address the court in French as well as the English language." Thereafter as well, the council's minutes indicate that petitions were received in both French and English. It was, simply, a necessity. After all, more than half the population spoke French and the government had to communicate with its Métis and Canadian-origin population. All enactments of the governor and council were published in both languages and bilingual or dual appointments to public offices were made to ensure service to both linguistic groups. Thus, in May 1856, for example, there was a demand for a francophone surveyor because "the Canadian population were dissatisfied with the present surveyor, that they could not understand him.'" [14]

Red River's duality was mirrored in religious affairs as well. There were an equal number of Anglican (Protestant) and Roman Catholic parishes and this equality became the basis for the distribution of public funds to the missionary schools, which evolved into parochial schools. When the Presbyterian settlers at Kildonan eventually obtained their own minister, they

THE DUAL LANGUAGE DUEL

petitioned the Council of Assiniboia for funding for their school. They were given a modest sum, but the council was at pains to point out it was not to be a permanent grant stating that it was "without prejudice, however, to the recognized equality in the premises between the Protestants as a whole and the Catholics." [15] To drive home the point, the council immediately increased the grant to the Catholic schools by the amount accorded the Presbyterians. The principle of equality between the two sectors of the community came to mean that on all major issues – timber-cutting, customs duties, liquor sales, defence – there was an attempt to obtain dual French and English majority support.

Dualism and equality may have been the rubric of governance in Assiniboia, but the perception of a pastoral idyll of tolerance and goodwill is deeply misleading. The cultural divisions between French and English visible in the very different natures of the Bay and Montreal fur trades bedevilled the colony from its inception, setting up an ugly hierarchy that would eventually have tragic consequences for it and for the new nation of Canada.

In his book, *The Canadian Prairies: A History,* historian Gerald Friesen says the French "pedlars" built up "a century of … experience with native marriages as a tool of trade and diplomacy" and "delighted in establishing close personal liaisons with their native customers." [16] The French had set down permanent roots in Native country by the late 1690s and throughout the next century, their progeny formed a distinct culture blending European and Aboriginal customs. They controlled the middle rungs of the fur trade as guides, interpreters, ferrymen, oarsmen, mail carriers and brokers between eastern companies and Aboriginal traders. They developed a distinctive mode of dress reflecting their dual heritage: utilitarian Aboriginal moccasins and leggings and modish European ruffled shirts and waistcoats. Neither Aboriginal nor French, they became the Métis, a distinct group with distinct interests whose homeland stretched from the southern tip of Lake Michigan to Red River.

It was very different with the English. While British men and Aboriginal women did form liaisons, creating what came to be called the "home guard", "half-breed" or "mixed-blood" people, they did not acquire a separate social status like the Métis. Continues Friesen:

> If they lived with the natives and travelled in their hunting
> bands, they were native. On the occasions when fathers par-
> ticipated in their upbringing, encouraged their education
> and perhaps aided in securing company positions for them,
> they usually became English. A middle racial category did
> not develop in the eighteenth century British fur trade. [17]

In her biography of Louis Riel, journalist and historian Maggie Siggins provides a vivid description of the vital role Aboriginal women played in the early fur trade:

The fur traders who ventured early into the wilderness of
the Canadian Northwest could never have survived without the help of Indian women. These marriages, *à la façon
du pays* (according to the custom of the country) were
encouraged by Natives and Europeans alike for they
established an economic symbiosis which fuelled the St.
Lawrence-based fur trade. The Indian woman ground corn
… chopped firewood, collected berries, snared hares and
partridges and caught fish, which frequently saved the
white traders from starvation and scurvy. She also provided her man with a never-ending supply of moccasins from
deer or moose skins, and she netted the intricate webbing
which gave the essential snowshoe its support. She
collected wattappe (roots from the spruce tree) and with
the resulting twine repaired his canoe, she dressed the
beaver and otter furs and prepared the staple food of the
Northwest – the famous pemmican, a mixture of buffalo
meat, fat and berries. She also acted as a guide, a language
teacher, and perhaps most important, an adviser on the
traditions and customs of various Indian tribes with which
her husband must deal. Some of these marriages were long
and happy, even after the husband had left the fur trade.
More typically, the Native woman was unceremoniously
dumped as soon as the white had no further use for her;
she and her children would simply melt back into her
family's clan – at an emotional and physical sacrifice that
can only be imagined. [18]

According to historian Arthur Morton, the "unceremonious dump-
ing" became ever more frequent as European colonization advanced. Not
only were Europeans becoming acclimatized to and skilled in the ways of
the wilderness, but first mixed-blood and then white women were becoming
more numerous. It then became apparent that racism had only been held in
check by necessity. The attitudinal shift was personified by George Simpson,
the hard-driving, domineering "little emperor", who ran the Hudson's Bay
Company in North America for almost forty years. Simpson's personal life
"at least until he was nearly forty, was disordered in the extreme. He had one

mistress after another, fathering at least one child in Britain before 1820 and several more in Canada." [19] His first position with the company was as factor at Fort Wedderburn in 1820-21. Arthur Morton tells us in his book *Sir George Simpson: Overseas Governor of the Hudson's Bay Company: A Pen Picture of a Man of Action,* Simpson "accepted the customs as he found them". In fact, he pushed these customs to, and sometimes beyond, the socially accepted norms. He fathered a child by Betsey Sinclair, a mixed-blood, and stayed with her for five years. Later, he referred to her, entirely ungraciously, as "an unnecessary and expensive appendage".[20] Subsequently, he took to himself Margaret, the fifteen-year-old mixed-blood daughter of George Taylor, captain of the schooner at York Fort. At the same time, he retained Margaret's brother Thomas as his personal servant.

George and Margaret had four children, three boys and a girl. The eldest, Maria, was sent to Scotland to be educated and there, at the age of sixteen, met and married Donald McTavish. The McTavishes emigrated to Cobourg in Upper Canada. Simpson frequently visited the couple and when Maria was widowed, oversaw her finances until she secured a second husband. His three sons were educated "as far as their dispositions would allow" and given their chances in the company service. Still, as Arthur Morton writes, however much he cared for his children, he steadfastly refused the blandishments of Red River's Anglican clergy to marry any of his country wives. It just would not do for a man of his station to enter into the holy state of matrimony with someone of Aboriginal, or even mixed, blood.

In fact as early as 1823, two years after he began his cohabitation with Margaret Taylor, Simpson wrote to Andrew Colvile, HBC governor, proposing a visit to England during which he might be married – to an Englishwoman. Colvile dissuaded him, not out of any moral considerations but because his company duties involved too much travel. Reluctantly, Simpson concurred, and delayed his marital ambitions for six years all the while continuing to co-habit, whenever duties allowed, with Margaret. Then, in 1830, his travels largely completed, he and two other chief factors, James McMillan and John George McTavish, sailed home. All three were embarked on the same "gentle errand" of matrimony.

At the age of forty-three and now the HBC governor, Simpson married his eighteen-year-old cousin, Frances Ramsay Simpson. His friend McTavish married a Miss Turner of Turner Hall, Aberdeenshire, while

The Canadian Crucible

McMillan chose a Scottish bride.

The Simpsons and the McTavishes crossed to Canada on the same ship. McTavish took his bride to his new charge at Moose Factory while Simpson gave Frances a royal tour of her new homeland. He and Frances were paddled and portaged by canoe 13,000 kilometres from Lachine to the Selkirk Colony, to York Factory and then back to Red River. The Simpsons' arrival at Lac la Pluie forced an ugly little scene. Margaret was bundled out the back door as young Frances walked through the front of the post that would soon be renamed in her honour. Frances, however, was not long fooled or kept from learning of her husband's many dalliances. It scarred their relationship and eventually led to an unofficial separation.

Once ensconced at Red River, Simpson faced the unpleasant task of getting rid of Margaret and also of McTavish's common-law wife of seventeen years. There was no dispute as to the method; it was the usual thing in the country. According to the custom, "dowries must be provided sufficiently large to promote speedy and satisfactory marriages …" [21]

McTavish's former partner presented Simpson with an especially ticklish situation. She happened to be the niece of Assiniboia governor Donald McKenzie. Furious at the slur being cast on her, McKenzie used his clout as a senior company official to demand a large dowry. After much haggling, the dowry was set at 100 pounds for each of the two children still with her. Simpson located a prospective bridegroom "of good character", a Fort Garry trader by the name of Pierre le Blanc, signed a contract with him and gave him a week's leave to "court" the rejected woman. Simpson's own former partner, Margaret, was also put on the market with a generous dowry and married off to one Amable Hogue.

> The repercussions of these events continued long and con-
> tributed to the isolation of the Simpson couple in a land in
> which there were none too many with whom they could
> associate. McKenzie and [James] Stuart [chief factor at Fort
> Alexander, where both jilted women resided] could not for-
> give Simpson. They intrigued and gossiped, and the feeling
> engendered made impossible any cordiality … Simpson's
> setting aside of the woman of his first connection seems to
> have been taken as casting a slur on those who had half-
> breed wives, duly married. [22]

At Moose Factory, McTavish and his English bride refused to have anything to do with Chief Factor Joseph Beioley's "woman". This, continues Arthur Morton, was something new in Rupert's Land society. At Red River, too, all was different now that the governor was married to an English lady and thus had demonstrated that a mixed-blood woman was beneath him. Having isolated himself and his bride and restricted their social relations to the "puritanical circle" composed of the missionaries and their wives, Simpson then had the insensitivity to write McTavish to say he had become utterly bored with the haughty pretensions and posturings of Red River society.

> I am most heartily tired of Red River, or rather of its good
> inhabitants, and should be delighted to join you at Moose
> next Fall; indeed, my better half is constantly entreating me
> to take her there, in order that she may enjoy the society of
> her Friend to whom she is most warmly attached. Here she
> has formed no intimacies: McKenzie's wife is a silly ignorant
> thing, whose commonplace wise saws, with which we are
> constantly persecuted, are worse than a blister; Mrs. Jones
> [the parson's wife] is a good unmeaning woman whom we
> merely see for half an hour occasionally, & Mrs Cochran
> [another parson's wife] whose assumed puritanism but ill
> conceals the vixen, shines only when talking of elbow
> Grease & the scouring of pots and pans. [23]

Simpson was not alone in his snobbery. As noted earlier, Adam Thom, the first recorder (judge) of Assiniboia, appointed in 1834 when the Hudson's Bay Company resumed jurisdiction over the colony at the end of the Selkirk era, refused to use French in court and was notorious for his savage attacks on French Canadians. Thom once wrote, in a letter to Simpson, that "the French (let alone the Métis or the Canadiens) possessed only one-hundredth of the intelligence and abilities of the Anglo-Saxons." [24] Thom was obviously regarded with extreme suspicion by the Métis, who finally petitioned that he be removed from "any charge of affairs in this colony" and threatened that he would be physically prevented from presiding at the general quarterly court.

Simpson persuaded Thom to step down from the bench for one year, but allowed him to continue in his job as chief counsel for the HBC and Assiniboia. The Métis presented another petition. "We have often been called

The Canadian Crucible

a band of savages and at this time, it may be said with truth, for we are now without justice …" They threatened to burn Thom's house down. Finally, Simpson relented. In June 1854, Thom sailed from York Factory to Edinburgh, a fresh wind in the form of a generous company pension at his back.

Racial and religious bigotry was most marked in the Anglican clergy. In his book, *Snug Little Flock: The Social Origins of the Riel Resistance of 1869-70*, historian Frits Pannekoek describes an inbred little society riven with all forms of intolerance, traceable largely to the ingrained snobbery and arrogance of the British element, particularly the clergy of England's established church. University of Manitoba historian Denise Fuchs says the snobbery and incipient racism was a product of the dismal science of the day.

> Eighteenth and Nineteenth Century pseudoscientific discourses used race as a means of describing differences in language, belief systems, artistic traditions and gene pools. Race was often confused with culture … Scholars of the time believed that humankind had evolved into a hierarchy called the Great Chain of Being that placed Europeans on top and Aboriginals on the bottom. Mixed-races were placed lower than Aboriginals because it was believed they inherited the vices of both races. [25]

Members of the Anglican clergy were firm in their conviction that civilization must go hand in hand with Christianity. The virtues of mid-Victorian England were preached as fervently as the Gospel since without the former the latter could not take root. A sedentary life tied to the soil was mandatory. Agriculture was to be the pillar of society. The Reverend David Jones refused to minister to the English-speaking half-breeds on the plains because he believed that "the habits of the hunter were inseparable from 'prodigality and idleness', and that his constant condition was one of 'beggary and extreme want'." [26]

Needless to say, these priggish gentlemen perceived Red River to be "barbaric and fallen". [27] They were determined to put an immediate end to marriages à la façon du pays. The Reverend William Cochran, who arrived in Red River in 1825 and stayed until his death forty years later, was typical of the breed. He believed the English to be "the dominant Race of this Continent" and hard work the path to salvation both spiritual and temporal. "Natives" and mixed-bloods in his opinion would always be "immoral, capricious, intractable, indolent, callous, prideful, wayward, extravagant, ungracious, improvident and careless." Buffalo hunting, fur trading, fishing were all pastimes of the "indolent Catholic Savages"; a pious "Christian" would dedicate his life to tilling the soil and raising his numerous offspring "in the service of the British empire". [28]

Pannekoek says the values of the Métis and mixed-blood communities were the exact opposite of the missionaries. A man's worth was measured by his freedom and his ability as a tripman, buffalo hunter and horseman.

> Commitment to the plough and the church, demanded by
> the missionary, was alien and not likely to be viewed as con-
> tributing to status. Those central activities that were critical
> to Métis status and identity, the cult of the horse and the
> hunt, were precisely those the missionary identified with
> leisure and idleness … the first step to Hell. [29]

While there is little doubt the Anglican clergy's racial, religious and sexual bigotry damaged the colony's social fibre, their prejudices did not infect everybody or characterize all relationships. Historian Irene Spry challenges Pannekoek's bleak view of Red River. In her 1985 article, "The Mixed-Bloods and Métis of Rupert's Land before 1870", she points to examples of marriages between English-speaking mixed-bloods and French-speaking Métis and provides a wealth of evidence of cooperation and interaction between the two in buffalo hunts and freighting expeditions. She argues that Red River's initial societal divisions had more to do with affluence, education and social status than with language and race. The latter antagonisms certainly existed within the clergy, she agrees, but she warns "such sources … must be used with great reserve". [30] Spry says that towards the end of the nineteenth century, the source of conflict and tension changed dramatically with the equally dramatic change in the economy and way of life.

> Western Canada, as we know it today, was indeed born of
> conflict, conflict not between Métis and mixed-blood, but
> between a wandering, free life and settlement; a conflict
> between agriculturalists, especially the flood of newcomers
> in search of landed property and wealth and the old way of
> life that both Métis and mixed-bloods had in common with
> their Indian cousins, a way of life based on adjustment to
> the natural environment and the shared use of the free gifts

of nature. That way of life was doomed with the coming of
surveyors, fences, police, organized government, settlers
and the private rights of property ... With it went the prosperity and independence of all but a small elite of Métis and
mixed-bloods alike. [31]

Still, that state of affairs was far in the future when, following
Simpson's example and egged on by the clergy to re-establish their Christian
"respectability", many retired Hudson's Bay Company men sloughed off their
Aboriginal wives and sent east for younger, whiter, daintier brides, equipped
with English tea services and silver dinnerware, women considered appropriate to take their marriage vows in the Anglican faith. The Aboriginal
and mixed-blood wives who did remain – many of whom where the most
inteligent, enterprising and influential women in Red River – were brutally
aware of the disdain and prejudice towards them.

In 1850, a steamy sex scandal split the English-speaking community
along strict racial and religious lines – the mixed bloods against the British
ruling class, the Presbyterians against the Anglicans. Sarah Ballenden, the
beautiful mixed-blood wife of HBC chief factor for Red River, John Ballenden,
somehow managed to insult two matrons of the British upper crust. They
took revenge on her by beginning a salacious rumour to the effect she was
having an affair with Captain Christopher Foss and was carrying his child. In
a strange twist of fate demonstrating the complexity and extremely personal
nature of the little colony's social rifts, Adam Thom sided with Mrs. Ballenden
and posted a notice on the front gate of Upper Fort Garry announcing that
charges of defamatory conspiracy would be brought against the scandal-
mongers and their husbands. Adding spice to the whole affair was the fact
one of these husbands had made sexual advances to Mrs. Ballenden and
been rebuffed.

The trial rivetted the entire community. The Anglican clergy supported
the gossip-mongers, but the jury was padded with Ballenden sympathizers
and the defence's chief witness was spirited out of the colony before the trial
started. Sarah Ballenden was vindicated and the defendants were required
to pay her the then-hefty sum of 400 pounds. However, the two factions
continued to snub each other socially for years.

According to Pannekoek, the missionaries of the established church
were determined to turn the Red River community into "A Little Britain in

the Wilderness" and were instrumental in creating a crisis of social division in Red River society because of their "slavish devotion to the creation of a society that they believed was European" and their bigotted opinion that inter-marriage between whites and "degenerate" mixed-bloods and Aboriginals was especially disastrous.

The Anglican clergy's virulent race pride was totally missing in the other major church of the colony. Pannekoek says the homogeneity of the French Catholic portion of Red River (with only a tiny number of French Canadians, it was almost exclusively Métis) allowed it to escape the racial conflicts plaguing the Protestants. Also, there was little social interaction between Catholic clergy and laity because the clergy had no wives and the church largely failed to recruit priests among the Métis. However, a serious split did develop beginning in the late 1830s between what Pannekoek refers to as the "sedentary" and the "nomadic" clergy, specifically between Bishop Provencher and Father G.A. Belcourt. The bishop tended to support the HBC, causing the Métis to turn against him and his establishment at The Forks and look instead to Father Belcourt and other members of the nomadic priesthood.

> The Métis were only expected to comply with the moral and
> ethical rules of the Church as enunciated in the catechism
> … The priests made no emphatic demand for civilization,
> since Christianity, not civilization, was at the heart of the
> gospel. In essence their attitudes were simply those of
> French Canada. The French-Canadian priest did not
> see himself as the scion of a great empire, and he rarely
> possessed the racial arrogance of his nineteenth century
> Anglican counterpart. More importantly, as a French-
> Canadian, he had long ago come to terms with the river
> lot, the bush, and the mixed-blood marriage. The fur
> trade, the hunt and the fisheries were hardly alien. [32]

Although mixed-bloods from both sides of the linguistic/religious divide participated in the buffalo hunt, it was the defining institution of their nationality for the Métis, while for the English mixed-bloods it was just another way to make a living. These two contrasting outlooks probably arose from the fact the Métis saw themselves as a distinct racial group, while the anglophone mixed-bloods had always faded into one or another of their two parental societies.

The English-speaking mixed-bloods, mostly Orcadian on their father's side, didn't fit exactly into the pattern of the Selkirk settlers at Kildonan, but still won the approval of the Scots, who were content that others should try to follow the Calvinist path. John McLean was prepared to write: "Very few resort to the plains, unless for the purpose of trafficking the produce of their farms for the produce of the chase; and it is said that they frequently return home better supplied with meat than the hunters themselves." [33]

According to some historians, the signal event giving birth to Métis cultural consciousness was the incident at Seven Oaks, called by some Scots settlers a "massacre" and certainly the bloodiest day in Red River history. In January 1814, Miles Macdonnell, the insensitive Scot chosen by Selkirk to be governor of his colony, issued what came to be known as the Pemmican Proclamation. Designed to protect the settlers from starvation, it banned the export of pemmican and other foodstuffs from Assiniboia. Historian W. L. Morton says that the proclamation confirmed the suspicion of the Nor'Westers that the Red River colony was deliberately planted across their supply route to thwart their trade and give the HBC total command over the furs of the northwest. They were determined to extinguish it.

In that endeavour they knew they could count on the support of the Métis, many of whom had worked for the North West Company and harboured longstanding hostility towards the HBC and *les anglais* of the Selkirk settlement. The Métis had as their leader the English-speaking Cuthbert Grant, the twenty-three-year-old son of a Scottish North West Company wintering partner and a Cree mother. Educated in Scotland and Montréal, he had returned to the west as a "bourgeois" (factor) for the North West Company. Later, he established a Métis community at St. Francois Xavier on the White Horse Plains that over time became known as "Grantown". By the time its founder was in his fifties, the settlement boasted about 170 families.

But all this was yet to be in the seminal year of 1816. That year, Robert Semple, described by W.L. Morton as "a sincere and earnest, but impulsive and indecisive gentleman" took charge of the Red River colony. In the spring, a series of skirmishes began between the HBC and the colonists on one side and the NWC and Grant's Métis on the other. Semple demolished the NWC's Fort Gibraltar, captured the previous year by his immediate predecessor, interim governor Colin Robertson, and rafted the stockades downstream to the HBC's Fort Douglas. In retaliation, Grant, who had wintered on the Qu'Appelle River in what is now southern Saskatchewan, captured and plundered Fort Brandon on June 1st. He then moved east across the plains, his men divided into two parties, one escorting a convoy of carts loaded with pemmican and the other planning to link up with the North West partners coming from Fort William to the east.

The first party reached Frog Plain, *la Grenouillère,* undetected. But the second Métis force was spotted from Fort Douglas and Semple went out to intercept them with a band of just twenty-five men, "a group too large for parley and too weak for fight," according to W.L. Morton.

On June 19th the two sides met at a place known as Seven Oaks, where the woods jutted into the plain. The Métis and Aboriginals, some in warpaint, fanned out on either side of Grant. Semple went out to meet the Métis envoy, François Boucher. Boucher taunted Semple; calling him a "damn rascal" for his destruction of Fort Gibraltar. Semple tried to grab Boucher's gun while seizing his horse's bridle. Boucher slid from his mount and ran back to the Métis line. Shots rang out. The other half of the Métis force suddenly swooped in, cutting off any avenue of retreat for Semple's men. Huddled together, Semple and nineteen of his company were killed. The Métis suffered but one casualty. The victors "washed the blood-stained cloaks of the slain in the Red ... Infantry on the open plain were helpless before the mounted marksmen of the buffalo hunt." [34]

The quasi-military structure of the buffalo hunt had provided the power behind the Métis' defiance of the HBC monopoly and, in 1869-70 would challenge the government of Canada itself. But to the English set-tlers, an increasing number of whom were arriving from Canada, the hunt cemented the popular impression "back East" that the Métis were half-savage, more Native than white, and indifferent to civilization as defined by individual land ownership, thrift, hard work, agriculture and the accu-mulation of personal wealth and material possessions. In other words, they were not only not Anglo-Saxon, they weren't even European. John Palliser probably reflected an all-too-common attitude when he commented about the Métis in 1857: "They hunt during three months of the year and beg, borrow and starve during the remaining time." [35] Despite the disparaging sneers of *les anglais,* the Métis knew what their foes refused to concede, that it was their hunts and their pemmican that kept the colony from

The Canadian Crucible

MANTON MARBLE / PROVINCIAL ARCHIVES OF MANITOBA

starving to death more years than not. To them, it was not just a way of life, it was the cultural and economic badge of their pride and identity.

W.L. Morton's seminal *Manitoba: A History* still provides one of the best and most colourful descriptions of what became the national symbol of the Métis of Red River:

> The occupation of the hunt had not only kept alive the
> corporate sense of the Métis, their belief in themselves as

a "new nation"; it had also ... given them character as a
people, a kind of government, and a very definite discipline.
Hunts ... had come in Red River to be organized as seasonal
migrations of the Métis people, men, women and children,
to the plains of the Souris and the Coteau of the Missouri,
far out on the borders of the Sioux. The movement of so
many into territory beset by hereditary enemies ... necessitated ... discipline on the march, in camp and during
the hunt. Founded on the forms and usages of the plains
Indians, the organization of the hunt became the framework of Métis society, their mode of corporate life. [36]

There were two annual hunts, one in spring and the other in fall.
The spring hunt was the important one. In June, the hunters prepared their
outfits – guns, ammunition, a hunting horse, a pony and a Red River cart.
Entirely of wood construction, this lumbering vehicle needed nothing for
repair that couldn't be picked up along the way. However practical, it pro-
duced from its dry wooden axles, "a shriek more piercing than howl of coyote
or cry of loon". [37] All went on the hunt except the old and the disabled.
W.L. Morton says the main river party assembled in Fort Garry and the
White Horse Plain party at St. François-Xavier. Both followed the Pembina
trail south of the Assiniboine to the Rivière aux Ilets de Bois (now the
Boyne River), with its groves of Manitoba maples, and then moved on to the
Pembina Hills. Once encamped, a president or chief of the hunt was elected
along with twelve councillors, a public crier and guides. In turn, "captains of
tens" were elected by ten hunters or soldiers who then attached themselves to
the leader of their choice. All decisions about the hunt, including the marches,
the choice of camping sites and the regulations governing camp life, were
decided by the president and his council and enforced by his soldiers. This
structure would be adopted by Louis Riel for his provisional government of
1869-70. Quasi-military and orderly though it was, it still produced an aura
of plains wildness. After all, it required a semi-nomadic lifestyle and in its
execution, it reminded the English Canadian settlers of nothing so much
as the much-feared and lightning-swift raiding parties of the plains tribes,
particularly the fearsome Dakota, called by many, the "Sioux" (a word that
meant "snakes" in the Algonquian language).

When the bison herds were sighted, the hunters would sneak up on their prey from a position upwind. Each, mounted on his best horse, would carry his gun slung across the steed's neck, powder loose in his pocket and his mouth full of balls. Once in position, at a signal from the captain, the riders charged in a line.

> As the buffalo turned to run, each picked his animal, usually a young cow, and rode alongside. The gun was fired across the horse's neck, aim being taken by the angle. Up to fifty or even a hundred yards, the Red River hunter could bring down his prey, though usually the shot was fired from close range … And so it went in the thunder of the hooves, the snorting and roaring of the herd, in the dust and glare of the summer plains, until each hunter had left behind him a string of kicking beasts … As the hunters trotted back to camp, the women, most of them wives and daughters but some hired for the work, came out with the carts to strip the carcasses of their robes, the fat humps, tongues and other choice bits. The rest was left for the coyotes and the crows. [38]

While the spring hunt was about pemmican, the smaller fall one was to harvest fresh meat and hides for robes. Those who wintered in the colony would bring in what the birds, the neighbours and their own absence had left of the crops they had planted in the spring. Then they would be set for a winter round of masses, horse races, dances and festitivies.

Nor was the buffalo hunt the only cultural and economic difference between Red River's two solitudes – the predominantly French Métis and the English settlers. When the HBC and the NWC amalgamated in 1821, many Métis, out of economic necessity, became free traders and once again found themselves in confrontation with "les anglais" and the HBC monopoly. This tension led to another battle, this time played out in the courtroom rather than on the plains. In 1849, HBC Chief Factor John Ballenden ordered Pierre Guillaume Sayer, the son of a Nor'Wester and a Métis mother, and three others arrested and charged with illegal fur trading with the Americans in violation of the HBC monopoly. The trial was set for May 17th, Ascension Sunday. Jean-Louis Riel, father of Louis, stood on the steps of Saint-Boniface Cathedral that morning and exhorted his fellow parishioners to "come armed and fully prepared to assert your rights." [39]

About 400 Métis did exactly that. Just as the trial started, a delegation led by the senior Riel pushed its way into the room to declare that if the accused were punished, force would be used to free them. Sayer was found guilty, but no penalty was imposed. Charges against the others were dropped. As Riel left the courtroom, legend has it that he uttered a victory cry that would echo throughout the North West. "Le commerce est libre. Vive la liberté!" The HBC monopoly was effectively dead.

Little Louis was only five at the time of the Sayer trial but, as a bright and impressionable child who adored his father, it affected him deeply. The father's courage created a son determined to be a crusader for his people.

2

Louis Riel and the Dream

I
N THE EARLY WINTER OF 2001, CBC-TV News carried an hour-long program on the great "What Ifs" of Canadian history, featuring a studio audience to ask the questions and a panel of history professors to provide the answers. Not for the first time or likely the last, one of the most important, intriguing and imponderable questions from this nation's past was posed, this time, by Will McLellan of Cantley, Québec: "What if Louis Riel had not been hung?" Responding, Jean Claude Robert of l'Université de Québec à Montréal said the evolution of Québec nationalism would have been quite different. Riel's execution created a "rift" in Confederation and while the population influx from Ontario might have been the same, "maybe with better constitutional power for the Métis it could have been different". In other words, more Québécois might have come west, counterbalancing the Ontarians and bringing the dream of a bilingual/bicultural North West shared by Riel and Sir George-Étienne Cartier closer to reality.

Still, perhaps the real question to fathom the Métis leader's impact on Manitoba and Canada is "What if Thomas Scott had not been shot?" The Scott execution was the beginning of a trail of tragedy, for Riel and for Canada. In his masterful, 900-page PhD thesis on the administration of Adams Archibald, Manitoba's first lieutenant-governor, N.E. Allen Ronaghan argues that Riel would have become Manitoba's first premier and entered the history books a Canadian statesman, had it not been for the execution's exploitation by Ontario's Loyal Orange Order, the Canadian Party's "reign of terror" in Fort Garry and Colonel Garnet Wolseley's "army of occupation".

> The Red River Expeditionary Force did not bring law and order to Manitoba. The Ontario Rifles at Fort Garry became an unruly army of occupation, providing protection for the "Canadian" party and a "reign of terror" for the Métis. This army of occupation prevented ... Archibald from succeeding in his policy of conciliation and from establishing responsible government in Manitoba ...

> Far from engaging in civil war, the people of Red River entered Confederation peacefully and, to a remarkable degree, united. Thereafter ... the exceptional efforts of a small, selfish clique undermined the authority of the lieutenant-governor ... and destroyed the harmony of the community. The consequence was not merely a divided Manitoba but a divided Confederation. [1]

George F.G. Stanley, author of the respected biography of the charismatic Riel, writes that the shots that rang out in the yard of Winnipeg's Upper Fort Garry on the cold morning of March 4, 1870 led inevitably to that chill morning of November 16, 1885 when the hangman waited for Louis Riel on the scaffold at the Central Police Barracks in Regina. "By one unfortunate error of judgement – this is what the execution of Scott amounted to – and by one unnecessary deed of bloodshed – for the provisional government was an accomplished fact – Louis Riel set his foot upon the path which led not to glory but to the gibbet." [2] Adds Ronaghan: "Louis Riel, who should have been Archibald's premier, was executed for treason in 1885, after a rebellion that could have been predicted at the time of Archibald's departure from the province." [3]

During the fifteen years and eight months between the two executions, Riel endured the life of an outlaw fugitive, always on the run and facing destitution, a $5,000 bounty on his head placed by Ontario's Liberal premier, Edward Blake. At the same time, he thrice received the singular honour of being elected as their Member of Parliament by the citizens of Provencher,

only to be prevented from taking his seat in the House of Commons on each occasion. Riel was a conscious and deliberate sacrifice to racial and religious bigotry and to the political expediency of successive federal governments, particularly that of Canada's first prime minister, Sir John A. Macdonald. And he knew it.

According to Ronaghan, Riel and the Manitoba Métis emerge as the only honourable and patriotic actors in the drama of Manitoba's entry into Confederation. They formed a provisional government that had the active support of a majority of the parishes and the acquiesence of the rest. That, he says, is "all that can be said of any government that has taken the trouble to win majority support … [N]o account [of the so-called Red River Rebellion] makes sense which does not show the success of the Métis forces and

Provisional Government in keeping the peace and in administering the Settlement's affairs over a ten-month period." [4] Their loyalty to Canada and willingness to provide a military force for the protection of Red River when it was threatened by a Fenian invasion likely prevented a civil war within the colony and the possible loss of the entire North West. Finally, their "making order triumph" with the execution of Scott and exile of the chief agitators of the Canadian Party inaugurated a six-month period of peace in Red River that only ended with the arrival of Wolseley's troops, a peace that would not be restored for another two years.

Yet the sad fate of the Red River Métis was to be dispersed by "terror", have their lands taken and distributed to Ontario farmers and Wolseley's irregulars and their leader forced into exile with a price on his head. "The tragedy of the events of 1869-1872 was that Canada lost the services of a people who were a bridge, both between English and French and between Indian and white." [5]

By the time of the North West Rebellion, the combination of all these pressures and stresses had taken their toll on Riel's psyche as, indeed, they would on anyone's. But Riel's personal fate, sad and terrible though it was, pales when compared to its impact on the new nation, Canada, a nation then colourfully characterized by Macdonald as "still in the gristle … not having hardened into bone". The uneasy binational pact achieved in 1867 between French and English Canada was almost torn asunder. The already entrenched mutual distrust and dislike between Canada's "two founding races" once again burst into open recrimination and antagonism. Canada's "two founding races" resumed their chilly relationship, kept at peace by the immense linguistic, social and cultural chasm separating the "two solitudes". Meanwhile, Canada's great founding Conservative Party saw itself condemned to nearly a century of suspicion in and exclusion from Québec.

Newspaper editorials captured the intensity of French Canadian feeling. On August 15, 1885, at the conclusion of Riel's trial, *Le Courrier de St-Hyacinthe* wrote: "If the sentence is carried out … Riel will have been hanged because he's not English; and because the French-haters of Ontario wanted to see him … dance at the end of a rope." Other newspapers were equally condemnatory. "The people [English Canadians] who demanded Riel's execution were 'those who hate everything which is French Canadian and Catholic.' For such people, 'Riel is only a name. It's the whole French-Canadian and Catholic population that they'd like to see dancing at the end of a rope.'" [6]

But most important of all to Canada's future, from that time forward, the Canadian West was to have far less appeal to French Canadians than to Ontarians and Maritimers, bringing to an end the pan-continental bilingual and bicultural dream of Riel, Cartier and others. Already labouring under the social and economic pressures of distance, remoteness and industrialization, the dream was fragile enough without the powerful deterrent of racial and religious bigotry. Even before the 1869-70 events, the Québec press had been portraying the North West as "wild" and the Métis as savages. Thus, the New Canada, the Canada of the West, would henceforth be an entirely different country with a different, much more American, ethos and outlook than the Old Canada, the original Canada; setting loose the myriad tensions and strains that bedevil the country's political, economic and social cohesion to this day.

Stanley, one of Canada's leading military historians, was head of the History Department at the Royal Military College at Kingston, the man who researched the heraldry for Canada's flag and finally, the lieutenant governor of New Brunswick. He could hardly be described as a champion of outlaws and traitors, a fact that makes his obvious sympathy for Riel all the more compelling. A scholar of undeniable credentials, he bases that sympathy on solid and powerful historical evidence: Riel's provisional government was legitimate under international law and that legitimacy was recognized and acted upon by Macdonald. The bilingual-bicultural provisions of the Manitoba Act of 1870, advanced by Riel's emissaries and accepted by the Macdonald cabinet, stand as proof. The prime minister's speedy betrayal of the Métis leader was an act of political expediency dictated by the Anglo-Protestant passions ignited by the Canadian Party's assiduous exploitation of the Scott affair.

Louis Riel was born October 22, 1844, the first child of Jean-Louis Riel and Julie Lagimodière. All his ancestors were French Canadian save his paternal great-grandmother, who was a Franco-Ojibwe Métisse. The very day of his birth, the baby was taken from his thatched-roof home near where the Seine River joins the Red River, to the cathedral at St. Boniface were he was baptised by Bishop Norbert Provencher.

Jean-Louis Riel was, at various times, either the leader or a prominent member of the ongoing agitation of the Métis against the restrictions of the HBC trade monopoly and the intolerance and bigotry of the English hierarchy of Assiniboia. He may have been the Métis who led the shouts of "Le commerce est libre – Vive la liberté!" when Guillaume Sayer was released after his conviction for illegal trading in furs in May 1849. He also was one of ten men who signed the petition to Sir George Simpson demanding the removal of Adam Thom and the appointment of a bilingual judge. In 1857, he chaired a meeting at which William Kennedy, the mixed-blood son of an HBC chief factor, spoke in favour of annexation to Canada. And in 1861, he protested the anti-Catholic bias of the *Nor'Wester* newspaper, then owned by William Coldwell and William Buckingham, shrill opponents of the HBC and the Council of Assiniboia. On one occasion, the paper referred to the Métis as "indolent and careless" and said they must "fall back before the march of a superior intelligence". [7]

Jean-Louis Riel's advocacy for his people earned him the enmity of Eden Colvile, the Governor of Assiniboia. Colvile destested him and, labelling him a dangerous radical, ensured that he was denied all government appointments. The young Louis worshipped his father and undoubtedly learned from him to take pride in his race and religion and to suffer humiliation and anger when that pride was disdained and ridiculed by others. Journalist and biographer Maggie Siggins writes: "Louis was a handsome child with a mop of thick brownish-auburn hair and huge saucer eyes which were nearly always serious. He was quiet and introspective, almost too thoughtful, too caring, for his age." [8]

As a boy, Riel was closest to and even more influenced by his deeply religious mother, Julie, the daughter of Jean-Baptiste Lagimodière and Marie-Anne Gaboury, the first white woman in the North West. As a child, Julie had experienced visions and at one time planned to become a nun. She transmitted her strong faith to her first-born. Louis' first words were reported to have been "Jesus, Mary and Joseph". In a letter later in life to Bishop Alexandre-Antonin Taché, he spoke of the centrality of his parents' devout Catholicism to his formative years.

> The first time I received the Holy Eucharist I was trembling,
> but, with the respect that I felt for my adorations, I also felt
> feelings of love rise in my heart. The priest had opened to
> me the road of my aspirations towards God ... My first
> years were perfumed with the sweetest scents of the faith for
> my beloved father would permit no one to speak evil in my
> presence. Family prayers, the rosary were always in my eyes
> and ears ... The calm reflective features of my mother, her

eyes constantly turned towards heaven, her respect, her
attention, her devotion to her religious obligations always
left upon me the deepest impression of her good example. [9]

Louis began his formal education at age seven, initially attending
the girls' school run by the Grey Nuns. Bishop Taché, recognizing that Métis
sons were not being educated "because the Métis do not like to be governed
by women", [10] prevailed on the Christian Brothers to come west to begin a
boys' school and gave them a room in his own house. Louis moved to the
brothers' establishment, but the classroom made available by the bishop was
so small the teacher had to go into an adjoining room if he wanted to sit
down. Taché kept a close watch on the little pupils because he was interested
in training local and particularly Métis boys as priests. Louis was an excellent
student and, on June 1, 1858, he and three other boys were sent east to attend
le Collège de Montréal, founded a century earlier by the Sulpician Fathers.

The trip west took five weeks. The children travelled by oxcart to
St. Paul where they boarded a Mississippi River steamboat to Prairie du
Chien. The rest of their journey was by train, through Chicago and Detroit
into Canada. In Hamilton, they ate their first oranges and gorged themselves
to the point of becoming sick. The trip was singular for another reason. At
Red Lake River, Louis met his father who was returning from Montréal with
machinery for his textile mill, a mill that was never to be built because of
financial difficulties. It was to be the last time father and son would see each

WALTER BAKER / NATIONAL ARCHIVES OF CANADA / C-106728

**The Sulpician Seminary
in Montreal**

other because Jean-Louis died in 1864 at Red River, four years before his son's return to the colony.

Life in the Sulpician college was cloistered, spartan and strict. The eight-year course followed classical French training: Latin, syntax, method, versification, belles-lettres, rhetoric and philosophy. The subjects included religion, Latin, Greek, French, English, mathematics, philosophy and the elements of physics, chemistry astronomy and botany. Initially, Louis placed in the bottom half of his class, still an achievement considering the hardscrabble education available in the crowded little room in Bishop Taché's house. However, by his third year and for the remainder of his time at the college, he led the class or was very close to the top. He was popular with his classmates but, as Stanley writes:

> there were other traits in Riel's character that did not win
> such outspoken praise: his pride, his quick temper, his incli-
> nation towards broodiness. He was too ready to argue with
> his teachers whenever he thought their orders unreasonable
> or arbitrary. Moreover, in arguments with his schoolfellows,
> he was not prepared to brook their contradictions. [11]

His father's death, in February 1864, changed everything. The young Louis went into a deep depression and began missing classes and disobeying other rules. In March 1865, four months before the end of his course of studies, Louis and the college came to a mutually agreed-upon parting of the ways. The college's director, M. Lenoir-Rolland, wrote a letter to Bishop Taché that, in light of future events, was both poignant and prophetic:

> … [W]e have no regret for having given him his education.
> It is true that we would have been happier if we had been
> able to return to you, in his person, a good missionary. But
> God does not seem to have called him to that estate. I am
> very much afraid that the poor boy was not worthy of it. In
> any case, it is a thousand times better that he should be an
> ordinary Christian than become a bad priest. [12]

Louis remained in Montréal for another year, living with his aunt, Mrs. John Lee. During this time he became interested in politics and involved himself in the rising ferment in Québec over the talk of Confederation. The romantic in him sympathized with the anti-confederates, les rouges, but it was the idea of a Métis, not a French-Canadian, republic that appealed to him. In any event, his strong religious faith kept him from embracing *les rouges*, because they were the anti-clerical party. He had been present when Canada's future first deputy prime minister, George-Étienne Cartier, came to the college in 1860 and the choir sang the patriotic song the French Canadian statesman had composed, *O Canada, mon pays, mes amours*. On two occasions, in 1864 right after his father's death and again in 1865, Riel unsuccessfully sought interviews with Cartier. At one point, he wrote several verses to Cartier praising his stand and urging him to "work for us who are your brothers, crush every obstacle before you, defeat your enemies and their noxious schemes, close your ears to the vulgar spite of those who are carried away by their own foolish ideas". [13]

Ironically, the young Riel finally found his first job as a law clerk in the office of Cartier's great opponent, the nationalist and anti-clerical Rodolphe LaFlamme, a staunch opponent of Confederation. But Riel was indifferent to the law and had fallen in love. On June 12, 1866, Riel and Marie Julie Guernon, the daughter of neighbours to the Lees, secretly concluded a marriage contract before a notary but without telling her parents. When the banns of marriage were published, Marie's parents objected so fiercely because of his Métis background that the match was broken off. Hurt and angry, Riel left Montréal, travelling first to Chicago, where he took up residence with the Canadian poet, Louis Fréchette, author of some vicious tracts against English Canada. There, Riel practised his own writing talent, composing poetry in the romantic and florid style of Alphonse de Lamartine. But it wasn't a living, so he gradually worked his way west, arriving in Red River on July 28, 1868, a decade and a month after he had left. As Stanley writes: "Louis Riel was home again. But he was not wearing a soutane. He was almost twenty-four years of age, educated, clever, imbued with a strong sense of pride in himself and his own people and unemployed. It was an explosive mixture." [14]

Confederation the year before had brought some major changes to Red River. To its traditional linguistic, racial and religious factions had now been added political ones. Moreover, south of the border, the Civil War was over and Americans were once again free to pursue their dream of Manifest Destiny. In 1867, United States Secretary of State William Seward told a Boston audience: "I know that Nature designs that this whole continent, not merely these thirty-six states, shall be sooner or later, within the magic circle of the American union." [15] The nature of Red River's economy and trade lent force to the United States's dreams of annexation, especially for those involved in the fur trade and the buffalo hunt, for the paths of both now trekked south.

Countering the American siren song were a new and sizeable number of Canadian emigrés, largely from Ontario, who were equally determined to make Red River a part of Canada, although in what form they never made clear. This prompted Métis suspicions that Red River would become a mere colony of Ontario and they would be left to drown in an English Protestant sea. The unofficial leader of these Canadians was Dr. John Christian Schultz, an imposing figure who had come to the colony in 1861. It was said of him that "fate had manufactured a scoundrel out of material meant by nature for a gentleman". [16] As an Orangeman and a Mason, Schultz was certain to come into conflict with the French-speaking and Roman Catholic Métis, whom he considered a lesser race. He had no desire to see Red River continue either as "a half-breed community" or as a colony under the thumb of the Hudson's Bay Company.

Schultz had his admirers, but also his detractors. Many considered him unscrupulous and ruthless. In 1864, he obtained a podium for his views by purchasing the *Nor'Wester* newspaper, whose editor was James Ross, the mixed-blood son of Assiniboia's sheriff and historian, Alexander Ross.

Ross, soon to be the unofficial leader of the English-speaking mixed-bloods, was already emerging as Louis Riel's great rival. The jealousy had actually begun with Jean-Louis Riel in the early 1860s. Ross used his editorship to agitate ceaselessly against HBC rule. He campaigned for an elected council and proposed either Crown colony status or perhaps even annexation. In November 1862, the elder Riel appeared at a public meeting in the parish of St. James to declare: "Mr. Ross is a deceiver and a misleader of the people for he says that dissatisfaction with the Company's rule is universal, whereas the truth is among my people there is no such dissatisfaction." [17] In 1868, Schultz sold his interest in the paper to Dr. Walter Bown, a dentist, who would become his private secretary when Schultz was appointed lieutenant governor of Manitoba some twenty years later.

In his seventeen-page biography of Louis Riel in the *Dictionary of Canadian Biography,* historian Lewis Thomas says that what Riel found at Red River upon his return in July 1868 was "an Anglo-Protestant Ontario community hostile to Roman Catholicism and the social and economic values of the Métis." [18]

Soon after Riel's arrival, the colony learned that to counter the annexationist aims of the Minnesotans, Prime Minister Sir John A. Macdonald was negotiating with the Hudson's Bay Company for the transfer of Rupert's Land to Canada. Neither the people of Red River nor their political representatives, the councillors of Assiniboia, were informed, let alone consulted about the negotiations. Further agitating the local population was the Canadian government's decision to build a road from Upper Fort Garry to Lake of the Woods. Ostensibly begun to provide relief to the colony after the devastating grasshopper plague of 1867-68, the road was, in fact, part of the government's annexation plans and the people suspected as much.

The construction of the Dawson Road, named after its engineer, Simon James Dawson, was bad enough. But making matters worse as far as the Métis were concerned was its personnel. The survey party assembled in

GRIP/ TORONTO / GREAT CANADIAN POLITICAL CARTOONS: 1820–1914

Justice still unsatisfied.

the settlement by John Allan Snow, head of the project, and Charles Mair, its paymaster, had no French-speaking members. And Mair, a friend of Macdonald's minister of public works, William McDougall, had been one of the founders of the Canada First party. Dedicated to instilling patriotism in the population of the new country, the Canada Firsters also had a dark side. Imperialist, the party was committed to spreading "superior" Anglo-Saxon values and stamping out the influence of all values that were French-speaking and Roman Catholic. According to Maggie Siggins, the Canada Firsters considered Aboriginal people "so inferior in the human hierarchy that they were simply not acknowledged". [19]

Mair wrote poetry. In fact, just before his arrival in Red River he had published a volume of verse, *Dreamland and Other Poems*, that earned wide critical acclaim. Newspapers accorded him the title of The Canadian Poet. Initially, Mair was lionized by Red River society and was invited to the homes of, among others, the free trader and postmaster A.G.N. Bannatyne, whose wife, Annie, the daughter of Andrew McDermott, was mixed-blood. But while Mair was enjoying the hospitality of the Bannatynes and other members of the colony's establishment, he was sneering at them in letters home to his brother, some of which were published in the Perth *Courier* and later picked up by the Toronto *Globe*.

> I received hospitalities to my heart's content and I left the place thoroughly pleased with most that I had met. There are jealousies and heart-burnings, however. Many wealthy people are married to half-breed women, who, having no coat of arms but a "totem" to look back to, make up for the deficiency by biting at the backs of their "white" sisters. The white sisters fall back upon their whiteness, whilst the husbands meet each other with desperate courtesies and hospitalities, with a view to filthy lucre in the background. [20]

Mair's bigotted opinions quickly made their way back to Red River. Annie Bannatyne, educated by the Grey Nuns and accustomed to considering herself one of Red River's leading citizens, decided on revenge. She found out when Mair went to the local post office to retrieve his mail and met him there one Saturday afternoon. According to Siggins, with the place packed with onlookers, Annie "grabbed him by the nose and, pulling a large horsewhip from under her shawl, she smacked him five or six good ones. 'There,' she scolded him, 'you see how the women of Red River treat those who insult them.'" [21] Within the hour, the entire settlement had heard of Annie's humiliation of Mair. Relations between the Canadians and the Métis as well as the English mixed-bloods were strained further. Riel penned a little piece of doggerel to celebrate Annie's spunk:

> Let us proceed to wring the nose of the dog-fish
> Down there!!!
> It is a lady who shows us
> It is a lady who shows us
> How we should treat them
> Down there!!! [22]

In a more serious vein, Riel wrote a letter to the editor of the Montréal newspaper, *Le Nouveau Monde*, to counter another of Mair's letters published in the *Globe*, in which he attacked the Métis for their unwillingness to farm and their devotion to the buffalo hunt. "The half-breeds are the only people here who are starving," Mair had written. "Five thousand of them have to be fed this winter and it is their own fault, they won't farm." [23] Replied Riel: "I am a half-breed myself and I say there is nothing falser than those words. I know almost all the names of those who received help this winter, and I can assure you that they were of all colours. There are some half-breeds who do not ask for charity, as there are some English, some Germans and some Scots, who receive it every week." Riel went on to attack Mair and others for "mocking the distress of our country" by making those driven by hunger to work "dirt cheap" on the Dawson Road. Later, Riel accused Mair and the entire Snow party of intending to "chase us from our homeland. They assume that after fifty years of civilization, our society has borne no fruit." [24]

Then, in March 1869, Canada and the HBC reached an agreement. The company would receive 300,000 pounds sterling for Rupert's Land, no restrictions on its trading rights, one-twentieth of all township lands opened for settlement and retain 45,000 acres (18,200 hectares) around its trading posts. The transfer was to take place December 31, 1869.

Not until the end of April did the people of Red River learn of the deal and then it was through an announcement that appeared in the *Nor'Wester*. No one, whether lowly bureaucrat or senior official, from the British Crown through the Canadian government to the Hudson's Bay Company, thought it necessary to inform, let alone consult, them. Little wonder Bishop Taché was incensed: "The people cannot tolerate the idea of having been sold." [25]

Even more frightening for the Métis was the form of government planned for Red River and Rupert's Land – a lieutenant-governor with an appointed council. They realized they could easily be excluded from the levers of power and their fears were compounded when it was learned that the new lieutenant governor was to be none other than William McDougall, the public works minister who had sent the Snow party to Red River. Macdonald had been anxious to get rid of the former Liberal, one of the leaders of the Clear Grits who had defected to the Conservatives in 1867. A morose and arrogant Ontarian, McDougall, also known as "Wandering Willie" because of his habit of changing his mind on matters political, was an Orangeman from North Lanark and a close friend of Mair and the Canada Firsters. He had once suggested that annexation to the United States would be one way to curb French power.

In July, McDougall ordered a survey of the settlement, although William Mactavish, the governor of Assiniboia, warned that it was premature and unwise. "As soon as the survey commences the Half breeds and Indians will at once come forward and assert their right to the land and possibly stop the work until their claim is satisfied," he said. [26] Robert Machray, the Anglican bishop of Rupert's Land, and Bishop Taché also warned the government, but the prime minister ignored them all.

As tensions mounted, the Métis began to look for a leader. In late August, Riel declared the survey a menace from the steps of Saint-Boniface Cathedral and on October 11th, he and a group of about eighteen Métis stopped the survey party in its tracks by standing on the surveyor's chain measuring André Nault's "hay privilege", the land extending behind his homestead just south of Fort Garry. Nault was Riel's cousin. Riel biographer and former Manitoba archivist Hartwell Bowsfield points out that the Métis had every reason to be concerned that the Canadians not only threatened their way of life, their language and their religion, but also their very presence on the land because their system of land ownership was customary rather than the formal, deeded property rights of British law.

The defiance at Nault's farm made Riel a hero. It was the first act of resistance to Canada's acquisition of the North West. A week later, the Métis formed the National Committee with John Bruce as president and Riel as secretary. L'abbé Noel-Joseph Ritchot became its advisor on matters

both spiritual and temporal. On October 21st, the committee built a
barricade on the road south of Fort Garry upon the news that McDougall
was on his way with cases of rifles and ammunition. Then it sent a missive
to the new governor, who was approaching Pembina: "The National Committee
of the Métis of Red River orders William McDougall not to enter the Territory
of the North West without special permission of the above-mentioned committee." It was signed "Louis Riel, Secretary."[27] This was the second act of
resistance to Canada.

Riel was summoned to appear at the Council of Assiniboia, still the
legal government of Red River, on October 25th to explain himself. The council
called the Métis actions "outrageous" and tried to assure Riel that Métis rights
were not in danger. It also warned Riel that the committee's actions were
"criminal" and might have "distastrous consequences". But Riel was adamant.
He said the Métis were satisfied with the HBC government and wanted no
other. In particular, Riel continued, they objected to the imposition of any
new government without their consent and they "would never admit any
Governor no matter by whom he might be appointed", unless delegates
were sent first with whom they might negotiate terms and conditions. Riel
explained the Métis were resisting the transfer of the country because they
feared mass immigration would crowd them out of their own country. He
insisted they were not breaking the law but instead defending the liberty of
all. He expressed the hope that the English-speaking colonists would join
the Métis in securing what he called their "common rights".[28] Riel possessed
Red River's only armed force – the buffalo hunters. So the council, fearing
civil war if it attempted to raise an opposing one, also sent a messenger
to McDougall advising him to remain at the border outside HBC territory.
It was the last time the council was to meet.

On November 2nd, two momentous events took place. An armed
Métis patrol commanded by Ambroise-Dydime Lépine met McDougall just
inside the Canadian border at Pembina Post near today's West Lynne,
Manitoba, and ordered him to leave the country. McDougall produced his
commission as governor to no avail. When he asked Lépine who had sent
the order signed by Riel, the Métis used the language of the buffalo hunt to
reply: "The government." Witnesses reported McDougall used language that
was contemptuous, insulting and racist. But he had no choice but to go back
across the border. As he did so, he heard Lépine say: "You must not return
beyond this line." Meanwhile, a member of McDougall's party, Captain D.R.

Cameron, son-in-law of Sir Charles Tupper and the man charged with setting up a police force in the new Canadian colony of Red River, had driven his buggy as far north as the barrier at St. Norbert in the company of J.A.N. Provencher, the nephew of the former bishop. Cameron, a stiff-backed military man, imperiously ordered the Métis guards to "Remove that blasted fence". When that didn't happen, he whipped his high-spirited team, attempting to force his way past. But the guards grabbed the horses' bridles. The guards treated Cameron politely and even gave him "a bumper glass of whisky" to settle him down, [29] but then he and Provencher were escorted back to the border by the horsemen.

While this was happening, Riel, accompanied by about 400 men recruited from the recently-returned fur brigades, walked quietly through the unguarded gates of Upper Fort Garry and took possession without firing a single shot. Challenged by Chief Factor Cowan, Riel said he was there to protect the fort. Here, as in his previous actions, Riel was proving to be no rebel. At no point had he committed any acts of rebellion against the Crown and on several occasions he scrupulously turned aside the temptations offered by the French-speaking American consul at Red River, Oscar Malmros. One was a promise or more accurately, a bribe, of $25,000 from the United States government. At all times, Riel displayed his belief that he and the Métis were loyal subjects of Queen Victoria, obliged to defend their rights against those who would unlawfully take them away. Even his order to McDougall did not prohibit the governor from ever entering Red River, but made his entry conditional upon negotiation between the colony and Canada. "He would not refuse outright to enter confederation, but he would do so only on terms that would be satisfactory to the little colony with which he had so completely identified himself." [30]

Nor did Riel consider himself to be acting solely in the interests of the Métis. He quickly appreciated that he needed the support of as many members of the colony as possible to legitimize his demand for negotiations with Canada. He believed quite rightly that he would have a far more compelling argument in Ottawa if he could demonstrate that both the English-speaking and the French-speaking people of Red River were united concerning the transfer of their country to Canada. And he did not want the entire burden of political resistance to be borne by the Métis. On November 6th, Riel issued the following proclamation:

The President and Representatives of the French-speaking population of Rupert's Land in Council (the Invaders of our rights being now expelled) already aware of your sympathy, do extend the hand of friendship to you, our friendly fellow inhabitants; and in so doing invite you to send twelve Representatives from the following places [and here were the names of eleven parishes, with two representatives being alloted to the 'town of Winnipeg'] in order to form one body with the above Council consisting of twelve members, to consider the present political state of this Country, and to adopt such measures as may be deemed best for the future welfare of the same. [31]

The English mixed-bloods had thus far been aloof from the grow-ing confrontation, but they were watching events closely. Both they and the Selkirk settlers considered Riel impetuous, and many of his actions, espe-cially the seizure of the fort, uncalled for. However, they had no real objec-tion to meeting. So, the English parishes elected their twelve representatives and sent them to Fort Garry. Unfortunately, Riel hadn't left himself time and was insufficiently prepared both in terms of an agenda and the rules of parliamentary procedure. Though the meeting convened on November 16ᵗʰ amid military pomp and circumstance including cannon salvos and the firing of a *feu de joie*, it quickly degenerated into a bitter row between Riel and James Ross. The two language groups split on just about everything. The English disliked Riel's parade of military power. The French considered it only fitting for an important ceremony. The English wanted a new chairman and secretary elected. The French would accept no one other than Bruce and Riel until the two groups forged some measure of agreement on matters of basic policy. The English objected to the barring of McDougall. The French said letting him in would allow the Canadians to take over the government.

The temperature of the meeting rose abruptly as a proclamation drafted by Governor Mactavish, at McDougall's behest, was read. The governor listed "unlawful" acts committed by the Métis and enjoined them to disperse themselves peacefully "before they are irretrievably and hopelessly involved". He concluded by warning them that "you are dealing with a crisis out of which may come incalculable good or immeasurable evil; and with all the weight of my official authority and all the influence of my individual position, let me finally charge you to adopt only such means as are lawful and constitutional, rational and safe." [32] Ross seized on Mactavish's language to proclaim that no further debate was necessary because the Métis were in a state of rebellion. Stung, Riel sprang to his feet.

> If we are rebels, we are rebels against the Company that sold
> us and is ready to hand us over and against Canada that
> wants to buy us. We are not in rebellion against the British
> supremacy which has still not given its approval for the final
> transfer of the country ... Moreover, we are true to our
> native land ... We want the people of Red River to be a free
> people. Let us help one another. We are all brothers and
> relations, says Mr. Ross, and it is true. Let us not separate.
> See what Mr. Mactavish says. He says that out of this meeting
> and its decision may come incalculable good. Let us unite.
> The evil that he fears will not take place. See how he speaks.
> Is it surprising? His children are half-breeds like ourselves. [33]

The Canadian Crucible

Riel's response was astute, playing on the colonists' distrust of
Canadian motives, devotion to the Crown and common mixed-blood heritage. Despite this, the convention adjourned without conclusion, a cleavage
between the two language groups having been opened although the convention continued to meet.

On November 23rd, Riel proposed the formation of a provisional government. This threw the English settlers into confusion. While some wanted
to reject it outright and withdraw from the convention, others realized that
unity was essential if there was to be any chance of getting a hearing from
Canada. A small group led by Dr. James Bird and including A.G.B. Bannatyne
and Alexander Begg, proposed the election of a new executive council with
the power to negotiate with Canada. Riel initially accepted the idea, but an
action by McDougall, still sitting in Pembina, caused him to change his mind.

The official date of the transfer of Assiniboia and Rupert's Land to
Canada was set for December 1st. However, the Canadian government had
heard of the unrest at Red River and Macdonald had decided he wanted
nothing to do with the mess. He would put off the royal proclamation of the
incorporation, leaving it to the HBC and the British Crown to sort out the
colony's affairs. But the prime minister informed McDougall of the delay
by regular post. Schultz's Canadian group, including Snow and Mair, who
had been busy rousing the English-speaking colonists to resist Riel with all
sorts of stories and deliberate misinformation about the supposed real
intentions of the Métis and Ottawa, had also been busy misleading the hapless McDougall, telling him that all the English of Red River needed to rally
to his cause and drive out Riel was to learn of the official transfer of the
colony to Canada.

McDougall had still not received the official documents, but neither
had he received the prime minister's letter announcing the delay. So, on the
bitterly cold evening of December 1st, he, six assistants and two hunting dogs
piled into sleighs and drove across the border to the abandoned HBC post.
There, McDougall got out, handed a flag to an aide, fumbled with his over-
coat to extract a parchment page – not the real proclamation, but one he had
drafted himself at the encouragement of the Canadians – and read it into the
teeth of the icy gale. Then, in the words of American writer Joseph Kinsey
Howard, the putative governor and his men "scrambled back into the car-
riages … Before they were back in Pembina the wind and snow had effaced
their tracks in Rupert's Land." (34)

The Canadian Party had had copies of the spurious proclamation made in advance and ensured their wide dissemination throughout the colony beginning November 23rd, the day Riel proposed his provisional government. Indeed, Schultz had plastered the front door of his home with them and a *Nor'Wester* extra was published. When news finally came that McDougall had actually issued it, Riel believed the English side would now abandon the Bird-Bannatyne compromise. So he withdrew his support for it. That same day, December 1st, the convention reconvened. Riel didn't know whether McDougall's proclamation was legitimate or not, but, in yet another attempt to placate the English, told Ross that the colony's chances might actually be better if McDougall really had become governor. "He has no more to do than prove to us his desire to treat us well. If he guarantees our rights, I am one of those who will go to meet him in order to escort him as far as the seat of his government." [35] Ross then asked Riel to outline his demands for McDougall. Riel and his group withdrew to prepare the first of what would eventually become four lists of rights, rights that would go on to be the Manitoba Act.

The list had fourteen points, including an elected legislature with the power to override the executive by a two-thirds vote, the official status of the French and English languages in the legislature and courts, a bilingual chief justice, full representation in the Canadian parliament, treaties to be concluded and ratified between Canada and the Aboriginal people, a rail connection for Winnipeg, the appropriation of public lands for the building of schools, roads, bridges and public buildings, free homesteads and the payment by Canada of all the expenses of public administration for four years.

Not even Ross could quibble with the reasonableness of the list. But trouble quickly brewed over the nettlesome issue of McDougall. The English wanted him immediately admitted into the colony. Riel was insistent that he not be allowed entry until he granted the demands or promised to secure Ottawa's consent for them. The convention foundered. Furious, Riel told the departing English: "Go ... Give this example to your children. But watch us act. We are going ahead to work and obtain the guarantee of our rights and yours. You will come to share them in the end." [36]

Having succeeded in rupturing the colonists' unity, the Canadians then trained their sights on overthrowing Riel. They began plans to raise a military force composed of surveyors and road men to attack Fort Garry at night. When Riel learned of this, he closed the offices of the *Nor'Wester* newspaper, emptied Winnipeg's stores of all guns and ammunition and mustered

PROVINCIAL ARCHIVES OF MANITOBA / MG3A1–18

his own force to prepare to meet the assault. None, however, came because the Canadians couldn't rally enough men. Nevertheless, Riel decided to put an end to the threat of the Canadians' ceaseless plotting and agitation once and for all. On December 7th, he marched his soldiers to Winnipeg where they surrounded Schultz's house. Schultz and his group were given fifteen minutes to surrender. Then they were led off to the cold cells of Fort Garry.

On December 13th, realizing his own government had left him high and dry and his erstwhile allies were unable to command support, McDougall returned to Ottawa, the enormity of his blunder beginning to dawn on him. He had learned, too late, that while the Hudson's Bay Company had signed the deed of transfer of Rupert's Land to Canada on November 19th, the governor general of Canada had informed the Colonial Office in London on November 26th that "Canada cannot accept transfer unless quiet possession can be given." (37)

McDougall's foolish declaration before receiving the official proclamation and letters of transfer had accomplished one thing. It had delivered the death blow to the Council of Assiniboia. While Canada's refusal to complete the deal with the Hudson's Bay Company didn't give lawful basis to Riel's government, it did leave the provisional government as the only effective administration. No less a person than the prime minister had fearfully divined just such an outcome. In the letter that arrived too late to stave off the impetuous action of his lieutenant-governor designate, Macdonald wrote these momentous words:

> An assumption of the Government by you, of course, puts an end to that of the Hudson's Bay Company's authorities ... There would be, if you were not admitted into the country, no legal Government existing and anarchy must follow. *In such a case ... it is quite open by the law of nations for the inhabitants to form a Government ex necessitate, for the protection of life and property ... and such a government has certain sovereign rights by the jus gentium, which might be very convenient for the United States but exceedingly inconvenient for you.* (author's italics) [38]

Thus, no less a person than John A. Macdonald acknowledged the legitimacy of Riel's actions under international law. Nor would this be the last time he or a member of his ministry gave Riel's administration tacit recognition. Indeed, it could be argued that the prime minister's refusal to accept the land transfer while the local population was in disorder, expecting the British Colonial Office to set things right with them, was a further acknowledgement of the legitimacy of Riel's position. Adding to McDougall's already considerable discomfiture, no doubt, was the receipt of a letter dated December 8th from Macdonald in which the prime minister warned him away from the Canadians in no uncertain terms. The friends and employees of his former department of public works, Schultz, Mair, Snow and others, had been "indiscreet and offensive", Macdonald wrote. "You must bridle those gentlemen or they will be a continual source of disquiet to you." [39]

On the same day the prime minister was penning his missive to McDougall, Riel issued *The Declaration of Independence of the People of Rupert's Land and the North-West,* offering to "enter into such negotiations with the Canadian Government as may be favourable for the good government and prosperity of this people." The ennobling phrases of the United States Declaration of Independence echoed through the young man's prose: "We, the representatives of the people in council assembled in Upper Fort Garry ... mutually pledge ourselves on oath, our lives, our fortunes, and our sacred honour to each other."

On December 10th, Riel, Lépine and W.B. O'Donoghue hoisted a white flag with a fleur de lis, the provisional government's flag, on the big

pole at the centre of the square of Fort Garry as Bannatyne and Governor
Mactavish watched. Mactavish, who had been gravely ill throughout, muttered prophetically: "Oh the fools! The fools!" Seventeen days later, Bruce
resigned and Riel became president of the provisional government. As Stanley
writes, Riel's star was in the ascendant. He had gone from being a discontented
young man with no apparent future to being the head of the colony's only
effective government. While he had removed the threat of civil war, he still
had not constructed a broad-based and firm foundation for his rule.

Now it was Ottawa's turn to try to exploit Riel's inability to forge a
union between the colony's English and French. On December 6th, Macdonald
had sponsored a proclamation by the Canadian governor-general for an
amnesty to all in Red River who would lay down their arms. He appointed a
two-member goodwill mission to the North West composed of l'abbé Jean-
Baptiste Thibault and Colonel Charles-René-Léonidas d'Irumberry de Salaberry.
But more importantly – and ominously for Riel – he also despatched Donald
Smith, later to be Lord Strathcona, president of the Canadian Pacific Railway
and, in November 1885, the same month that Riel would be executed in
Regina, the man who would drive the last spike in that transcontinental ribbon
of steel. Smith, the HBC's chief representative in Canada, had called upon
Macdonald and offered him the cooperation of the company to restore and
maintain order in the colony. Impressed, Macdonald made him a "Special
Commissioner to inquire into and report upon the causes and extent of the
armed obstruction offered at the Red River ... to the peaceful ingress of the
Hon. Wm. McDougall" and to "explain to the inhabitants the principles on
which the Government of Canada intends to govern the country, and to remove
any misapprehensions that may exist on the subject." [40] That was Smith's
written instruction. Two days later, according to Stanley, Smith was approached
privately by the prime minister and given the authority to buy off some of the
Métis leaders with money or jobs. Ironically, Smith's wife, the lovely Isabella
Hardisty, daughter of the chief trader of Labrador, was of mixed blood herself
and had once been married à la façon du pays to a fur trader. Smith, the chief
factor of the HBC's Montreal district, was also an inveterate and accomplished
land speculator. He immediately began using his position in Red River to
amass nearly 10,000 acres of valuable land.

Five years later, Smith told a select committee of Parliament that he
had distributed 500 pounds sterling among the Métis "whose assistance had
been absolutely necessary in my position as Canadian Commissioner in 1869

and 1870". It was money well spent from the federal government's standpoint, as some of the leading Métis did in fact withdraw their support for the provisional government and remain aloof from politics. Bitterest of all for Riel, his cousin Charles Nolin, who had walked out of the provisional government on Christmas Eve, began himself plying Smith's money among the Métis. According to tradition, Smith also tried to bribe Riel directly, but if he did, Riel never alluded to it in any of his writings. Smith left behind this cryptic statement in his report to Joseph Howe, Secretary of State for the Provinces: "On January 6th I saw Riel and soon came to the conclusion that no good could arise from entering into any negotiations with his Council." [41]

Riel quickly came to see that Smith was Macdonald's real emissary and, determined to find out whether he had the authority to negotiate with the people of Red River, placed him under guard and ordered his credentials seized. Smith declared he had left them in Pembina. Richard Hardisty was despatched to retrieve them and Riel offered to send one of his men along. Suspecting Riel's intent, Governor Mactavish ordered three half-breed scouts to intercept Hardisty first. When Riel and Ritchot in turn tried to intercept Mactavish's men, the Métis leader found himself looking down the barrel of a gun. Temporarily outmanoeuvred by Smith, Riel had to accede to his demand to hold a mass meeting of the colonists on January 19, 1870. Smith read out his official documents to the crowd. One, a letter from the governor general to Governor Mactavish, assured the inhabitants of Rupert's Land that "Her Majesty's government has no intention of interfering with, or setting aside, or allow others to interfere with the religions, the rights or franchises hitherto enjoyed or to which they may hereafter prove themselves equal". [42] Another, from Joseph Howe to McDougall on December 7, 1869, ordered him to assure the people of Red River that Canada would respect "all their civil and religious liberties" and that "all their properties, rights and privileges of every kind as enjoyed under the government of the Hudson's Bay Company will be continued"... and that McDougall's government was "merely provisional and temporary". [43]

While the colonists cheered, at least some were well aware that the assurances were vague platitudes lacking any specifics for implementation. The next day, Riel, with the backing of Bannatyne, proposed that twenty representatives each should be chosen by the English and French populations and they should meet on January 25th "with the object of considering the subject of Mr. Smith's commission, and to decide what would be best for the

welfare of the country." The meeting ended in cheers and such was the goodwill all round that on January 22nd, most of Riel's soldiers were sent home.

The ensuing elected convention of forty presented the young politician with some thorny problems. The American annexationists won a seat in
Winnipeg and Charles Nolin, the rallying-point for the anti-Riel Métis, managed
to get three of his candidates elected. Nevertheless, the convention struck a
committee of six – three from each language – to draft a new List of Rights.
Completed on January 29th, it was largely unchanged from the original except
for several new and substantial additions: a steam connection between Red
River and Lake Superior within five years and more specific democratic rights
such as universal male suffrage at age twenty-one, two seats in Parliament
and one in the Senate, recognition of "local customs, usages and privileges …
under the control of the local legislature" and "common" usage of French and
English in the courts and the legislature.

The list was debated for several days and the convention delivered
Riel a setback when it defeated his amendment to have it demand provincial
status immediately and not at Canada's discretion. He also lost on a proposal
to have the agreement made between Canada and Red River, not between
Canada and the HBC. On February 7th, the convention discussed the new list
with Smith, who confirmed what Riel had feared: that he had no power to make
commitments on behalf of Canada. However, Smith did propose the sending
of a delegation to Ottawa, assuring the convention that it would receive "a very
cordial reception". Riel's fundamental objective from the very beginning of the
resistance – direct negotiation between the duly elected representatives of Red
River and the federal government – had finally been achieved. Once again he
extended an olive branch to the English settlers, proposing that both language
groups participate in the provisional government. The English acceded when
Governor Mactavish agreed with Riel's proposal. According to the February
18, 1870 edition of *The New Nation,* the HBC governor, very ill with tuberculosis, "growled from his sick bed, 'form a government, for God's sake, and
restore peace and order in the settlement.'" Thus came the second official recognition of the *de facto,* if not *de jure,* legitimacy of Riel's actions and government.

It is quite probable that Donald Smith assured Riel that, in the opinion
of the Hudson's Bay Company, the provisional government was the only legitimate authority during the "interregnum"; certainly James Wickes Taylor (special
agent of the United States Treasury Secret Service Branch directed to work for
Red River's annexation) had this impression and reported it to his masters. [44]

The six-member committee that had drafted the second list of rights was commissioned to submit a constitution for the provisional government. Its proposals, accepted on February 10th, called for an assembly of twenty-four elected representatives drawn equally from the French and English-speaking parishes. Meanwhile, the General Quarterly Court of Assiniboia would continue to administer the law. Recognizing Riel's now-unassailable position, the committee proposed he be president. The new president, in turn, chose his executive and nominated a three-man delegation to proceed to Ottawa: l'abbé Ritchot representing the Métis; Judge John Black, the English settlers and Alfred Henry Scott, the Americans.

Riel had reached the pinnacle of his hopes and ambitions, and he could afford a gesture of generosity – he promised to release all the prisoners held at Upper Fort Garry. [45] Unfortunately for the aspiring statesman, the three most worrisome of those prisoners, Schultz, Mair and Thomas Scott – the last an impetuous young man who had come west with the Dawson Road crew – had already escaped. All had vowed never to tolerate the fact that "a damned depraved half-breed" had become president. Recognizing that their time to rally the English-speaking populace was running out, if, indeed, they ever had the chance, the threesome was now more than ever determined to foment civil war to overthrow Métis power.

Schultz had headed downstream along the Red River to drum up support in the English parishes and among the Ojibwe at St. Peter's. Scott and Mair had gone to Portage la Prairie, where they raised a force of forty-eight Canadians. Planning to link up with Schultz's party at Kildonan, the "army" left Portage on February 12th. Meanwhile Riel had released the last of the prisoners at Fort Garry on February 15th. When news of the Portage expedition reached Fort Garry, all knew its intention was to overthrow the provisional government and every available man was called in to defend the fort. On February 17th, as the Canadians approached Fort Garry, a small force of some fifty men arrested them and took them to the newly-emptied cells. Schultz, however, escaped and took off through the United States to return to Ontario.

This was the second time the "Canadian" or "Orangist" party had attempted to use force to overthrow him and Riel understandably was now certain it and its stalwarts were at the root of his political woes. Someone had to be punished and punished severely to send a message. Captain Charles Arkoll Boulton, head of the 46th Militia regiment and a member of the road survey crew, who had been pressured to lead the Portage force, was condemned to death. Smith prevailed upon Riel to show mercy and Riel agreed, on condition that Smith lend his voice to persuading the English parishes to elect representatives to the provisional government. Scott, apparently, saw Riel's mercy as a sign of weakness and decided to show his contempt for the Métis by heaping insults and slurs upon his jailers. They were about to give Scott a severe beating when Riel intervened and warned Scott to behave.

Scott was not the obscure and unfortunate young Irishman shot in cold blood for no good reason, as Canadian history books have presented him for almost a century. He was, according to Ronaghan and others, "a key actor" in the activities of the Canadians or Orangists, the perpetrators of the real Red River rebellion, if not outright civil war, given the general support the provisional government enjoyed among the colonists. Who was this bellicose and belligerent individual whose death fractures the Canadian state to this day? An Ulsterman, he was born on Lord Dufferin's estate in Clandeboye, County Down, in 1842. He emigrated to Canada in 1863, settling in Hastings County. His hero was Arthur Wellesley, the "Iron" Duke of Wellington. Scott had caused trouble from the moment he arrived in Red River in 1868. He was fired from the Dawson Road crew after he had been found guilty of assault and had survived doing odd labouring jobs and working as a barkeep in Winnipeg. He became deeply embroiled in the intrigues of the Canadian Party, was a strong supporter of Schultz and was thought to have been the chief player in the plot to assassinate Riel. Stanley writes that added to Scott's sense of racial superiority and contempt for all mixed bloods, was the "narrow bigotry of the Ulster Orangeman." [46]

> He certainly had a deep, almost psychotic hatred of the
> Métis leader, perhaps because Louis did not conform to
> Scott's stereotype of a Half-breed as stupid, dirty and duplic-
> itous. Once, on the streets of Winnipeg, he had accosted
> Riel, hurling racial slurs at him. [47]

After escaping from prison on January 9, 1870 and fleeing to Portage la Prairie, he was one of the most eager members of Boulton's army. He beat Norbert Parisien to death with an axe after the mentally-challenged Parisien, arrested as a spy by the Canadians, had escaped and, terrified that he was being pursued, mistakenly shot and mortally wounded colonist Hugh Sutherland, the son of one of the members of the convention. Ronaghan's account has Scott and a compatriot tying a scarf around Parisien's neck and dragging him behind a horse "as one would drag a toboggan". [48]

Re-incarcerated at Fort Garry on February 17[th,] Scott, who was apparently suffering from diarrhea, kept up an almost constant racket, hurling obscene insults and racist hatred at his captors, threatening them ceaselessly with being hanged. Henry Woodington, another member of Boulton's army, attested to Scott's offensiveness. Scott, he wrote in his diary, "was very violent and abusive in his actions and language, annoying and insulting the guards and even abusing the President. He vowed that if he ever got out he would shoot the President." [49]

Once, Scott and Murdoch McLeod overpowered two of their guards and attempted to foment the other prisoners into rebellion. They were unsuccessful and the Métis guards hauled Scott out into the courtyard and began beating him. Riel stopped them and tried to reason with the young hothead.

> When Riel came in, Scott says, "Where are my papers?" Riel
> answered, "I do not know anything about your papers,
> what sort of papers did you have?" Scott then cursed, "You
> God damn son of a bitch, I will have my papers in spite of
> you." He was awfully mad. Riel answered very quietly,
> "That's no way to speak to a human being, a man like you
> coming from a civilized part of the country should know
> better than use such language, you will all get your papers
> and letters back before you leave here." [50]

Riel's placating of Scott did nothing to lessen the anger of his soldiers, who still regarded their military status as that established by the customs of the buffalo hunt, where the leader serves at the suffrance of his men. The Métis guards thus warned their président that if Scott was not executed, they would shoot the young Orangeman themselves. Riel relayed the warning, but Scott reportedly sneered. "The Métis are a pack of cowards. They will never dare shoot me." Riel tried again to reason with him. "Ask me anything at all for a punishment." But Scott would have none of it. "I want nothing; you are nothing but cowards." [51]

On March 3rd, Thomas Scott was tried for treason in the Fort Garry council chambers, Ambroise Lépine presiding. It was a court empanelled to convict. The other members, all appointed by Riel, were Janvier Ritchot, the man who had put his foot on the surveyor's chain; André Nault and Elzéar Lagimodière, relatives of Riel; Joseph Delorme, Elzéar Goulet and Baptiste

Lépine. The trial was speedy and Riel himself acted as translator for the unilingual Scott. It isn't known whether Scott was able to present witnesses or cross-examine those of the prosecution. Despite evidence of Scott's threats to kill him, Riel pleaded with the military tribunal to show mercy. Still, Ritchot, Nault, Goulet and Delorme voted for the death sentence while Lépine and Lagimodière were opposed.

> Scott's obstinacy persisted even when he was on trial for his life. When Elzéar Lagimodière suggested it would be better to exile Scott, and offered to take Scott to the border, Scott replied: "Take me there if you will. I will be back as soon as you." [52]

All that night and into the morning, prominent members of the English-speaking community including, most notably, Donald Smith, tried to save Scott's life. If Riel could spare the life of Boulton, the commander of the insurrection, they pleaded, he certainly could show mercy to this impetuous young private. But Riel respected the democratic traditions of the buffalo hunt. Under enormous pressure from his Métis guards, Riel determined to proceed with the execution. He may even have feared a mutiny had he tried to stay it.

Smith's intervention was prophetic. The Canadian commissioner appealed to Riel's sense of history. Smith told the young politician that the one great merit of his insurrection to date had been that it had been bloodless except for the Sutherland-Parisien tragic "accident". He implored Riel "not now to stain it, to burden it with what would be considered a horrible crime". But Riel retorted that "we must make Canada respect us". [53] Riel also told several people, including Major Boulton, that he had to take a life to save many future lives because Scott's behaviour indicated he would not stop his violence and agitation against the government.

Riel's own accounts demonstrate that he agonized long and hard over Scott's fate. In a 1874 memoir penned in the third person, Riel writes:

> Scott did not fail to distinguish himself in prison by the violence of his conduct ... On March 1ˢᵗ ... (he) renewed his outrageous conduct and the soldiers made a great outcry demanding that the matter should be left to the military court
>
> All demanded that Scott be taken before a Council of War.

It must not be imagined that Scott was at once delivered to a court-martial. The President of the Provisional Government sought to avoid that extremity by having Scott brought before him. He invited him to consider his position seriously, begging him, so to speak, whatever his convictions, to be silent and remain quiet in prison; so that, said the President, I may have a reason for preventing your being brought before the Council of the Adjutant-General, as the métis soldiers loudly insist …

Riel did all he could to extract from Scott a promise of peaceable conduct: Scott jeered at him and insulted him … [He] scorned everybody, and persisted in his defiant conduct. [54]

At noon on March 4th, Goulet and Nault took the prisoner from his cell to the Fort Garry courtyard. Scott was permitted farewells with the other prisoners and said a short prayer with Reverend George Young. Then a piece of white cloth was tied over his eyes and he was led before the firing squad. His non-stop insults and bravado had now completely evaporated. "This is horrible. This is cold-blooded murder," Scott sobbed as he was pushed down to kneel in the snow. Nault gave the signal and all six executioners fired. Only two or three bullets struck Scott. With a ghastly groan, he sank to the ground in a pool of his own blood. François Guillemette stepped forward and with his revolver put Scott out of his misery with a bullet to the brain.

Riel, who had watched the execution, ordered the crowd to disperse and for Scott's body to be placed in a wooden casket. Young appealed to Riel to allow the young man to be buried in the Presbyterian cemetery, but the president refused, fearful that the grave would become a shrine for Orangemen looking to worship their first Canadian martyr. To this day, Scott's body has never been located. This led to another form of martyrdom for the young firebrand and even more woe for Riel. Rumours, some fantastic, flew for years. Siggins recounts that the favourites among the English-speaking population were that Scott hadn't died before the firing squad but had been buried alive or that Scott's body had been hacked to pieces by the "savage halfbreed". The Métis had their own myths, the most prominent being that Scott was not killed at all, but allowed to escape to the United States, never to be heard from again. The most colourful, and the one that probably comes closest

The Canadian Crucible

to the truth, is that Elzéar Lagimodière and Elzéar Goulet dressed the body in Métis garb, propped it up between them in a sled and drove at midnight to the Red River, where "the fishes soon had a feast". [55]

Thomas Scott's execution has long been regarded as murder, based on the assumption that Riel's provisional government was without legal foundation. The view of Prime Minister Macdonald that citizens who find themselves without constituted authority have the right to set up a government under international law would appear to challenge that assumption. So would the fact that, by the date of the execution, the provisional government had had men under arms for more than 134 days and had dealt with the repeated marches and insurgencies of the Canadian Party without the loss of a single life in the areas under its control. The two deaths at Kildonan were the responsibility of the Canadian party operating from Portage la Prairie. But the penultimate endorsation of the legitimacy of Riel's administration arises from one unimpeachable historical reality: within weeks, Macdonald and his Québec lieutenant, Cartier, would be negotiating Manitoba's entry into Confederation with his provisional government's emissaries, using the terms outlined in that government's List of Rights.

Ronaghan says that while Scott's execution was unfortunate, it has to be seen as Riel and the prime minister himself apparently saw it at the time – nothing more than a *raison d'etat*; the obligation on all governments throughout history for "reason of state" to preserve law and order.

> Uppermost on the minds of Riel and his councillors was the formation of a Provisional Government with the widest possible base to negotiate with Canada … It is impossible to view the available evidence without admiring the restraint with which the only functioning government in the Red River Settlement dealt with problems…[56]

Ronaghan argues persuasively that the Scott execution was in itself unremarkable and only became an issue because of the conspiracies of the Canadian Party aided and abetted by the Loyal Orange Lodges of Ontario. He notes that the Macdonald government decided to send the expeditionary force to Red River on February 11th, almost a month prior to Scott's execution, and not to quell the "rebellion", but to protect the settlement from possible incursions from the United States. It cannot be stressed enough that three months after Scott's death, Macdonald was meeting daily with Riel's emissaries to draft Manitoba's constitution.

Riel's pre-eminent biographer, George Stanley, looks at the execution from the perspective of its overall impact on Canadian history. He says it was Riel's only major mistake to date. But it was to prove fatal.

> The execution of Scott was a political act: and as such, it was a political blunder … The English-speaking parishes were stunned by the news of Scott's death. They would co-operate with the Provisional Government for the sake of the settlement which they all loved; but there could be no warmth, no sincere affection in their co-operation, no real unity of spirit. Riel gained his immediate end; but in the long run he opened a breach between the French and English-speaking elements of the population of Red River which has never been entirely closed. If henceforth there was little love lost between them, it was because there was little love left to lose. Else-where in Canada the Scott affair stripped from the underlying bitterness of race and religion, the veneer of co-operation with which it had been covered by Confederation in 1867. In the years to come, both Scott and Riel ceased to be … human beings with human frailties; they became political symbols … around which men rallied and for which they argued and fought with little knowledge of the real strengths and weak-nesses of the men whose names they bandied to and fro. [57]

Four days after Scott's death, Bishop Taché, who had been attending a conference at the Holy See in Rome, arrived back in the colony with good news. When he had disembarked from his trans-Atlantic ocean voyage in Portland, Maine, he was invited to come to Ottawa by no less a personage than Cartier. Macdonald's Québec lieutenant was by now only too familiar with the affairs transpiring at Red River and quite penitent about Ottawa's many errors of omission and commission. The French Canadian leader gave the bishop a copy of Ottawa's December proclamation of amnesty at Red River, which the latter interpreted to cover all acts, violent or not, that had taken place prior to his return to Red River. Once there again himself, he immediately so informed Riel and Ambroise Lépine. On March 15th, he met with the newly-elected Council of the Provisional Government and read a telegram from Macdonald's secretary of state for the provinces, Joseph Howe,

NATIONAL ARCHIVES OF CANADA / C-69922

PROVINCIAL ARCHIVES OF MANITOBA / N5413

Riel and his government.

saying that the List of Rights was "in the main satisfactory" [58] and that the Red River delegates should come to Ottawa.

On March 22nd, the third list of rights, this one prepared by the executive of the provisional government, was sent to the three delegates. It contained some interesting additions. It specified that the lieutenant governor as well as the chief justice be bilingual and that an amnesty be extended to all members of the provisional government and its servants. Two clauses suffice to demonstrate the pervasive commitment to the new province's duality:

16. That the English and French languages be common in the Legislature, and in the courts, and that all public documents, as well as all Acts of the Legislature, be published in both languages.

17. And whereas the French- and English-speaking people of Assiniboia are so equally divided in numbers, yet so united in their interests, and so connected by commerce, family connections, and other political and social relations, that it has happily been found impossible to bring them

into hostile collision, although repeated attempts have been made by designing strangers, for reasons known to themselves, to bring about so ruinous and disastrous an event.

Then, just before the mission to Ottawa departed, a fourth list was drafted. Like all its predecessors, its Article I established Manitoba as bilingual with linguistic duality and equality guaranteed. To this was added Riel's longstanding demand for entry as a province. Probably bearing the imprimatur of Bishop Taché, it also specified a second chamber like Québec's to protect minorities and Québec's dual system of confessional schools. Historian W.L. Morton says the provisional government's final list of rights was momentous, historically and constitutionally, for Canada:

> (It) would create within one province that union of French and English institutions that had been accepted as between Ontario and Québec, but not within Ontario. Thus, the demand for the status of a province had become one freighted with great significance for the future of the North West and indeed of the whole Dominion. [59]

All in all, the climactic events of 1869-70 had been a stunning accomplishment for a young man of just twenty-five years. Riel had begun concerned only with defending the rights of the Métis. But he had quickly grown and developed as a political thinker and actor. Early on, he grasped the need to legitimize his movement by including the English-speaking people of Red River. Then, he began to see the settlement as a political entity with its own ethos and finally, as a province capable of taking its rightful place within Confederation. As Riel himself put it to the provisional government council at its inaugural meeting on March 9th: "The people generally now have, for the first time in the history of this land, a voice in the direction of public affairs." [60] Democracy had come to the North West.

Riel's will and tenacity established a template for acquisition of a territory and its transition to provincehood no future Canadian government would attempt to change or deny. The transition would have to reflect the democratic will of the residents and be the outcome of open and full negotiation with them. It was Riel who chose the new province's name. He decided to call it Manitoba – "the God who speaks – the speaking God", as the prime minister was to translate it to the House of Commons on May 2nd, not

The Canadian Crucible

Assiniboia, as had originally been planned. He wanted it seen as something new and greater than the old HBC colony. The status of first premier of Manitoba and revered Canadian statesman could have awaited him – but for Thomas Scott and the schemes of the handful of men belonging to that shadowy and elitist organization known as Canada First.

Throughout the fall and early winter, events at Red River had aroused little interest or concern in Canada. Indeed, William McDougall's embarrassments had actually sparked amusement and derision. Even the anti-Tory, anti-French Toronto *Globe* contented itself with blaming McDougall for the resistance. Then, on March 26th, the *Globe* and the Montreal *Herald* published the first detailed accounts of Scott's execution. Edward Blake, the Liberal Party's rising hope from Ontario, demanded an official statement from Macdonald in Parliament. Still, there was no general outburst of racial antagonism. All that would soon change, thanks to the linked activities and ambitions of the Canada First group, Red River's Canadian Party and the Loyal Orange Order.

The Loyal Orange Order was founded in County Armagh in Northern Ireland in 1795. A political-religious society, the order stands for the defence of Protestantism and loyalty to the British monarchy. In Canada's case, that loyalty was extended to the maintenance of Canada's constitutional arrangements with Britain. Orangism spread to most British colonies but nowhere outside Ulster did it find the widespread acceptance it enjoyed in Canada. "There it was comfortably accommodated within the framework of a Protestant, British and Tory society which had refused to join the United States and was in an uneasy association with a French and Catholic province." [61] By 1870 there were more than 900 lodges in Ontario, to be found in all but twenty-five of that province's more than 400 settled townships. Manitoba's first Orange Lodge was reportedly founded in Winnipeg on September 18, 1870, on board the steamship *Jessie McKenney* anchored on one of the rivers, likely the Assiniboine. Initiations were carried out twice a week thereafter and by February 1871, there were at least 110 members. [62] By the spring of 1871, the Canada First group included Schultz, Mair, George Taylor Denison and William Foster of Toronto, Robert Haliburton of Halifax, Joseph McDougall, brother of the putative lieutenant governor and, significantly, George Kingsmill, the editor of the *Toronto Daily Telegraph*. They seized this podium to strike against Roman Catholicism and French power in Canada. The *Telegraph* published a series of inflammatory editorials penned by Foster.

Alexander Mackenzie, the leader of the Official Opposition in Ottawa, took up the cries of "murder" and "treachery" and demanded that there should be no dealings with the "traitors" of Red River. Other English newspapers began to add their voices to the cries for vengeance and retribution.

When Schultz and Mair arrived in Toronto on April 6th, they were met at the railway station by a large crowd that escorted them to their hotel. A meeting had been planned at St. Lawrence Hall to hear their stories but the numbers were so huge that the event was moved to the open area in front of City Hall. According to the *Globe* more than 5,000 people were present for "one of the most enthusiastic meetings in many a day". Toronto Mayor S.B. Harman told the assemblage that the names "of those gallant men who stood up for British supremacy in Red River ... would live in history, and be handed down side by side with those who led the gallant charge at Balaclava to uphold the dignity of Britain ... [T]he same power which had been able to make itself felt at Lucknow and Delhi would be sufficient to put down that miserable creature who attempts to usurp authority at Fort Garry and establish again the supremacy and glory of the British flag." The mayor wound up his speech by asserting that the meeting would demonstrate to the authorities in Ottawa that the people of Toronto were "prepared to uphold British supremacy on this continent".

After an equally inflammatory speech by Schultz recounting the horrors of his imprisonment in Louis Riel's "dungeon", the meeting adopted a series of resolutions, one of which said it would be a "gross injustice to the loyal inhabitants of Red River, humiliating to our national honour and contrary to all British traditions" for the government to receive or treat with the emissaries of "those who have robbed, imprisoned and murdered loyal Canadians whose only fault was zeal for British institutions, whose only crime was devotion to the old flag." [63]

The Canada Firsters then decided to fan out across Ontario to hold demonstrations and foment rage in the heart of Orange territory – Cobourg, Belleville and Prescott. They also sent a delegation to Ottawa but there the reception was chilly. Macdonald's government was concerned about the reaction building in Québec to the racist rhetoric and taunts emanating from Ontario and Riel's Québec friends had influence with Cartier. Each salvo Ontario fired at the Catholic Church and French Canada drew a spirited volley of return fire from Québec against the Orange Order and English Canada. Denison's threat to withdraw support for Macdonald was not enough to budge the prime minister, who not only needed votes in Québec as much as in Ontario but was facing the threat from his Québec lieutenant that he would resign if matters were pushed to extremes.

So the Canada Firsters took matters into their own hands. Foster and Hugh Scott, the brother of the dead man, applied for a warrant from the police magistrate in Toronto for the arrest of Manitoba emissaries l'abbe Ritchot and A.H. Scott for aiding and abetting the "murder" of "loyal subject" Thomas Scott. The warrant was sent to Ottawa's chief of police and Riel's delegates were arrested upon their arrival in the capital. The Canadian authorities retained the services of a lawyer and when the case came before the court, the Crown prosecutor declined to proceed due to lack of evidence.

By now, Judge John Black, the representative of Red River's English colonists, was also in Ottawa. The preliminary meetings with Macdonald and Cartier began. It soon became apparent that, of the three delegates, it would be Ritchot who would carry Riel's dreams and demands forward. Black was a compromiser and Scott preferred the bar at the Russell House to the negotiation table in Cartier's office. On April 26th, Ritchot obtained his central demand – official recognition for the delegation and, by extension, the provisional government that had sent it. The recognition came in the form of a letter from Joseph Howe extending a formal invitation to open negotiations with the prime minister.

That was just the first of Ritchot's victories. In short order, Macdonald conceded provincial status, language equality and confessional schools, but refused to hand over public lands. So Ritchot then demanded three million acres (1,210,000 hectares) be set aside for the mixed-blood population. Macdonald countered with 200,000 acres (80,400 hectares) and they finally settled on 1.4 million acres (567,000 hectares). The bickering and arguing finally got to the prime minister.

> This obdurate priest was enough to drive a man to drink; and on the 28th, Sir John took to the bottle, leaving Cartier to settle whether or not Portage la Prairie should be included within the boundaries of the new province. By May 2nd, sufficient progress had been made for the Manitoba Bill to be introduced into the Commons for first reading. [64]

However, an ominous black cloud continued to hang over the process: the thorny issue of amnesty. Significantly, Sir Clinton Murdoch, the special representative sent by the colonial office in London to watch over developments concerning the tiny new province, verbally assured Ritchot that there was nothing Queen Victoria desired more than the re-establishment of peace and "to pass the sponge" over events at Fort Garry. [65] Macdonald, who by now was dried out and keeping a wary eye on the shrill outbursts in Ontario newspapers against the government's truck with "rebels" and "murderers", wanted Ritchot to be content with the old December 6th proclamation of amnesty for those who would lay down their arms.

When debate on the Manitoba bill began in the Commons on May 2nd, the crafty prime minister had to choose his words carefully. It was a masterful speech, managing to steer his government and the bill between the Scylla of Ontario and the Charybdis of Québec, now both in full cry. The prime minister attempted to downplay the granting of provincial status to what was now being seen in English Canada as a rebel and revolutionary government, claiming the word "territory" was an American usage and "we thought it would be better … (to) not bring a new description into our statute book". Then he continued:.

> It was not, of course, a matter of any serious importance whether the country was called a Province or a Territory. We have Provinces of all sizes, shapes and constitutions, there are very few Colonies with precisely the same constitution in all particulars, so that there could be anything determined by the use of the word. Then the next question discussed was the name of the province. It was thought that was a matter of taste and should be considered with reference to euphony and with reference also as much as possible to the remembrance of the original inhabitants of that vast country. Fortunately, the Indian languages of that section of the country give us a choice of euphonious names and it is considered proper that the province which is to be organized shall be called Manitoba … which is euphonious enough in itself and is an old Indian name, meaning the God who speaks – the speaking God … [66]

Macdonald, having carried his work of consolidating the northern half of the North American continent one significant step further, collapsed in his office on May 5th, suffering from gallstones. He was initially so ill there were fears for his life. He recovered but had to spend the rest of the summer recuperating in Prince Edward Island.

The task of steering the Manitoba bill through Parliament thus fell largely to Cartier. W.L. Morton writes that the debate was generally uninspiring. Alexander Mackenzie, the leader of the Liberal Opposition, didn't oppose the settlement of the North West because his party "had always looked upon that territory as their own". [67] However, he said the government's whole course had been disastrous and "calculated to bring our government and people into disrepute with Imperial statesmen". Had the acquisition of the territory been carried out with good faith, he continued, "that insurrection, with all its consequent troubles, disasters and murder would have been avoided. In consequence of this conduct of the government, they had been threatened with a war of races and nations." He also called "ludicrous" according a "little municipality" of 10,000 square miles (26,000 hectares) and 15,000 people two senators and two MPs, saying it reminded him of "some of the incidents in *Gulliver's Travels*". [68] The Liberal leader questioned the exclusion of the Portage la Prairie settlements, which were Protestant, English and under Canadian influence. Initially, these colonists had wanted to stay out of a Métis-dominated province, but subsequently dropped their resistance. The government agreed to an amendment including them. Earlier, Mackenzie had protested about concessions to "Riel and his gang" to which the prime minister replied that "if [he] wishes to lose that country, he will pursue this course." [69] In the debate on the bill, neither Mackenzie nor any other MP touched on or opposed the provision for confessional schools, the use of the French language or the provision of a legislative council.

Joseph Howe, secretary of state for the provinces, spoke about his trip to Fort Garry, lamenting his inability to speak French. "How was it possible for me to address [the settlers in Winnipeg] intelligibly however anxious I might have been, when in early life I neglected to do what I advise every young man in Canada to do, to speak the French language fluently." The Commons record notes calls of "hear, hear". He found the intelligence of the Red River inhabitants "remarkable" and said he disliked the term "half breed", noting that at the time of the Norman Conquest, that was what the English had been called. "Let us not mar the glorious work of founding a province which would one day be an honour to the empire, by any reference to each other's religion," he continued, again to cries of "hear, hear". [70]

Cartier and Adams Archibald were the only other members to

elevate the debate to the level due its import to the nation. Historian W.L. Morton had high praise for Archibald, the Nova Scotian soon to be chosen by Cartier to be Manitoba's first lieutenant-governor, writing this in his 1965 book, *Manitoba, Birth of a Province*:

> Archibald's speech was a plea for the need for reconciliation and the acceptance of the Bill as a deed of partnership between French and English Canadians in the development of the North West. It was a speech of moderating wisdom by a gifted man of much common sense, and the first example of the role the Atlantic provinces had been expected to play in the working of the new Dominion, that of the creative third party. [71]

Noting Red River's relative seclusion from the rest of the country, Archibald said it wasn't surprising the people should fear for their rights "as Britons and freemen" when "they see their country about to be entered by strangers …

> I deplore as much as any man in this House, I can blame with as much severity as any man in this House, the fatal results which have followed, but I can not say I am astonished that under the circumstances in which these men were placed, and with the fears they entertained, just such things should occur as have occurred, and that they should have culminated in the sad event which we all alike deplore and condemn. [72]

Archibald eloquently enunciated his bilingual-bicultural vision for Manitoba and, by extension, the Canadian West:

> … in Manitoba, there is hardly an acre that is not cultivable. It is capable of sustaining a population of millions from the soil alone … It is true the present population does not exceed fifteen to seventeen thousand, but they will not remain long at that figure. One of the first results which will follow the organization of the country, will be a large influx of immigration. Québec will contribute its share, Ontario will do the same, many will come from beyond the water. [73]

He closed with an equally eloquent tribute to the loyalty of French Canadians in general and Riel's Métis in particular:

> In the country at this moment there are no more loyal sub-
> jects of the Crown than our fellow citizens of French
> descent. There are no men more truly British in their feel-
> ings, in their attachment to the Sovereign, in their love of
> British connection than are the French Canadians. And in
> this respect, the half-breeds of French origin in the territory
> reflect the loyalty which they inherit from both races. They
> have no sympathy with republican institutions, and if at this
> moment we have but little fear from Filibusters and Fenians
> in the West, it is due to the fact that the men who are fright-
> ened, unnecessarily frightened, into an aggresssive attitude,
> have no ... regard for the institutions of their Southern
> neighbours. [74]

The deputy prime minister also made it clear that Manitoba, with a constitutional provision for bilingualism and a separate school system mod-elled on Québec's, was to be the template for the creation of new provinces in the Canadian North West. Cartier described Manitoba as the *"key to the whole territory"* (author's italics) and stated the Manitoba Act "disclosed the policy of the government, for it was evident there was room between Ontario and the Rocky Mountains for several provinces and Manitoba was made the model ... for the provinces to be erected to the Pacific Ocean.[75]

> There are beyond its boundaries vast regions out of which
> later may be created provinces, and it is necessary that its
> political machinery should be as perfect as possible ...
> [M]ay the new province always speak to the inhabitants of
> the North West the language of reason, truth and justice. [76]

Cartier's vision was to be fulfilled – temporarily. The North West Territories Act of 1877 did provide for bilingual French and English institu-tions and confessional schools, a measure proposed by Marc-Amable Girard, Manitoba's first premier with real power, who subsequently became the MP for St. Boniface.* Cartier then turned his attention to the events at Red River.

---

* In 1890, the anti-French, anti-Catholic Ontario Conservative MP, D'Alton McCarthy, attempted to have the bilin-gual clause removed from the 1877 North West Territories Act. For the first time since Confederation in 1867, the political controversy split the House of Commons along straight French-English lines. In the end, Prime Minister Sir

While he did not approve of what the colonists had done, he also did not approve of their always being termed rebels and insurgents "for they never pretended that they were opposed to the sovereignty of the Queen". Macdonald's lieutenant agreed that "there was a prospective rebellion against Canada, but as Canadian authority did not exist there, the rebellion did not affect them, except by preventing them from exercising that power which they were to claim under the Act". Parliament, he continued, "ought to drown those difficulties by liberal measures", adding that "the people in the territory were educated and the conference at Red River would contrast favourably with [Canada's] at Québec". He reminded the House that "the original inhabitants of Upper Canada were only 10,000 when the Province was formed; and the settlers now at Red River Territory would contrast favourably with them". [77]

Finally, Cartier defended the land grant of 1.4 million acres to the orphan Métis children. At a time when passions were running high in Ontario over the shooting of Thomas Scott, Macdonald's lieutenant boldly stated the Métis case: "Is it not just, and at the same time wise to aid in the establishment of those who have contributed in such a notable measure to the prosperity of the Red River?" [78]

The bill passed on May 12th by a vote of 120 to eleven; the completion of the transfer from the HBC to the Crown of Canada occurred June 23rd and the Manitoba Act was proclaimed on July 15th. But three vexing questions were still unanswered: the amnesty, the creation of the new provincial

---

John A. Macdonald forged a compromise. The covenants in respect of the French language were restated and reaffirmed, the use of the French language in the territorial courts would continue to be permitted and the territorial ordinances would be printed in both French and English. However, after the next general election, the territorial assembly would have the right to regulate the conduct of its own proceedings, both oral and written, and would have the authority to determine the language of its own records and debates. When Saskatchewan and Alberta were carved out of the territories and made provinces in 1905, official bilingualism was retained in their constitutions, but, unlike Manitoba, not entrenched. With French-speaking populations smaller even than Manitoba's, institutional bilingualism quickly became a dead letter from a lost past, although confessional schools fared better in both provinces than they did in Manitoba. A diluted form of official bilingualism was reaffirmed in 1988 when the Supreme Court, in a six-to-two ruling arising from a 1980 speeding ticket given to Father André Mercure, said citizens had the right to speak French in court and the legislatures and ordered the laws to be printed in both English and French. Because, unlike the Manitoba Act, the bilingual requirement had not been entrenched by an act of the Imperial Parliament, both provinces were left free to repeal it by simple legislation. Both speedily did so.

The Canadian Crucible

J.W. BENGOUGH / GRIP / TORONTO /
GREAT CANADIAN POLITICAL CARTOONS, 1820–1914

**Two official languages are as useless as two tongues
on a North-West cart.**

government and the nature of the military expedition to Red River initially
planned to forestall the threat of a Native rising and/or American intervention. Significantly, the man who would go on to lead that military expedition,
Colonel Garnet Wolseley, was being pressed upon Macdonald by Donald
Smith as the best choice to become Manitoba's new lieutenant governor.
Cartier vetoed the idea, prevailing instead upon a reluctant Archibald. Cartier's
biographer, John Boyd, says it was an astute move. Cartier recognized that
the appointment of a military governor under the circumstances would be
a fatal politial error. Wolseley was furious and attacked Cartier publicly in
England, likening him to the fops satirized in Molière's *Le Bourgeois Gentilhomme*.

The passage of the Manitoba Act made the likelihood of a peaceful
transfer at Red River so great that it was possible for the government to consider
cancelling the expedition, except, of course, for the ever-rising tide of anger
being whipped up by the Orange Lodge and the Canada First group in Ontario.
Although the government knew a punitive expedition would contradict the
purpose of the Manitoba Act, it also knew the potential political price to be
exacted if none was sent. So the government caved in. It was the quintessential
Canadian trade-off at work. Québec obtained a province fashioned in its own
bilingual, bicultural image; Ontario obtained a military action.

The Red River Expedition had three purposes: to reassure the
Aboriginal inhabitants, to make it clear to the Americans that the Imperial
government intended to hold the North West for Canada and to establish
order in Red River. But, writes W.L. Morton:

> ... so fierce was the temper aroused against Riel, so many
> eager English Canadians entered the two battalions of
> militia, one from Ontario, one from Québec, which with
> the 60th Rifles made up the Expedition that the whole
> Expedition, including its commander, Colonel Garnet
> Wolseley, seems to have thought that it had been sent to
> fight and capture Riel. The English belief in the misnamed
> "Red River Rebellion" was already firmly planted. [79]

Ritchot, meanwhile, had returned to Red River, encouraged to believe, by
both the British emissary, Murdoch, and Cartier, that full amnesty would be
granted by Imperial authorities. According to Cartier's biographer, Alastair
Sweeny, Ritchot had finally become convinced of Cartier's position that any
Canadian commitment on amnesty would be either foolish or extra-legal and
that it would be better to maintain silence about it until Ontario had cooled
off or Queen Victoria had made her decision. [80] Ritchot passed these assurances on to Riel, who allowed his Métis to set off on the buffalo hunt and
the boat brigades while he waited unarmed to complete a peaceful transfer.
Ritchot brought other news, which strongly reinforced the first and was even
more explicit evidence of the legitimacy of the provisional government in
the eyes of the Macdonald government.

> At one point in the negotiations, the priest had asked
> Cartier, the acting prime minister ... "Who was to govern
> the country pending the arrival of the lieutenant governor?"
> Cartier had abruptly answered, *"Let Mr. Riel continue to
> maintain order and govern the country, as he has done up to the
> present moment."* (author's italics) Surely that was the recog-
> nition of all that the young Métis leader had accomplished. [81]

But things were unravelling fast. Taché, frightened to hear that
responsibility for the amnesty had now apparently shifted from Ottawa to
London, left for the nation's capital, determined to nail down the thorny
issue, once and for all. Cartier affirmed what Ritchot had said and led the
bishop to believe the amnesty was in the mail. As minister of militia, Cartier
had to go to Camp Niagara to inspect the troops and invited the cleric along
so he could introduce him to the governor general, Sir John Young. But
when the two arrived in Kingston, they were confronted with startling news.

The Canadian Crucible

Mair, Schultz and the others were planning another huge rally in St. Lawrence Hall and inflammatory placards were all over Toronto:

SHALL FRENCH REBELS RULE OUR DOMINION? MEN OF ORANGE, SHALL SCOTT'S BLOOD CRY IN VAIN FOR VENGEANCE! [82]

Ironically, considering all the high-flown rhetoric about insurrection and rebellion, Denison threatened to take over the armoury and said he was ready to fight it out on the streets of Toronto. "A half continent is at stake, and it is a stake worth fighting for," he cried. [83] Among the props Denison was using to whip up the passions of the Orange Ontario crowds packing "indignation meetings" was a piece of rope allegedly used to bind Scott's wrists, a rope he said he would personally deliver to the acting prime minister, Cartier. [84] To avoid embarrasing Cartier, Taché went to Buffalo, bypassing Toronto. When he finally met with the new governor general, the latter was cold to the point of rudeness. What Taché and the others were to learn much later was that Young sided with the Canada Firsters. Attached to a petition to Her Majesty from Canada First opposing any pardon for Riel and the other Métis leaders was a memorandum from the governor general. It advised the Imperial government that an amnesty would be "injudicious, impolitic and dangerous". Scott, he added, had been "led out and murdered in cold blood". [85] Says Sweeny:

> This deliberate misrepresentation by the Queen's Represen-
> tative in Canada was nothing more than an act of treachery
> and betrayal of Young's own duty, of Cartier, one of his chief
> ministers, and of the French Canadians. It was an act of
> irresponsible government, because, in spite of Cartier's
> assurances to Ritchot, an amnesty was not forthcoming
> from the Queen of England. [86]

Sadly, Taché's mission seemed only to accomplish one end – it permanently alienated the cleric from Riel and his family, all of whom concluded he had sold the Métis leader out to the Canadians.

The 1,200-man military expedition, billed as merely a "police force" and "a friendly expedition to ensure the safety of the Red River settlement" turned out to be anything but. Its leader, Wolseley, an Ulsterman with a long career in the British Army in India, Crimea and China, was a typical British imperialist of his age, a man who regarded anyone with Native blood as a "savage". Nevertheless he sent a proclamation to the colony at the start of his march on July 22nd pledging that he would represent no party either in religion or politics and afford equal protection to the lives and property of all races and creeds.

Riel had copies of the proclamation distributed throughout Red River and planned a big celebration to welcome the province's first lieutenant governor, Adams Archibald, the astute and conciliatory Nova Scotian who had spoken of English-French partnership in building the North West during the parliamentary debate on the Manitoba Act. On August 23rd, Taché, still unaware of the governor general's duplicity, arrived back in Red River. He promised that the amnesty was on its way and that it and Archibald would arrive before the troops. Riel, who knew Wolseley's force was already encamped at Lower Fort Garry, was so astonished he didn't even reply. He decided he and his government were in dire peril and made plans to evacuate Fort Garry.

His fears were confirmed the next day when an English settler, James G. Stewart, arrived on horseback, shouting: "For the love of God clear out, the soldiers are only two miles from the city and you are going to be lynched." [87] Riel left his meal on the table and crossed the Red River to Taché's house to confront him. When the bishop, completely unaware of what was happening, asked why he had left the fort, Riel replied that it appeared he had been deceived. "No later than last evening we were told by Your Lordship that there was no fear ... Rather than run the risk of being killed or murdered we prefer to leave the fort ..." [88] Riel turned and walked out while the bishop gazed across the river at Wolseley's soldiers. Before setting out for St. Vital to say goodbye to his mother and brothers and sisters, Riel cast a glance at the celebration going on at the fort and said: "No matter what happens now, the rights of the Métis are assured by the Manitoba Act; that is what I wanted – My mission is finished." [89]

When Wolseley found that Riel had abandoned the fort and fled, he expressed bitter regret:

> It was a sad disappointment to all ranks ... Personally, I was glad that Riel did not come out and surrender, as he at one time said he would, for I could not then have hanged him as I might have done had I taken him prisoner when in arms against his sovereign. [90]

Donald Smith, in his capacity as the representative of the Hudson's

Bay Company, the old order, was installed as the civil government, precluding the necessity for Wolseley to impose martial law. Governance was transferred

Artist's conception of Wolseley and the fleeing Riel at Fort Garry

to Archibald when he arrived nine days later, on September 2nd. The governor's council was constituted on September 17th. Archibald appointed Alfred Boyd, a merchant, as provincial secretary and Marc-Amable Girard as provincial treasurer, pointedly excluding Schultz, whom the new lieutenant governor was determined to isolate and marginalize. The principle of duality was thus established in the first cabinet. A census was held and the boundaries of the twenty-four electoral divisions set down in the Manitoba Act were drawn. Manitoba's first legislature was elected in December.

It is significant to note here that Manitoba's lieutenant governors acted as their own premiers until at least 1874 and a formal party system did not really take hold for almost a decade. However, out of common usage and because certain individuals did dominate legislative debate and government admin-istration, Canada's *Parliamentary Guide* recognizes three as the province's de facto premiers during its first four years: Alexander Boyd, September 16, 1870 to December 14, 1871; Marc-Amable Girard, December 14, 1871 to March 14,

1872 and Henry Joseph (Hynes) Clarke, March 14, 1872 to July 8, 1874.

The first Manitoba election was a crushing defeat for the Canadians and the Orangists and a victory for the moderates and old settlers. Seventeen of the twenty-four members were sympathetic to Riel and two, Louis Schmidt and Thomas Bunn, had been secretaries in the provisional government. Archibald expanded his cabinet by adding to Boyd and Girard two men from Québec, Clarke as attorney general and Thomas Howard as minister without portfolio. Fur trader James McKay was appointed to the Legislative Council so that he could join Archibald's cabinet as the representative of the mixed-blood population. The prickly problem of Schultz was settled by the voters – he was defeated in Winnipeg and St. John, occasioning a riot by members of Wolseley's Ontario militia.

According to the Census of 1871, the new province had 11,963 souls, of whom 5,757 (forty-eight per cent) were Métis; 4083, (thirty-four per cent) mixed-blood; 1,565, (thirteen per cent) European – 747 native-born and 294 Canadian – and 558, (five per cent), Aboriginal. Fifty-two per cent of Manitobans defined themselves as Protestant and forty-eight per cent as Roman Catholic.

Riel, the young man whose emissaries had recently sat in the high offices of the prime minister and the deputy prime minister and negotiated the terms for the new province's entry, whose ideas were embedded in an act recently passed by the Canadian Parliament and were soon to be ratified by the Imperial Parliament in the British North America Act of 1871, was now running for his life. Henceforth, he would live largely as a fugitive and outlaw, an existence punctuated with evidence of the linguistic/religious trauma that scars Canadian life to this day. Driven by political urgency and necessity, as well as expediency and often simple opportunism, the Canadian government dealt and then betrayed, betrayed and then dealt. Ottawa couldn't forgive him because of Ontario. But Ottawa needed him because of Québec.

After a brief stop to see his family on the evening of August 24, 1870, Louis Riel fled to the United States. The journey was marked by one mishap after another. On the first night, his horse and those of his three companions wandered away. The fugitives proceeded on foot. To cross to the west side of the Red River, they ripped apart a rail fence and bound its logs together with strips from their own clothing. In the process, Riel lost a shoe and had to continue barefoot. At home in St. Vital, his mother, Julie Lagimodière, prayed for her son. "My poor boy – my little Louis! He is everything to me; he is my life." [91]

3

The Dream Denied

Sir Stafford Northcote, the new Hudson's Bay Company governor, described the dilemma the difficult and danger-fraught birth of Manitoba posed for the Macdonald government in a perceptive and prescient letter to British Prime Minister Benjamin Disraeli dated April 28, 1870. Manitoba's crisis, he wrote, had inspired "the almost open raising of a national struggle" between French and English, which threatened to undermine Sir John A. Macdonald's government by shattering the prime minister's hold on Ontario and that of his deputy, Sir George-Étienne Cartier, on Québec. Québec, Northcote continued, wanted to neutralize the growing power of Ontario in Confederation "by creating a French Catholic province in the North West", while Ontario, particularly as a result of Thomas Scott's execution, "has been for war and forcible measures from the first". Had Macdonald sought to cancel Colonel Garnet Wolseley's expedition, the governor predicted, the House of Commons would have fractured along racial lines with the English imposing their "large majority" on the French.

> [T]he result would have been either to make a split between
> Macdonald and Cartier, or to destroy the influence of the
> latter with his own party – either of which results must

soon have destroyed the present combination and ... produced
permanent hostility between the two races. The two leaders
have shown great skill and tact in avoiding the catastrophe. [1]

Canada may have avoided catastrophe, but racial and religious
animosities pacified by Confederation were roused. They have never since
been completely laid to rest.

Louis Riel, the ex-president of the provisional government, was to
live the personal consequences of the Canadian dilemma every day. His treatment by the Canadian government was disordered, disconnected and above
all, dishonest. The first few weeks after Riel's flight to St. Paul, Minnesota, was a
period of lawlessness and debauchery in the new province. Wolseley couldn't –
or wouldn't – control either the local civilians bent on revenge or the members
of his militia who had enlisted with no other purpose than to give free rein to
their racial and religious bigotry.

> The Red River Expeditionary Force under Wolseley did not
> establish law and order in the new province of Manitoba.
> The men of the Ontario and Québec regiments of volunteers
> became a badly-behaved army of occupation giving support
> and force to those who, like [Canadian Party leader] J.C.
> Schultz, were deliberately fomenting disorder ... [A] large part
> of the Métis people were cleared from the province by terror. [2]

Elzéar Goulet, a member of the Scott court-martial, was identified and
singled out on the streets of Winnipeg on September 13th. Two soldiers and a
civilian chased him to the banks of the Red River. Goulet, whose brother Roger
had been an HBC magistrate, plunged in and tried to swim to St. Boniface as
his pursuers hurled rocks at his head. One found its mark and he sank beneath
the muddy waters. His body was recovered the next day and although the
culprits were identified, feelings were so high it was decided to take no action.
François Guillemette, whose revolver had administered the *coup de grâce* to
Scott, was killed near Pembina by vengeful Canadians whose identities never
became known. André Nault, another member of the court martial, was beaten
and left for dead. Thomas Spence, the editor of *The New Nation*, the paper
which had been sympathetic to Riel, was assaulted. Father Kavanagh, who had
been very critical of Riel, barely escaped assassination at White Horse Plains.

The new lieutenant governor of Manitoba, Adams Archibald, wrote
to Macdonald on October 9, 1871: "Unfortunately, there is a frightful spirit of

bigotry among a small but noisy section of our people … who really talk and seem to feel as if the French half-breeds should be wiped off the face of the globe …" He went on to say:

> With some (I cannot say how many) of the volunteers who went up, a desire to avenge the murder of Scott was one of the inducements to enlist. Some of them openly stated that they had taken a vow before leaving home to pay off all scores by shooting down any Frenchman that was in any way connected with that event … The great bulk of the French population having been, one way or another, concerned in the troubles, the feeling gradually grew to be one of intense dislike towards the whole race, which was heartily reciprocated by the French. [3]

In time, Riel began moving back and forth across the border himself, always avoiding Winnipeg but frequently visiting St. Boniface and the French parishes. That he could do this was testament to the strong support he continued to enjoy. Very few Manitobans of either language were interested in hanging Riel or any of the Métis leaders.

Not surprisingly, Riel was closely following events in Manitoba. Of particular interest was the first provincial election, which had delivered a stern rebuke to the Canadian Party, including the defeat of its leader, Dr. John Christian Schultz, in Winnipeg. Over half the members of Manitoba's inaugural legislature had been members of the two conventions of 1869-70. Riel also was impressed by the conciliation and even-handedness of the new lieutenant governor, who was quickly demonized by the men of Canada First. George T. Denison, one of the party's Ontario leaders, began describing Archibald as a "tool" of Sir George-Étienne Cartier and the new Manitoba government as the work of Bishop Alexandre-Antonin Taché and the deputy prime minister.

Meanwhile, a threatened Fenian invasion of the new province sparked the first of several occasions the Canadian government turned to Riel for help while continuing to refuse him amnesty and leaving him in continual fear for his liberty and even his life. The Fenians were members of an Irish nationalist secret society founded in 1857 in the United States to secure Irish independence from Britain. It reached its zenith in the immediate aftermath of the American Civil War, when it had raised about $500,000 and recruited some ten thousand Civil War veterans organized in military clubs. The movement split into two factions, one favouring an uprising in Ireland and another, an American invasion of Canada. The invasion planned for Manitoba turned out to be a chimera, but not before it exposed both the awful legacy of the Canada First agitation in Ontario and the decency and honour of Archibald. The Fenians believed the Métis would rise as one to assist in throwing off their oppressors and join the American union. Instead, thanks to Riel's intervention, the scattered Fenian soldiers who managed to elude the United States Cavalry and cross the border found themselves arrested by Métis horsemen.

Riel, of course, was not entirely altruistic. He saw the Fenian threat as an opportunity to prove his loyalty to Canada and place Ottawa under an obligation to him. He and his central committee voted twelve to one to unite their forces with those of the Manitoba government. Archibald subsequently reviewed the 200 Métis troops and thanked and shook hands with their leaders, including Riel himself. When news of this reached Ontario, another round of rage ignited and Archibald's recall from Manitoba was demanded.

> From the day the news of Thomas Scott's execution reached
> Ontario, Manitoba's politics became the business of both
> Ontario and Québec. The agitation that had been directed, if
> not provoked, by Denison and Schultz was never allowed to
> subside and feelings against Riel were not permitted to subside. [4]

Macdonald himself became convinced during the summer and fall of 1871 that the troubles in Manitoba were a result of agitation by Roman Catholic priests unwilling to submit to Canadian authority. Archibald sent Macdonald his letter of resignation in November, but privately warned him that the prime minister's rejection of his conduct showed a complete misunderstanding of the situation in the province. Archibald "spiritedly defended his actions in the speech from the throne at the opening of the Manitoba Legislature in January, 1872." [5] It passed with an overwhelming majority. His resignation wasn't acted upon until October 1872, however, because Macdonald had difficulty finding a replacement.

So long as the agitation continued, the Canadian government wouldn't move on its amnesty. And the agitation was not only continuing, it was becoming deadly. In his doctoral thesis on Archibald, Allen Ronaghan says this period in Manitoba and Canadian history is one of the most famous yet most imperfectly known thanks to the assiduous efforts of that powerful trio, the Loyal Orange Lodge, the Canadian Party and Canada First. The images of Riel as a violent and bloodthirsty "half-breed" and of the events of 1869-70 at Red River as a "rebellion" by "outlaws" had their beginnings in the prolific propaganda churned out by these groups. Thanks to their ready access to the English press of the day, the images were soon accepted as gospel and persisted in Canadian school history texts throughout much of the twentieth century.

Edward Blake, now the Liberal leader in Ontario, tried to force through the legislature a motion demanding that the "murderers" of Scott be brought to justice. Sandfield Macdonald, the Ontario Tory premier, attempted to turn it aside, arguing it was a federal matter. But Blake persisted, proclaiming that the Conservatives were running Manitoba "in the French and rebel interest". [6] Blake's appeals to racism and bigotry paid off at the polls. The Ontario Liberals won the spring election and the new premier proposed another resolution urging the apprehension and punishment of Scott's "murderers", offering a $5,000 reward to any person bringing about their arrest and conviction.

Sir John A. Macdonald was about to have to face the electorate himself and Ontario's political temperature as measured by the Blake thermometer was hardly inviting. The prime minister knew Blake's reward money would tempt someone, sometime, into seizing Riel and bringing him into a courtroom on a murder charge. That would spark an outburst of anger in Québec. Using the good offices of Taché, now an archbishop, Cartier and Macdonald offered to pay Riel to go into temporary voluntary exile.

Macdonald had only been willing to hand over $1,000, even though Taché had pointed out that Riel was the sole support for a family of a widowed mother and seven children. The archbishop had to wheedle and eventually go to Donald Smith to obtain an additional $600. Riel might not have acceded had a group of armed men, perhaps responding to Blake's lure, not forced their way into the Riel home in St. Vital, turned it upside down and threatened his sister, Marie. Riel's mother appealed to the authorities for protection but no arrests were made. The Métis leader's exile was a godsend for Macdonald. He was able to face an angry Ontario electorate with the disclaimer, "Where is Riel? God knows; I wish I could lay my hands on him!" [7]

But it was bitter as gall for Riel. He had formed and headed a government legal under international law, as conceded by the prime minister of Canada; his representatives had been received by and had negotiated with the prime minister and the deputy prime minister of Canada; his ideas had formed the basis of the constitution for Canada's first new province; he had

A CASE OF RIEL DISTRESS!

BENGOUGH, OCT 1873 / PROVINCIAL ARCHIVES OF MANITOBA / N5409

administered the soon-to-be-born province for months with the explicit consent of the deputy prime minister of Canada; he had rallied his people to help the governments of Manitoba and Canada in an emergency. He had long been promised an amnesty. He had an opportunity now to reflect and he wrote to a contemporary: "Lower Canada … is our whole support … it is the land of our fathers". [8] As a final blow, he soon felt no more safe in St. Paul, Minnesota, than at home in Manitoba. He once saw Schultz on the street there and found out the good doctor had offered someone $50 cash and another $1,000 to try to steal Riel's papers. On another occasion, Riel and Ambroise Lépine, who had gone into exile with him, overheard two men discussing what steps they should take to earn the Ontario government's $5,000 bounty. They fled across the state to Breckenridge, on the other side of the Bois de Sioux River from Wahpeton, North Dakota. Eventually, however, Riel returned to St. Paul. "I am uneasy. I place myself in the hands of God," Riel wrote the archbishop. [9] Lépine decided to go back to Manitoba.

Meanwhile, many in the Métis community began to think the unthinkable; that their leader should run for Parliament in the upcoming 1872 elections in the constituency of Provencher. Riel liked the idea. But Henry Clarke, the province's first attorney general, now its de facto premier, urged on by Riel's opponents within the mixed-blood community, decided he would contest the nomination. Clarke worked hard to woo the Métis, but he didn't stand a chance against Riel. Riel and Clarke had two public debates. Although Clarke warned his audiences that Riel would be killed if he ever went to Ottawa and railed that Riel's election would be prejudicial to Manitoba and to "our friends in Ottawa", it was to no avail. His candidacy simply paled when compared to that of Manitoba's former président. Clarke ended up in the ridiculous situation, as provincial attorney general, of challenging a presumed outlaw to a duel. It never happened.

Instead, Riel once again was called upon to sacrifice himself for his country and for the government that couldn't and wouldn't help him. Early in September 1872, Cartier was defeated in Montréal East. In those days, different parts of Canada voted at different times in a general election. Macdonald sent a telegram to Archibald: "Get Sir George elected in your Province – do not, however, allow late Provisional [President] to resign in his favour." [10]

Archibald, who, with Riel, had recently been burned in effigy in Winnipeg at the behest of Schultz, quickly arranged a meeting with Taché. Both men were in complete agreement. Here was the opportunity "to bind Sir George so tightly that he could not help doing even more afterwards than he had done towards the amnesty". [11] Riel was less enthusiastic. Though he was prepared to leave his amnesty to Cartier's good will, he wanted the deputy prime minister to pledge himself to secure the delivery of the promised lands to the Métis. This condition was telegraphed to Macdonald whose reply was dangerously ambiguous. Provencher ought to elect Cartier promptly and without stipulation, comforted by the fact that promises already made couldn't be strengthened by repetition, Macdonald replied. But it was enough for Riel. On nomination day, September 14th, Riel's name was not on the rolls. Cartier was declared elected by acclamation. Riel congratulated the electors for their good judgement and returned to St. Norbert with his supporters in a cavalcade of flags. He and Lépine sent a telegram of congratulation to the deputy prime minister.

While Archibald and Taché felt Riel had now placed Ottawa under deep obligation, the wily and nimble Macdonald saw it differently. To the prime minister, all that had happened was that Riel and Clarke had stepped aside for the good of Manitoba, and to guarantee it a direct voice in the cabinet.

Elsewhere in Manitoba, the election was considerably less peaceful. A rabble-rousing Canadian lawyer by the name of Francis Evans Cornish, later to be mayor of Winnipeg, harangued a crowd on the misdeeds of Archibald and all his French and HBC supporters and urged them to cross the river with him to attack the polling booth in St. Boniface. Donald Smith tried to quiet them and received a barrage of mud and worse for his pains. The rioters then took it out on the two newspapers that favoured the Métis and established authority. The offices and the presses of *The Manitoban* and *Le Métis* were smashed. The crowd tried to run Clarke out of town on a rail and Donald Smith barely escaped a thrashing with axe handles and stones.

Riel went home to await Cartier's gratitude. But the deputy prime minister was deathly ill with Bright's disease or nephritis, well enough only to board ship to England, where he was soon to die of kidney failure. By this time, Archibald had been replaced as lieutenant governor of Manitoba by Alexander Morris. As the MP for Lanark, Morris was a staunch supporter of Macdonald and had made his mark by introducing such liberal reforms as the abolition of public executions and the municipal registration of vital statistics. He left electoral politics due to ill-health and financial problems. At his own request, he had been sent to Manitoba as a judge, being made the first chief justice of the Manitoba Court of Queen's Bench in July 1872. Although not a well man, he agreed to take over the job of lieutenant governor, receiving his appointment on December 2, 1872.

Morris' goal was to create "a peaceful, stable Manitoba based largely on the Ontario model, with an acquiescent and cooperative French population". [12] Over time, however, he acquired a rather jaundiced view of his subjects. Although he achieved responsible government in Manitoba in 1874, lightening his burden of "managing the animals composing his Ministry" [13], Manitoba's second lieutenant governor penned this doleful assessment of the state of political affairs in the new province:

> Was there ever before a responsible ministry resting on a
> House of whose constituents more than half were liable to
> be hanged or sent to penitentiary ... [A]re the electors to
> exercise their functions with ropes around their necks ...

[Y]ou can hardly hope to carry on responsible government
by inflicting death penalties on the leaders of a majority of
the electors. [14]

Almost as soon as Morris took over, an attempt was made to arrest
Riel, but he escaped. Riel and Lépine penned a letter to Morris to summarize
the Métis situation. Morris made no reply but simply forwarded the document to Ottawa. However Ottawa, in the person of Macdonald, was suddenly
too busy to worry about Manitoba and Riel. His government was wading into
the swamp of the Pacific Scandal, the malodorous dealings around the
planned transcontinental railroad, and specifically, the payoffs to the Tory
party and its senior ministers in exchange for the contract to build it.

Riel decided on a pre-emptive strike. Cartier's death had created the
need for a byelection in Provencher. Riel, this time with the backing of
English Manitobans like Winnipeg free trader and merchant A.G.B. Bannatyne
and prominent French Manitobans such as Joseph Royal and Joseph Dubuc,
decided to run. By now, Riel's views of Canada were sharply etched. The only
friends the Métis had were in Québec and French Canada. From Orange and
Protestant Ontario, they could expect only hostility, abuse, submergence and
eventual extinction. Morris telegraphed Macdonald in August warning that
Riel's election was a certainty. Macdonald replied that he "cannot suggest any
way of avoiding evil".

On September 14th, some Canadians met in Cornish's office to discuss how they might collect the Ontario government's reward. They found a
member of Boulton's Portage la Prairie militia from February 18, 1870 and got
him to swear out a warrant for Riel's arrest. By the time they got to St. Vital,
Riel had fled but Lépine was still at home. They found him playing with his
small child and arrested him. He soon would be on trial for his life. Warned
by Bannatyne, Riel went into hiding, taking refuge in the woods at Vermette's
Point across the river from St. Norbert, where he was guarded by friends.
Lépine's arrest and the threat to Riel aroused deep anger among the Métis
population across the province. A large delegation including many prominent
English-speaking citizens met with Morris to urge amnesty. Morris promised
them nothing, but in a letter to Macdonald, wrote: "My sympathies have been
strongly with the mixed population … If the supporters of Riel had remained
quiet, and if they do now, it is a question whether it would not be best to
secure an amnesty." [15]

Riel was declared elected by acclamation on October 13, 1873. He didn't attend his own nomination meeting, wisely, as it turned out, because several armed men came to St. Norbert prepared to arrest him. On October 21ˢᵗ, Riel, accompanied by several bodyguards and using an alias, left St. Vital for the United States border determined to go to Ottawa via Montréal. Once there, he was met by Honoré Mercier, then member of parliament for Rouville.

As the first French Canadian politicial leader to assert that the government of Québec is the national government of the people of that province, Mercier is considered one of the founders of Québec nationalism. His early and ongoing affinity with the Métis leader and the fact that affinity went on to inform his entire political career provides yet more evidence of the powerful reverberations Manitoba and the fate of Riel send through Canadian history. Mercier was to take up Riel's cause as that of French Canada at large and to ride it to huge provincial political success. In 1883, he became leader of the Québec Liberal Party and after Riel's hanging in 1885, he headed a group of Liberals and dissident Conservatives who rejected their parties' positions on the execution. He then took over the leadership of the Parti National, Québec's common front political response to Riel's fate. By keeping alive the sense the

It was the destruction of the rights of French Canadians
that gave birth to Québec nationalism.

Canadian Crucible

execution gave Québécois of being isolated and alone within Confederation, the Parti National won the 1886 provincial election and Mercier was sworn in as premier on January 29, 1887.

But in 1873, with their two so opposite yet intertwined fates far in the future, Mercier kept urging the Manitoban to take his seat in the Commons as he and Riel travelled to Hull. On the appointed day to make his appearance in the House, Riel and his companions only got as far as Parliament Hill. There the Métis leader lost his nerve. Instead, he fled back to Montréal and on to Plattsburg, New York, where he took refuge with the Oblate Fathers.

By now, the Pacific Scandal had driven Macdonald from office and the new prime minister, Liberal Alexander Mackenzie, had called an election. Mackenzie's French-Canadian lieutenant, Antoine Dorion, sent a telegram to the Manitoba lieutenant governor asking him to tell Archbishop Taché that "in order to avoid excitement, Riel should not be a candidate". [16] Morris sent his secretary to the archbishop's house with the telegram. This – and the telegram's contents – were the final straw for the distinguished clergyman. Taché drafted a stinging reply to Dorion:

> The whole Province of Québec ask you to do an act of justice on behalf of men who have been shamefully deceived, and the only answer is to request me to manage so that their leader shall not receive a proof of the respect and confidence of his fellow countrymen. This man is within two or three hours' journey of Montréal, and an eight days' journey from me, and I am to take steps to induce him to hide himself and to continue with his family in misery! What is to be offered to Mr. Riel as a recompense for the sacrifices which he is called upon to make? Misery, exile, or a jail if he returns to his native land … I cannot act unless, I repeat, I have something certain to offer. If you knew all the indignities to which our poor people have been subjected, you would not be annoyed at my experiencing the painful feelings which I do. [17]

Riel let his name stand a third time and although his opponents, with Liberal support, fielded Joseph Hamelin against him, Riel won the riding easily. Riel again went to Hull and tried to get an appointment with Dorion, but the latter refused to see him. Although the government had changed in Ottawa, its attitude to the ex-president of Manitoba's provisional government stayed exactly the same. In fact, Mackenzie had campaigned on an anti-Riel platform, attacking Macdonald for promising an amnesty in the first place.

Still, this time Riel was determined to claim his seat in the Canadian House of Commons. In the company of Romuald Fiset, the member for Rimouski and a former schoolmate, the Métis leader entered a side door of Parliament and walked to the office of the Clerk of the House, Alfred Patrick. Fiset asked Patrick if he would swear in a new member. Patrick did not even bother to inquire the name, noting only that he wore "a heavy whisker, not exactly black". [18] He administered the oath of allegiance and heard the new MP repeat: "I do swear that I will be faithful and bear true allegiance to Her Majesty Queen Victoria." Patrick produced the roll and Riel and Fiset signed. Then they turned to leave. Recounted Patrick later: "I did not pay particular attention and did not look at the roll until they were leaving the room. To my astonishment I saw the name 'Louis Riel'. I looked up suddenly and saw them going out of the door. Riel was making a low bow to me." Patrick, astonished, finally recovered and rushed down the hallway to inform the justice minister that Riel, despite the efforts and plans of his enemies, had not only eluded capture but had entered Parliament and signed the register as the member for Provencher.

The newspapers were onto the story immediately. When the session opened on March 30th, it was largely given over to a pitched battle on the floor of the House between Riel's supporters and opponents. J.O. Mousseau and Rodrigue Masson moved an amnesty motion, which was defeated. The premier of Manitoba, Henry J. Clarke, Riel's bitter enemy from the first nomination, appeared before the House of Commons with the indictment against Riel for murder and declaring him a fugitive from justice. This gave an opening to Mackenzie Bowell, the Orange leader from Ontario, to move that "Louis Riel be ordered to attend the House tomorrow". Joseph Schull, the biographer of Canada's first French-Canadian prime minister, Sir Wilfrid Laurier, sketches the intensity of the political drama afoot:

> Under the baleful power of that name Riel, party allegiances
> were dissolving. Liberals and Conservatives alike were dividing
> and reforming as English and French. To Québec, Riel was
> the duly elected member for the constituency of Provencher
> in Manitoba. To Ontario he was a rebel and indicted murderer

with a warrant out for his arrest. Around that single shabby figure all the resentful frustrations, all the hopes and fears of the seven-year-old Dominion lay ready to meet and clash. [19]

The next day, a huge crowd showed up in the public galleries, including Lady Dufferin, wife of the governor general. Riel, however, did not come to claim his seat in the Commons and it adjourned for a week. During the recess, the French Canadian MPs went into caucus regardless of party to establish solidarity on the amnesty issue. Public meetings were held to express complete sympathy with the Métis leader and the determination of French Canadians everywhere to protect him from arrest.

When Parliament reconvened, a select committee was appointed to look into the causes of the "difficulties" in the North West in 1869 and 1870 and into those which "have retarded" the granting of the amnesty. But Bowell wasn't prepared to wait. He moved that "Louis Riel, having fled from justice and having failed to obey an Order of this House that he should attend in his place, Thursday, the 9th day of April, 1874, be expelled [from] this House". The motion was seconded by Riel's arch-nemesis, John Christian Schultz, now a Manitoba MP. It carried after a bitter debate in which the French Canadian Liberal MPs found themselves caught between their loyalty to party and their loyalty to Riel, whom they now saw as one of their own. In the end, party loyalty won out because the prime minister was emphatic that Scott's death had been a crime against humanity, justice and the law.

By now, Alexander Mackenzie was so vexed by the situation that he wrote Morris in Winnipeg that "it was a mistake" that Manitoba should ever have been made a province. [20] Riel, in ever more fear for his life, went back to St. Paul. Meanwhile, a parade of high-powered witnesses had been giving testimony to the House select committee, including the former prime minister. Macdonald insisted he had never recognized the Red River delegates, never given any undertaking to use the good offices of the federal government to seek an Imperial amnesty and was certain Cartier hadn't either. Despite Macdonald's verbal assertions, Cartier's secretary, Major Futvoye, and Cartier's own letters and memoranda supported the testimony of Archbishop Taché and l'abbé N.J. Ritchot. The archbishop couldn't restrain his anger. "Le Très Honourable John A. Macdonald a menti – excusez le mot – comme ferait un voyou" (The Right Honourable John A. Macdonald lied – excuse the word – like a trooper), he fumed in a letter to an old friend, Monseigneur

LaFlèche, the Bishop of Trois Rivières, formerly a member of the Council of Assiniboia. [21]

The committee met for thirty-seven days and heard twenty-one witnesses. Dramatic personal testimony and an avalanche of letters, documents and diaries made it absolutely clear amnesty had been promised not once but many times. Macdonald tried to wriggle out, insisting he had never officially recognized the Red River delegates so no promise of amnesty was official either. But this wasn't credible.

Newspapers in both Ontario and Québec gave exhaustive coverage to the proceedings of the select committee. Not surprisingly, their slants were quite different. The Québec press printed some of the testimony verbatim. Ontario's newspapers, especially *The Globe*, highlighted evidence showing Macdonald and his colleagues engaged in what the editors considered questionable dealings with priests and "halfbreeds" and downplayed anything that suggested the Red River troubles had some moral justification. The committee included parliamentarians who were both friends and foes of Riel and so deadlocked. Its report was a mere compilation of facts containing no recommendations. It was to be up to Parliament "to consider whether under the circumstances stated, any other steps shall be taken". [22]

In Montréal, a special Manitoba Committee had been formed to assist Riel. It agitated on behalf of the Métis at every opportunity, viewing the cause of the French mixed-bloods and the French Canadians as one and the same. Although André Nault and Elzéar Lagimodière had also been arrested for Thomas Scott's murder and Ambroise Lépine's case on the same charge was still pending, politically, things were looking up for the Métis in Manitoba. Henry J. Clarke's government had been defeated and replaced by a new administration with Marc-Amable Girard as premier and Riel's friend, Joseph Dubuc, as attorney general. Emboldened, Riel determined to once again contest the Provencher seat from which he had been expelled by the House of Commons. He was re-elected by acclamation in September 1874 but did not bother to seek to take his seat in Parliament. According to Stanley:

> Riel was convinced that his re-election was something more
> than just the vindication of his own personal stand. It was
> the symbol of something far more significant; it was the
> answer of French Catholic Canada to Orange Ontario; it
> was the assertion of the principle of equality of the two

races in all Canada. He therefore urged that there should be no more bowing to political threats, no more temporizing with bigotry, no more compromising with fanaticism. If Ontario wanted to battle it out on the field of race and religion, French Canada would accept the challenge and would abandon the meaningless struggles of political parties. All men who spoke French and accepted the Roman Catholic faith would unite to safeguard French influence in Manitoba and the North West. To defend Riel would be to defend French culture and the Catholic Church on the prairies.[23]

Red River had become a touchstone of the traditional rivalries between French and English Canada. The temperature was raised a notch in that simmering cauldron when, in November, Lépine was convicted of Scott's murder and, despite the jury's recommendation of mercy, sentenced to death. Reaction in Québec was immediate and furious. *Le Nouveau Monde* demanded that all Alexander Mackenzie's Québec ministers either secure an amnesty

Macdonald and Mackenzie – "Unanimous for once".

or resign. Other newspapers took up the cry. Adolphe Chapleau, a Québec attorney and Lépine's lead defence lawyer, was greeted as a national hero on his return home. Across the country, petitions poured into the offices of federal cabinet ministers. The archbishop of Québec and six of his bishops added their prayers in addition to those of Taché for a pardon. The Québec legislature passed an unanimous resolution asking the governor general to grant an amnesty to Riel and Lépine.

Mackenzie was, like Macdonald before him, caught in "a cleft stick" [24]. If he granted the amnesty, he would enrage Ontario; if he did not, he would infuriate Québec.

So, just like Macdonald, Mackenzie thrust the responsibility onto the shoulders of the colonial secretary, Lord Carnarvon, and the Imperial Government in London. He stated frankly to the governor general that he did so due to "the obvious embarrassments attending the settlement of a controversy … so seriously complicated by the vehement international antagonism which they have excited in this country". [25] For his part, Dufferin, who had been in Canada long enough to draw his own conclusions about the country and the centrality of its linguistic faultline, recommended commutation of Lépine's death sentence to the colonial secretary. In a long despatch to London, Dufferin made this caustic but correct observation: "This is the most thorny business I have ever had to deal with thanks to the imbecility of almost everyone who has hitherto meddled with it." [26]

The governor general reviewed the whole story of the amnesty. While he did not agree Riel's provisional government had even de facto status, let alone a quasi-legal basis, he was impressed with the Métis loyalty at the time of the Fenian raids. He based his decision to commute the sentence on Lieutenant Governor Adams Archibald's trust of Riel. He doubted, he wrote, that once the representative of the Queen in Manitoba had "put arms in the hands of a subject and … invited him to risk his life with the full knowledge that the individual in question is amenable to the law for crimes previously committed, the executive is any longer in a position to pursue that person thus dealt with, as a felon." [27] Carnarvon agreed but proposed Lépine be stripped of his political rights for life.

In February 1875, Prime Minister Mackenzie finally screwed up his courage and grasped the Manitoba nettle. He introduced a motion to grant a full amnesty to all persons involved in the North West troubles with the exception of Riel, Lépine and W.B. O'Donoghue, the erstwhile Manitoba Fenian leader. These three would gain amnesty "conditional on five years banish-ment from Her Majesty's Dominions." [28] This stand placated Québec some-what, while encouraging Ontario to blame Macdonald and the Conservatives. The prime minister was at pains to say his government was morally obliged to honour the promises the Tories had made. Still, as Stanley observed: "It was a poor sort of amnesty. It removed the threat of hanging; but it gave Riel only the freedom of an outlaw. For five years, he would be a man without a country." [29]

The sense of betrayal, hopelessness and persecution it engendered was likely a major ingredient in Riel's eventual decision to abandon his Canadian citizenship and become an American in 1883. Just prior to Mackenzie's motion, Riel, who was already writing friends about his religious visions of a divine mission for himself, gave a speech in Worcester, Massachusetts, calling on all Franco-Americans to go to Manitoba to assure a French and Catholic victory in Canada's North West.

> Justice will triumph over oppression. The sound of Lépine's and Nault's chains have aroused the sympathies of every French Canadian and every Catholic. The time must pass when those who have defended their liberty and their homes should suffer hanging ... Come, come to our land. The Métis extend the hand of welcome, come work on our soil and assure the victory of the French-Canadian nationality in the vast territory of the North-West. [30]

In a letter to Québec's Cardinal Taschereau, Riel declared: "... it is certain that Upper Canada will try to crush the little group of Métis and ... our safeguard, after Heaven, will always be the province of Québec ..." [31] But the subsequent years of banishment had their desired effect. With Riel out of action and out of the news, Canadians moved on to other things.

All that was to change in 1885 with the North West Rebellion and Riel's capture and subsequent trial, conviction and death sentence on the charge of treason.

> As he had been fifteen years before, Louis Riel once more became the symbol of the French-English quarrel in Canada. To those in Ontario, Riel again became a figure of criminality; to those in Québec, a figure of innocence. And

as before, the Riel question became the battleground of
Canadian party politics. [32]

The 1885 rebellion brought together all the dispossessed of the Western
plains: the Cree, Blackfoot, Blood, Peigan and Ojibwe, all fearing starvation
because of the disappearance of the buffalo; the white settlers along the North
Saskatchewan River angry that the Canadian Pacific Railway was taking a
southern route, and the Métis, who had grown desperate that their rights would
never be recognized. Riel was brought back from the United States in the
summer of 1884 and embarked on a familiar path. At a meeting in St. Laurent,
Saskatchewan, in March 1885, the Métis passed a ten-point Revol-utionary Bill
of Rights asserting their right to possess their lands and on March 18th and 19th
at Batoche they formed a provisional government and an armed force with
Riel as president and Gabriel Dumont as military commander. After some
initial successes, the rebellion was crushed by the sheer strength of numbers
of the often ineptly-led Canadian forces. Riel surrendered May 15th, while
Dumont fled to Montana. Cree Chief Big Bear's surrender to the North West
Mounted Police at Fort Carleton on July 2, 1885 ended armed resistance to
Canada's westward expansion and dealt a defeat to Western Canada's Aborig-
inal and mixed-blood population from which they have never fully recovered.

For an illustration of the extent once-moderate English hearts had
hardened towards Riel and the Métis cause, one has only to consider this comment on Riel's capture by Hugh John Macdonald, son of the now re-elected
Prime Minister Macdonald. Hugh John would go on to become Manitoba's
ninth premier in 1900, but fifteen years earlier, he was a young officer in the
90th Battalion, Winnipeg Rifles. This is what he said:

> Riel unfortunately was taken by three Half breed scouts from
> Prince Albert. Had our fellows taken him he would have
> been brought in a coffin and all trouble about his trial would
> have been avoided. [33]

Riel was charged, tried and convicted of high treason and sentenced
to death. As the political storm raged, the government granted several stays of
execution and, under pressure from its Québec ministers, appointed a three-
man medical commission composed of two English Protestants and one French
Catholic to look into Riel's mental condition. None had any training in psychiatry.
Dr. Michael Lavell, a staunch Methodist and Conservative, recently appointed

warden of Kingston Penitentiary, was a professor of obstetrics at Queen's University. Dr. F.X. Valade, a French Catholic physician from Ottawa, specialized in testing food samples for adulteration. Dr. Augustus Jukes, a North West Mounted Police surgeon, had been attending Riel all along. [34]

Of the three, only Lavell had no qualms about exacting the ultimate penalty. Valade wrote the prime minister that Riel "suffers from hallucinations on political and religious subjects", although he found him of sound mind on everything else. And Jukes, who had grown fond of the Métis leader and

Privately and publicly, Québec's leaders pleaded for Riel's
sentence to be commuted

GRIP/TORONTO / *GREAT CANADIAN POLITICAL CARTOONS: 1820–1914*

clearly did not want his blood on his hands, urged the prime minister to appoint a commission to study Riel's writings. But Macdonald had only added Valade and Jukes as a political sop to Québec. Lavell was the man he wanted and trusted and Lavell was the man to whom he listened. The prime minister was so set on his course he even bowdlerized Valade's and Juke's reports to make them agree with Lavell's, when, responding to opposition and public pressure, he had to table them in Parliament the next spring. Historian Tom Flanagan bluntly calls Macdonald's action a "forgery, even if done for *raison d' etat*". [35] Just as blunt is Flanagan's comment that "the doctors were only pawns in the game of political chess. Macdonald manipulated them to stiffen the resolve of his wavering French ministers." [36]

Macdonald's cabinet met on November 11, 1885 to deal with the deeply fraught issue of execution or commutation. The French Canadian ministers were hesitant, especially J.A. Chapleau, Riel's old schoolmate, now the secretary of state. He had stayed up all the previous night composing his letter of resignation, but at the last moment decided against presenting it because he feared it might provoke "a racial war".

For some reason, the Québec ministers accepted Macdonald's assertions that the three doctors really agreed. They also accepted Macdonald's argument the finding of sanity would provide them with all the ammunition they needed for the hustings in Québec where many believed Riel was mad and deserving of clemency. An important individual disagreed with the prime minister's assessment. Rodrigue Masson, the son of Riel's old patron, was lieutenant governor of Québec. While he couldn't speak publicly, he approached Macdonald privately and pleaded with him to commute the sentence. He warned the prime minister that Riel's death would so alienate French Canada it would provoke a basic political realignment, causing Liberals and Conservatives to come together to forge a nationalist movement in Québec. And he predicted, accurately, the obliteration of the Tory party in Québec for a hundred years. Macdonald was unmoved. Declared the prime minister: "He shall hang though every dog in Quebec bark in his favour." [37] The execution was set for the morning of Monday, November 16, 1885.

Virtually the entire front page of the *Manitoba Free Press* of Tuesday, November 17, 1885 was devoted to the hanging and its aftermath. Under the headline: THE FINAL ACT – LOUIS RIEL'S TRAGEDY COMPLETED YESTERDAY, the paper's correspondent wrote:

Canadian Crucible

Regina, Nov. 16 — The morning of the day fixed for Riel's execution dawned clear and calm, with a frosty keenness in the air ... About eight o'clock the prisoner was summoned by Deputy Sheriff Gibson from his cell where he had spent the night chiefly in prayers and devotion with his confessor, Père André. Mass had been celebrated by the latter assisted by Rev. Father McWilliams and the Last Sacrament had been administered to the doomed man. Supported by the two priests and preceded by the Deputy Sheriff, Riel walked steadily across the guard room and climbed the ladder which led to the gloomy loft at the back of the building. This the party crossed in like order to the door, outside of which the scaffold, with the empty noose depending from the beam ... The condemned man wore an appearance of unshaken fortitude and firmness, although his face was pale and his look earnest. He was dressed in a black coat, woollen shirt and collar, grey tweed trousers and moccasins. His head was uncovered. When Riel and the priests reached the doorway they kneeled down and engaged in prayer. Father André recited the Litany, the prisoner making the responses in firm and unbroken voice. The spectators were visibly affected by the pathetic scene and gave a sigh of relief when it was ended. At 8:15 prayers were finished, Riel arose to his feet and was kissed by the priests. The masked hangman stepped forward to pinion the prisoner, who prayed incessantly during the operation, at one stage lifting his hands heavenward and saying "Father, I am ready." When the pinioning had been completed Riel and the fathers proceeded towards the scaffold, the prisoner walking with steady step and repeating in French the declaration, "In God I put my trust."... Riel exclaimed as he took his stand on the fatal platform, "I ask the forgiveness of all men, and forgive all my enemies." When the executioner had taken his place, drawn the white cap over the prisoner's head and adjusted the noose, Father McWilliams repeated the Lord's Prayer. As he finished the bolt was drawn, the drop fell and all was over. The hangman's work had been well done;the neck was broken and in the short space of two minutes the heart had ceased to beat. The legs were drawn upward two or three times in this space of time and then the body was still. After hanging half an hour the body was cut down and placed in a coffin beneath the scaffold. The result of the post mortem by Dr. Jukes was as follows: The execution was most cleverly performed The neck was entirely dislocated from the bone of the two upper joints of vertebrae, thus paralyzing all the lower portions of the body. He could have felt no pain whatever ... The coroner and jury then viewed the body and found the features much distorted. One juryman had to retire from the sight ... The rope used has been destroyed by Deputy Sheriff Gibson, according to orders, to prevent relic hunters getting hold of it. It was a stout hempen cord five-eighths of an inch in diameter ... (T)he hangman was Jack Henderson of Winnipeg who was one of Riel's prisoners at the time of the Red River rebellion.

In a separate story headlined "Last Moments", the *Free Press* correspondent reported that Riel had prayed for the prime minister at the urging of Father André, asking God to forgive his sins, give him wisdom and justice and, when the time came, to take him quickly. Riel told the priest: "I don't wish Sir John any evil. I have prayed for him but I don't think he prays for me."

Riel went to his death believing he was being executed, not for taking up arms against the Canadian state in 1885, but for the execution of Thomas Scott. And his belief was founded in one of his last moments. The *Free Press* recounted: "As the hour of execution drew near Riel said to Father McWilliams, 'Father, you are from Ontario and I want to make a statement in regard to Scott. I have been reproached for the murder of Scott.' Father McWilliams: 'It is for that you are dying.'" Riel, the story continued, then made this statement:

> Well, perhaps so, but I was pardoned for that in my conscience. I feel and I swear, as I am about to appear before God, that I speak the truth that the shooting of Scott was not a crime; it was a political necessity. The carrying out of the sentence was mismanaged, but I was not to blame for that. I commended the shooting, believing it necessary to save the lives of hundreds of others. There is no particle of self-reproach in my conscience for that act.

George Stanley's account notes that Sheriff Chapleau, a French

Canadian, refused to play his role in the ancient and, from today's perspective, grisly, ceremony of state-inflicted death, leaving to his deputy, Gibson, the task of unlocking the cell door and walking the condemned man to the gallows. But Stanley also writes that not all present felt sympathy for the tortured Métis leader:

> As the moment of execution approached, there was silence. Then a dull heavy sound as of a body falling. "The God damned son of a bitch is gone at last," said one voice. "Yes," said another, "the son of a bitch is gone for certain now." There followed heartless laughter. But it was thin and brittle. [38]

In the words of Macdonald's secretary of state, J.A. Chapleau, "the storm … raged. An electric current is running through Québec, the force of which is not known even to those using it." [39] *La Minerve*, "the staunchest of *bleu* organs", opined: "They've put cruelty in the place of justice." Not even twenty years after its opening, the great book of Confederation had been "soiled by a stain of blood". Riel's execution had "scandalized an entire people in a shocking manner". The hand that passed the rope around Riel's neck had "insulted a whole nation". [40]

The same November 17th edition of the *Manitoba Free Press* carried reports from Montréal and Québec City. The paper's Montréal correspondent wrote:

> The city council this afternoon [Nov. 16] adopted a resolution to adjourn 'as a protest against the odious violation of the laws of justice and humanity in the execution of Riel.' Portraits of Riel, Hon. Mr. Chapleau and Col. Ouimet were exposed in windows and an excited crowd kept the sidewalk blocked all day. Riel's picture was framed with crepe and had a French flag for a background. The other two portraits were prostrate and each had a drop of red sealing wax on the forehead to represent drops of Riel's blood. There is a movement on foot to have requiem masses celebrated in all the Catholic churches through the Province next Monday for the repose of Riel's soul.

From Québec City the *Free Press* carried this dispatch:

Black bordered columns in the nineteenth century were an expression of deep mourning.

Top image: "The bloody drama is played out."
Bottom image: "Victim of fanaticism, Orangism and his own devotion to the cause of the Métis.

The excitement here is almost beyond all restraint ...
Tonight 200 or 300 students with their friends have been
marching through the streets shouting "Glory to Riel"
and cursing the Orangemen. Crowds are gathered near
Sir Hector Langevin's house ... and it is feared that they
intend mischief. The police, however, are patrolling in large
numbers. Hand bills have been distributed to all passers-by
calling on them to meet tonight. These bills are headed in
large letters and read as follows – "Riel hanged". "Infamie
Consommé" – [Consummate Infamy]

The triumph of Orangemen over the Catholics and French
Canadians ... [P]rotest against the terrible murder committed this morning by Sir John Macdonald, Sir Hector
Langevin ... L'Electeur, the Liberal organ, appears to-night
draped in mourning and all its articles are most stirring.
All its columns are devoted to the Riel matter and it calls
upon French Canadians not to forget the martyr who was
murdered for the French cause.

But the paper's Toronto bureau found a much different atmosphere. Crowds
gathered early in the morning around newspaper offices, many expressing
doubt the execution would actually proceed. One man actually bet $200
against the hanging. "The excitement here over Riel quickly subsided after it
became known that he had been executed. The courage displayed by Riel
on the scaffold was admired, but no expression of pity could be heard at
his fate."

The Riel execution helped bring to public prominence an eloquent
young French Canadian politician. Wilfrid Laurier, Liberal MP for Arthabaska,
then an up and coming opposition backbencher, knowingly took his career
in his hands in several speeches in Parliament and in public on Riel's fate.
On July 7, 1885, he rose in the House of Commons to put the entire blame
for the tragedy squarely on the callous indifference of the Macdonald
government:

To tell us that Louis Riel, simply by his influence, could
bring these men from peace to war; to tell us that they had

no grievances, to tell us that they were brought into a state of rebellion either through pure malice or through imbecile adherence to an adventurer is an insult to the people at large and an unjust aspersion on the people of the Saskatchewan ... I have not heard it stated, but it is in the minds of men that if these men have rebelled it is because they are to a certain extent of French origin. This I say and I say it coming from a province where less than fifty years ago every man of the race to which I belong was a rebel and where today every man of that race is a true and loyal subject: I say give these men justice, give them freedom, give them their rights, treat them as for the last forty years you have treated the people of Lower Canada, and you will have contentment, peace and harmony where today discord, hatred and war are ruining the land. [41]

On Sunday, November 22, 1885, Laurier was one of thirty-seven French Canadian leaders from all parties who took their places on the rostrums in Montréal's Champ de Mars to address a crowd of forty thousand people. Honoré Mercier, soon to be the leader of the Parti National, proclaimed in a "great voice ... like a tolling bell, 'Riel, our brother, is dead.'" [42] Laurier followed him with this bold and politically dangerous cry: "Had I been born on the banks of the Saskatchewan I would myself have shouldered a musket to fight against the neglect of government and the shameless greed of speculators!" [43] It was a comment the English-speaking press would haunt him with for years.

But Laurier made his most memorable oration in Parliament the next spring, during debate on a motion to censure the government for Riel's execution. He spoke for two hours on March 11, 1886 and the Commons, with almost all MPs present, was so silent all that could be heard during his pauses was the ticking of the chamber clock.

> What is hateful is not rebellion, it is the despotism which induces that rebellion; what is hateful are not rebels but the men who, having the enjoyment of power, do not discharge the duties of power; those men who when they are asked for a loaf, give a stone.

> I will not receive any lectures on loyalty. I am a British subject and I value the proud title as much as anyone in this House.

But if it be expected of me that I shall allow fellow country-men, unfriended, undefended, unprotected, and unrepre-sented in this House to be trampled under foot by this gov-ernment, I say that is not what I understand by loyalty and I would call that slavery ...

Sir, we are a new nation, we are attempting to unite the dif-ferent conflicting elements which we have into a nation. Shall we ever succeed if the bond of union is to be revenge, if we are to rake up old scores and launch them at the heads of one another?" [44]

While Riel's life and death shook the country to its foundations, the Riel family's personal tragedy continued unabated. Less than a month before his execution, Riel learned that his third child, a little boy, had been born but had lived only a few hours. The grieving father wrote to his sister Henriette:

The misery that I feel in seeing my little one taken from me without ever being able to embrace him, without ever being able to give him my love strikes to the innermost depths of my soul. I can only thank the good Lord in his charity, for having given the baby several hours of life, long enough for it to be baptized. The pure water poured on its infant fore-head, the sacred words on its little spirit, have made it one of the children of God. My dear little one came into two worlds in a single day; this world and the next. He appeared on earth only long enough to receive the sign of our faith [45]

His wife, Marguerite, would die of tuberculosis on May 24, 1886, just six months after her husband. His daughter, Marie-Angélique, died of diphtheria at the age of fourteen. Jean, Riel's eldest child, went to school in Québec and married the daughter of a prominent Québec family. Newly graduated as a civil engineer, he returned to Manitoba to work for the Grand Trunk Pacific Railway. That same year, 1908, he suffered a rib fracture when his buggy overturned. He died in St. Boniface, childless, at just twenty-six.

One of Riel's most poignant and powerful defences of his actions in 1869-70 and perhaps the most succinct outline of his cause and political philosophy was contained in a petition he sent to United States President

Ulysses S. Grant in the fall of 1870. Free and democratic people everywhere would find it hard to disagree:

> ... learning through the public press, our only media, that we had been sold by a company of adventurers residing in London, England, with our lands, rights and liberties as so much merchandise to a foreign government; and further learning through the same medium, the press, that the Parliament of the Dominion of Canada had organized a Government for our country as if it had jurisdiction over us, and that we were to have no voice in the Government, and that a Governor appointed to rule over us, clothed with "almost despotic power" had started from Canada en route to our country, accompanied by a band of unscrupulous and irresponsible followers, who were to form his Council, and fill other offices in the Government and thus plunder and eat out our subsistence ... [46]

He revived the argument in the last interview he gave before his hanging. Riel told W.W. Harkins of the Montréal *Weekly Star* about his religious visions. Then he continued: "And the province of Manitoba? Without our Provisional Government it would still be nothing more than a colony tied to the apron strings of Canada. I deserve to be called the Father of Manitoba." [47]

The legacy of Louis Riel is in two parts, although he identified it as one. His struggle for the rights of the Métis people remains largely unfulfilled. They obtained official recognition in the 1982 Canadian Constitution but their legal battles to regain their land, or at least, financial compensation for it, continue to drag on in the courts more than a century and a quarter after passage of the Manitoba Act. The apparent extreme polarity in the published research and arguments of respected academics like Tom Flanagan and D.N. Sprague on the Métis land question masks a surprising commonality. Whether the lands were legally sold (often at firesale prices) or denied and/or stolen, the same historical reality remains. After Confederation, the Métis quickly became unwanted strangers in their own land. Swamped by an alien and hostile culture that engulfed and overwhelmed them almost overnight and lacking formal title to the lands they had occupied for nearly a century, they felt forced to leave.

A somewhat different perspective is offered by Alberta historian Gerhard Ens who casts the Métis land issue in a broader light. He says that while both dispossession and alienation were definite factors in the Métis diaspora, they began their movement out of Red River long before 1869-70 in response to new economic opportunities created by the emerging capitalist economy. Like their European neighbours, the Métis were recognizing the importance of land and property and abandoning subsistence life to earn money either as traders or full-time farmers. But to do so, they had to leave Manitoba, either because their river lots were too small for profitable agriculture or the bison herds and the buffalo robe trade were by now too far away. Still, Ens acknowledges that the sudden and dramatic shift in Red River's demographics following provincehood was a powerful incentive behind the Métis departure, filling them, as it did, with "an invincible repugnance." He continues:

> Too many changes, at odds with their customs and morals, had taken place in both social and political realms. The arrival of the Wolseley Expedition in 1870 had, in fact, instituted a reign of terror in the settlement … It was not safe for a French Métis to be seen near Fort Garry … and those who did venture into Winnipeg risked life and limb … If there was an element of coercion in the Métis exodus from Red River, it was the intolerant actions and behaviour of the incoming Protestant settlers from Ontario. [48]

Archibald's biographer, Allen Ronaghan, takes yet another view. The Macdonald government's decision to withhold control of public lands from the infant province turned Manitoba into a federal colony and delayed responsible government. Ronaghan believes that the reservation of Manitoba's lands "for purposes of the Dominion" was a conscious act designed to force the Métis out of Manitoba and cripple any future attempt by them to block European settlement in the North West. Whether one attributes such malicious and Machiavellian motives to Macdonald or not, that was the practical effect. The brief flare of the 1885 Rebellion aside, the Métis were defeated and dispersed and the Canadian West was opened to the railroad and the march of "civilization". The Dominion Lands Act of 1872 made the promise of 1.4 million acres for Métis children "subject to" rights "defined or created under this Act". This meant, Ronaghan says, that "any volunteer who had come to Manitoba in August of 1870 was as entitled to a grant of land as a Métis whose family had been in the province for decades." [49]

By 1881, eleven years after Confederation, Manitoba's population had almost tripled and switched from a slight plurality of French speakers to a massive English majority. Fully 59.7 per cent of Manitoba's 62,260 citizens claimed English as their first tongue. Those of French mother tongue represented only 15.6 per cent. Closing fast on the Franco-Manitobans were the German-speaking Mennonites at 13.6 per cent.

The second part of Riel's legacy – Manitoba's bilingual and bicultural character as the intended template for the westward expansion of the nation – is the one that concerns this book. It has fared scarcely better than the first. As history testifies, the bilingual-bicultural flame was illegally snuffed out in 1890 and kept extinguished for almost ninety years. When the Supreme Court finally re-ignited it, times and circumstances had so changed that it was far too late to make much if any difference to Manitoba, and no difference at all to her three western provincial sisters. René Lévesque, the separatist premier of Québec, noted sardonically in response to the 1979 constitutional judgement that the Supreme Court had moved with amazing speed to uphold the rights of dead francophones in Manitoba and live anglophones in his province.

The Ottawa River may represent the geographic boundary between Canada's two major language communities, but it is the Red River that has proven to be the nation's bilingual and bicultural faultline. As Franco-Manitobans lost, one by one, their linguistic, cultural and educational rights – not just for themselves but for all the other threatened French Canadian enclaves in the rest of Western Canada – their defeats revived and stirred the nation's primal passions, driving the wedge ever deeper between the two "founding races" and confounding the nation's ability to define and govern itself.

As mentioned before, the bilingual/bicultural dream for Canada was not the sole purview of a lone, unbalanced prairie revolutionary. It was shared by none other than the new nation's first deputy prime minister, Macdonald's Québec lieutenant, Sir George-Étienne Cartier.

During the Confederation debates of 1865, Cartier and others repeatedly stated that equality and fair dealing between English and French Canada had to be the foundation of Confederation. Historian Arthur Silver argues in his book, *The French-Canadian Idea of Confederation 1864–1900*, that even if Confederation did not mean equal status for French and English in the four original provinces, it could well be expected to imply equality in the North-West. "[W]as not the North-West a new and empty territory, not yet settled, not yet developed?" [50] The fact it was financed out of taxes paid by all Canadians added weight to the argument it was as much the property of French as English Canadians. Silver goes on to say it is only reasonable to assume that Cartier and other federal leaders "anticipated a French-Canadian presence on the prairies." [51]

John Boyd's biography of the second most influential Father of Confederation reminds us again that Cartier handled most of the negotiations with Riel's emissaries, conducting them "with rare tact and ability, maintaining his calmness in a period of intense popular excitement and passion even when the most violent attacks were levelled at him personally as well as at those of his own race and creed." [52] It was Cartier who ensured Manitoba entered Confederation as a province with representative institutions, not as a federal protectorate as had been originally intended. It also was Cartier who piloted the Manitoba bill through Parliament and, says Boyd, "he performed the responsible duty in an exceptionally able manner." [53] Boyd accepts the analysis that it was Cartier's purpose to make Manitoba a French Canadian province, noting the province's constitution was largely modelled on that of Québec and the fact the province's first fully-empowered premier, Marc Amable Girard, was a close personal friend of Cartier's. Boyd goes even further, saying Cartier's purpose was "perfectly legitimate ... French-Canadians had been amongst the earliest pioneers of the Canadian West." Even more compelling was the fact the deputy prime minister was watching his compatriots emigrate in large numbers to the United States. "Was it not patriotic policy on his part to desire that instead of the country losing its people, if they desired to move they should go to the Canadian West?" [54]

But, Boyd goes on to note, French Canadians did not fulfill Cartier's wish, instead continuing to flow to the "nearer and more civilised centres" of the United States, leaving Manitoba to be peopled by English-Canadians from Ontario and new Canadians from countries such as Russia and Iceland. Cartier's early death doomed any hope of realizing the dream of pan-Canadian duality. His successors as Québec lieutenants shared neither his vision nor his political power and skill.

Still, a new spirit was rising among Québécois because of their sympathy and identification with the travails of Riel and the Red River Métis in the North West, not to mention their intensifying alarm over the anti-French hysteria running rampant in Ontario and the anti-Catholic outburst in New Brunswick. In April 1870, a number of Québec newspapers wondered "How much hatred there is in these Anglo-Saxons' souls against everything which is French and Catholic!" [55] Silver says French Canada's political leaders were drawn ever deeper into the national project as they sought ways to use Québec's political power at the federal level to fight on behalf of their "brothers" on the western plains. On April 18, 1870, *Le Journal des Trois-Rivières* wrote:

> [T]hese indignation meetings in Ontario, this determination to make a war out of the affair … must teach us Lower Canadians that the inhabitants of Ontario want to see a policy adopted that will undermine French influence in the North-West. Ah, but on that point the Province of Québec will have only one answer: to protect and assist our brothers out there. [56]

Indeed, by the time the Manitoba Act was passed, some Québécois, like Cartier, had begun thinking of the North-West, not as an extension of their homeland, but as a second French-Catholic province which would become an ally of Québec within Canada. When Elzéar Goulet was murdered, it looked for a time that French Canada would have its own Thomas Scott. Opined *L'Opinion Publique* on October 13, 1870:

> Unless the culprits are pursued vigorously and punished severely, unless Upper Canadians express a unanimous and energetic disapproval of this act of barbarism, there will be a dark feeling of dissatisfaction among the whole French and Catholic population of the Dominion. [57]

In 1872, French Canadian newspapers warned that Ontario's offer of a reward for the killers of Thomas Scott could mean "Confederation will become impossible before long." [58].

The blows on Québec's unfortunate compatriots outside the province rained down hard and fast: the arrest of Ambroise Lépine in 1873, Riel's election to the House of Commons and expulsion in the spring of 1874, the refusal of Ottawa to provide a full amnesty, the inconclusive report of the Commons select committee on the Red River troubles. Throughout, the Québec press waxed ever more indignant. It certainly didn't help that, while the North West was simmering, New Brunswick repealed the rights of Roman Catholics, largely French-speaking Acadians, to their own schools and failed to publish official documents in French. Two died in riots in Caraquet.

On October 1, 1873, *Le National* wrote: "The wind of persecution is blowing through both of those provinces [New Brunswick and Manitoba]. In one, it's a war of religion; in the other, it's a race war." [59] On November 14, 1874, the "bleu" *Courrier de St-Hyacinthe* attacked its own party: "Sir John A. Macdonald, to avoid displeasing the Orangemen, whose grand master he used to be, shamefully abused Mr. Cartier's good faith …" [60]

Québec, says Silver, had become aware of French elements elsewhere in Canada, aware, too, that they were under attack and was now seeing that attack as directed at Québec itself. On February 3, 1875, *Le Canadien* warned: "One is tempted to believe that there is an immense conspiracy against the French race in the dominion. Trampled underfoot in Manitoba, crushed in New Brunswick, we are threatened with annihilation." [61]

As their compatriots in language and religion continued to suffer at the hands of *les maudits anglais,* French Canadians developed a tautology. The more their language and religion was threatened within Canada, the more they identified with the francophone minorities elsewhere but the more determined they became to stay in or near Québec to protect and reinforce French Catholic language, culture and power at its base. Silver writes:

> This view of Québec as a province with a special mission to defend French and Catholic minorities in Canada not only explains the concern displayed for those minorities, but it does so in a way that is consistent with the autonomist approach of Lower Canadians towards Confederation in the first place. It enabled Quebeckers to express their natural sympathy for fellow French Catholics while retaining their fundamental belief that Québec, after all, was the essential homeland of the French-Canadian nation. [62]

Defending the minorities in Manitoba and New Brunswick became Québec's "noble and lofty mission". [63] Because Québec felt honour-bound to protect the minorities against the depredations of the Anglo-Protestant majority, it followed, ominously, that whenever those aggressions succeeded, Québec itself suffered defeat. Lépine's treatment was, therefore, "an insult to our province"; Riel's expulsion from the House of Commons was "to sacrifice the Province of Québec"; the refusal to grant full amnesty to Riel and Lépine flouted the earnest wishes of "a whole province … an entire people". [64]

Still, as noted before, throughout this period, a strange and seemingly counter-intuitive phenomenon was underway. Just as the second sons of Ontario headed west in search of land and opportunity, the second sons of

French Canada were also on the move, but to a truly "foreign" land, to the United States, where neither their language, their culture nor their religion had even the slightest constitutional protection.

Why didn't French Canadians come west? Why did they prefer the United States? There were several reasons, all working to reinforce one another. Most fundamental was *la survivance*, the importance, particularly among its elites, to maintain Québec's strength as the homeland and bulwark of the French and Catholic race in North America. Arthur Silver says the only thing that made Canada acceptable to French Canadians in the first place was their understanding that it was to be "an association of national states, called provinces, united in a federal alliance ... And in that alliance, the province of Québec was to be the national state of the French Canadians." [65] The survival of the French fact in North America depended on the preservation of the French and Catholic character of Québec.

To the overarching importance of *la survivance* to Québec's elites was added the perception of the average Québécois that English Canada was a growing threat to the French Canadian nation. That perception took a quantum leap with the events of 1869-70 and their aftermath. The apparent persecution of Riel and the French-speaking and Catholic Métis, followed by waves of "bigotted and racist" Ontario emigrés flooding into Manitoba, made western settlement almost unthinkable to the vast majority. Why would anyone make the enormous personal and financial sacrifice of pulling up stakes to travel to an unfamiliar, distant place knowing that he or she would suffer discrimination, denial of language and religion, and daily intolerance and bigotry?

Finally, in the latter half of the nineteenth century, *la survivance* was being threatened as never before by the world-wide phenomenon of industrialization brought on by the growth of capitalism. As mentioned earlier, in the period between 1870 and 1900, close to 400,000 Québécois felt forced to leave the province to find work in the textile mills and factories of New England.

In his study of industrial migration, *On The Move: French Canadian and Italian Migrants in the North Atlantic Economy, 1860-1914*, Bruno Ramirez argues that Québec could not seal itself off from the impact of the industrial revolution and the resulting mass population shift from country to city and from farm to factory. The newspapers and the province's elites bemoaned the exodus, warning those departing that they and the entire French Canadian nationality would be "buried alive" in the United States. Ramirez, however, does not explore why, by the 1886 Census, Manitoba's English-speaking population had increased more than elevenfold, from 6,500 in 1870 to about 76,000, in the process swamping the 11,000-strong French-speaking population that had not even doubled since Confederation. Of Manitoba's 109,000 citizens counted in that Census, sixty-eight per cent were of British (English, Irish and Scottish) origin while just ten per cent were French-speaking. [66] Franco-Manitobans, the majority at the time of Confederation, were now a threatened, tiny minority. Most of the Manitoba newcomers were the second sons of Ontario farmers, lured west by the English-only advertising campaigns of Canada First and other British imperialist organizations – campaigns that began even as Riel's provisional government still held power – promoting the new province's vast stock of cheap prime farmland.

Ramirez notes, but only in passing, how the simultaneous mass southward movement of French Canadians – he uses the number of 351,745 between 1870 and 1900 – impacted Canada's "fragile nation-building and acute ethnic tension between the two founding groups". [67] He does not examine the reasons for that fragility and tension nor does he probe how it might have dictated the preferred destination of French Canadian migrants. The small towns and rural countryside of the New England states bordering the French Canadian homeland offered, at once, three protective differences not available anywhere in Canada outside Québec. They were within a short distance of home and family; they were small and easily made over into informal French-Catholic communities and, perhaps most important of all, they were not part of the truly alien "conquering race" of insensitive, imperialist, racist and bigotted Anglo-Canadians.

A whole new citizenship of sorts arose known as "franco-américain". This group soon became the subject of regular entreaties from the church, from French Canadian colonization societies and even, occasionally, from the Québec press to pack their bags and families and return "home"; home being the North-West along with their native province. *La survivance* meant it was to these expatriates, never to residents of Québec itself, that French Canada's elites turned to try to find the numbers to bolster the French minority in the West. As seen earlier, even Louis Riel lent his name and credibility to the effort.

The late Robert Painchaud, a Franco-Manitoban who wrote his MA and PhD theses on French Canadian colonization issues, points to a complex and contradictory web of reasons – social, religious and economic – for the failure of French Canada to prevent, in W.L. Morton's memorable phrase, "the triumph of Ontario democracy" in Manitoba and the North West.

Painchaud argues that it was a combination of many forces – Ontario English Protestant hostility on the ground in the West and within the corridors of power in Ottawa; the opposition to emigration within Québec's establishment; the perception of English persecution and the wildness and remoteness of the Canadian North West among ordinary French Canadians, and the world-wide phenomenon, especially in this period, of population migration from rural, agricultural communities to urban, industrial centres – that effectively destroyed the dream of Canadian duality. In his last scholarly work, published posthumously in the December 4, 1978 edition of the *Canadian Historical Review*, Painchaud weaves all of the threads together to produce a sobering account of an opportunity lost and a country forever changed. Noting that Québécois historians, for the most part, have approached the issue of French Canadian colonization only indirectly through their examinations of individual flashpoints like the fate of Louis Riel and the Manitoba School Question of 1890, Painchaud gives his readers an exhaustive review of their varying interpretations. Québec historians of the 1950s, 1960s and 1970s had a common analysis.

> Briefly, their reasoning is that English Canada was determined, at the time of Confederation, to limit the French fact to the province of Québec and that it demonstrated that resolve in 1869-70 by persecuting the Métis people who were seen as symbols of French Canadian expansionism. Ontario's hostility was especially evident in its dispatch of settlers to the Red River Valley, where the new arrivals promptly challenged the bilingual and bicultural framework contained in the 1870 Manitoba Act and the 1871 Education Act. Once the institutional arrangements conformed to their image of Western Canadian society ... English Canadians undertook to introduce a "foreign" immigration which would completely end any dreams entertained by French Canadian leaders both in the West and in Québec. Inherent in this general thesis ... is the view that, faced with a prejudiced, fanatical, anti-French and anti-Catholic majority, French Québec could not possibly hope to play a major role in the development of the West and that it would certainly not encourage the Québécois to go there. [68]

LOUIS RIEL,

CHEF METIS,

Exécuté le 16 Novembre 1885.

MARTYR POLITIQUE !

Coupable d'avoir aimé ses compatriotes opprimés,

Victime du fanatisme orangiste, auquel l'ont sacrifié des politiciens sans âme et sans cœur.

QUE LES VRAIS PATRIOTES S'EN SOUVIENNENT !!

Imp. L'UNION, St. Hyacinthe.

The "martyrdom" of Louis Riel was one factor that discouraged many Québécois from making Manitoba a western homeland.

What Painchaud refers to as the "plot mentality" historical school became dominant after 1920. It has a number of variations. Jean Bruchési's *Histoire du Canada pour tous. II: le régime anglais* argues that the Métis fears for their future in 1869-70 were justified because of "le voisinage d'une minorité anglaise aggressive" (the proximity of an aggressive English minority). [69] Furthermore, annexation to Confederation "ouvrirait la porte à des milliers d'immigrants". (Canadian annexation of the North West would open the door to millions of immigrants.) Defeat was probably assured, since Métis influence was replaced by French Canadian influence, "elle-même rapidement submergée par la vague anglo-saxonne" (itself rapidly being submerged by the Anglo-Saxon wave). [70]

In his 1959 *Québec-Canada: Histoire du Canada. II 1763-1958*, Monseigneur Albert Tessier said Ontario feared being hemmed in by a French-Catholic pincer movement represented by Québec on the east and Manitoba on the west and that was why it was determined to erase Manitoba's character as a second French-Catholic province. Ontario, he said, felt it necessary to promote "une forte immigration ontarienne afin de noyer l'element français et d'assurer la matrise économique et politique" (a strong Ontario immigration in order to drown the French element and assure its own economic and political domination). [71]

In 1961, Robert Rumilly wrote in his scholarly work, *Le problème national des Canadiens français*: "Il fallait à tout prix éviter la constitution, dans l'Ouest, d'une autre province canadienne-française, qui eût, avec Québec, encadré Ontario et peut-être assuré au Canada une population de majorité française – peut-être livré aux Canadiens français le contrôle de la législation fédérale". (It is at all costs necessary to avoid the creation, in the West, of another French Canadian province which could have, with Québec, surrounded Ontario and perhaps assured Canada of a majority French population, perhaps surrendering to French Canadians control of the federal law.) [72]

Michel Brunet, in his *Québec-Canada anglais – deux itinéraires – un affrontement*, published in 1969, said "Canadians" were determined to prevent the expansion of "French and Popish domination" and achieved their goal by refusing to promote the repatriation of hundreds of thousands of Franco-Americans and instead subsidizing the immigration of foreigners from Europe who had "la plasticité psychologique nécessaire pour se soumettre à leur Canadian domination" (the psychological plasticity necessary to submit themselves to Canadian domination). [73] States Painchaud:

[H]ad the French Canadians desired to heed George-Étienne Cartier's dictum to go West, they would have encountered more obstacles in the form of discriminatory transportation rates. Bruchési pointed out that it was more expensive for an inhabitant of Rivière-du-Loup to get to Alberta than for "un Juif Galicie ou ... un paysan du Danube" – a Jew from Galicia or a peasant from the Danube". [74]

Similar special treatment was given to British immigrants. According to Rumilly, the 1925 Empire Settlement Act made it cheaper for an English family from England to go west than for a French Canadian family from Montréal.

Tessier, for his part, says the great French Canadian nationalist Henri Bourassa saw in Ottawa's immigration favouritism "une manoeuvre destinée à noyer les Canadiens français, à reduire leur importance proportionnelle dans l'ensemble du pays" (a manoeuvre destined to drown French Canadians, to reduce their proportional importance in the whole of the nation). Concludes Tessier: "Il y a longtemps que les orangistes, inquiets de la forte nationalité des Canadiens, cherchent à faire contrepoids à leur trop grande expansion" (For a long time the Orangemen, disquieted by the strength of the French Canadian nationality, have searched for a counterweight to their too great expansion). [75]

Painchaud says another common theme in French Canadian historiography is that French Canadian westward migration was effectively dammed by the abolition of the French language and confessional schools in Manitoba, relegating French, in one observer's words, to the same status as Russian or German. For sociologist Philippe Garigue these decisions "signalent le déclin de la participation canadienne-français au développement du Canada" (signalled the decline of French Canadian participation in the development of Canada). [76]

Painchaud sees the "plot" school as incomplete, not wrong. While it is tempting to dismiss these analyses as traditional Québec nationalism, he continues, "it is probably more appropriate to view them as the expression of the defensiveness which characterized French Canadian society after what appeared to be repeated humiliations in Confederation, from the first Riel troubles of 1869-70 to the conscription crisis of 1917." [77] Where the "plot" historians err, according to Painchaud, is in ignoring the role that Québec elites – the church, the press and the politicians – played in discouraging

French Canadian emigration westward .

Soon after Manitoba's admission into Confederation in 1870, Bishop Taché went to Québec City to present his case for western emigration to the general council of the province's religious hierarchy. The resulting "Lettre circulaire de 1871" was endorsed by all bishops present and sent to all parish priests throughout Québec. Later missions to Québec in 1873 and 1876 were undertaken by l'abbé Ritchot and l'abbé Albert Lacombe. They reported to Taché that they had received support for emigration from Bishop Bourget of Montréal and, in 1876 a "bureau de colonization" was set up in Montréal that enjoyed the apparent blessing of the highest clerical and political authorities.

It foundered on several jagged rocks of reality. Many of the families willing to relocate to Manitoba were unacceptable to the Manitoba clerics because they had neither the agricultural experience nor the savings to buy lands in or near existing Manitoba parishes where their reinforcement was most needed. Over time, it also became apparent to the Manitoba clergy that the colonization society was never intended to promote emigration among French Canadians living in Québec, only among those residing in New England. The society did succeed in repatriating to Manitoba several hundred families from New England. But even that effort petered out once an economic recovery in the United States made remaining in the manufacturing towns and villages bordering their native province far more appealing to French Canadians than the thought of homesteading in the remote and barren North West.

Meanwhile, as Silver also notes, the Québec press was almost universally hostile to western emigration. Québec City's *La Minerve* editorialized that it couldn't encourage any regular emigration from Québec to Manitoba "parce que ce serait travailler à diminuer la force de notre nationalité ici, sous prétexte de l'augmenter là bas" (because it would work to diminish the strength of our nationality here under the pretext of increasing it out there). [78] The few times newspapers sent out calls for emigration to assist beleaguered French communities in the North West, it was apparent they, too, were appealing only to those living in the United States.

As for the political elite, Lacombe was told by Québec Premier C.E.B. de Boucherville in 1876 that he would do everything in his power to prevent French Canadians from going to Manitoba, a message Lacombe immediately transmitted to Archbishop Taché.

La survivance was, indeed, a powerful, emotive force at the elite levels of Québec society. "Québec leaders were concerned primarily with provincial autonomy and with the retention of French Canadians within their province," says Painchaud. "In the face of a massive exodus of Québécois to the United States, they were not about to encourage their population to migrate to Western Canada. Nor were they convinced that the future of French Canada lay in expansion." [79]

As evidenced by the ongoing flood to New England, however, *la survivance* hadn't quite the same resonance among ordinary French Canadians who had their own personal economic survival to consider. Still, their overwhelming choice of New England over the North West was logical, driven as it was by the comparison of distance and cost between the two destinations, the growing appeal of urban factory work over rural farm labour and the entirely legitimate impression gained from the popular press of the day that Manitoba and the entire North West were implacably hostile to French Canada, linguistically, culturally and religiously.

As Painchaud states in his PhD thesis, Ottawa also showed initial interest in repatriating French Canadians as one way to populate the North West. In 1873, an English Canadian MP told the Commons that it was "important to adopt a policy which would encourage these French Canadians to migrate to our own North West Territory". [80] The Commons struck a committee on immigration and colonization and the agriculture department commissioned Father P.E. Gendreau to investigate the Franco-American situation. Gendreau reported there were about 400,000 French Canadians living in New England. Many, he found, only stayed long enough to earn some money before returning to their native province. Others were content to remain in the United States, either because they lacked the means to return to Canada or because they had gone into business or the professions. Gendreau told Ottawa it would find better prospective recruits for the North West among those French Canadians who already had signalled an interest in the pioneer life by going to the American West.

Bruno Ramirez provides an interesting counterpoint to Gendreau's findings. As noted earlier, he says that 351,745 Québécois moved to the United States between 1870 and 1900, [81] indicating the French Canadian exodus to the mills and factory towns of New England not only tapered off but actually contracted as the nineteenth century drew to a close.

Beginning in the mid-1870s, Ottawa began a policy of group settlement, attracting Mennonites and Icelanders to Manitoba. When Franco-Manitobans set up their own colonization society in 1874 and requested similar financial assistance, Ottawa refused. Painchaud argues the government's action was not animated by hostility towards expanding the French fact in Canada but merely reflected reality – French Canadian reluctance.

One who attempted to overcome that reluctance was Joseph Dubuc. Born in Châteauguay, Lower Canada, in 1840, he was one of those Québécois who went to New England to "learn the English language and find a well-paying job in a factory". [82] Returning to Canada, he enrolled at the Collège de Montréal where he met and befriended Louis Riel. He graduated from McGill University Law School in 1869 and within a few months, received an invitation from Riel to join him in the North West. From his vantage point in Manitoba during Riel's provisional government, Dubuc not only met l'abbé Ritchot, but contributed many articles to the Québec newspaper, La Minerve, defending the Métis cause in his native province. He encouraged Riel to run for Parliament and with his law partner, Joseph Royal, leader of the French Métis in the Manitoba Legislature, founded the Manitoba newspaper, Le Métis, in 1871. Because of his close connections to the Métis leader, he was accosted and beaten by thugs on the streets of Winnipeg in 1872 and left blinded in one eye.

Sharing Riel's determination to draw French Canadians to Western Canada, Dubuc became the director and president of La Société de Colonisation, the organization that worked to repatriate French Canadians from the United States and encourage settlement from Québec. By the 1901 Census, the number of Manitobans listing their "origin" as French had risen to 16,021 from just 9,688 in 1881. Impressive as that number is, it has to be put in context with the province as a whole. In percentage terms, Manitoba's francophone population plummetted from 15.6 per cent to 6.3 per cent in the twenty years between 1881 and 1901. And this even though their numbers had almost doubled from 9,688 to 16,021.

His close ties to Riel did not bar Dubuc from a distinguished legal career. He was appointed to the Manitoba bench in 1879 and in 1903, was made Manitoba's sixth chief justice, a post he held until his retirement in 1909.

As the Census figures demonstrate, even with the best efforts of people of Dubuc's stature, French Canadian immigration to Manitoba was never sufficient to match the ongoing Anglo-Saxon and European influx. As a result, by the 1880s, the Catholic church began narrowing its focus to its own survival in the West. Once bishops like Alexandre-Antonin Taché, his even more conservative successor, Adélard Langevin and Alberta's Vital Grandin realized they could not achieve the dream of Canadian duality and save the French language in the West, they determined to at least save their church by recruiting Catholics from Europe, particularly Ireland and Belgium. The latter had the added advantage of being French-speaking.

The entire frustrating and disheartening colonization experience instilled a profound sense of betrayal in the Western Catholic clergy. Resentment towards the Québec hierarchy was deep and bitter, leading to frequent clashes in public and private. The fact that most Western church leaders were ultramontanes, conservative-minded, made their defeat all the more painful.

> Given their belief in agrarianism, the exodus of French
> Canadians from Québec to the towns and manufacturing
> centres of New England distressed them greatly. They could
> not understand why their French Canadian compatriots
> failed to take advantage of the opportunities awaiting them
> on the Canadian prairies. They considered the West to be
> a natural extension of the patrimoine of French Canada,
> a romantic vision which had its roots in the 18th century
> travels of the la Vérendrye family to the country beyond
> the Great Lakes ... [83]

Taché's dream of Manitoba as "a little Québec" was stillborn. In the first decade of Confederation, twice as many Ontarians moved to other provinces than did Québécois. In the 1880s and 1890s, the proportion for Ontarians became three times what it was for Québécois. In a few short years "la vague anglo-saxonne" did indeed wash over and submerge Manitoba's tiny French beachhead. As we saw earlier, from enjoying a slight plurality over the English and half-breed population at the time of Confederation, Manitoba's French and Métis community barely doubled from what it had been in 1870 to a mere 11,000 in 1885-86. Meanwhile, those Manitobans claiming British or Irish origin had climbed over tenfold to 73,000.

As it had in the United Canadas in the 1840s, the dramatic demographic shift meant that even the vocabulary changed. Father Louis Drummond, a French-Irish priest, gave this retrospectively significant language lesson in an address to the Manitoba Historical Society in 1886:

> Thirty years ago, we who speak French were called by every
> one purely and simply "Canadians"; others were known as

English, Scotch or Irish. Lately the fashion has grown up of calling others Canadians and distinguishing us as French. [84]

In fact, francophones in Manitoba did not call themselves Franco-Manitobans until the late 1960s. Prior to that, their term of choice was either Canadiens or, as noted earlier, Canayens. [85]

A report compiled for La Société St. Jean-Baptiste de Manitoba in 1900 provides a dramatic summation of the extent of the failure of the duality dream. That year, a grand total of just 941 French-speaking immigrants arrived in Manitoba, of which 560 were from Québec, 153 were Franco-American repatriates and 228 came directly from France and Belgium. These numbers paled into insignificance when compared to the overall Canadian immigration into the province of 31,937. But it is important to recall Father Gendreau and Bruno Ramirez and the some 400,000 French Canadians who went to the United States rather than to the North West. It is equally intriguing to ask how 400,000 French-speaking homesteaders would have dramatically altered the foundation and culture of the North West and, by extension, the essential character of modern Canada.

It was not to be. And not just because of Riel or because of *la survivance*, the attitudes of Québec's religious and political hierarchy and the lure of industrialization. It was also because of ongoing and relentless anglophone bigotry, a bigotry that, ironically, marched in lock-step with increasing French Canadian engagement with Confederation.

4

The Death of the Dream

MANITOBA'S ENTRY INTO CONFEDERATION IN 1870 prompted French Canadians to believe they deserved the same access as English Canadians to Canada's new territories in the North West. Simultaneously, French Canada's view of Confederation was evolving from a mere pact among provinces to a compact between two races as well. Historian Arthur Silver says that after entering Confederation as a means to preserve Québec, French Canadians were gradually brought by the tragedy of Louis Riel and the Métis to turn their attention outwards, to the survival of their language and religion elsewhere in Canada, particularly, in Manitoba and the North West. They did not expect the prairie West to be completely bilingual, but they were asserting a right to share in its future. Like deputy prime minister Sir George-Étienne Cartier, they felt French Canadians should have "a little province of Québec" set aside for them in the West, even if the vast majority didn't want to go to live there. Continues Silver: "[T]he Riel affair, by bringing to such an intense pitch French Canadian feelings of concern about events in the West, helped them move *toward* a bilingual-dual nationality theory of Confederation." [1]

This editorial comment, appearing in the Québec newspaper *La Patrie* on August 7, 1885, captures the sentiment exactly. "Let it be understood that we have the right, in the North West just as on the banks of the

St. Lawrence, to work to set up a French Canadian state [2] "

French Canadians interpreted the hanging of Louis Riel in 1885 as a denial of their right to participate in the development of Canada's West. Historian Tom Flanagan writes about the Métis leader: "Small wonder that his career – particularly his lonely appearance in the prisoner's box in Regina – has captured the Canadian imagination. He symbolizes in one way or another many of the great issues capturing our national agenda." [2] The execution triggered a conflicted, contradictory response among French Canadians. It reinforced their traditional determination to build a Fortress Québec as the sole guarantor of *la survivance* and encouraged French Canadians once again to heed warnings like this uttered by *L'Opinion Publique* on June 25, 1874: "United together we can accomplish great things; dispersed to the four corners of the continent, our efforts are half-paralyzed." Yet it also engaged them in finding ways to use their political power within Canada to try to ameliorate the harsh conditions afflicting their fellow citizens elsewhere in the nation.

Opinion-makers in Québec and a prominent Franco-Manitoban colonizer agreed that the execution led to the belief it was unsafe for French Canadians to go west. One Liberal pamphleteer wrote: "I ask you what security one can have in a country whose Government authorizes the plundering of its inhabitants, ignores their requests, and hangs madmen!" [3] T.A. Bernier of St. Boniface, who worked tirelessly to bring French-speaking settlers to Manitoba, added the hanging to the list of obstacles he faced. "We often hear people reproaching the Anglo-Saxon races for wanting to take over the North-West and make it into English provinces." Since the French element was already almost completely drowned out in Manitoba, "'why, then should we go there?' several of our compatriots have asked." [4] On three occasions in the spring and summer of 1886, *La Vérité* commented: "Those of our compatriots who are already settled in those vast territories have been mistreated, pushed into rebellion by the civil authorities; and then, instead of being given justice, they've been massacred, hanged, imprisoned." [5]

If the Riel execution cemented French Canadians' resolve to preserve the integrity of their Québec homeland, it also brought to a climax their concern for the fate of the harassed Métis. It was to be a major turning point for Canada. States Silver:

> This growing involvement with the Métis had gradually led
> Québécers to feel that they – that French Canada – had

> something important at stake in the West ... Ultimately,
> some of them at least would be led to a redefinition of
> Canada itself – to a novel view of the dominion as a
> bilingual, dual nationality. [6]

In the end, French Canadians were given many reasons aside from Riel's unhappy fate to decide to personally avoid – yet to have to pay rapt attention to – Manitoba throughout the first thirty-six years of its history.

As noted before, Manitoba entered Confederation as a province made in Québec's image. Its first three lieutenant governors – Adams Archibald, Alexander Morris and Joseph Cauchon – were chosen by Ottawa in part because all were fluent in English and French. The province was governed and administered in two languages from 1870 to 1889. The debates were not recorded in an official "Hansard", but a nearly verbatim account of the legislative sessions appeared in French and English in two local newspapers. The Journals of the Legislative Assembly, the official records of its business, were published in two versions, one French and one English, from 1871 to 1889. So were the statutes. The cabinet, usually a five-person group, always contained French-speaking representatives in this period. And the boundaries of the constituencies were drawn to ensure linguistic and religious as well as regional representation. [7]. But the province's ethnic makeup was rapidly being transformed, in part as a result of a deliberate strategy by the Orangist Canada First movement to drown Manitoba's French, Catholic and Métis character in a tidal wave of English Protestantism. Historian Allen Ronaghan reports that as early as the summer of 1870, Charles Mair of the Canada First group was placing advertisements throughout Ontario inviting farmers to consider emigrating to Manitoba. Even before Archibald had arrived at Fort Garry on September 2, 1870, the North-West Emigration Aid Society was organized and pressing the Dominion government to assist Manitoba-bound settlers. Urged on by the province's first legislature, Archibald petitioned Ottawa to proceed in the granting of the promised 1.4 million acres. But the federal government did just the opposite. It sloughed off onto the lieutenant governor's shoulders the responsibility to make good on the Métis land allotment and instead passed an order-in-council guaranteeing that "bona fide" settlers who had staked claims on unsurveyed land would have them confirmed and respected. Meanwhile, Mair's advertisements and circulars were bearing fruit. The leading edge of Canada First's planned

Anglo–Saxon wave began arriving in the spring of 1871. States Ronaghan:

> There were no facilities to receive them; land had not been
> surveyed; there was no agent to give them information.
> These settlers … squatted wherever the land looked attrac-
> tive … Settlers were staking claims everywhere and nothing
> had been done about the 1.4 million-acre grant of the
> Manitoba Act." [8]

Manitobans, both English- and French-speaking, were alarmed.
The situation almost turned violent in a confrontation along the banks of the
Boyne River (Rivière aux Ilets de Bois) near present-day Carman. Ronaghan
explains that the people of the parish of St. Charles had been in the habit of
using this area to cut hay, keep bees, pasture cattle and cut logs for many
years and while they had erected little permanent settlement there, they considered the land theirs and proceeded to blaze trees and post signs to protect
it. Within days, a party of Ontarians, following Mair's directions to locate
good land with wood handy, cut across country from Pembina and quickly
found themselves standing nose to nose with the stakeholders. The St. Charles
people informed them the land had been claimed and warned them off.

> Threats were made; angry words were uttered. A less
> disciplined people than the Métis would have massacred
> the newcomers. Instead, the Métis appealed to their leaders
> and to Archibald, and he, seeing that he could not force
> the Ontarians to go elsewhere for land, advised the Métis
> to give way. The Métis obeyed, but with a deep feeling
> of having been betrayed both by Archibald and by the
> Canadian government. [9]

Soon new immigrants were added to the Ontarian flood. Icelandic
and Mennonite group settlements were established in the mid-1870s. Fully
7,000 Mennonites arrived between 1875 and 1880. The province's original
bilingual and bicultural institutions quickly fell under sustained pressure.
Historian W.L. Morton says the balance of population steadily turned against
the French from the establishment of civil government in September 1870
on and it wasn't long before the principle of duality was imperilled, too.

The land issue was only one area of French-English discord. Racial
and linguistic tensions soon arose over the electoral map, the province's

appointed upper house and, finally, sectarian schools and official bilingualism itself. Standing in defiance of historical inevitability, historian Lovell Clark argues eloquently that the fate of Franco-Manitobans should not have been a foregone conclusion. The fact they quickly found themselves in minority was no excuse for the violations of their rights. Further, there should have been nothing inevitable about the attack on Manitoba's dualism. In *The Manitoba School Question: Majority Rule or Minority Rights,* he says:

> If French Canadian (and Roman Catholic) immigration to the West had been on a sufficient scale to make them a political force to be reckoned with, so the argument runs, then interference with their rights would never have been attempted. This last statement is undoubtedly true, but it does not necessarily follow that the converse is true, that a group which is small, and of little political importance locally, inevitably suffers oppression and loss of rights. Or rather it is not inevitable unless one assumes that the words "tyranny" and "majority" are inseparable. [10]

Unfortunately, as we shall see, the history of Manitoba from 1870 to 1985 was one where "tyranny" and "majority" became and remained inseparable. Making matters worse, the province for most of that period was blatantly operating outside constitutional law, a fact it would periodically tacitly acknowledge by an ingenious form of legal subterfuge.

Manitoba achieved full responsible government in the summer of 1874. [11] Robert Atkinson Davis won a byelection and introduced a motion of non-confidence in the government's attorney general and former premier, Henry Joseph Clarke. The motion passed and the government resigned. The MLAs insisted on a voice in selecting the new cabinet and Lieutenant Governor Alexander Morris acceded. "For the first time, a lieutenant governor deferred to a premier, Marc-Amable Girard," writes historian Ruth Swan. [12] Girard chose a cabinet with equal representation of Catholics and Protestants and was sworn in on July 8, 1874.

A Franco-Manitoban thus became the first Manitoba premier with real power. The lieutenant governor himself proudly noted the accomplishment in a letter to the federal secretary of state. The government, he wrote, had been formed by means of a premier, a practice that "has introduced responsible Government in its modern type into the Province – the previous ministry was selected personally by my predecessor and none of its members were recognized as first minister". [13]

But the race issue quickly raised its head. Historian G.O. Rothney says Girard's "great misfortune" was that his premiership coincided with the period when Riel was waging his several campaigns for a parliamentary seat. Not only did Girard's presidency of the L'Association Saint-Jean-Baptiste de Manitoba identify him with the Riel side of the ongoing controversy, but his attorney general, Joseph Dubuc, affronted the English because he had defended Ambroise Lépine against Thomas Scott's capital murder charge. When two English-speaking ministers refused to fight the next election led by Girard and Dubuc, all but one member of the cabinet resigned on December 1, 1874. Morris called on Davis, the remaining minister, to head a new government. In the coalition that emerged two days later, Davis was the spokesman for the English Canadian element, Joseph Royal represented the French Canadians and Colin Inkster acted for the original Red River settlers. The ministry went to the polls at the end of December and won enough seats to form a minority government. [14]

Davis' four-year term as premier (1874-1878) was marked by strong racial divisions which he, as a bilingual Anglophone originally from Québec, was uniquely positioned to both attract and deflect. "He could speak French and was able to convince Royal and Dubuc that he supported French rights as established in Manitoba," says Swan. That, of course, complicated his attempts to gain the trust of the English. To win their backing, he offered a cabinet seat to John Norquay, the leader of the "old settler" English group. Norquay dropped his demand for the abolition of the French language and educational rights in return for the promise of a bill giving more seats in the assembly to the growing English community.

In 1875, the principle of legislative duality – twelve French constituencies and twelve English constituencies established by the province's original electoral law – was abandoned and replaced by eight French, eight English (old settlers) and eight English (new settlers) ridings. This was sufficient for Norquay, but left offside the English radicals – the Canadian Party under the leadership of John Christian Schultz and an Orange rump led by Francis Evans Cornish. Davis' "softness" on French rights also earned him the enmity of the province's leading newspaper. Writes Swan: "Because of his willingness to form a coalition with the French party, the *Daily Free Press* of Winnipeg denounced him as disloyal to Canada." Historian Gerald Friesen

refers to the newspaper's outburst "as Liberal and WASP bile not representative of the majority of English-speaking Manitobans at that point." [15]

In 1876, as an economy measure, the federal government offered
Manitoba a larger grant if it would agree to abolish its upper house. The
legislative council, as it was called, was an exact duplicate, even to the name,
of Québec's second chamber and like it, had as one of its roles the defence of
minority rights. But to many Ontarians, whose legislature was unicameral, it
was unnecessary and foreign and altogether too close to French Canada and
Roman Catholicism for their liking. The members of the legislative council,
not surprisingly, were vehemently opposed to the loss of their incomes and
positions and defeated the first two bills designed to abolish the chamber.
The third bill passed but only after Davis bought off enough councillors with
promises of other government sinecures. The council's demise did not immediately become an English-French flashpoint, but may have been a waystation
along the road to an attempted political coup three years later. At the time,
however, Joseph Royal told the *Free Press* that Manitoba's French community
relied on the guarantees in the British North America Act, that is, they were
"henceforth dependent for the special position of their group in Manitoba on
the courts and the political weight of Québec in Confederation." [16] Both were
to prove frail reeds, indeed.

Davis retired from politics in 1878 and was replaced by Norquay.
The new premier was popular in all sections of the province's diverse population with the exception of John Christian Schultz and his Orange Ontario
radicals. Norquay was a six-foot, 300-pound giant of a man of Orcadian and
Aboriginal ancestry. In fact, he had the same proportion of Aboriginal blood
as Louis Riel. His grandmother was the daughter of a "country marriage".
But the important difference was that in his case, the "country marriage"
was between an Aboriginal woman and a Hudson's Bay Company man.
That meant he was much better positioned, as were all Manitoba's English
mixed-blood citizens, to win acceptance by the dominant English-speaking
white society than were the increasingly small minority of Métis.

Norquay went on to become Manitoba's most successful early premier, serving from October 16, 1878 to December 12, 1887. He presided
competently over a period of rapid growth in the province. As noted earlier,
Manitoba's population was burgeoning, rising from 12,000 in 1870 to 30,000
in 1877 to 60,000 in 1881 to 120,000 by the time he left office. Government
spending also increased dramatically, soaring from about $90,000 in 1876 to

about $700,000 in 1886. Historian Gerald Friesen writes in the *Dictionary of Canadian Biography*: "His forceful negotiations and urgent representations at Ottawa won larger subsidies and enlarged boundaries for Manitoba, and his cabinets were competent in the administration of justice, public works and agriculture." [17]

Although a federal Conservative, Norquay opposed the introduction of federal party politics into the provincial legislature mainly because he believed that a non-partisan front would strengthen the province's hand in negotiations with Ottawa on a host of vital outstanding issues including control of public lands and the granting of railway charters. In the spring of 1879, Norquay was nearly the victim of a political coup launched by his cabinet colleague, Joseph Royal, and a leading Conservative opposition member by the freighted name of Thomas Scott. "This incongruous alliance of a French Canadian Roman Catholic from Québec and an English-speaking Orangeman from Ontario was intended to cause a shift in support from the English-speaking mixed-blood premier to Royal and a new coalition cabinet," Friesen recounts. [18] Royal likely believed he could control the introduction of eastern party politics while Scott wanted to see the Conservative party firmly established in Manitoba.

University of Ottawa historian Cornelius Jaenen sees the event as an attempt by Royal to gain some recognition of "French power" based "on a consciousness of the erosion of the role of the Francophones in provincial affairs". [19] Just five years after entering Confederation, the linguistic majority of 1870 had lost not only its right to an equal number of seats in the legislature, but also an equal voice in the cabinet. Continues Jaenen:

> Was it an assertion of the principle of "double majority", or the need for both founding communities to give their consent on major legislation? Or was it an attempt to introduce the national party system into provincial politics? It seems that behind Royal's attempt to overturn the Norquay government … there was a growing disagreement between Francophone Métis and French Canadians about appointments to public office, land policy, and political representation. [20]

Jaenen notes that, even by the mid-1870s, the face of francophone Manitoba had changed. A small but steady trickle of Québécois and Franco-Americans were arriving to offset the Métis diaspora. According to the 1881 Census, the actual number of French-speaking Manitobans had risen by more than three thousand to 9,688 from 6,500 at the time of Confederation in 1870. This modest increase paled in comparison to the massive English influx. The number of anglophone Manitobans had soared from 6,500 to 37,155 over the same time frame. The percentages paint a stark picture. From a position of parity in 1870, the two linguistic groups had gone in opposite directions, the English, to 59.7 per cent of the province and the French, to a mere 15.6 per cent.

Norquay outmanoeuvered the attempted francophone coup by hastily assembling a caucus of all the English-speaking MLAs. "Norquay condoned, if he did not actually initiate, a round of anti-French speeches, and then offered to lead an 'English' ministry which would be committed to a curtailment of French language rights and political representation." [21] His majority secured, Norquay demanded Royal's resignation from the cabinet and subsequently accused him of "treachery" in a letter to the prime minister. In quick succession, he pushed through an electoral law further reducing French representation and introduced a bill to cease printing all government documents in French save the provincial statutes. Entitled *An Act Respecting Public Printing*, it reads:

> Her Majesty, by and with the advice and consent of the Legislative Assembly of Manitoba, enacts as follows:
>
> I. From and after the passing of this Act none of the public documents shall be printed in the French language except the statutes of the province.
>
> II. This Act shall not prevent the printing of any of the public documents in the French language which shall be considered necessary and advisable by the Lieutenant-Governor in Council and in all matters required to be printed in the Manitoba Gazette the same may be repeated in the French language immediately following the same in the English language. [22]

Lieutenant Governor Joseph Cauchon reserved it as possibly *ultra-vires* (beyond the powers) of the legislature. He informed the governor general, the Marquis of Lorne, of the situation:

> Inadvertently the Bill had been carried through the Assembly before it was shown to me or I had ever seen it at all, otherwise

the difficulty might probably have been averted; but as the case then stood there was no other alternative left to me but to run the risk of producing a possible graver result, or to reserve it for the signification of your Excellency's pleasure, believing it wiser under all the circumstances, to submit it to the better judgement and greater knowledge of your Excellency's government, and thus to obtain, for all time a guiding precedent and permanent rule for all the Legislatures of the Dominion, simularly situated in relationship to the same question. [23]

The Macdonald government followed the path of avoidance and procrastination that earned the prime minister the sobriquet "Old Tomorrow" and let the matter die. Some historians believe Manitoba, then nearly bankrupt and having argued for the measure by saying that cheaper was better, was pacified by Ottawa's increased subsidy. Official bilingualism remained, but Ottawa issued no "guiding precedent and permanent rule" that would serve for all regions and "for all time". [24]

In fact, it would be exactly 100 years before the "guiding principle and permanent rule" serving all regions "for all time" would be enunciated by the Supreme Court of Canada in the Georges Forest judgement handed down in December 1979. A full century would pass before the nation's highest court would validate Cauchon's concern. The Manitoba Act couldn't be altered by a simple act of the legislature because it was passed by the Canadian Parliament in 1870 and re-enacted in 1871 by the Imperial Parliament and so constitutionalized. As we shall see, there is only one way for a province to amend its constitution and that is through a majority vote in its own legislature and the passage of the amendment through both houses of the Canadian Parliament.

Those long-ago debates on electoral redistribution and language exposed all the racial and linguistic prejudices that lurk to this day in the province's bosom. With astonishing durability, consistency and repetition, the essential arguments animating them persisted for at least the first 115 years of the province's history, and perhaps well beyond, ever ready to leap out and stain anew Manitoba's public life. The *Journals of the Legislative Assembly, First Session of the Third Parliament of Manitoba, 42 and 43 Victoria, begun and holden at Winnipeg on the first day of February, 1879 and closed by prorogation on the twenty-fifth day of June, 1879* provides taste and flavour.

The committee of the whole debate on Bill 32, an act to provide "an equitable distribution of the Electoral Divisions for the Province of Manitoba" took place on Wednesday, June 18, 1879 at three o'clock in the afternoon. Joseph Royal, MLA for St. François Xavier West, seconded by Pierre Delorme, MLA for St. Norbert, moved that the report of the committee "not now be received", but amended with a stinging eight-point rebuke to the government. It pointed out, among other things, that the measure had neither been discussed in the last election nor mentioned in the Speech from the Throne and that there was no proper list of electors upon which to base the new redistribution.

Then the amendment ripped into the government for its unjust, unfair and "unBritish" attack on minority rights. It was "entirely destitute of justice and fairness towards the population of this Province speaking the French Language" and lacked "due regard to the various classes of interests which it is the duty of the Government and the Legislature in a mixed community to promote and harmonize ..." Noting that the legislation was a product of "all the representatives of English-speaking electoral divisions," the amendment stated flatly that "the minority composed of all the members representing French-speaking electoral divisions, was expressly and systematically ignored and excluded ... on account of sectional prejudices ..." As a result, "no alternative is left to the minority who were not treated with British fairness by a hostile majority " [25]

The amendment was lost in a vote of twelve to eight and the bill, which reduced French representation to just six seats out of twenty-four from a status of equality in 1870, was passed.

Second reading debate on Bill 25, "respecting public printing", the language bill, began the following day, June 19, 1879 at three o'clock in the afternoon. Joseph Royal was again on his feet, this time objecting to the legislation on the grounds it was unconstitutional. The speaker refused to rule, saying he hadn't the right or the responsibility to pronounce on constitutionality "as I consider it beyond my sphere". [26] Royal, again seconded by Delorme, moved the traditional parliamentary killing motion, the six-month hoist. Like their amendment on the electoral boundaries, this also contained a stirring appeal for justice and minority rights:

> Whereas the keeping of the public records of this province
> of Manitoba, in both the French and English languages is a

part of the written Constitution of Manitoba which was obtained by the people of the country and granted by the Dominion of Canada under the sanction of an Imperial Act; and

Whereas all the members representing the English-speaking electoral divisions, being the majority in the Provincial Legislature, have lately entered into a certain political compact, chiefly to carry out certain radical measures calculated to annihilate the legitimate influence of the oldest, and to-day one of the two principal elements of the population of the Province; and Whereas under the fallacy of economy, the so-called English party have, in the said compact determined upon the abolition of the printing in the French language of all the public documents, except the statutes of the Province; and Whereas such a measure will have the effect of depriving an important class of her Majesty's loyal subjects in Manitoba, of one of the rights and privileges granted by the Manitoba Act most endear [sic] to them" [27]...

The amendment failed by a vote of twelve to six. The *Manitoba Free Press* carried an exhaustive two-column report of the June 19th debate on page three of its June 30, 1879 edition. The bulk of the coverage was devoted to the premier's speech. He was at once antagonistic and sympathetic to the Franco-Manitoban cause.

Norquay insisted his government had absolutely no intention of abolishing the French language. The legislation was being pursued solely in the interests of "true economy" and was "undertaken by those who entertained nothing but the most friendly feelings for their French neighbours – undertaken as a matter of necessity and duty which they would prove false to the Province at large to neglect". He had no desire to do anything "which would grate harshly on the feelings of any section of the people of our Province". Nor, he believed, was there "the slightest wish on the part of any one section of the people to do injustice to the other".

The reason his cabinet had no French representation was not his fault, he said. He had "made overtures to the French member remaining in the Cabinet to stay and finding he would not, sought elsewhere to fill the vacancies with a view to a fair representation of both sections". Those who refused his advances were unjust now to accuse him of allying himself solely with the English. When Royal questioned why similar economies were not being sought in the printing of English government documents, Norquay said he was opposed to unnecessary printing in either language.

Addressing the issue of the bill's constitutionality, the premier advanced a narrow interpretation of the province's official language requirement. The Manitoba Act, he insisted, only required that the laws be in both languages "while in reference to the other printing, it was a matter of option". He argued further that his government was only "keeping pace with the growing wants of the country". As for the usage of the French language in the legislature, that would continue to be protected by the presence of a French as well as an English clerk of the house, he said. "He had stated before – and he desired to repeat it – that he should be sorry, indeed, to see the day when on the floor of that House any member would be interdicted from expressing his opinions on the public questions of the day in his native language." [28]

Then suddenly Norquay dropped his conciliatory and tolerant tone. Obviously still stinging from what he saw as Royal's treachery, the premier indulged himself in what could be seen as anti-French prejudice. He accused the Franco-Manitobans of demanding "exceptional rights" at a time when their numbers were so diminished they had nearly "passed away – become a thing of the past – scarcely a vestige of them being now found" while an equally historically important community in Manitoba – the Selkirk settlers – "never seem to have demanded any special rights". Further, the premier "waved the bloody shirt" by recalling the Seven Oaks massacre when the Selkirk settlers "were nearly all swept away on one memorable occasion, particularly, by men speaking the French language coming from the Saskatchewan." He continued:

> Coming to this country when it was a wilderness, they [the Selkirk settlers] located on the banks of the Red River where they became a thrifty, flourishing community, contributing materially to the progress of the country and the development of its institutions. And while they could be set down side by side with the early explorers of the country – those in whose behalf rights were now claimed – these people had not demanded any exceptional rights – did not clamour for any imaginary vested interests – because they felt the

claim would not be in accord with the progress of the age. It was the business of legislators to deal with the practical questions coming before them and not with mere questions of sentiment such as this about French rights. [29]

In 1878, the printing of all government documents in French had cost the provincial treasury $4,712.56. Despite requests from the French-speaking MLAs, the government did not provide the House with the cost of the English printing. According to the newspaper report, Joseph Royal contented himself with correcting the premier's version of the events surrounding the Battle of Seven Oaks. "He went on to confute the statement that the early Scotch colonists had been almost annihilated by a party of French colonists. The action was between the servants of two rival fur companies – not between the colonists of two different nationalities as such." [30]

The 1879 affair didn't go unnoticed in Québec. By then, Québécois much more readily identified themselves with the embattled Franco-Manitoban minority than they had in the cases of the Métis and the Acadians. While not that many had moved to Manitoba, thanks to the diaspora of Métis, most of the French Canadians still in the province were now of Québec origin, if more recently from the United States. When wind of the Norquay government's twin blows against Manitoba's duality first reached Québec, Le Nouveau Monde proclaimed it "a declaration of war against the minority" [31] while Le Courrier de St-Hyacinthe called it "a persecution of our race in Manitoba". [32]

It never flowered into a genuine cause célèbre because it met a speedy demise with Cauchon's reservation. Still, some Québec newspapers took the occasion to warn English Canada. On June 17, 1879 La Minerve wrote: "Naturally, they [the Franco-Manitobans] are assured of our sympathy and of our most loyal co-operation, and we are confident that this struggle, carried on by peaceful means, and with the aid of the laws and institutions of the country, will end to the shame of the perpetrators of fanaticism." [33]

Those 1879 events in Manitoba strengthened French Canadians' resentment against Anglo-Québécois. Manitoba's treatment of its minority "stood in bitter contrast to the situation in the province of Québec where the Franco-Canadian element is such a big majority and yet treats the Anglo-Canadian minority in such a different manner" [34]

W.L. Morton, in his Manitoba: A History, entitles the chapter covering the period between 1881 and 1888 "The Triumph of Ontario Democracy". The speed and totality of the province's transformation within twenty years was astounding.

> The old Manitoba of 1870 had been engulfed by the new Manitoba of 1881. In one decade of swift change, the province had seen the fur trade give way to the grain trade, the cart brigade to the railway train. The *métis* had withdrawn to the wooded river lots or trekked to the plains of the Saskatchewan to shoot down the last bands of buffalo. The loose beauty of the park belt, the landscape of shimmering meadows flowing around the clumped poplar bluffs and down ragged willow runs, was giving way to a new pattern, the rectangular pattern of ploughed field and quarter-section farm. The new Manitoba was confident of its future. (35)

BIRD'S-EYE VIEW OF MANITOBA.

The extension of the province's boundaries northwards and westwards in 1881 added 16,000 people to the province in one stroke. Pressure to escape from the bonds of apparently outdated and costly official bilingualism began to mount. Along with economic and cultural transformation came political change. Gerald Friesen says a new political entity had developed in opposition to Norquay in the 1880s representing many of the Ontario settlers. It could be described as the forerunner of the Liberal Party because it was an offspring of the southern Ontario political movement led in the House of Commons by George Brown, Alexander Mackenzie and Edward Blake, the man who put the $5,000 price on Riel's head. The Manitoba offshoot was led by Thomas Greenway and Joseph Martin, both of whom represented the heartland of Orange Ontario in the province, the southwestern Manitoba constituencies of Mountain and Portage la Prairie respectively.

Entangled in a railway scandal, Norquay was forced to resign in 1887. He was succeeded by D.H. Harrison, one of his own ministers. But Harrison's administration failed in its first test, the re-election of new ministers on their acceptance of office as the law then required. One of these byelections spoke again to the enduring issue of linguistic duality. Joseph Burke, the French representative in the new ministry, sought re-election in St. François Xavier. His Liberal opponent was F.H. Francis of Headingley. The Liberal candidate assured francophone voters a new Liberal government would treat them exactly as they had been in the past. Caught up in the "time for a change" atmosphere building in the province, St. François voters took him at his word. The byelection victory in one of the old Red River districts as well as the defeat of two of its other ministers brought the enfeebled Harrison ministry "to a swift and timely end". writes W.L. Morton. [36] Harrison resigned on January 18, 1888 and the Liberal leader, Greenway, was asked to form a new government. True to the pledges given in St. François Xavier, after consultation with Archbishop Alexandre-Antonin Taché, Greenway brought Franco-Manitoban James Émile Pierre Prendergast, the member for Woodlands, into his cabinet, making him provincial secretary. W.L. Morton says the Liberals were motivated only by political necessity.

> The Liberals at that time were not committed to the elimination of the French from the government of the province or to any measure a French representative could not accept. The decisive factor was the narrow division in the legislature, in

which the Liberals had been in a minority until the events
of December and January. Even with the victories in the byelections, they could be sure of controlling the House only
with the support of the French members. [37]

The new government was unlike any Manitoba had seen before. It signalled,
as W.L. Morton and other historians have written, the end of the old Red
River order. Springing not out of the soil of Manitoba but from the modern
political culture of progressive reform and individual rights then sweeping
through North America, the government had five main objectives – economy in public administration, railway extension, increased immigration by
all practical means, redistribution of electoral ridings on the basis of strict
representation by population and universal manhood suffrage.

Redistribution was the first order of business when the legislature
convened in March 1888. The province was divided into thirty-eight electoral
districts the boundaries of which were to reflect as nearly as possible the
standard unit of 2,600 people each. The significant feature of the bill was
that it completely ignored the old concept of communal representation. The
former Red River districts of the "old settlers" and the French survived, if they
survived at all, only by happenstance, that is, through population density.
Only Kildonan and Provencher remained to represent the Selkirk settlers and
Franco-Manitobans respectively. The "colony" seats like Gimli also disappeared.
Gimli, the centre of Manitoba's Icelandic "Republic", was swallowed by St.
Andrew's. For the first time, the recently settled areas of the "new Manitoba"
were fully enfranchised.

What had happened could be seen as a long-overdue acknowledgement of the province's new reality, its maturation from colony to modern
democracy in keeping with the phenomenal growth – and shift – in its population. That growth had been nothing less than astonishing, burgeoning from
62,260 in 1881 to 152,506 in 1891. And as for the shift, successive Census
data were to show that between 1881 and 1901, the portion of the population
identified as French-speaking would plummet from 15.6 per cent to just 6.3
per cent. Nonetheless, the transformation of 1888 constituted a revolution and
tended to intolerance of difference and non-conformity. Says W.L. Morton:

> ... [T]he triumph of Grit democracy in Manitoba was com-
> plete. The old order, whether the dual system in language
> and schools with all it meant to the French, or the influence

the old settlers had exercised through their communal constituencies and their own representatives led by John Norquay, now existed at the discretion of the new majority, largely Ontario-bred and Protestant by creed. " [38]

The election of 1888 was a sweeping victory for the Liberals. Eleven, including the premier himself, were returned by acclamation. The government captured thirty-five seats. Only six MLAs were French-speaking. According to W.L. Morton, the election "marked the triumph of Ontario over Québec in Manitoba. The decision of 1870, the work of Riel's daring and Taché's diplomacy, was tacitly undone." [39] The table was now set for the second Manitoba crisis based on language and religion, one that would easily rival and possibly even surpass the Riel tragedy in the potency of its threat to the uneasy French-English partnership that underpinned and sustained Canadian Confederation. Prime Minister Sir John A. Macdonald best captured the mood and motivations of the events of 1889-90 when he described them as driven by "one of those insane crazes which can only be compared to the Popish plot ..." [40]

Historians disagree on whether the Public Schools Act and its less profiled but more important fraternal twin, the Official Language Act of 1890, were provoked from without or an inevitable evolution within the province itself. To bolster his perspective of outside agitation, historian Lovell Clark, editor of *The Manitoba School Question: Majority Rule or Minority Rights*, quotes no less an authority than the lawyer for the Roman Catholic school cause, John Ewart. He told the Canadian Privy Council in 1895 that the Greenway government's initial school reforms intended merely to replace the dual board with a department of education. Only the "craze" generated by the anti-French firebrand, D'Alton McCarthy, goaded it into the complete abolition of sectarian schools. But Clark's colleagues, W.L. Morton and Donald Creighton, say the forces were already in motion within Manitoba for the assaults on the province's duality. For their proof, they look no further than the fact McCarthy was accompanied on his platforms in Manitoba by none other than Greenway's attorney general, Joseph Martin.

Joseph Hilts, in his 1974 University of Manitoba PhD thesis entitled *The Political Career of Thomas Greenway*, agrees the Manitoba School Question was an entirely made-in-Manitoba development and McCarthy merely jumped on a bandwagon that had already started rolling by the time he arrived in the province. "The origins of this conflict were based in Manitoba as James Smart, with Greenway's concurrence, precipitated the controversy prior to the speeches of D'Alton McCarthy and Joseph Martin." [41] Hilts says the driving force behind the laws was the government's concern for economy in provincial and municipal taxation and its need to divert public attention from the accumulating railway and land speculation scandals the *Manitoba Free Press* was busy sniffing out. The paper's editor, W.F. Luxton, a fierce opponent of railway monopoly and the Liberal member for Rockwood, had accused Greenway and Martin of agreeing to lease the Red River Valley Railway to the Manitoba Central in return for a political donation. The government then turned around and leased it to the American-owned Northern Pacific, this time, the paper said, in exchange for personal bribes. Martin brought a libel suit against the paper, but a disagreement within the grand jury prevented the case going to court. A royal commission was appointed and on November 15, 1888, reported that no evidence had been advanced to support the charges against the premier and his attorney general. Still, the paper was loath to let go of something that had the potential to produce a Manitoba rival to the Pacific Scandal. In editorials published August 29 and September 12, 1889, the paper claimed Martin wanted to start "a row over the schools between the Dominion Government and the Province in order to bury the strong-smelling past in connection with the Northern Pacific corruptions and general infamies". [42]

As far as the nation was concerned, it didn't matter what "corruptions and infamies" the Manitoba legislation was designed to cover up or whether its inspiration was homegrown or imported. The speeches by McCarthy and Martin immediately made the twin bills about anti-French and anti-Catholic prejudice and nothing else but anti-French and anti-Catholic prejudice. Prior to this, peace had reigned between English and French Manitobans since the attempt to disestablish the French language was quietly buried by the lieutenant governor and Ottawa in 1879. However, even though "the opposition to dualism was quiescent and might long have remained so, the prairies were dry, the grasses dun and grey after summer's heat [and] a spark would set the fires running." [43]

The spark was not long in coming. In 1888, Québec Premier Honoré Mercier's government passed the Jesuits Estates Act to settle the long-standing question of the Canadian lands of the Jesuit Order that fell to the British Crown at the time of the Conquest and went to the province at

Confederation. The act directed that the order use the majority of the monetary compensation for educational purposes, but requested the Pope, as the head of the Church of Rome, to arbitrate certain disputed claims. None of the English Protestant MLAs voted against the measure, a noteworthy fact immediately subsumed in the instant conflagration of racial and religious bigotry.

The spectre of papal intervention in Canadian affairs created an overnight outpouring of rage in the Orange Lodges of Ontario and southwestern Manitoba. McCarthy, a Toronto lawyer and a rising young Conservative star in the House of Commons, saw his chance to attack one of the features of Canada – French-English dualism – he firmly believed was holding it back from its great destiny. The Equal Rights Association was formed to press for federal disallowance of the act and in March 1889, the "Noble Thirteen" or the "Devil's Dozen", depending on your perspective, staged a formidable attack on the Québec legislation in the House of Commons.

A natural platform orator with a talent for eloquent and incisive argument, the handsome McCarthy had entered politics as a protégé of the prime minister's and come to be regarded as the great new hope of the Tory party. He had been offered but had declined the justice portfolio, being too ambitious to be content with a small ministerial salary and too independent-minded to be tied to the discipline of caucus and cabinet solidarity.

> The events that followed the execution of Louis Riel – the sudden rise of Mercier and his Nationalistes [in Québec] – had convinced him that English-Canadian supremacy and Canadian national unity were threatened. French Canada, he believed, had become a far too distinctive, exclusive and powerful bloc in Canadian life. [He regarded] the Roman Catholic Church and its institutions suspiciously as manifestations of a separate and impermeable French-Canadian culture. He refused to accept dualism as a principle of Canadian life. He wanted unity achieved and maintained through English-Canadian supremacy. [44]

He told the prime minister that the defining question of Canada's existence was not annexation to the United States but "whether it is to be English or French". [45] He urged Macdonald to abandon the historic English-French alliance that had been the Tories' foundation since 1854 and abolish the official status of French in the Canadian West. Macdonald refused even to consider such a risky and revolutionary course. Said the prime minister:

> I have no accord with the desire expressed in some quarters
> [that] there should be an attempt made to oppress the one
> language or to render it inferior to the other; I believe that it
> would be impossible if it were tried, and it would be foolish
> and wicked if it were possible. [46]

So a defiant McCarthy simply went his own way, determined to
awaken English Canada to a sense of its "extreme peril". From a platform
in Stayner, Ontario, in July 1889, McCarthy prophesied that the problem of
French Canada would either be settled by ballots in his generation or by bullets in the next. Having whipped up his own province to a fever pitch, he
decided to carry his crusade on to Manitoba and the North West Territories,
new regions of the country that had, in his view, been unjustly and inappro-
priately burdened with sectarian schools and official bilingualism.

His appeals weren't to fall on stony ground. In early 1889, Joseph
Royal, the former Manitoba MLA who had fought John Norquay's attempt
to abridge the official status of the French language in 1879 and was now
the lieutenant governor of the North West Territories, a region that included
the future provinces of Saskatchewan and Alberta, provoked "astonishment
and annoyance" when he opened the Territorial Council with a speech in
English and French. [47]

In Manitoba, this *bouquet garni* of the Jesuits Estates Act, the Pope
and D'Alton McCarthy infused the long-simmering anti-Catholic, anti-French
pot with a pungent new flavour. These prejudices were particularly strong in
Brandon and Portage la Prairie and their surrounding rural areas, all now
almost exclusively Ontario Protestant and Orange. "In all the province from
the Assiniboine River south, and from the foot of the Pembina Escarpment
westward, in that south-central and south-western Manitoba which was a
new Ontario, the anti-Catholic cry was certain to set the echoes ringing." [48]
The Jesuit historian, Paul Crunican, observed:

> Along with strong men, strong prejudices came from the
> East. Ontario was transplanting the most virulent of its
> opinions onto a relatively peaceful Manitoba scene. But
> Ontario was not alone to blame. The whole escalation of
> events that followed the execution of Riel was exacting a

bitter price. Honoré Mercier had come to power in Québec in the long shadow of Riel's hanging and had angered Orangemen and Protestants everywhere by his overly demonstrative Catholicism. [49].

In May 1889, the Liberal *Brandon Sun* sounded the first salvo for the abolition of the old dual order. In July, Premier Greenway, representing the Mountain riding, Joseph Martin, his attorney general and member for Portage la Prairie, and James Smart, the public works minister and member for Brandon, decided to abolish the dual school system. This decision they reached without consulting their other two colleagues, Col. D.H. MacMillan (Winnipeg Centre) and Provincial Secretary James E.P. Prendergast (St. François Xavier), the cabinet's francophone representative. Smart announced the plan in a speech in Souris on August 1st. He sold it solely as an economy and efficiency measure, making neither racial nor religious references.

Then on August 5, 1889 D'Alton McCarthy came to Portage la Prairie, an Orange Lodge stronghold, and made what W.L. Morton calls "a fiery, anti-Catholic speech". As MLA for the district, Martin shared the platform with McCarthy. Reportedly carried away by the Orangeman's oratory, he rushed to the front of the platform at the conclusion of McCarthy's speech to pledge himself – and by implication the government – not only to abolish the dual system of schools but also the official use of the French language in Manitoba. This was the first time the French language had been mentioned, but legendary journalist John W. Dafoe, in two articles published in the *Winnipeg Sun* later that year, wrote that the Greenway government had decided a year earlier, in 1888, to abolish official bilingualism. [50] The *Manitoba Free Press* of August 7, 1889 carried lengthy extracts of McCarthy's and Martin's speeches.

McCarthy told the crowd he had been in Parliament for a dozen years and had watched what he called "this [French] movement" grow year by year. "He declared that the people were more French now than ten years ago, and if this thing were not stopped they would be more French ten years hence than now." He pointed to the American experience. "They had French people in the State of Louisiana; but did they allow French to be spoken in the courts, the schools and the legislative halls? The flag was lowered and the people became American citizens." There was, he continued, "silence on both sides of the House of Commons when this curse of the dual language was coolly planted upon this province. We were to be brought up with two languages in our midst." He had pledged to his constituents that he would:

> move at Ottawa to expunge the dual language out of the
> Northwest Territories Act. There was something for the politi-
> cian to live for; we have the power to save this country from
> fratricidal strife, the power to make this a British country in
> fact as it is in name This is a British country and the sooner
> we take up our French Canadians and make them British, the
> less trouble we leave for posterity.

To loud applause, Joseph Martin took the stage. He told the crowd he hoped the government would act to "once and for all settle" the two great questions of separate schools and language. Then he matched McCarthy's intolerance:

> He had no antipathy towards the French people, he had
> many friends amongst them [he] considered that they pos-
> sessed many great qualities, and were ... valuable citizens.
> Along with Mr. McCarthy and he trusted, with the audience,
> he was an Englishman and he believed this was an English
> country. French was a most beautiful language, but to him it
> was beautiful at home, to him it was a foreign language; and he
> maintained we should speak the language of the country. He
> had no more disagreeable duty as a minister than that of sign-
> ing documents and vouchers for public documents and
> statutes printed in a foreign language. He would cease soon to
> be a minister of the crown or cease soon to sign those vouchers.

Martin put the government in a difficult spot. Greenway had been an Ontario Conservative MP before coming to Manitoba in 1879 as the leader of a group of settlers and had shown sympathy for the New Brunswick Acadians who had lost their school rights in that province's Common Schools Act of 1871. His biographer, Keith Wilson, wrote that the premier "was an astute politician but he was not a bigot. Early in his career he had shown a marked sympathy for the Catholic cause and, though himself a Methodist, he held no rigid beliefs. He initially worked hard for the support of French Catholic voters ..." [51]

While Greenway was always to use the arguments of economy and equity in taxation to justify his government's actions on language and schools, Martin didn't bother with such sensibilities. His Portage la Prairie outburst revealed the anti-French animus that drove the government's policy. He was privately rebuked and publicly repudiated by Greenway for proposing the abolition of the official use of French, but the attorney general, along with McCarthy, had let the genie out of the bottle and neither the premier nor anyone else was to persuade it to return. [52] Prendergast, Greenway's sole French-speaking minister, seeing what was coming, resigned from cabinet. Later he was to tell the legislature why the government acted the way it did: "The country was ablaze with a prairie fire and a strong wind was blowing." [53]

The issue immediately seized the province. The newspapers loaded their editorial muskets and fired round after round at the issues and each other. The Manitoba *Free Press* weighed in on the side of unconstitutionality. Separate schools, it wrote, cannot be taken away without "a gross violation of faith, a cowardly exercise of accidental power, and a serious menace to the whole fabric of Confederation". [54] But the *Winnipeg Tribune* took the opposite tack. "And this is our answer to Québec. We shall not allow the state to support religion, we shall not allow the church to control the state, we shall not return to the Dark Ages, we shall not recognize Rome. We shall hold to the principle of equal rights for all, and that principle shall be dearer to us than Confederation itself." [55]

Le Manitoba was, of course, also extremely vigilant and throughout the summer carried editorials and lengthy articles about "La question des écoles". The articles quoted the *Free Press* and presented rebuttals to the government's rationale. Archbishop Alexandre-Antonin Taché was not above the fray and wrote letters to the newspapers, opposing the government's plans. [56].

The clergy both inside and outside the province and of all denominations commenced an ecclesiastical war of words that went on for years, turning their pulpits into political platforms. The Reverend George Bryce, principal of Manitoba College, railed against the pope's interference in Canadian affairs in his sermon at Knox Presbyterian Church as reported in the *Free Press* on August 12th. Quoting the English Bill of Rights of 1689 that prohibited "any foreign prince, potentate or prelate from having power within the realm", Bryce continued:

> We have in this nineteenth century in a British province an
> act passed which introduces the Pope of Rome as a party

having jurisdiction. I don't care anything about the letter of the constitution, there's the fact. It is a society alien to new world civilization, but unfortunately recognized, as a priest told me the other day as its advance guard by the Papal Church that has forced this question on us. When men deliberately state as they have done that they aim at building up a French Canadian nationality, what is that but a blow at our hopes as one Canadian people. Language and separate schools are being used to build up what is really destructive to our hopes as a people and we should be unworthy of our name if we permitted such aggression.

In one letter published in *Le Manitoba*, the ailing and aging Taché uttered this prophetic appeal: "One cannot, without danger, or impunity, deprive [a people] of rights that were granted and are dear to their hearts." [57]

The fate he had always feared for his people had come to pass with appalling suddenness. Despairing, he fought on all fronts – the letter and spirit of the constitution, appeals to honour and fair play, refutations of the financial and legal arguments being advanced to justify the creation of a single public school system. He even laid bare the fundamentals of Manitoba history and the negotiations between Ottawa and the provisional government in 1870 in newspaper articles published in December 1889. But it was all to no avail. The wider public had been convinced that times had changed, a single Canadian nationality had to be built out of a multiplicity of nationalities and no injustice was being done to Franco-Manitobans by treating them the same as everyone else in a common democracy.

Defeated but still battling on three years later, the archbishop penned a pamphlet to argue that Manitoba's public schools had actually become extensions of the former Protestant schools and thus constituted a complete injustice to the Catholic minority who were now subjected to a form of double taxation – required to support the public schools through their taxes and their own childrens' education privately. He closed with this poignant cri de coeur:

> The sun of Canada has smiled upon my cradle. I hope
> it will also shine over my grave. For six generations, my
> ancestors were born on the banks of the St. Lawrence.
> Canada is my country. I never had and never will have
> another home. Manitoba and the Northwest have had my
> life, my labours and my affections for nearly half a century,
> they will have them until my last day. I am a Canadian. [58]

Bishop La Flèche of Trois Rivières, Québec, who a year earlier had publicly instructed French Canadians "forced by harsh circumstances" to leave their province for Manitoba, [59] put his shoulder to the wheel on behalf of Franco-Manitobans. In 1891, after the passage of the school and language laws, he wrote to J.A. Chapleau, the federal secretary of state, requesting the disallowance of both. They were laws, he argued, that had been passed "at the instigation of a few fanatics".

> Today it is in the name of the federal compact that the
> Manitoba minority ask for protection against an unjust law,
> which is a violation of the federal compact, for that compact
> guarantees the official use of the French language on the same
> footing as the English language. The manliness with which
> you repelled a similar attempt in the Northwest Territories
> inspires me with confidence that you will not fail to take a
> firm stand in this case also. In my humble opinion this is a
> far more serious matter than the Riel question, inasmuch
> as it involves a direct violation of sentiments dearest to the
> heart of man, his love for his native tongue and his religion. [60]

Canadian Crucible

The third session of the seventh Manitoba Legislature opened on January 30, 1890 with the Speech from the Throne read in the gravelly voice of the province's lieutenant governor, none other than Louis Riel's nemesis, John Christian Schultz. Schultz's appointment on July 1, 1888, had been one of those quintessential Macdonaldisms. A testament to the prime minister's political genius or his political elasticity, or both, it was yet another instance of the wily Macdonald's ability to balance precisely on Canada's taut racial/linguistic/religious tightrope. Here he was choosing Schultz to represent the Queen in Manitoba one minute and eloquently defending French Canada the next. Schultz had not only been the leading light of the Canadian Party in Manitoba who helped forge the Equal Rights Association that whipped Orange Ontario into an anti-French anti-Catholic frenzy in 1870, but had been once described as "indiscreet and offensive" by Macdonald himself.

In 1869, the prime minister had warned the hapless William McDougall, the man who never became Manitoba's first lieutenant governor, to avoid him. Schultz and his Manitoba cohorts, the prime minister had written McDougall as he sat in Pembina, North Dakota waiting to cross the border, need to be "bridled". Now, twenty-one years later, Schultz was about to play an interesting role in the second Manitoba linguistic and religious war, a role that demonstrated a shift either in his views or Macdonald's or perhaps both.

The House had barely begun its deliberations before the six French MLAs began a sustained attack on the government for its cabinet order the previous September to stop printing the Manitoba *Gazette* in both languages. Every day, they brought numerous petitions to the House from all Manitoba's French-speaking communities protesting the government's assaults, both current and anticipated, on their rights. Prendergast, the former provincial secretary and new unofficial leader of the Franco-Manitoban caucus, issued a warning to his former colleagues.

> The French members could do nothing against what might be called the "brute majority". In view of the opposition against everything French Canadian and Catholic, he would say to members opposite that whenever they went beyond their powers they would find the French members trying to obstruct them in their nefarious work as much as they could. He would show the honourable gentlemen what they

were doing in their usual way – the coarsest possible way regardless of minorities. (61)

On February 11th, Prendergast moved a motion of censure against the government for ignoring the constitution and the law and abolishing a right guaranteed in the Manitoba Act by a mere cabinet order. Martin Jerome (Carillon) told the government its action was unconstitutional:

> There are others who know well the full meaning of the
> constitution but are only acting with an aim in view, that
> of trampling upon everything that is dear and sacred to us.
> The French are not alone. All the just and right-minded
> men of Manitoba who have peace and justice at heart, will
> resent the outrage and speak out boldly their repudiation of
> the government at the first occasion. (62)

But Attorney General Joseph Martin wasn't moved. In fact, he was dismissive, almost rude. He insisted the cabinet was perfectly within its rights because the *Gazette* was not specifically mentioned in the the Manitoba Act of 1870. He ridiculed Jerome's call to respect Manitoba's twenty-year bilingual precedent by comparing it to keeping government offices filled "as full as possible with supporters of the Government whether their services were needed or not just because that was a former practice". He was satisfied that anyone who took an interest in the *Gazette* was also quite capable of reading it in English. There was

> no more justification for the French-speaking people asking
> to have the proceedings of the House in French than there
> would be for the Germans, who in point of numbers were
> equal to if they did not exceed the French. The Icelandic
> immigrants might as reasonably ask the House to provide
> the statutes and journals in Icelandic.

At that juncture, to the accompaniment of much laughter in the chamber, Kenneth McKenzie (Lakeside) called out: "Put in Gaelic as well." Once the laughter had subsided, Martin continued:

> In the republic to the south of us where there were all the
> different nationalities of the world, they adopted the plain,
> simple and reasonable rule that the country is English-

speaking and English is the official language, no matter
how numerous some foreigners might be. We wish to have
a Canadian nation, not French or German, but a colony of
the great British Empire. [63]

The floor turned over to another Franco-Manitoban, Alphonse Fortunat
Martin (Morris). Citing the St. François Xavier byelection, he tore into the
attorney general for misleading Franco-Manitobans solely to get their votes
and then, once elected partly on the strength of their trust and numbers,
turning on them. He challenged the minister's attempts to equate other languages with Canada's two constitutional languages.

> The position of Germans, Italians and Scotchmen was not
> the same as that of the French, who had been the discover-
> ers of this country, the first pioneers, the first Christians.
> The British flag would not have been over this country but
> for the French Canadians. The treatment of these people
> today was persecution. The French Canadians would take
> the best means to obtain their rights. [64]

In the end, Prendergast's point of privilege was defeated by a vote of twenty-
four to eleven. Greenway immediately moved a motion "amending the rules
of the House so as to make it unnecessary to use the French language in
transacting the business of the House." [65] This went on to become the bill
that abolished the official use of the French language in the Legislative
Assembly, the civil service, government publications and the provincial
courts. As a result of the last of these, Franco-Manitobans even lost their
right to trial by a French jury. The Official Language Act of 1890 subsequently
became Chapter 14 of the Revised Statutes of Manitoba 1890. The premier's
speech must have been very short. According to the newspaper accounts he
made only one salient point which was that "if this Province were two-thirds
French it would be proper as a matter of business to make the official language French". [66]

Prendergast and the other Franco-Manitoban members drew on
200 years of history and legal and constitutional arguments to confront the
government. But historian W.L. Morton said they knew their cause was lost.

> The French members, led by A.F. Martin and Prendergast,
> made a spirited defence of the rights of the French language,

but they received no support and no overt sympathy. It is plain from the reports of the debates that they expected none, and had no hope of altering the determination of the majority, but were speaking for the record and for posterity. [67]

A.F. Martin asked the premier to reflect on what the response would be among Québec's English-speaking official minority if the premier there were to bring in a bill abolishing English as an official language, even though there were proportionally far fewer English in Québec than there were French in Manitoba. Prendergast told the House that the contention that the country became an English domain when Charles II granted the charter to the Hudson's Bay Company in 1670 was "an absurdity. This country was English, or Dutch or French according to actual occupation." [68] He pointed out that Manitoba's bilingual requirements were identical to those in the federal Parliament and in the Province of Québec. The legislature, he said, "cannot touch this act; they go beyond their power." Recalling earlier attempts to encroach on Franco-Manitobans' rights, Prendergast reminded members:

> They (Franco-Manitobans) had certain rights and privileges as a minority just as the English had in Québec. They asked that the Legislature should recognize rights which had been declared to be one of the bases of the constitution. In conclusion, they would find a means of appealing against this injustice to higher tribunals and, if necessary, to the foot of the throne. [69]

The attorney general came back to accuse the French MLAs of using the constitution "to clog the wheels of progress."

> Mr. [Joseph] Martin: If the constitution is against us it is our duty, right and privilege to agitate and argue for a change in the constitution. The majority of this province have no desire to antagonize the minority; but they will not allow the minority to hold them to a condition of things which is practically obsolete. There is no justification in Manitoba or the Northwest ...

> Opposition members: D'Alton McCarthy again?

> Mr. Martin: Yes D'Alton McCarthy again. When he introduces

a motion abolishing the dual languages in the Territories,
I am with him whether he be Grit or Tory. Some people
seemed to think it was disloyalty to amend the British
North America Act which was only a compromise of
Canadian politicians, ratified by Imperial legislation. He
was in favour of taking these steps in Manitoba, and any
steps in the Parliament of Canada that would tend to make
Canada a homogeneous nation. [If Manitoba can't amend
its own constitution] then everything that has been done by
the legislature since the abolition of that useless legislative
council in 1876 has been illegal. That is reducing the argument to an absurdity. The sooner the French members
abandoned their factious opposition, which meant stopping
the work of the House, the better it would be in their own
interests and the general interests of the country. [70]

The abolition of the French language carried, in one eight-hour day of
debate, by a vote of twenty-seven to six. The only nays were from the six
French-speaking members. The premier never spoke after moving the original motion.

The language bill was followed in short order by the legislation to
create a public school system operated by local elected school boards under
a provincial department of education with a minister reporting to the legislature. Patterned generally after the School Act of Ontario, it differed in two
important ways. Although the new school system would be supported by all
taxpayers, Ontario's provision to allow parents to designate their taxes for
either Protestant or Catholic schools was omitted. As a consolation, so was
Ontario's requirement for compulsory attendance. The government was prepared to allow its Roman Catholic citizens the right to keep sending their
children to their own schools so long as they were prepared to pay for them
out of their own pockets and also pay their taxes to the provincial system.
The public schools were to be non-denominational but not secular. Religious
exercises were permitted, though not required, under certain conditions. As
a final humiliation to Manitoba's official langue minority, Catholic feast days
were eliminated as public holidays.

At one point during the debate, James Smart, the public works minister, used the 1886 Census to defend the government's actions. While those

of British (English, Irish and Scottish) stock had doubled since 1881, those of French ancestry had gone up a mere 12.5 per cent. As well, the Icelanders and the Germans had both outstripped the French in growth and the German population was now almost equal to the French.

At the end of every session, then as now, the lieutenant governor is called into the chamber to give royal assent. The clerk calls out the number and title of each bill passed, concluding with the ancient and ornate formulaic that turns legislation into law in the British parliamentary system. On March 31, 1890, the last day of one of the most rancorous and momentous sessions in Manitoba history, "a wild hope rose in the breasts" of Franco-Manitoban MLAs during the royal assent. The titles of the language and school bills were not read out in the order in which they had been voted upon. Could it be a repeat of 1879 when the lieutenant governor of that day had reserved the first attempted encroachment on their rights? Their joy was short-lived. The clerk of the house had inadvertently placed them at the bottom of the pile. At the end, the clerk of the house intoned: "In Her Majesty's name His Honour the Lieutenant-Governor doth assent to these bills." Schultz did reserve two bills, An Act respecting Sales of Land for Taxes and An Act affecting arrears of Taxes in the City of Winnipeg. After they, too, were read out, the clerk said: "His Honour the Lieutenant-Governor doth reserve these bills for the signification of the pleasure of His Excellency the Governor-General."

Then the gravelly voice of Schultz filled the chamber. He congratulated the members for their "zeal and energy".

> The various measures you have passed during this session
> will long be pointed to as marking important changes in the
> existing laws, and will, I have no doubt, tend materially to
> advance the best interests of the country. The Consolidation
> of the Municipal Act, the School and other Acts will, I am
> sure, meet with the hearty endorsation of the people of the
> Province, and when brought into operation will fully justify
> the care and consideration given them. [71]

The session concluded. It was over. "[T]he work of Taché and Riel was swept away." [72]

Schultz, functioning as lieutenant governors did in those days as the eyes and ears of Ottawa, had been keeping Macdonald fully informed of the Liberal government's activities. Schultz's relations with Greenway on the school and language legislation demonstrated "a long record of weakness and deceit on the part of the premier," writes Schultz's biographer, Lovell Clark. "According to Schultz, the attorney general, Joseph Martin, was 'the ruling spirit in the cabinet and bull dozes Greenway into doing what he pleases'." [73] Greenway apparently complained regularly to the lieutenant governor that Martin was always getting him into trouble and seeking to replace him as premier. For his part, the lieutenant governor became convinced Martin, who went on to become, briefly, premier of British Columbia and then a British MP, was using the language and schools issues to cover up his corrupt land speculation activities. [74] This was not to be a repeat of 1879, when Cauchon reserved the language bill passed by the Norquay administration with Ottawa's consent. This time, the federal cabinet instructed the lieutenant governor to assent to both the schools act and the language legislation and reserve only two comparatively trivial bills to do with land and taxes. Ever the canny politician, "Old Tomorrow" smelled the political wind blowing ever

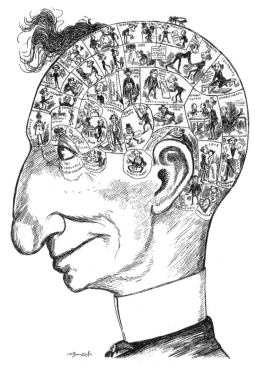

Phrenological Chart of the Head of the Country.

stronger on the Manitoba prairie and, indeed, the West. Macdonald rejected the disallowance option, not because he had backed away from the principles enshrined in the Manitoba Act, but because he was, as always, a consummate politicial survivor.

According to Hilts, the prime minister feared Greenway was actually hoping Ottawa would disallow the two laws, giving the Manitoba premier a pretext to call an election, sweep the province and once again force the divisive issues of language and religion to the top of the national agenda. Macdonald's suspicions had been alerted by Schultz. According to the lieutenant governor, Greenway kept mentioning to him that he believed the two acts were unconstitutional and would be disallowed. In a letter to Noah Chevrier on March 25, 1890, Macdonald made this observation.

> If the bill were disallowed, the game of Greenway and Martin would be played successfully. They would probably summon the legislature again, and carry the bill over again, and then dissolve and go to the country. The excitement would be tremendous and the question would remain unsettled. [75]

Both the prime minister and his justice minister believed the issue was best decided by the court. In a letter to Schultz dated March 21, 1890, Justice Minister John Thompson advised the lieutenant governor to let the law stand and the courts judge it, saying:

> The power of the provincial legislature to amend or repeal this section of the Manitoba Act ... admits of great doubt. The validity of the act under consideration may be very easily tested by legal proceedings on the part of any person in Manitoba who is disposed to insist on the use of the French language in the pleadings and process of the courts or in the journals and acts of the assembly. As it is apparent that a large section of the people of the province desire that English alone shall be used in such matters and that a very considerable section desire the provisions of the Manitoba Act upheld in this particular, there can be little doubt that a decision of the legal tribunals will be sought at an early date ... A judicial determination of that question will be more permanent and satisfactory than a decision of it by the power of disallowance. [76]

Hilts recounts that "Macdonald's method of avoiding an immediate dispute with the Greenway government was adopted". [77] The federal government encouraged one of its employees to test the law's constitutionality and paid his legal costs. John Kelly Barrett, inspector of inland revenue for Western Canada and a Roman Catholic ratepayer of Winnipeg, refused to pay his school taxes.

Although Macdonald and Thompson clearly hoped otherwise, Canadian dualism was crumpling under the onslaught of majoritarian political pressure. Dualism's driving force, Sir George-Étienne Cartier, had by now been gone nearly two decades. No one had ever replaced him. States Hilts: "The Manitoba School Question ended efforts to attract settlers from Québec." [78]

The acts of 1890 struck a devastating double blow at Manitoba's French minority. *Le Manitoba*, the province's French language newspaper,

*A list of odious measures
unknown in Canada prior to this day.*

catalogued the list of what it called "mesures odieuses" in its April 2, 1890 issue. The editorial's last sentence summed up the community's overwhelming sense of loss and powerlessness: "Le mot du *Free Press* est le mot juste, et nous le répétons: NOT LEGISLATION, BUT PERSECUTION" (The *Free Press* is accurate and we repeat it: NOT LEGISLATION, BUT PERSECUTION).

On April 23rd, *Le Manitoba* followed with an even more poignant cry from the heart: "One thing is for certain ... We will not let them take away our rights in silence ... These unspeakable acts embitter us and in some instances bring back sinister memories of our worst days living under British rule." And just a little more than a year later, Archbishop Taché, writing in the same newspaper, prophesied the course of action that would finally return their constitutional rights to Franco-Manitobans. "As soon as the school question will be resolved, it will be imperative to pursue the French language issue and that will not be long." [79] Unfortunately, his advice would not be heeded for almost a century.

Writes Gabrielle Roy's biographer, François Ricard: "No less than the entire dream of a bilingual Manitoba embodying an extension of the old French Catholic civilization of the St. Lawrence Valley had been dashed at a single stroke, transforming the vanquishers of yesterday into a community under seige and those who had believed they had a homeland into foreigners." [80]

The beseiged Franco-Manitoban community which had, in less than a generation, moved from equality to minority, felt it had to make a choice. Franco-Manitobans decided their best chance for preservation lay in fighting for their schools rather than their language. From the perspective of a century later, the decision emerges as a tragic and fatal error. But at the time, it made eminent sense. Historian Gerald Friesen explains why:

> Because their children's religious instruction was so important to them, because French might remain a language of instruction in the schools, and because they could establish a powerful political alliance with the English-speaking Catholics of Winnipeg, they chose to fight the school law rather than the language law. [81]

In his 1969 MA thesis, *The Minority and the Ballot Box: A Study of the Voting Behaviour of the French Canadians of Manitoba, 1888-1967*, Roger Turenne, who would go on to become Manitoba's first director of French language services in 1981, was blunt:

The attack on the French had fallen short of physical violence; it had been aimed at the subjugation of their social
values, at their cultural assimilation. It had not been violent
enough to obviate all causes of discord among them. Their
unanimous opposition to the Schools Act still left some
room for recrimination, personal ambition and hawk-dove
debates over what their response to the attack should be. [82]

For the second time in two decades, the tiny province of Manitoba
had sent shock waves through the nation. The issue put minority linguistic
and religious rights on a collision course with the growing muscle of provincial rights. Neither Macdonald nor Wilfrid Laurier, the Liberal Leader of
the Official Opposition, would speak publicly of disallowance although "it
was well within the federal power and they had ample precedents". [83] To disallow would enrage Orange Ontario and provincial rights proponents everywhere. The schools issue – not the language issue –went to court in three
separate cases and produced two conflicting decisions by the British Privy
Council. One, known as the Barrett Decision, rendered in 1892, supported
the province's right to create a tax-supported school system. The other, the
Brophy Decision, handed down in 1895, backed the right of Manitoba
Catholics to seek redress from Ottawa. Contrary to popular opinion, the
British North America Act doesn't grant the provinces absolute jurisdiction
over education. Section 93 Subsection 3 allows an appeal to the Governor-
General in Council if a provincial act affects "any right or privilege of the
Protestant or Roman Catholic Minority". However, the Manitoba Act has a
slight difference in wording, a difference the anti-compact historian Donald
Creighton stresses. Section 21/2 of the Manitoba Act adds "… by law or custom at the time of union". Different, perhaps, but as the Brophy judgement
demonstrated, not conclusively so.

Brophy obliged the Conservative administration of Sir Mackenzie
Bowell to try to bring Manitoba to heel with some agreement on remedial
legislation. But the Greenway government, standing firm on its provincial
rights, refused to yield. The federal cabinet and the Conservative Party fell
apart. Seven ministers resigned. The government was patched together again
under the leadership of Sir Charles Tupper who had to be recalled from his
post as Canadian High Commissioner to London. Tupper tried to drive a
remedial bill through the House in the teeth of opposition from Wilfrid

Laurier's Liberals and a group of dissident Conservatives led by D'Alton McCarthy. The opposition blocked it until the life of the Parliament elected in 1891 ran out, thus ensuring the Manitoba Schools Question would be the fulcrum of the federal election of 1896.

In the lead-up to that race, Laurier, using the Aesop's Fable of the competition between wind and sun to get a wayfarer to remove his coat, coined the felicitous phrase "sunny ways" to symbolize "Liberal effectiveness, friendly if possible, coercive if necessary". [84] He managed to maintain French-English equilibrium while simultaneously defending the doctrine of

WHICH SIDE ?

Laurier (to Bowell): "I'd enjoy your predicament if I didn't have to get past it myself.

provincial rights and offering hope to Manitoba's Roman Catholic minority. He won a resounding victory by playing up the divisions over remedial legislation within the Conservatives – Hugh John Macdonald opposing it in

Canadian Crucible

Manitoba and Tupper and his lieutenants in Québec supporting it – and keeping his own prescriptions as vague as possible. That vagueness cost him the support of the powerful Catholic hierarchy in his own province but it barely mattered in the outcome. The Liberals captured 53.5 per cent of the vote and forty-nine seats in Québec. In Manitoba, surprisingly, the Conservatives captured five seats to the Liberals' three. W.L. Morton says this was hardly a case of Manitobans "voting for their own coercion"; rather, it was evidence the electorate felt the schools issue was long settled. "With such indifference did Manitoba treat the question that wrought a revolution in the federal politics of Canada." [85]

The "sunny ways" negotiations between Liberal Ottawa and Liberal Manitoba produced the Compromise of 1897. In its language provisions, it opened the door to elevating all the other tongues of Manitoba's burgeoning ethnic mosaic to the same status as French, that is, languages of instruction in the public system where numbers warranted. The so-called Laurier-Greenway Compromise resulted in Clause 258 of Manitoba's School Act. It stated:

> When ten of the pupils in any school speak the French
> language, or any language other than English as their native
> language, the teaching of such pupils shall be conducted
> in French, or such other language and English upon the
> bilingual system.

University of Ottawa historian Cornelius J. Jaenen says the Compromise of 1897 "could be interpreted as shifting the emphasis from confessionalism to ethnicity". [86] However, in an editorial published on January 13, 1916, on the eve of the compromise's demise, the *Manitoba Free Press* stated that the extension of the bilingual provision to other languages was designed to "avoid exciting anti-French prejudices in Ontario and elsewhere", the expectation being that only the French and perhaps a few Mennonites would take advantage of it. But Archbishop Adélard Langevin, who had not been consulted in the framing of the compromise, saw its purpose as quite the opposite. Not only would it not benefit Franco-Manitobans, it would lead to their submergence. In a sermon delivered in his cathedral church reported in the *Winnipeg Tribune* of November 23, 1896, he uttered this prophetic warning:

> [W]e who came as the pioneers into the country ... have
> not more than the last arrivals; we whose rights are guaran-
> teed by the constitution, are placed on the same footing as

those who came from Ireland or the depths of Russia, we are not better apportioned than the Chinese and Japanese.

It took only a decade for his fears to be proven right. In 1916, another Liberal government, alarmed at what it considered a Tower of Babel in public education – not only classrooms but teacher training institutions in at least four languages – brought in the so-called Thornton Act repealing Section 258. According to the provincial education department's statistics, 16,720 of the province's 100,963 pupils as of June 1915 were enrolled in bilingual schools for a ratio of about one-sixth. While that doesn't seem large, the bulk of the bilingual schools were the much-romanticized rural one- and two-room "little red school houses". Fully one-quarter of all rural students attended a bilingual school and some of these schools were trying to function in as many as three languages. As of the end of the school year in 1915, Manitoba had 126 French schools employing 234 teachers, sixty-one German schools employing seventy-three teachers and 111 Ukrainian and Polish schools employing 114 teachers. In some districts, Ukrainian had already crowded out French as a language of instruction.

The legislators of that day dressed up their actions in the best progressive and egalitarian clothes. One unilingual non-sectarian public school system available to all and supported by tax dollars from all was essential to forge a single Canadian nationality, build social cohesion, create economic progress and ensure equality of opportunity and upward mobility for every immigrant child within a generation. But others saw a darker impulse at work. Canada was then at war. The government of T.C. (Toby) Norris judged "the English language to be threatened by the invasion of 'foreign' languages" and distrusted "in particular the French Canadian and German minorities who were suspected of harbouring only half-hearted loyalty to the British Empire". [87] There is a story, which is perhaps apocryphal, that the law's proclamation was accompanied by a mass book-burning on the Legislative Building lawn to dispose of the thousands of French, Ukrainian, German and Polish textbooks.

In the end, Laurier's "sunny ways" compromise was not only bizarre and bedevilled; it created even greater strife and turmoil. Worst of all, when it fell apart, the last vestige of French constitutional rights in Manitoba were extinguished. Any thought that the entire mess had been caused by two clearly unconstitutional and illegal acts taken twenty-six years earlier in 1890 now seldom if ever crossed a single mind outside the small and embattled Franco-Manitoban community.

Not surprisingly, the crisis' twenty-six-year tortured and twisted path had major legal and political repercussions nationally. In Québec, it not only roused indignation, but sowed doubt about the very future of Confederation itself. Manitoba's attack on its own official bilingualism was accompanied by D'Alton McCarthy's unsuccessful attempt to strike down the bilingual clauses of the North West Territories Act. Both became inextricably linked in the minds of French Canadians. According to historian Arthur Silver, McCarthy's bill set the tone of debate for the 1890s. Laurier called it "a declaration of war against the French race" and said that it was not by eliminating one of the

NATIONAL ARCHIVES OF CANADA / C29606

Mr McCarthy: In the language of the poet, " Where am I at?

races in Canada that unity could be brought about between them. [88]

The reaction of the Québec press was instant and furious. On January 27, 1890, *La Patrie* wrote that "the abolition of French in the territories is only the prelude to the general abolition throughout the dominion, not only of the official use of French, but also of the separate school system …

> [T]he most solemn guaranteees, the most sacred rights of
> the minority are at the mercy of the first political intriguer
> who takes it into his head to remake the constitution
> according to his own whim … Is there a caste of conquerors
> here and a caste of conquered slaves? Are we not all British
> subjects in the same right?". [89]

On February 11, 1890, *L'Étendard* warned that it would cause "the complete anglicization of the North-West, the complete exclusion from it of French-Canadian and Catholic influence"; on February 13th, *La Presse* said that to pass it would be "an infamy" and "a defiance of the French-Canadian nationality", and on February 18th, *L'Électeur* said it meant acceptance of "domination and intolerance towards the French minority".

Interestingly, however, at least some within Québec were prepared to accept part of the blame for this latest Anglo-Canadian outrage. *Les bleus* believed the aggressive Catholicism of Premier Mercier had helped to bring it on. Said *La Minerve* on March 5, 1890: "Having sown the wind of nationalism, French Catholics must now reap a whirlwind of fanaticism, intolerance and prejudice." Even non-*bleu* papers took the premier to task. Said the anti-clerical *La Presse* September 14, 1889: "The English majority continues to give its answer to the useless and senseless provocations of the national movement and the so-called Catholic party!"

La Presse, however, sounded a welcome note of balance and conciliation five months later, on February 13, 1890: "The two nationalities should live in perfect harmony, but in order to reach that goal they must not treat each other unjustly." Similarly, *L'Électeur* allowed in an editorial published on February 18th that it might be desirable for Canada to form a single great nation, "but that does not mean that this nation must not speak any other language than English." Instead unity could only be based on duality, on a recognition that both races "are equal before the constitution and before the law".

The 1890 crisis marked another major step in the evolution of

French Canada's view of Confederation. While Québec remained the French Canadian homeland, its people now had a special responsibility for French minorities in other parts of Canada. As Henri Bourassa's newspaper, *Le Nationaliste*, said in editorials published April 4, 1904 and March 5, 1905: "The entire edifice of the Canadian Confederation rests on the equality of the races" and on the "duality of origins, language, and religion of the Canadian people." [90] Arthur Silver puts it this way:

> To the continuing English-Canadian demand for a single-unhyphenated Canadianism, people like [Henri] Bourassa responded with a dualist theory. Confederation, they said, was the result of an agreement between two races to live together on the basis of equality and co-operation. To ensure this equality they had established minority rights as the keystone of their system. [91]

****

THE LAWS

THE BRITISH NORTH AMERICA ACT 1867

> Section 133: Either the English or the French Language may be used by any Person in the Debates of the Houses of the Parliament of Canada and of the Houses of the Legislature of Québec; and both those Languages shall be used in the respective Records and Journals of those Houses; and either of those Languages may be used by any Person or in any Pleading or Process in or issuing from any Court of Canada established under this Act, and in or from all of any of the Courts of Québec.
>
> The Acts of the Parliament of Canada and of the Legislature of Québec shall be printed and published in both those Languages.

THE MANITOBA ACT 1870

Section 23: Either the English or the French language may
be used by any person in the debates of the Houses of the
Legislature, and both those languages shall be used in the
respective Records and Journals of those Houses; and either
of those languages may be used by any person, or in any
Pleading or Process, in or issuing from any Court of Canada
established under the British North America Act 1867, or in
or from all or any of the Courts of the Province. The Acts
of the Legislature shall be printed and published in both
those languages.

AN ACT TO PROVIDE THAT THE ENGLISH LANGUAGE SHALL BE THE OFFICIAL LANGUAGE OF THE PROVINCE OF MANITOBA 1890

Her Majesty, by and with the advice and consent of the Legislative Assembly
of Manitoba, enacts as follows:

1. Any statute or law to the contrary notwithstanding,
the English language only shall be used in the records
and journals of the House of Assembly for the Province
of Manitoba, and in any pleadings or process in or issuing
from any court in the Province of Manitoba. The Acts of the
Legislature and of the Province of Manitoba need only be
printed and published in the English language.

2. This Act shall only apply so far as this Legislature has
jurisdiction to so enact, and shall come into force on the day
it is assented to.

5

La Survivance Franco-Manitobaine

O N FEBRUARY 23, 1916, LIBERAL MLA P.A. TALBOT, imbued
with Henri Bourassa's vision of Canadian unity in duality, rose in the Manitoba
Legislature to challenge the province's final assault on minority rights – the
Thornton Act creating a single, English-speaking, non-sectarian public school
system in Manitoba.

"If any single member expects the English to assimilate the French
in this Dominion I might give them friendly advice to disabuse themselves.
The French are a distinctive race and we will not be assimilated whether you
like it or not. We have been given our rights as a separate nationality and
we will hold them." [1]

Talbot's impassioned defence of the status of his nationality in
Canada was echoed by some Conservative opposition members who also
pleaded eloquently for the rights of French as the language of the first
Europeans in Manitoba and the West. It was to no avail. T. C. (Toby) Norris'
Liberal government was convinced that Manitoba, with a population of
500,000, where 30,000 spoke French and another 100,000 spoke languages
other than English or French, could face a social crisis if the issues were not
addressed. Premier Norris even went so far as to equate "French" and "foreign". In March 1914, he told the legislature that "the bilingual privilege had
been placed in the school law for the benefit of their [Franco-Manitobans']

foreign-born friends". [2] "Foreign" was, of course, a particularly freighted term given that the premier was speaking mere months before World War I began.

The government's alarm was undoubtedly accelerated by the on-going demographic revolution occuring in the province. Manitoba's population doubled and then almost tripled from 255,221 in 1901 to 461,394 in 1911 and to 610,118 in 1921. The absolute numbers of all ethnic groups increased dramatically across the board, but their relative strengths shifted. The English declined from 64.4 per cent in 1901 to 57.2 per cent in 1921 while the relative proportions of Ukrainians, Germans, Dutch, Polish and Scandinavians shot up by as much as four- or five-fold. The francophone community – by this time including many French-speakers from Belgium – almost tripled in absolute numbers, from 16,021 to 40,908, but relatively, stood almost still, rising from 6.3 per cent to 6.7 per cent.

The Compromise of 1897 was originally designed to permit only French and German in addition to English as languages of instruction where numbers warranted. Time and the ongoing pressure of new arrivals from all over Europe meant other languages were able to find shelter under the 1897 umbrella.

Indeed, there were grounds for thinking that efforts had been made, under the cover of the (Rodmond) Roblin government's defence of the bilingual system, to unite the Ukrainians and Poles with the French to resist any change. The result was to confound French with languages the clause had not been intended to cover. [3]

In 1914, the *Manitoba Free* Press launched its own inquiry into the province's school system and reported not only the presence of additional languages besides French and German, but also that English was often not even being taught. The paper also claimed that the so-called "bilingual" schools provided inferior education regardless of language used. The language and schools issue was of special interest to John W. Dafoe, the paper's editor, a passionate Canadian nationalist, but a man of his time and place. Dafoe went on to make the *Free Press* one of the most famous and respected newspapers in the English-speaking world. He was a visionary on domestic and international affairs and one of the authors of the report of the Royal Commission on Dominion-Provincial Relations appointed in 1937 to address the vast inequalities in provincial wealth and power exposed by the Great Depression. Its defining principle, underpinning Confederation to this day, was that the wealthier parts of the federation have a responsibility for the less fortunate, a principle that is now enshrined in the Canadian Constitution and fulfilled through the federal equalization program. By it, Ottawa uses the federal tax system to distribute revenues from "have" to "have-not" provinces.

However enlightened, Dafoe nevertheless reflected the prejudices of his period, although they lessened over time. Born near the staunchly Orange community of Belleville in eastern Ontario, he began his newspaper career in Montréal where he "identified himself very early with the English, commercial, Protestant ethic and absorbed completely the prevailing ... attitude that the French, as a minority, had certain ... privileges ... but their status was ... one of grace and favour, for which they ought to be duly appreciative." [4] Once in Winnipeg, Dafoe's views hardened. "He had no doubt at all that abolition of the official use of French in Manitoba was justified." [5] As his Canadian nationalism grew, so did his conviction that there should be only one language in Canada and that it must be English. Political scientist Murray Donnelly says Dafoe's inherited suspicion of Catholicism was given a new focus and direction in Winnipeg. "He accepted the doctrine that the Cathedral in St. Boniface was not just Catholic but was an outpost of French Canadian control from Québec." [6] He was not just a supporter of the Norris government's decision to create a single, compulsory, secular, English-speaking public school system, but an early and tirelesss proselytizer. "He turned his reporters loose and whenever they turned up an interesting item, he followed it up the next day with an editorial." [7] He savaged counter arguments made by Joseph Bernier, a Franco-Manitoban MLA, as "ludicrous, reactionary, fossilized". [8]

However, while the *Free Press* was determined to abolish the confessional school system, it was careful to acknowledge the special position of French. In an editorial published on February 19, 1916 entitled "Cutting the Gordian Knot", the paper wrote that the teaching of French "is an essential part of a liberal education".

A year earlier, a Department of Education report claimed that "linguistic chaos" was the order of the day in many school districts. [9] "The situation is just about out of hand," Robert Fletcher, the deputy minister of education, told his minister, Dr. R. S. Thornton. [10] The minister decided that French and German were inextricably involved with the newer languages and decided the only solution was to abolish the bilingual system entirely. In his speech to the Legislature, the education minister cloaked the bill in the raiment of progress. His words nevertheless must have sent shudders of apprehension through the Franco-Manitoban MLAs and across the entire French community.

> It is necessary to deal with this law [the bilingual clause] both in our own interests and in the interests of the strangers within our gates who have come to make their homes with us with the purpose of becoming a part of this nation. The first essential to individual progress in any land is to know the language of the country. In an English-speaking country, as this is, a knowledge of English is more necessary than a knowledge of arithmetic. No matter what a man's attainment may be, the doors of opportunity are closed to him if he had not a knowledge of English, the common tongue …
>
> A grave injustice is being done to the children who do not receive a satisfactory education in English. Without that knowledge, they grow up under a continuous handicap. We wish to give them the same consideration as is accorded our own children, to fit them to earn their way through life and to take their place as citizens in our Canadian nationality … We are building today for the Canada of tomorrow, and our common school is one of the most important factors in the work. In this Dominion, we are building up, under the British flag, a new nationality. We come from many lands and cast in our lot and from these various factors there must evolve a new nationality which shall be simply Canadian and British. [11]

The government marshalled authorities from across Canada and the United States to help make its case for educational unilingualism as a unifying and liberating tool. Toronto school superintendent R.H. Cowley said immigrant children taught in English only are able "in a few months to hold their own, according to age and class, with any native children." [12] J.M.H. Frederick, Cleveland's superintendent of schools, said his city had a very large percentage of people who were "ignorant of the language of our land. Our experience is that the best way to assimilate these new elements is to assist them to acquire the use of the English language as soon as possible. It would be quite impossible with our multitude of languages to use the bilingual system in Cleveland." [13]

David Sheddon, commissioner of the Massachusetts Board of Education said that "assimilation in the direction of true citizenship is otherwise impossible" without the sole use of English. And W.A. Maxwell, superintendent of schools for New York City, said teaching in English only is "the best plan, both for citizenship and for academic training". [14]

The 1916 schools legislation cost the Norris government two francophone members, Joseph Dumas (St. Boniface) and Talbot (La Vérendrye) who resigned from the party to sit as independents. In their speeches, both men spoke of their deep sense of betrayal by their party and leader. Talbot allowed his fury full rein:

> I used to believe the declarations of my party but I have been greatly deceived ... The government's sycophants are saying to the government that its decision is courageous. No, it is cowardice of the worst type ... It is folly to believe that the French-speaking people of this province are going to abandon that which they regard as their sacred right ... In a letter signed by his own hand Mr. Norris assured me personally that no one would touch the Laurier-Greenway settlement. Now Mr. Norris lies about his promise and his word. He has thrown away his hypocritical mask and shown himself for what he really is: a traitor. I will not follow such a man. [15]

St. Boniface MLA Joseph Dumas called the legislation the worst injustice ever to be perpetrated in the province and hinted at his own future plan of action.

> I regret that after fifteen years of loyal and faithful service to my party I must rise to oppose a law I consider the most unjust ever to have been inflicted on this province. I would fail in my duty to my voters if I were not to stand to fight this legislation in front of those previous speakers who claim that we [Franco Manitobans] have no rights. To these members I reply by citing Article 23 of the Manitoba Act. The legislature does not have the right to repeal that clause. And I say that French too is an official language of Manitoba. [16]

Aimé Bénard (Iberville), called "the Sphinx" by his colleagues because he had never uttered a word in ten years in the House, was spurred into an emotional appeal by the government's action:

Au Reichstag du Manitoba

M. Talbot, député de La Vérendrye, et Jos. Dumas, député de Saint-Boniface rompent avec leur parti. Discours de MM. Préfontaine, Hamelin, Bénard et Parent.

Les galeries applaudissent énergiquement le vigoureux et éloquent réquisitoire du député de LaVérendrye.

" Français nous sommes, Français nous demeurerons."

LE CENTRE DU PATRIMOINE / FEBRUARY 2, 1916

The denial of Franophone rights, at a time when Europe was at war, spurred charges of authoritarianism in *La Liberté*.

> No government has the right to act in defiance of the British constitution and its spirit. It will be a very grave injustice on the part of this chamber to vote for a law which violates the principles of the constitution and all the principles of honour, especially since this chamber has not received a mandate from the people to do so. (17)

The debate maintained this intensity over a period of several weeks. It was frequently haunted by the spectre of the Great War then being fought in Europe. That bloody conflict inspired a moving appeal by the francophone leader of the Official Opposition to recognize the common nationality of French and English Canadians who were at that very moment sharing trenches at the battlefront. But once again, like its two predecessors in 1879 and 1890, the debate exposed the frailty of constitutional law when threatened by aroused majoritarian power.

Conservative leader Albert Préfontaine (Carillon) led off the Official Opposition's attack on the legislation on February 23rd. Franco-Manitobans, he said, had not come to the legislature to ask for favours but to ask for their constitutional rights. He read out the sections of the Manitoba Act making the province bilingual. He asked the government not to proceed with such a divisive measure when the country was at war.

> Now it seems that the Laurier-Greenway settlement is to be looked on as the Germans looked on their treaty with other nations – as a scrap of paper. It is unfortunate that a question like this should come up in a time of war. The English and the French are fighting side by side in the same trenches and we at home are divided on a question of importance. I have a son now being trained for the front in Nova Scotia. Soon he will be on the firing line. It may be he will be in the same trench with my honourable friends from Virden or Assiniboia or Lakeside. While that is happening we at home will be fighting. While they are fighting for liberty we at home will be fighting about our constitutional rights. [18]

But J.W. Wilton (Assiniboia) accused the Franco-Manitoban MLAs of being "nationalists like those in Québec". Reminding the House of Talbot's assertion that French Canadians would never be assimilated, Wilton continued: "If this meant that the French Canadians wished to build up in Canada a nationality separate from the Canadian nationality, he had no sympathy with the aspiration … If the sowthistle has to be eradicated, so has bilingualism." Wilton went on to say European discovery and original occupation of Canada was not enough to confer constitutional rights. "If Canada had not been conquered, then Wolfe was not a hero … It was necessary also to have the power to hold." Wilton then proceeded to utter the cry of every bigot before and since. He "denied he was actuated by any motive against the French Canadians. He had many personal friends among them." [19]

The debate featured one emotional exchange between Préfontaine and Wilton. Préfontaine asked Wilton how he would feel if he were to encounter the opposition leader's son fighting in France, adding: "It would be unfortunate for him to have to report that back in Manitoba the French and English were at strife." Wilton shot back: "I should tell him that English is now going to be adequately taught in all the schools – the language of the country which has spread liberty over the earth. That is something to be proud of." [20] The premier adopted some of Wilton's opinions and language. Norris said Talbot had made a big mistake by declaring the French would never be assimilated. "He was sorry to discover they had a separatist in the party all these years. Mr. Talbot had placed himself in a class by himself as a separatist which meant the same thing as a nationalist." [21]

Two members, George Armstrong (Manitou) and John Williams (Arthur) made the most significant and historically accurate contribution to the debate by pointing out that the Manitoba Act enshrined French and English languages as official in the legislature and courts but enshrined not language but denominational rights in education. As events almost sixty years later were to demonstrate, this was the Achilles heel of the decision by the Franco-Manitoban community in 1890 to pursue their constitutional rights to Roman Catholic schools rather than their constitutional rights to their language.

With regard to the abolition of French as an official language of Manitoba, there must, Mr. Williams said, be some good reason for the fact that no effort had been made to recover this privilege. If the privilege had been guaranteed by the constitution or an act of parliament one would have thought that an effort would have been made to reclaim it. As far as he knew, no such effort had been made. [22]

The Liberals defeated Préfontaine's six-month hoist motion and passed the bill by a vote of thirty-five to eight on March 8, 1916. The last vestige of Franco-Manitobans' constitutionally-entrenched rights were swept away, not to be fully restored until 1985 and only then through a legal challenge based not on schools but on the unconstitutionality of the 1890 act making English the sole official language of the province. Although the popular impression has long been that the Thornton Act specifically made English the sole language of instruction, that was not the case. Instead, by simply repealing the clause of the School Act that allowed languages other than English to be used as teaching languages where numbers warranted, the Norris government returned the province to what one historian calls "a legal vacuum because no language of instruction was set forth ... It was not contrary to the law to teach in French." [23] While it may not have been illegal to teach in French, neither was it legal, as subsequent generations of Franco-Manitobans were to discover.

Thus the very institutions to which Franco-Manitobans had turned for deliverance – their faith and their schools – had led to their downfall. The Roman Catholic church, despairing of sufficient French-Canadian migration, had sought to maintain itself by recruiting European co-religionists. It was to these new immigrant communities – primarily Ukrainian and Polish –

Even large families couldn't save Franco-Manitobans.

Franco-Manitobans looked for the population weight to sustain their own language and schools. In the end the supposed instruments of their salvation led to their entrapment. They were reduced to being regarded as just one among many minorities instead of the official minority in a province founded on the principle of duality.

Franco-Manitoban historian Paul Ruest believes the Norris government was highly influenced by American melting-pot theory predominant at the turn of the twentieth century. It was determined to break up and assimilate immigrant groups and settlements and, especially, to turn their children into English-speaking Americans steeped in Anglo-Saxon values and culture within a single generation. In his doctoral thesis, Ruest wrote that, for the Orangemen, the 1916 law had the added advantage of being "a victory over hated Catholicism and a quick way to eradicate the French fact in Manitoba." [24] The minority linguistic and religious protections contained in the Manitoba Act of 1870 were rendered null and void in practice; the concept of constitutional language rights was not simply ignored but forgotten; the twenty years of leather-bound statutes and legislative and court proceedings in French were left to gather dust on the shelves of the Legislative Library, a mere curiosity from a long-dead and – for most Manitobans – unmourned past.

Donald Creighton, the biographer of Sir John A. Macdonald and one of Canada's most famous historians, never accepted the duality principle as having any basis in historical fact. In Volume Two of that biography, *John A. Macdonald – The Old Chieftain*, Creighton's disdain for French Canada, Louis Riel and the Métis is palpable. Saying Manitoba's status as "a little French

Canada in the west" had been achieved through "the arrogant dictatorship of Riel", he continued:

> Riel and his spiritual advisers had sought, in the interest of the Métis in particular and French Canadians in general, to determine in advance the structure and institutions of the first western Canadian province ... This determination of the constitution of Manitoba in advance of the unmistakeable assertion of its real character had not been an easy matter even in 1870. It had been accomplished only through the deliberate falsification, by Riel and his advisers, of the known wishes of the inhabitants of Red River. [25]

Creighton repeated the assertion, somewhat more diplomatically, in *Canada's First Century*, published in 1970:

> The institutions of the prairie country, including sectarian schools and official bilingualism, had been imposed prematurely under heavy pressure and without much forethought in the 1870s; but by the end of the next decade, English-speaking and Protestant immigration had overwhelmed the bilingual character of the fur-trading days and determined the permanent character of the west. [26]

Certainly, historical inevitability would agree with Creighton. And the forces of historical inevitability working against the French language within Canada, strong as they were particularly in the West, were amplified everywhere by the mythic and messianic siren songs of the great republic to the south – one nation, one unhyphenated nationality, one flag, one language, *E Pluribus Unum*, out of many one – siren songs perpetually seeking to seduce Canadians to abandon the complexities of two languages and two cultures, indeed, to abandon Canada itself.

Historical inevitability, however, is "might makes right" sanitized. The Norris government was legitimately concerned about a Tower of Babel school system. But a school system of two languages is hardly Babel. It exists successfully in many countries around the world, in Canada, including the Province of Québec and for some years now, once again in the Province of Manitoba.

The 1890 crisis and its baleful legacy of making Franco-Manitobans over in the image of "just another minority" played into the hands of the Anglo-Saxon assimilationists in two important ways. It all but erased from collective memory Manitoba's bilingual constitutional status, thus keeping it hidden from generations of new Manitobans who reacted with their own sense of justifiable outrage when it was subsequently made manifest. And it handed to the English-speaking majority the powerful divide-and-conquer weapon by which all other minorities could be marshalled against any attempt by Franco-Manitobans to redress the wrongs done them. This would reach its apogée in the constitutional amendment cataclysm of 1983-84.

There was, of course, one community in Manitoba whose collective memory was never erased. Labouring under external discrimination and a deep internal sense of communal injustice, French Manitoba dedicated itself to *la survivance* (survival). Although assimilation ate away steadily at its numbers, it was quite unable to humble its pride, erase its institutions or eradicate the unique historical qualities and cultural enrichment its presence lent to the life of the province and its largest city. Franco-Manitobans retained a sufficient critical mass to maintain their community. Indeed, the community's numbers actually grew in relation to the rest of the province after the initial plunge fom 15.6 per cent in 1881 to 6.3 per cent in 1901, reflecting that particular tenacity and vibrancy that often accompanies external threat. In 1911, the francophone community comprised 6.8 per cent of Manitoba's population; by 1941, its strength had risen to 7.3 per cent and by 1961, it soared to a peak of 9.1 per cent. [27] This increase was, however, achieved through higher birth rates, not through immigration.

Franco-Manitobans supported an unbroken string of lively newspapers – *Le Métis* from 1871 to 1881; *Le Manitoba*, from 1881 to 1926 and at least eleven other papers and journals in the ensuing decades, the best known of which was *La Liberté*, founded in 1913. It joined forces with *Le Patriote de l'Ouest* in 1941 to become *La Liberté et le Patriote*. In Collège Saint-Boniface (later to become Collège Universitaire de Saint-Boniface), the community boasted a highly-respected institution of higher learning that had been one of the founding colleges of the University of Manitoba in 1877. The City of St. Boniface also contained the oldest major hospital in Western Canada, operated by les Soeurs Grises de Montréal. Literary and political institutions arose that won respect across the province and the nation, including a lively theatre, Le Cercle Molière; a historical society and, as an immediate outcome of the 1916 debacle, l'Association d'Éducation des Canadiens-Français du Manitoba, which had as a founding purpose the "just reclamation of all the rights of the French Canadians of Manitoba" [28]. Originally split between laity and clergy, l'Association became la Société franco-manitobaine in 1968, an entirely secular organization regarded as the official voice of the province's French community. After a public subscription, which the Province of Québec pledged to match dollar for dollar, raised some $260,000, St.Boniface became home to Western Canada's first all-French radio station, CKSB Radio Saint Boniface on May 27, 1946. "For the first time since the laws of 1890 and 1916, Franco-Manitobans were able to see the French language almost legitimized in a cultural and informational sphere." [29] CKSB subsequently was made part of the CBC Radio-Canada national network, paving the way for CBC French television in 1960.

****

The story of one of Canada's greatest authors, Gabrielle Roy, traces the form and strength of Franco-Manitoban *survivance*. Her ancestry and early life were archetypical of French Manitoba, a template for the community and its times. Marie Rose Emma Gabrielle Roy was born the youngest of eight surviving children to Léon and Mélina Landry Roy March 22, 1909 and baptised the very next day in Saint-Boniface Cathedral. Her father, then sixty years of age, was one of the Franco-Americans the bishops of Québec and Manitoba had solicited and encouraged to come West, arriving to homestead in the region known as Pembina Mountain, about 160 kilometres southwest of Winnipeg, in March 1883. Life as a sodbusting farmer was quite different than that of a restauranteur in Lowell, Massachusetts. But the restaurant had fallen on hard times, his partner had died and Léon felt himself sliding into alcoholism. He was part of the largest-ever influx (about 400) of French Canadians into post-Confederation Manitoba in the late 1870s and early 1880s, prepared to take their chances on a quarter-section of cheap land. Like the others, Léon and his two brothers Majorique and Édouard chose Pembina Mountain because it was where Monseigneur Alexandre-Antonin Taché, the second bishop of St. Boniface, had persuaded the authorities to set aside two counties for French Canadian repatriates. Léon quickly became a well-known figure in the new community. By 1885, his neighbours in St. Alphonse, most of them also former Franco-Americans, had elected him to the council of Lorne. The government had also appointed him justice of the peace. That next year he found a wife in the neighbouring parish of St-Léon.

Mélina Landry Roy had been born in the hills of St-Alphonse-de-Rodriguez northwest of Joliette. In 1881, when Mélina was a girl in her mid-teens, her father, a logger and log-driver, had succumbed to the blandishments of "recruiter priests" sent by Taché to Québec to persuade French Canadians to help hold the prairies for French Canada and as a bonus, find an easier, more rewarding life with more opportunity for their children. When Léon and Mélina married on November 23, 1886, he was thirty-six and she, nineteen.

Léon, by now a shopkeeper, involved himself in politics, becoming a convinced and very active Liberal both provincially and federally. [30] At first glance, it would seem an odd choice – Roy's biographer calls it "not without ambiguity" – due to the Liberals' passage of what the francophone community came to call the "spoiliatory laws" abolishing the use of French in the legislature and courts and forbidding public support of Roman Catholic schools. As Ricard points out, the laws roused indignation and sowed doubt over the future of Confederation itself in Québec, but in Manitoba, the impact "was far more severe". [31]

If being a provincial Liberal meant discomfort, however, being a federal Liberal for a Franco-Manitoban or indeed, any French Canadian, in those days was something else entirely. Not only did that allow Léon to do battle against the "hangmen" of the Tory party who had allowed Louis Riel to be executed in 1885, but it also meant rallying to the support of the first French Canadian to lead a federal political party, Wilfrid Laurier, then the leader of the Official Opposition. Léon, who met the future prime minister in 1894, was convinced that Laurier would right the grievous wrongs committed against Franco-Manitobans by his provincial cousin.

Léon's labours on behalf of the Liberal cause in the 1896 federal election won him one of two jobs that Clifford Sifton, Laurier's right-hand man and patronage chief in the West, had earmarked for "Frenchmen", that of French interpreter at Winnipeg's Immigration Hall. The appointment was effective April 1, 1897 and it necessitated the Roy family's relocation to Winnipeg or rather, to the oldest community on the Red River, St. Boniface.

At that time, the centre of Franco-Manitoban life had fewer than two thousand inhabitants, the majority of whom were French-speaking. While St. Boniface was small in relation to Winnipeg, it, too, was a metropolis because it played a central role in French Catholic life throughout the Canadian West, a role that strengthened after the turn of the century. In addition to its historic hospital and cultural and educational insitutions, St. Boniface had been the see of an archbishopric since 1871 and boasted all the industry, shops, services and amenities of urban life at the time. It was, says Ricard, "the home of the French-speaking elite. It was the image of a peaceful, well-ordered and pleasant society." [32]

The family settled first in a rented house at the corner of La Vérendrye and Du Collège (now Langevin) Streets in the north end of town, a poor, predominantly Métis, working-class neighbourhood known as "la Pointe". In 1904, Léon, a rising and successful civil servant and the father of eight children, purchased a large lot at the corner of Deschambault and DesMeurons streets. He used his influence to have the area landscaped and serviced with a sewer system and wooden sidewalks and personally oversaw the construction of a large and attractive new home. In August 1905, the Roys moved in to 15 Deschambault Street, now a musée.

In the early days of the twentieth century, Franco-Manitoban life differed hardly at all from that of the average Québécois of the time. It revolved around the church which was seen as the bulwark against the English and Protestant forces arrayed against the community. St. Boniface was culturally homogeneous, its life centred on the Cathedral, the Grey Nuns' hospital, the religious orders and their teaching institutions. Although St. Boniface was, in reality, a kind of ghetto and Franco-Manitobans were increasingly targets of discrimination, Gabrielle's childhood memories were ones of security created by "having a past sustained by stories, by memories and a proven moral and social order.

> I remember that you could hear a convent or chapel bell
> ringing almost all the time in one corner of the city or
> another ... There were always children walking two by two
> on the sidewalks of our city ... led by nuns whose rosaries
> would chink as they walked. While over the sluggish brown
> waters of the Red River flew the call of cathedral bells, gulls
> ... flew practically among the cemetery's tombs, which
> crowded almost down to the river's banks ... to bring us a
> feeling of open sea, a kind of island complex. For it was as
> though we of St. Boniface really were on an island, rather

alone in an ocean of prairie and surrounded by the
unknown on every side. [33]

Gabrielle started school at the Academie Saint-Joseph in 1915-16,
the same year the Thornton Act was adopted. The Academie had been founded
in 1898 by the Soeurs des Saints Noms de Jesus et de Marie. The nuns bent
to the new law, officially changing the language in which they taught and
devoting more class time to English grammar and literature. They also took
advantage of an aspect to the new school regimen allowing one hour a day
for instruction in another language to continue to teach French during regular
school hours. This French instruction was supplemented with additional
classes given during their own unpaid time. The sisters were convinced they
were right to take on the law because they believed they were combatting
fanaticism and they knew they had the blessing of the new archbishop of
St. Boniface, Monseigneur Arthur Beliveau.

The difficulties created by such a situation in the years immediately
following the adoption of the anti-French law are not hard to imagine, particularly for little French-speaking children like Gabrielle who were just
beginning school. Confusion reigned in the classrooms and the quality of
teaching suffered. Furthermore, for children raised in an almost entirely
French-speaking family environment, school became a foreign, if not hostile,
place, making their adaptation even more difficult. Throughout their first
years of classes, the children had to direct most of their efforts to learning
English, since that was indispensable to following the official curriculum of
the Department of Education and also to passing the various examinations,
which were all held in English. [34]

One of the first acts of l'Association d'Éducation des Canadiens-
Français du Manitoba was the creation of an unofficial French curriculum.
In fact, the AECFM simply adopted the Québec curriculum and textbooks.
Senior education department officials including Dr. Robert Fletcher, the
deputy minister of education, knew this was going on and turned a blind
eye to it. Dr. Fletcher and his senior bureaucrats were sympathetic to the
Franco - Manitoban cause and waged a continuous battle against the more
zealous school inspectors determined to wipe out any trace of languages
besides English. "There was ... a recognition among the bureaucrats, who
were almost all of Anglo-Celtic origins, that the "French" were Canadians
of long standing and not immigrants." [35] So French instruction continued,

sometimes unpaid on the part of the teachers, and often clandestinely, throughout Franco-Manitoba from 1916 on. Father Jean-Paul Aubry, then editor of *La Liberté et Le Patriote*, recalled his school days in Ste. Agathe vividly in an interview published in the *Globe and Mail* in December 1970:

> We were all French-speaking and so were our teachers. We learned in French every day except the day the school inspector came. That day, we put our French books away and brought our English ones out. Most inspectors knew it was going on and they turned a blind eye. But the occasional one made trouble. The system meant French students had to write two exams in every course, one in French and one in English. The French exams were held on Saturdays late in May each year. It was tough going and a lot of students dropped out because of it. [36]

School was daunting for Franco-Manitoban children because they effectively had to learn every course twice, once in English and once in French, so they could write both sets of exams. Gabrielle recalled with some amusement the extent of the subterfuge to foil the inspectors.

> If at the convent we were celebrating the visit of some church dignitary, red carpets would be laid on the floor of the big reception hall, ferns would be placed on pedestals, and portrait photographs of the archbishops of the West would be prominently displayed on the walls all around us. All day long we would speak the language of survival, and of the French Canadian cause. A while later, another celebration would bring us a visit from some gentlemen from the Manitoba Board of Education. Then the principal, la mère directrice, would have the pictures of archbishops taken down; the Fathers of Confederation would take their place; we would have learned some very decorous compliments for the occasion, appropriate songs; all that day there would be nothing but British allegiance, loyalty to our sovereign, and a Canada stretching from sea to sea. The gentlemen from the Board of Education would leave enchanted, bowing low to our mère directrice and calling her Madame. [37]

Canadian Crucible

ENCHANTMENT AND SORROW

The Autobiography of Gabrielle Roy

Translated by Patricia Claxton

I

WHEN DID IT first dawn on me that I was one of those people destined to be treated as inferiors in their own country? I don't think it was during any of the frequent forays that Maman and I made to Winnipeg, leaving our little French city of St. Boniface and crossing the Red River by the Provencher Bridge. It would be easy to suppose so, since our capital city never really received us otherwise than as foreigners, but when I was a child I rather liked the feeling of crossing a border and being in a strange place, light years away but right next door to home. I think it opened my eyes, trained me to observe things and stimulated my imagination.

Generally we set out early, Maman and I, and it was summer because all of us were natural walkers and loved to stride along with our eyes free to roam, our minds wherever they wished and our thoughts unfettered – and so we do still, those of us who are still of this world.

We almost always set off in high spirits and full of expectation. Maman would have read in the paper or heard from a neighbour that Eaton's was having a sale of curtain-lace, or printed cottons suitable for making spoons or house-dresses, or maybe the children's shoes. Always, as we began these shopping expeditions, we were drawn by the hope that so warms the hearts of poor people, that of turning up a real find at the bargain counter. It occurs to me now that we hardly ever ventured into the rich metropolis next door except on buying trips. This was where a good portion of our hard-earned money went – and it was pennies from the pockets of poor people like us that made the city such an arrogant and intimidating neighbour. Later I often went to Winnipeg for a lot of other

3

The provincial department of education regarded l'Academie as one of the top girls' schools in the province. But if the suppression of the French language was relatively benign in reality, this was thanks to the informed open-mindedness of senior civil servants, certainly not to the attitude of the community at large. The department was often beseiged by linguistic "snitches", who had heard about the French language being spoken in a particular school or seen a French textbook in some child's hands. Such public pressure necessitated periodic crackdowns to satisfy "fanatics". Urban legends arose, among the most durable of which was the fable of the supposed false bottoms in school desks in French communities for hiding the contraband French texts.

Nor did the bigotry stop at the schoolhouse door. Chapter One of *Enchantment and Sorrow*, Roy's last book and her autobiography, begins with this all-important question:

> When did it first dawn on me that I was one of those people
> destined to be treated as inferiors in their own country? …
> The humiliation of having someone turn to stare when I
> was speaking French in a Winnipeg street was something
> I'd felt so often as a child that I no longer realized it was a
> humiliation.

We hear about her mother's tales of the homelessness and endless succession of hardships suffered by her people. Recognizing that Franco-Manitobans are a second-class, scorned community, Gabrielle discovers that "there was no cure for the misfortune of being French Canadian".[38] Further on, Gabrielle recounts the response of the visiting English school inspector once he uncovered her knowledge and love of Shakespeare, particularly *Macbeth*.

> He seemed moved. Perhaps he sensed a significance in that
> classroom scene which was as strange as that of the witches
> on the heath. Perhaps he had an inkling of what it was like
> to be a little French Canadian in those days in Manitoba,
> and perhaps he felt compassion for us ... He studied me
> with touching benevolence. That was when I first discovered
> how dearly our English-speaking adversaries can love us,
> providing we play the game and show what good, obedient
> children we are. [39]

Gabrielle's recollections of her mother's and her own early experiences were so poignant and powerful that when the original French edition, *La Détresse et l'enchantment,* was published posthumously in 1984, it was considered a belated stand in support of French Canadian nationalism, something Gabrielle had always abhorred.

The shy and withdrawn girl who would go on to become one of the most internationally-famous Canadian authors of all time, initially determined to enter one of the few professions open to any woman of her era regardless of language – teaching. Thanks to the Thornton Act, which had resulted in the closure of L'Ecole Normale de Saint-Boniface, she had to go to the English-speaking Provincial Normal School in Winnipeg.

This was a fiercely English and non-confessional institution; the few French Canadian students who dared venture into its halls adapted with great difficulty and were made to feel like foreigners or inferiors. Not only was instruction given entirely in English but a good many of the teachers were Scots, who, Ricard says, were known among Franco-Manitobans for anti-French fanaticism. The students were furthermore required to do two practicums in the city's elementary schools where all the classes were in English. Hardly ever were they sent to St. Boniface or a French village. Not surprisingly under these conditions, francophone candidates were rare and hard-pressed to succeed. [40]

Of some 500 students in Gabrielle's 1928-29 graduating class, only five had French names. She was the only one whose graduation recommendation was "unconditional". Three of her francophone classmates were among the twenty-two whose recommendation was "conditional" and the last was one of six who were not recommended.

While the department of education retained control over the curriculum and the training and certification of teachers, their hiring was the purview of individual school boards. L'Association d'Éducation des Canadiens Français du Manitoba used its influence in francophone communities to see to it that the school boards recruited teachers capable of serving the cause of *survivance*. In effect, the AECFM determined the placement of teachers throughout francophone Manitoba. Gabrielle Roy taught in rural and northern Manitoba for twelve years, during which time she was active with le Cercle Molière. Leaving Manitoba in 1937, she lived for two years in France and England working as a freelance journalist before returning to Canada to settle in Québec and begin her writing career. All her life, she kept coming home to St. Boniface to the big white house on Deschambault Street where her mother and sisters lived. In later years, she supported them.

Gabrielle Roy was a passionate French Canadian and one of the greatest Canadian writers of either French or English origin. Her first and most famous novel, *The Tin Flute*, published in 1945 in French as *Bonheur d'Occasion* and under its English title in 1947, won the Prix Fémina in France and the Literary Guild of America Award. It has been translated into fifteen languages. Other famous works include *Where Nests the Water Hen, Rue Deschambault, The Road to Altamont, Garden in the Wind, Children of my Heart and Enchantment and Sorrow*. She was the first woman to be admitted to the Royal Society of Canada and her literary prizes include three Governor General's Awards, the Lorne Pierce Medal, the Prix Duvernay and the Prix David. Some of her early works were written in English but, as she explained later, she returned to her maternal language for it was in French that she truly lived and breathed and where her ideas achieved their fullest form. All of her works were published in Canada's two official languages, first in French, then in English. She worked closely with her translator in each case. Her themes centred on humanity's solitude and pain leavened by hope for human reconciliation. She has been described as "one of the most important writers of the post-war period". [41]

Her extraordinary gift was her own but her birthplace moulded her understanding of Canada and the place of her community within it. This understanding is shared by the majority of French Canadians in the diaspora and one at decided odds with Québec nationalism. Her identity with the plight of her people and their language in Canada made her an ardent anti-separatist. She fiercely objected to the famous "Vive le Québec Libre" cry of French President Charles de Gaulle from Québec City's Hôtel de Ville in 1967, Canada's Centennial Year, writing this powerful letter published in Québec City's *Le Soleil* and Montréal's *Le Devoir*:

> I protest the lesson that General de Gaulle presumes to teach our country. I can see in it only disdain for the noble efforts undertaken in Canada with a view to real progress which resides nowhere if not first in a desire for under-standing and mutual respect ...

> As a French Canadian writer I have never suffered from a lack of freedom when I have wished to have it, either in Québec or elsewhere in Canada. The fact that I was born in Manitoba and having spent my early years there I learned French well enough to be recognized later as writer of the French language even in France proves it sufficiently, it seems to me ...

> With all my faith in the future of humankind, with all my strength, I enjoin my compatriots who consider themselves not as French in Canada but as French Canadians to demon-strate in favour of true freedom in Québec. For it is in grave risk of being taken from us if by inertia we let it slip little by little into the hands of extremists or visionaries held back by dreams of the past rather than with eyes open to the realities of our human condition on this continent. Grandeur for us will consist not in undoing our ties but in perfecting them. (42)

Gabrielle Roy's biographer, close friend and literary executor, François Ricard, says she saw the independence movement as a retreat into intolerance and hatred that reminded her of the "stifling atmosphere of her birth milieu, backward-looking, vengeful, immobilized by distrust and resent-ment". She herself said she dreaded it like "the worst evil". After the Parti Québécois came to power in 1976 she was torn. She did not want to have

Mme Gabrielle Roy
dénonce de Gaulle

L'écrivain Gabrielle Roy a
fait enregistrer sa protestation
contre les propos tenus par le
général de Gaulle, affirmant que
le président français a fait preu-
ve de mépris pour les nobles efforts entrepris au Canada en vue
du véritable progrès "..."
side nulle par
bord

LE DEVOIR

50 CENTS

..., dit-
.... plein de digni-
....gme par le premier mi-
nistre Pearson."

Souhaitant la "vraie liberté"
au Québec, Mme Roy signale
qu'elle "risque fort de nous être
ôtée si nous la laissons aller no-

to choose between her loyalty to Québec and her affection for "the rest of Canada where we as a people have wandered and suffered, yes, but throughout which we have left our mark". [43]

Ricard concludes his extraordinary biography of this extraordinary Manitoban with an assessment of the significance of her literary achievements and their meaning for her country and natal province:

> In the Canadian context, her work was and still is unquestionably universal, for it has been read, admired and studied as much in English-speaking circles as in French-speaking, as much in Toronto and Winnipeg as in Montréal, which at the time could be said of very few authors either French Québeçois or English Canadian. To this day, Gabrielle Roy is probably the only true "Canadian" writer in the federal sense of the word, meaning the only one whose work genuinely transcends the language barrier and is embraced unreservedly by the two communities as their own – and by the two literary establishments. [44]

That Manitoba could have produced this genius at the height of its repression of its bilingual and bicultural constitutional heritage is a testimony not only to the individual herself and to the indomitable qualities of the human spirit, but also to the unique Canadianness forged in the fire of the Manitoba crucible. Certainly, Roy's international stature puts the lie to the 1916 Norris government's attack on Manitoba's confessional French schools. Indeed, as Université d'Ottawa historian Cornelius Jaenen says: "The bilingual schools were beginning to turn out bilingual students in 1916!" [45] Journalist and author Jacqueline Blay says that Gabrielle Roy epitomizes the quality of teaching that was decried so much in 1916. "Her language skills were flawless – in English and French – and yet what was the reason invoked by the government to repeal the Laurier Greenway compromise? The poor quality of education in the schools." [46]

Gabrielle Roy's life entices us to engage in the perilous game of second-guessing history. At the very least, we are tempted to use her as a potent rebuke both to the francophone Roman Catholic and political hierarchies of Québec who feared their language and nationality would perish outside that province and to the anglophone Orange Order imperialists who feared a bilingual, bicultural west would deny Canada its greatness.

Her life also serves to remind us that individuals frequently have a more profound impact on the course of history than religion, ideology, governments and armies. This was to be especially true in Manitoba.

Although the organic francophone community decided to mobilize behind restoring its school rights, five individual Franco-Manitobans over the course of ninety years went to court to fight what they were certain was the illegal abolition of their language. Two won pyrrhic victories. The third was blocked by his own compatriots. The fourth and fifth made constitutional history in Canada as well as in Manitoba.

Collège Universitaire de Saint-Boniface political scientist Raymond Hébert argues the French community in Manitoba acquired a jaundiced view of the legal system for the very valid reason that "the first fifty years after Manitoba's entry into Confederation had demonstrated how easily the Manitoba constitution could be ignored as a source of protection of their basic rights; the Anglo-Saxon majority simply did what it wanted starting in 1890 regardless of the constitution or its judicial interpretation." [47]

The first legal challenge against the Official Language Act of 1890 was launched in 1892 before County Court Judge Louis-Arthur Prud'homme in La Broquerie, a tiny francophone community south of

Winnipeg. The lawyer bringing the action was none other than James Emile Pierre Prendergast, the former provincial secretary in the Thomas Greenway Liberal administration, who resigned his cabinet post to lead the legislature's francophone members in their battle against the 1890 laws that abolished French as an official language and Manitoba's separate school system. Prendergast represented a man by the name of Pellant who contested the mayoral candidacy of one Joseph Hébert on the grounds he was semi-literate and incapable of representing his electors. Prendergast submitted his documents in both French and English. Hébert's lawyer contested Prendergast's deposition on the grounds English was the sole official language of the province. The judge found for Prendergast and Pellant, declaring the Official Language Act of 1890 unconstitutional.

"There is no doubt that Section 23 of the Manitoba Act and Section 133 of the British North America Act are identical. The word Manitoba is substituted for the word Québec, that's all," the judge declared. [48] He also disagreed that Section 92 of the BNA Act gave the provinces the power to alter their own constitutions.

> The consequence is that the legislature does not have the right to legislate on the subject ... The delegation of power in the BNA Act is limited ... The provincial legislature, fully sovereign when acting within its own sphere, cannot enlarge at will the fluctuating opinions of the legislature. It can redo or modify its methods of operating but it lacks the power to legislate on matters outside its jurisdiction.

> Provincial legislatures do not possess any inherent power outside what is given them by statute.

> I am therefore of the opinion that (the Official Language Act of 1890) is *ultra vires* of the legislature of Manitoba and that Section 23 of the Manitoba Act cannot be changed let alone abrogated by the legislature of that province. [49]

The victory was total and complete. It was also immediately squelched by a clever but odious ruse to subvert both justice and the law that would nevertheless be used by two successive governments of different political stripes when other Franco-Manitobans attempted the same challenge. One man's perseverance and ingenuity finally put an end to it some eighty-four years later. The first attorney general to employ the ruse, Joseph Martin's replacement, Clifford Sifton, simply ignored the judge's ruling, neither acting upon it nor appealing it to a higher court. Pellant and Judge Prud'homme were frozen in their tracks. Such was the regard for the law, the constitution, conscience and duty to be displayed at intervals over the next eighty years by three senior cabinet officers who by virtue of their position carry the title of "Chief Law Officer of the Crown and Keeper of the Great Seal of Manitoba".

Seventeen years later, in 1909, Judge Prud'homme returned to the fray in *Bertrand vs. Dussault and Lavoie*. This case lay buried for sixty-eight years, surfacing again as part of Appeal Court Justice Alfred Monnin's 1977 dissenting opinion regarding Georges Forest's precedent-setting long legal battle with the City of Winnipeg and the Province of Manitoba over unilingualism. Forest's lawyers had dug it out and employed it in their court arguments. Similar to the issue to be raised by Forest, the 1909 case involved an attempt to quash a statement of claim because it was written only in French. Monnin, upholding Forest's plea to begin his case against the Official Language Act of 1890 at the appeal court level, included Prud'homme's judgement in its entirety in his written dissent. He did so, he said, because it had lain "unknown or ignored" for nearly seventy years and "so that [it] may not be lost forever to posterity".

In his 1909 ruling, Judge Prud'homme once again established the parallel between the official bilingualism decreed by Section 23 of the Manitoba Act and that enforced by Section 133 of the British North America Act. Once again he declared the Official Language Act of 1890 abolishing the constitutional status of the French language in Manitoba to be beyond the powers of the provincial legislature.

> ... the standing of the French language in Manitoba is the same as that of the English language in Québec or to be more correct, the evident intent of those sections is to perpetuate both languages in those provinces ... I then hold that ... Section 23 of the Manitoba Act 1870 cannot be amended and still less repealed by the provincial Legislature. I could not come to a different conclusion without doing violence to both the letter and the spirit of the British North America Act of 1867 and the Manitoba Act of 1870 ...

Section 23 is an organic provision of the Manitoba Constitution. There is not authority given in the Manitoba Act 1870 to touch it in any way ... The fathers of Confederation wishing to settle that vexed question once and for all, have advisedly placed it dehors [outside] the control or legislative power of provincial Legislatures. The same privilege as to their language is conceded to the French minority of Manitoba as to the English minority of Québec by provisions which the Legislatures of these provinces cannot alter in any shape or form ...

The evident intent of the framers of both acts was to perpetuate English and French in these two provinces and place them beyond the reach of their respective legislatures. [50]

But once again, the government of the day, this time the Conservative government of Sir Rodmond Roblin that had otherwise demonstrated some sympathy for the francophone cause, subverted the court decision. Attorney General C.H. Campbell employed Clifford Sifton's clever strategem. He simply pretended the judgement hadn't been rendered. By ignoring it, he deprived the successful litigant of the justice awarded him by the court.

Then in June 1916, a few months after the passage of the Thornton Act, Joseph Dumas, the St. Boniface MLA who had resigned from the Liberal Party over the abolition of French language school rights, brought an action in Court of Queen's Bench to recover a debt of $525 from Donat R. Baribault. Albert Dubuc, Dumas' lawyer, submitted his documents in both English and French. The court clerk refused to accept them. Realizing that this was going to create a confrontation over the constitutional status of the French language in Manitoba, La Liberté reacted with a stinging editorial strongly condemning, not the law nor the actions of the court clerk, but Dumas.

We would have preferred by far to have learned that the action taken by Mr. Dumas would have been taken in conjunction with l'Association d'Education des Canadiens Français du Manitoba but it seems that the opposite is true. The MLA for St. Boniface is lacking the most elementary discipline necessary to a cause like ours. This cause is so sacred and the decision of the Privy Council on the topic will be so final that it is very important to touch it only after much reflection even if the rights are very clear. We have to look at it only after making sure all the legal guarantees are in place first. Did the MLA for St. Boniface do this? We can't deny it absolutely but we have to say that we doubt it. When we have to put together a defensive plan once the fight is committed we run a bigger chance of being wrong. We doubt very much that Mr. Dumas exercised this caution. We feel it is more a diversion to divide us. [51]

The editorial captures the essence of how embattled and fearful Franco-Manitobans had become after two decades of constant assaults and defeats at the hands of anglophone governments, laws and courts. It also illustrates part of the reason why the community chose to fight for its schools instead of its language.

Franco-Manitoban journalist Jacqueline Blay, whose coverage of the French language crisis of 1979-1984 for *Radio-Canada* led to a master's thesis and subsequently, the book, *L'Article 23, les péripéties législatives et juridiques du fait français au Manitoba 1870-1986* (Article 23, the legislative and judicial zig-zag of the French fact in Manitoba 1870-1986), says the French community saw Dumas as "a lone ranger" doing his own thing and thus potentially dangerous. The St. Boniface MLA may also have suffered prejudice because he was Métis. In any event, he abandoned his action. The community insisted upon drawing its first line of defence around schools because, Blay continues:

> [S]chools created religion and religion in those times was the main driving force. We used to say "la langue gardienne de la foi" – language is the keeper of the faith – so if you teach the language you keep the faith. That is why leaders of the time went to court for the schools, because the language issue seemed to be less favourable for a good ruling. Yes, you had leaders in the community, judges, lawyers, and they were involved with the law and yet they didn't fight [the Official Language Act] and that's the mystery. Bishops Taché and Langevin wanted to take care of the schools issue first because if you are teaching you might also convert ... The Catholic faith mattered more than the language issue. [52]

In her book, Blay describes the period 1916 to 1968 as "the crossing of the desert" for Franco-Manitobans. They turned inward, focusing on *la survivance*, politically, educationally and socially. Roger Turenne's thesis on Franco-Manitobans' voting behaviour from 1888 to 1969 shows that Franco-Manitobans trod the well-worn path of threatened minorities throughout history in their relationship with political power: They sought protection by cooperating with the government of the day.

> The constant pressure brought to bear on the Franco-Manitobans put them on the defensive and psychologically conditioned them to accept that any of the democratic niceties could be done away with if it would help *la cause*. Similar phenomena can be seen in the Southern United States' adopting the one-party system to protect its "way of life" and in Québec's turning upon itself, "protected" by authoritarian governments and clergy. [53]

Members of majorities take for granted their right to individual political opinion and dissent. Both are luxuries that members of oppressed minorities cannot afford. For oppressed minorities, the survival of the group takes primacy over the interests and preferences of the individual. Turenne describes it graphically as "the stifling of the democratic spirit in a threatened minority". [54] But as is often the case with marginalized groups, even their political subjugation wasn't enough to protect Franco-Manitobans.

Because Liberal governments had authored the deadly assaults on their rights, the Franco-Manitoban political party of choice at first was the Conservatives. But the Conservatives, while certainly more sympathetic than the Liberals, also betrayed them, supporting the Greenway government's schools legislation in the 1892 election and the Norris government's Thornton Act in 1920. Turenne reports that in 1899, Premier Sir Hugh John Macdonald even ruminated about amending the franchise law to restrict the right to vote only to those who could speak and write English. He later "clarified" himself to indicate he was only referring to Slavic immigrants. But, says Turenne, "it was not very reassuring to the French Canadians." [55] In any event, Macdonald left office to run federally before anything was done.

His successor, Sir Rodmond Roblin, emerged as a friend to the embattled francophone community. Premier from 1900 to 1915, Roblin had been the only Protestant MLA to vote against the schools act in 1890. His government was sensitive to francophone interests to the point the *Manitoba Free Press* darkly ruminated about an unholy alliance between the premier and the Archbishop of St. Boniface, Adélard Langevin.

As noted earlier, it was under the Roblin government that the lenient administration of the schools act – turning a blind eye to the use of French texts and the French language – began. As well, the Roblin government built a French normal school, started construction on a highway from St. Boniface to the little French communities that dotted the east side of the Red River south of Winnipeg and gave the Franco-Manitoban community a fourth constituency, Assiniboia (the other three were St. Boniface, La Vérendrye and Carillon) where they would enjoy a majority. And finally, Turenne reports, "the premier himself made a hundred dollar donation to the St. Boniface Hospital". [56]

But perhaps of greatest importance, in 1913, Roblin appointed the first francophone cabinet minister in twenty-four years – Joseph Bernier. Not since J.E.P. Prendergast resigned in 1889 had the Manitoba cabinet included a member of the province's official language minority. With this step forward there was an offsetting step back, initiating a baleful tradition that carried through to the middle of the century. Until the advent of the NDP government of Edward Schreyer in 1969, francophone ministers were restricted to lesser portfolios, seated "below the salt" so to speak. Initially, they were ministers without portfolio and unsalaried ones at that. Then they were moved up a notch to the grab-bag post suitably titled "provincial secretary". Sir Rodmond's grandson, Dufferin (Duff), who became premier in 1958, would have broken the mould before Schreyer but was prevented by a distressing turn of fate, of which more later.

With the formation of the l'Association d'Éducation des Canadiens-Français du Manitoba, (AECFM) in 1916 and the election of Premier John Bracken's United Farmers of Manitoba in 1922, the francophone community's political strategy shifted as well. Says Turenne:

> Since Manitoba had decided that it would not tolerate
> cultural duality, the only way the French could maintain
> this duality was out of sight and out of mind of the rest
> of the province. This they did through the AECFM, whose
> task it was to look after the *survivance* quietly and by
> keeping minority issues out of electoral politics. [57]

In 1952, a small seed sprouted in the desert. The Liberal-Progressive government of Douglas Campbell, in a late evening session just prior to prorogation, included a new Section 240 to the Public Schools Act among its many amendments to that massive and ever-changing legislation. Astonishingly, there was no debate. Section 240 allowed a school board to authorize a language other than English in three limited areas: during a period for religious instruction, a period authorized for teaching a language other than English and before and after school hours "as prescribed by regulation and applicable to that school". At the same time, the government authorized teaching a *Français* course for one hour a day from Grades Seven to Twelve and, after thirty-six years, the Department of Education took over responsibility from the AECFM for curriculum, textbook development and inspection relating to Grades Seven to Twelve Français.

In 1963-64, Campbell's successor, Conservative Duff Roblin, the first open and acknowledged francophile premier of Manitoba since Marc-Amable Girard, appointed and consulted an Advisory Committee on Bilingualism and Biculturalism chaired by University of Manitoba historian W.L. Morton. "The provincial authorities came to the view that though provincial society constituted an ethnic mosaic, the Franco-Manitoban community occupied an historically distinctive role along with the Anglo-Celtic founders." [58] In 1963, following the introduction of a private member's bill by Laurent (Larry)Desjardins, the Liberal MLA for St. Boniface, the Français program was legalized by regulation starting from Grade One. [59] In 1965 and again in 1966, Desjardins attempted two more private members bills to make French a language of instruction for all subjects but, as is usual with such bills, they died on the order paper.

In January 1964, Reverend Raymond Durocher, editor of the weekly *La Liberté et Le Patriote*, gave an important and prophetic address to the Roman Catholic Parent-Teacher Federation. Durocher, who was also chairman of the Bishop's Advisory Committee on Catholic Education, said any solution to the problems of parochial schools in Manitoba must come from a united legislature. "Any governmental decision on the matter will have to represent a vast majority of the province's public opinion if it is to be durable," he said. "Partisan action will have faster results but won't last, even if made by the party in power."

Then Durocher walked his audience through the bed of thorns known as the Manitoba School Question. The Schools Act of 1890 did not create public schools, rather it suppressed the Catholic schools, a much easier task to accomplish, he said. "Manitoba's school system is modelled after that of the United States: a deliberate attempt to impose a predominantly Protestant, exclusively Anglo-Saxon pattern on a horde of ignorant quarrel-some foreigners."

The *La Liberté* editor used humour to chide the premier for his long silence on the issue. "Is Roblin wobblin' or has Duff got the stuff? Is there ineffective goodwill or dissimulated indifference behind that wall of silence? Look at those rare phrases. Is there any beer below the foam?" Manitoba, he concluded, was "odd man out", the only province in the nation not to pro-vide some form of aid to parochial schools. The others all "carry out the spirit of the British North America Act". [60]

In May 1965, Roblin's advisor and noted historian W.L. Morton appeared before the federal Royal Commission on Bilingualism and Biculturalism during its Winnipeg hearings. English Canada had treated French Canada with injustice and intolerance and unless something was done about it, the country's survival would be in danger, he said. Warning that French Canada must never be equated with Québec, W.L. Morton said Québec must never be granted special status because French Canadians out-side that province would then lose their linguistic and cultural rights. Special status, he continued, "is the abandonment of the Canadian ideal of equality of the founding peoples in language and culture just when it has become possible to make the ideal a reality". If Canada is to be kept together on the basis of free consent, the historian continued, it is essential "to give the fullest practical application to the principle of bilingualism." [61]

That year, the Roblin government established a system of shared services between public and private schools as a kind of back-door way to return some level of public funding to Manitoba's Catholic schools. Under it, parochial schools could contract with neighbouring public schools to teach their students core but non-cultural courses such as the sciences, mathematics and physical education that their tight budgets left them hard-pressed to offer. As with all compromises, both sides were unhappy. A group of militant Protestants formed a Committee to Save our Public Schools while the Roman Catholics rejected it as totally unacceptable. St. Boniface Archbishop Maurice Baudoux said the Catholics had asked the premier for bread and been given a stone. [62] But the majority of Manitobans accepted it on the premier's sensible observation that, were there no parochial schools at all, the public education system would be teaching all their pupils their entire course of studies.

Finally, on March 27, 1967, Roblin's education minister, George Johnson, introduced Bill 59 in the Legislature to allow French as a language of instruction "in social studies and for such other subjects as the Minister may by regulation stipulate". [63] The significance lay not so much in what was done, because all of it was still a long way from returning French to its original status as an official language of Manitoba co-equal with English. Rather, it lay in the fact it was done at all and in the open, tolerant spirit that accompanied its doing. Two NDP MLAs gave speeches that were almost radical in the Manitoba context. Russ Doern, the bilingual member for Elmwood who, sixteen years later, would emerge as one of bilingualism's most implacable foes, took the national perspective.

> I think that the people who phrased the Bill, the Minister and his advisors, have attempted to look at this very complicated question which tore this province apart many years ago, with some depth and some insight and I think they put it in a national context. They apparently did not look upon Manitoba as an isolated province or as an isolated area, but they seemed to regard our province as it should be; namely a part of the Canadian framework. [64]

Sidney Green, also bilingual, gave the step its historical and constitutional context, a context freighted with import for the monumental clash to come sixteen years later.

> Mr. Speaker, the people who are interested in maintaining some ties with their background, some tie with their language and some tie with their traditions, are wrong to argue that French is a minority grouping like every other minority grouping and should have the same privileges and rights as these minority groups. I think it is to the benefit of the ethnic minorities that we recognize that Canada is not a homogeneous country, it's a heterogeneous country, that it is a country which makes possible the living together of two founding nations, two founding people, in this case the French and English founders of our country ... [65]

Bill 59 passed unanimously. Reflecting back on his accomplishment some twenty years later in an interview, Roblin stressed the exceeding delicacy he knew the issue required: "In the French question the doors had been locked and barred for about forty years. When we made our move to restore French as a language of instruction, it had to be done on what someone thought was a minimum basis, and I won't argue with that description, but it was what people felt was fair and proper at that time." [66]

The year 1967 marked Canada's centennial as a nation and the 365 days of celebrations, including Montréal's exciting World's Fair, Expo '67, seemed to throw open all the country's doors and windows. Canadians were feeling proud, even jubilant, about themselves and their country and ready to jettison the attitudes, prejudices and strictures of the past. After all, the future seemed full of hope and opportunity. Unfortunately, in Manitoba, the bright year opened with the clash of controversy – over the place of the French language in Canada and the province.

The Manitoba Historical Society's major fundraiser is its annual Sir John A. Macdonald Dinner, held on or near the first prime minister's January 15th birthday. In 1967, in honour of Canada's Centennial, the society invited the great man's most eminent biographer, historian Donald Creighton, to be guest speaker at the gala affair held in the ballroom of the Fort Garry Hotel on January 11th. Creighton used the occasion to label the bilingual-bicultural policies of the federal Liberal government "a misuse of history" and outright historical revisionism. He scandalized the Franco-Manitobans in the audience, including Maurice Arpin, a lawyer and close personal friend of Premier Roblin's. Roblin attended the dinner but left before the speech, leading some to wonder if he knew what was coming.

Creighton's address received front page coverage in the *Winnipeg Free Press,* as did Arpin's furious response. Creighton said there was no evidence the Fathers of Confederation ever intended Canada to be bilingual or bicultural. Indeed, the whole idea was merely an invention to advance what he called the "revolutionary aims" of French Canada. Nor was Creighton content to stop there. Louis Riel, he said, was a dictator who had no intention of permitting democracy to have its way in Western Canada. The theory that Confederation was a pact between French and English was a recent invention of French Canadian nationalists "and their English-Canadian associates", Creighton said. Because Canadians are not historically minded, it was easy for those advancing the bilingual-bicultural theory to "sell this new and spurious invention." He continued: "It would be a tragedy if ... Canadians were led on to damage their futures through a serious misunderstanding of their past."

While Riel demanded that bilingualism and biculturalism should prevail in the West, "it was a claim of Riel – not the other citizens of Red River," the historian continued. The last thing the Fathers of Confederation wanted to perpetuate was duality. The Manitoba Act was imposed by a set of circumstances, he said, describing it as "a hasty appeasement". Macdonald wanted to win the West for Canada and since he feared the United States might prevent Canada's expansion, he had to agree to Riel's demands. But it all fell apart within twenty-five years. He advised the audience to judge the then-forthcoming report of the Royal Commission on Bilingualism and Biculturalism accordingly. He warned:

> We are now confronted with radical new ideas about a new version of Confederation … [Many French Canadians] seem to believe in bilingualism and biculturalism for Canada but a virtually independent Québec which – if it decides to remain in – wants a special position. History has a lesson. The methods of a revolutionary are to dismiss the past or to reinterpret it to provide justification for a cause. [67]

Alongside its story on the Creighton speech, the *Free Press* reported the reaction of Arpin under the headline "Arpin's blood boils at speech". Arpin, whose ancestors came to Canada in 1648, had confronted the historian at a reception after the dinner and, according to notes he made later, told him: "Bon soir, Monsieur Professeur. I've read too much history of Canada and of Manitoba and studied too many of the historic and constitutional documents to be able to give any credence to your interpretations and theories." Then, he said, he turned on his heel and walked out. Noting that Premier Roblin had been at the dinner but left before the speech, Arpin told the newspaper that "I have reason to believe he doesn't subscribe to (Creighton's) theories." [68]

Two days later, the paper carried a long response to Creighton's attack written by a young history professor at United College, now the University of Winnipeg. Cornelius Jaenen, who would go on to become professor of history at l'Université d'Ottawa and the author of many articles and papers on French-English relations, exhaustively reviewed all the historical evidence from the Confederation debates and official British documents to demonstrate that indeed, a bi-national compact was at the core of the British North America Act, Canada's first constitution.

[Creighton] repeatedly cited the BNA Act, for example, as a
document devoid of any reference to a compact between
English and French Canadians. To be perfectly honest with
his audience he might have added that if Section 133 gives
no official status to French throughout Canada then it also
gives no legal status to English ... What is sauce for the
French-Canadian goose is sauce for the English-Canadian
gander. If anglophone Canadians may assume that their
presence in a region entitles them to the official use of their
language, why should not francophone Canadians operate
on the same assumptions?

Just as disconcerting and disheartening was Creighton's analysis of
Louis Riel and the events of 1869-70 in Manitoba, Jaenen continued. Riel's
second bill of rights was drawn up, not by a dictator, but by a democratically-
elected convention of Fort Garry colonists.

Professor Creighton views our history from a Toronto bas-
tion and does not see French Canadians as participants ...
[Creighton is an] imperialist-nationalist Tory interpreter and
it is hard to believe that [the biographer of Canada's first
prime minister] would turn around and reduce considerably his stature by making him the dupe of Red River Métis
and priests. [69]

In an interview thirty-six years later, Jaenen recalled the event with
a chuckle. Creighton threatened to sue him but never followed through. He
had been at the dinner and had challenged Creighton from the floor. He was
subsequently approached by Arpin to write the piece for the newspaper. [70]

Despite being openly francophile, Roblin's efforts at political/electoral
rapprochment with the Franco-Manitoban community were rebuffed from
the start. In his thesis on Franco-Manitobans' voting behaviour, Roger
Turenne put the community's apparent disregard of its own best interests
down to the repression and fear inculcated by minority status.

A respect for minority rights as understood in the "moral
pact" of Confederation, is a prerequisite in a pluralistic society
in order to have meaningful democracy. Denied what it
considers its inalienable rights, a minority tends to become

defensive and insular to the degree that its participation
in the democratic process is inhibited. Its capacity for and
tolerance of dissent within its ranks and, to some extent,
its flexibility in voting, depend on a certain sense of security.
If Duff Roblin found the voting behaviour of the Franco-
Manitobans somewhat frustrating, he might have been
reminded that it had its roots in 1890 and 1916. [71]

During the thirty-plus years of non-partisan coalition government in
Manitoba, Franco-Manitobans had once again placed their political support
with the incumbent regime, namely, with the ever-shifting alliance of parties
composing it. It was a strange creature indeed, an amalgam of agrarian protest,
Conservative, Liberal, Progressive, Cooperative Commonwealth Federation
(the forerunner of the New Democratic Party) and Social Credit. In other
words, it had at the same time every shade in the province's political rainbow
save the bright red of Communism and it was stridently non-partisan and
non-political. The legislature operated like a large municipal council and it
was not unusual during those years for ministers – including Premier John
Bracken himself – to run for and win all the party nominations in their constituencies. As the coalition gradually migrated from its non-partisan original
United Farmers roots to become first Progressive, then Liberal-Progressive
and finally Liberal, the majority of francophones migrated right along with
it. Francophone support of the Liberal Party was cemented in 1961 when
Gildas Molgat, a French-speaking Manitoban of Belgian ancestry, succeeded
Douglas Campbell to become Liberal leader and leader of the Official
Opposition in the Manitoba Legislature.

The gradual transfer of francophone allegiance from Conservative to
Liberal occasioned by the lengthy non-partisan period in Manitoba politics
was exemplified by one of Franco-Manitoba's first families, the Préfontaines.
Albert Préfontaine, the unofficial leader of the small group of francophone
MLAs who battled the Norris government's Thornton Act in 1916, had repre-
sented the constitutency of Carillon from 1903 to 1935 with only two brief
interruptions in 1914-15 and 1920-22. In 1935, he was succeeded by his son,
Edmond. Albert had first been a Conservative, then a Progressive and then
a Liberal-Progressive. Edmond began as a Liberal-Progressive, joined the
Manitoba Democratic Movement for a while, but remained a Liberal. Says
Turenne: "The Préfontaines were a large, close-knit, influential family with a

strong sense of duty and which took its politics seriously." [72]

Two of Edmond's four sons were active in public life: Gilbert, president of the La Vérendrye Liberal Association and René, secretary of the AECFM and secretary-general of the Manitoba School Trustees Association. These positions put René in close personal contact with the new young Tory premier soon after Roblin broke his party out of the old coalition and, in 1958, formed Manitoba's first Conservative government since that of his grandfather. The young Franco-Manitoban quickly became convinced of the premier's sincerity in wishing to improve the lot of the official minority. Adds Turenne: "He also became aware at this time of the crying need for a francophone spokesman in the cabinet." [73] Roblin, too, wanted a Franco-Manitoban in his cabinet, in part for the practical political reason of breaking the Liberals' hold on four constituencies.

The time seemed right at the end of 1962. La Vérendrye, one of the province's four historic francophone ridings, was vacant. Roblin asked René to enter the cabinet as minister of municipal affairs so that he could face his prospective voters as a candidate with clout. The ensuing events were charged with high drama, fraught as they were with great personal angst and political opportunity lost. The swearing-in was to be in French for the first time since the language had been banished in 1890. As a Tory minister, René would not only be sitting opposite his father – a man revered in the Franco-Manitoban community – in the legislature, he would have to fight his brother's Liberal campaign organization in La Vérendrye.

René accepted the premier's offer. The ceremony was set for the morning of November 7, 1962 and the press release was printed and issued. The lieutenant governor and the press were assembled and waiting. Under intense pressure from his family, René decided at the last minute he simply couldn't proceed. The ceremony was cancelled. The lieutenant governor's chamber emptied and the press raced to their telephones and typewriters. The public embarrassment was intense for the premier and his protegé.

Roblin called a general election for December 14, 1962. "Caught between the bitter-end partisanship of his father, and his devotion to *la cause* which he had learnt from childhood, (René) chose the latter and entered the fray as Conservative candidate in La Vérendrye." [74] But there had been too much damage. To many he was seen as a turncoat, worse, as an indecisive and unreliable turncoat. The family's searing split was out in the open. His father – who was retiring from politics – and his brother both

Canadian Crucible

repeatedly accused him of being misled and called for his defeat. At the Liberal convention in La Vérendrye one delegate claimed that "René was lured away with promises that he could serve the French Canadian cause. This is hog-wash ..." [75] The Liberal candidate won a majority of the French polls and took the seat by a margin of 300 votes. The Préfrontaine debacle hurt the Tory hopefuls in the other three francophone ridings too. All went Liberal. States Turenne:

> Duff Roblin had been handicapped by the lack of a French
> Canadian spokesman, frustrated in his attempt at getting one,
> plagued by the school question and opposed by a French
> Canadian leader of the Liberal Party. Yet none of these factors
> should have prevented a politically aware electorate conscious
> of its true interests as a group to give him some measure of
> support. In 1962, the Franco-Manitobans did not constitute
> a politically aware electorate conscious of its true interests.
> The long years of being "non-partisan" on matters of concern
> to the minority had dulled its political instincts. [76]

Despite its rebuff from francophone voters, the Roblin administration had managed to stir the sands of the Manitoba language desert and new life sprang up all over. What had caused the fresh, moist breezes to blow? Journalist Jacqueline Blay and political scientist Raymond Hébert agree it was part and parcel of the quasi-revolutionary decade of the 1960s, a time when established order was under attack or serious questioning across the western world, from the civil rights movement in the United States to the "Prague Spring" in Czechoslovakia and from the popular student uprising in the streets of Paris to Canada's coming of age with the famous "B&B" Commission, Montréal's Expo 67 and the election of "philosopher king" Pierre Elliott Trudeau as Liberal leader and prime minister in 1968.

> A new spirit of renewal and militancy within the francophone
> community brought about by the election of the Trudeau
> government in 1968 and adoption of the Official Languages Act
> in 1970 led a growing number of francophones to believe that
> perhaps the impossible could come true; perhaps instruction in
> the French language could be fully legalized in Manitoba. [77]

The 1960s also cracked Manitoba's political mould. Fresh out of university and only twenty years of age, Raymond Hébert, whose family tree includes Sir Wilfrid Laurier, Canada's first French Canadian prime minister, became the editor of the the new community newspaper, the *St. Boniface Courier*. His first editorials were challenges to the Franco-Manitoban community to press for non-sectarian French-speaking public schools. Hébert's journalistic career was short. He soon abandoned it to become a senior provincial civil servant and subsequently, a professor of political science at le Collège Universitaire de Saint-Boniface. But his editorials were emblematic of a sea-change in the Franco-Manitoban community. The clergy and the elite of the AECFM recounted in Roger Turenne's thesis were losing their decades-long grip on Franco-Manitoban thought and action. Franco-Manitobans were ready to enter the political mainstream. In fact, they were in the forefront of the wave of political change about to wash across the province.

Winnipeg had long had a solid base of democratic socialist support. Gradually and imperceptibly, Clifford Sifton's fabled "men in sheepskin coats", the Germans, Ukrainians, Jews, Poles, Hungarians and Russians who wove the vivid tapestry of Manitoba's swelling ethnic mosaic, had been shifting their political allegiance from the Liberals, the party that had thrown open the nation's doors to them in the first decade of the century, to the CCF and its successor, the NDP. Ed Schreyer, a farm boy from Beausejour, was uniquely positioned to fuse left-of-centre politics and ethnicity into a potent electoral force. Fluent in English, French, German and Ukrainian and a professor of political studies at the University of Manitoba's St. Paul's College, he became Manitoba's youngest-ever MLA at the age of twenty-two and subsequently, the MP for Selkirk. He returned from Ottawa to be elected leader of the NDP at a televised leadership convention held in the middle of the provincial election campaign of 1969.

To wring maximum advantage out of its new young leader – the first of neither English nor French parentage in Manitoba history – and his photogenic family, the NDP chose "Ed Schreyer's New Democrats" as its campaign slogan. Schreyer carried the party from third to first place in one bound on election night, June 25, 1969, decimating the Liberals and humbling the Tories whose spark had sputtered after Walter Weir, a small-c conservative funeral director from Minnedosa, was chosen to replace the retiring Duff Roblin. Harkening from another political time and place in comparison to the urbane and progressive Roblin, Weir favoured black Homburgs and bulky black coats and smoked stogies. He freeze-framed his short career as first minister by remarking upon his election as Tory leader in late 1967 that a Manitoba premier had to be able to "kick manure (actually, sh..) off tractor wheels". He also was one of the first premiers to challenge Pierre Trudeau over official bilingualism and constitutional reform.

Schreyer was only thirty-three when he became Manitoba's sixteenth premier, making him the province's youngest leader save Louis Riel, the twenty-five-year-old president of the 1869-70 provisional government. Ed Schreyer's New Democrats captured twenty-eight seats, one shy of a majority. Almost immediately, Larry Desjardins, the longstanding Liberal MLA for St. Boniface, became the NDP's unofficial twenty-ninth member and subsequently joined the Schreyer ministry as a "Liberal Democrat,"maintaining his ties to the federal Liberal party but sitting as part of the NDP cabinet and caucus. He stated his reasons in a speech to the House on June 27, 1970:

> The day after the election, I chose to support Mr. Schreyer in order that he could form a majority in the House and consequently form the present government of Manitoba. In short, the question for me was to make a choice between two men rather than two parties: Mr. Weir, leader of the Conservative party who had not shown himself to be sympathetic to the French Canadians or to the idea of a bilingual Canada; and Mr. Schreyer, who had during his campaign and on many other occasions, stated without ambiguity his desire to see a bilingual Canada which would allow all Canadians to progress according to one or the other of the two official languages of Canada. [78]

Desjardins' decision, decried in some political quarters as a tawdry backroom deal between two Roman Catholic francophiles, was enthusiastically endorsed at a large public meeting of the MLA's St. Boniface constituents. [79]

The political cynics had their worst suspicions confirmed when, on June 1, 1970, the Schreyer government introduced Bill 113, yet another amendment to the Public Schools Act, legalizing French as a language of instruction for all subjects except English from Kindergarten to Grade Twelve. But once again, it stopped short of fully restoring linguistic equality in education because it was permissive, not universal. Access to French as a language of instruction depended on a classroom-by-classroom opting-in formula: twenty-eight students at the elementary level, twenty-three at the secondary.

Since a course in English for Français students was made compulsory from Grades Four to Twelve, in practice that meant the language of instruction could be 100 per cent French from Kindergarten to Grade Three and up to seventy-five per cent of total instruction time from Grade Four to Twelve. [80] For Franco-Manitobans, who found themselves stranded on a tiny atoll battered on all sides by a relentless English ocean, this meant a succession of long, uphill climbs to create the long-sought-after totally French-speaking milieu only achievable in a total school setting. But it was one more step towards the ultimate redress of what were now known as "the years of injustice".

Education Minister Saul Miller cast the government's action in the light of the Canadian constitution and – a must in Manitoba – addressed the link between Canadian dualism and multiculturalism:

> … needless to say we believe that the extension of official language rights in the province is both correct and a necessary measure geared to strengthening the bonds of Confederation and of course as long as the Canadian Federation remains, and so long as Manitoba is a part of it, the two official languages of Canada must be enhanced as official languages in Manitoba …
>
> The bill is a simple and straightforward attempt to provide French-speaking Manitobans and others who are interested … with their established right to be instructed in the official language of their choice within the framework of our public school system.
>
> Just as we recognize our commitments to do our part in following the federal lead in helping to strengthen Confederation and at the same time recognizing the virtue of promoting our two official languages for the sake of building our national unity, our national identity, we also recognize the necessity of following the lead of the people of Manitoba … We favour no melting pot philosophy. We don't believe that it works; we don't believe that it can succceed. Rather we wish to encourage the development of what is now commonly known as our cultural mosaic. [81]

Bill 113 passed the House unanimously June 26, 1970 and became Section

258 of the Public Schools Act. All MLAs present spontaneously stood and sang *O Canada*. But while the politicians were busy patting themselves on the back, for many Franco-Manitobans, it was a case of too little, too late.

Desjardins, now the legislative assistant to Schreyer responsible for federal-provincial relations and cultural affairs, acknowledged in an interview published in the *Globe and Mail* on December 16, 1970 that "the future of French-speaking minorities outside Québec in Canada is on trial right here in Manitoba". Both he and Reverend Jean-Paul Aubry, the editor of *La Liberté et Le Patriote*, warned that the legislation had been overtaken by time and circumstance. It was too late to stop assimilation's inevitable course. On the one hand, many Franco-Manitobans of the current generation felt they had been held back by an insufficient knowledge of the majority language and so were reluctant to sign their children up for French-only schooling. On the other, the 1961 Census revealed that 24,000 of the 80,000 Manitobans who claimed French as their origin also stated that their first language was now English.

The *Globe* reported that a visit to Collège Universitaire de Saint-Boniface found English and French used interchangeably in the student common rooms. Worse, the legislation triggered tension within the francophone community, pitting parents who wanted bilingualism against those seeking French unilingualism. The St. Boniface School Board faced two opposing factions: the Parents' Committee for the Preservation of Bilingualism, led by Edwin Fitch, a Ukrainian lawyer with a French-speaking wife, in a stand-off with a group of Franco-Manitoban students demanding an entirely French milieu. In a brief to the school board on November 24, 1970, the parents' committee said French unilingualism was segregation and warned it would undermine relations between the two language communities. Continued the committee's brief: "While we accept the use of French as a language of instruction for [French courses], geography and history, [we] are opposed to the use of French as a language of instruction for mathematics and science." The parents argued this would put students at a disadvantage if they wished to pursue science and maths at university or community college. The students disagreed, arguing that most Franco-Manitobans were already more comfortable in English than they were in their own language and no matter what language was used to teach them a subject, they could practice it in English. Stated one:

> The bilingual school system does not favour an adequate
> knowledge of the French culture because in one school,
> where both English and French students attend, all activities
> outside French classes are in English in order to respect
> unilingual students ... If we accept the concept of equality
> of the two cultures [we must accept unilingual schools]
> since without this change, there is no equality.

Jean Hébert, the students' leader (and brother of Raymond), told the *Globe*
that without Bill 113 and the creation of French-only schools, the Franco-
Manitoban community faced total assimilation within twenty years.

> The process of assimilation is so advanced now that it is
> impossible to predict whether, even with French-only
> schools, French-speaking Manitobans would stop using
> English in their everyday conversations with one another.
> But it is our only hope. Mr. Fitch worries about segregation
> and the necessity to transport pupils to the school of their
> language. He is not even on our wavelength. What we are
> talking about is the survival of our language in Manitoba.

Albert Lépage, president of la Société Franco-Manitobaine, agreed.

> After fifty years of repression, we have to do something to
> redress the past imbalance. The bilingualism Fitch speaks
> about isn't bilingualism. We live in an entirely English-speak-
> ing milieu and we have to have a French environment in our
> schools if we are to remain in a position to be bilingual. [82]

At that time, the St. Boniface School Division had three French-
speaking and two English-speaking trustees. It presided over a community
where French-speaking citizens were now in a minority. Because it included
the entirely English-speaking suburb of Windsor Park, there were only
2,400 French-speaking children in a total school population of 9,000. Nor
were things any better even where there was a higher concentration of
Franco-Manitobans. Four other school divisions south and west of Winnipeg
were between seventy and ninety per cent French-speaking and thus affected
by Bill 113. Still, the community had to fight for every one of its Français
schools.

Much more than local-option permissive legislation was needed to recover almost ninety years of lost ground. "Permissive" meant exactly what it said: parents had to ask for the permission to have a Français class and that permission was dependent upon the goodwill of trustees, many of whom were reluctant if not actively hostile.

Bill 113 was far from a success. Three years later, only one or two French language schools had been established. It was obvious that even with financial assistance from the secretary of state in Ottawa and generous assistance from France in the form of cultural exchanges, textbooks and other educational materials negotiated by Desjardins, [83] administrative backing from the provincial department of education was essential. The Schreyer government obliged. Le Bureau de l' éducation française and l'Institut pédagogique at Collège Universitaire de Saint-Boniface were established in 1974 and two years later, an assistant deputy minister responsible for French-language education was appointed. [84] He was Raymond Hébert, the former young newspaper editor who had first advocated secular French schools in Manitoba.[85]

Over the years, however, many pitched battles were waged and some communities were torn apart thanks to the permissive aspect of the legislation. Trustees feared cost, controversy and above all, public backlash. And backlash there was. The long and debilitating struggle fuelled the creation of la Fédération provinciale des comités de parents Inc. (FPCP) and court action. Two decades later, in 1994, the Conservative administration of Gary Filmon created La Division Scolaire Franco-Manitobain, the province-wide French school board which administers the province's twenty-two Français schools. The board draws its trustees from French communities across Manitoba.[86]

The other "spoiliatory law" – the more fatal of the two – the abolition of the official status of the French language, was a battle that had not been joined since 1916 when Joseph Dumas, MLA for St. Boniface, was spurned by his own community for launching a constitutional challenge on the language issue itself. How it was soon to be taken up and battled through to its triumphant conclusion is the final tortured tale of Manitoba and Canada, French and English.

6

Forest v. Manitoba

I've always been a Don Quixote but this time I've caught a windmill.
—Georges Forest, June 2, 1978 [1]

GEORGES FOREST WAS PROUD OF THE FACT his grandmother had harboured the fugitive Louis Riel during one of his many dashes south along the Red River to safety across the American border. He was proud of his Franco-Manitoban-Métis heritage. But above all, he was a proud, passionate – almost fanatical – Canadian and Manitoban. "Manitoba," he said in the midst of his battle to redress what Franco-Manitobans called their ninety years of injustice, "can now be the birthplace of a new Canadian identity". [2]

Born eighth in a family of eleven in the rural municipality of La Salle just south of Winnipeg in 1924, Forest received his primary schooling in English but remembers "being sent to bed without supper often for not speaking only French at home." But high school in St. Norbert cultivated a deep pride in his language and cultural inheritance.

> Grandmother Degagné would take me to the site of "la barrière" where Louis Riel had resisted federal troops and I listened fascinated to her tales of Riel and the Red River

Rebellion. Of Métis stock herself, she had once hidden Riel behind a large kitchen cupboard. It was from her that I first learned of the rights that Riel's Provisional Government had gained from Canada before Manitoba joined Confederation in 1870. [3]

Like every other Franco-Manitoban schoolchild of his era, Forest had vivid memories of "having to hide our French textbooks when the school inspectors dropped in. I began asking myself, 'If we have the rights guaranteed Riel, why do we have to hide our books?' The answer I was to learn much later." [4]

Forest served in the RCAF during the war, returned to university and became a teacher. All the while, he grew increasingly aware of and concerned about rising disunity and animosity between French and English Canadians. In 1948, he established an insurance agency in St. Boniface, hoping to find in Western Canada's largest francophone community "a vital, growing French-Canadian culture which English-Canadians would be eager to share". [5] By 1949, he had solidified what he called his "basic belief in Canadian identity" – compelling but too idealistic for the vast majority of his more cynical or prejudiced fellow citizens.

I realized how an English-speaking Canadian, either native or of immigrant descent, had the opportunity to share or at least recognize the French language culture of modern Canada. At the same time, the French Canadian would naturally embrace the dominant language and culture of the North American continent. Such a sharing would give all Canadians a distinct identity, founded on dualism but producing – the Canadian … I think of myself as totally bicultural, as a Canadian should be. Particularly francophones don't realize how close I feel to Shakespeare, for instance. [6]

As the years passed, Forest became disillusioned with the "passivity" of Franco-Manitobans in the face of creeping assimilation. He also had learned much more about the laws and history that had deprived French-speaking Manitobans of their basic rights.

We had hidden our books in St. Norbert, for example, because French education had actually been abolished by

the Thornton law of 1916! As students we had never known
this. The Franco-Manitoban educators and other leaders
had obviously been content with compromises from sympathetic (sic) governments for over half a century and the
populace remained blissfully ignorant. I wanted to cry
aloud: "What happened to the rights secured by Riel?" [7]

"Necessity" forced him to resort to drama and theatrics to jolt
Manitoba francophones out of their quiesence. "The French people have
been lulled into an attitude 'there's nothing we can do about it.'" [8] The first of
many Forest tilts at Manitoba's English-only windmill began in 1959 when he
received a note of congratulation in English from Winnipeg mayor Stephen
Juba on the birth of his baby daughter, Nicole. Since St. Boniface was its
own city at that time, Forest publicly expressed his objection and alarm for
its survival. In a 1960 photograph preserved in the Forest household, Juba was
seen with the year-old Nicole in his arms maintaining that the birthday greeting had been a clerical error and promising never to "gobble up St. Boniface".

That same year, Forest led a sedate invasion of the Manitoba
Legislative Building to protest the Roblin government's bill to set up the
Metropolitan Corporation of Greater Winnipeg, creating a second governmental tier for the Manitoba capital's twelve area municipalities including,
of course, St. Boniface. Correctly, Forest perceived Metro as the first step
towards complete amalgamation of the Manitoba capital. He ran for mayor
of St. Boniface on an anti-Metro ticket but lost.

A decade later, when the Schreyer government introduced legislation
to make Winnipeg and all its surrounding municipalities one big city, Forest
decided on a more direct and attention-getting approach. One January
evening in 1971, a bearded, snowshoed voyageur boarded a flight from
Winnipeg to Montréal. Forest was on his way to Mount Royal, Winnipeg's
twin city, to protest Unicity, as it was then called, a move he warned meant
"assimilation, not amalgamation" for St. Boniface. A newspaper account of
the day called the gambit "vintage Forest". He snowshoed thirteen kilometres
from his home to the airport and twenty-six more kilometres from the Montréal
airport to a downtown hotel. En route, he told everyone who would listen
how one big Winnipeg would make St. Boniface a folkloric "French quarter"
instead of a living, developing city – French Canada's outpost in the west.
In fact, however, by the 1970s, only "old" St. Boniface, north St. Boniface,

retained its historic French character. Thanks to Norwood and St. Vital, St. Boniface had an anglophone majority.

On his return from Montréal, Forest dressed up in the same costume to trudge to every one of the government's public hearings. He always made a dramatic appearance and said his piece about the importance of preserving Manitoba's French fact. Finally, he went on a twenty-one-day hunger strike. As well as trimming thirty-two pounds from his portly frame and alarming his family, Forest accomplished at least part of his objective. St. Boniface became part of Winnipeg but the St. Boniface community was guaranteed communication in French in the City of Winnipeg Act of 1971.

Just prior to his last battle for St. Boniface independence, Forest was made the first voyageur of St. Boniface's new annual winter event, *Le Festival du Voyageur*, celebrating Franco-Manitoban life, culture, music and sports. It was launched in 1970, Manitoba's Centennial Year. He and his wife Anita researched the exact clothing of Louis Riel's maternal grandparents, Jean Baptiste Lagimodière and Marie Anne Gaboury. And they wore it to the first festival gala held on New Year's Eve 1969. A *Winnipeg Free Press* society page story on January 1, 1970 reported:

> As well as their New Year's costumes and festival costumes, Mr. and Mrs. Forest are planning a summer outfit. By that time they hope also to have complementary costumes for their children ages two to fifteen. Included in the couple's nineteenth century wardrobe are other outfits which the couple have been wearing for the last two months. They include a simple housedress, shawl and bonnet for Mrs. Forest and "outdoor wear" for her husband. Mr. Forest's New Year's Eve costume will include a royal blue double-breasted coat which features puffed sleeves and a wide red sash. All outfits were designed by Mrs. Henri Lane of the St. Boniface Historical Society.

Much later, Forest was to explain why he did all this. "I wanted French and English-speaking Manitobans to realize that I represented the spirit of the original voyageur and that the modern voyageur was a living entity, not just a relic of the past to be seen one week every year and stowed away until the next festival." [9] But the francophone populace of St. Boniface decreased steadily between 1971, the year Bill 113 passed, and 1976. Enrolment in

French schools also declined because of fear of loss of access to the majority community and a lack of a formal provincewide administrative framework.

"Something very basic caused this reluctance to develop a modern French-Canadian pride," he reflected several years later. [10]

Forest's determination to keep trying to make his dream of Manitoban and Canadian unity in duality a reality took on new life in March 1975. He went out one morning to find on his car's windshield a ticket for illegal overnight parking on the street in front of his home at 44 Champlain Street in St. Boniface. Despite the promises of the City of Winnipeg Act of 1971, Forest's ticket was in English only. He couldn't resist the temptation to tilt at yet another anglophone windmill. He decided to challenge Winnipeg's right to issue summonses in English only, hanging his hat on the clause in the City of Winnipeg Act his earlier antics had helped create: "All notices, bills or statements sent or demands made to any of the residents of St. Boniface community in connection with the delivery of any service, or the payment of any tax, shall be written in English and French." [11]

In April, he appeared before City Council to argue that Winnipeg must respect this aspect of its charter. He received his answer from city solicitor Duncan Lennox in October. Lennox said the City of Winnipeg Act did not apply because it did not cover a summons, which was a police service. In November, Forest returned to City Council and requested it ask provincial Attorney General Howard Pawley for a legal definition of the extent of Section 80(3). The city did not respond.

That might have been the end of it except on February 6, 1976, Forest's daughter Nicole left her father's car parked past the one-hour limit in front of his insurance office at 160 Marion Street. The car, a red 1968 Oldsmobile, was ticketed a second time. Forest decided he needed a lawyer and chose the St. Boniface law firm headed by Rhéal Teffaine. Teffaine regarded the case as routine and minor and transferred it to his junior partner, Alain Hogue. [12]

Some months later, Lennox reiterated his position: the parking ticket did not come under the City of Winnipeg Act and since it had not been paid, Forest received a summons to appear in provincial judges' court, traffic division. Finally, the lonely crusader got a break. Justice J.S. Walker ruled on July 27, 1976 that the ticket was not a mere notice from the City of Winnipeg. It was a judicial document and as such, came under the Official Language Act of 1890. Stated Walker: "The specific provisions of the Official

Languages (sic) Act take precedence over the more general provisions of the City of Winnipeg Act" and fined Forest $14.90 (the original ticket plus costs.) [13]

By invoking the law making English the only official language of Manitoba, Walker gave Forest the opening for which he had long been looking. Blay and Hébert both say the judge had "not only given him a cause, he had also given him a solid legal argument for taking the case to superior courts."

Three years later, Forest described his feelings in a lengthy interview with Charles Bolster, former professor of English literature and director of French theatre at le Collège Universitaire de Saint-Boniface, published in two articles in *The Winnipeg Tribune* on July 21 and 23, 1979:

> ... it all came together in that courtroom in July 1976. I was now up against a statute which crushed the basic language rights granted Franco-Manitobans by the British North America Act of Confederation itself, the Manitoba Act which in Section 23 entrenched the use of "the English or the French language ... in the debates of the House of the Legislature and ... in all or any of the Courts of the Province" and the British North America Act 1871 which confirmed Manitoba's entry into Confederation. The combination of these three acts firmly entrenched Franco-Manitobans' language rights and it had been a borderline-criminal action of the Manitoba government to deny those rights in 1890!

Forest called on La Société franco-manitobaine to "enlist in a struggle which concerned all Franco-Manitoba". The society, according to Forest, told him "a parking ticket was not enough to justify such a battle". It remained focused on its longstanding fight for French schools. For once furious, Forest asked if "they wanted another hanging".

The SFM's response was an epiphany for Forest. He suddenly realized that his community may have been fighting the wrong battle ever since 1890. The basic reason for their insecurity had been laid bare.

> What is the sense of forcing Franco-Manitoban children to be educated in French when all they can do is speak it in the schools, at home, in a poorly-attended play at le Cèrcle Molière or as a federal civil servant here or in Ottawa? The courts and the Legislature are such fundamental institutions

of any province, and if the Franco-Manitoban cannot plead
for his life, or participate in his native tongue in the shaping
of laws which will govern him and his offspring then, frankly,
he doesn't have freedom – he doesn't have the basic rights
which existed when Manitoba became a Canadian province. [14]

The appeal before St. Boniface County Court was heard November
17 and 18, 1976, two days after the overwhelming victory of the separatist
Parti Québécois under its charismatic leader René Lévesque. The Crown
attorney warned Justice Armand Dureault to carefully consider the consequences of a ruling in favour of Forest – a clear indication the province, this
time under an NDP government, was up to its old tricks of trying once again
to bury the now ninety-year-old question mark it realized hung over its constitutional conduct.

Dureault was not to be intimidated. His decision, issued December
14, 1976, was later described by Charles Bolster in *The Winnipeg Tribune* as
"twenty-nine pages of firm, authoritative reasoning". Dureault, like Judge
Prud'homme in 1892 and 1909, ruled the Official Language Act of 1890
unconstitutional and "beyond the power" of the Manitoba Legislature. The
newspaper called the ruling "monumental in Canadian law". It ranged far
and wide, especially given that it came from a county court.

Dureault knew he was making history. He quoted Bora Laskin,
then the chief justice of the Supreme Court of Canada, in matters regarding
bilingualism. He cited the Privy Council decisions on the schools question.
And he referred to an article written by noted Canadian constitutional expert
F.R. Scott published in the University of Toronto Law Journal in 1950. In it,
Scott said the Official Language Act of 1890 had never been tested in the
courts "and the better view would seem to be that it was beyond provincial
jurisdiction". [15]

The judge said he had concluded that Section 23 of the Manitoba
Act, being an exact copy of Section 133 of the British North America Act,
was intended as a substitute for it and "accordingly beyond the reach of the
Legislature's amending power". [16] The judge also classed as "repugnant"
arguments by the provincial attorney general to use the BNA Act's Section 92
– the one specifying the rights enjoyed by the provinces – as a tool to dig
entrenched language rights out of the constitution. Further, he said the fact
the Manitoba Act had been validated by the Imperial Parliament, elevating it

to the status of an Imperial statute, clearly put it beyond the reach of the legislature and of Section 92's provision that provinces can amend their constitutions except for the office of the lieutenant governor. Finally, Dureault responded with defiance to the Crown attorney's patronizing admonition to consider the political and governmental impact of a ruling favourable to Forest by quoting in its entirety Lord Mansfield's famous 1770 dictum in the case of *Regina versus Wilkes*. The great English jurist was answering the huge crowd demonstrating outside his courtroom demanding he release the prisoner:

> The constitution does not allow reasons of state to influence our judgement: God forbid it should! We must not regard political consequences, howsoever formidable they might be: if rebellion were the certain consequence, we are bound to say, *"Fiat justitia ruat caelum"* – Let justice be done even though the Heavens fall ... Once and for all, let it be understood that no efforts of this kind will influence any man who at present sits here. [17]

Concluded Dureault: "So much for the consequences." [18]

Reaction to Dureault's ruling was immediate – and predictably it was fiercely hostile. Hate mail started arriving within days, cursing Forest as the "Frenchman" and urging him either to "go back to Québec" or "speak white" if he wanted to stay in Manitoba. The hatemongering wasn't to stop for the rest of Forest's life.

Vic Grant, a former sportswriter and city columnist for *The Winnipeg Tribune* wondered why Forest had waited so long to challenge Manitoba's English-only status, noting the law was nearly ninety years old. "Was it not until he was tagged with a parking ticket that he realized that the language thing in these parts isn't the way he thinks it should be?" While Grant said he didn't begrudge anyone championing their rights, Forest was "nitpicking". The columnist then concluded with the two most popular – and specious – arguments to be used against Franco-Manitobans for the next decade: first, that French Canadians have more rights in the rest of Canada than English Canadians have in Québec; and second, that recognizing the historic place of the French language and culture in Canada took rights away from Canadians of non-English, non-French background.

> If a bilingual $5 parking ticket is all the minority has to scream about these days then this country is in pretty good

shape. I believe that George (sic) Forest can read, write and speak English. He lives in Manitoba where the predominant language is English. By his own action he suggests that St.Boniface have its own special allotment of parking tickets, printed in two languages. That might also suggest that our Ukrainian community have its allotment of English-Ukrainian tickets, ditto our German community, Chinese community, etc. etc. I wonder if George Forest would battle as hard in Québec where legislation is being prepared by the Parti Québécois government which will restrict freedom of choice in the language of education to citizens whose mother tongue is English. [19]

A subsequent lunch arranged between the columnist and Forest by a friend of the latter did nothing to improve Grant's view of the matter. Noting that Forest "couldn't even afford to fight over the lunch bill" and had admitted his battle had cost him about $12,000 in lost business, Grant concluded: "Who the hell really cares if a parking ticket is presented in one language or two? What is so difficult, especially in Manitoba, about reading the English language?" [20]

What Charles Bolster would call "English Canada's standard blunt weapon against Confederation's dualism" [21] – creating a zero sum rights game between French Canadians and everyone who wasn't of British extraction – was also advanced by city councillor Ray Brunka. He urged the city ignore its act and adopt an English-only policy out of respect for "the Polish, Ukrainian and German residents" in his Riverton ward.

Some English Manitobans rallied to Forest's cause. Frank Muldoon, QC, a friend of former premier Duff Roblin and later chair of the federal law reform commission, wrote a letter to the editor of *The Tribune* to point out:

> There is no province which is either historically or principally Ukrainian-speaking, Polish-speaking, or German-speaking … To learn French in Canada as a Canadian is to learn much about Canadian realities … It takes nothing away from the rights and respect which are accorded to Canadians of other diverse languages and cultures to recognize the reality of French in Canada. [22]

But perhaps the most telling and poignant response came from the Franco-Manitoban community itself. While some donated money to assist Forest's past and future legal costs and wore buttons proudly supporting "L'Affaire Forest", others were disdainful and angry. One close observer of French Manitoba put it this way:

> Georges should have been in theatre. He's tried everything to be in the limelight. He wants to be a new Louis Riel. But the French-speaking people of Manitoba don't care too much about a bilingual court system. They worry about other things, like paying off their mortgage, a second car and their kids' education. [23]

As for the francophone leadership, it ran the gamut from tepid applause to hostility as virulent, for its own reasons, as the vast majority of anglophone Manitoba. It was to be as virulent as Joseph Dumas' experience in 1916. Jean-Jacques Le François, editor of *La Liberté*, wrote that "Monsieur Forest has put on Messiah's robes and walks about us as ... the Saviour of the Race to whom everything concerning the future survival of Franco-Manitoba was consecrated." Like La Société franco-manitobaine, Le François stressed the "priority of developing a French school system". [24] In an interview two days after Dureault's ruling, SFM president Gérard Archambault told CKSB Radio a gradualist approach was required. While it would be nice to reclaim all the community's rights and institutions, he continued, Franco-Manitobans' first priorities must be to work in cooperation with the wider populace for the benefit of the laws and institutions already in place.

Journalist and author Jacqueline Blay says the SFM was driven by two considerations – one, being the cost of a court challenge of that magnitude, and the second, its desire for the bread and butter of French language services over the symbolism of translated statutes. Forest was also to suffer the same fate that befell Dumas over half a century earlier. He was viewed as a dangerous "lone ranger" operating outside the community's consensus. "He was thinking too much outside the box and they [the SFM] were not ready for him," Blay says. [25] Nevertheless, on December 16, 1976, the SFM announced the creation of a special fund:

> For more than three months, the SFM has provided moral support to Mr. Forest's struggle. It is obvious that that strug-gle directly concerns all Franco-Manitobans attached to their

language. That is why the SFM believes it essential to put in place a special fund to permit Franco-Manitobans to financially support Mr. Forest's legal battle. [26]

In the end, however, the SFM fund raised only $5,500 towards Forest's legal costs. The balance was covered by himself ($3,000) and the federal government (more than $70,000).

Political scientist Raymond Hébert writes that much of the francophone community's hesitancy towards Forest stemmed from its desire and need to be "good neighbours" in daily life with the overwhelming English-speaking majority. French Manitoba was again confronted with the same "fundamental dilemma" that had faced it virtually since the province's founding. "In pressing for respect of its rights, it would raise the ire of the majority which is either ignorant of or antagonistic to these rights." [27]

Undaunted, Forest kept trying to convince his fellow francophones that "language rights should be the prime concern of modern Franco-Manitoba. A Franco-Manitoban who has accepted crumbs for eighty-nine years, and mutters when he doesn't get more, will have far less respect than one who insists on a full meal." [28] Forest attributed the mixed feelings about him within his own community to a "new elite" of businessmen. They had replaced the clergy as the driving force in St. Boniface and elsewhere in the province but, like the church, put education ahead of language rights. [29] For its part, the supposedly francophile Schreyer government dug back to the offensive precedents of 1892 and 1909 to frame its reply to the Dureault ruling. Attorney General Howard Pawley refused either to appeal or to accept it. In mid-January 1977, his department issued the following press release that even got the title of the 1890 law wrong:

1. The Crown is prepared to proceed to hear the merits of this particular case. We do not intend to appeal the court's ruling on the preliminary objection at this time but do not accept the ruling of the court with respect to the constitutionality of the Official Languages (sic) Act.

2. The Crown specifically indicates that it does not accept the ruling of the Court vis-à-vis the Official Languages (sic) Act and is proceeding without prejudice to its position concerning this question.

3. The Crown wishes to indicate that in any case where the Act is brought into question it will not regard this ruling on a preliminary objection, which it now waives, as creating a binding precedent and reserves the right to argue the question in a case where it is material in issue. [30]

The government not only put itself in contempt of court, but was treading where no executive had walked since the days of the divine right of kings. Forest, a perennial optimist who seldom if ever responded to setbacks and attacks in anger, put the government's response down to an imminent provincial election. Determined to see goodwill wherever he could, he said he was sure that there were 500 reasonable anglophones in the province for every unreasonable one. [31]

But the government's dismissive stance revived all the old fears for *La Liberté*. In an editorial published February 17, 1977, the paper reflected its predecessor's alarmist denunciation of St. Boniface MP Joseph Dumas' planned court challenge of the language law sixty years earlier in 1916. Like Dumas, Forest was a maverick, acting on his own and without regard for the possible consequences of failure for the French community. Continued the editorial: "Mr. Forest adopts the attitude of a patriarch, the Chosen One ... in whom all knowledge about francophone Manitoba, its future and survival, has been conferred."

The Schreyer government's decision may have been illegal, unethical and unconstitutional. But it was smart politics for the time and the NDP was coming up to an election. To the latent but ever-simmering anti-French anti-bilingual prejudice that roiled just under the surface of Western Canada, particularly Manitoba, had been added Pierre Elliott Trudeau's Official Languages Act of 1970. By the mid-1970s, the language pot was once again ready to boil over. The prime minister was now widely detested in the parts of Canada that had voted for him in 1968, hearing he would "put Québec in its place", but not understanding that his plan to do so meant extension of and support for the French language in all federal institutions and from coast to coast to coast. That the prime minister had an equal determination to defend English rights in Québec counted little in the West.

The Progressive Conservative Official Opposition in Ottawa under Robert Stanfield had supported the 1970 legislation but seventeen of his MPs – all from Western Canada, including five from Manitoba – had voted against it. Still loyal to former prime minister John George Diefenbaker, whose trademark was "unhyphenated Canadianism", these MPs did their best to stir up anti-French, anti-bilingual feeling in their ridings. Not only did it play well with their constituents, they fervently believed it themselves. Every alleged excess by so-called federal "language zealots" determined to "shove French down our throats" received high-voltage coverage from open-line radio shows, local newspapers and MPs' mailings. All kinds of fears were fed, from the understandable concern about the increased difficulty unilingual westerners would face getting federal jobs to the hysterical conviction that the prime minister was engaged in a plot to turn Canada into a unilingual, French-speaking puppet of France.

The anti-French fever reached its peak in the 1974 federal election. All federal Tory candidates in Manitoba – including Duff Roblin's former attorney general, Sterling Lyon, who unsuccessfully challenged Defence Minister James Richardson in Winnipeg South – sought to ride the anti-French, anti-bilingualism tide. A favourite Tory theme was defeating "French power" in Ottawa.

RÉAL BÉRARD (CAYOUCHE) / LA LIBERTÉ / SEPTEMBER 14, 1990.

Manitoba's language zoology.

One of Lyon's campaign brochures simply listed the names of all the Québécois ministers and senior bureaucrats in the Trudeau government. Manitoba returned only two Liberals, Richardson and Joe Guay (St. Boniface).

Bilingual Today, French Tomorrow, a rabidly anti-French, anti-Trudeau tract written by war veteran J.V. (Jock) Andrews, alleged there was a conspiracy to make Canada entirely French. It was published shortly after the election and soared onto the bestseller lists, becoming – with 120,000 copies sold – the point of reference for every prejudiced English-speaker in the nation. It was quickly followed by another, titled *French Power: The Francization of*

Canada, written by Montréal high school teacher Sam Allison. This tract was more explicitly racist, claiming the English were inherently superior to the French in every way.

It was in this atmosphere that Schreyer, trailing in the polls, would have to call a provincial election in the fall of 1977. He told a group of reporters on tour with him that he held former prime minister John Diefenbaker largely responsible for the anti-French feeling across the West. The premier recalled his own family's stories of how The Chief sowed a bitter seed along the highways and byways of Prairie Canada, warning everyone of non-English, non-French heritage that the restoration of rights for French Canadians would push them down to third-class status. Implicit but unstated in Diefenbaker's thesis was his acceptance of a pyramid of rights in Canada with the British co-founding group at the apex.

The decision by the Schreyer government to ignore Judge Dureault's decision left Forest, just like Pellant and Bertrand, Dussault and Lavoie before him, "in a bind. He could not appeal his own case, having won it; yet the victory was meaningless." [32] A way had to be found to force the case to a higher court, making it impossible for the attorney general to continue his defiance of the rule of law. Forest's lawyer, Alain Hogue, hit upon a plan. Using the two Prud'homme judgements of 1892 and 1909 and the Dureault ruling, he wrote the Queen's Printer, with a copy to the minister responsible, Consumer Affairs Minister René Toupin, requesting the French versions of four laws. Toupin agreed on condition that Forest personally pay for the entire cost of translation, which the minister pegged at $50,000. Adding insult to injury, on February 23, 1977, Pawley said that "nothing in the Dureault judgement prevents the pursuit of the case in English only and that includes the use of English statutes". [33] Eventually the province reduced its translation bill to $17,000.

Then began an almost comic-opera chain of events which saw Forest and his case volleyed back and forth between Manitoba's two highest courts like the ball in a tennis match. On March 17, 1977, Hogue filed documents in French with the clerk of the Court of Queen's Bench. The clerk initially accepted them but after discussion with the court's chief justice, A.S. Dewar, refused them. The documents requested the court to order the attorney general of Manitoba and the minister of consumer affairs to translate the laws relevant to his case.

That left Hogue and Forest with only one remaining avenue – the province's highest court, the Court of Appeal. That court's clerk, also after consultation with the chief justice, Samuel Freedman, refused Hogue's documents.

On April 5ᵗʰ, Forest's lawyers filed a request for a writ of mandamus to force the government to give Forest satisfaction and to apply the Dureault judgement. They also informed the court that a constitutional matter would be placed before it. (34)

On May 13, 1977, with a provincial general election looming ever closer and the hot breath of anti-French bigotry scorching his back, the premier announced he had no intention of abrogating the English-only law of 1890, "a gesture which again had more than a whiff of the authoritarian intolerance demonstrated by earlier Manitoba governments". (35)

On June 22, 1977, the Court of Appeal handed down its decision on Forest's application. In a ruling of four to one, it directed that the case should first be heard – in English – by a lower court, the Court of Queen's Bench where Forest had begun. Justice Alfred Monnin, the court's only francophone, dissented. The Court of Appeal can exercise original jurisdiction in exceptional circumstances and the fact "the accused had found all openings barred in his attempt to enforce his constitutional rights" made this an exceptional circumstance, he wrote. Justice Monnin then issued a scathing rebuke to the province for its "arrogant" attitude to the law.

> I am at a loss to understand how the custodian of the constitutional rights of this province, the attorney general, can indicate that he will not accept a ruling of a properly-constituted tribunal … and how he can state that he does not intend to appeal the ruling, and that in the future he does not regard the ruling as having created a binding precedent. A more arrogant abuse of authority I have yet to encounter. Moreover, it was highly discourteous to the trial judge … The issue is real and not academic. It should not be longer ignored. The Dureault decision warranted review. It may be sound, it may be unsound, but it should not be allowed to remain in limbo. A course of conduct such as that of the attorney general ought not to be allowed. If a private citizen attempted to ignore a court when unhappy with its decision he would be quickly brought to his senses. So must the attorney general. (36)

Writing for the majority, Chief Justice Freedman advanced an important new argument that would become a counter-intuitive but central element in the Court of Appeal's definitive judgement on the Forest case some months later. While confirming Judge Dureault's decision that Section 23 of the Manitoba Act, the section making French and English official languages of the province, was indeed part of the Canadian constitution because it had been adopted by the British Parliament, he used the weakness of the 1890 English-only law to save it. The second section of that statute says it "applies only so far as the Legislature has jurisdiction to enact". Freedman reasoned it would be inappropriate for a court to judge the law unconstitutional when the law itself admits it cannot go where the legislature has no authority. In this situation, Freedman continued, a court would more appropriately find that the 1890 law was either inoperative or not applicable to the matters covered by Section 23. Perversely, therefore, the strict limits surrounding the 1890 English-only statute were all that kept it constitutional.

Still, the chief justice acknowledged the significance of the case. "… the very importance of the issue here involved makes it desirable that it receive the attention and consideration of every available court in the ordinary functioning of the judicial process." [37]

At last, Forest was to have his day in court, even though he couldn't be heard in his own language in the proceedings. But Hogue and Forest now faced a new government and a new attorney general, one even less sympathetic to their cause. Ed Schreyer's New Democrats went down to crushing defeat in the October 11, 1977 provincial election to be replaced by the Progressive Conservatives under Sterling Rufus Lyon. Lyon, brought up in Portage la Prairie, had little sympathy for official bilingualism, constitutional charters of rights or any of the other ideas and works of Pierre Elliott Trudeau, whom he once described publicly as having a "mid-Atlantic Gallic mind".

Lyon's attorney general, Gerald Mercier, a unilingual English-speaker of French Canadian heritage, was in charge when the province filed its statement of defence against Forest in the Court of Queen's Bench on December 8, 1977. The province said it would be "inequitable and contrary to the public interest" to repeal Manitoba's Official Language Act of 1890. It charged further that Forest "has no real or substantial interest in the determination of the legal effect" of the English-only statute. It claimed that the legislature had been well within its powers to enact the language law eighty-seven years earlier and it demanded that the court dismiss Forest's case. [38]

Hogue told the media it appeared the government was now determined to drag its feet as much as possible, noting it had already asked for two extensions to file its defence. But on the bright side for the St. Boniface crusader, Ottawa's new court challenges program on behalf of official language minorities announced it was coming on board bringing with it pockets deep enough to go all the way to the Supreme Court of Canada if necessary. Manitoba's days of constitutional defiance were drawing to a close.

While he waited for the court proceedings to begin, Forest gave speeches and frequent interviews to the media. On February 20, 1978, he told Kelvin High School students that Manitoba may be the key to holding Canada together. If Manitoba had not overthrown official bilingualism in 1890, he continued, Manitoba, Saskatchewan and Alberta would all be bilingual provinces. "Canada would be an altogether different nation if that act had not been put into place." He also denounced the campaign by Winnipeg South Liberal MP James Richardson to make Canada English-speaking and only Québec bilingual. "It's so unworkable, like trying to put an elephant into a mousehole. We might as well say we don't want Québec and we might as well become an American state." (39)

The Forest case was heard in Court of Queen's Bench at the end of May 1978. The plaintiff, Forest, posed five questions to the court:

1. Is the 1890 Official Language Act *ultra vires* [beyond the jurisdiction of] the Legislature of Manitoba?

2. If it is not, is it inoperative by reason of the constitutional paramountcy of Section 23 of the Manitoba Act?

3. Is the 1890 act invalid by reason of its having been introduced, passed and assented to in the English language only?

4. Is Section 23 of the Manitoba Act the subsisting law in the province in whole or in part?

5. If the 1890 act is valid and operative does it prohibit the oral use of the French language in all or any of the courts of Manitoba?

John Scollin, the lawyer representing the federal government, said "language rights are personal rights for minorities … They cannot be altered by the usual democratic process of majority rule". Section 23 of the Manitoba Act "is not a transient provision but a firm and fixed part [of the act] that got the province under way." Forest's lawyer Hogue said the Manitoba Act could only be amended by the Imperial Parliament at Westminster.

But Kerr Twaddle, representing the province, argued that although the Manitoba Act originally allowed and sometimes required both French and English to be used in the legislature and the courts, there was never a "guarantee the law would remain forever". Language rights of the nineteenth century were not the same as minority rights of the twentieth century, he said. "It was contemplated [in 1870] the population would grow and the province would be settled. In consequence one would permit the people … to make their own decisions as to such basic questions as the language of the government." Twaddle was at pains to point out that by 1890 the province's population had risen to more than 100,000 and the francophone portion was only 7.3 per cent compared to the majority it held among just 13,000 residents when the province was formed in 1870. "The inevitable happened," Twaddle continued. The province passed the English-only act. The province's lawyer also noted that Ottawa could have used its power of disallowance to stop the province and the fact it did not demonstrated that the federal government recognized the temporary nature of Section 23.

The Manitoba Act, he said, dealt with "the organization of unorganized territory". The concern of the lawmakers of 1870 "was the way Manitoba would be organized, not its relation with the dominion". History made it clear that certain matters, including language rights, "would have to be left until the people of Manitoba themselves could make the decision." He quoted Prime Minister Sir John A. Macdonald saying in 1870 that "it will be quite within the power of the legislature" to deal with language rights.

In the end, Twaddle revived the argument of the Crown attorney who had infuriated Judge Dureault and urged the court to consider the consequences of finding the Official Language Act of 1890 unconstitutional. But Scollin, representing the federal government, recalled Judge Dureault's point, saying the "fundamental question" is the validity of Section 23 of the Manitoba Act. "It is not a question that can be avoided simply by worrying about the consequences." Court of Queen's Bench Chief Justice A.S. Dewar reserved decision on the case May 31, 1978. [40]

Two days later, Forest received this missive from an anonymous letter-writer: "Just a troublemaker … Never ran into a bigot as small as you, you runt. No way am I going to pay extra taxes for a silly looking old jackass. Hope you lose your business, too." [41]

For once, Forest got a speedy answer. But it was hardly what he wanted. Mr. Justice Dewar dismissed the action in a July 18, 1978 ruling on the grounds that the plaintiff already had a decision on the constitutionality of the 1890 law from the county court. The Queen's Bench chief justice stated that he had no "standing" to argue a constitutional matter based on a parking ticket.

The judge described the background and genesis of Forest's action as "notorious" and criticized Judge Dureault's ruling as "perhaps broader than was required for the purposes of the matter before him". [42] Dewar ducked all but one of the questions put to him. He refused to answer the first on the grounds the plaintiff already had his answer from the county court. "Questions 2, 3 and 5 do not [therefore] require answers and the answer to question 4 is an obvious affirmative." [43] Finally, the Queen's Bench chief justice sent Forest back to county court to continue his litigation against his parking ticket there.

> Having obtained a declaration in favour of his position (on the illegality of the English-only statute) why does the plaintiff abstain from prosecuting his appeal and sue in this court? A declaration made in this court in this action cannot affect the results in the county court ... The conclusion of the plaintiff's county court appeal and subsquent appeal proceedings, if any, will produce ample opportunity for the plaintiff if the question of the constitutionality of the statute requires further judicial consideration ..." [44]

It seemed the courts as well as the government were simply running Forest around in circles, using ever more inventive and specious arguments, rulings and evasions to mock him, frustrate him and tie him up in knots, hoping to wear him down and make him give up. But Forest was far from giving up. On August 22nd, Hogue filed an appeal of Dewar's ruling to the province's highest court. As grounds for appeal, Hogue said the chief justice had erred in not allowing Forest to raise the constitutional questions in his court, in not ruling on the constitutional issues and in not exercising his discretion to give Forest the right to pursue the case in French. Hogue's appeal notice further stated that Dewar's decision was contrary to law, the evidence and the weight of evidence. [45]

The Court of Appeal heard Forest's appeal in late February 1979. Once again, Forest's lawyers asked the five justices to find the Official Language Act of 1890 unconstitutional because it was beyond the powers of the provincial legislature. Scollin, again appearing as intervenor for the Attorney General of Canada, said the 1890 statute was "a complete and utter nullity" because French language rights are entrenched and beyond provincial jurisdiction.

But this time, Forest's legal team offered to settle for less than a declaration the English-only law was beyond Manitoba's powers. Co-counsel M.B. Nepon said that if the court was reluctant to strike down the law totally, thus forcing an immediate return to full bilingualism in the courts and the legislature, his client would be prepared to settle for a half-loaf: official French versions of the four provincial statutes at the same cost as the English versions and a ruling that he should have been allowed to submit French documents in his previous hearings in lower courts. Justice Joseph O'Sullivan told Nepon the court had no authority to order the province to print the statutes in French.

Provincial government lawyer Kerr Twaddle borrowed Dewar's Queen's Bench judgement. Since Forest had received a favourable ruling from county court two years ago he didn't have the right to argue his case in a higher court. But Twaddle was rebuked by Chief Justice Samuel Freedman and the court's sole francophone judge, Alfred M. Monnin. Saying the Dewar decision "clamours for review", Freedman noted Forest had been trying to have his case heard for nearly two-and-a-half years and then was suddenly met with the argument that he didn't have the status to argue the matter. The chief justice said he found the negative attitude of some officials towards Forest puzzling. For his part, Monnin called Twaddle's argument that Forest didn't have the right to be before the appeal court a "red herring". The constitutionality of the 1890 English-only law had been an unresolved issue in the province since it was passed, Monnin continued. "The Crown has been avoiding the issue ever since. You are trying to delay it further."

The Court of Appeal gave Forest a partial victory in its decision handed down April 25, 1979. It maintained the constitutionality of the 1890 law with regard to the legislature but struck it down as far as the province's courts were concerned. Franco-Manitobans had the right to use their language in any court proceeding, but the province's statutes needed to be printed in English only. In a written decision, the chief justice said – wrongly – that statutes were not always adopted in French even before 1890. However, he noted that the French -speaking residents of Manitoba had been induced to put an end to their "insurrection" during Manitoba's formative years "on the basis that their rights would be ensured for the future". The enactment of the Official Language Act deprived them of the linguistic rights which were safeguarded. Writing for the court, Chief Justice Freedman said:

> Georges Forest's Odyssey towards an authoritative judgement dealing with the validity or invalidity of the Official Language act 1890 ... is now approaching an intermediate goal. En route he has had to move with care between a present-day Scylla and Charybdis, these being sometimes of his own making, oftener erected in his course by others. His prolonged effort in an important cause lawfully merits the judgement of this court and I would not deny it to him." [46]

Freedman rebuked Dewar for ordering Forest to go back and argue his parking ticket in county court. For the Queen's Bench chief justice to suggest that "the heart of the dispute between Mr. Forest and the Crown is the traffic ticket is to ignore the realities of the situation," he wrote. "There has never been any mystery about the plaintiff's desire and attempt to have the language question litigated in a superior court." Freedman went so far as to say Dewar's ruling was "fundamentally unfair" in that Forest was effectively penalized for having won in county court. "Had he been the loser he could have found an avenue to access to the Court of Appeal. But the Attorney General of Manitoba, the loser in county court, neither accepts that decision nor appeals against it." [47] The province's chief justice then quoted from a noted authority, *Canadian Constitutional Law*, to argue the fundamental importance of language in Canada:

> All communication between people depends on language Accordingly, culture and education, business and government, private and public life generally in many aspects, may be vitally affected by mandatory provisions about language in statutes or constitutions. Such matters are delicate and sensitive simply because they are so basic and all-pervasive in everyday life ... Of course a person's native language is not the gift of a government or a law, rather it is primarily a matter of family, community and cultural inheritance. Customary usage is the main and the massive social force in matters of language. Nevertheless, legal intervention at certain critical points by mandatory language requirements

or guaranteed language options is a feature of Canadian constitutional and legal development. [48]

Freedman noted the "striking similarity" between Section 133 of the BNA Act and Section 23 of the Manitoba Act and said no one would contend that it was the product of coincidence. He marshalled rulings from Supreme Court chief justice Bora Laskin and Québec Superior Court judge Jules Deschenes to argue constitutional language rights are beyond the scope of provincial legislatures and the Canadian Parliament to amend or abolish. Laskin, in the case brought by Moncton Mayor Leonard Jones against the federal Official Languages Act, said the Parliament of Canada is empowered to extend minority language rights but it cannot just limit them. Deschenes, ruling against Québec's French Language Charter, stated:

> It was the intention of the Fathers of Confederation to remove the question of the use of the two languages, English and French, from the possibility of the arbitrary or capricious or even very simply of the wish perceived legitimate by the majority, whether English in the central parliament or francophone in the legislature of Québec. They intended that this provision remains intangible and secure from all legislative intervention by one or other of the elected assemblies. [49]

Freedman said that to argue Manitoba could diminish rights conferred by Section 23 of the Manitoba Act would be to negate the very reason for the section's enactment in the first place.

> The French-speaking citizens of Manitoba, including not only the famous Louis Riel but all the representatives of the French–speaking parishes (who, it must be mentioned, reached a remarkable unanimity with their English-speaking representatives) were induced to put an end to the Red River Insurrection and to support the creation of a province and its union with Canada only on the basis that their rights would be ensured for the future. The enactment of the Official Language Act deprived them of the linguistic rights which were safeguarded, or thought to be safeguarded, under Section 23. [50]

Despite his ringing endorsement of Forest's position, however,

Freedman stopped well short of giving him the complete victory much of his ruling seemed to portend. He did not agree that Section 23 required all statutes to be passed in French to be valid, even though the Deschenes ruling had adopted that view regarding the use of English in the passage of legislation in Québec. One reason may have been the statute creating the chief justice's own court would thus be in jeopardy.

> I would not be prepared to declare that all the statutes of Manitoba since 1890 are constitutionally invalid. Indeed, an agreed statement of facts suggests that, so far as can be ascertained, statutes were not adopted in French in Manitoba even before 1890. Since this court was established by a statute enacted wholly in English after 1890, it could hardly be that we could make any declaration at all if the statute providing for our existence were not valid ... [51]

While it may be the province is required to print and publish in both languages, he continued, its failure to do so should not nullify the laws.

> In our earlier encounter with this matter I indicated our awareness of the practical problems that would arise from a judgement holding the [1890] Official Language Act to be inoperative ... I do not think I go beyond my judicial function to suggest to all concerned that constitutions can be made to work only if the spirit of them is observed as well as the black letters they contain, and if there is a disposition on the part of all concerned to make them work in a practical and reasonable way without, on the one hand, intransigent assertion of abstract rights and without, on the other hand, a cutting down and chipping away of those rights. [52]

The chief justice struck down the 1890 law as "inoperative as far as it abrogates the right to use the French language in the Courts of Manitoba ..." and ruled that it "may be necessary" for the province to "make regulations for the purpose of bringing about the implementation of the provisions of Section 23 in a reasonable and practical way." Forest was awarded costs.

The actions of the appeal court were being watched by one of Québec's most distinguished editorialists and opinion-leaders, Lise

Bissonnette, editor of *Le Devoir*. In an editorial appearing on April 30th, she wrote that the decision

> … confronted Canada squarely with the injustices of its history. We are overwhelmed by a feeling of absurdity because to give back to Franco-Manitobans, today, the right to speak French in the courts and the legislature, and to give a copy of the debates and laws in their language, will not bring back a dynamism that was, purposely, meant to be destroyed.

It was important that the intentions of the Fathers of Confederation regarding the language rights of minorities were confirmed, she continued. But what she found ironic and shocking was the "collusion" between the governments of Lévesque and Lyon, who "is the most openly intractable towards all those who speak French".

On May 6, 1979, a little over a week after the appeal court judgement, the Forest household received this letter: "You French are a bunch of troublemaking bastards. Go back to Quebec." It was followed by a warning that the Battle of the Plains of Abraham could be repeated if necessary to make it clear to French Canadians who had won and who had lost. The letter was signed by a Yugoslav naturalized Canadian. That same day, Forest spoke to a Grade Eleven history class at Dakota Collegiate in suburban south St. Vital, which neighbours St. Boniface. He read the letter out and told the students he received similar mail all the time along with frequent death threats. He had been advised to report all incidents to the RCMP.

Forest also said the same thing was happening to the anglophone minority in Québec and it was just as dastardly and regrettable as what had happened to the francophone minority in Manitoba. Many students raised their hands when he asked them if they were taking French. He compared being satisfied with just one language to being satisfied with black and white television when colour was available. "If I lose, it's the end of Canada," he told them. He asked for questions but there were none. "Okay, let's bring on the food," a student called out. Lunch, at least as far as this class was concerned, was more important.

As he started to leave, a student came up, introduced herself as Ukrainian and asked him why Québec felt alienated when "they have alienated themselves". Forest replied that the rest of Canada can do much to make French Canadians feel welcome in their country. "Why should we do that? It's their problem," she replied. Forest turned to an accompanying journalist to say sadly: "It's discouraging if that is all they know."[53]

Despite Forest's partial victory, La Société franco-manitobaine remained lukewarm. Its president, René Piché, said that while it recognized that "the principles involved in Georges Forest's struggle will affect all Franco-Manitobans,

> for the moment, however, and indeed for the last three years, we cannot actively contribute to an individual's court case. We have limited means and these must be concentrated on our prime objective – the conservation and development of French language education in this province. We cannot invite discomfort for many years even if the act of 1890 were declared unconstitutional. We must live as a minority which will always be a minority. [54]

La Liberté at last warmed to the lonely crusader. Shortly after the Court of Appeal verdict was in, this editorial appeared:

> One cannot imagine the majority of Franco-Manitobans continuing to ignore the possible consequences of the event. Think only a moment of the situation one or two generations hence if "L'Affaire Forest" received a favourable ruling in the Supreme Court of Canada. [55]

As mentioned earlier in July, the St. Boniface language rights crusader gave an interview to Charles Bolster of le Collège Universitaire de Saint-Boniface. It formed the basis of two lengthy biographical articles published in the Winnipeg Tribune. In the second of the two, on July 23rd, Forest expanded on his favourite theme of Manitoba as "the key to Canadian unity":

> Take St. Boniface and the rest of Winnipeg. Imagine the real sharing of the dual cultures if the francophones continued being part of the English community while having no fear of being eventually assimilated. They would not have this fear if the language rights granted by Confederation were reaffirmed. Then [as we see increasingly now at St. Boniface College and all school divisions] those anglophones who wished would learn French, later urging the same for their

children and so on. Those who, for whatever reasons, chose to carry on only in their native language would still have the pride of being distinctly Canadian, not just other North Americans who spoke English.

Forest's dream of a truly tolerant bilingual and binational nation in which all Canadians could move at will between the two official languages and cultures to the enrichment of all, was soon to be openly and vehemently opposed by one of the strangest and certainly among the most cynical alliances ever forged in Canada. It was quickly dubbed "the union of the two bigots" by a respected Franco-Manitoban. The anti-bilingual Manitoba Conservatives and the anti-bilingual Parti Québécois, their unilingual laws having both been struck down by their high courts, were readying appeals to the Supreme Court of Canada; appeals in which each would have intervenor status in the other's case to defend and advance their right to deprive their official language minorities of their constitutional language rights.

The Parti Québécois government of Premier René Lévesque, which had been preparing to hold a referendum on sovereignty-association with Canada since its election in November 1976, passed Bill 101, Québec's Charte de la langue française on August 26, 1977. Chapter III of Title 1 of the charter provided that French alone would be the official language of the legislature and the courts. However, it was a good deal more generous to the English minority than Manitoba's Official Language Act had been to Franco-Manitobans. Under the Québec law, English Quebeckers would still be able to communicate with their government in English, receive services in English and have all statutes and regulations provided in English.

The section of the charter entitled "The Language of the Legislature and of the Courts" reads as follows:

7. French is the language of the legislature and the courts in Québec.

8. Legislative bills shall be drafted in the official language. They shall also be tabled in the Assemblée Nationale, passed and assented to in that language.

9. Only the French text of the statutes and regulations is official.

10. An English version of every legislative bill, statute and

regulation shall be printed and published by the civil administration.

11. Artificial persons addressing themselves to the courts and to bodies discharging judicial or quasi-judicial functions shall do so in the official language, and shall use the official language in pleading before them unless all the parties to the action agree to their pleading in English.

The governments of Manitoba and Québec decided to jointly appeal the defeats dealt them by their top courts and to work together to crush minority rights. Québec planned to argue that Section 92 of the British North America Act gave the provinces the right to amend their constitutions unilaterally, including the issues of language rights. [56] However, Ottawa was to argue that Section 133 – and by extension, its exact copy, Section 23 in the Manitoba Act – were inviolable, the basis of the 1867 Confederation pact. [57]

Québec's and Manitoba's respective language minorities found themselves in league too. The next step, the final chapter in Georges Forest's "odyssey", would be taken in concert with a group of English language activists from Montréal and would play out before the Supreme Court of Canada in the summer and fall of 1979.

Peter Blaikie, Roland Durand and Yoine Goldstein had challenged Québec's French Language Charter, Bill 101, for the same reasons Forest had long challenged Manitoba's 1890 law – that both were *ultra vires* (beyond) the power of the province. Blaikie's victory had been complete at Québec Superior Court; Forest's had been more equivocal. Canada and New Brunswick had intervenor status in the two cases. A Montréal lawyer with the distinguished name of Henri Wilfrid Laurier was also an intervenor in the Québec hearing.

The Québec case went first. The arguments covered a day and a half in June and drew a capacity crowd to the august Ottawa courtroom. Lawyers for Manitoba and Québec sought unsuccessfully to bar as evidence extracts from the parliamentary debates and conferences leading up to Confederation. The minority language litigants and New Brunswick argued that statements by both Sir John A. Macdonald and Sir George-Étienne Cartier in 1865 clearly intended to guarantee the use of English and French in Parliament and the Québec Legislature and put language rights beyond the reach of the ordinary legislative process. That intention would be translated into Section 133 of the BNA Act and become one of the fundamental principles upon which Confederation was established.

Chief Justice Bora Laskin found for New Brunswick, noting the court itself often used the Confederation debates to "draw inspiration from the course of events leading from 1840 to 1867". He took exception to Manitoba's argument that nothing in the BNA Act is a fundamental law. Manitoba's contention that no one outside Québec was affected by the language used in its institutions also was challenged. Robert Litvack, lawyer for the Blaikie group, said the demography of the entire country was affected by the restriction of language rights within one province. Forest's lawyer, Hogue, said Section 133 of the BNA Act "confers very important and vital civil rights and ... its provisions cannot be diminished except by an act of the British Parliament." Laurier's lawyers argued that the object of Section 133 was plainly to protect the francophone minority in Canada from abuse by the federal government and the anglophone minority in Québec from abuse by the Québec government. The purpose would obviously be frustrated if the two majorities in question were free to amend the article. [58] The bulk of the arguments in both the Québec and Manitoba cases revolved around how far the provinces could go to amend and shape their own constitutions.

Meanwhile, the SFM was finally coming to the realization that Forest's crusade was everyone's crusade. In October, knowing the court decision was looming and would have enormous repercussions, it struck an ad hoc committee under the chairmanship of Armand Bédard to examine what the court might do. It settled on the two most likely outcomes. The committee agreed the decision would be politically charged and as a result, expected that, to avoid a confrontation with Québec over Bill 101, the court would not push Manitoba too hard:

> It is very doubtful that the Supreme Court will attack Bill
> 101 directly for fear of provoking a reaction in Québec ...
> Lyon will be able to use this to his advantage by saying that
> he will respect the court decision by putting in place the
> mechanisms necessary to implement the judgement. After
> all, that doesn't amount to that much: (1) a bilingual legis-
> lature; (2) translation of the legislative journals (3) bilingual

courts (already established under federal law). [59]

There was one aspect of the outcome that was alarming for the SFM because it concerned the attitude of English Manitobans: "Wrapped as they have been in the Union Jack since 1890, English Manitobans are likely to take very badly the news that their province henceforth must be officially bilingual." The SFM wisely decided to demand the Lyon government immediately pass legislation:

> ... finally blotting out the 1890 law and also making the Manitoba Act of 1870 and particularly, Section 23, the basis upon which the SFM and the provincial government would be able finally to negotiate to ameliorate and guarantee the legal status of the Franco-Manitoban minority.

> Unless the judgement is mandatory, which isn't likely, it will be a Pyrrhic victory; a defeat. The Manitoba government will not be under any obligation to act any more than it was after the Durrealt decision ... In any case, we will have to start all over again at square one. [60]

The Supreme Court delivered its verdict on December 13, 1979,

Manitoba's 1890 law is also unconstitutional.

simultaneously striking down both Manitoba's Official Language Act and the sections of Bill 101 making French the only language of the legislature and courts. The court declared the two laws in contravention of Section 23 of the Manitoba Act and Section 133 of the BNA Act and thus beyond the powers of the legislatures of Manitoba and Québec.

While Section 92 of the BNA Act allowed provinces to amend their constitutions in certain areas, it did not permit them to change or abridge constitutionally-entrenched minority language rights, the court said. In Manitoba's instance, the verdict was summed up in this short and succinct sentence: "The Manitoba Legislature has no more power to amend Section 23 of the Manitoba Act, 1870, than Québec had to amend Section 133 of the BNA Act 1867." [61]

When Georges Forest heard the news, he was lecturing on the Manitoba constitution to a Grade Eleven class at the Français high school then located in le Collége Universitaire de St. Boniface. (Louis Riel Collegiate was subsequently made the Français high school and renamed Collége Louis Riel.) The students gave him a standing ovation.

Later that evening a *Winnipeg Free Press* reporter found him at home. He was sitting in his living room at 44 Champlain Street, where he had just uncorked a bottle of champagne.

7

Prelude to Cataclysm

WHILE GEORGES FOREST WAS UNCORKING CHAMPAGNE in St. Boniface, Premier René Lévesque was ordering Québec's Assemblée Nationale to sit all night if necessary to rescue its two years of illegal unilingual French laws. And Manitoba, with eighty-nine years of illegal unilingual English laws – virtually the entire legal structure of the province – was doing and saying as little as possible publicly while plotting privately how to perpetuate its longstanding political strategy of constitutional denial and defiance.

Some comments by leading political figures are instructive. Reflecting back five years later, former premier Duff Roblin had this to say:

> From 1890 up until 1978, everyone believed that the constitutional position was OK ... Everyone! No one had apparently tested that. It never occurred to me. It just came out of the blue as far as I was concerned ... It seems to me when looking at it now, it should be clarified because if you don't, you always get the thing ticking around ... For many, many years, we got along without anyone complaining about it, and I think that a lot of people probably thought that Georges Forest was being a bit fussy in complaining about it, but it appears it led to a very important constitutional decision. [1]

Former premier Howard Pawley, the then-attorney general, had written this to an unknown correpondent two years' prior to Forest's first victory in St. Boniface County Court:

> Thank you for your letter of May 29, 1974, advising me of your intention to request a declaratory judgement from the Court of Queen's Bench with regard to the official language of Manitoba. I want you to know that in the province of Manitoba we have more populous groups of people that speak Ukrainian or German than those who speak French. Therefore, you will note that from an administrative point of view, it would create a very difficult situation for Manitoba to provide statutes in the French language without providing for statutes in other languages. I regret that I cannot be more accommodating to you. [2]

Even after the nation's highest court had rendered its judgement, Pawley, now the leader of the Official Opposition, still did not grasp the issue. He had opposed official bilingualism as attorney general, he told the *Winnipeg Free Press*, and he only reluctantly accepted the decision. "We fought this case because there was no blatantly obvious need when we had so many other alternative needy programs. Now I have to accept that there have been considerable changes in Canada in regards to the unity issue." [3] But the most foreboding comments came from Premier Sterling Lyon the day after the decision. Manitoba accepted it, he said, but would only do the "practical" things required to implement it. He subsequently was more specific. Language rights were better left as a matter of "common courtesy", not "legislative action":

> There is absolutely no question that the government accepts the judgement of the Supreme Court and we will now assess the ramifications on the procedural changes resulting from it. We intend to do the practical things to give effect to the spirit of the judgement without doing things that are impractical in pursuit of abstract rights. [4]

Lyon never defined what he meant by the phrase, "abstract rights", a phrase he had plucked from Manitoba Chief Justice Samuel Freedman's balanced and nuanced Court of Appeal decision, which had also warned against "a cutting down and chipping away of those rights". It was a phrase the premier would employ over and over again both with regard to Manitoba's official language obligations and also to Ottawa's desire for a constitutionally-entrenched charter of rights. The premier, a firm believer in parliamentary supremacy and ardent foe of what he called "judge-made law", knew his audience well. It sent just the right message to a cranky public already aroused by politically-inspired scare stories of faceless federal bureaucrats with long skinny arms shoving French down the throats of hapless English Canadians.

Three Manitoba premiers, two with no basic understanding of, and the third with scarcely concealed hostility towards, the province's history and constitution added up to an all-too-familiar English Canadian arrogance, an arrogance that fuelled the fury Lévesque expressed to reporters the day the Supreme Court ruled on December 13, 1979:

> This judgement … seeks to redress a situation in Manitoba
> after eighty years (almost ninety, in fact), after assimilative
> forces have had lots of time to erode the francophone pop-
> ulation, but imposes on us the same type of correction
> urgently after only two years in a context where I see no
> threat anywhere for Québec's anglophone minority … [It is]
> an insulting and a cruel wrong to French Québec which
> was trying through Bill 101 to prevent the kind of massive
> assimilation that has taken place in Manitoba. [5]

Despite his anger, the Québec premier not only instantly obeyed the court by calling an immediate special session of the assembly, he said he never considered not obeying it. He also insisted it did not tempt him either to bring forward the date of his long-planned referendum on Québec sovereignty to be held in May or to call a snap provincial election.

Phillipe Bernard, president of the national council of the Parti Québécois, said the superficial balance and equality of the Supreme Court decision masked a fundamental inequality. The court had reinforced anglophone domination. "Yes, the Supreme Court made the same ruling about the Manitoba law as it did on Bill 101, but ninety years later, which allowed ample time for the francophone element of Manitoba to shrink from fifty per cent to four per cent of the population." [6] Political commentator Marc Laurendeau agreed. By placing Québec on the same footing as Manitoba, the court tried to leave the impression that its judgement was equitable but it fooled nobody. Québec had been brought before the court within two years, while Manitoba had been able to defy the law and the constitution for eighty - nine years, suppressing the French language and leaving the Franco-Manitoban minority on the verge of extinction. The wrong, Laurendeau wrote, was "irreparable".

Federal Conservative Justice Minister, Senator Jacques Flynn, said Ottawa would not intervene if Manitoba and Québec failed to act on the court decision. This brought a sharp rejoinder from Senator Jean Marchand, a former Liberal cabinet minister. Pointing to Manitoba, he asked if Ottawa was going to wait another ninety years before acting. Flynn replied that if he were Franco-Manitoban he wouldn't be impressed by shouting from the rooftops about a century of martyrdom. "I would simply demand my government conform to the judgement as rapidly and as well as possible." [7]

La Presse editorial writer Vincent Prince described the judgement as a "great victory for democracy … In both cases, the highest court in the land has stated that the provinces concerned never had the right, by virtue of the constitution, to impose unilingualism." Yet it was important not to exaggerate the scope of the decision in either instance, he warned. Despite Lévesque's attempt to cast it as an insult to the province, "in practice, the French fact has already triumphed almost 100 per cent in the courts and the assembly." As far as Manitoba was concerned, he said, Forest was overlooking a number of realities when he declared the decision to be the greatest triumph Manitoba's francophone community had ever known. The redress has occurred so late that it had more symbolic than real value. There are many other areas of life where respect for the French language would touch much larger sectors of the community and have more immediate consequences. Still, "for the moment, it is interesting to note that the Manitoba government appears to want to move swiftly on the court judgement in spite of the enormous difficulties the task brings."

Prince concluded: "Without looking to rush things, it should now be possible to count on its [Manitoba's] cooperation to always respect fully the cultural duality that history and the constitution imposes on our country." [8]

La Presse also gave prominent play to Forest's reaction under the headline: "Les Québécois doivent comprendre que le Manitoba leur appartient!" (The people of Québec must understand that Manitoba belongs to them!) He described his victory as better late than never and called on all provinces to join to build a truly bilingual nation. "I'm not surprised because my lawyer and I foresaw this to be the outcome," he said. He hoped the Lyon government would realize that Manitoba now is "the king-maker of national unity, that Manitoba now holds the key". A positive response by Manitoba to the court ruling would be important in the referendum debate in Québec, he continued. "The Québec people now can be sold effectively on their belonging to Canada and that Manitoba belongs to them." Equally important was the way the decision would finally open the doors to Franco-Manitobans. "Up to now the need to learn French in Manitoba was limited." Forest added. Franco-Manitobans who wanted to use their language in their work "may have had to exile themselves to Ontario or Ottawa to seek jobs in the federal civil service."

Forest was right. The desire to speak French and to ensure a francophone environment for their children had led to a Franco-Manitoban "brain drain" to Ottawa, Eastern Ontario and Québec, particularly in the 1970s. In the view of some, it weakened the community's leadership and may have been one explanation for Forest's lack of support.

The thoughts of Harry Daniels, president of the Native Council of Canada, the national Métis organization, went back to Manitoba's founder, Louis Riel. The man who had brought the province into Confederation would be "happy as hell" with the Supreme Court's ruling that the province acted beyond its power when it passed the 1890 law taking away French language rights, he said. "It's only fitting and proper that the courts should have ruled in favour of French language rights. Riel would have been ecstatic." The court had affirmed everything for which Riel and the Métis had fought, Daniels continued. "We were in the vanguard of a big movement then and Canadians didn't know it." [9]

The next day, Québec's Minister of State for Cultural Development, Camille Laurin, told l'Assemblée Nationale that the province would be happy to receive federal aid for translation just like Manitoba. But he noted that the federal government so far had not indicated it would treat Québec the same as Manitoba. Robert Gaulin, president of the province's teachers' federation, said the court had demonstrated the "anti-democratic and anti-Québec" character of the Canadian constitution. Not only did the constitution prevent the government from developing the culture and language of its majority, but worse and more seriously, it obliged the majority to turn itself into a minority just as if assimilation had already completed its work as it had in Manitoba. The judgement, Gaulin concluded, was a "supreme insult to the popular majority of Québec".[10]

Under the headline "Le ciel écroule" (the heavens fall) – *Le Devoir* editor Lise Bissonnette recalled Judge Armand Dureault's use of Lord Mansfield's famous dictum, "Let Justice Be Done if the Heavens Fall" to point out that the problems now facing the province were huge. She wondered if it would be necessary to translate every law passed since 1890 and how bilingual Manitoba's courts could actually be given the fact only four judges and twenty lawyers spoke French. But she went on to note that with goodwill and a desire to compromise, anything would be possible. "If the government of Manitoba wanted to show that it is truly eager to redress the wrongs of 1890, it would be in no one's interest to require it meet unrealistic objectives in impossible time frames." For the court decision regarding Manitoba's language rights to have any value, she continued, it should apply to all francophones outside Québec. The ruling, she said, clearly demonstrated the "anachronism" of the British North America Act on the issue of language rights. Here was the constitution protecting the rights of 50,000 Franco-Manitobans but not the rights of Acadians (more than a third of the population of New Brunswick) or the rights of the 500,000 Franco-Ontarians.

> Should we amend (the BNA Act) by extending that protection
> to provinces where there is an important official language
> minority, or even to all provinces? Or, on the contrary, like
> the recommendation by the Pépin-Robarts Commission on
> Canadian Unity recommended, would it be better to release
> the provinces from this obligation and leave them free to legis-
> late on linguistic matters, which, according to the Lévesque
> government, is the most rational way to fix the anachonism?
> … Their good old constitution, it's its real imbalances that
> now stand out, not its supposed wisdom of 1867. [11]

In Winnipeg, Manitoba's Attorney General Gerald Mercier was more forthright than the premier about the government's definition of "abstract rights". Displaying the same ignorance of the constitution and the law as his predecessor, Pawley, Mercier said it would be up to the legislature to decide how far to go in implementing the decision. While all persons would have the right to speak in either English or French in debate and all records and bills would be printed in both languages, more expensive measures such as simultaneous translation of debate would have to be approved by the legislature, where the Tories held a healthy majority. While Mercier believed Manitoba's English-only laws "appear to be valid", a final determination would have to await analysis of the judgement, a judgement he admitted had not been "unexpected". In other words, the government would do only what it was absolutely forced to do and take its time even about that.

Mercier had no interest in offers of advice and assistance from Forest. He launched what would become Manitoba's mantra: a demand that Ottawa help, not only with the estimated $15 million in translation costs, but also in the provision of translators. The province seemed to assume the whole matter was somehow the federal government's fault. In sharp contrast to Québec, no time limit was deemed necessary and no urgency was sounded. Mercier saw no need to advance the legislature's spring session, then two months away, let alone recall the house immediately. Any decisions about the functioning of the province's courts could wait until the government made up its mind, he said. "Even with the judgement, obviously the vast percentage of business in the legislature and courts will still be conducted in English, so that in implementing the decision we would want to be as practical as possible." [12]

The legislature's two Franco-Manitoban MLAs, perhaps fearing a backlash, were subdued. "I don't feel it [simultaneous translation] is really necessary in the house. I'm not really hung up on it," said Pete Adam (NDP, Ste. Rose). Larry Desjardins, the NDP MLA for St. Boniface, said he wouldn't rely on French in debate much either. "I don't want people to leave the House when I'm talking in French," he said. While the Supreme Court righted an historic wrong, Desjardins said it was too late to make Manitoba truly bilingual. "Some Manitobans will think French is being shoved down their throats," he warned prophetically. [13] But Desjardins said the decision was very important for national unity.

The other two bilingual MLAs had even lower expectations. Former NDP cabinet minister Sidney Green feared the Supreme Court ruling would fuel Québec separatism. "Canada cannot be bilingual and Manitoba cannot be bilingual unless there is a place in Canada where French is the official language," he said. Yet the judgement would have only negligible effects on Manitoba since so few Manitobans spoke only French. "We won't see people using French any more than they did before," Green continued. "You can lead a citizen to a language but you can't make him speak it." Abe Kovnats, the only bilingual Conservative MLA, said he wouldn't use the language any more than he had in the past.

Forest's lawyer, Alain Hogue, naturally believed the judgement was clear and sweeping in its implications. All provincial legislation passed since

1890 would have to be translated into French and given retroactive royal assent. All new legislation would have to be introduced, passed, printed and published in both French and English. Simultaneous translation and the printing of all legislative and government documents such as Hansard, Votes and Proceedings and the Manitoba Gazette in both French and English would be required. French litigants would be able to speak their language in Manitoba courts, have their lawyers and witnesses also speak French and have the court proceedings recorded for transcript purposes in that language. Those unable to understand French would have to obtain translators. The "$64,000 question", Hogue said, was whether the Supreme Court's decision invalidated Manitoba's body of unilingual laws. "Our position is that it ought not to make [them] void." But translation and re-passage including royal assent would be necessary to avoid "literally throwing the province into chaos". [15] This was the second time a constitutional lawyer uttered the word that would gain ever-greater importance as the next chapter of Manitoba's constitutional malfeasance unfolded.

In January, Mercier announced the province would spend about $500,000 over the following fourteen months to begin the task of translating 10,300 pages of statutes and an unknown number of pages of regulations and other documents. He also revealed the province intended to expand its new translation unit from the initial four to eleven positions. He estimated the mammoth job could take up to five years. Asked if the demand for bilingualism justified the expense, Mercier said that was a difficult question and once again made the government's reluctance apparent for all to see:

> Certainly there will be residents of this province who will say
> only five per cent of the population of Manitoba at the pres-
> ent time is French-speaking and therefore the requirement
> to spend $500,000 over the next fourteen months shouldn't
> be done. But it is part of the constitution of the country and
> it has been determined by the court that way and we have an
> obligation to live up to its requirement." [16]

Mercier also announced there would be no simultaneous translation or bilingual Hansard. "At the moment every MLA can speak English and work in English. I'm not using that as an excuse but I'm saying we're taking signifi-cant steps initially and can only work along and determine this as time goes by." He noted Québec didn't have simultaneous translation. Pawley gave the Official Opposition New Democrats' consent to the government's plan.

Forest smelled the wind. "I think the government is trying to sweep this whole issue under the rug again," he told reporters. "I don't find any satisfaction whatsoever in Mr. Mercier's remarks today." The language crusader said he intended to write to the Queen's Printer for a subscription to a French version of Hansard anyway "and we will see how much it will cost – I hope it's not $17,000". [17]

Two months later, on March 24, 1980, Mercier appeared before la Société franco-manitobaine to ask for patience. "I hope everyone will bear with us." When the attorney general spoke of the difficulty of finding French translators schooled in the common law, one member of the audience said the province had only itself to blame because it had illegally extinguished the legal status of the French language. Manitoba was reaping the whirlwind from its "ninety years of injustice". [18] When a lawyer complained about his continuing inability to have papers in French accepted in Manitoba courts, Mercier reminded him: "This is part of the overall problem. This can't be administered overnight."

Despite the January promise of eleven positions, he was obliged to tell the SFM that Manitoba had just three translators at work and was still expecting a fourth. He announced translation services would be offered in the courts "at no cost to litigants" and that there were three or four judges bilingual enough to conduct a trial in French. Then he made a surprising admission. Asked when Manitoba might get a bilingual attorney general, he said that had the 1890 law not been passed "you would have a bilingual attorney general". Despite his name, Mercier spoke no French. His family had been totally assimilated. The SFM obliged him by conducting his portion of its annual meeting in English. As soon as he left, the meeting reverted to French.

Without doubt, Manitoba faced a much more onerous and daunting task than Québec in implementing the Supreme Court's sweeping and unequivocal judgement. But in law, individuals are not allowed to use the degree or the duration of their felony to argue for more lenient treatment. It should therefore be unconscionable for a government – the foundation of law and order – to base its policy on extracting the maximum possible benefit from the excessive extent of its misconduct.

The nature of the judgement played into Manitoba's hands. The court was silent on how the province should remedy the situation because the court had not been asked to provide one. This silence aided the government in pursuing its familiar old ways of denial and evasion and invited a second, more pointed legal challenge to determine the remedy. It would not be long in coming. Still, the judicial void inspired wild hope in some quarters of the Franco-Manitoban community. Some dared to dream the impossible dream – full government services in French in addition to official bilingualism in the legislature and courts. Other sectors of the community advised prudence. Fiscal verities and public opinion needed to be recognized and respected.

The first to step into the volatile and potentially dangerous gap left by the court was McGill University constitutional law professor, Stephen Scott. It had so happened that the same day of the Supreme Court ruling, Joe Clark's seven-month-old Tory administration in Ottawa fell on a budget vote. That evening, Scott sent a telegram to former Manitoba premier, now governor general, Ed Schreyer:

> Respectfully recommend that before dissolving parliament you require government to secure joint resolutions of Senate and House of Commons in the following or like terms: resolved that the government be authorized to secure from the United Kingdom Parliament such legislation as may appear urgently required to render valid some or all of the laws or purported laws of the province of Manitoba, during such reasonable time as may be required to bring the province into compliance with Section 23 of the Manitoba Act and to deal with related matters. [19]

Scott perceived that with the defeat of the federal government the potential existed for all Manitoba's laws, indeed, its entire governmental structure, to be in peril. The province stood on the brink of legal chaos. This freighted idea would gain ever-increasing currency and importance as time went on. A few days later Scott was informed that the governor general and the government were familiar with the situation and asked Scott for his arguments.

Manitoba's two largest daily newspapers took decidedly different tacks in response to the judgement. *The Winnipeg Tribune* was first to speak, the day after the decision came down and its views were generous:

> Justice is a long time coming sometimes but it comes in the end; wrong can be dethroned … Québec remains a bilingual province and Manitoba goes back to being bilingual. The comparison of the two is an eye-opener for even after Québec

ruled that French was its only official language, it continued
to translate its laws into English … In effect, it remained
bilingual. Things were different in Manitoba and the
Supreme Court ruling will exact a heavy price …

Saying the provincial government had "already acted badly" by
fighting the case right up to the Supreme Court, the paper said it must correct the "rude message" it had sent its French-speaking citizens by embracing
the judgement and welcoming "the chance to correct an old, festering wrong
… Franco-Manitobans will be reasonable if the government is responsive. But
right and justice are on the side of French. There can be no argument there." [20]

On December 22, 1979, the *Winnipeg Free Press* gave its interpretation of the court decision. It took its cue from the Lyon government: caution
and delay, playing for time while doing as little as possible. The paper saw no
need for simultaneous translation in the legislature and no need for Hansard
in both languages. It thought it necessary for only some courts to be bilingual
and, as far as the civil service was concerned it allowed only that "someone
ought to be around in branches of departments which deal with the public to
cope (author's italics) with French-speaking citizens." Concluded Manitoba's
largest daily:

> All of this, of course, adds up to a good deal less than a bill
> of linguistic rights for Manitoba's French-speaking commu-
> nity. The real essentials for the survival of that community
> are not translations of government documents but govern-
> ment support on the economic, educational and cultural
> fronts. Action in those areas is not imposed by the Supreme
> Court. It should be imposed by the provincial government
> upon itself as a basic recognition of the rights and needs of its
> own citizens.

La Liberté added its voice on January 17, 1980: "Having decided
that the French language is an official language of the courts of Manitoba,
it remains that there is a large chasm between theory and practice."

One of the first straws in the wind that would eventually attain hur-
ricane force appeared in a letter to the editor in the *Tribune* on March 1, 1980.
Written by one George H. Hambley, it urged Manitobans to prepare "to fight
the battle for our long-cherished linguistic freedom and rights in Manitoba":

We nail our colours to the mast and believe in equal rights
for all, special privileges for none. For now, the very existence of those rights has been challenged and probably
destroyed by the recent action of the Supreme Court of
Canada … Now the Supreme Court … does the unbelievable thing of declaring a law made a century ago unconstitutional, therefore null and void. I doubt if any court anywhere in Canada or England has ever done this and got
away with it. Why not go a step further and declare that the
Battle of the Plains of Abraham or even the Bill of Rights
were unconstitutional?

On March 17th, the Lyon government introduced Bill 2, its formal
response to the Supreme Court judgement. It was a slap in the face to the
province's francophone community. While it repealed the 1890 statute making
English the only official language of Manitoba and re-established that "'official
language' means the "English language or the French language" in the legislature and the courts, it explicitly and repeatedly established English as the
pre-eminent language. Section Two of the two-and-a-half-page bill stated that
wherever a conflict arose between the French and English versions of statutes,
the "official language in which the bill for the act was [first] printed … prevails
over the corresponding provision in the other language". Since it would be
highly unlikely any government bill would first be printed in French, the
English version would almost always be paramount. In cases where bills were
printed in the two official languages simultaneously, "preference shall be given
to that meaning of the provision that, according to the true spirit, intent and
meaning of the act as a whole best insures the attainment of its objectives".
Again, the English version would be the one more familiar to most lawmakers
and so would retain ascendancy. The bill was also unequivocal that English and
English alone would remain the authoritative language as far as the province's
entire body of existing statutes were concerned even after the translation
process was completed. Section Three (ii) stated:

> For greater certainty in the interpretation of the statutes of the
> province heretofore enacted, the bills for all the acts hereto-
> fore enacted shall be conclusively deemed to have been
> printed in the English language when copies thereof were first
> distributed to members of the assembly in the assembly.

To justify its action, the government was at pains at every opportunity to remind Franco-Manitobans that all MLAs understood English perfectly and their language group now accounted for just five per cent of the province's population. The bill fell well short of the bare minimum required. A legal case could easily have been made that it was as much in violation of Section 23 as the 1890 English-only statute. Neither Section 23 nor Section 133 of the British North America Act even hint that Canada's two official languages can be placed in a hierarchical order. NDP front-bencher Saul Cherniack was subsequently to put the matter into a national context by looking at Canada's other three bilingual jurisdictions. According to his research, the federal government and New Brunswick specify that both official language versions of all bills, laws, records and reports are considered equally valid. However, Québec, in the mirror image of Manitoba, accorded preeminence to the French language in its emergency 1979 legislation

DALE CUMMINGS / WINNIPEG FREE PRESS

Premier Lyon's view of bilingualism.

flowing from the Supreme Court judgement.

It is important to note that Manitoba's begrudging reaction to its newly-restored bilingual status was occurring in the midst of the most serious threat to Canada's survival since Confederation – the first attempt by a Québec government to separate from Canada. One of the Parti Québécois major election promises in 1976 had been to hold a referendum on what it called "sovereignty-association" – full political sovereignty coupled with an ongoing economic association with the rest of Canada. The referendum was set for May 20,1980 and the question simply asked for a mandate to negotiate sovereignty -association with Ottawa and presumably, the other provinces. It was to be defeated handily – fully sixty per cent, including a majority of francophones, voted No – but polls right up until the last week and a series of climactic and powerful speeches by Prime Minister Pierre Elliott Trudeau showed a tight race.

Manitoba's legislators, with one major exception, appeared either unaware or indifferent about the impact of their words and deeds on the battle to save the country. Introducing debate on the language bill's second reading April 7, 1980, Lyon tried to be statesmanlike, but in the end betrayed his deep-seated opposition to what he saw as constitutional dictat and judge-made law. He pointed out that the French community in Manitoba had quickly diminished from a majority to a tiny minority between 1870 and 1890 because "most of the French-speaking Québec immigration preferred to settle no further than the New England states to the south of that province". Only four of the thirty-five MLAs elected in 1888 had been born in Manitoba, he noted. He also tried to undermine Manitoba's official bilingualism by falsely claiming that it had often been breached even before 1890.

> The legislature elected in 1888 apparently found it cumber-
> some to continue to work the bilingual administration which
> had been in effect since 1870 even though its observance
> was certainly far from complete. The consequence was that
> the 1890 act was brought before the house and adopted ...
> During the intervening years, after 1890, there were certain
> informal or unofficial accommodations made under which the
> French language continued to be used, more through a spirit
> of fair play and compromise which motivated, as I suggest,
> Mr. Speaker, and continues to motivate most Manitobans,
> rather than by legal decree ...

The premier once again approvingly quoted Freedman's admonition against "intransigent assertion of abstract rights" this time including the chief justice's similar warning about "a cutting down and chipping away of those rights". Then he continued:

> Those wise words clearly relate to what I have already said about the spirit of fair play and reasonableness which has generally motivated the people and the governments of Manitoba over the years, and which should certainly guide us today in giving effect to the Supreme Court judgement ... Because a period of ninety years has elapsed since the adoption of the 1890 act, there are a number of questions which must be resolved in that spirit of reason and fairness in order that we may give full effect to the Supreme Court decision ... I recognize, Mr. Speaker, that not all Manitobans will support wholeheartedly the actions which the government is now bound to take. Those actions, however, I suggest are absolutely necessary in the national interest and in fairness and equity to our fellow Manitobans whose mother tongue is French. [21]

The opposition leader echoed the premier's cheese-paring tone. It was an unpalatable obligation to be fulfilled reluctantly because of necessity. Pawley noted that the legislation "must be introduced because there is no option". The Supreme Court ruling meant "that the statutes and regulations at least to some extent, must be translated into French ..." The bill's "decree" was "fine insofar as it goes but certainly it is limited insofar as its effectiveness [in] developing the ... Manitoba that we wish ... to see grow. There is the need for ... a fuller, richer Manitoba [embracing] all the varied sectors of the population ... contributing towards [Manitoba's] overall mosaic.

The legislature, Pawley continued, should keep in mind the need to "grow to a better understanding, a better means, better facilities ... to deal with peoples in Manitoba in both French and English and as far as that is concerned, Mr. Speaker, in other languages where same is practical and feasible". [22]

St. Boniface's longstanding MLA, opposition frontbencher and past and future cabinet minister, Laurent Desjardins, spoke next and began in his mother tongue. He chastised the government. "I must express my disappointment and dissatisfaction towards the Manitoba government following the

Supreme Court ruling." He had spoken French in the debate on the Speech from the Throne on February 26th, and had been waiting ever since for a translation of his remarks to appear in Hansard. "It seems that I have the right to speak French but I do not have the right to be understood. You will admit, Mr. Speaker, that this isn't progress." Under such circumstances, the right to speak French in the legislature is a gesture of such futility that it is insulting, he continued. How, he asked, could he exercise his rights as a member to participate meaningfully in debate on issues and bills in his own language if other members couldn't understand what he was saying and wouldn't find out until the matter had long since been concluded? Switching to English, Desjardins said the province had actually taken a step backwards from the days when using French in the chamber was a privilege. At least then, Hansard eventually did provide a translation.

The veteran MLA also took the government to task for giving English paramountcy in the bill before the house, reminding members that Franco-Manitobans had for far too long been pushed into what amounted to a ghetto. Noting that the Québec referendum date of May 20th was drawing ever closer, Desjardins referred to "this important time for our country" and continued:

> I feel that this government has the unique opportunity to demonstrate true leadership to the rest of Canada, not just take something to the letter of the law, and to make amends for an injustice perpetrated for over ninety years … It seems to me that the government instead chose to buckle under the pressure from the rednecks … I think, Mr. Speaker, that the true test of greatness for politicians is to lead and to think of the future, not … fly kites and think of political expediency…

> Diversity is what made us what we are today. There is nothing wrong with diversity. You can be united in diversity. This is what democracy is all about …

> I don't want this country to separate. I don't want to become an American. I am very pleased and happy to be a Canadian, a western Canadian and a Franco-Manitoban, but that doesn't mean that I'm going to give up fighting for the rights that I think I have and I think I should have and that should be respected …[23]

Sidney Green, another NDP frontbencher and former cabinet minister, said Canada's duality depended, not on laws and constitutions, but on its citizens' recognition of duality's advantages. As someone of neither French nor English extraction who had taught himself French, Green said all the other ethnic groups in Canada owe their ability to maintain their identities to the fact the country was founded, not on a single nationalism like the United States, but instead on the principles of diversity and tolerance arising from its bi-national character. Tory Government Services Minister Harry Enns took Green's argument a step further. In one of the few public criticisms ever levelled by a Manitoba Tory at former prime minister John Diefenbaker's thesis that French Canadian rights stole rights from all Canadians of non-English and non-French background, Enns stated:

> I think those of us who have some role of leadership in representing these different ethnic groups have perhaps been derelict in not expressing that very clear understanding that I have that there is a substantive difference between the rights as accorded the French and English founding groups within our country in the language sector as compared to the rights of language with other ethnic minorities ... The honourable member for Inkster is again dead-right when he says that by preserving the very unique feature of this country I have a better opportunity and my association of German-speaking people have a better opportunity ... [24]

However, the senior Conservative minister finally defined exactly what the government meant in its frequent references to the one phrase in Freedman's judgement. Forest's constitutional crusade stemming from a parking ticket was "taking the law to the abstract extreme". Enns vigorously defended both the speed and scope of the province's response to the court ruling, a ruling he clearly regarded as socially disruptive and counter productive. "Mr. Speaker, proponents wishing to legislate by law ... what we as a society ... are not prepared to evolve into and do over a period of time do the present status of Canada, linguistically speaking, no justice." [25]

NDP frontbencher Russ Doern was now half way through his personal and political journey from being an unabashed francophile in the 1960s to a trenchant opponent of bilingualism in 1983-84. He echoed the Diefenbaker position that French Canadian language rights were a zero-sum game and used data from the 1971 Census to argue that the court judgement flew in the face of current western and Manitoban reality. While francophones accounted for only four to six per cent of Manitobans, forty-one per cent claimed British heritage, twelve per cent, German and eleven per cent Ukrainian. "I simply say that when you are talking about cultural rights ... linguistic rights, when you start to move in that area, then there are many groups ... who may feel correctly that they have particular rights in certain areas, whether they are embedded in the constitution or not." While he supported the bill, he said, language rights are only one small part of a whole.

> It's not good enough to say that the laws will be translated into one or more languages. What must ultimately be sought is equality of opportunity. It's not a linguistic question, it's even more than a cultural question, it's a social and an economic question ... It means that we must attempt to do away with hyphenated Canadians. When people feel they are under attack; when people feel that they are not welcome; when people feel hostility, they resort to their hyphenated heritage. When the environment and the milieu is warm and friendly, then the hyphens disappear and the Canadians come out in full force. [26]

A.R. (Pete) Adam, the NDP backbencher from Ste. Rose and the legislature's only other Franco-Manitoban, levelled the strongest attack of all on the bill, although he said he had no choice but to support it . He slammed the government for its constant loud complaints about the translation costs and criticized the proposed legislation for being "very insignificant" and therefore completely unsatisfactory to Franco-Manitobans.

> We have to go much further, much further, than that ... The minister has missed his opportunity to do something, to demonstrate his goodwill, but the minute that he introduced this bill ... he started talking about $500,000 ... and that really hurt the French people, Mr. Speaker, It's the reluctance on the part of the government to have to spend $500,000 to try and help the French people. Mr. Speaker, the French people have been robbed for ninety years; they've been robbed of a right that was theirs. They have been robbed of their culture

and the damage is irreparable. We'll never be able to undo the damage that's been done over the last ninety years. That's the sad part of it and the government is dragging its feet …
That's where the attorney general made a serious mistake when he started talking about money because we'll never be able to repay the French people what has been stolen from them. [27]

The legislation passed second reading but at the third reading stage in early July, Desjardins moved the six-month hoist, the legislative killing blow. During debate, he insisted he didn't seek to defeat the bill, merely to give the government more time to demonstrate its sincerity in obeying the court decision by setting a public timetable for the task of statute translation and the provision of basic government services in the French language. The lone Liberal in the legislature, June Westbury, echoed the St. Boniface MLA. She wanted the government at least to commit to give translation priority to the most important laws such as the City of Winnipeg Act, the Summary Convictions Act and the Highway Traffic Act. Pete Adam again chastised the government for not consulting with Franco-Manitobans before determining its course of action. Calling Desjardins' amendment "perverse" and "non-under-standable", the premier personally attacked the Franco-Manitoban MLA:

It makes it difficult to deal in a rational way with matters of this sort when you sometimes are being faced with flights of emotional fancy which really have no bearing upon the sub-ject matter at hand. We want to get under way with the implementation of the Supreme Court judgement …"[28]

The government used its majority to defeat the motion and pass the bill on July 8, 1980. Only Desjardins and Adam supported the hoist motion, which failed by a vote of thirty-seven to two. No recorded vote was taken on third reading. Bill Two received Royal Assent the next day.

Playing counterpoint to the entire debate had been La Société franco-manitobaine's controversial decision to support the Yes side in the Québec referendum. The SFM insisted its position was tactical only and not an endorsement of separation. French minorities outside Québec have had to straddle two uncomfortable realities ever since the independence movement took hold. They need Québec to be strong enough within Confederation to force the federal government to support the official language minorities in the English-speaking provinces, but not so strong that it achieves actual separation, regarded as the death knell for the francophone cause within Confederation. The SFM feared a No vote would seriously weaken Québec and, by extension, its bargaining power for constitutional change and francophone rights. While its support for the Yes position was probably better stated as a "Yes But", it was a public relations disaster at home. It forced the francophone community on the defensive and split it deeply. Both Forest and Desjardins instantly denounced it. Further, it poisoned whatever goodwill Manitoba's tiny French-speaking community enjoyed from its fellow citizens.

Québec's resounding No vote on May 20, 1980 inspired the City of Winnipeg to make all traffic tickets bilingual once its current supply of unilingual English tickets was exhausted. The motion was introduced by Taché councillor Guy Savoie on May 22nd as a goodwill gesture to Québec. Communist councillor Joe Zuken called it a "modest and symbolic way" to recognize Manitoba's recently-restored bilingual status. And Councillor Harold Piercy supported Savoie, saying that "to deny this motion and send it back … would be to kick the people of St. Boniface, St. Pierre and the French communities and say we don't give a damn". However, Elmwood coucillor Alf Skowron voted against the motion, arguing "the city can show greater homage other than having another language on our parking tickets". [29]

Manitoba's premier was on a very different tack than City Hall, however. When he met reporters to comment on the No victory the night of May 20th, Lyon was asked about Manitoba's plans for federal constitutional reform and specifically, Manitoba's own constitutional obligations. Six months after the Supreme Court ruling, the premier finally made public his real feelings and intentions concerning Manitoba's constitutional obligations. They were not matters of law, but of manners.

> Services in French are a matter of simple courtesy and it
> is impossible to legislate courtesy. I think there has been
> far too much talk of individual rights and so on, and not
> enough talk about the fundamental responsibilities that we
> all have to the other and to the nation in particular, so I
> would prefer to use the term courtesy although some
> may choose to call it a right. [30]

At a news conference several days later, SFM president Gilberte Proteau

DALE CUMMINGS / WINNIPEG FREE PRESS

said Lyon's attitude was insulting and a clear sign the society would not get a fair hearing from the province. "We're not asking the government to provide French services for all areas of Manitoba tomorrow morning," she told a news conference. But language services are not a courtesy, "they are a matter of principle". The SFM wanted Manitoba's francophone community involved in the upcoming constitutional negotiations. And the society also had proposals for "concrete, reasonable and practical services in French such as French schools, community, social and recreational services and legal documents ...

"We do want to believe in the good intentions of our prime minister, but find it difficult to do the same for the premier of Manitoba," she continued, adding that Lyon's attitude was "disquieting". Proteau predicted – accurately – that the Manitoba premier and Alberta Premier Peter Lougheed would be major stumbling blocks to real constitutional reform. [31]

The combination of Manitoba's foot-dragging, both real and perceived, and the Supreme Court's silence on just what Manitoba's obligations were and how the province should proceed to fulfill them led inevitably to a small procession of Franco-Manitoban lawyers deciding to follow in Georges Forest's footsteps and force the province's hand the only way they could – by going to court.

The single most important case actually began before the December 13, 1979 Supreme Court ruling. On October 10, 1978, Rémi Smith, vice-president of the SFM and a lawyer, received a speeding ticket. He decided to use it to go to court to argue it was invalid because the authority for it stemmed from an illegal, English-only statute, the Highway Traffic Act. Smith's act was deliberate. Well before the Forest decision was handed down, a group of young Franco-Manitoban lawyers had gotten together and determined that even if Forest won, the issue of the province's body of unilingual laws and the necessity to translate them would probably have to be confronted directly. They drew up an informal action plan to do just that. Smith appeared in provincial court July 13, 1979 and in county court on February 5, 1980. County Court Judge Gerald Jewers ruled that Section 23 was directory, not mandatory. And he did so using the ingenious argument of unintended negative consequences for an innocent public:

> In my opinion Section 23 of the Manitoba Act imposes duties ... upon the elected members of the Manitoba Legislature and those persons serving it, to enact, print and publish laws in both English and French and should be considered directory if the duties are not met ... The Manitoba Highway Traffic Act and indeed all provincial laws were passed for the benefit of all citizens ... and are obviously essential to the proper regulation and welfare of society ... The public had nothing to do with the failure of the legislature and those serving it to comply with Section 23 of the Manitoba Act. If the striking-down of the Manitoba Highway Traffic Act [and the implication of a decision to do so being virtually all provincial laws passed since Confederation are invalid] would not create chaos, at the least it would lead to serious inconvenience to an innocent public. In my opinion, it cannot have been the intention of the Parliament of Canada that laws passed by the Province of Manitoba in pursuance of the powers conferred upon the provinces by the BNA Act and otherwise properly and validly enacted, should be set at nought by the failure of the legislature and other public servants to comply with Section 23 of the Manitoba Act. [32]

Smith decided not to pursue the issue for personal reasons but the torch was quickly picked up and carried by another member of the young lawyers' group. Like Forest before him, this young man was going to stick with it for the duration. He would go on to become the deputy attorney general of New Brunswick.

On May 29, 1980, Roger Bilodeau, a University of Moncton law student and son of a respected *bleu* Franco-Manitoban family, received a unilingual English-only speeding ticket as he was driving from Winnipeg to his parents' home in Ste. Agathe. On August 14th, he and his lawyer, prominent Winnipeg barrister and Progressive Conservative Party supporter, Vaughan Baird, acting *pro bono*, held a news conference to announce they were going to use the speeding ticket to challenge both the unilingual English Highway Traffic Act and the Summary Conviction Act and, by extension, the validity of Manitoba's entire body of English-only statutes and regulations.

Calling Bill Two a small step that neglected many other aspects and wondering how long it was going to take Manitoba to bring the French language into all areas of its jurisdiction, Bilodeau said:

> There's been no position taken, no public measure announced. I think they're still delaying some points. How do you compensate the French people for having their rights subrogated? I want the government to provide us with additional criteria. I want to know how this law will be applied and in what fashion … Our argument is, if Section 23 is law, and it is because of the Supreme Court ruling, all laws in Manitoba are invalid. [33]

Baird said the summons was invalid because it was not issued in both languages. He had informed the attorney general that he would be proceeding on a notice of constitutional question rather than simply contesting a speeding ticket to allow the government to prepare its case. "We are stating that the Supreme Court has declared the Manitoba Act valid. The government of Manitoba must obey it. If it doesn't it is acting *ultra vires* [beyond its jurisdiction]". [34]

SFM president Proteau welcomed Bilodeau's decision, saying it would force the province to clarify its position. "There seems to be a lack of political will. As far as we're concerned, the Progressive Conservative government doesn't want to get involved with a minority group." [35]

Desjardins agreed. "This government is stonewalling,'" he told the *Free Press*. "Obviously, it's going to give the very minimum it was ordered to give. It's done nothing else." But Manitoba's legislative counsel, Rae Tallin, said that in his opinion the government was under no legal obligation to translate regulations and specific documents and forms like speeding tickets and maintained Bilodeau was fighting over language rights.

In an editorial on August 19th, the *Free Press* took a swipe at both sides. It noted that when the Supreme Court judgement had come down in 1979, the Québec legislature sat all night to re-adopt its two years of French-only laws in English.

> No such matching effort has been made in Manitoba, with its immense backlog of English-only laws, to ensure that the statutes of this province stand on an equally solid linguistic footing ... The government has moved toward compliance with the Manitoba Act, but it has not yet done what the constitution says "shall" be done ... Constitutional language rights in Manitoba are still plagued by the twin evils of which Mr. Justice Freedman warned: intransigent assertion of abstract rights and a chipping away of those rights. The courts can determine what the law means, what is legal and what is not and what, if anything, the citizen can do about it when the government fails to do promptly what the law requires. But the courts alone cannot make the constitution work ... The chief justice sought to raise our eyes beyond "the black letters" of the constitution to find its spirit. The province has not yet heeded that advice.

Bilodeau's case was heard before Chief Provincial Court Judge Harold Gyles on August 19, 1980. Baird argued the two laws were invalid because they were published in English only and therefore, the summons was also invalid. "In not having acts passed in the French language, the French people's rights have been systematically violated by successive Manitoba governments from 1890 to 1980," he continued. But Crown counsel Wayne Myshkowsky asked Gyles to dismiss the motion. While conceding the Supreme Court ruling, Myshkowsky argued that not all provincial statutes were adopted in French prior to 1890 and noted that Chief Justice Freedman had stated in his Forest decision that non-compliance with Section 23 did not make laws invalid.

The chief provincial court judge pointed out to Baird that his argument would mean all Manitoba laws, including his court and his appointment to its bench would be invalid. "I don't know what any of us are doing here," Gyles said. Baird replied that those issues could be decided at a later date. He employed the same Lord Mansfield quotation used in the 1976 judgement on the Forest case delivered by St. Boniface County Court Judge Armand Dureault: "Let justice be done though the heavens fall." (36)

The heavens did indeed fall – on Bilodeau, Baird and the entire Franco-Manitoban community – when Gyles delivered his verdict August 29, 1980. Gyles ruled that the Manitoba Act did not enjoy the same constitutional status as the British North America Act. Because the BNA Act took precedence over the provincial constitution, only the federal government and the Province of Québec were constitutionally obligated to be bilingual. The British Parliament would have had to add Manitoba to Section 133 of the BNA Act to put it in the same category as Canada and Québec as a jurisdiction with two official languages. "Even if the requirement of Section 23 of the Manitoba Act dealing with the printing of the acts of the legislature in both the English and the French languages were valid, it is my view that it would be directory and not mandatory," the chief provincial court judge ruled. Myshkowsky was relieved because "to rule otherwise would have invalidated all provincial laws and the courts themselves". Saying he was "shocked" that Gyles would "disregard" Section 23, "the Gilbraltar of our constitution in Manitoba", Baird immediately announced his intention to appeal. (37)

On November 6, 1980, the province announced that only fourteen legislative bills or 500 pages had been translated by the end of September. At that rate, it would take at least another six years to translate the remaining almost 10,000 pages. Mercier blamed the difficulty in finding qualified translators. The government had advertised in five major Canadian cities and received only thirty-four applications of which just one was successful.

Later that month, the SFM appeared before the parliamentary committee studying Prime Minister Pierre Trudeau's constitutional patriation package to lambaste the provincial government's response to the Supreme Court judgement and to call for a constitutionally-entrenched charter of rights beyond the reach of popular majorities. The SFM's language was powerful and unequivocal:

In the last session of the legislature, of 115 bills submitted, only nine were submitted in both languages. The government of Manitoba has no known plans to provide a bilingual court system or to train necessary legal personnel. In short, Franco-Manitobans have been faced for the past ninety years with concentrated, deliberate legislative subversion of their constitutional rights … It is not enough that French minority rights be dependent on the will of the government of Canada and the English majority in Parliament. Franco-Manitobans are acutely aware that it is desirable to offer greater protection to minority rights through a charter-based judicial review system. The rights of minorities are not best protected by legislatures, since legislatures are primarily responsible to the majority. Therefore, the Société strongly supports entrenchment of minority rights … conditional upon a guarantee of access to the courts and inclusion of an enforcement mechanism to ensure constitutional behaviour by public authorities. [38]

As if to justify the SFM's fears, Manitoba joined Québec before the Supreme Court November 27, 1980 to argue for strict limits on how far a province had to go in translating laws and regulations into the other official language. Québec had gone to the high court to seek clarification on the scope of constitutional bilingualism. Manitoba was an intervenor on Québec's behalf as was Forest for the three English-speaking Montréalers who had joined him in the successful 1979 assault on Québec's and Manitoba's unilingual laws. While the latter favoured the widest possible bilingualism, Manitoba and Québec argued that translation should be confined to the courts and legislative proceedings only.

The two provinces were afraid that, without limits, the entire scope of government activity, including municipalities and school boards as well as all government bodies, Crown corporations and professional, social, economic and political associations, would be caught in the translation net. The costs would be huge and the task practically insurmountable. "The Manitoba government would grind to a halt," Kerr Twaddle, the province's lawyer, told reporters outside the court. "It would be an impossible and impossibly expensive task." Québec's lawyer, Henri Brun, told the court that municipalities and school boards of either language should be exempt. He gave the court a list of 118 organizations and types of organizations the province felt should also be excused, including Hydro Québec, the Québec Bar Association, the major universities, provincial boards and professional associations. Twaddle told the justices Manitoba supported Québec's position "completely". [39]

On February 23, 1981, the Manitoba Court of Appeal heard Roger Bilodeau's challenge to his $35 speeding ticket based on the claimed invalidity of the laws undergirding it. Bilodeau's lawyer, Baird, had a heavy hitter partially in his corner: John Scollin, representing the federal government. Scollin and Baird told the court that the language requirements of Section 23 of the Manitoba Act were mandatory and statutes passed in English only were null and void. In his presentation to the court, however, Scollin conceded an important point: that the English-only statutes enacted prior to the December 13th, 1979 Supreme Court ruling must "on the basis of necessity" be considered sound. But the federal lawyer chastised the province because only nine of the ninety-eight bills passed by the legislature in its 1980 session were translated into French despite the fact the Supreme Court ruling meant all bills had to be translated simultaneously with their passage. The province was well aware of the court's decision and it had no right to continue legislating in English only, Scollin continued. "If your constitution has certain basic requirements ... it doesn't permit you to make laws except in accordance with those requirements. It seems to me that if you can't make laws lawfully, you don't make them at all." [40]

Baird pointed out six months had elapsed between the court judgement and his client's unilingual ticket, yet the province still hadn't started translating the two statutes in question. "I suggest the rights of French-speaking people have too long been denied by the province of Manitoba," he said. Baird appreciated the difficulties the government was facing in finding translators but stated it was important the court remind the government that its bilingual obligation was mandatory. "They've had time but we'll give them more time knowing that you have the whip to crack," he told the judges.

The province's lawyer, Kerr Twaddle, said the court should confine itself to the validity of the two statutes before it and not stray into other legal areas. Citing the immense task and difficulties facing the province, Twaddle argued that as long as it "moves towards compliance as quickly as possible" it was meeting the requirements of the Manitoba Act and the 1979 Supreme Court decision. But the court's sole francophone judge, Alfred M. Monnin, noted that at the pace set by the 1980 legislative session, "it will take us half a century before we get full compliance with the Supreme Court ruling. Surely there comes a time when somebody will step in and say 'enough'", adding that Franco-Manitobans had been fighting to obtain recognition of their rights for almost a century. [41]

The next day, the province scrambled to defend itself and once again draw attention to the enormity and difficulty of its predicament because of the severe shortage of qualified translators. The attorney general warned that the provincial government and legislature would grind to a halt if all new legislation had to be in both languages. Enactment of all new laws in French as well as English is "impossible without severely reducing the government's legislative program," Mercier said. The province had managed to translate twenty-eight statutes totalling about 750 pages. "It's wrong to say we're not doing what we can to translate. We're doing all we can, with priority to acts used most by the public or involved with the courts." [42]

André Martin, director of translation services, said eleven of the twenty -seven full statutes passed by the legislature in 1980 had been translated, including the Public Schools Act and the Education Administration Act. But he acknowledged no attempt had been made to translate sixty other bills which amended existing laws. "There's no question of translating them. There's no sense translating the amendments when the basic act hasn't been translated." Another twelve statutes were private members' bills which had "less priority" for translation, he continued. In addition, Martin said all the province's financial statutes had been translated and about 600 pages of court statutes and forms have been contracted out to the translation centre at the University of Moncton in New Brunswick, one of only two universities in Canada offering common-law courses in French. "We probably will end the present fiscal year with about 1,000 pages done," he said. "With any kind of luck we can double that rate to about 2,000 a year. We're not too far off the mark." Martin estimated the "catch-up" translation of Manitoba's 10,300 pages of unilingual laws on the books as of December 13, 1979 would take between five and six years. In addition to the contract work given to the University of Moncton, Manitoba had seconded a senior federal translator to Winnipeg, sent work to three translators in Ottawa and hired a fifth locally. [43]

Martin's – and the province's – hopes for understanding and relief were dashed on April 6, 1981 when the Supreme Court handed down a unanimous 7-0 judgement on the scope of translation required in Québec and Manitoba. In what is called the "Blaikie II" decision, the court exempted municipalities and school boards, but ruled that virtually everything requiring cabinet or ministerial approval – in other words, all Crown corporations, boards, agencies and commissions operating within the provincial government's scope – had to be bilingual. Mercier characterized the ruling as "about as favourable as it could have been toward the argument put forward by the province", noting that municipalities and school boards were let off. He noted that Crown agency regulations are easier to translate than entire statutes but warned that "if this decision requires any additional work in both languages, we're in some difficulty because we've been unable to get sufficient translators as it is".

Twaddle, the province's lawyer, sought to put the best face on things and in the process, once again tried to downplay Manitoba's constitutional obligations. Noting the ruling dealt with Québec and that Manitoba was only an intervenor, Twaddle said "there has not been a direct decision vis-à-vis Manitoba. I'm not saying Manitoba would not be subject to a similar rule but I'd want to study the judgement first." The case had involved institutions operating under "delegated legislation" and, Twaddle continued, "the court said the test is whether the government is in fact participating in the making of the law or simply authorizing it ..." [44]

Reacting to the court's judgement in an editorial published April 8, 1981, the *Free Press* blistered the province for its interminable whining and foot-dragging under a headline proclaiming "Obey the law on French".

> The grudging effort the Manitoba government has made
> so far to provide the French language services required by
> the constitution is nowhere near adequate to the needs of
> the case. Rather than moaning about the difficulty of com-
> plying, Attorney-General Gerry Mercier and his colleagues
> should be finding ways to carry out their duties ...
> Willingness to comply with the law and the constitution is
> the least that can be expected of a provincial attorney-general.

The paper returned to the topic the very next day

> The French language in Manitoba is not going to go away.
> It is rooted in history, in the constitution and in contem-
> porary social reality. Government, business and public bodies
> should recognize the opportunities opened to them by the
> province's bilingual character and make the most of them ...

The editorial, entitled "French is here to stay", went on to say that the province requires a core of lawyers, judges, law professors and court officials able to handle all phases of judicial proceedings in French and interpret Manitoba's French statutes. In addition, the province's civil service needs to be able to respond in French where requests from the public for service in French most often arise. All the government's most frequently-used forms and documents should be available in French and the offices that receive them should be able to process them without the need for a translation bureau.

The newspaper's spirit of tolerance and openness was having little impact on the government. A week later, The *Winnipeg Sun*, the new tabloid that arose to fill the void created after the ninety-year-old *Tribune* folded in August 1980, reported that the provincial government's pamphlet on the constitutional patriation issue was available in English only. Entitled "Constitutional Issues for the People of Manitoba", it was destined for distribution to every Manitoba household at a cost of $38,000. Columnist John Drabble minced no words:

> No one probably cares if the government publishes unilingual pamphlets on hog marketing or mine safety. But the constitution is different ... If any document should be bilingual, this pamphlet should be ... Premier Lyon has always maintained he is a staunch defender of the rights of Manitoba citizens including the rights of Franco-Manitobans. Yet his government doesn't even publish its constitutional position in French. [45]

However, the province did take one important step. On March 20, 1981, an interdepartmental memo from the premier announced that the government's new French Language Services Secretariat within the Department of Cultural Affairs and Historic Resources was "now operational". Its first director, Franco-Manitoban and former federal diplomat, Roger Turenne, was charged with responsibility to "give substance to the government's announced intention of applying the spirit as well as the letter of the Supreme Court's ruling on bilingualism in Manitoba". The government saw the need to provide "at least some of their services to Manitobans in both official languages". With the benefit of today's hindsight, its final words were portentous indeed. "I trust," the premier's memo continued, "that a pragmatic, imaginative and common sense approach will be applied to a policy which I consider to be very important for the province of Manitoba.".[46]

The government talked the talk sometimes, but it walked the walk rarely unless forced. Its ambivalence often crossed into intransigence. The famous basic principle of physics – that each action triggers an equal and opposite reaction – became the *modus operandi* of what was quickly becoming Manitoba's emerging linguistic standoff. The government's apparent stubbornness inspired a similar inflexibility in some quarters of the Franco-Manitoban community. Chief Justice Freedman's warning was turning into a sad reality: the government's "chipping away" at the constitutional language rights of Franco-Manitobans was beginning to goad a few into pursuing those rights to the point of abstract obduracy.

In early May, St. Boniface lawyer Renald Guay, son of Joe Guay, St. Boniface's former mayor and longtime Liberal MP, took the cases of two francophone clients charged separately with speeding and littering offences. He asked provincial court judges Sam Minuk and Robert Trudel to authorize trial proceedings entirely in French – with a French-speaking judge, Crown counsel and court reporters. Guay argued the provision of translators was insufficient because the restoration of Manitoba's bilingual character by the Supreme Court meant the province's official language minority was entitled to full French court proceedings. Minuk said he would consider the request while Trudel, the only French-speaking provincial court judge in the province, said it would create havoc with his trial schedules. Deputy attorney general Gordon Pilkey said Manitoba had the facilities to provide translation services for French-speaking persons but "we can't really take it any further than that. Manitobans have the right to use either language in court, but I don't think we should have to do everything in French. English is still one of our official languages. It would be absurd to bar English-speaking prosecutors from the court, for example," he said.

Assistant deputy attorney general Gil Goodman pleaded for time and reasonableness. "In time we might get to the point of complete bilingual service but right now we just don't have the resources." Goodman added that his department had just the one French-speaking judge, Trudel, one Crown attorney, Georges de Moissac, and only one court reporter and legally trained translator. Guay was unimpressed. Manitoba is "way behind" Ontario and New Brunswick, both of whom have bilingual "court teams" able to function in either French or English, he said. [47]

But in early July, the province moved. Even though Minuk had ruled that the Section 23 constitutional requirements could be met by the provision of translation services, the government announced that beginning October 17, 1981 it would provide a full-service French court – judge, Crown attorney and court reporter – in St. Boniface that would be available on certain dates to try traffic, bylaw and minor criminal matters. Goodman said the decision was meant to defuse Guay's double-barrelled case. Although Guay was appealing Minuk's decision, he welcomed the province's move as "a big shift, a 180-degree turnaround. Things are moving along." [48]

But one of Guay's clients wasn't mollified. Claude Aubin, who had recently moved to Manitoba from Québec, committed a second traffic infraction at La Broquerie on June 20th by failing to stop at an intersection. Appearing in provincial court in Steinbach, Aubin insisted on his right to a trial in French and refused to address the judge in English. When Judge Mike Baryluk asked for his plea, Aubin responded in French. The nonplussed judge turned to Crown counsel and requested an interpreter. One was called but Aubin wouldn't talk through him. Baryluk registered Aubin's French plea as "not guilty" and begged the thirty-three-year-old resident of St. Vital to recognize that "this is only a traffic case". After initial objections, the attorney-general's department agreed to transfer the case to its planned St. Boniface court. This also didn't satisfy Aubin. Institutionalizing the French court in St. Boniface was a ghetto-ization of the province's francophone community. "This service is my right, not a privilege," he said. "Whether I am in Churchill, Thompson or The Pas I have the right to have my case heard entirely in French. So that's all I'm asking." A frustrated Goodman claimed the province's French-only court went beyond the constitutional requirement. Aubin was driving past practicality right through to rigid and abstract principle. "How far do we go along with him?" Goodman asked. "Who knows if he'll go and speed up in Thompson? What then?" [49]

Meanwhile, the City of Winnipeg had been moving at a slightly faster pace. As of early summer 1981, sixteen of its twenty-two departments had some bilingual capacity. The major ones with extensive French capabilities were social services, parks and recreation, fire, police and operations. Others providing French services only in the St. Boniface-St. Vital area were land surveys and real estate, streets and transportation, waterworks, waste and disposal, civic properties and transit. Bilingualism was not deemed to be necessary in the remaining six that had little contact with the public: audit, law, computer services, budget bureau, personnel and purchasing. [50]

It was perhaps fitting that the first Franco-Manitoban to have his trial conducted in French in more than ninety years was none other than the son of

Georges Forest. Pierre Forest had been charged with going through a red light in connection with a March traffic accident. He pleaded "pas coupable" (not guilty). Forest waived his right to simultaneous translation because he was fluently bilingual, as were his lawyer, Vaughan Baird, the judge, Robert Trudel and the Crown attorney, Georges de Moissac. Throughout the trial, all participants slipped easily back and forth between the two official languages. The younger Forest was acquitted. "Justice was done," he beamed at the conclusion. But his father was off on a new crusade. A sign in the St. Boniface courtroom said "No Smoking". The elder Forest declared he planned to write a letter asking that it be supplemented with one saying "Défense de Fumer". [51]

While all this signalled progress – albeit at a snail's pace – the big issue, the one being tested by Roger Bilodeau, received a stunning setback when the Court of Appeal handed down its verdict on July 7, 1981. Chief Justice Freedman had been convinced by the combined reasonings of Jewers and Gyles. And Justice Gordon Hall sided largely with him. The chief justice found that Section 23 was directory and not imperative for the simple reason that to agree with Bilodeau and declare invalid the Highway Traffic Act and the Summary Conviction Act – and by implication, Manitoba's entire body of unilingual statutes as well – could set loose the forces of "chaos and pervasive social disorder" on the province. Freedman said that "one of the tests for determining whether a statute is mandatory or directory is the degree of hardship, difficulty or public inconvenience that will result from treating it as mandatory". Because the legislature could not have intended chaos, he would impute that the legislature intended for Section 23 to merely be optional. The chief justice used the status of his own court as a basis for his ruling. All Manitoba's courts, including his own, were set up by English-only statute. Yet, he noted, Georges Forest and now, Bilodeau, had gone to them for redress, by implication, confirming their validity.

> I speak of the courts because they are close to me. But what applies to them applies to everything else … Virtually every statute in Manitoba is invalid if we give to Section 23 a mandatory effect. The result is indeed chaos …[52]

The court's sole francophone judge, Alfred M. Monnin, disagreed and as usual, neither minced words nor hid behind legalese but wrote in lucid, powerful prose. While he didn't support any outcome that would "create chaos and disorder of great magnitude" he found no excuse for the province's conduct since December 13, 1979.

> The legislature of Manitoba is still in breach of the clear
> requirement of Section 23. The Attorney General of Manitoba,
> the chief law enforcement officer of the province, allows this
> breach to continue and through counsel, claims he is not in
> breach since the legislation is only directory … I am of the
> view that his argument is untenable as the legislation is clear
> and speaks of "shall be used" and "shall be printed." There is
> nothing of a directory nature in that language. Furthermore,
> entrenched linguistic rights are by nature mandatory and
> never directory. If they were directory only, the risk is that
> they never would be enjoyed or be of any use to those to
> whom they were addressed … I have difficulty understanding
> the problems which Section 23 of this Act seems to raise in
> the minds of some persons. It is forceful but plain language
> which needs no interpretation. It reflects the history of
> Canada … To allege that Section 23 is only directory in
> order to avoid the drastic result that all laws since 1870 are
> invalid is to make the wrong use of an otherwise good prin-
> ciple but one which has no application to this case. All laws
> since 1890, since they were not enacted in both English and
> French, failed to comply with Section 23 … Since (Dec. 13,
> 1979) the invalidity can no longer be excused. The statute is
> clear – it gives rights which must be complied with … [53]

Monnin drew the court's and the public's attention to a broadside delivered at the Manitoba government by the Commissioner of Official Languages in his 1980 annual report. "The Attorney General and his subordinates ought to read and re-read what Canada's linguistic ombudsman … wrote about the situation," Justice Monnin stated. Then he included it in his judgement just to make sure that they did.

Max Yalden had written that the province appeared to regard the Supreme Court decision as a burdensome administrative challenge rather than an opportunity to make amends for the past. "One has the impression that things are moving very slowly in a situation which cries out for imagination and innovation." French-speaking minorities in Canada faced what the commissioner referred to as "Kafkaesque" difficulties. They continued to encounter "one set of hurdles after another" when they tried to obtain justice "as though there were a deliberate intent to wear them down". This was especially true for Franco-Manitobans who had finally been vindicated in their "long struggle to assert their French identity in the face of prejudice, suppression and neglect". [54] Yalden went further. Even on its chosen ground, Manitoba had only made modest inroads into the mountain of translation, it hadn't begun to introduce simultaneous translation in the legislature or started to publish legislative records in French.

Justice Gordon Hall agreed with Freedman that he "wasn't prepared" to declare all of Manitoba's laws since 1890 invalid. "As to whether this court should request or order the government and the legislature to give practical effect to the printing and publishing of statutes, that is a matter for them and does not require or invite intervention by the court." [55]

The appeal court decision was brought into question by Joseph Magnet, a professor of constitutional law at the University of Ottawa who was retained as counsel by the SFM. Magnet referred to a "profound atrophy of will" to promote bilingualism among Canada's political leaders. The appeal court's fear that finding for Bilodeau would cause chaos "completely misunderstands the issue," Magnet said. "The issue is not whether Manitoba's statutes are valid or invalid. The issue is: in view of Manitoba's admitted breach of its constitutional obligation, what is the proper remedy?" [56]

In September, Bilodeau's lawyer petitioned to appeal the decision to the Supreme Court. "It is more than a question of civil rights," Vaughan Baird told the *Globe and Mail*. "We are at a crossroads in our history as a nation. Manitoba has a chance of being a bilingual province and giving leadership to the West in this regard and bringing unity to our country." But if Manitoba stays unilingual, Québec may choose to become independent. "And if that happens, we will see the West joining the U.S. … We are moving towards a separate nation in the West and that bothers me. It bothers me a lot." [57]

Baird vented his anger against the Manitoba Court of Appeal decision. "To me, if our constitution is to mean anything and if we are to have a future bill of rights that will mean anything, this decision must not be allowed to stand." It would give a green light to all provincial governments to refuse to obey the constitution by claiming constitutions are directory and not mandatory. "In other words, governments can violate the law, but individuals can't.

It's like saying 'Yes, we are a bilingual province but the legislature doesn't have to act on it.'"

Noting that Québec was abiding by the Supreme Court ruling of December 13, 1979, but Manitoba remained in breach of the law, he asked: "Where is Canada if Québec has to follow one law and Manitoba can follow another?" When governments "in their hearts" really don't want to do something, they usually can avoid the issue, he continued. "They mustn't be allowed to avoid this one."

The *Globe* also reported that a year earlier NDP MLA Wilson Parasiuk had learned that the province's motor vehicle branch had done all the necessary computer programming to issue bilingual licences, but the Lyon government had blocked the move. At the time, Highways Minister Don Orchard said compliance with the Supreme Court was a major undertaking and the government didn't want to "ad-hoc, do one thing here and one thing there". A year later, the government still had done nothing. Also, Orchard had refused bilingual traffic signs even to municipalities that had asked for them. He told the legislature they would be too costly and "might antagonize the ninety per cent of the people who don't speak French".

Politics infused every facet of the bilingual file. Having helped to raise the public temperature against bilingualism, the Manitoba Conservatives did not intend to "shove French down Manitobans' throats" by putting the French language on driver's licences, especially in the run-up to a fall provincial election. Having sowed the wind, they feared reaping their own whirlwind.

Despite their caution on language, the Lyon Tories became the first government in Manitoba history to lose after a single term. They were badly beaten in the election on November 17, 1981, dropping ten seats to twenty-three. The New Democrats won decisively, taking thirty-four of the legislature's fifty-seven ridings and capturing forty-seven per cent of the vote.

The election's timing meant Manitoba and Québec found themselves once again twinned on a constitutional matter. Since the fall of 1980, Canada had been caught up in Prime Minister Pierre Trudeau's attempt to patriate the constitution from Britain with a charter of rights. It had been his response to Québec's resounding rejection of sovereignty-association in the May referendum. Lyon had been one of the most articulate and passionate spokesmen among the so-called "Gang of Eight" premiers opposed to the package. The "Gang" boasted every province except Ontario and New Brunswick. Its recruitment of Québec's Lévesque was regarded as a major coup. In fact, it

DALE CUMMINGS / WINNIPEG FREE PRESS

merely confirmed that cynical truism that "the enemy of my enemy is my friend" no matter how antithetical that "friend" may be.

Nor was the irony of The Gang confined to the unlikely and unholy alliance of Québec separatists and anti-French westerners. In one of the great ironies of recent Canadian history, The Gang, all of whom championed parliamentary supremacy over entrenched constitutional law interpreted by courts, turned to the courts to derail the prime minister's plan to bring the constitution home from England with or without provincial consent. The Supreme Court found that Ottawa's unilateral initiative, while legal, defied convention. Thus partially vindicated, The Gang crafted an amending formula that, unlike Trudeau's, abolished Québec's historic veto. Lévesque signed on to the loss of his province's hammer because he was convinced the constitutional initiative was ultimately doomed. The Gang also sought to temper the ability of the charter to trump Parliament and the provincial legislatures by a "notwithstanding" clause that empowered what its opponents called "temporary political majorities" to override unpalatable court judgements.

The final first ministers' constitutional conference held to forge a compromise began November 2, 1981 just fifteen days before the Manitoba vote. Although he represented Manitoba at the table, Mercier correctly thought it improper to take any specific action on behalf of the province under the circumstances. As a result, Manitoba was the only province other than Québec not to sign the constitutional accord on November 5, 1981. Trudeau accepted The Gang's amending formula (seven provinces with fifty per cent of the Canadian population) in return for a constitutional charter with rights and freedoms made subject "to such reasonable limits … as can be demonstrably justified in a free and democratic society", as well as to the premiers' notwithstanding clause.

The Québec delegation was staying across the Ottawa River at a hotel in Hull. Shortly after midnight on November 5th, the justice ministers from Canada, Saskatchewan and Ontario came together in the kitchen of the old Ottawa railway station where the conference was held to horse-trade the final compromise. It came to be known as "the night of the long knives" and it left Lévesque convinced the English provinces had betrayed him. They had, but only because they felt he had betrayed them first. In an attempt to peel Québec away from the English provinces, Trudeau had offered to submit the charter to a referendum. The Québec premier, who prided himself on being a great democrat and who obviously believed in referendums having held one a year earlier, was temporarily put off balance. He soon rebuffed the prime minister, but his momentary waffle was enough for the English-speaking members of The Gang to feel free to break ranks with him.

Learning the next morning of the overnight deal that had excluded his province, a furious Québec premier stormed out of the conference, warning the nation of "incalculable consequences". Stripped of its constitutional veto power and denied final consultation, let alone input, Québec, under successive governments, still has not signed the new Canadian constitution. Manitoba's signature was added as soon as the new NDP administration of Howard Pawley was sworn into office.

The change in government in Manitoba did not, however, mean any immediate change on the bilingual file. On March 8, 1982, the *Free Press* reported that, two years after the court judgement, only twenty-four of the province's 450 statutes had been translated into French at a cost of about $400,000. Meanwhile, the provincial legislature was still carrying on almost entirely in English, with only occasional speeches and parts of speeches in French. Thanks to equipment purchased by the Lyon government, the Pawley administration was prepared to offer some simultaneous translation – provided prior notice was given by those wishing to use the French language. Simultaneous translation would require seven translators a day and the NDP had ruled it out, at least for the time being. SFM president Gilberte Proteau seemed to have acquiesced, albeit reluctantly. "There isn't much point when we know it isn't feasible," she said. [58]

Behind the scenes, however, there had been a substantial shift in government attitude. While the NDP was aware of the need to tread carefully on the language file given the volatility of public opinion, it didn't want to begin its term by picking a fight with a minority – Franco-Manitobans – it knew had voted for it. And as a law professor, the new attorney general, Roland Penner, understood the constitutional issue and was committed to putting right what he recognized as a legal and moral wrong. In fact, initially, he was even prepared to let the Bilodeau case proceed to the Supreme Court precisely because he expected Manitoba to lose, but was talked out of it by the federal government. Throughout the entire ensuing constitutional trauma, Ottawa was to view all Manitoba's legal and political manoeuvrings almost exclusively through the prism of their impact in Québec.

One of the major players in influencing and channelling the shift in attitude was Roger Turenne, who had been appointed the first director of Manitoba's French Language Services Secretariat by the Lyon government. On January 15, 1982, only a month and a half after the swearing-in of the Pawley administration, Turenne sent a memo to Penner on "the political implications of the Bilodeau case" that charted a whole new path for the government, the Franco-Manitoban community and, eventually, the province and nation. The three-page memo proposed the province make the Supreme Court appeal of the Roger Bilodeau case unnecessary by dropping its legal position that Section 23 of the Manitoba Act was directory (optional) only, the position that had been upheld by a split decision in the Court of Appeal. Turenne proposed the government accept that Manitoba was indeed constitutionally required to use two languages in its legislature and courts and go on to "indicate what we see as the practical consequences of such a decision and clearly spell out a realistic plan of implementation". [59]

As Turenne was to recall more than twenty years later, his diplomatic background had taught him to defuse confrontation and try to bring two opposing sides together by first helping them to find their common ground, however small. He began by telling the attorney general that, win or lose, Manitoba – and Canada – would be the ultimate losers if the Bilodeau case went to the Supreme Court. "We could in fact find ourselves in a situation of 'if we lose, we lose – if we win, we still lose.'" [60]

If the province lost and the Supreme Court declared Section 23 to be mandatory, Manitoba's difficulty would depend on how the court addressed the validity of Manitoba's body of English-only laws. He described as "serious" the consequences of the court possibly declaring all post-1979 laws invalid and setting unrealistic translation deadlines, pointing out that only ten statutes were currently published in French with another fifteen "in the pipeline".

> On the other hand, if we do win the case, our administrative
> life will be easier and we will no doubt save some money on
> translation in the long run, but this might be accomplished
> at a heavy price for Canada as a whole, and could strengthen
> Manitoba's undeserved and unfortunate reputation as a red-
> neck province … [A] judgement that Article 23 is directory
> only would be final confirmation by the highest court in the
> land of the double standard in the treatment of minorities.
> We would be in a situation where "shall" means "shall" for
> Québec but "you may if you wish" for Manitoba … It would
> add salt to Québec's wounds.

Turenne urged the new government to establish its own position on official language rights in Manitoba as its first priority, adding the trenchant historical context of the times. Canada was about to formally enact its new constitution with its enhanced linguistic guarantees.

> It would be pointless to enter into a discussion of the tactics
> to be employed in the Supreme Court if we do not have a
> clear idea of our objectives. Before November 30th, 1981, the
> objective of the government of Manitoba was to nullify what
> it considered to be unfortunate consequences of the Supreme
> Court judgement in the Forest case. Little thought appears
> to have been given to the political consequences outside of
> Manitoba. Is this still the Manitoba government's objective? [61]

The government shouldn't "blandly assume" it would win its case simply by pointing to the "absurd" situation of losing its laws, he warned. And he highlighted the province's "vulnerable position" should the court find against it. Suggesting the government should look at the dissenting opinion given by

Justice Monnin in the Court of Appeal ruling, Turenne said Manitoba would strengthen its position if it went before the court with a "reasonable" program of implementation and "realistic" delays.

> ... I believe that a change in objectives and tactics would bring benefits to both the province and the country. Because the political costs would be greater than the financial and administrative advantages gained, our objective should no longer be to have Article 23 declared directory ... Manitoba's 180-degree turn on this question would not go unnoticed. At this critical juncture in Canada's constitutional evolution, Manitoba would seem to have accomplished a very statesmanlike act ... It would also underline the clear difference of approach between this government and the previous one on constitutional questions. [62]

Turenne sent a copy of his memo to Michael Decter, the new clerk of the executive council and the province's top civil servant. Decter, the husband of Lucille Roch, a Franco-Manitoban and the executive director of the SFM, was more than sympathetic. Less than a month later, on February 5, 1982, Turenne sent a further memo to the attorney general that set out to correct an error that had crept into legal arguments and from there into judgements from the province's two highest courts. The error was that Manitoba had often not bothered using French as an official language even before 1890. Wrote Turenne:

> Throughout the course of the Forest and Bilodeau cases, there has been a general assumption that there is no firm evidence as to the actual practice ... of the Manitoba Legislature between the years 1870 and 1890. In his majority opinion of last July, Justice Hall quoted approvingly from a statement made by Justice Freedman in the Forest case that "an agreed statement of facts suggests that so far as can be ascertained, statues were not adopted in French in Manitoba even before 1890". This seems to have been taken as gospel by everyone since. Indeed, as recently as two weeks ago, officials in your department believed that statutes were not even translated in Manitoba before 1890. I have since

discovered otherwise. In fact, all of the pre-1890 statutes were published in French, as well as all the journals, and the Manitoba Gazette. All are available in the Legislative Library … The real point of this discovery is that it demonstrates clearly that there was never any doubt in anyone's mind that Section 23 was mandatory, given the enormous, and successful efforts to comply with it. [63]

Turenne told the attorney general that the real import of this discovery was to undermine the Court of Appeal majority judgement that Section 23 was directory (optional) only. Writing for the majority, the chief justice had said that since the legislature could not have intended widespread chaos to be the result of non-compliance with a particular law, the legislature must have intended that the statute was voluntary and not obligatory. But, Turenne stressed, intentions can only be ascribed if there is no contrary evidence. And Manitoba's strict adherence to its official bilingualism between 1870 and 1890, verified by its body of French statutes, was proof positive of that contrary evidence.

It was yet more ammunition for a government already disinclined to risk a humiliating loss before the nation's highest court, a further rending of the fabric of Canadian unity and yet another black mark on Manitoba's reputation. The attorney general struck an ad hoc committee to develop a new constitutional position. As Turenne recalls, he became one-third of what became known as the "Terrible Ts". He was the political strategist; Rae Tallin, the province's legislative counsel, was the legal technician, and Kerr Twaddle was the constitutional adviser. Held over from the Lyon era, Twaddle never abandoned his conviction Manitoba was not constitutionally obliged to function in two languages, a position he firmly believed would be vindicated by the Supreme Court. A Scottish immigrant, Twaddle nursed a personal peeve against bilingualism. He was very fond of a particular variety of Scottish marmalade that he could not import because it didn't have a bilingual label. Turenne never ceased reminding the lawyer that the point wasn't about winning or losing. It was about "doing what was right … I kept telling him, we aren't doing it because we have to; we're doing it because we want to." [64]

On other fronts as well, the year 1982 was a fitting presage to the climactic events to come, which would rip asunder the province's political and social fabric. For Franco-Manitobans, nothing much changed. There were steps forward and steps back; goodwill displayed and intransigence exhibited.

On March 10th Winnipeg police had to be called to escort the chairman of the St. Boniface School Board from a meeting. The dispute, centered on the board's plans to go ahead with a controversial school reorganization that included the conversion of an all-English school to one dedicated to French immersion, had been simmering for more than a year. A crowd of about 500 irate parents complained that the reorganization favoured French immersion at the expense of the English program. As if to confirm the allegations, the board members split along French-English lines, with the two francophone trustees voting for it and the two anglophones opposed. Jim Garwood, the board chair, broke the tie both in the vote and in the perception of linguistic division. But it was to prove incendiary.

When trustee and lawyer Renald Guay moved the motion to approve the reorganization, the meeting erupted. Calling him a "turkey", one member of the crowd warned Guay: "If there's any blood spilled, you're responsible." Several parents made obscene gestures at Garwood and called him a fink and one man even crumpled up a piece of paper and threw it at him after the vote was taken. "Help him away," a man yelled as Winnipeg police escorted Garwood through the throng of furious parents. Trustee Joan Barker said it was "nothing less than criminal that this board [could] create a blood bath in this community". But Guay argued that after fourteen months of debate, it was time to make a decision. (65)

The linguistic tension was a product of the demographic shift in St. Boniface. The city considered the capital of the French fact in Western Canada had become predominantly anglophone by the middle of the century. The percentage of French-speaking residents gradually shrank from a majority in 1900 to just thirty-one per cent when the City of Winnipeg was amalgamated in 1972. (66) That year, francophones comprised slightly more than twenty-two per cent of the population of the cities of St. Boniface and St. Vital combined and just under six per cent of the new City of Winnipeg. Franco-Manitobans were concentrated in the northern end of St. Boniface. Norwood was English-speaking, Protestant and hostile to its French neighbour. It demanded and got its own school board. Meanwhile, the City of St. Boniface itself functioned almost exclusively in English. Services and communication in the French language were an informal hit and miss affair. The situation actually improved for Franco-Manitobans after amalgamation, since the City of Winnipeg Act guaranteed a minimal level of bilingual communication.

The ominous evidence of linguistic friction, if not outright bigotry, before the St. Boniface School Board in the spring of 1982 was soon countered by the most dramatic move taken by the province since the court ruling more than two years earlier. Addressing his first meeting of the SFM as premier, Pawley won a standing ovation when he announced that the province's 80,000 francophones would be able to have all criminal trials conducted in French by July 1ˢᵗ, that birth and marriage certificates and drivers' licences would be bilingual by October and that simultaneous translation would be available starting with the fall sitting of the legislature. The premier further pledged that provincial government services would be offered in French and English in francophone areas. It was a complete about-face for the former attorney general, who had once considered Franco-Manitobans just another minority group: "The French language has a unique historical and constitutional position in Manitoba," he proclaimed. "Not only is it the province's obligation to implement an official languages policy, it is a task to which we are committed because Franco-Manitobans are an essential and vital part of this province." The throng of 500 serenaded him with the traditional French salute: "Il a gagné ses épaulettes" (He has won his spurs). [67]

Less than a week later, a meeting of Interlake mayors and reeves, by "an almost unanimous show of hands" condemned Pawley's decision to expand French language services. David Harms, president of the Union of Manitoba Municipalities who attended the Stonewall meeting but didn't vote, told the *Free Press* that "when the French population in the province was only about three per cent, we're particularly unhappy that he'll be spending tax money on translation". [68]

The schools issue stayed in the headlines, too. Police had to be called to another rowdy St. Boniface School Board meeting in April. In August, Beliveau junior high school announced it would provide separate staff rooms for its English and French teachers. St. Boniface trustee Joyce Patterson, an opponent of the board's expansion of French language education, said the situation bred prejudice and "is a visible display of people trying to separate because of their language". Joan Barker, another opponent of the French immersion initiative, said she thought teachers could be more "professional. Since when can't staff have a cup of coffee together?" However, the former acting superintendent, Roger Millier, said that "when you have two schools within a school, you have two of everything" and trustee Renald Guay said he couldn't fault the idea. He noticed that every time two different groups are put together they often "end up separating anyways". [69]

Language also roiled the waters in the River East School Division, where parents feared a French immersion program planned for Springfield Heights School would squeeze out its English and Ukrainian bilingual programs. And Bob Rose, president of the Manitoba School Trustees' Association, said bilingual education needed reassessment because of its costs, particularly in rural school divisions. A group of Swan River parents announced plans to go to court to stop a French immersion program planned by their board.

Feeding the turmoil around the education controversy were continued rumours and allegations the SFM had a "master plan" to foist French education on Manitobans – an accusation heatedly denied by the society. But the schools issue was always more than simple linguistic prejudice. It pitted francophones against francophones and anglophones against anglophones as much as francophones against anglophones. Some francophones wanted their children to be educated in English while others wanted, not French immersion, which they feared led to assimilation, but the Français program where the school ambience was entirely French. The anglophone community was similarly split, running the gamut from parents who wanted no part of French to those who campaigned to have their children enrolled in the all-French Français program. Added to that were parents from the other strands in the province's rich ethnic mosaic who pressed to have their children learn their mother tongues.

By the summer, there were signs the premier's March speech to the SFM may have been more sizzle than steak. Although Official Languages Commissioner Max Yalden had praised the government on a trip to Winnipeg in June for its "major step in the recognition of the rights of Franco-Manitobans", in early July, the attorney general limited the right to French criminal trials to federal charges only, excluding those heard in provincial, municipal and traffic courts. Georges Forest told the *Winnipeg Sun* the policy was "too narrow … Either French is equal or it is not equal in the courts of Manitoba. We can't have these changes made piecemeal." [70]

Also that month, Penner announced his department had drafted an amendment to the province's constitution to eliminate its requirement to translate all its laws. The amendment required that all new legislation be bilingual while the translation of existing statutes would be, in the language of the Freedman judgement, directory (optional) and not mandatory. Its purpose was to permit the province to devote its scarce translation resources exclusively to the province's active body of laws and avoiding wasting them on statutes that were either dead or dormant. The government had estimated that there were about 450 "core" active laws out of a total of some 4,500.

The NDP's amendment subjected it to harsh criticism from an unlikely source. Mercier, now the Official Opposition Conservatives' justice critic, became an overnight champion of constitutionally-entrenched rights and attacked Penner for violating the Manitoba and Canadian constitutions. Pointing to the 1979 Supreme Court decision, Mercier correctly stated Manitoba had lacked the power in 1890 to amend its own constitution unilaterally and pass the English-only law and it still lacked it now. Worse, he continued, the Penner amendment, by restricting the French language, defied the new Canadian constitution as well. But Mercier was off-base. He missed the point that what was being proposed was a constitutional amendment and a constitutional amendment does not "defy" the constitution unless it is attempted by unconstitutional means. Manitoba fully intended to observe the amending formula in the 1982 Constitution, which required the consent both of the legislature and the Canadian Parliament.

Bilodeau's lawyer, Vaughan Baird, said the amendment would "destroy the Gibraltar of English and French language rights in Manitoba". He also warned it would almost certainly be declared beyond the province's power by the Supreme Court. Publicly, Penner had argued the amendment was necessitated by the threat to Manitoba's legal framework posed by the Bilodeau appeal to the Supreme Court, a threat he frequently and eagerly bandied about, claiming it could create "chaos". In fact, the chaos the government feared was administrative, not legal; difficult and costly but not a constitutional meltdown. Nevertheless, the government found the portentous and terrifying idea of legal chaos useful in helping convince a dubious public, confident that lawyers and judges would, for their own purposes, be a sufficient echo chamber to make it compelling.

And all the time the government, or at least its attorney general, was committed to trying to find a solution that would correct the "ninety years of injustice" without setting loose the anti-French tiger within the Manitoba population. On August 26th, Penner announced he had abandoned the amendment after consultations with the SFM. The SFM and the government agreed to leave Section 23 of the Manitoba Act intact "because of its historical significance" and add a clause that would give the government five years to complete the mammoth translation task. [71] It was the beginning of a perilous bargaining process that would lead both the province and the body representing its official language minority – and by extension, the nation itself – to terrible grief.

The Canadian Crucible

8

The Gathering Storm

THERE WAS A SCENT OF FEAR AND LOATHING in the Manitoba air as 1982 closed and 1983 began. In the summer of 1982, Dan McKenzie, the veteran Progressive Conservative MP from Winnipeg South Centre, sent out a constituency leaflet accusing the Liberal government of having wasted $4 billion since 1969 promoting bilingualism. That was the year the Trudeau government, with the almost-unanimous support of Parliament, passed the Official Languages Act. Seventeen backbench Tory MPs, five of whom were from Manitoba – Walter Dinsdale (Brandon-Souris), the former postmaster-general in the cabinet of John Diefenbaker; George Muir (Lisgar); Gordon Ritchie (Dauphin); Bud Simpson (Churchill) and Craig Stewart (Marquette) – defied their party to vote against the bill on second reading. Official bilingualism became one of the hottest issues of the 1972 election, particularly on the prairies, propelling McKenzie, an employee of the Crown-owned Manitoba Telephone System, into Parliament. He easily defeated Liberal E.B. Osler in Winnipeg South Centre after only one term.

McKenzie's 1982 pamphlet also attacked the Liberals for giving preference to francophones in hiring and promotion, often at the expense of the merit principle. McKenzie told the *Canadian Press* the language program was "an attack on anglophones" and an insult to francophones because it suggested they needed the government "to hold their hands". He announced he had asked the Canadian Human Rights Commission to investigate two cases of alleged discrimination in government hiring, arguing that francophones were given an unfair edge. The mailer went on to say that three government departments – energy, agriculture and employment and immigration – were hiring francophones who were less qualified than candidates from other ethnic groups. [1]

McKenzie then levelled a broadside at his own party and its leader, Joe Clark, saying the Tories had no policy on bilingualism and demanding they support the holding of nation-wide hearings on the issue. He told the *Winnipeg Sun* he was taking his party to task for the good of the country. "I'm doing this on behalf of the Canadian people. It's very important. I can't ignore them. My motto is country first, constituents second and party third ... I have constituents who are affected – people who have applied for the RCMP and the armed forces and have been turned down because they don't speak French." [2]

The *Winnipeg Free Press* took McKenzie to task in a tart editorial headlined "Sniping at Bilingualism". He was simply wrong to charge discrimination because a French-speaking candidate was picked for a particular civil service job over a unilingual anglophone applicant because

> ... if the government does not examine the language abilities of civil service candidates in French and English and insist upon a certain number who speak French, the departments or agencies will not achieve or maintain the ability to serve the country in both languages and French-speaking people will continue to be under-represented, relative to the general population, in the federal service.

> Mr. McKenzie has not yet made out a case that the policy of the Official Languages Act is damaging to the civil service or is wrong in principle ... Nation-wide hearings on bilingualism ... would elicit complaints from those of the Gordon Kesler [an Alberta separatist who a year earlier had won a surprise byelection victory in the southern Alberta provincial riding of Olds-Didsbury] stripe who believe bilingualism is part of a vile plot to subvert the country ... Until Mr. McKenzie comes up with some more substantial material, he can safely be ignored. [3]

The Canadian Crucible

McKenzie, one of the most vocal right-wingers in the Tory caucus, had been a thorn in the side of his party's federal leadership throughout the terms of both Robert Stanfield and Clark because of his high-profile, relentless attacks on official bilingualism. He scarcely allowed a constituency mailing or an appearance on a radio talk show to go by without sounding alarms over federal bilingualism's gross waste of taxpayers' dollars and egregious unfairness to English-speaking Canadians. It was a message that sold well in a constituency that a senior provincial Conservative once referred to as "the Alabama of Manitoba". The leafy and relatively affluent communities of St. James and Charleswood flanked both banks of the Assiniboine River from the edge of downtown Winnipeg west to the Perimeter Highway at the border of the Portage Plains. Predominantly Anglo-Saxon, many of their residents were descendants of the Ontario Orange pioneers who flooded into Manitoba in the years immediately following Confederation, changing forever the ethnic and cultural ethos of the province.

Thanks to a dedicated staff who daily sifted through the city newspapers' obituary, birth and wedding notices and a voluminous card index, McKenzie, a former Winnipeg city councillor and handsome, silver-haired legionnaire, also never missed remembering a constituent's birthday or wedding anniversary with a greeting card or a spouse's or close relative's death with a sympathy note.

He didn't consider himself in any way extreme or bigotted. He could point to his whopping majorities in four successive elections (1972, 1974, 1979 and 1980) to argue convincingly he was a good representative of his voters, a faithful mirror of the overwhelming public sentiments in his riding. In the summer of 1973, McKenzie and fifteen other Tory MPs bolted caucus to vote against the federal bilingualism program. In the 1974 federal election, McKenzie laced his door-to-door campaigning with stories about a federal program "costing millions" to install bilingual doorhandles on all federal buildings in Western Canada and thirty-dollar ashtrays for the prime minister's residence.[4]

As another indication of the mood of the times, in that same election, former Conservative attorney general Sterling Lyon also made anti-French, anti-bilingual sentiment a subterranean theme of his unsuccessful effort to unseat Liberal defence minister James Richardson in Winnipeg South. Lyon distributed a pamphlet featuring the names and pictures only of cabinet ministers and senior federal officials who were French Canadian, an unsubtle way of claiming the government of Pierre Trudeau directed all its policies and dollars to Québec. "I'm not running against the Liberals," Lyon proclaimed in his mailer. "I'm running against the Trudeau Liberals. There really is a difference …"[5]

McKenzie's controversial views didn't end with bilingualism. He was a vocal supporter of South Africa's apartheid regime and was once quoted saying blacks made good mechanics and were noted for their musical rhythm. He also backed the far-right Canadians for Foreign Aid Review (CFAR), a shadowy organization founded by white supremacist Paul Fromme that opposed foreign aid to African and other "socialist" states.

While McKenzie's prejudices appalled many Manitobans, they tapped into a rich vein of populist sentiment. That sentiment was rapidly turning into all-out linguistic hatred by the early months of 1983, fuelled by the launch, after a two-year delay, of bilingual drivers' licences the previous October and periodic media reports of negotiations between La Société franco-manitobaine and the government involving the extension of French language rights in the province.

The rampages leave their traces on St. Boniface.

The Canadian Crucible

The exterior walls of businesses and schools with French signs and names in St. Boniface and even the bilingual sign on the site of the new Air Canada building in downtown Winnipeg were subject to an increasing barrage of racist graffitti: "No More French" – "Canadains (sic) want to speak English. Let the majority rule" – "Join the majority. Speak English." – "No More French, NMF" – "Reserved for Frogs". The office of the French language weekly newspaper, *La Liberté,* was broken into and a camera stolen. Its editor had a window of his car smashed as it stood outside his home. Language crusader Georges Forest was by now reconciled to an almost daily routine of painting, washing and wiping epithets like "Frog" and "Go back to Québec" off the walls and windows of his Marion Street insurance office. He had recently had to contend with a more threatening assault – his office windows were sometimes smashed as well.

But the fire-bombing of La Société franco-manitobaine offices on January 30, 1983, gutting the $100,000 building on Provencher Boulevard, frightened the society, the entire francophone community and beyond and prompted a shocked editorial in the *Free Press* entitled "Inexcusable". Léo Robert, the new SFM president, called a news conference to warn the public that while it might only be the actions of a small fringe group, the crescendo of harassing late-night phone calls to society members, the vandalism and graffiti and finally, the fire, threatened all Franco-Manitobans. "There is an anti-French campaign organized by a very small but well-organized group inspired by feelings of hatred," Robert continued. "We won't give up. We are supposed to be living in a civilized society." [6] Robert was joined on the podium by representatives of the B'nai B'rith League for Human Rights and Parents for Ukrainian Education. League chairman David Matas explained: "Violence directed to one of our [minority] groups is an assault on us all."

Even as Robert was holding his news conference, maintenance staff were at work at Louis Riel Collegiate painting over new "Speak English. No More French" graffitti on the school's exterior. Principal Roger Druwe was upset and worried. The moment he saw the slogans, he had inspected the school and the grounds to see if there had been any attempt to start a fire. "I've got 500 students in this building. We don't know what we did to get involved in this … This is an educational institution." [7]

On February 13th, the *Winnipeg Sun* carried a story under the headline "Secret Gang Confesses to Graffitti". It reported that a group calling itself The Painters had sent the paper a letter followed by a phone call to editor

Paul Sullivan claiming responsibility for the spray-painting but denying any role in the fire. The group said its members were of Ukrainian, English, Polish, Japanese and French origin ranging in age from sixteen to nineteen. It insisted its actions were political and not racist. "We want to draw attention to the fact that the Franco-Manitoban Society is having great success in bluffing the current provincial government into a pro-French campaign," the one-page letter said. "Only since Hitler has a small minority had so much success." The group's spokesman said the idea stemmed from the experience of two members who felt forced out of Louis Riel Collegiate when it switched from French immersion to the total Français program. The Painters, its spokesman explained, considered themselves too old to learn "proper bilingualism" and feared their chances in the job market were threatened.

For his part, SFM president Robert told reporters he believed the vandalism was a result of negotiations between the SFM and the government on bilingual services. But St. Boniface MLA and NDP health minister Larry Desjardins said the negotiations would continue and the government would not be intimidated by a few "red-necks". [8]

The talks between the government and the SFM were about a lot more than the expansion of French services, although that would not become clear until later and in a way that would cause Manitoba's ever-simmering language cauldron to boil over. That both sides would seek negotiations was inevitable – and sensible. As noted earlier, the NDP had been elected in part thanks to the support of the Franco-Manitoban community. While small in numerical terms, the province's official language minority tends to be concentrated geographically. Eleven of Manitoba's fifty-seven electoral ridings – St. Boniface, St. Vital, Seine River, Riel, Niakwa and St. Norbert in Winnipeg and La Vérendrye, Emerson, Ste. Rose, Lakeside, and Morris in rural Manitoba – have a francophone population of between ten and fifty per cent. In Manitoba's highly-polarized and competitive political culture, this is far more than enough to determine who wins government.

Also as noted earlier, a small core within the new government, centred on its erudite attorney general, Roland Penner, a law professor, saw an opportunity for positive action on Canada's always supercharged linguistic front and to make amends for Manitoba's past behaviour.

In light of the new constitution of 1982, there was a certain desire for Manitoba to be the author of its first amendment, an amendment that would represent French-English reconciliation from a province that had done so much damage in the past. [9]

The decision to pursue a constitutional amendment was taken in the spring of 1982 over the objections of the province's constitutional advisor, Kerr Twaddle, who remained convinced that the Supreme Court would not foist official bilingualism on Manitoba. The SFM was equally interested in the idea of a constitutional amendment. It was more concerned with the provision of government services in the French language to members of Manitoba's shrinking official minority in the communities in which they lived than it was in the costly translation of thousands of pages of laws few people had ever heard of, let alone deemed vital to their lives. On its own, of course, the SFM had no constitutional standing, but Ottawa's bottom-line insistence that any settlement be acceptable to the province's linguistic minority gave it a *de facto* constitutional veto.

Because any amendment to a province's constitution requires Canada's consent, the federal government had been party to the negotiations from the outset. From start to finish, Ottawa viewed the Manitoba language file primarily through the prism of its mirror-image boost to anglophone rights in Québec. Despite the identical nature of their constitutional protection, the difference in the power of the English minority in Québec and the French minority in Manitoba could hardly have been more stark. The former lived on a continent of some 250 million English-speaking people, had always been able to reinforce and enrich itself through a panoply of its own institutions and had commanded the heights of the Québec economy for two centuries. The latter had been under siege almost from the day Manitoba joined Canada. Fearful that a Supreme Court victory for Roger Bilodeau and francophones in Manitoba, and thus anglophones in Québec, would feed the separatist flame, Ottawa immediately seized upon the out-of-court settlement idea. At first, Ottawa concerned itself with ensuring that the Franco-Manitoban community was being adequately represesented and consulted. Later, it had to apply its seal of approval on the outcome and grease the wheels of the deal with federal personnel and money for the mammoth translation task.

For its part, the provincial government was worried about the potential for Roger Bilodeau's speeding ticket to impose a sweeping and draconian translation obligation on Manitoba going well beyond statutes to include regulations and journals at a cost the province couldn't afford – the much-feared "administrative" chaos. [10]

The SFM was prepared to drive a hard bargain. After ninety-three years' experience with the bona fides of successive Manitoba governments elected by non-francophone and implacably hostile majorities, the SFM wasn't about to turn its back on its hard-won legal victory and run the risk that the French language could be swept under the rug again. The government had to enhance Section 23 of the Manitoba Act with a constitutional amendment that neither its successors nor the general public could ever again ignore or repeal.

Negotiations had started in the summer of 1982. Larry Desjardins, the venerable MLA for St. Boniface, now the province's minister of health, didn't want to be the point man on the language file. Not only was he pre-occupied with the government's heaviest portfolio, he had no desire, as a francophone himself, to be viewed as the "person pushing French". While neither side went public with what was on the table, there was no real secrecy. Snippets of various bargaining positions were sprinkled through the English-speaking media in the fall and early winter of 1983 and the French-speaking media, both *La Liberté* and CKSB, had been on the story from the start, publishing and broadcasting numerous articles and reports as the negotiations proceeded. On January 13, 1983, the *Globe and Mail's* Manitoba correspondent, Richard Cleroux, made the most detailed report so far in the English media – and in Canada's self-styled "national" newspaper. He wrote that:

> Attorney-General Roland Penner wants to make a deal with Manitoba's 50,000 francophones to enshrine their language rights in the new Canadian constitution. He's willing to toss in some expanded French-language services in return for more time to translate Manitoba laws into French ... He's been negotiating behind closed doors for the past six months with the Société franco-manitobaine. Both sides are close to an agreement ...

Penner was worried about the Bilodeau case, the article continued, because the last time the province had tried to fight a traffic ticket case based on language at the Supreme Court it had lost. A key aspect of the SFM-Manitoba negotiation was that Bilodeau agree to drop his appeal, due to be heard later in the spring. As a result, Bilodeau and his lawyer, Vaughan Baird, were also party to the talks. Cleroux reported the province had agreed to state in the constitution that both French and English are the official languages of Manitoba and to provide government services in French where numbers warranted. There were still some unresolved issues. The SFM wanted the duality clause enshrined in the Charter of Rights as well, full versions of Hansard in both languages and completion of all translation by 1990. The government was pushing to follow Québec's plan, adopted in 1979, for a single bilingual Hansard printed in the language used by the member speaking. It also sought an extension to 1995 of the grace period to finish legal translation.

Penner had decided not to bring the Official Opposition Conservatives into the negotiations, although there was ample precedent in Canada for bipartisan accord and action on constitutional matters. He told a reporter much later he had kept Tory leader Lyon and his justice critic, Gerry Mercier, informed on an ongoing basis about the course and content of the discussions and never received nor asked for their opinion. However, as Lyon was to state in the legislature on May 18, 1983, Mercier had had just one communication concerning the negotiations from the minister and that was back in mid-December 1982. At that time, Mercier had warned the government not to proceed down that path.

The exclusion of the opposition was one fatal error by the government. Another was Penner's failure even to keep his francophone colleagues – Desjardins and NDP Caucus Chair Gérard Lécuyer – fully apprised of developments. He told Roger Turenne, the province's director of French language services, that he didn't want "too many cooks" negotiating with the SFM, fearing negotiations would bog down. It was a fateful decision that was to leave the government flat-footed, unprepared and almost defenseless when the storm finally broke.

On January 16, 1983, more than 150 members of the SFM came to a public meeting with the society's leadership in St. Boniface to get more details about the closed-door negotiations. According to Cleroux's report in the *Globe* the next day, some told their executive in no uncertain terms that they didn't want to trade constitutional rights for language services. Georges Forest was highly critical of the strategy. The man whose parking ticket had finally ended the "ninety years of injustice" in the 1979 Supreme Court judgement said Franco-Manitobans should have the right to demand services in both languages everywhere in the province, not just in areas of high demand. Forest's arguments did not carry the day in the end, however. The membership of the SFM gave its leaders a strong mandate to continue with the negotiations.

Jacqueline Blay, the journalist who wrote her masters thesis on the language crisis, was at the meeting and today calls it a "key ... in the history of the province and the Franco-Manitoba community. The respective camps were defined that day."

On one side, you had the negotiators who were so aware of the full import of what they were negotiating; it was without precedent in any province in Canada ... On the other side you had Roger Bilodeau who triggered the whole episode in court and was basically holding the ace card: if the province did not comply with what needed to be done, he would proceed with his court case. However, he put a caveat to his plans: he said that he wanted what was best for the community and he would agree to whatever the community wanted. And then you have Georges Forest who had been saying for months that he had won the whole case, lock, stock and barrel. Suddenly, on stage the negotiators are saying, albeit politely: no, not everything was won, in fact everything has still to be done. That is why Forest behaved the way he did that day and during the language crisis. He went from being opposed, incensed, in agreement one day, in disagreement another day. His zigs and zags were very troubling for anybody who had followed and believed him. He would never shy away from a sound bite that would chastise the government – Gérard Lécuyer was often the target of his comments, or the SFM ... His accusations of "rape with consent" stung and were unwarranted. It was a very difficult time for Georges because he felt that his victory had been obtained in vain. I remember discussing this with him and he was adamant: he had won and the whole province was bilingual; no designated areas; no piecemeal programs, nothing. He found an audience, and at some level provided leverage for those who opposed the package.

In a way, it affected the outcome. The Sterling Lyons, the Russell Doerns and all the people who did not want bilingualism felt that they could oppose the deal because Forest opposed it. It was awful. And it gave credence to Donald

Creighton, who had always said that a minority was imposing its will on a majority while it was the opposite, the minority of today was the majority of yesterday and vice versa: the francophones had first protected the anglophones. The SFM was unable to achieve the all-important Franco-Manitoban unanimity. [11]

Forest kept up the heat. His "rape with consent" remark came during a March speech at the University of Winnipeg's Exposure '83 conference. The SFM's negotiations with the province, he added, would lessen the impact of his court decision and "limit the development of French in Manitoba". He singled out the delay in translation, the partial extent of French services and the proposal for a single bilingual Hansard rather than one in each official language. He promised to organize a public fight against the proposal once it went before the legislature. "In Manitoba, we must struggle not for survival but for development that will allow the two languages to become equal." [12] Lucien Loiselle of the Office of the Commissioner of Official Languages in St. Boniface told the *Winnipeg Sun* that francophones were not being "bullheaded or fanatics ... We're just being what we want to be ... [Manitobans] here in Canada."

But the less tolerant members of Manitoba's silent majority were making their feelings known in many direct and at times, amusing, ways. An elderly woman began a unique weekly protest at the Safeway store at the corner of River Avenue and Osborne Street in Winnipeg's trendy Osborne Village. Humming cheerfully to herself, she would march up and down the aisles wheeling a grocery cart and turning cans and packages around so that only the English side was visible. She never berated the clerks nor offered any comment on her one-woman crusade to restore Manitoba to its unilingual senses. Another woman phoned the province's Motor Vehicles Branch to complain about the province's new licence plates emblazoned with the phrase, "Friendly Manitoba" in English only. "They're in French," she shouted angrily at the startled clerk. When the clerk protested they were not, she refused to listen. "The numbers precede the letters this year. Anybody knows that means they're in French," she huffed. [13] Funny as these vignettes were, they stood as chilling testimony to the irrational fear and intolerance that can overtake otherwise sensible people when they perceive a threat to their security of person and place.

In early April, *Free Press* editorial writer Terry Moore, armed with material from Turenne, published a two-part series laying out the framework of the final agreement between the government and the SFM. In an interview almost twenty years later, Turenne recalled that he wanted the newspaper articles to appear during a crucial negotiating session with Roger Tassé, the federal deputy minister of justice. He felt the articles would have a positive impact on Ottawa's view of the talks, a hunch that turned out to be accurate. The newspaper's backgrounder pieces gave the issue its political dimension. French Manitoba, Moore noted, had voted for the NDP. The attorney general was not only concerned about legal chaos, he also wanted to avoid going to the Supreme Court of Canada to argue against the rights of Franco-Manitobans.

Section 23 of the Manitoba Act would be amended by several new clauses. The first would make the printing and publishing of acts of the legislature in both languages mandatory and not directory, as the Manitoba Court of Appeal had ruled. This was the nub of Bilodeau's appeal to the Supreme Court and with that language, Bilodeau was prepared to abandon it. The second was the clause that would set Manitoba on its ear. It said English and French were the official languages of Manitoba. Moore noted, however, that the clause did not go as far as the amendment to the Canadian Constitution did in making the two languages official in New Brunswick. There, they have "equality of status and equal rights and privileges as to their use in all institutions of the legislature and government of New Brunswick." Moore also noted that the reach of the New Brunswick wording was unclear and added: "It seems unrealistic to expect that the French language would loom as large in official literature and speech in Manitoba as it does in New Brunswick." [14]

The next clauses of the amendment "saved" the existing body of unilingual English laws from future court challenge and provided a timetable for translating them and enacting new ones in both languages. January 1, 1987 was set as the date by which all bills in the legislature would have to be "enacted, printed and published" in French and English. Laws passed before that would not be invalid if their process and publication had been in English only. December 31, 1995 was the date at which all old statutes would have to be translated and made part of a new general revision of Manitoba's body of laws. 1987 was also used as the cutoff year for the validity of unilingual English regulations and the requirement for bilingual ones. The province won its victory over Hansard. There would be one Hansard which would use the language of the MLA speaking.

The final paragraphs dealt with French language services and largely copied Ottawa's formula. Any Manitoban was given the right to communicate in French with head offices of government departments and agencies and with local offices where there was significant demand or where the nature of the office made it reasonable that service be available in both languages. But the clauses on services also waded into dangerous waters, spelling out in detail what would happen if a service failed to be provided. The matter would go before the Court of Queen's Bench and the government would be required to produce a plan to ensure respect for the right to be served in French. The court could then approve or change the plan or develop its own plan and direct the government or agency to fulfill it.

Moore said the government believed the detail was required to ensure the court would remedy the problem and not simply punish the government. It was also designed to ensure the court understood it had the power to order the government to spend money – something Canadian courts, unlike their American counterparts, have traditionally been loath to do.

In an accompanying unsigned editorial, the *Free Press* correctly pinpointed the one big criticism of the amendment proposal. It attempted to constitutionalize what the paper referred to as the "settling of old scores" and to burden a document designed to set out "the fixed and fundamental terms of the social and political arrangement between the Canadian state and its people" with housekeeping minutia. Constitution-makers, the paper intoned, should not assume that judges are fools "who need to be led by the hand. Nor should they assume that, in every detail, they know better than their grandchildren ... how shoelaces should be tied and faces washed". Constitution-makers, the editorial continued, should also recognize that they have only a "hazy view of what uses the Manitobans of the next century will make of the constitution they inherit".

Although the paper had a point, its analysis overlooked Manitoba history. "Fixed and fundamental terms" hadn't been sufficient to protect the French community in 1890. From its perspective at least, constitutional guarantees of a "paint by numbers" specificity were not only reassuring but required. The French community had suffered precisely because a hostile majority had taken upon itself the right to "make" its own "uses" of the constitution. But the editorial was clairvoyant on one fundamentally important point:

The amendment is unlikely to pass smoothly through the

Manitoba legislature or through the federal Parliament if it is not well understood and generally accepted by the Manitoba public. If its subsequent implementation produces nasty surprises for the non-French Manitoba public, serious ill-will is likely to result which will not benefit the French-speaking minority. [15]

Surprisingly, neither the media attention nor the growing focus of the opposition Conservatives on the language question in daily question period did much to raise the overt public temperature. The issue smouldered, but never caught fire. Something dramatic and catalytic – either a person or an event – would be required to strike the match.

Prime Minister Pierre Elliott Trudeau was the matchstick and he ignited himself. On May 16, 1983, he came to Winnipeg to address a crowd of Manitoba Liberals at the Fort Garry Hotel. As usual, he switched back and forth between French and English. He chose the French language in which to announce that Manitoba was about to be declared officially bilingual as a result of an agreement in principle reached that week between the federal and provincial governments and the SFM. It took a day for the province's English media to get on top of the story. The prime minister's words were confirmed by all the major actors of the piece.

Other than announcing that the deal to forestall the Bilodeau case, slated to proceed before the Supreme Court on May 26, 1983, had finally been concluded, there was nothing new in what Trudeau said in Winnipeg. The proposal was out there, had been out there, for some time, including the declaration that the province was officially bilingual. It had been explained and assessed in detail by Manitoba's largest daily newspaper more than a month before. But with the intervention of Pierre Trudeau, the fatal link was forged between what Manitoba was proposing to do and the Trudeau Liberals' hated and despised "forced bilingualism" complete with its imagined platoons of skinny-armed bureaucrats forcing French down hapless English-speaking throats and seizing jobs and opportunities away from unilingual anglophones, their children and all generations to come.

On May 19th, the prestigous Québec newspaper, Le Devoir, gave Manitoba's decision to make itself officially bilingual a banner headline on Page One. "Le Manitoba accédera en 1987 au statut de province bilingue" (Manitoba will become a bilingual province in 1987), it said. In a lengthy article datelined Winnipeg, François Barbeau pointed out that the announcement had been made in Winnipeg the previous Monday evening by none other than the prime minister, but because he spoke in French, the largely English-speaking media missed it. Official bilingualism was the basic component of an agreement in principle reached between the federal and provincial governments and the SFM, although all would have to ratify it, he continued.

The newspaper offered its opinion in a front-page editorial published on May 21st illustrated by Manitoba's coat of arms and written by Jean-Louis Roy under the headline "Une obligation historique et morale" (A historic and moral obligation).

After exhaustively reviewing both the terms and reasons for the proposed amendment and noting the criticisms of former premier, now opposition leader, Sterling Lyon, Roy wondered if it wasn't all too late:

LE DEVOIR, MAY 21, 1983

"By waiting almost a century, this type of justice is finally being given back to a minority once important but now reduced to little more than a group limited to the survivors of well-known, exhausting and tragic struggles."

Roy went on to point out the number of Manitobans claiming French as their first language had sunk from fourteen per cent in 1971 to just 12.8 per cent in 1981 and continued:

> Will the new constitutional guarantees be enough to slow
> down assimilation, reclaim the indifferent and, who knows,
> slowly regain the lost ground? The response from one of the
> minority's spokespersons comes spontaneously: we haven't
> waged this long historic battle and this demanding negotia-
> tion only to give up just at the exact moment when at last the
> protections we have so long waited for have finally been
> acquired. The new agreement will apply the brakes to assimi-
> lation, return confidence and bring out of the shadows the
> 50,000 bilingual francophones who will be added to the 30,000
> Manitobans who still declare French as their first language.

> Unaccustomed to making history, Manitoba's cabinet ministers
> retort that they will have done whatever was in their power.
> For them, henceforth, the French community will have access
> to some essential tools for its survival and development ...
> There have been decades of struggle from a community,
> diminished and hurt by unfairness, but still able to be assertive,
> as could be seen in the agreement tabled yesterday in Winnipeg.

La Presse's Vincent Prince wrote that it appeared Manitoba was about to embark on the most ambitious promotion ever of its French fact. Under the headline, "Gains du français en sol manitobain" (French gains on Manitoba soil), his editorial walked readers through the details of the consti-tutional proposal, saying that in exchange for a less onerous statute trans-lation regime, Franco-Manitobans had taken some interesting strides forward.

> Thus, they have ensured that Section 23 of the constitution
> of Manitoba cannot be modified. Above all, they have
> ensured that the province will proclaim itself officially bilin-
> gual in 1987 and, most important, that it is committed to
> provide government services in French where warranted,

also by 1987. This promise would bind the province's central administration and its departments, commissions and
Crown corporations ... In short, the SFM wanted to give
the government time to adjust to the new situation but,
in compensation, has not only safeguarded Section 23 of
the Manitoba constitution but also obtained the means to
enlarge it substantially. Therefore, the Pawley government
demonstrated evidence of an open mind. What remains
to be seen is what will be the concrete meaning of these
changes for the province. [16]

The political opportunity of a lifetime opened before the Manitoba
Conservatives. With a skilled and powerful orator in the person of former
attorney general and premier Sterling Lyon at their helm, they neither hesitated
nor once paused for a second thought. They played the status political card,
plucking the language issue, the government and public opinion like strings
on a guitar. Coded trigger words and phrases designed to evoke maximum
fear and loathing from the body politic dominated daily question period in
the legislature: "secret" negotiations, in which a pampered and undeserving
small minority was cosseted and listened to and from which the vast
majority of Manitobans was excluded; the ignored and mistreated majority
who would be called on only to pay the bills, financial and linguistic; the granting of undeserved and unnecessary constitutionally – entrenched rights to
a few that would be used to trump the democratic rights of the many; and
finally, manipulation by a hated exterior force (the Trudeau government)
with no regard for Manitoba's interests beyond using them as a pawn in a
wider political game.

On May 18, 1983, the day the *Free Press* and other news organizations carried stories on the prime minister's remarks of two days earlier,
Lyon rose at the beginning of question period to ask Premier Howard
Pawley to confirm the prime minister's statement. Superficially, the Tory
leader sounded almost statesmanlike. Noting the negotiations had been in
the public domain for "some several months" he asked if the government
had the "entirely happy" intention to submit the matter to the legislature
for full review and public hearings before proceeding further in order that
"the people of Manitoba might voice their opinions". Pawley replied that
the matter would have to come before the House and added that the

government would consider public hearings.

His voice then dripping with irony, Lyon inquired further whether the legislature and the public would at least see a draft bill "before it is finally sanctified by the Executive Council of Manitoba". Noting that the matter has "been discussed at this stage privately only with the Franco-Manitoban Society" he thought it only proper that "this Legislature and the people of Manitoba" be allowed to be "of whatever help they can to the government in completing a negotiation which is an important one for the people of Manitoba, and one that all parts of Manitoba society will wish to be familiar with before it is finally approved". He concluded by stressing once more the "privileged" position the SFM enjoyed over all other Manitobans and making this trenchant point:

> Can the first minister give the assurance to the House that the Opposition and the people of Manitoba will be able to see what is envisaged in this new agreement that is being contemplated between Canada and Manitoba, which is now being discussed with the Franco-Manitoban Society, but which I suggest, with respect, needs to be discussed even more fully before it is finally ratified?

Pawley only committed to examine ways for "fuller and more complete consultation". [17] The premier, often inarticulate to the point of incomprehensibility when on his feet in extemporaneous debate, was as usual his own worst enemy. He emerged from the exchange looking elitist and anti-democratic and even ignorant of the legislature's rules. Manitoba is one of the few provincial jurisdictions to routinely refer all major bills to an outside legislative committee for public hearings. While not a statute, a constitutional resolution could easily qualify as a matter requiring public input.

Reflecting on the climactic moment from the vantage point of twenty years, Roger Turenne recalled that the attorney general was out of the province at the time of the prime minister's speech and he was the only member of the cabinet really familiar with the file. "Penner wasn't there and that made things ten times worse. We weren't ready. And Trudeau had spilled the beans." [18]

Nor was that the only ineptitude on the part of the government. Its initial handling of the issue was thoughtless and reckless and as much a contributor to the coming crisis as the irresponsible and inexcusable political games-playing by the opposition. Stripped of their loaded trigger words and phrases, Lyon's points were valid. And the government had recent history to tell it so.

The public would no longer tolerate exclusion from a matter as important as a constitutional amendment, whether it was about language or anything else.

During the constitutional patriation struggles of 1981-82, the Trudeau government was forced finally to open up the process beyond the provincial premiers to allow public debate and input, an outcome that gave an enormous boost to Canadians' embrace of the new Canadian constitution and especially, its Charter of Rights and Freedoms. But Manitoba didn't get the message. Less than a year later, it blithely tried to turn back the constitutional clock. Neither Manitoba, nor subsequently, Brian Mulroney's government, first with the Meech Lake Constitutional Accord of 1990 and then, the Charlottetown Accord of 1992, realized that the charter had changed everything. It has transformed the constitution from a musty tome of arcane nineteenth century legalese used by courts to referee Canada's endless federal-provincial turf wars into the peoples' document. Thenceforth, elite accommodation – men in blue suits meeting behind closed doors – as a method of constitution-making or altering had gone the way of the bowler hat. As former NDP cabinet minister Sidney Green observed during the public hearings much later, a constitution cannot be negotiated with a private body, but only with the people.

The provincial government repeatedly cited the looming court case as the reason for the secrecy and haste of the negotiations. But it could have asked the Supreme Court to delay the Bilodeau hearing scheduled for May 1983, a delay the court would have been hard-pressed to refuse since it was being requested to allow a full public debate on a constitutional remedy. Equally vital to securing public legitimacy for a solution to the most volatile and vexatious issue in Manitoba history, the government should have made the opposition a full party to the negotiations from the start. Even the Fathers of Confederation had recognized the value of bipartisanship, arriving for the Charlottetown Conference of 1864 with members of their legislatures' oppositions in tow.

From a historical perspective, though, the behaviour of both political players was only too predictable and familiar. Like the Bourbons in Talleyrand's famous comment, Manitoba's political parties had learned nothing and forgotten nothing when it came to the most vexed question of the province's history. Their behaviour descended in direct line from the truculence and bigotry (Conservatives) and misunderstanding and insensitivity (NDP) of 1890, 1916 and 1980. But this time, the stakes were much higher, because this time, the issue was to be fully joined by the Franco-Manitoban community and a national political consensus, with the whole nation watching.

The government quickly went into crisis mode. "A decision was taken to isolate the premier from the storm. One of his aides was quite blunt: 'The attorney general got us into this. He can twist in the wind.' Unfortunately, this meant the government began to act as though Lyon was right." [19] The attempt to isolate the premier was as inadvisable as it was impossible.

Two days later, on May 20th, Penner stood up in the legislature to unveil the constitutional amendment in a short, unemotional speech reciting the tangled legal history of all the court cases that had brought Manitoba to its current crossroads. Georges Forest had come to hear the attorney general and the leader of the opposition but decided to eschew the public gallery and to listen instead with a small group of journalists in the second floor *Winnipeg Free Press* gallery office. Penner noted at the outset that the Manitoba Act of 1870 "made Manitoba bilingual in certain respects". Still, he was at pains to assure English-speaking Manitobans that their lives would be unaffected.

> (The agreement) seeks to correct anomalies created by breaches of the constitution for over ninety years in Manitoba. It seeks to address the long term question of the status of the French language in Manitoba in a reasonable and practical manner that does not affect the situation of any Manitoban who does not want to be affected ... It seeks to assist the francophone community to maintain itself as a viable entity in this province without imposing any obligation whatever on the vast majority of Manitobans who do not speak French ... It is important to point out again and to emphasize that this obligation (the provision of services in the French language) is one undertaken by the government and does not affect any individual, any corporation, or any non-governmental institution; nor does it apply to any school board.

The attorney general told the legislature the federal government had agreed to provide Manitoba with $2.4 million over the next eight years to assist in translation and personnel and help those municipalities who wished to establish their own bilingual municipal services. Franco-Manitobans, he concluded, are an essential and vital part of Manitoba's diverse and cosmopolitan culture. The agreement, he said, "is an achievement of which all Manitobans

can be proud". It was slated to come into effect December 31, 1983. This
deadline and the government's repeated insistence that nothing in the
amendment or the agreement could be changed because it would require
the consent of the other parties was to become another major flashpoint of
public anger. Yet the lesson wasn't learned. Seven years later, Prime Minister
Brian Mulroney and the ten premiers would try to play the same kind of
High Noon politics over the Meech Lake Constitutional Accord, only to
find they had only intensified Canadians' anger and resistance.

Lyon's reply started with a ringing defence of his government's
actions in 1980 in response to the 1979 ruling striking down the 1890
English-only law. He, of course, was never to concede that those actions had
been deeply flawed, as the pursuit of further court actions testified. In
essence, they perpetuated the injustice of 1890 by making English legally
superior to French and deeming constitutional language rights mere "courte-
sies" to be granted or limited at will by the majority. Warming to his topic,
Lyon launched into his denunciation of the government's proposed amendment by tearing apart the rationale for it in the first place. The premise of
the Bilodeau case, that all unilingual laws passed since 1890 were invalid
thus throwing the province into chaos was a "practical absurdity ... Mr.
Speaker, the law does not permit an absurdity ... the courts cannot impose
the impossible, any more than King Canute can hold back the tides". Why,
then, he asked, was the government so concerned about the case that it went
ahead and negotiated an agreement that would be "more onerous" than anything the court might order?

The Conservatives were prepared to pay the money required to do
the translation, he continued. Certainly it was preferable to the "trouble" that
lay ahead in the agreement. Then he played the status politics card on the
issues of official bilingualism and judge-made law, even drawing a comparison with the race issue in the southern United States:

> I suggest, with respect, Mr. Speaker, that Section 23 did not
> make Manitoba a bilingual province. It provided for bilin-
> gual services to be provided in certain stated institutions in
> Manitoba, period, paragraph ... I suggest, Sir, that the pro-
> vision ... about the court being available to persons who
> feel aggrieved under the agreement, that is a very dangerous
> provision. Deciding how this will be implemented should

be a decision made by the legislature, not by the courts and
I foresee grave problems, such as arise in the United States,
where court-ordered busing and so on has caused grave
social disorder in that country. This kind of court-ordered
bilingualism, Sir, is a violation of our whole tradition of
parliamentary supremacy in this country, and I can regrettably foresee the kind of social divisiveness arising out of
this section, if it were ever to be implemented; inviting
people to go to court to litigate this very agreement … that
should be intended to bring about unity in our country and
our province.

But the former premier was not finished. He still had two more
status-issue grenades to throw onto the chamber's blue carpet in the expectation their explosions would reverberate throughout the length and breadth of
the province. Manitoba, he said, had "capitulated" to the federal government
and set up a "tyranny" of a tiny minority. This was all about the linguistic
rights "for six per cent of our citizens in this province.

[W]e must be ever vigilant that we do not create a tyranny
by that very minority, because that, Sir, in some ways, is
what has happened with respect to the implementation of
the Official Languages Act in other parts of this country.
Legislation that could lead to the kinds of administrative
excesses seen elsewhere must be studiously avoided in
Manitoba. I suggest, Sir, that the social fabric of the province
cannot and should not be made hostage to what Chief Justice
Freedman referred to in his judgement in the Forest case as
'intransigent assertion of abstract rights' by language zealots.

The legislature, Lyon concluded, cannot "inflict on our province
some form of locked-in constitutional change which the people may well
reject". All action on the agreement should be immediately suspended and it
should be sent to an intersessional all-party committee to hold province-wide
hearings and report back to the legislature at its 1984-85 session. He and his
party were, he said finally, prepared to be called anti-French, "to take that
abuse if, indeed, it is forthcoming".

A shocked silence fell over the House, broken only when the speaker

called for the introduction of bills and Tory backbencher Abe Kovnats
stood up to introduce an act to amend an act to incorporate Winnipeg
Bible College and Theological Seminary. [20] Later, outside the chamber,
Penner told reporters that Lyon's response was "expected, skilled and
disappointing". [21]

In the second floor press gallery office, a dejected and white-faced
Georges Forest was gathering his papers, his usual cheery good humour
gone. He had been quiet throughout most of Lyon's peroration. But when
the former premier made his references to school busing in the American
South and the creation of social disorder, he couldn't stay silent any longer.
"He has opened Pandora's box," he said, more in sadness than in anger. Earlier
in the week, Forest had told the *Winnipeg Sun* he had seen the constitutional
agreement and was now prepared to endorse it. Calling the proposals, particularly the declaration that Manitoba was officially bilingual, a major step in
the right direction, Forest continued: "I'm beginning to develop a feeling of
enthusiasm." [22]

Some 600 members of the Franco-Manitoban community ratified
the proposed constitutional agreement by an overwhelming vote of 576 to
eleven at a meeting called by the SFM on May 24th. The atmosphere was cele-
bratory, almost tumultuous, with SFM president Léo Robert receiving two
standing ovations. "Being able to live in French in one's home is something
special," Robert told his audience. "We'll be able to deal with our provincial
government in our maternal language." [23] Recalls Jacqueline Blay: "The joy
and pride are still difficult to express even after so many years." [24]

Meanwhile, the Conservative opposition in the legislature was daily
discovering new ways to fan public fears about the agreement, the government's motives and competence and, by implication, the supposed linguistic
intransigence and zealotry of Franco-Manitobans. Tory justice critic Gerry
Mercier told the House the translation costs would likely top $20 million,
while only twenty-five copies of French statutes had been requested from the
Queen's Printer since 1979. Both claims were refuted by the government.

On June 4th, federal Tory leader Joe Clark, in the midst of a leadership campaign, waded into the language imbroglio with a warning to the
Manitoba government that it risked a backlash by moving too quickly to
restore official bilingualism. He told *Le Devoir* that the government should let
the Supreme Court decide on the Bilodeau case to demonstrate to Manitobans
that the government had no choice but to make Manitoba bilingual. The

same day, the *Winnipeg Free Press* published a spate of letters that were, if anything, a mild rendition of what was to come.

"Linguistic equality leads to dissension and to heavy costs," wrote Travis McCullough of Carman. "Bilingualism in Canada is a passable French and a bastardized English like that of Jean Chrétien and Marc Lalonde. English is, without question, the best language from all points of view." French was a language in retreat around the world, the language of the cradle and priests. Canada would be set back 100 years if it were made bilingual, wrote Mary McGimpsey. French immersion fosters elitism, not a spirit of brotherhood and understanding. Ian MacPherson said Pawley was ready to betray the English-speaking people of Manitoba. And Mike Krycun said Manitobans should decide whether the province becomes bilingual or not. The NDP government didn't have a mandate to make the province bilingual. "If we have need of another language in Manitoba, it should be Ukrainian or German, not French."

The temperature was steadily rising in the legislature. Penner accused Lyon of deliberate distortion and scare tactics. Lyon said Penner had "sold the farm". The Tories made lavish use of the word "bilingualization". The issue quickly ran ahead and away from the government, which gave every indication of having blundered into it without the slightest comprehension of what might happen, with no strategy and without even the ability to see it needed one – and fast. A partial explanation for this came nearly two decades later. At an historic symposium at the University of Manitoba in the fall of 1999 involving all four of Manitoba's surviving premiers, Pawley said he had canvassed Duff Roblin and Ed Schreyer and had been assured by both of them that their experiences with the French language issue indicated its incendiary propensities had finally died away.

There were major reasons for the difference in 1983-84. Both Roblin and Schreyer had built consensus as they moved forward with their policy changes. Neither was dealing with a constitutional change. Perhaps most important, neither was facing a Sterling Lyon as opposition leader. As well, the two former premiers were accomplished and skilled in the art of political leadership in sharp contrast to the soft-spoken country lawyer from Selkirk about whom one Young New Democrat once cracked: "Howard's idea of fun on a Saturday night is to go down to Eaton's and try on gloves." Pawley never had a taste for hand-to-hand political combat and was constantly taken to the floor of the legislature, verbally battered and bloodied, by the astute and articulate Lyon.

In the early going, the attorney general was the government's point man on the language issue. Roland Penner was a political neophyte, who had been in the legislature for less than two years. Of Jewish and Mennonite background, he was the son of Jacob Penner, one of Winnipeg's small but influential band of Communist city councillors and school trustees. Penner served in the Royal Canadian Artillery during the Second World War and entered the University of Manitoba in 1946. He was a member of the university's debating teams who won the McGown Cup and the Dominion Debating Championships in 1949. That same year, he was awarded the university's gold medal in English. Upon graduation from law school, he articled with and subsequently became a partner in the law firm of Joseph Zuken, another Communist city councillor who won wide admiration and respect for his measured and informed opinions on civic affairs in a career that spanned almost forty years. In 1979, Zuken came close to being elected Winnipeg's mayor.

Penner joined the university's law faculty in 1967, achieving full professor in 1972. Although a dedicated Communist in his youth, he slowly cut his ties to the party, accepting a Queen's Counsel from the Schreyer government and eventually joining the NDP. First elected in 1981, he represented the trendy small-l liberal constituency of Fort Rouge. The Conservatives were appalled and scandalized to see a "Marxist-Leninist" take his seat in the government front bench. They never missed an opportunity to excoriate him for his past political affiliations and the premier for his effrontery in making him a minister of the Crown. He was called "Red Rolly" and the "Rouge from Fort Penner". As an urbane and sophisticated intellectual, Penner immediately grasped and identified with the constitutional and moral force behind the Franco-Manitoban case. As a lawyer, he saw the language issue as a legal problem to be solved in the normal way legal problems are, by negotiations between the two parties. He simply assumed all other Manitobans would see the eminent good sense in helping people (language services for a historically-abused official minority) in exchange for saving money (federal help with translation and associated costs). He recognized immediately what the Conservatives were up to, but demonstrated his political inexperience and historical oversight by being genuinely shocked when it paid off so handsomely.

There was no doubt the constitutional amendment went beyond the actual words of the original Manitoba Act. University of Ottawa constitutional lawyer Joseph Magnet, who had assisted the SFM in its negotiations, told the *Globe and Mail* the accord would make Manitoba almost as bilingual as New

Brunswick, certainly more bilingual than either Ontario or Québec and a model for the rest of the country in minority language rights. [25] However, given that the scope of government was much broader in 1980 than in 1870, a case could be made that the intent of the language of Section 23 in 1870 did require bilingual services in 1980. Certainly the identical language in Section 133 of the British North America Act was the basis for the historic rights of anglophone Québécois to speak to their provincial government in their own language as well as to their own schools, universities, hospitals, churches and other historic social and economic institutions. Certainly, too, it had been the rationale behind the federal Official Languages Act of 1970. It is illogical to suggest the framers of the Manitoba constitution believed the francophone majority of 1870 was to be allowed to use its language in the legislature and courts only and nowhere else in public and everyday life.

The loaded language reverberating in the legislature throughout the month of June 1983 was having its own impact on Manitoba's everyday life. On June 9th, veteran NDP MLA Russ Doern announced he was prepared to break ranks and oppose his own government on the constitutional amendment if the public was not consulted. He said he was sending a mail-in poll to 7,500 homes, apartments and businesses in his northeastern Winnipeg constitutency of Elmwood. Average Manitobans had a right to be heard, he told reporters. "All we know to date is that (the agreement) has the overwhelming approval of the French community ... If the poll is overwhelmingly against and there is no provision for the public to be heard, I would certainly be opposed." [26]

Doern, a history teacher, had long been sympathetic to Franco-Manitoban causes. Like Lyon, however, he was adamantly opposed to entrenched rights, willing only to provide them in regulations and legislation readily repealed or amended. He embraced the Diefenbaker view that constitutional rights for French Canadians turned all other non-anglophones into third class Canadians. There also was more than a suspicion that his actions were motivated by political revenge. A cabinet minister in the Schreyer years, he had run for the leadership against Pawley and been furious when he was relegated to the back benches by his former nemesis.

Alone or as the leader of the growing army of anti-bilingual crusaders, Doern was as important in fomenting and sustaining the crisis as the Tories. He quickly became as potent an opponent of the constitutional agreement as all the Tories put together He had a populist flair, was effective at crafting

The Canadian Crucible

grassroots campaigns and slogans (he coined the oft-used phrase "the Pawley-Penner-Pierre deal"), glib on radio talk shows and adept at blowing up and riding "waves" of public anger. As such, he was an invaluable complement to the Tories, creating the populist half of a two-pronged assault to bring the government to its knees procedurally in the legislature and politically in the all-important arena of public opinion.

On June 15th, Pat Maltman, a fifty-two-year-old registered nurse who, with her husband, ran a small Scottish imports shop, delivered a petition with 250 names to the premier's office demanding a plebiscite. She insisted she wasn't against bilingualism, just to the high-handed attitude of the government. But then she went on to express sentiments that became the signature of the anti-bilingual movement:

> I'm not against bilingualism. I am against the fact the
> government is not going to ask us if we want bilingualism.
> The government has not got the right to say we do. I feel
> very strongly that for a very long time, we have sat by
> and watched things pushed on the country with very little
> thought about how people feel … Manitobans will have
> their due right to vote for or against this province being
> declared bilingual. It is costly and favours the minority. I
> don't believe minorities should have the right to override
> the majority. [27]

Joined by Bill Hutton, a former provincial NDP president, Maltman began a drive to force a civic referendum on the issue. Two days after she launched her campaign, the Conservatives, stealing a leaf from their federal counterparts' strategy book, accused the government of imposing bilingualism on Manitoba, challenged the premier to call an election and walked out of the house on an adjournment motion and stayed out, leaving the bells summoning the members to vote on the motion to ring for ninety minutes before re-entering the chamber. Bell-ringing, in effect a parliamentary strike or work stoppage, was a unique invention of the federal Tories. They had used it in 1981 to force the Liberals to break up an omnibus bill.

Bell-ringing is the nuclear bomb in the arsenal of parliamentary tactics, the ultimate weapon, the coup d'etat. Through it, the opposition seizes power. With parliament shut down, the government is prevented from proceeding with the public's business, in effect, prevented from governing.

L'NOUVEAU LIVRE DE L'EXHIBITIONNISTE

RÉAL BÉRARD (CAYOUCHE) / LA LIBERTÉ

The new book of the exhibitionist

Under parliamentary and legislative rules, the speaker cannot call a vote unless the whips of both the government and the opposition come into the chamber. Bell-ringing was to become the Tories' chief weapon in the weeks and months ahead, culminating in a full-blown governmental and constitutional crisis. In the Manitoba Legislature, bell-ringing is more than an assault on parliamentary democracy; it is an actual physical assault. Manitoba's bells are fire alarms and they reverberate through the cavernous marble floored and stone hallways at a decibel level unbearable to be near. There was a striking irony to the tactic: one (legislative) minority crushing a majority to ensure that another majority could continue to crush a (linguistic) minority.

The increasing fury of the opposition – at one point Lyon accused the government of saying "to hell with the people of Manitoba, we'll pass it anyway" – [28] was met by equal intransigence from the government in the crucial early going when public opinion was being formed. Fixated on avoiding the court challenge and keeping the parties to the constitutional compromise together, the New Democrats fashioned a rod for their own backs which the opposition was only too glad to seize and apply. The political optics were terrible, especially for a party of the left – a constitutional change arising from a "secret" negotiation with a small private organization most

Manitobans knew little or nothing about, no public consultation and no possibility of change.

On June 17th, the *Winnpeg Sun* reported that fifty of Manitoba's 200 municipalities had passed resolutions condemning the agreement even though it only called for twenty-nine municipalities to provide services in French on a voluntary basis. Worse still for the government, Reeve Francis Benoit of the heavily-francophone RM of Ste. Anne south of Winnipeg said the agreement had not sparked any interest in his community and so "we left it neutral". René Maillard, mayor of Ste-Rose, another francophone community in western Manitoba, said he never had any requests. "We wouldn't have the funds anyway. It's bad enough for us to go metric." John Rankin, reeve of the RM of Hamiota, called it "highly unnecessary ... How soon ... until two people can demand it?" By June 23rd, about half of Manitoba's municipalities had adopted resolutions condemning provincial bilingualism proposals. A spokesman for the Union of Manitoba Municipalities tallied ninety and projected the number would reach 110 by the next week. "We simply believe this is the tip of the iceberg," said one official. "We're opening up something here." [29]

The government bent a bit. It would hold "informational" meetings around the province to explain the purpose and extent of the proposed amendment. They would be chaired by Jack London, dean of the University of Manitoba law school. This angered the Conservatives even more. They quickly branded the information sessions "propaganda" and cast aspersions on the character and political affiliation of the law school dean.

Radisson NDP MLA Gérard Lécuyer, the NDP caucus chair, became the target of particularly venomnous attacks in the legislature. He infuriated the Tories because, as NDP backbencher Don Scott explained, he was "the only francophone MLA who's kept his roots. He speaks French at home and in the House and he fights for his rights". [30] During one heated exchange, Lyon shot across the House at him: "Do we hear something from the lily pad on the far bench there?" Tory backbencher Don Orchard called him "Kermit the Frog" during one heated exchange. And in his major address on the amendment July 12th, the Tory leader labelled Lécuyer a "zealot" and a "zealot fool". [31]

On June 22nd, the *Free Press* weighed in with an editorial entitled "A Narrow View":

"We love you to death".

The Canadian Crucible

Conservative leader Sterling Lyon proposes a narrow, defensive and mean-spirited policy on the protection of language rights for French-speaking Manitobans. In scarcely a year and a half, he has lost touch with the social and political realities which led his government to adopt a line more consistent with the history and ethnic makeup of this province, with the requirements of constitutional logic and with the role Manitoba plays in Canada …

The spirit of Section 23 involves a kind of symmetry between Québec and Manitoba. It invites Manitoba to do unto its French-speaking citizens as it would have Québec do unto its English … The same narrow, angry spirit which led René Lévesque and Camille Laurin and their colleagues to try to wipe English off the official face of Québec leads Sterling Lyon to try to contain within the tightest possible limits the place of French in the institutions of Manitoba. A group of 60,000 or so in a population of a million poses no threat to Mr. Lyon and his language. There is no danger that his children or his children's children will be dragooned into Francization by swarming hordes of Franco-Manitobans …

The same day that editorial was published, Doern left the NDP caucus on the basis of a mutual agreement. He had appeared on an open-line radio show without advance notice. He told reporters he would continue to support the government on all other matters but would use his freedom to oppose the bilingual measure. The next day he called a news conference to announce 93.3 per cent of the 433 responses he had received to his constituency canvass opposed the government's position while just twenty-six signalled support. He warned the constitutional amendment wouldn't help the Franco-Manitoban cause. "People in Manitoba are going to resent this privilege and this expenditure." [32]

Organizations representing Québec's anglophone minority began to speak out in defence of the embattled Manitoba government, its agreement and Manitoba francophones. McGill University constitutional law professor Stephen Scott, who provided legal advice to the Positive Action Committee, told the *Free Press* that Manitoba was playing a role in the renewal of Confederation. He accused the Tory leader of stirring up "fears and hatreds. He has done a great deal of damage." [(33)].

The major English rights group, Alliance Québec, sent its its president, Eric Maldoff, to Manitoba to plead for understanding and generosity towards linguistic minorities in both provinces. In an interview, Maldoff warned that the actions of the opposition Conservatives were being reported widely in Québec and were helping to "fuel the fires" of separatism and French unilingualism in that province. He also said English-speaking Manitobans should be aware that even with the Parti Québécois' restrictive Bill 101, the English minority in Québec still enjoyed far more rights than the French minority anywhere else in Canada. [(34)] Maldoff told the *Winnipeg Sun* the Manitoba language battle was "just the kind of issue Lévesque has been praying for. In the face of what would be seen as a massive emotional outpouring against the French language from Manitoba, French-speaking Quebecers, who've been moving towards a much more open attitude towards Canada and Québec, would step back and ask if they'd been mistaken." [(35)]

The *Winnipeg Sun* delivered a stern rebuke to the government's foes on June 26th:

> The Tory-Doern opposition seems to be based on a belief that Manitoba is a unilingual province whose government has decided to extend official language rights to a linguistic minority. If that were true, the opposition stand would have some credibility …
> But Manitoba is not a unilingual province and never has been …
> For Doern and the Conservatives to assail the negotiated settlement as a giveaway shows a disregard for the facts of Manitoba's history.

By the end of June, the government was signalling it would consider a free vote and changes to the amendment if the other parties would agree. Still, the pressure from the Conservatives and from Doern increased. The Tories wanted intersessional public hearings; Doern was siding with the Maltman forces to demand a plebiscite. On June 29th, a noisy band of eighty angry protesters, all wearing tags bearing the single word "No", jammed a committee room at the legislature to oppose the extension of French language services. One woman, claiming to be French Canadian, left in angry tears after telling the attorney general that the SFM didn't represent her, it only represented the federal government. Dennis Epps of the Canada Western Federation, an Alberta-based right-wing protest movement and one of the few protesters prepared to give his name to reporters, said bilingualism was "a helluva waste of money ... All we want to do is have Québec leave us." [36] The Tories staged a second bell-ringing "strike" against the legislature, this time keeping the house adjourned for nearly an hour in a further protest over Jack London's informational meetings, slated to begin on July 7th.

The government chose Dauphin, Brandon, Thompson and Winnipeg for the meetings. The crowds were generally small in the first three communities, perhaps because they conflicted with the beginning of summer holidays. Dauphin attracted eighty, Brandon 150 and Thompson, sixty. Most presenters tended to grumble and complain, in sharp contrast to the emotional binge going on in the legislature. Teacher Earl Moberg of Dauphin said entrenchment of the right to services in the French language would promote disunity with Manitoba's other ethnic groups. Moberg, of Swedish descent, said, "I see money spent on French and there's no opportunity for me to bring up my kids in my culture." Clarence Kiesman, the reeve of Grahamdale, said he had "no sympathy, no time and no money" for minority groups. No other group was pressing for rights except "the Indians, and who are they learning it from?" The day he had to translate his municipality's bylaws into French

RÉAL BÉRARD (CAYOUCHE) / LA LIBERTÉ / JULY 1, 1983

OYÉ! OYÉ! CANADIENS... QU'NEZ VOUS BEN! CAR VOUS ÊTES À LA VEILLE DE VOIR APARAÎTRE DE NOUVEAU, LE COMBLE DE LA BASSESSE AU MANITOBA; LE MÊME SALE JEU PAR LE MÊME PARTI POLITIQUE.

C.C.: BRIAN MULRONEY

OYE! OYE! French Canadians ... HOLD ON TIGHT! Because you are about to witness again, hate on the verge of exploding in Manitoba; the same dirty games by the same political party.

would be the day he would resign, he said. A man sitting in the front row at the Dauphin meeting said Kiesman should be elected premier. [37] In Winnipeg, however, more than 800 showed up and the crowd booed London roundly when he made the mistake of opening the meeting with a few words in French.

In the legislature the next day, maverick New Democrat Russ Doern appealed to the premier to permit a province-wide referendum on the constitutional proposal, an idea that was dismissed with a curt "no" from Pawley. Then the Elmwood MLA accused the province's French language weekly newspaper, *La Liberté,* of bigotry for a cartoon (previous page) published in its July 1st edition. The cartoon, which Doern distributed in the chamber, showed himself and the Conservative caucus dressed in Ku Klux Klan garb desecrating Louis Riel's grave, burning down the SFM headquarters and cavorting about wielding ropes, axes and lances. Lyon was portrayed as an Anglo-Saxon burning the Canadian flag. Doern said he wouldn't sue. "If they want to get in the gutter and fight, then I'm not going to get in the gutter and fight with them." [38]

On June 24th, under a cartoon of a caveman Lyon holding an ``English-only`` bat over the bruised head of a downed Franco-Manitoban, *La Liberté's* Bernard Bocquel wrote: "The valiant leader of the Opposition, who recently announced his pending departure from public life, has done it again. It's official. Sterling Conservative Lyon firmly intends to make the anti-French of 1916 look like amateurs."

But Franco-Manitobans soon learned that they weren't alone. Beginning with a meeting on July 12th, individuals representing a cross-section of the province's major ethnic organizations started speaking out in favour of the government initiative and the official language minority. Those favouring the agreement between Ottawa, the province and the SFM included members of the Ukrainian, Jewish, Métis, German, Portuguese, Italian and Chinese communities. "If the rights of the francophones are denied (in Manitoba) then the rights of any other multicultural group in Canada could just as easily be denied," said Terry Prychitko of the Ukrainian Canadian Community Development Committee. "If French rights are denied, then it's much easier to deny the Ukrainians, the Germans and the Jews," added Dany Waldman, chairman of Manitoba Parents for Hebrew Education. "Twenty-five per cent of Canada is French," said Harry Schellenberg, president of the Manitoba Parents for German Education. "Like it or not, they're here. Historically and constitutionally, they have this right [to a more bilingual province]." [39] Dr. Yantai Tsai,

The Canadian Crucible

past president of the Winnipeg chapter of the Chinese National Council came on board after attending the rowdy standing-room-only government informational meeting at the International Inn where Penner was repeatedly shouted down and London's use of French and any mention of the French language brought loud choruses of boos. Dr. Tsai told the *Globe and Mail* he was "taken aback … If this sort of thinking prevails, then it is very easy for a government to take away the rights of other minorities." [40] SFM lawyer Remi Smith, the adopted son of Senator Joe Guay, a former federal cabinet minister, was heartened. "The day of the rule by the pure WASP is over," he said.

Doern attempted to discredit this support in a letter published in the *Free Press* July 30th as only a "handful" who were "unrepresentative" both of their associations and their members. Doern had a point. The organizations representing Canada's ethnic mosaic derive much of their funding from Ottawa and Ottawa was keen to assist them in their pro-Franco-Manitoban campaign.

On July 4th, Penner opened second reading debate on the constitutional resolution, declaring that minority language rights for the English in Québec and the French in Canada were "one of the foundation stones upon which Confederation was built … and without which Confederation, in my judgement, would not have been possible." He offered three reasons for seeking the constitutional amendment rather than, as the opposition wished, letting the Bilodeau case proceed to the Supreme Court. The first was Canada's new constitution and Charter of Rights and Freedoms, both of which enhanced the original guarantees of minority language rights in Canada.

> … [G]iven that we were now living in a new constitutional era … it would have posed an enormous difficulty for the Supreme Court to find that the word "shall" in Section 23 of the Manitoba Act merely meant "may". It would have destroyed, within less than a year of the enactment of this new constitutional regime – and remember all the agony that went into forging this new constitutional regime – it would have torn that fabric apart at one fell blow. It did not seem likely to me that the Supreme Court indeed would do that …

Secondly, Manitoba already had a record of "zero for two" in the Supreme Court fighting language rights. But most important of all to the attorney general would be the dire consequences both provincially and nationally for Manitoba to once again seek to ignore and repeal its constitutional responsibilities to its official language minority.

> There would be no victors, there would be only losers. It would be a blow to constitutional guarantees ... It would be open for people to say [the constitution] is a piece of paper; it's worthless because it's unenforceable; "shall" only means "may"; there is no remedial strength to the constitution; it would be a blow – let there be no doubt about that – to Canadian unity. It would leave ... a residue of bitterness we could not possibly dissipate in our lifetime; indeed, that would be a victory, would it not? It would be a Pyrrhic victory and we could all keep our hands warm over the ashes of constitutional guarantees. So we sought an agreement – not a dishonourable thing to do – the kind of thing that one does day in and day out when faced with a particularly complex or difficult issue before the courts ...

Penner walked the MLAs through the agreement and then read into the record the Lyon government's cabinet memorandum of October 6, 1980 detailing the Conservatives' plans for French language services. They were indistinguishable from the amendment except, of course, that they were ordinary regulations and not constitutionally entrenched. The memo stated all government departments should equip themselves to serve the public in French. This would entail the hiring of bilingual civil servants where circumstances warranted as well as language training opportunities for civil servants. Speaking directly to the Tory benches opposite, the attorney general continued: "These are your own words and your own decisions. They are, they are. Now they have come to haunt you ... when it suited you politically. That, Sir, in other places is called hypocrisy." [41]

Lyon shouted over the din in the House: "You have entrenched it, you fool. Don't you see that?" [42] Penner shot back that Lyon couldn't have it both ways. He couldn't argue that the Supreme Court would be reasonable about the legality of Manitoba's body of unilingual laws while claiming that other courts would be completely doctrinaire when adjudicating the rights to French language services.

The attorney-general closed by appealing to history and magnaminity

– finally giving the issue the historical, constitutional and national importance that was its due.

> Sir, there is one final issue ... the most important issue, and that is the issue of Canadian unity, a fragile thing throughout our history but under severe strain now. Let no one underestimate the strain that Canadian unity is under, and no more so than with our fellow Canadians in Québec ... beguiled, all too many of them, with the notion that they cannot exist as a culture in Canada. These people are looking to the leadership that Manitoba can give ... What we say and what we do here will play a tremendous role ... in countering the divisiveness which exploits the notion of two solitudes, exploits that which apparently divides us, ignores that which clearly unites us ... Let us, I implore, deal with the real issues ... Let us rise above narrow political advantage ... Let us pay that debt which we owe to our history. Let us pay it with dignity. Let us pay it with responsibility. Let us rise above the negative and paranoic politics of linguistic conspiracy ... Let us tell Manitobans you have nothing to fear. Let us tell Manitobans you have everything to gain. You will have not only paid history's debt ... you have done something for Canadian unity that will live long in the history books, long after we have left this place of noise, strife and turmoil." [43]

If the attorney general harboured any illusions that his words might make a difference, he was quickly disabused. The Conservative leader was not about to let go of the issue. Each of his successive lengthy orations on the subject honed his legal and political rhetorical knife to greater sharpness. The government members visibly crumpled before the onslaught. The public galleries that grew fuller every day often had to be admonished by the speaker to cease their demonstrations of enthusiastic approval. It was as though the first premier in Manitoba history to be defeated after only one term in office was, by the power of his oratory and the certainty of his convictions and the effect they were having on public opinion, wresting the premiership back from a leader and government he clearly viewed as weak and inferior.

Decisions over the extension of French language services would be removed forever from the legislature and placed in the hands of non-elected and non-accountable judges, he declared again and again. Taxpayers would face paying for endless litigation by "language zealots" to "keep the socialist hive buzzing".

The agreement would "hold one million Manitobans hostage … It never was a constitutional imperative that French and English are the official languages of Manitoba," he said. And he played the Trudeau/bilingualization card. "The Trudeau government and the Société franco-manitobaine can't dictate the policies of this province. This legislature does." He accused the Pawley government of capitulating to the federal government and adopting the "official bilingualism policy of the Trudeaucrats" that had been implemented in a "ham-handed and bull-headed" way. The amendment, he said, went far beyond what was needed, insisting no court would throw the province into legal chaos, let alone compel Manitoba to establish a costly and unnecessary program of French services. And he demanded that the views of all Manitobans be heard, punctuating his insistence with caucus walkouts and lengthy episodes of bell-ringing that shut the legislature down and prevented the government from carrying on any business.

Penner at class.

His main response to the constitutional resolution was given on July 12th, eight days after Penner's moderate and moving speech. It was vintage Lyon, a tour de force that was polished, scornful and crafted to awaken every racial and linguistic antagonism in the body politic:

> Mr. Speaker, are we only here in the minds of these socialists talking about costs? I thought we were here debating principles. I know, Mr. Speaker, that principle is a stranger to their

The Canadian Crucible

thought processes most of the time but they are going to
debate principle today whether they like it or not ... A court
... cannot order the impossible. I know that is new to a zealot
like the member for Radisson [Lécuyer] ... In their coarse
and gutteral [sic] and bovine approach to this matter, all
they have done is stirred up Manitobans, they haven't tried to
explain anything and I'm attempting to explain to Manitobans
how this incompetent government got themselves into this
pickle ... That statement of Manitoba being a bilingual
province just isn't true, it's not true historically, it's not true
politically; it's not true legally. It has never been true that
Manitoba was conceived as a bilingual province ...

To explain the origins of the constitutional amendment, Lyon read
into the record a speech federal Secretary of State Serge Joyal gave to the SFM
on March 19, 1983. In it, Joyal told the SFM it "held the keys to restoring the
equal status of French in Manitoba ... to make French a language equal, not
only in law but in fact as well". Joyal spoke of the need to keep Canada's
special character "as fundamentally French as it was English", to strengthen
French language cultural and educational institutions and to support a greater
French presence in muncipal and school board governance. Continued Lyon:

We find a kind of coalition between the Trudeaus and the
Pawleys of this world with respect to what they are going
to do with Manitoba ... Mr. Speaker, I suggest after reading
those quotations to you from the federal minister ... that we
can see the guiding hand with respect to the agreement ...
an agreement that was consummated in a form of political
perfidy between the Trudeau government and the socialist
government of this province ... I hate to use the street phrase,
Mr. Speaker, but this NDP socialist government has demonstrated that it is in bed with the Trudeau Liberals ...

Lyon said the government had no more business negotiating a fundamental constitutional change with the SFM with a membership of about
600 or 700 people than it would with the Interlake Committee of Ukrainian
Canadians or the Selkirk Legion.

Mr. Speaker, I say to you as humbly as I can, does this

government realize what it is doing? I'm afraid they don't. I'm afraid that in their zeal to accommodate Mr. Trudeau and to accommodate Mr. Joyal and to accommodate the Franco-Manitoban Society or anybody else, Mr. Speaker, who may come along and say "boo" to them; that they have not ... sold the farm, they have given the farm away. There is no need in any constitutional amendment to Section 23 to state what has never been stated before, that English and French are the official languages of Manitoba because they never have been except as provided in Section 23 for the purposes of the courts and the legislature and the printing of the statutes ... So we're left to conjure that my honourable friends opposite in their zeal to co-operate with the federal government ... are trading off the birthright of Manitobans, trading off the constitutional history of this province, trading off, Mr. Speaker, the total history of this province for their own petty, partisan purposes and trying to leave this province with an entrenched irreversible constitutional amendment which is not in sympathy with or in accord with the background or the history or the tradition of this province in any way whatsoever ...

He said he had no doubt the SFM had asked for bilingual rights as a matter of negotiation, never dreaming any government would be such a "doormat" as to agree. "But they found one". He closed by again demanding public hearings or failing that, a provincial election. "Let the final judgement on this matter be that of the people, not of a disintegrating majority of a socialist government in this House. [44]

On July 11th, Roger Turenne, head of the government's French Language Secretariat, announced that implementation of the French language services policy initiated by the former Lyon government was one-third completed and both it and the amendment would leave ninety-seven per cent of the province's civil service jobs unilingual. Nothing was new except the entrenchment. "We're giving a constitutional foundation to a program that's been ongoing." Bilingual services will not cost the taxpayer because many civil servants are already bilingual and can be transferred into jobs requiring their language skills. "It's a gradual, systematic approach. Much is in the organization of existing resources." Many Franco-Manitobans felt intimidated if not frightened by the growing backlash because they are a steadily-diminishing minority, he continued. They may even be prepared to give up rights to maintain peace for themselves and their families. "They're scared of people like Doern and Lyon because they are vulnerable." [45]

Turenne merely set out the pain and anguish that was already engulfing the francophone community, but in the process he infuriated Lyon. The next day in the House the opposition leader accused him of partisanship and threatened to fire him if the Tories returned to power. Turenne had become *persona non grata* to the government, too. Fallen victim to the NDP's frantic attempt to cool passions, he was ordered to become invisible and forbidden to talk to Penner. It was a decision that would boomerang on the government because it meant that the civil servant most familiar with the file was placed outside the loop just at the time decisions were being made about the delivery of minority language services. "I had all the information, but the people drafting the services legislation couldn't talk to me," he recalls. [46]

It was left to Lécuyer, the passionate Franco-Manitoban, the chair of the government caucus, the butt of slurs, to elevate the legislature debate to where it should have been all along and to attempt to hold back the intolerant majoritarian tide that was once again poised to engulf his community as it had twice before in Manitoba history. He set the issue in its proper historic context and in the process, gave expression to the feelings and attitudes of an embattled minority that hadn't been heard in public life since 1890. More than that, he tried to rekindle the Cartier vision for Canada that Manitoba had so abruptly extinguished.

He began in French. He linked the rights of Franco-Manitobans to those of all Manitoba's other ethnic minorities. "In adopting this resolution before us, Manitoba remakes its history and embarks on a new phase of a more united Canada." He reminded members that a brief review of Canadian history belies the claim that Canada has only one language and that the matter was settled on the Plains of Abraham in 1759. The Treaty of Paris of 1763 brought an end to the war between England and France by guaranteeing to the people of New France their language and their religion. Further, the Québec Act of 1774 secured the language and political rights of the anglophone minority even though they constituted only one per cent of the population at that time. Seizing upon Lyon's assertion that the agreement would bind the province "for generations to come", Lécuyer asked why anyone would want to sabotage the rights of Franco-Manitobans; why they were resorting to the "nefarious and illegal" laws of 1890 and 1916. "Why not finally redress the injuries and injustices of the past before it is too late for justice?"

The accusation that the amendment went too far too fast was nothing more than a pretence for those blinded and obsessed with their ignorance and bigotry, the MLA for Radisson continued. Then he switched to English:

> Some of those guilty of scare tactics ... sit right here in this House. These are people who ... see me and those of other ethnic backgrounds as people less worthy than they, who are of white Anglo-Saxon background. That is why we are sometimes told by members of this House that we are not worthy of sitting in this Chamber since – and I quote the words of the leader of the Opposition – "We don't have the right background" ... Lately many racist slurs have been shouted at me from members across ... Generally I ignore these remarks as they are, I hope, generally made in jest. But at the moment I cannot help but wonder whether they are meant jovially as words of endearment or are they really perhaps meant as disparaging racial expressions. At any rate, Mr. Speaker, let me assure you, these words do not shake me at all. I've heard those words and worse ones in the past but I know who I am and I'm proud of what I am. The fact remains that so far on this resolution, the opposition has done its best to fire up the rednecks and the bigots who have tried to hide their racial feelings behind such red herrings and unfounded arguments as entrenchments, costs, waste of money, etc. The obligations and the responsibilities we have as legislators to abide by the law, to exercise justice, to honour acts and treaties and to remain true and honest to history, should come first. Certainly we should not distort history ... and certainly we should make every effort not to be blinded by gross bigotry and flagrant injustice.

The Franco-Manitoban MLA questioned why Manitoba couldn't finally progress one small step and guarantee limited essential services to give his community some assurance they will not have to live under constant fear and harassment as they have for better than 100 years. Why can't we finally let them know that they will not be trampled over as they were in 1890 and 1916 and through countless other incidents of the past? Why can't we today when we have this great opportunity reduce social tension, reduce social discrimination and enhance Canadian unity?

The resolution signalled that linguistic duality was possible outside Québec. Every Canadian, he noted, was part of a minority. Translating laws while denying services would be an admission that the majority wanted more court battles with the hope of "bringing francophones to their knees in surrender" hoping they would give up the "nonsense" of their right to their culture and language.

Mr. Speaker, it cannot be true that for me to be a Canadian I must deny my heritage, renege on my culture and limit the use of my mother tongue to the home, to the courts, or the legislature. For me to accept to speak only English – or to speak "white" or speak "Canadian" as some ignorant people will sometimes tell me – would mean that I also have to accept that this country is forever divided. It would also mean that there is no place for me in this province and in this House. [47]

The Manitoba Legislative Building, constructed of the province's magnificent Tyndall limestone, which also graces the Parliament Buildings in Ottawa, is considered by some to be, with the White House in Washington, D.C., one of the two most beautiful public edifices in North America. But the grandeur of its towering vaulted ceilings, its white and black marble floors, its enormous sweeping staircases and splendid internal vistas defy any attempt to provide it with air conditioning. Its thick stone walls usually keep it pleasantly cool well into July. But once high summer arrives, those same thick walls trap and hold the heat, turning this magnificent work of art into a broiling oven for those who must work in it.

In 1983, the heat of the dog days of summer heightened the tension and acrimony in the House as the session dragged on. Day after day, the Conservatives simply stalemated. They came for question period, moved to adjourn and then simply walked out. For ten acrimonious days, the bells rang most afternoons, for thirty minutes, for forty-five minutes, for an hour, but most often, for the remainder of each sitting. A Tory MLA was ejected in mid-July for claiming the premier had misled the House. As the pressure mounted, the government continued its slow and humiliating retreat, a retreat that, with every step, only whetted the appetite of its opponents for more.

On July 22nd, the attorney general announced the government would allow the agreement to go to a legislative committee and said he would bring in some "clarifying" amendments to address the concerns expressed by the province's civil service union, the Manitoba Government Employees Association. But he would not change fundamental principles.

The MGEA had repeatedly demanded the government tighten up ambiguous terms like "significant demand" and "where numbers warrant" that its president, Gary Doer, feared could vastly expand the scope of French services and the need for bilingual personnel. As union president, he was under pressure to be seen to protect the interests of its members, and he was seeking assurances that unilingual civil servants would not have their careers jeopardized. The MGEA president, who would go on to replace Pawley as NDP leader in 1988 and be elected premier in 1999, took a moderate, problem-solving approach in his discussions with the government. Once he received those assurances and had a better understanding of what the proposed legislation contained, he softened his stand. In the end, the MGEA stayed neutral and did not oppose the legislation.

The fact that the province's public servants – the people most affected – were satisfied with the government's initiative had no effect whatsoever on the anti-bilingualism forces. They simply ignored the fact their trump card – the jobs issue – had itself been trumped, even ratcheting up their insistence that unilingual English-speaking Manitobans would be barred from civil service positions in their own province. Penner continued to promise that "we as a government will listen to those directly affected. We will listen to the public … We will listen to suggestions from the opposition." [48] This brought a warning from Léo Robert that the SFM would not accept major changes.

This was not enough for the Tories, however. They maintained their demand for intersessional hearings. To reinforce their displeasure, they allowed the bills to ring through the night of July 28th. The bells rang again, this time for twenty hours, after Lyon was ejected from the House just before the August long weekend, for repeated disruptions and accusing the premier of lying. Meanwhile, Doern was busy stoking the fires of public rage with a ceaseless stream of letters to the editors of both Winnipeg newspapers. This, from the *Winnipeg Sun*, was a typical example:

> Does the Supreme Court of Canada consist of a group of senile old men who make irrational decisions? … Manitoba's negotiating team believed that they were dealing with three separate organizations – the federal government, the SFM and Alliance Quebec, so that the odds were three to one against them to begin with. In fact they were only dealing with one team. A team with one voice. A team which was determined to not only force bilingualism on Manitoba, but also use this agreement as a lever to pressure the provinces of Ontario, Saskatchewan, British Columbia and Alberta. It is clear that the person who was really calling the shots behind the scenes was none other than the prime minister of Canada: the Rt.

BÉRARD (CAYOUCHE) / *LA LIBERTÉ*

PAWLEYON

Hon. Pierre Elliot Trudeau. [49]

The government backtracked once more with a major concession that was ominous indeed for the francophone minority. The premier said Manitoba municipalities were free to hold individual referenda on the language proposals if they wished in the upcoming fall elections. In a classic case of too little, too late, the government announced plans to send an eight-page colour brochure, costing $28,000, explaining the constitutional proposal to every household in the province.

On August 8th, Canada's national newspaper, the *Globe and Mail,* slammed both sides in an editorial entitled "Fear of Creeping":

Callers to Winnipeg radio hot-line shows often give the impression that Manitoba suffers from an incurable case of francophobia. Nor can the rancorous opposition to bilingualism which the anonymous callers express be dismissed as unrepresentative of the broader population, not if one is to judge by a brochure recently issued by the Department of the Attorney General. The Manitoba Government's aim in publishing "The Facts about French Language Services" is apparently not to win support for its extension of French language rights but rather to dampen opposition. It defends the wider provision of French language services in almost apologetic terms, explaining that the province's hand was forced by a Supreme Court legal challenge. There is no attempt to emphasize the virtues of providing services in both of Canada's official languages. "Manitoba is not becoming bilingual, nor introducing the Trudeau government's bilingual program," says the brochure reassuringly. "Nothing is being forced on people ... Limited services simply means most people will not be affected." Nor, it adds, is there any basis for the fear that entrenchment of French language rights in the constitution will be "the beginning of 'creeping bilingualism'". How sad that public incomprehension and animus requires such an essentially negative campaign by the government of Premier Howard Pawley. At best, Manitobans will be left with the impression that they are being infected with an unpleasant, but ultimately non-lethal, strain of hoof and mouth disease.

On August 12th, the government finally capitulated to the Tories' demand for province-wide public hearings. The committee on privileges and elections would visit eight communities – Swan River, Ste. Rose, Dauphin, Brandon, Arborg, Ste. Anne, Morden and Winnipeg – between September 6th and October 4th. For their part, the Conservatives agreed to finish debate on all other government business within six days and to a rules change that placed a two-week limit on bell-ringing for individual votes. The House finally recessed on August 18th, after a record 134 sitting days to return after Labour Day for the hearings. The session, which began in December 1982 and would not adjourn until February 27, 1984, is still the longest in Manitoba history, spanning three calendar years.

There was more than enough guilt to go around for the spectacle Manitoba was making of itself on the national stage. On the government's part, the guilt lay in its failure to understand or appreciate the province's history and the lesson of the 1982 constitution. Manitoba New Democrats take pride in the fact they don't have esoteric concepts like constitutional reform and minority language rights high on their priority list. As social democrats, their focus is always on the bread and butter issues of jobs, the economy and social programs. With a few notable exceptions, they presented the agreement to Manitobans as little more than a necessary evil to duck costs and possible chaos. Then they unwittingly helped open Manitoba's Pandora's Box by appearing elitist and intransigent, refusing to consult the public until it was too late and the all-important image of citizen inclusiveness and consent had been shattered. As for the opposition, its guilt centred on its eagerness to shout fire in a crowded theatre, use inflammatory political rhetoric and appeal to the very worst side of human nature with complete disregard for the social peace of the province and the unity of the country. And all for dreams of partisan gain. Lyon wasn't alone among Conservatives who believed the language issue was tailor-made to smash the broad ethnic coalition that was the base of the NDP's electoral support.

Lise Bissonnette, the separatist editor of Montreal's *Le Devoir*, put it bluntly in a highly critical July 23rd editorial entitled "Not a love story". She castigated the government for being so eager to conceal official bilingualism that it was running out of metaphors, and Lyon, for "sa campagne réactionnaire". She continued:

Communities do not make peace, just like that, acknowledging a wrong, accepting a principle and feeling generous. They move only out of self-interest or necessity … While we acknowledge that part of English Canada is changing, we have to be careful and not be too triumphant, or be fooled by the illusion of a great march towards equality … Anglophones learn French because there is an economic advantage. They do not necessarily subscribe to positive attitudes towards Francophones.

lise bissonnette

Not a love story

LE DEVOIR, JULY 23, 1983

son solliciteur général, M. Penner, se fait huer durant ses « séances d'information » et un député ministériel d'arrière-ban, Russell Doern, siège comme indépendant depuis que ses électeurs lui ont fait savoir, presque à l'unanimité par sondage, qu'ils ne veulent ni voir ni entendre cette langue si dérangeante.

Alarmé, surtout après avoir tant célébré cette affaire qui devait nous démontrer le contraste entre la générosité du Canada anglais et la mesquinerie du Québec, le président d'Alliance-Québec, M. Éric Maldoff, s'est rendu à Winnipeg le jour même de la Saint-Jean pour enjoindre les Manitobains à la sagesse. Intéressant, son plaidoyer repose surtout

The Canadian Crucible

9

Seasons of Rage and Sorrow

IN THE WEE SMALL HOURS OF THE MORNING OF SEPTEMBER 15, 1983, the moment of truth arrived for the members of Winnipeg City Council. Would they submit the language rights of Franco-Manitobans to the rule of the majority in a plebiscite to coincide with the October 26th municipal election?

After a ten-hour debate, the question was called at 3:30 a.m. Up for re-election, city council deadlocked, with Mayor Bill Norrie voting in favour. The mayor cast his second, tie-breaking ballot, again for the plebiscite.

Norrie knew the result would not be binding on either the city or the province, but because Winnipeg has about two-thirds of Manitoba's population, a negative decision would put enormous pressure on the government. The mayor had been inundated with thousands of irate letters and telephone calls demanding a voice on the "bilingualization" of Manitoba. The former Rhodes scholar was initially opposed, fearing it would rip the community apart. In the end, under what he called "tremendous pressure", he acquiesced, saying he felt he had no choice.

Veteran Communist city councillor Joe Zuken thought councillors had simply capitulated to a mob. He was furious. "You don't hold a referendum on the rights of any minority," he said. It would "open the door wide for the bigots to come out and unleash the emotional outburst that will swamp other issues." He expected the plebiscite would turn the municipal election "into another Keegstra affair". Alberta teacher James Keegstra had made national headlines when he was convicted under Canada's hate laws for using anti-Semitic and Holocaust denial material in his classroom. Zuken warned that racists and bigots would be given an invitation to vent their spleen on Franco-Manitobans. [1]

In the end, Winnipeg, Brandon, Thompson and twenty other towns all bowed to mounting public hysteria and fury and allowed plebiscites on minority language rights to accompany the province-wide biennial municipal and school board elections. A dozen municipalities were also holding plebiscites on nuclear disarmament.

Québec's two major newspapers – the mass circulation *La Presse*, with a masthead declaring it to be the biggest French daily in America, and the influential *Le Devoir*, the paper founded by legendary Québec nationalist Henri Bourassa – were now as caught up in the climactic events unfolding in Manitoba as their predecessors had been a century earlier concerning the fate, first of Louis Riel, and then of the Franco-Manitoban community in 1890 and 1916. Over the next year, both would regularly give the Manitoba story highlighted front-page play, often the Page One headline, and provide their readers with extensive analysis and editoral comment on its implications for Canada.

The analysis and editorials tended to reflect the papers' sharply divergent perspectives on the place of Québec in Confederation. *La Presse*, being federalist, supported the Franco-Manitoban cause and applauded the Manitoba government's language initiative and the efforts by the Trudeau government to bolster it. The nationalist/separatist *Le Devoir* sympathized with Manitoba's francophones, but used the crisis as powerful evidence that the Confederation bargain between English and French was simply unworkable. The Manitoba debacle proved that English Canadian hostility to the French fact was implacable, francophone minorities outside Québec were doomed and the homeland of French Canada must redefine itself to survive.

Thus, the charged atmosphere of the debate in Manitoba found a ready audience in Québec, just as it had one hundred years before. And just as it had then, Manitoba's linguistic intransigence imperilled Canada's always-fragile national consensus. Only this time, the behaviour was considered so damaging that the Parliament of Canada would twice be called upon to take the almost-unprecedented step of passing an all-party resolution to urge the province away from a course of action deemed a direct threat to the nation's unity. And on one of those occasions, the prime minister of Canada, Pierre Elliott Trudeau, would declare the Manitoba debate to be "le moment le plus important de ma vie parlementaire" (the most important moment in my parliamentary life).

In fact, the day after the Winnipeg city council vote, *Le Devoir* carried a front-page story providing the first indication that Trudeau wanted the other federal parties to join with the government in a united front to urge Manitoba to make French an official language of the province. "Il veut 'influencer' le Manitoba" (He wishes to 'influence' Manitoba), the story said. Trudeau was again playing his favourite card, language, the article continued, knowing that Brian Mulroney, the new and untried leader of the Official Opposition Progressive Conservatives, faced a bitterly divided caucus on the issue. Mulroney had beaten former Tory leader and prime minister Joe Clark in a leadership convention in June, chiefly on his pledge to capture the 110 ridings in Canada with a significant francophone population that he said the Conservatives had been automatically conceding to the Liberals in every elec- tion since the Manitoba Schools Question in 1896. Mulroney's determination to bring his native province into the new Canadian constitution "with honour and enthusiasm" was another major theme of his campaign.

At the end of August, *Le Devoir's* editor, Lise Bissonnette, had warned Franco-Manitobans that if the provincial government succumbed again to the menacing pressure confronting it, they must not hesitate to respond with all the means at their disposal. In an editorial entitled "Le Manitoba s'embourbe" (Manitoba bogs down), she continued:

> They could still obtain – quickly – from the Supreme
> Court of Canada, a final decision relative to the scope of
> Manitoba's obligations. They too would prefer an amicable
> agreement to this "chaos" that will force the translation of all
> the laws and the immediate bilingualization of the courts.
> But given the current conditions, to cave in again would be
> to confuse a reasonable compromise with naïveté. (2)

The democratic franchise turns from one of humanity's most noble inventions to one of its most odious when the rights of a minority are submitted to the brute electoral power of the majority. It is democratic vigi- lantism, an electoral lynching mob, a psychological pogrom that replaces the torch and the noose with the wounding and terrifying language of hate, prejudice and bigotry. In fact, it is more. In a constitutional democracy like Canada where minorities have defined rights protected by the fundamental pact that created the nation, plebiscites or referenda on minority rights are a flagrant denial of the rule of law.

The *Winnipeg Free Press* also wrote a trenchant editorial on September 16th, which read in part:

> Language and the status or honour accorded to one language or another are matters of passion, extraordinarily difficult to discuss calmly and tolerantly. Within the close-knit, almost clubby atmosphere of the council, insults and abuse were eschewed. But those who argue with spray cans and matches do not operate that way. The process which Mayor Norrie and fifteen councillors are inflicting upon the city is likely to hack deep wounds into the Winnipeg spirit for no good purpose. They must answer to their consciences and to their electors for that choice. The city and its people must live with the practical consequences.

Federal Transport Minister Lloyd Axworthy, Manitoba's representative in the federal cabinet, called the council decision "dangerous and unfortunate ... I think it could be very dangerous to have a majority vote on minority rights." [3]

The same day, the *Globe and Mail*'s Michael Valpy took the perspective of Canadian history:

> The Manitoba language issue ... represents the continued determination by anglophone Canadians to limit the French language to Québec.

> What is happening in Manitoba today is a rerun of what happened in 1890 — with the same political passions and misunderstandings unleashed ... Thus Canadians (Canadians, not just Manitobans) are again at one of the high moments of their history ...

The idea of a civic plebiscite was first floated at Winnipeg City Council in late July by Councillor Don Mitchelson, husband of Tory MLA Bonnie Mitchelson. On July 27th, Mitchelson moved, seconded by Councillor

Abe Yanovsky, that voters participating in the October 26th election have an additional plebiscite ballot asking: "Do you favour the proposal by the governments of Manitoba and Canada and the Franco-Manitoban Society to amend the Constitution by making English and French the official languages of Manitoba and entrenching French language services in government offices, boards and agencies?" Council referred Mitchelson's motion to its executive policy committee. Mitchelson told reporters that he had "heard a lot" from his constituents about "the French entrenchment question". He was in favour of assuring people of French language services "whenever and wherever needed", but opposed entrenchment. "It's both interesting and important to find out how the people feel about guaranteeing French language services," he said. [4]

The wording of the question finally hammered out at that marathon ten-hour city council meeting in mid-September was a little less loaded than Mitchelson's but at a cost of being almost incomprehensible. Winnipeggers would be asked: "Should the provincial government withdraw its proposed constitutional amendment and allow the Bilodeau case to proceed to be heard and decided by the Supreme Court of Canada on the validity of the English-only laws passed by the legislature of Manitoba since 1890." Greg Mason, director of the University of Manitoba's Institute for Social and Economic Research, said the question was so complicated and abstract its results would be almost meaningless. People would cast their ballot on the basis of emotion, not the question, he warned. Mayor Norrie, who chose the wording, said it had been deliberately crafted to avoid being racist. [5]

The plebiscite concept had been spawned in June by NDP MLA Russ Doern and Winnipeg ex-nurse and businesswoman Pat Maltman. In his book, *The Battle over Bilingualism*, Doern said he considered a plebiscite essential because only Franco-Manitobans had been consulted on the proposed constitutional amendment. Doern took his view to the streets in the form of newspaper ads. The first set, which ran on July 23rd in the *Free Press* and July 31st in the *Sun* under the headline "Against Bilingualism", made inflammatory, inaccurate and in some cases, nonsensical, claims: as many as 4,000 civil service positions would have to be bilingual; bilingual civil servants would be sitting around gathering "cobwebs" waiting for someone to need them; Manitobans would be excluded from working for their own provincial government unless they knew French, and municipalities and school boards would soon be forced into bilingualism.

The ads concluded with a coupon to clip and return and a request for donations to offset the $4,500 cost. They elicited some 17,500 responses. Then in late August and early September, using a mixture of his own money and donations, Doern bought two more sets of quarter-page ads in the weekend editions of the *Winnipeg Free Press* and the *Winnipeg Sun* again denouncing the amendment, giving the City Hall phone number from which councillors' telephones could be reached and providing a second coupon readers could clip and fill out, this one to be sent to the mayor's office. The ads had the big, black headline: "Let the People Speak" and prompted about 6,000 replies. The first municipality to agree to a plebiscite was the northern city of Thompson on August 15, 1983.

Manitobans had a brief lull from the charged emotions of the language dispute while the legislature took a recess from August 18th to September 6th, when it would return for the standing committee on privileges and elections

McKenzie: You know Doern! We succeeded with Riel and the sabotages of 1890 and 1916. Let's go with Article 23 ... that will be the end of the French Canadians! Then we'll attack the others ... as long as there's still some ... rope ... of course.

Doern: That's right McKenzie! Let's push for unity! ONE race, ONE language, ONE religion. The only one, OURS! MEN! Take up arms! Advance! to the public hearings.

Nothing is more terrifying than ignorance on the march – Goethe to criss-cross the province to listen to the people on the vexed constitutional amendment. The relative peace and quiet of the last days of summer had all the menacing calm of the stillness before a sudden and violent prairie thunderstorm. There was certainly no respite for Springfield NDP MLA Andy Anstett, the chair of the committee, or for the staff of the office of the Clerk of the House who were handling arrangements for the tour. "It's going crazy," a frazzled civil servant told the *Free Press* on September 2nd. She was being besieged by calls from the public and media. She added that many callers had asked: "Is this the Russ Doern French thing?" By that date, 150 groups or individuals had indicated their intention to appear before the committee, ninety-one in Winnipeg alone.

The first thunderclap of the oncoming storm shook and reverberated around the province the day after Labour Day, September 6th, when the hearings opened at the legislature. They promised to be hot in more ways than one. The temperature inside the Legislative Building was, if anything, higher than outside. The elegant second floor committee room featuring the portraits of Manitoba's premiers is graced with a wall of two-storey casement windows providing a sweeping view of the south lawn, the statue of Louis Riel and the Assiniboine River. The clerk's staff tried to compensate for the afternoon sun by drawing the blue velvet curtains and placing fans at strategic spots for the relief of MLAs and public alike.

Attorney General Roland Penner was the first witness and he introduced a series of major changes to the proposed constitutional amendment. The declaratory statement that English and French were the official languages of Manitoba was watered down by restricting it specifically to the courts, the legislature, the statutes and the institutions of the government. This was to reassure municipalities and school boards they needn't fear creeping bilingualization. Also to reassure local government and the Manitoba Government Employees' Association, the definition of "significant demand" to qualify for French language services was tightened up. The SFM's initial reaction was anger. Vice-president Rémi Smith said the changes created "the possibility of a tailor-made constitutional attack on us through a route very similar to Bill 101 (the language legislation of the Parti Québécois). (6) But later, the organization grudgingly fell into line. Still, the amendments did nothing whatever to quell what was building into a tempest of tornadic intensity about to whirl around the province.

One of the first witnesses after Penner was French language crusader

Georges Forest whose unilingual English parking ticket had brought an end to Manitoba's "ninety years of injustice" in 1979. His appearance served again to highlight the division he represented within the minority linguistic community, a division the English-speaking opponents were only too happy to keep exploiting. He was furious that the committee had made no provision for simultaneous translation into French. "It is a gross injustice," he said. And he found support from Opposition Leader Sterling Lyon, ever eager to confound the government. Forest then surprised the crowd by saying the government should scrap all plans to entrench French language services and proceed with a constitutional amendment simply declaring English and French to be Manitoba's official languages. The government's amendment was perceived as heavy-handed and was creating serious divisions in the province, setting back bilingualism. "I could live with entrenched services, but it would make bilingualism that much more difficult. It's got to flow from goodwill, from understanding. Too many people, both on the English-speaking side and the French side too, have been alienated. We could be in for something very, very disastrous." [7]

McGill University constitutional law professor Dr. Stephen Scott told the committee the previous Lyon government had invited the controversy by delaying living up to the 1979 Supreme Court ruling overturning Manitoba's 1890 English-only law. The former government, he said, should have immediately sought some legal breathing space from the court to translate its body of statutes. Since its dilatory conduct had sparked the challenge to that body of unilingual English laws posed by Roger Bilodeau's speeding ticket, Scott continued, the Tories were not in a position to attack the NDP government's negotiated agreement to avoid the laws being declared invalid by the high court. The agreement was the minimum that had to be given to a minority who had waited ninety years for redress. "It doesn't seem to me that the people who are responsible for the crisis should now attack the agreement in these terms," Scott continued. "The Opposition seems unwilling to leave a reasonable latitude to the government when in fact they had two years in office to deal with it in their own way." Scott warned that Manitoba's refusal to obey its constitution "can be, has been and is cited by French-speaking Canadians elsewhere that our constitution, our country, cannot keep faith with its citizens."

Lyon and Doern challenged Scott's claim there was a real threat the court might strike down Manitoba's laws. Scott replied the court would not and could not allow a situation that is unconstitutional to stand. "Why should [the court] tell all governments, present and future, that constitutional guarantees will not be enforced if the consequences of enforcement are made drastic enough? Everyone must be able to have confidence that the constitution will be respected and that, where breaches occur, remedies sooner or later will be found. Otherwise the constitution means nothing and simply breaks down." [8]

Raymond Poirier, spokesman for a French-speaking parents' group, accused Lyon and Doern of spreading "paranoia" and took Lyon to task for treating witnesses supporting the amendment as though they were on trial. Lyon replied he wasn't trying to make witnesses personally like him, he was just trying to establish facts. The Conservatives are asking Franco-Manitobans to trust governments, Poirier continued. "But what we are saying is 'Like hell we will.'" [9]

University of Winnipeg historian Donald Bailey placed the row in its wider Canadian and historical context. He condemned the country's English-speaking majority for having tried continuously for two centuries to "shove English down French throats" and for its absolute refusal to accept the simple historic truth that since 1759, Canada had had six constitutions and all of them affirmed the dual nature of Canadian nationality. "Canada is a country which is historically and constitutionally composed of two nations … Anyone is free to hold an opinion wishing that some other legal constitutional situation were so … but in the meantime Canada would be more united if everyone recognized and accepted the founding principles of the country." [10]

Not everyone was open to scholarly argument. Una Johnstone said the majority should not be ruled by a minority. "Governments are encouraging the hyphenization of the ethnic groups" instead of making English the common denominator in the country. "Let us all be just Canadians and not hyphenated Canadians." [11]

During its two days of hearings in Brandon, the committee got an earful from local reeves and councillors of surrounding municipalities. They denounced not simply the entrenchment of Franco-Manitoban rights, but the constitutional rights of all French Canadians. One was even prepared to sacrifice the rights of anglophones in Québec if that's what it took to keep Manitoba English-only. Some raised the spectre of a plot by the French to take over the country, while others said that if the Supreme Court made a decision the majority didn't like, it should simply be ignored.

Shellmouth councillor Gene Nerbas read a resolution from his council urging that the rights of all French-speaking people in Canada be abolished and a new constitution drawn up making English the sole official language. "Why is there minorities here?" he asked. "Why can't these poor, oppressed people be raised to the ranks of the majority and become like us? ... When are they going to accept the fact they're Canadian as I define Canadian?" [12]

Some presenters advanced the contradictory argument that Franco-Manitobans were too few to demand special rights, yet powerful enough to take over the province and force everyone to speak their language.

Einar Sigurdson, the reeve of Lakeview, adopted a philosophical approach. "This has been going on for ninety years and it hasn't hurt us yet." No language needs constitutional protection, he insisted. "For us country people it's like stirring up a hornet's nest. If you leave them alone, they don't bite and maybe you can control them." [13]

Sydney Lye, reeve of the Rural Municipality of Portage la Prairie, told the MLAs that "there are other things more important than keeping various cultures alive at public expense. What do we do with the minority? Do they not have to agree with the majority? ... We've had a wonderful and peaceful province for more than 100 years. Let us keep it that way and do not let cranks or radicals spoil our way of life." [14]

Committee chair Anstett, a native of Ontario who had been Manitoba's deputy clerk and deputy chief electoral officer before being elected as the NDP MLA for Springfield in 1981, was shocked at both the lack of understanding and the visceral antagonism he encountered at the Brandon meetings. "I've seen a face of Manitoba I didn't know existed," he told the Globe and Mail. [15]

The hearings in Thompson and Swan River were more balanced and reasoned. The Franco-Manitoban community received support from Arvind Aggarwal, representing the Indian Padan Bhartiya Cultural Club and the Sikh Society of Thompson and also from Farida Dharamshi of the Thompson Moslem Association. And in Swan River, the no-shows outnumbered speakers. Of the nine briefs opposed to the extension of French language services – one of which was accompanied by a petition with about 1,000 names – eight speakers said the government at the least should hold a province-wide referendum before enacting the changes. J.M. McIntosh, reeve of the Rural Municipality of Minitonas said that if the government was "so confident" that the agreement was in Manitoba's best interests, it "should be confident enough to take it to the public by way of a provincial referendum." The Manitoba Métis Federation said the protection of francophone rights offered protection

to all other minorities. Ron Richards, a member of the Camperville community council, urged the government to pass the constitutional amendment as
originally drafted and not to weaken it with the changes the attorney general
had announced. (16)

St. Rose du Lac, centred in a predominantly French-speaking part
of the Parklands in west-central Manitoba, offered graphic evidence of how
deeply the issue was tearing at the very hearts and souls of many Franco-
Manitobans. "I don't know. I don't want the English to get mad at the
French," a Grade Twelve francophone student replied when asked if she
supported the constitutional amendment. Of the twenty-nine presenters,
twenty-three backed the government and five were opposed. A fence-sitter
was Joe Van de Poele, the reeve of the RM of St. Rose. He said he had considered not even appearing before the committee because of his fears it could
create deep rifts in his community, which was forty-two per cent francophone. "I kind of sway both ways and I don't know where to go. I've lived
here for twenty years and I've never been as conscious of my last name as in
the last three or four months." But René Maillard, mayor of the village of
St. Rose, was both opposed to the package of French language services and
in favour of the entrenchment of the province's bilingual status. "Bilingualism
should be pushed as a pride issue, that we are proud to be bilingual, not as
something that should be forced on people," he said.

As would be the case throughout the hearings, a clear majority of
Franco-Manitoban witnesses said the SFM spoke for them and the amendment was simply correcting a ninety-year injustice. Claudette Gingras, one
of seventeen who addressed the committee in French, said that when she
moved to Manitoba from Québec twenty years ago, she had no idea how
difficult it would be to retain her language. If she wanted her children to
continue their French education after Grade Nine, she said, she would have
to send them to St. Boniface. "I would like to know what reward there is for
these sacrifices. We must receive services in French for our children to use
the language." Father Roland Tessier, pastor of the Roman Catholic Parish in
Ste. Rose, told the committee that "a great deal of noise is being made over
not much. There is a certain expansion of French rights in Manitoba but I
don't think it threatens the ninety-four per cent majority." However, Reeve
Russell Phillips of the RM of Dauphin disagreed. Claiming to speak for his
council and a majority of the people in his district, Phillips said "we live in
an English-speaking world" and if people would have patience, the language

issue would just disappear. [17]

The hearings in Morden produced what seemed on the surface to be a surprise: nineteen in favour of entrenched French language services and nine opposed. Morden, south and west of Winnipeg, might be considered part of Manitoba's WASP and Mennonite Bible belt. But it also is close to many of the historic Red River Valley Franco-Manitoban settlements. One of those historic communities, the Rural Municipality of Grey, opposed the government initiative because the desire of its councillors to control government spending trumped their desire for services in their mother tongue. Reeve Julius Petkau, who told the hearings that three of the five Grey councillors were French-speaking, said that during his six years on council, "not once has the staff come to us and said that there is a problem in that area". The reeves of the RMs of Rhineland, Thompson, Pembina, Louise, Roland and the mayor of Manitou also spoke out against the amendment.

Reeve David Harms of Pembina, the president of the Union of Manitoba Municipalities, said making Manitoba a bilingual province is "undesirable, unnecessary and really does not serve any useful purpose". Instead of entrenching French, Harms suggested a new provincial constitution be drawn up reflecting "all those who have made a contribution no matter what nationality or ethnic background, and give them all equal status as citizens of Canada".

But Albert St. Hilaire, reeve of the RM of Montcalm, neatly turned the tables on the opponents. Although his municipality was seventy-five per cent French-speaking, it had been offering services to its anglophone minority for decades and experienced no difficulty. "We offer this not as a courtesy, but as a right to our minority." St. Hilaire was strongly criticial of the idea of a plebiscite on minority rights. He asked the committee if they thought blacks in the United States would have been well-served by a slavery referendum in 1860 and whether the government would like to put the payment of taxes to a vote.

Travis McCullough of Carman was opposed to any measures that further divided people, including the expansion of French language services. "I don't like Folklorama. I don't like multiculturalism. I don't like anything that divides us and points out our differences ... If anything, let's all learn Esperanto." [18]

In the Interlake community of Arborg, the MLAs heard from seventeen witnesses – nine in favour of the amendment and eight opposed. Blanche Tully of Marquette, who delivered a brief that included a petition of 190 names, said for the government even to consider making Manitoba bilingual was "literally the last straw." The Georges Forest and Roger Bilodeau court challenges of English-only traffic tickets were "plain and simple blackmail". But Reeve Rens Renouy suggested the government consider creating bilingual districts in Manitoba along the lines of those mandated by the federal Official Languages Act. That way, the province could avoid superimposing bilingualism on the whole province and "turning neighbour against neighbour and husband against wife". And Rob Sarginson, a Selkirk school teacher, said the government would have the support of Manitoba's middle class because of the high demand for French immersion. During his nine years in the classroom, he had noticed greater tolerance developing among students towards ethnic groups other than their own. He predicted the extension of language services would allow the "French culture to flourish" and lead to an even more tolerant society. Finally, the Irish Canadian National Association of Manitoba Inc. castigated the Opposition Conservatives in a biting written brief. "We find it very difficult to tolerate the incredible and divisive backlash from a vocal minority in this province who would turn the clock back to 1890." [19]

The day-long hearings September 27th in Ste. Anne, the heartland of francophone Manitoba, were an emotional high point for the embattled Franco-Manitoban community. They came from every corner of the province, singing and carrying banners and flags, as if by all standing together they could impress their fellow citizens with the rightness of their cause and the continued strength and vitality of their language and culture. Fifty-one of the fifty-six briefs were delivered in French.

For the evening rally portion, about 650 people crammed into the legion hall and another 1,500 milled about outside in a dusty parking lot to show support for the SFM, which had advertised the meeting extensively, appealing to all Manitobans to come to what it billed as a "public gathering". Twenty buses, including chartered commercial buses as well as school buses from the Norwood and Red River school districts brought people to the parking lot, where two large tents and a stage and been erected. Placards proclaiming "Justice for one, Justice for all": and "Vivre en français chez nous" were distributed to the crowd along with flags and SFM buttons and T-shirts. Chairs and benches were supplemented by hay bales to provide seating to the throng and a closed-circuit television feed transmitted the proceedings inside to those outside. When the legislative committee members arrived, they were greeted with a song, "C'est une Histoire", that had been adapted especially for the Ste. Anne hearings. The singing began at the back of the hall and quickly spread. Committee chairman Anstett frequently had to ask the crowd to be quiet and refrain from public displays of approval, but it soon became a lost cause as audience and presenters alike were caught up in the poignancy and drama of the event.

SFM president Léo Robert, a burly, bearded but surprisingly soft-spoken educator, received a tumultuous standing ovation when he entered the legion hall at 8:30 p.m. He said the size of the crowd would impress the

"Mon NON est franco-manitobain"

Mes chers amis,

Le 27 septembre à Ste-Anne est aujourd'hui inscrit à un chapitre de l'histoire de notre longue lutte pour le respect de nos droits. Si cette manifestation a été une réussite incontestable, et, si elle se taille une place privilégiée dans les livres d'histoire de nos petits-enfants, cela est grâce à vous qui étiez présents en si grand nombre. Je profite de la présente pour vous exprimer mon plus vif sentiment de reconnaissance et mes plus sincères remerciements pour votre présence à Ste-Anne.

Mais si cette manifestation était le message d'une collectivité, le suivi de cet événement veut maintenant que vous exprimiez votre message individuel. Vous qui habitez la ville de Winnipeg, je vous encourage donc à vous prévaloir de votre droit de vote le 26 octobre prochain. Je vous invite à faire part de votre

message personnel dans le cadre du plébiscite sur le projet d'amendement de l'article 23. Dites-leur que votre "NON" est franco-manitobain.

Car celui ou celle qui vote NON à ce plébiscite appuie l'entente conclue avec le gouvernement du Manitoba et appuie donc une solution négociée entre manitobains, pour les franco-manitobains.

Le 26 octobre nous donne l'occasion de réaffirmer notre détermination et de faire respecter nos droits.

ALLEZ VOTER. VOTEZ NON.

Sincèrement,

Léo Robert, président
La Société franco-manitobaine

LA LIBERTÉ / OCTOBER 21, 1983

Un appel au ''non'' à l'occasion du référendum municipal sur le projet d'amendement de l'Article 23. (*La Liberté*, 21 octobre 1983).

legislative committee and proceeded to walk the audience through the negotiations and the fine points of the draft constitutional amendment. Once Robert's speech was over, musicians and actors took to the outdoor stage for a celebration of Franco-Manitoban culture.

Neither Lyon nor Doern attended the evening rally but were present for the hearings earlier in the day where all but three of the fifty-six presenters supported the constitutional amendment, criticizing the government only for having watered it down. Lucienne Boucher, a private citizen, called the amendments "mumbo-jumbo" that had failed to appease the critics but had "hemmed and boxed in" the two official languages. The government was "afraid of its own shadow", she said. And she warned the politicians: "It's all over for timid souls. The eyes of Canada are upon you."

The two most moving presentations came from a senior citizen and a student. M.J. Fisette, representing the residents of seventeen francophone senior citizens' homes, said the people of the older generation had made "enormous sacrifices" to protect their language and cultural heritage. Many parents had "bled themselves white" so their children could attend boarding school and be educated in French. Valerie Vielfaure, a Grade Eleven student at La Broquerie School, asked the MLAs for French language services so she and her fellow classmates could use the language they were being taught in school. "We are the adults of tomorrow," she said. "Give us back our rights." [20]

"This night belongs to the Franco-Manitobans," said Anstett. [21]

The committee returned to Winnipeg the next day to receive an abrupt reminder of the other side of Manitoba's two solitudes. So many people wanted to make presentations the two-day wrap-up hearings had to be stretched into almost a week. Witness after witness revived the old John Diefenbaker thesis – that any granting of rights to French Canadians made all other ethnic groups in Canada besides the inherently first-class Anglo-Saxons third-class Canadians. Over and over, MLAs were reminded that Franco-Manitobans had less claim on constitutional protection and entrenched rights to government services than German or Ukrainian Manitobans because the latter were more numerous than the former and their Canadianness was just as legitimate.

The author, a political columnist with the *Free Press* who wrote extensively on the language issue, received almost daily telephone calls throughout the crisis from enraged older Manitobans with mid-European accents. Why can't "we just all be Canadian, like the Americans are

American", they wanted to know. One elderly gentleman, fury in his voice, complained: "When my family came here from Germany, nobody told us we were coming to a French country. We were told we were coming to an English country." Another man identifying himself as Ukrainian in origin, was indignant: "My parents broke the soil here. They worked as hard as the French to build this province. Why should the French get special treatment?"

Again and again, MLAs heard that the constitutional amendment was tearing Manitoba apart, shattering the tolerance and goodwill that characterized relations among the nationalities of the province's rich ethnic mosaic. This idyllic view of the openness of Manitoba society flew in the face of a lot of ugly history, some of it quite recent, when those of non-Anglo-Saxon origin endured racial slurs and the north Main Street streetcar stopped at the CPR tracks, compelling the people of Winnipeg's legendary North End to get off and walk home – sometimes miles – no matter the weather. When Ukrainian Manitoban Steve Juba was elected mayor of Winnipeg in 1957, the city's elite was aghast, convinced that he would humilate the city because he wouldn't know how to conduct himself in polite society.

The hearings demonstrated just how profoundly the events between 1870 and 1890 had changed not just Manitoba's history, but the history and ethos of Canada. The concept of Canada as a two-nation pact between two founding races had been stopped in its tracks at the Manitoba-Ontario border. West of it, an entirely different Canada, one much more in the image of the United States, with one flag, one language and an unhyphenated identity, had been planted and taken firm root.

The hearings also confirmed the fears of those who for years had complained about the calibre of Canadian history as it had been taught for over a century in the nation's schools. Outside Québec, it was the British imperialist interpretation of Canada. In the pages of history texts from coast to coast, the most significant event and date next to Confederation itself in 1867 was the Battle of the Plains of Abraham in 1759. The six successive Canadian constitutions that all affirmed duality as the basis of Canadian nationality were glossed over if not ignored, as was the important legal and practical difference between Canada's written and Britain's unwritten constitutional structure.

A surprisingly large number of opponents to the amendment simply couldn't understand how, in a democracy, the will of the majority as expressed by Parliament or a legislature couldn't prevail. They were incredulous at the completely "undemocratic" notion that a law passed in 1870 couldn't be amended or scrapped to conform to new circumstances simply because it was "constitutional". These positions were expressed in language that ran the gamut from reasoned argument to hysteria.

One woman caused gasps when she strode to the microphone and began: "My name is Alice Richmond and I am a bigot. In fact, I am a red-necked bigot. I accept this appellation, not in the way Webster's Dictionary defines a bigot but in the way it is applied today to anyone who opposes the entrenchment of the French language in the Manitoba Constitution." She called Canada's two founding nations "a myth", objected to the cost and the "dissension it's causing. We've been told that entrenchment is necessary to preserve the French culture. All I can say is that the French culture must be pretty flimsy if it cannot be preserved without government assistance!" She noted her father had personally financed her Highland fling dancing classes when she was a little girl and other children went to their churches Saturday mornings to learn their parents' language and culture without government assistance. "I know I will be labelled as a bigot, but bigotry is not a criminal offence, blackmail is!" [22]

The attorney general had simply had enough and stalked out of the committee room during Fred Debrecen's presentation. Debrecen had arrived with two large E's pinned to his vest to declare his preference for the English language. The fact he was obliged to remove them before addressing the MLAs did nothing to improve his mood or cool his white-hot anger. "The issue is pure and simple, a French takeover of Canada," he stormed. He called the hearings "the most despicable, dishonest showing ever in Manitoba." Clarence Morris told the government that the path it was taking would destroy the NDP. "I'm a Manitoban, not a something-Manitoban, be it Ukrainian, French or German."

Elmer Greenslade, mayor of Portage la Prairie and president of the Manitoba Association of Urban Municipalities told MLAs that fifty-eight per cent of its members opposed the government's initiative and wanted the Bilodeau case to proceed to the Supreme Court. Penner asked him how much he knew about the case and Greenslade had to admit he only had an "overview". Pushed to explain that, he couldn't answer. "I don't know if I can put it into words at this time." But then he went on to appeal to the committee not to destroy Manitoba's harmony. "We have a harmony between the different ethnic peoples that is so precious. What we're doing is destroying the harmony. It'll cost us a lot of money. Heaven knows how far it will go." [23]

Once, the hearings degenerated into an exchange of bitter and personal insults between Penner and Lyon. The Tory leader had been trying to get spokesmen for the Canadian Union of Public Employees' local representing 850 Manitoba Hydro workers and 150 other provincial government employees to admit the only reason they were getting input into the language services issue which would affect their jobs was because of the fight the Conservatives were waging. When CUPE's Paul Moist refused to comment, Lyon asked whether his union sent delegates to NDP conventions. Penner, who had just walked into the committee room at that point, interrupted: "How does this arise from the [union's] brief?" During the ensuing shouting match, Lyon called Penner a "Communist ... who now parades as a New Democratic Party member" and accused the attorney general of "subverting" his country because of his Communist affiliation. "You're out of your cotton-picking mind," Penner shot back.

Herb Schulz, brother-in-law of former premier Ed Schreyer, said he hadn't spoken out on the issue because "I fear the label of bigot." He accused the government of using the Big Lie technique by trying to convince the public its amendment wasn't an expansion of French rights. He branded the constitutional amendment "politically stupid, socially disruptive and totally unnecessary." But H.S. Dulat, representing three provincial Sikh organizations, said the agreement would save money and serve people better. He said India had two official languages and his home province, three. "If a poor country as burdened with economic problems as India can afford these services for its peoples, why can't Canada?" [24]

Perhaps the most alarming presentation came from Clarence Kiesman, the Moosehorn farmer and reeve of the Local Government District of Grahamdale, about 180 kilometres northwest of Winnipeg. He had appeared at the earlier informational meetings. French Canadians were using politics, schools, churches and the media to attack "our traditions", he said. In seeking the right to be served in French in government offices, Franco-Manitobans are trying "to set themselves up as a superior race. To all the bleeding hearts, I say appeasement is no answer and will only make us look like morons ... For all we know" France was involved in the effort "to make us foreigners in our own country." As far as he was concerned, the Manitoba Act of 1870 was illegal because Métis residents outnumbered white Manitobans at the time and "the white minority had no voice in it."

He concluded by threatening the government that if French services were entrenched in the province's constitution, English-speaking Manitobans "will settle it on their own on the streets". [25]

Le Devoir's editor, Lise Bissonnette, had captured and reproduced for her Québec audience the sheer ugliness of the demons now unleashed in Manitoba in a mid-September editorial urging the federal opposition leader, Brian Mulroney, to join in the effort to exorcise them.

> The odiousness of Sterling Lyon's fight tends to make us forget it, but political leaders also have a moral duty. At the instigation of the Manitoba Conservatives, many Manitoba municipalities are tempted to hold referenda [on the constitutional amendment] even though they are totally untouched by it. Given the level of public passion, we can only fear how dire the outcome will be. Before things deteriorate even further, Mr. Mulroney, if for no other reason than his position, should try to calm things down. [26]

Earlier in September, organizations speaking for more than thirty ethnic communities, including Jewish, Ukrainian, Polish, German, Portuguese, Chinese, Irish, Italian, Sikh, Chilean and Filipino, had created an umbrella organization called Manitoba 23 to support the entrenchment of French and other ethnic language rights. Essentially, Manitoba 23 hoped to return to the pre-1916 days of the Laurier–Greenway compromise where significant minority languages as well as French were recognized in Manitoba schools. They joined the newly-formed Manitoba Association for the Preservation of Ancestral Languages in presenting their position to the committee.

Reflecting his party's deep dislike of Ottawa's multicultural policies and the understandable suspicion that federally-financed ethnic organizations could be made to dance to the tune of the federal fiddler rather than listen to their own grassroots, Tory MLA Harry Graham tried to have Manitoba 23 chairman Neil McDonald put under oath to force him to disclose the source of the group's funding to the committee. He was voted down by the NDP majority, but the Tories' hunch was right. Manitoba 23 was in fact secretly funded by the federal government, who laundered the money through the various member ethnic organizations.

Le Devoir trumpeted the creation of Manitoba 23 in a front-page story by Rodolphe Morissette on October 3rd, warning it would inevitably lead to demands from all the other ethnic organizations for the same rights as francophones.

> In a new, if not explosive, development in the Manitoba bilingualism affair, the SFM has concluded a secret agreement with a coalition of other cultural communities in the province, an agreement that will be a major embarrassment to the politicial players involved in this contentious issue. If provincial governments, like the federal political parties, take too long to agree and recognize the language rights of francophones, they run the risk of facing the same request from all ethnic groups, and this time, they will be supported by the francophone minorities.

Dissension was rending both of Manitoba's political parties. In addition to the noisy and destructive departure and antics of Elmwood MLA Russ Doern in June and the more recent criticisms of Herb Schulz, the government now found itself being upbraided and attacked by two more former high-profile members. Former cabinet minister Sidney Green, who had gone on to form his own political party, the Manitoba Progressives, and former NDP president William Hutton assailed both the agreement and their former colleagues. As a lawyer, Green said "no one would get me to amend our laws on the basis of threatening me with a court case. I'd say, let the case go ahead! I will not negotiate a constitutional change with a private organization. I will go to the public." Hutton said he was opposed to the SFM's efforts "to make Manitoba a lopsided bicultural province where, on one side of the coin there exists a small, powerful, monolithic French ethnolinguistic community and on the other side a heterogeneous, multicultural polyglot collection of assorted ethnic and linguistic communities." [27]

Meanwhile, two prominent Conservatives, both Winnipeg School Board trustees – Mira Spivak, wife of the former Tory leader, Sidney Spivak, and Elizabeth Willcock, a candidate for national Conservative Party president in 1982 – tried to have the board endorse the government's constitutional proposal at an October 4th meeting. Spivak, who would later become a senator, said the issue was important because of the division's many language programs while Willcock said the board should take public positions on major issues. The board referred the motion to the administration. [28] Later, Sidney Spivak, who had lost the leadership to Lyon in 1976, gave an interview to the *Free Press* to announce that he, too, supported the constitutional amendment. While he said the provincial Tory position was legitimate from a legal, practical and constitutional point of view, the constitutional amendment proposal "recognizes the reality of the country and the direction in which it is heading … The position of the federal party is correct." [29]

In all, the committee heard 305 witnesses and received another ninety-one briefs; all made it clear that the province was sharply polarized. The attorney general said he would make some changes to the accord but would not back away from its basic principles, citing the need to win the approval of the other signatories – the SFM, the federal government and Bilodeau. "I am more convinced than ever that our basic decision to resolve this if possible by a political settlement rather than a court decision is correct," Penner said. But Tory leader Sterling Lyon was equally adamant. "We remain consistent. Constitutional entrenchment is not the way to go." [30] He claimed the SFM was "an organization that's no more important than the Kiwanis Club … a fraternal organization without standing." He added it was best at organizing bazaars. [31]

La Liberté's Jean-Pierre Dubé dismissed Lyon's claim that the federal government and the national political parties were engaged in "blackmail", "unjustified intrusion in the affairs of the province" and "trampling democracy in the dirt". The question of language rights in Manitoba has always been a national question. "If Sterling Lyon will not accept the principles that permitted the creation of Canada 116 years ago, he has decisions to make." [32]

By now, the rest of Canada was sitting up and taking notice. The sovereignist Parti Québécois government of Premier René Lévesque split on

SFM good at bazaars: Lyon

By PAUL PARK
For The Sun   OCT 6 1983

OTTAWA — What do Germans, Chinese and Kiwanians have in common?
They're all no more important than francophones, according to Tories Sterling Lyon and John Crosbie.
During the Conservative leadership campaign, Crosbie said he didn't have to be bilingual since the language was no more important than "German or Chinese." Now Lyon has joined the chorus.
In a weekend interview with a Montreal French-language paper, the former premier took a shot at the Société Franco-Manitobaine.
"It's an organization that's no more important than the Kiwanis club or the Richelieu Club," Lyon said, "a fraternal society without standing."
He added the outfit was best at organizing bazaars.

THE WINNIPEG SUN, OCTOBER 6, 1983

the issue. Immigration Minister Gérald Godin said the attempt to make French an official language of Manitoba and increase its use in the province was "a stupid move" by the federal government. "It's a lost cause," said the minister who administered the province's controversial language law, Bill 101, and had responsibility for minority cultural groups. "They don't have any guarantee of surviving except as a folkloric community in the coming years … Only about four per cent of the population out there speaks French … It (the constitutional proposal) has set back the acceptance of the French fact in all of Canada."

Godin went on to note that Franco-Manitobans' assimilation rate had been forty per cent in the last decade. "In Manitoba you still have 50,000 people declaring French as their mother tongue and only 31,000 declaring that they still speak French at home. So in a number of years they simply are dead." The predicament facing Franco-Manitobans now was whether to send their children to "what's left" of the French school system and condemn them to unemployment or to "betray their roots" and send them to English schools so they could get jobs. Constitutional rights are not enough, the PQ minister continued. "Without institutions, they mean nothing. They simply mean you get your parking tickets in English and French. That's not what I would call a dynamic situation for any language."

Godin attacked Prime Minister Pierre Trudeau for clinging to his "pipe-dream" of a bilingual nation. A certain amount of protection is required for linguistic minorities, "but not full equality. The only solution is to recognize that Québec is French and the rest of Canada is English." However, he admitted the situation in Manitoba would colour his government's planned hearings on Bill 101. [33]

But Québec Education Minister Camille Laurin disagreed with his cabinet colleague and was not nearly so bleak. "I don't think [francophone rights in Manitoba] is a lost cause," he told reporters. Noting that the Québec government gives grants, technical assistance and scholarships to French minorities in the rest of Canada, Laurin said: "We hope all those measures will help the French fact not only in Manitoba but in all other English-speaking provinces." However he agreed with Godin that simply entrenching official bilingualism was not enough. "This is purely formal. The real problem for a group that wants to keep its language is to get control over school institutions and other economic measures to strengthen their place in the community." [34]

Lévesque told reporters he thought Godin's comments were "maybe too brutal … I think that what he meant to say, concretely, was that there isn't much hope for [French survival] if we think in terms of the year 2000. But in the short term … there should be solid moral support for those faced by the type of racism there." [35]

As always, Québec politicians, especially the members of the Parti Québécois, were not about to sacrifice provincial autonomy and rights even to support embattled francophones elsewhere in Canada. The PQ's sovereignist position depended in part on demonstrating that francophone minorities outside Québec were doomed. Both Lévesque and Intergovernmental Affairs Minister Jacques-Yvan Morin said they had no plans to extend moral support to the Manitoba government. "I don't think it would help for Québec to tell the Manitoba government 'You should do this' or 'You should do that'. It's their business," Morin said. He likened the province's policy towards francophones elsewhere in Canada to France's policy towards Québec: non-indifference and non-interference. "Non-interference because we don't intend to tell Ontario or Manitoba what to do. We don't want the other provinces or the federal government to put pressure on us. We have always wanted to help our francophone compatriots, but without the least trace of paternalism." Like Godin, he was skeptical the Franco-Manitoban struggle would succeed. "But despite our skepticism, we must help and encourage them and if ever the status of the French language in Manitoba improves, we must rejoice." He, too, used the opportunity to castigate the federal government, contrasting its advocacy for Franco-Manitobans to its indifference to Franco-Ontarians and French Québec. Ottawa, he said, "reinforces French where it is in a terminal phase; remains passive where it has real chances to affirm itself and weakens it where it is strong." [36]

New Brunswick Premier Richard Hatfield slammed the decision by Winnipeg and twenty-two other Manitoba municipalities to put the minority language rights issue to a plebiscite. "It's anti-democratic to have plebiscites on certain issues," he told the Canadian Club of London, Ontario. "It will destroy our political system. I am worried about a majority saying they are going to have their way in spite of the rights of a minority." Citing his own province's decision to become officially bilingual, Hatfield said "It's not too expensive and it works." [37]

During a meeting in Toronto the last week of September, Prime Minister Pierre Trudeau asked Premier William Davis to make French an official language of Ontario. Davis refused, saying he preferred to expand French language services gradually and not entrench them in the constitution. On September 29th, the *Globe and Mail* published an editorial urging Davis to take the prime minister's advice and, among other things, provide "moral support to the embattled Government of Manitoba". Under the headline, "No Better Time", the editorial said:

> There could hardly be a better moment for Ontario to become officially bilingual. It might head off court actions filed recently by Franco-Ontarians wearying of the long political struggle for educational equality. It would be a timely message to Québec, Ontario's neighbour, that French Canadians do not have to drown in the English sea – a gesture which might have an influence on how Quebeckers vote on independence in the next provincial election ... Moreover, unlike Manitoba's New

Democratic Premier Howard Pawley, Mr. Davis would have
the support of his opposition ... This is very different from
the case of Mr. Pawley who has faced an ugly public clamour ever since Conservative leader Sterling Lyon forced the
bilingualism issue to public hearings around the province ...

Meanwhile, the federal government, too, had long been considering
providing direct "moral support" to the "embattled" Pawley government. When
wind of it first surfaced in early September, it was roundly denounced in
Manitoba for being likely to make matters worse and, across Canada, for
being a brazen political gambit by the federal Liberals to split the Conservative Party and ambush and snare its newly-elected leader, Brian Mulroney,
a fluently bilingual Québécois, just as he arrived in the Commons as leader
of the Official Opposition.

On September 13th, Trudeau invited Mulroney to meet him for private talks about a multi-party strategy to save the threatened constitutional
amendment. Mulroney agreed on condition that NDP leader Ed Broadbent be
included. Telling reporters "my position on bilingualism is as clear as water
from a mountain stream", Mulroney said he didn't think Trudeau's invitation
was a Liberal plot nor did he believe it would cause internal dissension. "I
hope the prime minister is not using this as a partisan matter. All parties are
agreed upon this and it should be thoroughly depoliticized." Former prime
minister Joe Clark, Mulroney's predecessor as Tory leader, was not so sure.
"We anticipated that there might well be a planted decision, designed not to
aid Franco-Manitobans but to cause divisions within our ranks." Anti-bilingual crusader and Winnipeg South Centre Tory MP Dan McKenzie, who was
that very day appearing in the Federal Court of Appeal on a challenge to federal bilingualism policies, told the media through a secretary he would have
nothing to say until after Mulroney met Trudeau and then the Tory caucus.

Trudeau met with Broadbent first and the NDP leader reported he
and the prime minister discussed various options including a parliamentary
resolution supported by all parties. The prime minister told reporters he was
"at a loss" as to the best course of action and for that reason sought the advice
of the other leaders. The Manitoba situation was more than a provincial matter,
he continued:

It is true that it is being debated before the Manitoba
legislature, but [Mulroney] also knows that it turns on a

constitutional question ... It is a subject which concerns not
only the immediate province, but all Canadians and notably
all those [parliamentarians] who have enshrined bilingualism
law in the Constitution. (38)

Trudeau and Mulroney met the next day for forty-five minutes and
explored what Mulroney called "certain possibilities and working hypotheses"
regarding Manitoba. The prime minister said he would get back to the opposition leader. But the federal Tory caucus held the opinion that the matter
should clear the Manitoba Legislature before Parliament did anything. Neither
the New Democrats nor the Tories wanted to take any step that could be seen
as trampling on provincial rights. But the Liberals considered the Manitoba
initiative a constitutional act within the jurisdiction of the federal government
and hoped to find some way to stiffen Pawley's spine. Significantly, McKenzie
did not talk to reporters after the Tory caucus meeting, a signal to some that
Mulroney was already clamping down on those MPs whose views and statements he felt embarrassed and compromised the party.

In Manitoba, the ruminations emanating from Ottawa forged an
unlikely and, under the circumstances, almost unbelievable meeting of minds
between the attorney general and the Conservative leader. "The better part of
wisdom is to let us work it out in Manitoba and I am confident we will,"
Penner said. While no one would object to the three federal parties

encouraging Manitoba to try to find consensus ... that
should be the extent of it at this time ... Jurisidictionally,
the only thing the House of Commons can do is to vote on
a resolution amending the Constitution. That they don't
have ... nor does anyone know the final shape of it.

Lyon said it would be presumptuous for Parliament and Mulroney to
intrude on a purely provincial matter at this point and "express any opinion until
Manitobans decide ... Who knows if Parliament will be asked to deal with
any resolution?" Lyon told reporters at a news conference that he hadn't discussed
the issue with Mulroney but he had talked to some Tory MPs, whom he refused
to identify. "I believe our position on this is understood in the federal caucus in
Ottawa," he said, adding that he thought they agreed "as far as I'm aware." (39)

If Mulroney was trying to clamp down on his MPs, he wasn't successful with Manitoba MP Jake Epp (Provencher). Epp told the *Free Press* on

The Canadian Crucible

September 16th that Manitoba was a province with no majority group and harmony among the various nationalities shouldn't be disturbed by the prime minister. Trudeau's plan to put pressure on Manitoba was short-sighted and divisive and would create new separations among the many ethnic groups that had learned to live together in tolerance and mutual respect, he said. "I wish the prime minister could see his role as a unifying force."

Suspicions that the Liberals' move was inspired by partisan gain and designed to increase the pressure on Ontario to become officially bilingual were only fanned when Secretary of State Serge Joyal entered the fray. Joyal condemned the plebiscites in Winnipeg and hinted that Ottawa might weigh in with financial help to the SFM in the battle to sway public opinion. He also said increased provincial government services in French in Manitoba would have a profound impact on language rights in other provinces. "What happens to a minority in a province has an impact on the conditions of the minority in another province. Some other provinces might be tempted to improve the treatment of their minority following what has been done in a province or induced not to treat more fairly their minority because another province has taken another stance." The outcome in Manitoba could influence "Ontario in particular". ‾

Just how loudly the Manitoba issue was reverberating around the country could be measured by the leaks from the federal Tory caucus. While the importance of standing united with their new leader was sufficient to stifle even the fiercest among the anti-bilingualism western Conservative MPs, the caucus perceived only endless political woe flowing from its predicament no matter which way it turned. Some wanted to link support for the rights of Manitoba francophones to the rights of anglophones in Québec. That was ruled out when others said the inclusion of anglophone rights in Québec would automatically raise questions about how Ontario treated its 400,000-strong francophone minority. Not only could that damage the Ontario Tory dynasty at Queen's Park, but it might well jeopardize anticipated major federal Conservative gains in the ethnically-diverse Greater Toronto area in the upcoming federal election expected in 1984. All were convinced that whatever they did, Manitoba's provincial Conservatives would emerge the main losers. On the other hand, as one anonymous MP put it: "I suspect that when it's all over, we'll discover that we have been caught a bit in our own paranoia. We're suspecting a big blowout. It's like a death wish."[41]

As the date for the federal debate approached, the front, editorial and opinion pages of Québec's two major newspapers fairly steamed with rhetorical passion, both nationalist and federalist. Not surprisingly, the nationalist academics seized upon the Manitoba imbroglio as proof positive of the failure of Confederation to protect French Canadians outside their home province.

On October 5th, the day before the debate, *La Presse* published an open letter to Manitoba Opposition leader Sterling Lyon from Québec's leading nationalist historian, Michel Brunet. Brunet bitterly attacked the Trudeau government's policy of pan-Canadian bilingualism and backed the provincial Conservative position that the issue of language in Manitoba should be left to Manitobans alone to decide. Trudeau's vision of Canada was "unitary and anti-federalist" and demonstrated "flagrant ignorance" of Canada's history, he said. He congratulated Lyon for his opposition to the prime minister's patriation initiative that Trudeau "was unfortunately permitted to impose on the country". It "dangerously weakens our parliamentary institutions and provokes a fatal destabilization of Canadian federalism". His dismissal of Franco-Manitobans was almost brutal.

> As for the linguistic rights of the minute group of [Franco-Manitobans] who still have the illusion of survival, you should know that the Franco-Québécois are not interested in their fate at all. Only a few old-fashioned ideologues and some troublemakers interested in division still believe in French messianic nationalism. When a handful of Anglo-Québécois from Alliance Québec gathered and, pretending to be the official spokespersons of the Québec anglophone minority, asked for a more generous policy from the government of Manitoba for a few francophones, did you not notice that not one francophone Québécois organization thought it important to intervene in a debate of significance only to the citizens and Legislative Assembly of Manitoba?

Trudeau's language policies, Brunet continued, were confrontational and divisive and creating imbalance in the country – "a distrustful Maritimes, a bitter and isolated Québec, an ambivalent Ontario, a completely alienated Western Canada". He hoped that Québec, "once and for all" would correct its "absurd" situation where a minority within its boundaries considered itself a majority and that English Canada would finally realize that anglophone Québec was its "Achilles heel".

The next day, the newspaper carried a warning from Université d'Ottawa professor and demographer Charles Castonguay that regardless of the success of the Pawley government's language initiative, the Franco-Manitoban community was destined to fade away. "For Franco-Manitobans, the future only holds contraction. It's inescapable," he said. He noted that the number of Manitobans using French as their first language had shrunk almost twenty per cent between 1971 and 1981, from 39,600 to 31,000. [42]

Alongside the Castonguay story, *La Presse* featured another article, datelined Winnipeg, in which former NDP president Bill Hutton said the government's language plans would put Manitoba in a bicultural box. "For him, a bicultural Manitoba would be equivalent to cultural and social separatism. He opposes it as much as he opposes the PQ's dream to separate Québec from the rest of Canada."

After several meetings between Trudeau, Mulroney and Broadbent, the die was cast. An all-party resolution would be presented to the House of Commons on October 6th. Only the three party leaders would speak and the resolution would be adopted without a vote. The resolution contained nine clauses. Described by one columnist as "more Gallic than Anglo-Saxon in its pristineness" [43], its phrases delineated in clear and powerful language the essence of Canada's constitutional duality:

> WHEREAS a fundamental purpose of the Constitution of Canada is to protect the basic rights of all Canadians including Aboriginal peoples, English-speaking and French-speaking minorities, religious, ethnic and other minority groups;
>
> WHEREAS the constitution contains provisions respecting the status and use of the English and French languges in Canada;
>
> WHEREAS the Manitoba Act 1870 was enacted by the Parliament of Canada to establish the province of Manitoba and is part of the Constitution;
>
> WHEREAS in 1870 Parliament provided special protection for the use of the English and French languages in Manitoba under Section 23 of that act;

WHEREAS the Supreme Court of Canada on December 13, 1979 re-affirmed this constitutional protection under Section 23 of the Manitoba Act of 1870;

WHEREAS the Constitution is the supreme law of Canada and is binding upon Parliament and the legislatures of all the provinces;

WHEREAS it is in the national interest that the language rights of English-speaking and French-speaking minorities in Canada be respected and protected in a spirit of tolerance, civility, amity and generosity;

WHEREAS an agreement was reached on May 16, 1983 by the Government of Canada and the Government of Manitoba with the participation of the Société Franco-Manitobaine to modify the Manitoba Act 1870 so that the Government and Legislative Assembly of Manitoba can fulfill effectively their constitutional obligations under Section 23 of that Act;

WHEREAS it is in the national interest to support continued efforts by the Government and the Legislative Assembly of Manitoba to fulfill effectively their constitutional obligations and protect the rights of the French-speaking minority of the province;

(1) the House endorses, on behalf of all Canadians, the essence of the agreement reached by the Government of Canada and the Government of Manitoba with the participation of the Société Franco-Manitobaine on May 16, 1983 to modify the Manitoba Act, 1870;

(2) the House invites the Government and Legislative Assembly of Manitoba to take action as expeditiously as possible in order to fulfil their constitutional obligations and protect effectively the rights of the French-speaking minority of the province. [44]

Prime Minister Trudeau was in high spirits, but the *Free Press* reported that many of his Québec MPs were near tears when he began to speak. "I feel truly privileged to participate in this debate," the prime minister said. "I should like to say, not without emotion, that it is perhaps the most important day of my life as a parliamentarian." MPs had gathered to right a wrong. A nation's constitution, he continued, is the source of all authority. "If it is not obeyed, the human contract it represents is imperilled … The constitution must stand if we are to continue as a civilized society."

Franco-Manitobans were not being granted a new right. "This is a right which was given to them in 1870, which was unconstitutionally withdrawn from them in 1890 … this is a matter of re-establishing certain rights." It was an important day for Parliament because all three parties were agreed that

> no matter how old, how forgotten, and no matter how
> few people were protected by it, the constitution must stand
> if, indeed, we are to continue to exist as a civilized society.
> Wrongs must be righted … I think it is fundamental to
> our existence as a people and, indeed, to our survival as
> a nation that we say no matter how small the minority, if
> they have rights, those rights will be respected."

The prime minister put on the record Sir John A. Macdonald's famous reply to D'Alton McCarthy on February 7, 1890 when the Tory MP proposed to abolish the official status of the French language in Western Canada. Said Macdonald:

> I have no accord with the desire expressed in some quarters
> that by any mode whatever there should be an attempt
> made to oppress the one language nor to render it inferior
> to the other. I believe that it would be impossible if it were
> tried and it would be foolish and wicked if it were possible.

That, the prime minister continued, "is the spirit of Confederation which this resolution asks the House to endorse today. It is a spirit which goes to the very basis of our society.

> I believe that if the events in Manitoba turn out in the way
> we hope and pray … I have confidence that living in this
> country will be, for all those minorities and all those other
> people who are asking for greater measures of justice, a

turning point in the life of our nation. Our forefathers have built a country where life is not particularly easy but is based on tolerance and fraternity. [W]e would be unworthy of them if we failed to do everything in our power to make this nation survive and prosper, this magnificent country that was founded on the principle of reciprocity, of "cohabitation" of cultures and the principle of minority rights. [45]

Mulroney said the purpose of the resolution "is one which has touched the soul of Canada for decades". He recalled that as a boy growing up in Baie Comeau, Québec, he "knew an injustice had been done in Manitoba ... A francophone minority, which had enjoyed an historical protection of its language in Manitoba, was suddenly cut off – amputated – from this guarantee which was so vital." He described the Commons action as "noble" and the resolution, "a reminder of our wider obligations if the country is to have hope for the future ... Bilingualism is a valued principle and indispensable dimension of our national life." The Tory leader described the issue as one "of simple justice ... this resolution is about fairness, about decency, about an invitation to co-operate and to understand. It speaks to the finest qualities of our nation." He was aware of the feelings in Manitoba and didn't want to make the problems any more difficult. "But there is no painless way to proceed because there is only one issue at stake, the simple issue of ensuring that minorities can live at all times in justice." His MPs, he insisted, "stand with me in endorsing a fundamental tenet of our nation". [46]

Broadbent called the resolution an historic necessity. When a majority uses its power fairly, there is cohesion. When it does not, there is conflict. "We are now at such a turning point.

We have to see the history of Manitoba itself in the context of this resolution ... Led by Louis Riel, English- and French-speaking members of the Red River Colony alike forced the federal government by their own actions to take notice of the moral legitimacy of their claims to a government of their own ... It is this I want to emphasize today, Madam Speaker, that Manitobans set the trend for the historical development of Western Canada.

When the Manitoba legislature stripped away the language rights of

The Canadian Crucible

Franco-Manitobans in 1890, Franco-Manitobans became "strangers in their own country. They no longer had access to public education in French. Franco-Manitoban teachers who taught the French language and culture to their pupils were threatened with dismissal. They could not be themselves in public."

The NDP leader said it was important for Parliament to know that the constitutional resolution had the support of virtually all ethnic groups in Manitoba including the Aboriginal and Métis.

> We are now acting in the spirit of those who created Canada in 1867, who out of necessity and by imagination created our fundamental duality. We are supporting a spirit of tolerance and a respect for diversity which should always be the hallmark of Canada and Canadians. Never again should any Canadian say I am a stranger in my own country. [47]

Less than an hour before debate began in the Commons, a resolution asking Manitoba to take action "as expeditiously as possible" on plans to entrench French language services was presented in the senate by Government House leader Bud Olsen and seconded by Manitoba Tory senator and former premier Duff Roblin. It passed in twenty minutes. However, Roblin said it was important that Manitobans not feel they were being ordered to take action. "The federal government and Senate resolution leaves the ultimate decision in these matters where it belongs ... in the hearts and minds of the people of Manitoba." [48]

Meanwhile, in the corridor outside the Commons chamber, Winnipeg South Centre Tory MP Dan McKenzie muttered that the whole exercise was "meaningless". In Winnipeg, Lyon had gone hunting, leaving deputy Tory leader Bud Sherman to face the media. Sherman, who was planning to seek the federal Tory nomination in Winnipeg Fort Garry, was understandably on the horns of a dilemma. The speeches were "compelling Canadianism and inspirational ... lofty performances," he began diplomatically. But Canada extends beyond the rhetoric of the national anthem. The three party leaders had failed to get down to the "feelings running in the streets and avenues of Manitoba". [49]

Lyon had held a news conference the day of the debate. Ever true to his admiration of British parliamentary supremacy and his visceral dislike of entrenched rights, the Tory leader condemned the resolution for "trampling democracy in the dirt" and the Commons action for being "historically, legally and constitutionally inaccurate ... We regret the [federal] Conservative party takes this view. We think it is wrong. We will not be swayed by wrong-headedness whether it comes from the left, the right or the centre."

Also the same day as the debate, Sid Green lodged a formal complaint with the Law Society of Manitoba against the attorney general, claiming his handling of the Bilodeau case constituted unprofessional conduct by a lawyer that jeopardized his client's – Manitoba's – case. Green alleged Penner's public statements that a Supreme Court ruling in favour of the province would damage the credibility of constitutional guarantees was a critical prejudgement of the court. "By indicating the dangers of victory, Mr. Penner clearly indicates he does not want to win our case," Green said.

And on that day as well, John Shields, a twenty-five-year-old Winnipegger studying constitutional law at McGill University, lost his attempt to obtain an injunction to prevent the October 26th plebiscite on the constitutional amendment. His application, filed in Court of Queen's Bench September 27th, was based on the fact the City of Winnipeg Act, an English-only statute, was illegal. Doern had fumed to the media that he suspected the whole thing was a "sham" and Shields had been put up to it by his professor, Dr. Stephen Scott.

On October 8th, *Free Press* Ottawa columnist Joan Cohen dropped a bombshell. The prime minister had been prepared to pre-empt the Manitoba Legislature and introduce the constitutional amendment package in Parliament first. This, apparently, was the resolution Mulroney saw at his initial meeting with Trudeau. While Manitoba would also have had to pass the amendment before it could become part of the constitution, Ottawa, not Manitoba, would have been the one to start the constitutional amendment process, a step Cohen described as "a massive intervention in Manitoba's affairs" and proof of Trudeau's penchant for pre-emptive federal strikes and his intense concern over the Manitoba situation.

Parliament's intervention did exactly as its critics feared: it fanned the flames higher in Manitoba, where the municipal plebiscites were now less than three weeks away. Parliament's unusual action also received Page One banner headlines in Québec's two major dailies and lengthy editorial comment.

In his editorial entitled "Unanimité à Ottawa", published on October 6th, the day of the historic parliamentary vote, *La Presse* editor Michel Roy condemned the "deux nations" position of Michel Brunet and the asssimilationist pessimism of Godin and Castonguay. He asked Lyon if he really was prepared to listen to them, particularly in light of the fact that Franco-Manitoba had survived despite all that had been done to it. He wrote in part:

> Whatever bitterness has been left by memories and the weight of regrets, we should rejoice with all Canadians who speak French, wherever they live in this country. We should rejoice with everybody who is fighting to have minorities' rights recognized. Nobody can remain indifferent to the last phase of this struggle ... To truly support the cause of the French minority, to give its intervention a political and moral scope, the House of Commons had to avoid the agonizing discussions and differences of opinion based on ethnicity or language ...

> Now it behooves Pawley and Lyon to draw the necessary conclusions on behalf of Manitoba. Will the Tory leader, who has in his pocket the letter from Mr. Brunet – a letter that was published in *La Presse* yesterday – be able to put up barriers against francophone rights, thanks to that letter? Would he rather use Gérard Godin's arguments or the studies from Charles Castonguay, the demographer, and conclude that the Franco-Manitoban cause is lost? Mr. Brunet's statements prove his unspeakable lack of sensitivity towards a minority shamelessly pushed around by history which, painfully, after all those years and despite so much adversity, is finally having the rights denied it recognized. If Franco-Manitobans had not resisted history, they would have lost their cause a long time ago. Should we talk about about these men and women speaking French in Manitoba as if we are historians or scientists and they are mummies or lifeless objects? Just when they are given reasons to cling to life in their language, some academic from Québec writes to Mr. Lyon to say that they are sentenced to die. With such statements, la Société St. Jean-Baptiste is talking betrayal.

In an editorial page piece on October 8th, *La Presse* columnist Marcel Adam called the parliamentary debate "an event of great historical importance", which redeemed the past.

> People who are even just somewhat familiar with the history of this issue cannot help but be moved … if only because they would have sympathy for all the tribulations Franco-Manitobans have gone through in the last century. That, of course, excludes Gérard Godin, Michel Brunet and all the other Franco-Québécois who want no part of this sad story. They are *de facto* allies of those in Manitoba who oppose their brothers and sisters in Manitoba regaining their linguistic rights.

> What is the Canadian Parliament's impact on the Franco-Manitoban cause? The Canadian Parliament, speaking on behalf of all Canadians, is formally and unanimously stating the primacy of the country's constitution and that the rights of both official languages have to be respected, regardless of numbers or time spent since those rights were denied. Those who are blinded by fanaticism should think twice about this troubling aspect of the problem in Manitoba.

Adam concluded by saying that while the parliamentary debate wouldn't help the prime minister solve the problem in Manitoba, it was nevertheless "eminently useful".

Le Devoir's publisher, Jean-Louis Roy, weighed in with that paper's editorial on October 8, 1983.

> Despite the limitations of [Parliament's] adopted format, we should rejoice at the conclusion of something that began in a rather partisan context. The adoption of this resolution "on behalf of all Canadians" is without precedent. It does not erase history but it signals a substantial shift in the attitude of a Parliament whose behaviour at the end of the last century was notoriously abject towards this minority … A century later, it is not the courage of the current political leaders or their common determination that stands out … Against all logic and hope [the francophone minority], diminished as we can see in the last Census, managed to survive on its own. This courage took many forms and was rarely spectacular. It

was visible in the many small gestures from rather humble people who were moved by religious convictions and a strong belief in unwavering cultural values.

This anonymous and daily courage deserves to be noticed … [It] was deployed over more than a century, a century of abdication, partially compensated by an ancestral solidarity from Québec, a century of inequity and denial of the most fundamental rights, rights that were – for all intents and purposes – written in the constitution of the country. Even if the official speeches from the leaders of the federal parties demonstrate a clear change, it should not make us forget this history, a history where the heroes are perhaps not who we think they are.

In the case of Manitoba, we are not creating new protections, we are reinstating – partially – what was removed – outrageously – a century ago from the francophone minority of that province.

Manitoba also had been gaining attention from another quarter. On October 4th, some of the country's top religious leaders appealed to Manitoba municipalities to scrap the plebiscites and urged the government to press ahead. "A referendum or plebiscite is not an appropriate means of determining minority rights," they said. "What appears democratic is in fact deeply undemocratic."

Their statement was signed by Archbishop Edward Scott, Primate of the Anglican Church of Canada; Bishop John Sherlock, president of the Canadian Conference of Catholic Bishops; Right Reverend Clarke MacDonald, moderator of the United Church of Canada; Victor Goldbloom, president of the Canadian Council of Christians and Jews, and Alan Rose, vice-president of the Canadian Jewish Congress. Other signatories included John Humphrey, president of the Canadian Human Rights Foundation; William Siemienski, Québec vice-president of the Canadian Polish Congress; Eric Maldoff, president of the English-rights group Alliance Quebec, and André Cloutier, president of the French-Canadian Association of Ontario.

"We believe you don't do ethics or morality by referendum, any more than you do theology by referendum," said Reverend Tom Sherwood, the United Church representative at the news conference. "Respect of minorities is the very essence of our democracy," the statement continued. It cannot be subject to "'the shifting wind'" of public opinion. Asked why the group came forward in Ottawa instead of Winnipeg, Goldbloom said most of the organizations represented are national bodies "and this is the capital of the country".

Goldbloom, a former Québec Liberal cabinet minister who did most of the talking for the group, said they all were "very conscious" that their intervention could provoke a backlash in Manitoba and they took great care to try to avoid it by sticking to the principle of subjecting minority rights to a vote by the majority. [50]

On October 18th, SFM president Léo Robert and maverick NDP MLA Russ Doern faced off in a so-called Great Debate at Red River Community College. It was quickly clear that it was Doern's crowd. "Hundreds of millions are being spent to keep a dead language alive so that a few people can live in the past," fumed one man. "The French will have the pick of government jobs," claimed another. He wasn't mollified when Robert said not a single unilingual English-speaking civil servant would lose his job. Doern repeated several of his most evocative anti-Trudeau lines. "A bigot is anyone who doesn't support the NDP or the feds. It's nothing but a scare tactic ... About the only thing the feds haven't done is send fifty-seven Liberals into the legislature, occupy the building and pass whatever legislation they want." Bilingualism "is a slippery slope. You can't predict the outcome. So let's stop it now." About Québec he said, the threat of Québec separatism was "too often used as blackmail – and Western Canada is sick of it". [51]

Thanks to the fevered state of public opinion and the ineptitude of the government, Doern, Maltman, Hutton and the Conservatives had a clear and massive edge from the outset. As the plebiscite date neared, the language question came to dominate everything. It was all Manitobans could read or watch or hear about, in their newspapers and on television and radio. As is always the case in an emotional paroxysm, the voices of reason were drowned in the din raised by the voices of hysteria and hyperbole. They intensified with each one of their new and more outlandish claims, creating a vicious circle of fear, suspicion and loathing.

The SFM knew the size of the tidal wave that was about to sweep over and engulf its tiny community, but was still organizing feverishly in a frantic attempt to avoid total defeat and crushing humiliation. Its members clung to a slim hope they could obtain at least thirty per cent support in

Winnipeg. Francophone groups across Canada, with the exception of Québec's staunchly nationalist Sociéte St. Jean-Baptiste, rallied to their side. Funded by La Fédération des Francophones hors Québec, a group calling itself the Committee for Manitoba's Constitutional Amendment was created. It had a "war chest" of between $2,000 to $3,000 and volunteers from all English-speaking provinces and a number of Québécois who came on their own. Sylvia Mouflier, its spokesperson, said it didn't want to pick a fight with the other side, merely to try "to counter misinformation … a lot of people don't understand what the legislation says." In particular, Mouflier continued, the committee would try to tell Manitobans the amendment would restrict the rights of francophones more than a Supreme Court decision which could require the entire province to provide both languages at all levels of government. Its efforts were bolstered by Manitoba 23, the coalition of ethnic organizations. Maltman and former NDP president Bill Hutton, co-chairs of the "No" side, said they weren't concerned and hoped to get their message across with limited resources. (52)

The "No" committee's headquarters were located in three unused classrooms in the Collége Saint-Boniface where about 100 young people, including twenty-six from outside Manitoba, were put to work on telephones in an attempt to identify their supporters in preparation for the vote. The outsiders were billeted in private homes and in a nearby convent and ate their meals in the college cafeteria. Their travel expenses were paid by the various francophone provincial federations across Canada, which were asked by SFM president Robert to send either money or volunteers. Most were politically inexperienced, having never worked before at identifiying and getting out a vote.

"This is more than just a Manitoban thing," said Solange Bourgoin, twenty-five, a community organizer from Prince Albert, Saskatchewan. "If rights are denied to the minority here, they can be denied to all minorities everywhere in Canada." (53)

Six days before the vote, Robert travelled to Montréal to receive a $1,000 donation from La Société St. Jean Baptiste and to tell its members that a victory for French rights in Manitoba could only help the language's precarious future in the rest of North America. SSJB president Gilles Rheaume said its vision of an independent Québec had no bearing on its support for a bilingual Manitoba. He said the society would ask Québec newspapers to publish free ads appealing for donations to aid the Franco-Manitoban cause and set up a support committee of prominent Québécois to promote the issue in the province. (54)

Five days before the vote, Douglas Campbell, Manitoba's last Liberal premier, who was defeated by Duff Roblin in 1958, accused the Trudeau Liberals of wanting to make Canada a French state. He was supported by his former education minister, Bobby Bend. Stated Campbell: "I think [Secretary of State Serge] Joyal has said it publicly and Trudeau has said it publicly. I don't think [Trudeau] is looking at it politically as much as advancing something that is very dear to his heart."

Neil McDonald, chair of the Manitoba 23 group of thirty ethnic organizations branded the claims ludicrous and asinine. "It looks like these people are into a scare campaign of smear and fear. That's scary." All the prime minister or the secretary of state had ever said was that the French fact must be recognized in Canada, he continued. (55)

The SFM didn't get its thirty per cent. In Winnipeg, 155,408 – 76.5 per cent of those who cast ballots – voted against the constitutional amendment and to send the Bilodeau case to the Supreme Court while 47,771 – 23.5 per cent – backed the government. The amendment's defeat was even more decisive in the twenty-two rural communities. In total, 20,349 voters – seventy-nine per cent – opposed the amendment and just 5,440 – twenty-one per cent – supported it. The plebiscites produced one ironic twist. The staunchly Anglo-Saxon community of Carman southwest of Winnipeg gave the amendment its highest approval anywhere in the province – forty-four per cent. The wording of the question was different between Winnipeg and the other municipalities. In Winnipeg, opponents to the government's plan voted Yes, while elsewhere, opponents voted No. Carman's mayor explained Carman's exposure to heavy media saturation from Winnipeg confused a lot of voters. [56]

Penner remained undaunted. "We believe we have a duty to resolve Manitoba's present constitutional difficulties in a principled way by means of the legislative process," he said. "We further believe that a well-defined and carefully-safeguarded process for validating our laws, reducing the translation burden to manageable proportions and constitutionally guaranteeing certain French language services by the provincial government is preferable to a Supreme Court decision which could have disastrous consequences for all

RÉAL BÉRARD (CAYOUCHE) / LA LIBERTÉ

Manitobans." [57] However, he said the government was contemplating some changes to the amendment that would not be revealed until the legislature reconvened in mid- to late November. [58]

Lyon called on the government to abandon its plans for a constitutional amendment entirely. When challenged, he dismissed fears that the rest of Canada would regard Manitobans as anti-French. "The people of Manitoba are a better judge of what their future should be than other people," the opposition leader said. Speaking for the other side, Manitoba 23 chairman McDonald was philosophical. "Any time you put minority rights up for public opinion I think you can predict the outcome."

Again, Québec's two major dailies weighed in with saturation news coverage and editorials. The day before the plebiscite, *Le Devoir* carried a story from Winnipeg by Canadian Press correspondent Denis Lessard, under the headline, "Tomorrow's referendum is only the last in a long series of battles for Franco-Manitobans". It traced the sad history of Manitoba's official language minority from 1870 to the present. On October 24th, Lessard had written that the francophone community was preparing for the worst. The headline read "In Winnipeg, all that remains is to minimize the mess". Also on October 25th, *Le Devoir* had run a major story "The disturbing balance-sheet of assimilation" – tracing the slow but steady decline in the use of the French language in Manitoba.

On October 27th, the nationalist daily treated the overwhelming defeat of the Manitoba language initiative on Page One under the headline, "Manitobans reject unequivocally Pawley's project". The next day, October 28th, *Le Devoir* had no less than three stories and an editorial on the issue. One said the plebiscites had done nothing to settle the political crisis in the province. Another reported an interview with Québec's Intergovernmental Affairs Minister, Jacques-Yvan Morin, by the paper's Québec City reporter, Bernard Descôteaux. Morin said the Manitoba results were a "ressac" (backlash) against the policies of Prime Minister Trudeau who had chosen the path of constitutional bludgeoning to impose French services in English provinces. The Manitoba outcome, the Québec minister warned, showed that Trudeau must return to gentle persuasion, particularly if he wanted to get Québec's support for reciprocal agreements.

Morin said it would now fall to Québec to resume the dialogue with the other provinces. The referendum illustrates "the fundamental legal illusion of the Trudeau-Mulroney tandem". Both had a nineteenth century belief in the virtues of legal texts and constitutional obligations. But the Manitoba crisis showed that constitutional obligations imposed externally aggravate rather than solve issues. "Unfortunately, before the West forgets the bludgeon of French Power, there will be as much water flowing in the Red River as in the St. Lawrence."

It was almost eerie, the degree to which the linguistic views of Québec's most nationalist cabinet ministers meshed with those of Manitoba's reddest rednecks. Both, of course, wanted to be rid of the other. In fairness, the PQ response was at least cloaked in courtesy and concern, even if it was patronizing. Morin and Cultural Affairs Minister Gérard Godin pledged support to francophone minorities outside Québec but both also added they hoped these minorities would draw the obvious lesson from the Manitoba outcome: the French fact can only be protected and thrive within Québec. Godin also seized on the opportunity to contrast the plight of francophone minorities in English Canada to the "civilized attitude" his province displayed to its English minority.

Lise Bissonnette penned her paper's response to the plebiscites in an editorial published October 28th entitled "La vérité manitobaine" (The Manitoba Reality). Having to hear its leadership claim a "moral victory" from the "heart-rending" and "devastating" Winnipeg referendum was a sad commentary on the Franco-Manitoban community's isolation and frailty. She was even prepared to accord some credence to it, given that a quarter of the population of Winnipeg did support the Franco-Manitobans despite "the vicious campaign" of the opponents of French rights. But ten years hence, she predicted, the results would be even more devastating. She continued:

> Winnipeg is a capital open to all influences, including that
> of the Canadian media, the Canadian parliament and ethnic
> groups in the province, all of whom generally supported
> Premier Howard Pawley's project ... But all this only margin-
> ally countered the anti-French sentiment that surfaced after
> the announcement of the proposal ... It is to be hoped that
> the Pawley government disregards the results and proceeds
> with the entrenchment with Ottawa's blesssing. But even if it
> does so, the rejection on October 26th will not be forgotten.

La Presse gave the plebiscite result its front-page headline on

October 27th. The article by Gilles Paquin datelined Winnipeg provided graphic details of the "Strong Majority Against Pawley". Inside, the paper's assistant editor, Michel Roy, wrote the lead editorial entitled "Franco-Manitobans' Moral Victory". Even though Franco-Manitobans constituted just ten [sic] per cent of the population, their cause was backed by almost one-quarter of the province's citizens, he said. He praised the Pawley government for pledging to carry on. "This is a courageous decision that Québécois must view with respect and admiration." Roy noted the negative vote could also have been influenced by popular opposition to both the Trudeau and Pawley governments for other reasons. Although inspired by the best of motives, the parliamentary resolution hurt the francophone cause because it brought out that portion of the electorate angry at Ottawa for backing the constitutional entrenchment of French language rights in the province.

> History will never be able to say that Manitoba's NDP government was negligent in consulting the population: a travelling commission criss-crossed the province and listened to all points of view, including a range of prejudices against the francophone minority; finally, the muncipalities, as the law allowed them to do, proceeded to give voice through referendum. In all, fifty-two per cent of those eligible voted, an unprecedented level of participation at the municipal level in Manitoba.
>
> The consultation period, rich in demagoguery and propaganda, gave the opposition Conservatives the time and the means to influence public opinion far more than it provided the government the means to fully inform Manitobans. Because it wishes to avoid aggravating fanaticism and accentuating the currents of hostility, the government is too timid about getting information to the public.And that is the only thing for which we can reproach the government. But it could be quickly forgotten if the government rushes to honour its promise and ensures that the law is passed, a law that intends to restore linguistic rights for francophones, rights that were unfairly taken away.
>
> As noted earlier, SFM president Léo Robert adopted the "moral victory"

The Canadian Crucible

outlook of Québec's federalists, finding two silver linings in the cloud of deep gloom that, for the third time since Manitoba joined Confederation, again enveloped his community.

Because only six per cent of Manitobans were French-speaking, anything above fifteen per cent support was considered to be good news and anything over twenty per cent, a victory, he said. He claimed to be especially heartened by the fact that the residents of Brandon and Thompson had supported the entrenchment of French language services by twenty-six and thirty-one per cent respectively.

Robert's view was partially echoed by Jean-Pierre Dubé in the St. Boniface newspaper, *La Liberté,* on October 28th. He, too, highlighted the difference between the actual number of francophones and the vote their cause received. But Dubé was critical of the francophone community in general and the SFM in particular. The vote was not a categorical opposition to bilingualism because there was much confusion and ignorance at play, he wrote, noting that no less a person than language crusader Georges Forest had opted to vote against the constitutional amendment.

If a majority of Winnipeggers didn't even know the name of their own mayor, how could they be expected to know anything about "the Bilodeau case", Dubé wondered. He also blamed the SFM for sending as many confused signals as Forest.

> The disunity on the part of the francophones – Forest and Robert changed their opinions at least two times since May – created a certain impatience among the bigots, who are used to seeing things as black or white, yes or no …

> After having condemned this referendum as insensitive and anti-democratic, along with federal and provincial politicians of all parties, the churches, the judges, the journalists and the ethno-cultural groups, it was astonishing that the SFM would throw itself into a battle it couldn't win. It was not to the SFM's advantage to give power to ignorance.

Myron Spolsky, president of the Manitoba Association for the Preservation of Ancestral Languages, took solace in the fact that two weeks before the plebiscite, the supporters of the constitutional initiative felt they might only obtain ten per cent. Their ability to push the numbers up as high as they did in such a short time indicated minds were perhaps not closed. Had the Yes side been able to start earlier to counter the months of misinformation and hysteria, the outcome might have been very different. [59] Spolsky's assessment constituted another indictment of the government's handling of the issue. The government never recognized that an agreement negotiated behind closed doors had to earn popular consensus. It partnered with the deeply unpopular Trudeau government and the little-known and instantly-suspect SFM, never thinking it needed simultaneously to involve other credible groups in Manitoba society from the political opposition to ethnic organizations. It appeared intransigent when it needed to show flexibility. It sold the amendment as a necessity rather than an opportunity. In short, it never once got ahead of the issue, opening the door wide to its opponents' bigotry and political opportunism.

Angus Reid, head of a Winnipeg polling firm that subsequently would become one of Canada's most respected public opinion survey companies, said the Yes side spoke to people's "hearts and guts, to their underlying fears and anxieties" while the No appealed to the public's intellect and tolerance. The Yes group had been able to intensify the public's distrust of bilingualism by its constant reference to the Trudeau government. [60] An internal poll commissioned by the Pawley government probed the dichotomy – and the enormous success the Conservatives had had in exploiting reflexive English-speaking Canada's antipathy to "judge-made" as opposed to majoritarian law. It found that eighty per cent of Manitobans opposed the constitutional pact but sixty per cent supported the provision of French language services to Franco-Manitobans. [61]

New Brunswick's Conservative premier Richard Hatfield worried that the "battle for Canada" had been lost in Manitoba. He suggested the citizens of Winnipeg should reflect on the safety of their own rights now that they had denied them to Franco-Manitobans. Noting that fifty-eight per cent belonged to one of many different ethnic groups, Hatfield said: "I think each one of them should ask themselves are they next on the list to have their rights as Canadians taken away." Plebiscites, he continued, are "a corruption of democracy". [62]

La Société St. Jean-Baptiste told the standing committee of Québec's Assemblée Nationale studying the province's language policy that the Manitoba results proved that Bill 101 had to be strengthened because no one else in Canada would protect the French language. [63]

On October 28th, the editorial pages of several major Canadian newspapers outside Québec deplored what was happening in Manitoba and urged the government not to back down. The *Globe and Mail* said the "only legacy of the Manitoba plebiscites is bitterness and division. They settled nothing, and the councils that held them did their communities a disservice." The *Toronto Star* said the plebiscite outcome was "sad but not really surprising. When sensitive issues of minority rights are thrown open to a vote in a campaign in which opponents play on peoples' fears, there is always the danger that the spirit of tolerance will be lost amid the commotion." The *Vancouver Sun* wrote that "those who seek Canadian unity will do well to sympathize with and encourage Manitoba's NDP government in its course, as all three national political parties have already done."

One particularly potent commentary came from a Franco-Manitoban, Paul Daoust of Saint-Eustache. Published in *La Presse* the day of the referendum, Daoust excoriated Trudeau's dream of "coast to coast" bilingualism and endorsed the nationalist view that only Québec can safeguard French Canada. "Trudeau's language policy tries to put a shine on a rotten coffin. It's sad to say, but French in Manitoba is only folklore." He pointed out that when Manitoba entered Confederation with fifty per cent of its population francophone, the federal government paid the way for Poles, Germans and Ukrainians to come from across the sea to Manitoba but it "hadn't a sou" for Québécois who also wanted to settle in the new province. "And now that our people are either assimilated or on their way to assimilation – when even the lieutenant-governor of the province whose name is Jobin cannot speak a word of French – the federal government quivers with pride in talking about repairing the injustices of the past."

> Let's wish that in this whole issue, Franco-Manitobans – or whatever is left of them – are able to find some dignity before they disappear in the western anglophone melting pot. But we have to denounce with as much vigour as possible the federal government's illogical attitude of using francophones outside Québec for the political purposes of national unity. Actually, history will tell if such agitation around a Manitoba that was French a long time ago has negative consequences already; francophobia has already done some damage. In Canada, French will be saved in Québec or not at all. [64] ·

None of this had the slightest effect on the Official Opposition in

Manitoba. The Tory caucus announced that the magnitude of the Yes side's victory had handed it a mandate to use any and all parliamentary and procedural weapons available to stop the government in its tracks. The tactics it finally resorted to created a parliamentary crisis previously unknown in the Commonwealth and unique to this day in the annals of parliamentary democracy.

10

The Bells

IN A WAR OR ANY OTHER CONTEST, it is supposed to be the victor, not the vanquished, who is generous and magnanimous. Not, it seems, when it came to the French language question in Manitoba in the fall of 1983. The municipal plebiscites on the proposed constitutional amendment to make English and French official languages of Manitoba and entrench French language government services in areas of high demand were an exception to that noble tradition. The victors emerged mean-spirited. The vanquished were the ones to demonstrate grace and character.

Four days after voters in Winnipeg and twenty-two other municipalities overwhelmingly rejected the amendment by margins of between seventy-six and seventy-nine per cent, a group of about 100 members of an ad hoc group calling themselves Manitobans Against Government Bilingualism took to the streets near the legislature waving anti-French and anti-bilingual placards.

"They shoved French down our throats; now they're shoving it up our assets," said one. "Stop forced French. Just who won the battle [presumably of the Plains of Abraham]," opined another. And there was more: "English is the Language of Western Canada" – "Who's in charge of Canada, Russ Paulley [the name of the former leader of the provincial NDP was mistakenly used for the current premier, Howard Pawley] or Pierre Trudeau" – "No French nation in Canada" – "Two Nations is One Too Many".

Fred Cameron, one of the organizers, was cheered loudly when he told the crowd through a bullhorn: "Hurray for the English language and long may it live in this world." Despite the provocative sentiments on the placards, Cameron tried to keep the tone moderate. "We don't want any racial or slanderous remarks or other expressions of harassment."

But individuals were only too eager to abandon the caution in interviews with reporters. Middle-aged Ortha Marshall of Winnipeg said this was the first time in her life she had joined a march. "We have no business going back 100 years just to satisfy a few radicals." Giving language rights to a minority was like "having the tail wag the dog" and would simply create "a francophone elite". Allan Fostey, a customs broker from Sprague, said bilingualism had gone far enough. "The building we're standing in front of [the legislature] is not a private club for the elite. The people who serve here work for us. The majority have a right to expect representation … Why can't we say that English is the language of Western Canada? More than ninety-five per cent of the people speak English." Russ Maley, carrying a flag from the Second World War, said French was inadequate to express scientific and technical information and was also inefficient. French, he continued, "always takes several more lines to say the same thing as English". [1]

The contrast with the advertisement La Société franco-manitobaine placed in Winnipeg's two newspapers the day before the plebiscites could hardly be greater. "Whatever the outcome," the ad began, "life will go on. Winnipeg will still be our home, and we will still be friends." It appealed to the English-speaking community to help heal the wounds created by the language issue that had split the province and given it a black eye across Canada. It thanked those who intended to vote in favour of Franco-Manitoban rights and held out an olive branch to those who would reject the position of the province's 74,050-strong francophone community. "We understand your concerns, and respect your right to voice your opposition. We accept your vote as a mirror of your convictions," the ad continued.

Rémi Smith, the young SFM vice-president who headed the society's Winnipeg campaign, wasn't concerned about the wisdom of running an ad essentially conceding defeat the day before the vote. "We wanted people to know ahead of time how we felt, independent of the results,". Smith said. "We never wanted this referendum, we never asked for it, and we knew we would lose it before the campaign even started."

SFM President Léo Robert was blunt. "I think we lost it on September 14th when City Council decided to hold the referendum." It wouldn't have mattered which minority's rights had been on the ballot, he insisted. Whenever the rights of a minority are put to a vote by the majority the outcome is predetermined and inevitable. That, in Robert's view, was the mistake.

Smith said the referendum campaign, distasteful as it was, instilled a new spirit of vitality and enthusiasm in the Franco-Manitoban community and forced it to come forward and speak out for its rights. And he was pleased that so many leaders from the city's ethnic communities, particularly the Ukrainian and Jewish, had joined in solidarity with the Franco-Manitobans.

The ad ended on the same tone as it began: "And to those of you who will take your places at City Hall, we have but one request: let this be the last referendum on any issue that would divide our community, and force friends and neighbors to take sides against one another. Merci." [2]

Within days of the municipal vote, Provincial Court Judge Robert Trudel demonstrated that the referenda had solved nothing because, temporary electoral majorities aside, laws remain laws and constitutional rights remain constitutional rights. He acquitted two men charged with Highway Traffic Act offences because their summonses had been printed in English only.

While Trudel refused to discuss his decision with reporters, Michel Monnin, defence counsel for one of the two accused, CBWFT station manager Bernard Turenne, said the acquittals could trigger legal chaos if other judges followed Trudel's lead. But Crown attorney Georges de Moissac said Trudel's ruling appeared to run contrary to the Court of Appeal's decision on the Roger Bilodeau traffic ticket, which had launched the proposed constitutional settlement. In a split decision, the court had decided the obligation in Section 23 of the Manitoba Act to publish statutes in both languages was directory and not mandatory. However, Monnin, son of Court of Appeal justice Alfred Monnin, said that "notwithstanding the Bilodeau case" it appeared Trudel had based his decision on the 1979 Supreme Court ruling on George Forest's parking ticket, the case that restored the status of the French language in Manitoba after eighty-nine years.

Continued Monnin: "I guess he [Trudel] was saying it's been long enough, [that] sufficient time has elapsed and the province still hasn't done anything …"

On November 21st, the legislature's committee on privileges and elections released its report following province-wide public hearings at which 305 Manitobans appeared and another ninety-nine sent written briefs. It was a brief, vague document that read more like a declaration of principles than a committee recommendation. It proposed the government press ahead with its plans for the constitutional entrenchment of francophone rights and the expansion of French language services and suggested a few small house-keeping amendments. It wasn't to be the last time committee chair Andrue Anstett, a former deputy clerk of the House, was to try to use his extensive knowledge of parliamentary rules and procedures to outwit and outmanoeuvre his political opponents.

The report began by pointing out a fact that was often missed in the media coverage of the committee's tour. The majority of submissions supported the government's plan. Here is what the report said in part:

> Your committee was impressed with the interest shown and analysis of the subject matter demonstrated by many of the submissions. While there were a great many more briefs that supported the government proposal in principle than opposed it, a large number of the briefs noted specific areas of concern. While it may not be easy for the government to find the middle ground between conflicting views, it should seek to do so while protecting the broader public interest. In your committee's view a political resolution of Manitoba's present constitutional difficulties … is preferable to a court imposed solution.

Needless to say, the government's opponents were furious. Tory leader Sterling Lyon immediately accused the government of ducking debate, claiming its silence was due to deep divisions in the NDP caucus. Renegade NDP MLA Russ Doern, who had spearheaded the referendum drive along with businesswoman and retired nurse Pat Maltman, charged that it was unprecedented for a committee to draft such a meaningless report after extensive public hearings. He was "shocked" at "another slap in the face to the people of Manitoba". (3) The *Free Press* editorialized the obvious, that the government had simply found a way to sequester itself from another round of blistering opposition and public attack. But the SFM, too, was taken aback. SFM president Léo Robert was worried about what the report didn't contain.

As 1983 drew to a close, the major political actors on both sides of the drama changed. In November, Anstett was elevated to cabinet as minister of municipal affairs and government House leader. He took over responsibility for the language file from Attorney General Roland Penner. And at a mid-December convention, Gary Filmon, a Winnipeg businessman, former city councillor and minister of consumer and corporate affairs in the previous Tory government, assumed the leadership of the provincial Conservatives from Lyon, who had signalled his intention to retire from public life before the language row erupted. Filmon defeated two other challengers on the second ballot, but his victory was narrow – 291 to 241 – over his nearest competitor, Brian Ransom, Lyon's former finance minister. Ransom was widely perceived to have been the choice of Lyon and the party's old guard, especially its powerful and very conservative rural caucus. The narrowness of Filmon's victory, the perception that he was urban, progressive and a party outsider, plus the charges of vote-buying and "dirty tricks" that swirled around his leadership campaign, would severely restrict his freedom to manoeuvre in the months ahead.

Filmon was perceived to be a dove on the language issue, particularly in comparison to his predecessor. At a bearpit session during the early December leadership convention, all three contenders reiterated their opposition to the government's constitutional amendment route, but all also said their leadership styles would differ from Lyon's. Ransom said he preferred to deal with facts, not personalities, while Filmon promised to use "a calm and reasoned approach. The strength of my arguments will be logic and reason." [4]

The cheers had scarcely faded away from Filmon's victory party Sunday before the government decided to pounce, testing his mettle and hoping to exploit the inevitable post-leadership tensions within the Tory caucus. The government had arrived at its strategy for handling the constitutional file but – in a gesture of feigned accommodation – decided to withhold making it public before showing it to the new Tory leader literally on his first day on the job, Monday, December 12th. Emerging after a ninety-minute meeting, the premier and Filmon appeared to offer the prospect, if not of common ground, of Filmon's promised "calm and reasoned" political debate. "I think there is a real opportunity for consensus here," a happy Pawley told reporters. "There is a specific proposal that offers to do certain things in order to attempt to accomplish part of the government's objectives," Filmon said. He also undertook to present the government's plan to the Tory caucus the next day "for a full and complete review" and to meet again with the premier to report the caucus response.

The hoped-for accommodation was short-lived. Filmon didn't wait for his meeting with the premier. Stampeded by his MLAs, he wrote Pawley a letter, which he promptly released to the media, not only rejecting the government's proposal but claiming it would vastly increase the scope of bilingualism in Manitoba.

The government had told Filmon it would exclude municipalities and school boards from bilingual entrenchment. It wasn't enough for the Tories. They now shifted their opposition to the amended Section 23 of the Manitoba Act declaring English and French to be the official languages of Manitoba. This made Manitoba officially bilingual, they claimed, opening every part of the province's public life to attack by what they had long derided as "linguistic zealots" getting their way through "judge-made law". Said Filmon: "Entrenching Section 23 is a vast extension of constitutional rights beyond anything ever contemplated in the original Manitoba Act or thereafter." A furious Anstett accused Filmon of breaching an agreement he had with Pawley to keep details secret until his meeting with the premier. "The letter is signed by Gary Filmon but obviously it was written by Sterling Lyon," Anstett said. Filmon, now firmly in the clutches of his caucus, said he would not meet with Pawley again. "It is not in the best interests of Manitobans to attempt to deal with this in a closed manner." [5]

The prospects for the government had taken an ominous turn on another front as well. Earlier in the month, a group calling itself Grassroots Manitoba emerged under the leadership of Grant Russell, a federal civil servant on health leave from his job with Canada Manpower and Immigration. He was soon joined by Pat Maltman of Russ Doern-referendum fame. Dedicated to all-out war against any extension of francophone rights in the province, Grassroots soon became the banner under which all Manitobans opposed to the initiative rallied. As its membership burgeoned, it became a formidable extra-parliamentary force, able to mount intimidating phone blitzes that silenced any alternative viewpoint on open-line radio shows. But most importantly, its constant muscle-flexing finally drove the Tories into unprecedented parliamentary obstruction.

Over the next three months, it helped foment such a deeply polarized and angry climate in the province that the entire cabinet and leadership of the SFM had to be placed under round-the-clock police guard. Such was the concern for the safety of some of the major figures and their families that SFM president Robert sent his wife and children out of Manitoba. Meanwhile, many Franco-Manitobans were afraid to use their language in public and reports persisted of French-speaking children across the province being chased, beaten up and otherwise tormented before and after school. There were even stories of people being spat upon for speaking French.

On December 15th, Anstett made the government's revised plan public. It removed French language services from the constitutional amendment and put them in ordinary legislation capable of being repealed or changed in the normal fashion by the legislature alone. Anstett said the bill merely carried forward the previous Tory government's plans to provide French language services. The bill stated that every Manitoban had the right to use French or English in the "principal administrative office" of a department, court, Crown corporation, agency or quasi-judicial body of government. All offices would have to provide French language services in "designated service areas", defined as any municipality where the French language "is the language first learned in childhood and still understood by at least 800 residents or at least eight per cent of the residents."

The government still planned to have English and French declared the official languages of Manitoba in a revised Section 23, but amended the constitutional clause to make it clear municipalities and school boards were excluded. The new wording proposed for Section 23 was:

> English and French are the official languages of Manitoba
> and any right to use either of them as enjoyed under the
> law in force at the time this section comes into force shall
> not be extinguished or restricted by or pursuant to any act
> of the Legislature of Manitoba. This section does not apply
> to municipalities, school divisions or school districts.

A language ombudsman would be appointed to head off frivolous and unreasonable litigation over access to language services. Finally, as before, the number of statutes to be translated was set at 400 "core" laws, less than ten per cent of the province's body of 4,500 unilingual English statutes.

The SFM gave the revision only tepid support. While it stayed on board, it noted that the official bilingualism clause was so watered down and worthless the community would be better off with the existing Section 23 which mirrored exactly Section 133 of the British North America Act and thus formed the basis for minority language rights in Québec and at the federal level.

Once again, Filmon sounded open-minded and conciliatory. He termed the proposals "new" and said they were worthy of close consideration, requesting several weeks to study them. But only a few days passed before he once again flatly rejected them following a caucus meeting. The public and

the government got a taste of what was going on inside the Opposition caucus at the final meeting of the standing committee on privileges and elections on December 22nd. Filmon was deeply embarrassed. He delivered a strong but temperate criticism of the government's plan and sat down. Lyon immediately stood up and before long had launched headlong into his trademark histrionics and vitriol against not just the language plan, but any and all works of the

The Canadian Crucible

"godless socialists" as Filmon sat helplessly by. The NDP, who certainly had little to be happy about, took some brief solace in the obvious discomfiture of the new leader of the opposition and the apparent tensions and splits brewing inside the Tory party. Still, it was cold comfort for a government in as deep a political trough as the Pawley administration found itself.

Manitoba's fifty-seven MLAs finally headed home to their families for the Christmas and New Year's festivities. But rather than visions of sugar plums dancing in their heads, MLAs on both sides of the House entertained thoughts of nightmarish traumas awaiting them once the legislature resumed in early January.

The Tories' opposition was keeping them on the side of the people, but earning them opprobrium from opinion-makers. University of Winnipeg historian Donald Bailey attempted once again to remind Manitobans of the historic duality of their province and nation. If Canadians and Manitobans are generous and accepting to their official minority, they will enrich their nation and province but if they continue to "hammer down" their French compatriots, they will "cripple us all", he wrote in the *Free Press*.

> Manitoba itself has a longstanding, intrinsic French connec-
> tion ... It may seem artificial to attempt to save the language
> rights of only six per cent of the province's population ...
> but even the rights of one per cent are still rights ... The
> effort to save French in Manitoba is worthwhile for the
> other ninety-four per cent too, and for both our province
> itself and our place in Canada it is obvious that opposition
> to French is both futile and costly in both money and
> human dignity ...

> The land of Manitoba, like that of Canada and the Atlantic
> provinces, was first explored and settled by French-speak-
> ing people. Whether there is special merit in being Canada's
> "first-in province" may be doubted, but most Manitobans
> express pride in that fact and they owe that distinction to
> the French and Métis of the Red River Settlement. After
> 1870, then, there was a province rather than a territory to
> come to and that province had a constitution which made
> French and English the political languages of its inhabitants.
> Human memories can be short and gratitude often shallow;

only twenty years passed before a changed majority arbitrarily betrayed the province's creators and illegally changed the Manitoba Act ... Although the 1890 breach of the Manitoba Act was vigorously opposed by Franco-Manitobans, Québécois and a few others at that time, the struggle of power politics was won by Ontario and most non-French Manitobans accepted violence to Manitoba's constitution just twenty-four years before marching off to save the world for democracy ...

The tragedy of Manitoba is that persons of good faith have not been easy to find ... More rides on this than Mr. Lyon's last hurrah; more than the basic issue of respect for the constitution and Canada's history and identity is involved in Mr. Lyon's partisan hairsplitting and the destruction of the essence of justice while hiding behind verbal and legal superficialities ...[6]

The *Free Press* itself weighed in with an appeal to the new Tory leader to put aside the "disorderly, unreasoning and disruptive" conduct of his predecessor who was "appealing to vague fears and ancient hatreds" and instead provide constructive criticism of the government's new proposals. "They [the Tories] have tried gutter-level opposition and it has not stopped the government course. Mr. Filmon has his chance to show that a new hand is on the tiller." [7]

But Filmon, or at least his caucus, wasn't listening. Nor were they the only ones unwilling to rethink old habits and start afresh. The NDP had once again chosen to draft its new plan in secret behind closed doors, had once again given Manitobans the impression they were outside the loop, to be instructed, not consulted.

On January 3, 1984, the day before the House was scheduled to resume, Anstett released yet another revision of the language package. The changes were small but significant. The use of the English and French languages was to be described as a "freedom" rather than a "right". This, the House leader said, would further restrict the likelihood of frivolous court challenges and surprise judgements. Predictably, it did nothing to help the medicine go down with the anti-bilingualism forces. Maverick New Democrat Russ Doern said it wouldn't be acceptable to Manitobans. The word "official" was the real problem and it would have to go. "No matter what the qualifiers are, they are giving special, official status to French," he said. [8]

Once more, Filmon's initial reaction was positive, but once more, he rejected it after meeting his caucus. "There is a risk and a concern that [it] might be interpreted to bring about an expansion of French language rights," he told reporters. "I think that if you're expanding any minority rights at the expense of a majority, then you have to be concerned with the effects." While acknowledging that francophones have a special status in Canada, Filmon said "you have to look at the practicality. If it means duplication of positions, of services and additional costs, is it a priority … and what does it accomplish?" The Tory leader also drew a distinction between human rights and linguistic rights, questioning the need to entrench and expand French language rights in Manitoba. "I don't see how anyone is being harmed by not having an expansion of their linguistic rights." [9]

The opposition leader would not be alone in his belief that language rights were not the same as other human rights. In the early 1990s, the Supreme Court of Canada itself viewed language rights as merely political rights. The attitude undoubtedly arises from the fact Canada is a nation of immigrants. Many Canadians come here determined to improve their quality of life and that of their children and fully prepared, even eager, to learn a new language to do so. Because of the flawed teaching of Canadian history, many never learned about the centrality of language to Canada's ethos and therefore had difficulty fathoming French Canadians' determination to keep their tongue. But it is one thing to expect to learn a new language as an immigrant. It is another to consider your language to be a national language and then have it taken away from you. French Canadians believed their language, like English, was part of the compact that founded the country. Still, from the beginning to the end of Manitoba's tortured, century-long linguistic struggle, it apparently never occurred to more than a handful of anglophones to put the shoe on the other foot, to ask themselves how they would have felt if, by one stroke of the legislative pen, they had lost the right to use their language to teach their children, to debate the laws that governed them and to defend themselves in court when their liberty and perhaps even their lives were at stake.

The *Free Press* used stinging satire to rebuke the opposition leader in an editorial on January 6, 1984:

Gary Filmon has come up with his position on the fourth version of the Pawley government's constitutional amendment. He is opposed to it. But his work is not done yet for he has yet to produce a plausible reason for his opposition. By announcing he is against, Mr. Filmon keeps himself in the same camp with Sterling Lyon, whom he dare not contradict, with other members of his caucus, whom he needs more than they need him and with all those around the province who do not actually know what the government is proposing and who do not need to know in order to find out they are against. But to make his position plausible to a wider audience, Mr. Filmon should work out an argument that is related to what the government is proposing.

There is a risk, Mr. Filmon says, that the proposal might be interpreted to bring about an expansion of French language rights … There is a risk when Mr. Filmon gets out of bed each morning that he will fall and break his bones. But he does get up none the less … When a frightened child fears a monster in the closet, the parent can turn on the light, open the closet and satisfy all reasonable observers that there is no monster. But the child who enjoys being scared will not say where the monster is. The parent is powerless to prove the absence of a monster who is given neither a description nor a location … An opposition argument that has a basis in fact deserves a hearing … Mr. Filmon's whimperings cannot be taken seriously. He should be told firmly to be quiet and go back to sleep.

If the attack hurt the beleagured opposition leader, he could take solace in the fact a volunteer army was marshalling to march behind him, or at least, behind the Tory caucus. Grassroots Manitoba held a formal news conference to announce its stable of high profile supporters including former federal Liberal cabinet minister James Richardson; former Manitoba Liberal Progressive premier Douglas Campbell, and former prominent New Democrats Herb Schulz, brother-in-law of Manitoba's first NDP premier, Ed Schreyer, as well as Bill Hutton, once an NDP provincial party president and a federal NDP candidate. Grassroots head Grant Russell said the organization had formed "more or less spontaneously" and probably had at least 10,000 supporters. The NDP was committing political suicide, he said. "Until now they've been shooting themselves in the foot constantly. Now they're aiming at their head." [10]

Grassroots Manitoba brands French services back door bilingualism.

Grassroots' first shot across the government's bow would consist of large ads run in both the *Free Press* and the *Sun* calling on all Manitobans opposed to "official bilingualism" to fill out protest coupons and telephone their MLAs. SFM president Robert said the society had no plans to counter Grassroots. "I think we have said all we can say on this question. This has been dragging on for two years now and we're getting a little tired of it." [11]

On January 10th, the Tories gave further evidence that while their party leadership had changed, their policy and strategy stayed the same. Twice during the afternoon sitting, the Official Opposition brought business to a halt by walking out of the House, on one occasion leaving the bells to ring for forty minutes. Then after offering a deceptive olive branch – an amendment to the constitutional resolution proposing the entrenchment of statute translation only – which the speaker took under advisement, the Tories' bell-ringing ratcheted up sharply. For four successive days – January 16th, 17th, 18th and 19th – they walked out of the legislature immediately after Question Period and stayed out for the remainder of each sitting, stopping the government dead in its tracks and holding its entire legislative program hostage.

In the parliamentary system, bells ring for only as long as it takes the party whips to round up their members for a recorded vote. Then the whips enter the chamber, a signal to the speaker that the parties are ready for the vote to be called. By British custom and tradition, if one whip stays out, the vote cannot be called. But bell-ringing as an obstruction tactic is the mirror opposite. The opposition members don't intend to be available and the opposition whip isn't interested in rounding them up. Instead, this form of bell-ringing is designed not only to stop the vote but to shut down parliamentary government. All parliamentary business is halted and the core institution of parliamentary democracy is rendered silent, empty and impotent. Obstructive bell-ringing is usually set off by a motion to adjourn the House, which can be made at any time by any member and is not debatable. The speaker puts the question to a voice vote. The government usually wins. But any member, including a member of the opposition, can ask for a recorded vote. The speaker orders the sergeant-at-arms to "call in the members". The bells sound, the opposition leaves and stays away – sometimes for hours, but in Manitoba's case, soon for days and weeks at a time.

The Manitoba Legislature's bells are large electric buzzers – fire alarms, really – with their trademark strident sound. Dotted at intervals along the vaulted limestone corridors on all four floors of the building, they set up an echo and a reverberation that can inflict physical pain in the eardrums of those who must pass by or work near them. So, for almost thirty hours that week of January 1984, all occupants of the legislature – civil servants and politicians alike – sought refuge from the bells behind closed office doors in order to endure the sonic assault. The eerie stillness of the deserted hallways combined with the relentless, awful, cacophony of nether-worldly noise amplified the atmosphere of gathering crisis.

It was a mere dress rehearsal for what was to come. The *Free Press* weighed in with an editorial that was accurate but unfortunately, not prescient. Calling the Conservative bell-ringing "skulking" and "a little game" to avoid discussion, the newspaper said there comes a point "definable only as a matter of political judgement" when those seeking to avoid debate and decision by refusing to appear "can no longer prevent the vote from happening".

> It does not stand to reason that a minority of members should be able by running away to suspend indefinitely the work of the House. If the Conservatives intend to form a government later on, they should be more careful of the precedents they create … [A] system of government which relies on prolonged obstruction as a usual method of opposition does not serve anyone's interests. [12]

On January 21st, Filmon moved a six-month hoist on the language services bill, telling reporters that all twenty-three members of his caucus intended to speak on it and all would take their full forty-five minute time allotments. He claimed the hoist was to give an opportunity for passions to cool in the province. Reminding the House that the legislation was not to go into effect until January 1, 1987, he said: "We need that healing influence before venturing further into uncharted waters." The same day, Speaker Jim Walding ruled the Tories' translation-only amendment to the constitutional proposal out of order, because it changed the basic intent.

On January 23rd, the NDP served notice it would bring in closure on the services bill, first time a Manitoba government had used the parliamentary guillotine since the John Bracken administration forced a vote on the 1929 throne speech. Under Manitoba rules, once the closure motion has passed, debate cannot be adjourned until two a.m. the next day, extending the daily sitting by four hours after which the vote must be called. Anstett said the bell-ringing had forced the government's hand. "Obstruction became very apparent and we had no choice." But Conservative House leader Harry Enns disagreed. Manitobans "accept these tactics … they feel strongly about the issue." [13]

In his speech on January 23rd, Tory backbencher Arnold Brown (Rhineland) provided a representative sample of the tenor of the debate. He regaled the House with the perils of federal bilingualism and warned members to prepare for it or worse in Manitoba:

> Whenever you'll be phoning any of the Crown corporations, Crown agencies or whatever, the first thing that they're going to be doing is they're going to be answering

the telephone in French. This just happened in Winkler the other day when a lady came up to me and says, Mr. Brown, I cannot get through to Air Canada. I said, well, that seems very strange. She says all I'm getting is some kind of mumbo-jumbo whenever I phone. I said let me try for you. So I went and I tried to call the number and what happened? At Air Canada in Winnipeg over here, they were answering in French first and this lady hung up because she had no idea what they were saying ... People, especially in the prairie provinces, take great exception to this. [14]

Second reading of the services bill was given in the early hours of January 25th under closure. In a move that stunned the Tories, Anstett immediately announced the government was ready to use closure on the constitutional amendment, although he refused to say when he would invoke it.

The next day, January 26th, the Manitoba language debate took on a new and even more menacing tone. It was learned that security had been stepped up to protect the premier as a result of a death threat. Questioned at a news conference, Pawley was reluctant to talk about it. "There have been threats on my life. I don't think that should surprise you ... I don't take them very seriously," he said. Pawley's press aide, Garth Cramer, said the premier had received a large number of abusive calls during the summer when the language deal was revealed. "But this one was a death threat. We advised building security."

Government sources said other ministers were also receiving threatening calls. The government security chief, Jim Johnston, told reporters he was aware of the threats to the premier and "some steps have been taken". Winnipeg police and the RCMP had been advised. Filmon revealed he and his family had been getting harassing phone calls too, "saying things like 'you'd better watch out' to my kids." He hadn't reported them to police and thought the less said the better. "I am not sure if they are threats or emotional outbursts. The best way to handle it is to ignore it." [15]

That night an angry crowd of about 800 organized by Grassroots Manitoba descended on the legislature to protest the language proposals and to demand a meeting with the premier. Scheduled to use one of the largest rooms in the building, the rally's numbers were so great the overflow gathered

DALE CUMMINGS / WINNIPEG FREE PRESS

on the grand staircase between the two massive bronze bison, Manitoba's majestic symbol.

The crowd had to endure the cacophony of the bells because the Opposition Tories had walked out early that afternoon to object to Anstett's plans to use closure to force through the constitutional amendment. Speaker after speaker denounced the government. At one point, a member of the crowd shouted: "Bring us Anstett – we want to hang him." Some took up posts outside the premier's second floor office chanting: "We want Pawley" and "Howard is a coward." They threatened to smash down the door. The legislature's security staff took up posts outside Pawley's office.

Filmon told the angry mob the government had embarked "on a terrible course" and promised "we will do whatever we can to stop it". The government's use of closure, he said, demonstrated its contempt not just for the opposition and the institution of parliament, "but for all you Manitobans". He received a loud ovation. Lyon also played to the crowd. "The bells are ringing tonight because you have got a government that refuses to listen to the people. We are employing every parliamentary device … and we will continue to do that." Privately, however, one Tory MLA conceded that he was scared by the mood of the Grassroots mob because it might turn violent.

After his two-hour meeting with the premier, Grassroots leader Grant Russell told the assemblage he had had "no influence" on the government. "They don't feel the people of Manitoba understand." A loud chorus of boos temporarily competed with the ear-splitting clangour of the bells. They were finally turned off at the 10 p.m. adjournment hour. The last Grassroots stragglers departed the legislature at 10:30 p.m., promising to be back the next day to demand Lieutenant Governor Pearl McGonigal refuse to sign the language services bill into law and dissolve the legislature and call for an election. [16] Pawley told reporters later he attributed much of the difficulty his government was having to misconceptions about the initiative's intent and results. The protest had not shaken his resolve to pass the bill and the constitutional amendment.

True to their word, the Grassroots protesters were back the next day with petitions containing the signatures of about 28,400 Manitobans, which they presented to McGonigal, urging her to intervene to prevent the government from imposing "unwanted bilingualism" and if necessary, dismiss the government. One of the petitions given to the lieutenant governor had been circulated by Conrad Kelly of Winnipeg and endorsed by Ron Gostick, a known racist and anti-Semite, publisher of *The Canadian Intelligencer*, a far-right extremist magazine based in Flesherton, Ont. and founder of the Canadian League of Rights, an organization that distributed books and tracts peddling anti-Jewish conspiracy theories and Holocaust denials.

Manuel Prutschi, director of community relations for the Winnipeg Jewish Community Council of the Canadian Jewish Congress told the *Free Press* Gostick's literature propounded "an extreme right wing philosophy which believes white, Anglo-Saxon Protestant Christianity is fundamental to the survival of Western civilization". What interest would a far-right anti-Semite have in Manitoba's French language question? Prutschi replied it was usual for such people to value the British connection as the way to preserve civilized society. "There is no room for minorities and no rights for anyone but themselves."

Grassroots' Russell said he was shocked when he heard of the link between Kelly and Gostick. "I reject extremism in the physical sense and in the political sense … As far as his [Kelly's] relation with Canadian Intelligence

Publications, [sic]... I know nothing." Lyon also acknowledged he was bothered by the sudden appearance of a neo-fascist group. "But what can you do? It doesn't dim the value of the opposition to what the government is doing." [17]

Kelly insisted he had acted "strictly as an individual" in circulating the petition but refused to say whether he was linked to Gostick. However, a letter to Manitoba subscribers of the *Canadian Intelligencer* and League for Rights publications signed by Gostick urged members to circulate the petition "and get them back to Conrad Kelly without delay".[18]

Anti-French, anti-Catholic bigotry has long been one of the hallmarks of Canadian far right extremists. The American white supremacist Ku Klux Klan was active on the prairies throughout the early years of the twentieth century. While the white-sheeted cross-burners in the American South targetted their black fellow citizens, the Canadian version of the KKK had French Canadian Roman Catholics as their target of hatred and exclusion.

The Manitoba paroxysm wasn't going unnoticed in Québec. Writing in *Le Devoir* on January 28th under the headline "The parties and fanaticism", Jean-Claude LeClerc called what was happening in the province "disgraceful".

> From the disgraceful incidents dominating the headlines and concerning the recognition of French in Manitoba, [Premier] René Lévesque didn't take long to conclude that Québec is the one and only place where the French minority is safe and secure in Canada. And that, as a result, anglophone Québécois must get used to the kind of protection required to safeguard French, despite their difficulties with Bill 101.

> It is as true today as it was in the past that without a territorial and political base, no national group can feel truly secure. Manitoba's example doesn't necessarily argue in favour of Québec separation. But it eloquently demonstrates that nothing is easy or definitive when it comes to the matter of religious or linguistic national rights and that a charter alone lacks political force. Despite the cabinet's compromises in the midst of its ordeal, credit must be given to the Pawley government for its courage from the outset of this storm and its perseverance in adversity. If the NDP were a growing force in Canada, one could place upon it hopes for the final

resolution of this difficult question … What is striking at a
time when fanatics, both virulent and silent, hold the floor,
is the manoeuverings of the Liberals who are boasting about
having made Canada bilingual and having endowed it with
a charter of linguistic rights …What lesson can one draw
from this sad episode? Both federal and provincial parties
have already done too much damage to linguistic minorities.
They must now have the foresight to rebuke the fanaticism
that has arisen … In linguistic matters, in Canada and in
every province where this question might arise, the parties
must seek a multipartisan solution. Fanatics should understand, without any doubt, that they cannot put their vote up
for bidding, nor can they trigger a vulgarity contest which
would see minorities and the whole country pay the price.

The same day, Lieutenant Governor Pearl McGonigal met with
Pawley to tell him of the concerns expressed to her by the Grassroots representatives and turned the petitions over to him. "I told them I would bring
it to the attention of the first minister, but I won't advise him," McGonigal,
a Trudeau Liberal appointee, said. Grassroots ratcheted up the pressure on
Anstett, busing in a crowd from his constituency to confront him in the
legislature and then helping to organize a rowdy, threatening meeting at
Oakbank in the minister's Springfield riding on January 29th. One member
of the 100-strong constituency delegation that came to the legislature told
the minister he had been a life-long New Democrat, but was quitting the
party for good over the language issue. Nose to nose with Anstett, Gerald
Shields, sixty-eight, said: "I admired you but you let me down. I want to
disassociate myself from the NDP." Handing Anstett his party card, he
continued: "It grieves me, it hurts me, to do this to you." Replied Anstett:
"It hurts me, too."

The next day in Oakbank, a crowd of over 600 people repeatedly
yelled at the government House leader to "resign" as he attempted to defend
the government's language proposals. The riding, historically strong Tory turf,
contains a sizeable Franco-Manitoban population. But Anstett couldn't count
on support even from that quarter, at least, not from those who came to the
meeting. "I'm totally against what you're bringing in," Julie Blais told the minister. "It's going to turn my neighbours against me because I'm French. The

legislation is turning the English-speaking people against me." Lynn Beaudette called the bill "a very scary piece of legislation. It's discriminatory against everyone other than the French. The SFM doesn't speak for all the French people in Manitoba." But Anstett, a parliamentary scholar and political scientist in his own right, stood his ground, recalling eighteenth century British parliamentarian Edmund Burke's famous address to the electors of Bristol:

> When I ran in 1981 I said I would do my best to represent
> your interests. But I also said that in the final analysis I
> would have to use my own best judgement as to what's
> right and wrong. When you elect an MLA you elect the per-
> son because you have respect for their [sic] judgement. [19]

The Tories' walk-outs and bell-ringing were now a daily routine, commencing immediately after Question Period and running until the end of every sitting day. During the last week of January, the unbearable bells of the Manitoba legislature rang for a total of four days and fourteen hours. The Tories would often not return for the evening adjournment at 10 p.m., leaving the bells to ring all night until the next day at 10 a.m., when they would return for Question Period. The author warned about the threat bell-ringing poses to parliament and to the concept of responsible government and democracy itself:

> The parliamentary system is at once very strong and very
> fragile. The bell-ringing tactic first developed by the federal
> Conservatives is the most potent threat to its existence yet
> devised. It is qualitatively different from all other parliamen-
> tary manoeuvres because it renders the institution silent and
> powerless. Married to the sophisticated polling technology
> of the 1980s, it could end representative government.

> From now on, thanks to the precedent here and in Ottawa,
> an opposition obtaining an opinion poll majority on a single
> issue could force a duly elected government to give up its
> right to govern or face an election ... Eventually, parliament
> would become irrelevant. In its place would be a form of
> plebiscitary chaos with no government capable of governing
> past its first controversial decision ... [T]here would be per-
> manent political instability with all the dangers that poses. [20]

In the final week of January, the government and opposition reached a compromise. The government would hold closure in abeyance and the opposition would allow the services bill to go to an outside legislative committee for public hearings. However, the Conservatives signalled they would not allow the services bill to pass the House either before or at the same time as the constitutional resolution for fear that would entrench it, too, and vastly expand the legitimate use of the French language.

At the hearings, MLAs were treated to anti-French bigotry so vicious and extreme that even the Tories privately expressed disgust and refused to question witnesses. A succession of briefs claimed a francophone conspiracy was trying to take over the province and Canada and blamed French Canadians for everything but the assassination of President John F. Kennedy. "The French never stop pushing for more special privileges," said Ian MacPherson. Both the RCMP and the Canadian Armed Forces are controlled by the French and the western provinces are next, he said. To save itself, Western Canada will have to secede and join the United States. To back his fears, MacPherson said the French language was given the "preferred page" in the proposed legislation, the left-hand page. Vivien Friesen said the government's language proposal was part of "a French power takeover". She called the SFM a "bunch of racists".

Two former prominent New Democrats accused their erstwhile party of fomenting racism in Manitoba. "You don't understand what you've done. You've created racism in this province," said Sid Green. Bilingual himself, Green said the government's legal and constitutional approach had set the cause of bilingualism back 100 years. Herb Schulz charged the government with legislating "official racism" and pitting Manitoban against Manitoban, leading to the "gradual ghettoization" of the province into language districts. "Either withdraw this legislation or resign. That's the only honourable thing to do," he said. The committee room shook with the applause for every anti-government speaker. [21]

Grassroots was riding the wave. On the evening of February 2nd, it rented the Winnipeg Convention Centre for a mass rally against the government and the language proposals. A crowd estimated at 2,500 poured in from across Manitoba to hear eight speakers from four political parties. Two busloads came from Portage la Prairie and more from communities such as Roblin and Altona. Ten City of Winnipeg police detectives were on hand to watch the crowd for possible violent outbursts. Unlike the threatening affair at the legislature, this rally was orderly and quiet, except for the inevitable standing ovations for the anti-government rhetoric cascading from the stage. According to newspaper reports, most of the crowd was fifty years of age and over. A few Franco-Manitobans watched from the back of the hall. One, Jacques Forest, son of the French language crusader, said he found the spectacle frightening.

Grassroots head Russell said his group had support from Saskatchewan, Ontario and the United States. Lyon told the throng any injustices to Franco-Manitobans perpetrated in 1890 had been remedied by his government in 1980 . "No further restoration of rights is needed or called for." Maverick NDP MLA Russ Doern echoed Lyon. Franco-Manitobans aren't suffering and no additional rights need be extended to them, he said. Former Liberal party leader Bobby Bend warned the services law could result in job discrimination by favouring those who spoke French. Douglas Campbell, Manitoba's last Liberal premier and one of the most prominent members of Grassroots, called the legislation "dangerous for Manitoba. Never before in the history of Manitoba has the will of the people been so callously disregarded". Grassroots activist Pat Maltman told the media the number of names on petitions against the government's plan had reached 42,000. (22)

Meanwhile, Québec's influential daily, *Le Devoir*, had despatched one of its reporters, Jean-Pierre Proulx, to Manitoba where he would stay and write almost daily front-page stories until the saga of the bells reached its climax at the end of February. Proulx probed the issue from every angle and his long and detailed articles – sometimes two or three at a time – gave his readers blow-by-blow accounts of the crisis from the perspectives of all its players under the appropriately black-coloured logo, "The battle of the French in Manitoba". It was unbiased, straightforward reporting. Carried as it was almost always on Page One above the fold, it was also disturbing and dispiriting, especially for French Canada's federalists.

On February 3rd, Proulx wrote that the concept of Confederation as a pact between two equal linguistic groups so accepted in Québec simply didn't exist in Manitoba. He quoted one Joseph Schwartz, "an honest citizen" of Ashern, saying that the majority of Franco-Manitobans were quite happy with how things were, just as their ancestors had been for the past 113 years. "They have been excellent citizens and they are in step with the non-francophones of Manitoba. They are able to protect their culture, their religion and their language without interference by one person." Meanwhile, in

Québec, Léo Létourneau, the newly-elected president of la Fédération des Francophones hors Québec said that what really mattered was to revive the debate for French language services at the federal, provincial and municipal levels.

On February 4th, Proulx expanded upon the giant Grassroots rally, telling readers that Manitobans, "tired of being labelled 'bigots' and 'red-necks' by the Pawley government and the nation's editorialists", were now trying to proclaim themselves to be "the friends of Franco-Manitobans". He quoted former NDP cabinet minister Sidney Green saying that the French language didn't belong solely to Franco-Manitobans any more than the English language was the sole possession of English Canadians.

While the convention centre was reverberating to the applause of the Grassroots rally, the legislature's bells had once more resumed their unbearable clamour. After a brief truce, the Tories had walked out. This time, there appeared to be no end in sight to the tense political standoff.

The next day, a small, more militant group of Franco-Manitobans calling themselves l'Association des Pro-Canadiens du Manitoba announced it had hired former NDP cabinet minister Sidney Green to assess the legal possibilities of forcing the Supreme Court to rule on the intent and impact of the government's package. Saying the SFM "doesn't speak for us", spokesman Maurice Prince called the agreement a backward step. "French language rights were interrupted in 1890 in Manitoba when they were developing naturally here. French language development should continue where it left off. It is not up to the provincial government to say to what extent French can be used in this province." French, like English, is an official language of Manitoba to be used by those who can use it throughout the province, Prince continued.

Prince's view was echoed on February 4th in an anonymous letter sent to the *Free Press* editorial department from a man describing himself as a Métis Manitoban. The letter was a poignant cry from a people who felt long lost and forgotten. Its words brought the events of 1869-70 back into sharp focus. The Métis, not the SFM, should be negotiating French language rights, the writer said:

> Manitoba history reveals that the controversy between the
> Métis and French Canadians over French language rights
> has been around for a long while – since 1916 in fact! At
> that time, French Canadians were only trying to procure,

at most, the legitimacy of French as a subject of instruction in the schools, whereas ... the Métis argued that French should be a language of instruction, a big difference indeed!

As far as I'm concerned, the bilingualism issue has become nothing but un jeu de mots [a game of words] between the SFM, the Pawley administration, the opposition and the general public, hence my desire to have the Métis reassert their claim to being the only legitimate organization through whom the government should re-negotiate the 1870 constitution. We Métis represent the 'Silent Francophone Majority' who dwell, as social outcasts for the most part, on the periphery of a society which has too long been oblivious to our needs ... isolated and outnumbered by wave upon wave of newcomers ... Further to this, we also have anywhere from 100,000 to 200,000 people in this province who can legitimately claim, in varying degrees, to being of Métis blood ... As I am the father of three children, aged eleven, ten and seven years old, I am understandably very concerned over the issue of French language rights which, you may be certain, shall prove disadvantageous to future generations should the SFM acquiesce to the government's watered-down proposals.

In summation, I am disenchanted with the lack of decisiveness as currently being exemplified by the SFM, but, not least, angry over the fact that the Métis, who are descendants of the original negotiators of the 1870 constitution, have been denied a voice in the renegotiation of their constitution.

That same day, the government finally decided to try to break the impasse in the legislature. After the fifth Tory walkout in seven sitting days, acting premier and Health Minister Laurent Desjardins called on Speaker Jim Walding to act. "It can be settled very easily by the Speaker. After a certain time, the Speaker has a duty and a responsibility to step in," he said. Anstett, a parliamentary expert, had also on two previous occasions advised the speaker that he was within his powers to call a vote on the closure motion without the opposition in the House. Walding's only response was to rebuke Desjardins. "I hope [he] is not reflecting on the chair." [24]

The British-born Walding was first elected to the legislature in a 1971 byelection, one of two that gave the Schreyer government its first majority. An optician, he laboured in the government backbench until the NDP lost power in 1977 and then assumed a number of critic roles in the shadow cabinet, ending up with the prestigious post of energy. When the NDP returned to office in 1981, he naturally expected energy or, failing that, another equally important portfolio, but it was not to be. He was passed over and his consolation – the speaker's chair with all its accompanying prestige, pomp and opportunity to travel to Commonwealth parliamentary conferences all over the world – was not sufficient to assuage his wounded pride.

The language imbroglio gave him an opportunity to hit back at the premier he believed had slighted him and he seized it. It wasn't long before the government learned not only just how much malice he bore, but that his wife Valerie was very active in the Grassroots Manitoba crusade against its language policy.

Under the British parliamentary system, the speaker is seen as the servant of the House. But in many ways, he or she is its master, the interpreter, upholder and applier of its rules. Speakers who are elected by all members in a secret ballot, as is the case in the House of Commons in Ottawa and in Manitoba since the NDP came to office in 1999, enjoy real independence and the power and respect that goes with it. But an elected speaker is still a relatively new and rare phenomenon. Historically, speakers were chosen by the first minister from within the government caucus after consultation with the opposition parties. Not surprisingly, the vast majority of those individuals were mere servants of the government of the day. Walding's stalwart defiance of his party and government, therefore, was unique in Manitoba history. For whatever reason – personal animus, dislike of the constitutional amendment, belief he was reflecting the public will, conviction that his action best safeguarded the institution and the rights and privileges of its members – Walding refused to do the government's bidding. He followed the new precedent established two years' earlier by House of Commons Speaker Jeanne Sauvé when the opposition Tories for the first time used bell-ringing to bring Parliament to a standstill, a precedent that was soon superceded by a rule change in that house. Walding steadfastly refused to meet the House unless both government and opposition were prepared to be present and had signalled that intention by sending their whips into the chamber to answer the call to vote.

The same day Desjardins' appeal was rejected by Walding, a confrontation almost turned violent at the entrance to the government caucus room. The portly health minister and Natural Resources Minister Al Mackling blocked a group of about thirty-five of Anstett's Springfield constituents determined to go inside to confront him and demand his resignation. "What you are doing now is harassment and intimidation," Mackling shouted at Lois Edie, who described herself both as a "friend" of the government House leader and a loyal Conservative. Mackling tried to close the door on her but she blocked him with her foot.

Security guards arrived in time to stop the situation from getting out of hand. They cleared the area in front of the caucus room and stood guard while the government members met inside. When Anstett finally came out, he was flanked by two of the government's tallest ministers, Jay Cowan and John Plohman, who accompanied him up to his third floor office. Security guards then blocked the stairway. When the Springfield group got access to the office from another stairway, security guards ushered them away. Anstett met later with about fifty people from his riding. Once more, they called on him to resign.

On February 4th, the premier himself was swarmed by a mob shouting "Heil Howard" at a River East community event billed as an opportunity to discuss the economy and jobs. New Democrats present responded by yelling "fascist bigots" back at the gate-crashers, one of whom was Herb Schulz. They demanded a vote on whether to drop the economy as the topic and take up the language issue. By their own count, they won it by a split 60-40 decision. At first the premier tried to carry on with his economic message amid the catcalls and slurs. "This is ridiculous," Dorothy Johnstone shrieked at the premier. "This was a complete waste of time." Finally, he relented on condition "you are prepared to listen to what I have to say".

Pawley couldn't change their minds. They accused him of making "deals" with Prime Minister Pierre Trudeau. A new Canadian from Chile drew an unflattering parallel from his own country's fractious history. "I saw this happen in my country. When people don't listen to each other any more, it means danger," said Jaime Carrasco. [24]

Three days later, a man was ejected from the legislature's public galleries when he shouted "Throw 'em out" and twice called on the speaker to force an election. Henry Nichiporick said he wasn't anti-French but he opposed the government's plans because they were "just splitting people". [25]

A mixture of cheers and jeers met the premier at a rally in his own riding of Selkirk on February 8th. Pawley appealed for understanding. "Surely, friends, we don't require nine judges in Ottawa to impose a decision on Manitobans?" But his message fell largely on deaf ears. Selkirk Body Shop owner Hubert Pallaers assailed the premier from a floor microphone. "Wouldn't it be a lot cheaper to produce bumper-stickers that said: "Bilodeau. Public Enemy Number One?" Brandishing a $100 bill above his head, Pallaers extolled the virtues of established English words. "What's a hamburger in French? It's a hamburger." But others were supportive. Teacher Rob Sarginson called for tolerance. And Rosanne Hooker said "I'm a Canadian and proud of it and I'm proud of what's being done by the Pawley government." [26]

Through Le Devoir, Québécois were learning that even though the French language services legislation was "un tissu de compromis" (a pack of compromises), Franco-Manitobans still found it acceptable because they felt they had little choice but to continue to put their faith in the Pawley government. "They have been constant in their determination despite the Conservative assaults," SFM president Léo Robert told Proulx. [27]

As the rancour and outbursts grew louder, Manitoba's national image grew blacker. On February 13th, Le Devoir's Proulx reported that an increasing number of Manitobans were becoming fearful that no matter how the language crisis was resolved, the province's stature on the nation's stage would suffer severe damage.

> There is little doubt that this province of a million people from every part of the world has had its image tarnished … Every racist remark – and there have been many in public and elsewhere – seems to reverberate throughout all of Canada and overseas. Suddenly, Manitoba journalists are being questioned by their colleagues across Canada, the United Kingdom, France, the United States and West Germany. The topic is always the same: language.

The same day, the paper's editor, Lise Bissonnette, penned a stinging editorial headlined "The progress of the terror". She began with a reference to an interview the Manitoba premier gave in which he said "I am not particularly interested in the word 'official' in the constitutional resolution that is

The Canadian Crucible

meant to restore rights to the French language in Manitoba." She continued:

> Such a statement is a bad omen because it is expressed at
> a time when the Tory Opposition is keeping on with its
> procedural blackmail in order to block the adoption of the
> resolution in the Legislative Assembly. Tired, the govern-
> ment could drop the symbolic clause of this resolution that
> recognizes French as an official language in Manitoba. It
> would be one tumble, one too many.

Québécois, like the rest of Canadians, she said, are under the impression that the current debate in Manitoba was not meant merely to restore the rights of Franco-Manitobans, illegally abolished a century ago, but to expand them. But, she went on: "That is not the case and it is important to remember it." She reminded her readers that the SFM's own lawyer, Joseph Magnet, had opposed the December compromise removing French language services from constitutional protection. According to Magnet, the compromise "not only jeopardizes the rights won by the francophone population in Manitoba but opens the door to more damage". She also reminded her readers that the SFM ignored his advice and accepted the amendment anyway. Their reasons, she said, were obvious:

> We know why the SFM did not listen to its advisor and
> accepted the December compromise. The brutality of
> the reaction from the Tory Opposition and the hysteria
> it fed in some quarters were threatening to undermine
> any francophone life in Manitoba ...

She was still of the opinion that Franco-Manitobans would be better to go to the Supreme Court because she was sure they would win.

> But at what price of unbridled hostility and blatant racism?
> This victory by terror, which had and still has some impact
> on the government and the representatives of the SFM, is
> not just a speed bump ... Manitoba is shattering the old
> dream of the "Canadian duality". This historical concept is
> not valid any more over there and opponents to the French
> fact are saying it quite openly ... After the results of the last
> Census, a lot was said about the spectacular progress of

individual bilingualism, especially in the western provinces where immersion classes are successful. How is it possible to reconcile this fad and the show of irrational denial that we are currently seeing in Winnipeg? It is because the French language has become a discarnate language. A former member of the Pawley government, Sid Green, said "the French language does not belong to Franco-Manitobans". In other words, it is not linked to the historical rights of this very same community that is speaking it. And that is more and more the leading slant in English Canada … In Ottawa, some people are hoping that unanimous consent from all parties would bring speedy adoption of the resolution, therefore avoiding in the federal capital the disgraceful debate and the despicable agitation that we can see in Winnipeg. This is an unacceptable strategy … We cannot accept another radically diluted version [of the constitutional package] without another assessment unless we are ready to sacrifice – one more time and right in line with the spirit of Canadian history – the fate of the francophone minority to the electoral peace of each camp.

An increasingly tense set of negotiations between the provincial Tories and their new and staunchly pro-bilingual national leader continued to bear no fruit. Brian Mulroney had won his party's leadership determined to break the ninety-year political drought the Conservatives had faced in Québec, due in large part to the seminal national events begun by Manitoba's birth. But Manitoba Tories, a majority of whom had supported Mulroney's rival, Joe Clark, in the previous year's leadership race, were more interested in their own political fortunes than those of their federal cousins.

Speaking at a Manitoba federal Liberal gathering on February 5th, Manitoba's cabinet representative, Transport Minister Lloyd Axworthy was blunt. The language debate, he said, "is being taken over by a small core of extremists bent on depriving Franco-Manitobans of all their rights". The Conservatives had hijacked the legislature and were inflaming anti-French sentiment throughout the province. He defended NDP attempts to end the debate by invoking closure. "Closure is one of those things a government must do if they're ever going to make a decision."

Former premier Lyon posed as much a threat to national unity as Québec Premier René Lévesque, Axworthy continued. He noted that Lévesque was trying to advance separatism by telling Québécois the federal government wanted to force his province to provide bilingual services to its anglophone minority while Manitobans aren't prepared to protect their francophone minority.

> The unity of this country again is put into some peril because Mr. Lévesque is a dangerous man from that point of view, but no more dangerous than what Sterling Lyon is doing ... Sterling Lyon, in a strange, paradoxical way is doing the same thing Mr. Lévesque is doing, with the same attitudes and the same results ... You're talking about the provision of some very minimal services ... I'm getting very upset by what I've seen in the last two or three weeks. [28]

Unless Manitobans of goodwill started to come forward, the transport minister warned, severe damage would be done to the province, to its image in the country and to national unity. He concluded by quoting William Butler Yeat's famous poem, *The Second Coming*: "The best lack all conviction, while the worst are full of passionate intensity."

As the temperature of Axworthy's "small core of extremists" continued to rise, the SFM was reminded by its lawyer of just how weak the so-called protections of the government's constitutional amendment were. In a bluntly-worded opinion given to the society, Université d'Ottawa lawyer Joseph Magnet advised it to repudiate its deal with the province because under the proposals, Franco-Manitobans would be trading away most of the force of the original Section 23 of the Manitoba Act. Not only did the NDP changes remove the obligation imposed by Section 23 for the legislature to enact laws in both official languages, Magnet warned, it also explictly repealed what he considered the clear intent of the original Section 23 to cover municipalities and school boards. Also, because the government proposal allowed the Manitoba Court of Appeal ruling on the Bilodeau case to stand, changing Section 23 from mandatory to discretionary, some 163 quasi-judicial institutions such as the securities commission, the law society, the public utilities board, the labour board and the dental association would no longer have to be bilingual as Magnet believed they would have to be under the original Section 23. The trade-off, the proposed bill on French services, was just not worth it, the constitutional lawyer concluded. Continued Magnet:

> Legislatures respond to temporary political pressures. In the past six months, the provincial Conservatives profited greatly by provoking animosity against the Franco-Manitoban community. Political parties do not drop profitable issues. The SFM may expect recurring pressure from Conservative politicians or a future Conservative government, to dilute services provided in this act.

> Constitutional entrenchment protects minorities against temporary political crises. Ordinary legislation exposes minorities. If the provincial Tories stir up animosity against the Franco-Manitoban community again, the community will be defenceless. It will have bargained away its only legal weapon, the remedies of voidability and invalidity sought in Bilodeau. [29]

Although the SFM rejected Magnet's advice, it served as a timely reminder to Manitobans in the midst of all the sound, fury, hysteria and gross misinformation and scare-mongering that the government package was now actually much weaker than what was already in the constitution.

Periodically, Manitobans were also being reminded that the crisis was not going unnoticed in Québec, where the anti-French racism and bigotry emanating from the committee hearings and rallies were receiving wide media exposure. Premier René Lévesque said the Manitoba spectacle only served to prove that French Canadians could never be assured of their rights outside Québec. Eric Maldoff, president of Alliance Québec, the SFM's sister organization protecting the rights of anglophone Québécois, told the *Free Press* that with the interventions of former premiers Campbell and Lyon the impression in Québec now was that extremism was backed by important Manitobans and was therefore an accurate reflection of a majority of the citizens. [30]

As the Tories walked out immediately after Question Period each and every day and the agonizing bells continued their relentless clamour through the afternoon and evening until the 10 p.m. adjournment hour, the government tried to reach a peace. It attempted to get the previous summer's unofficial agreement between the two House leaders to limit bell-ringing to two weeks telescoped to two hours. The Tories said they wouldn't be bound by time limits. The government also offered to allow its members a free vote on the language package if the vote could be held immediately. The Tories hemmed and hawed.

At one point, the tortured and futile negotiations offered one humourous and very human sidebar. The parties' two House leaders, Anstett and Tory veteran frontbencher Harry Enns, developed a strange kinship, perhaps a variation of the so-called Stockholm syndrome where the kidnapped come to identify with their kidnappers. Certainly both men were skilled parliamentarians and steeped in parliamentary lore. This affinity prompted mutual respect and a sense of being equally trapped and bound together by the unprecedented exigencies of their joint situtation. When the premier sprang the free vote proposal before Question Period on February 9th, the two men adjourned to the men's washroom across the hall from the chamber to hold their negotiations. The frequent interrruptions eventually drove them to the relative peace of Anstett's office.

Still, there was no agreement. Not even the parliamentary knowledge and skills of Anstett could offset the unbroken line of blunders committed by the government from the very outset. It was becoming obvious that the more the government compromised and backed away from its original plan, the more it whetted the appetite of its opponents and the more determined they became to force it to total and complete retreat.

The NDP's central difficulty from the outset was that the defence of minority language rights was not part of its set of core political values. True to its social democratic roots, the party's primary interest is the economic aspects of human rights and power relationships within society. Indeed, the NDP's attitude was probably best articulated by Filmon's comment that language rights were different than human rights. Both positions unquestionably sprang from Manitoba's multi-ethnic reality. Many MLAs on both sides of the House came from families who willingly, even eagerly, sacrificed their maternal tongues and even anglicized their names to ensure opportunity for their children in a new land. The idea that the French language was different could be grasped intellectually, but not at the kind of emotional gut level essential to a government in a fight for its political life.

The government's best friends were losing heart because of its lack of spine and will. Myron Spolsky, executive director of the Ukrainian Canadian

Community Development Committee and one of the leaders of the ethnic coalition Manitoba 23 that had formed to fight the municipal referenda the previous fall, put it this way: "Many in the ethnic leadership don't want to go out on a limb again, when the government keeps backing off. We wonder if there is any purpose to backing a government which is not sure of its course and which seems to be unable to bring the hammer down in the House." Another, who wished to remain anonymous, said: "The destabilization has ceded the entire stage to Grassroots. The government's supporters find it difficult to defend and promote something that not even the government is defending and promoting." [31]

Sane and sober heads in the Tory caucus were also offering second thoughts on condition of anonymity. The apprentice was now controlling the sorcerer. The sudden emergence of Grassroots Manitoba and its undeniable political savvy and sway left the Tories fearful that unless they hung tough and kept the legislature bells ringing, a new right-wing party could emerge to threaten their base in the next election. The Tories were set to suffer political pain from another quarter – their federal leader. In mid-February, his initiatives to bring his provincial party onside in tatters, a frustrated Brian Mulroney publicly repudiated its opposition to the government's French language proposal. Asked if he supported the bell-ringing tactic, Mulroney was blunt. "The answer to that of course is no." While he stopped short of telling his provincial colleagues he would like to see them vote on the issue, he reiterated his position he set out the previous October. "This country has no obligation more compelling than to ensure that our minorities are treated with fairness and justice at all times. That includes Franco-Manitobans. It includes English Quebeckers." Two days later, Mulroney issued an ultimatum to longstanding anti-bilingualism crusader Winnipeg Assiniboine MP Dan McKenzie: either support the party's official position on minority language rights or quit the Tory caucus. McKenzie decided to stay with the caucus. McKenzie and Simcoe South MP Ron Stewart had been using a trust fund to pay legal expenses for Grassroots Manitoba head Grant Russell. Russell, a federal civil servant who was on long term sick leave from the federal department of manpower and immigration, had been called to account by his superior for violating the civil service conduct code. DMI's Manitoba director, T.H. Swan, had told Russell to either abandon his political activity or resign. Russell had hired an Ottawa lawyer to fight back.

Filmon tried to paper over the huge cracks that had appeared in

Tory unity. The federal leader was discussing minority language rights and that was not the issue in Manitoba, he said. In Manitoba, the government was "attempting to alter the balance of linguistic rights … It's one thing to protect those rights. It's another thing to attempt to change those existing rights. When you change rights, then what you are doing is shifting and altering the others in the minority and their rights." [32]

With that last comment, the opposition leader once again demonstrated that he didn't grasp the essence of the issue: the crucial constitutional difference between the French minority in Manitoba and the English minority in Québec, and all other minorities. He also demonstrated the indelibility of John George Diefenbaker's maxim, promulgated along all the highways and biways of Prairie Canada, that language rights for French Canadians pushed everyone else who wasn't a member of the British charter class down to third class status.

Meanwhile, a spate of public opinion polls showed continuing high opposition to the government's language proposal but only tepid support for the Tories' incendiary bell-ringing filibuster. One, conducted for the *Free Press* by the University of Manitoba's Institute for Social and Economic Research, found 67.3 per cent of Manitobans opposed to the language initiative and the Tories' tactics backed by only thirty-five per cent of Winnipeggers and forty-three per cent of rural Manitobans. Still, the Tories now held an overwhelming lead in the electoral race: 66.7 per cent compared to just 24.9 per cent for the NDP and 8.4 per cent for the Liberals, Progressives and other parties.

On Thursday, February 16th, the House met for what would be the last time in the session. After Question Period, Tory backbencher Albert Driedger rose on a matter of privilege to once again denounce the government's language package and intention to invoke closure. Then Anstett stood in his place to move closure, not on the services bill, nor on the constitutional amendment, but on the motion to limit bell-ringing to two hours, which he had introduced on February 6th. Anstett married his considerable political and parliamentary skills with his pent-up fury to deliver a speech withering in its rhetoric and intensity.

The NDP house leader called the Manitoba Conservatives "inglorious blackguards who have associated themselves with everything that is mean and mean-spirited, and some of the things that have been the meanest and most mean-spirited in the last century of this province's history". He accused

Hurry up sun! Melt that one as quickly as possible!

them of dredging from "the very bottoms of the extreme right of this province sentiments that should have stayed buried". Then he turned to the issue at hand, the government's motion to limit bell-ringing to two hours.

> Mr. Speaker, I believe the only way a Parliament can operate is if it has the authority to make decisions and Sir, no parliamentarian who believes in the British parliamentary tradition will say otherwise … We have two concerns, Mr. Speaker, the question of minority rights and the protection thereof [and] the British parliamentary tradition and the foundation it has in this province. That's what's at issue in this matter of privilege and for that reason I ask all members to vote and to vote in support of the motion.

The question was put, the government won on the voice vote. Tory

House leader Harry Enns demanded a recorded vote. Speaker Walding issued the order to "call in the members". Then he made this unusual address to the House:

> I have been advised by the Official Opposition whip that the Official Opposition will provide me with not less than two hours prior notice of their intention to return to this House. In view of this advice, I have informed chamber staff that they will not be required to remain on duty outside normal working hours. I have made arrangements to secure the chamber and the sounding of the bells will be minimized to the greatest extent possible. I am accordingly leaving the chair to return when the opposition advises me of their intention to return. [33]

Parliamentary history was about to be made and a ghastly precedent was to be set for the countries around the globe who adhere to the British parliamentary system. The opposition had staged a coup d'etat and the speaker of the house, sworn to defend its rules, procedures and traditions, had made himself its accomplice. The historic Manitoba Legislative Assembly *Debates and Proceedings* of February 16 to February 27, 1984 – the only one in the province's history to span eleven days – records it this way in black block letters:

(AND THE DIVISION BELLS HAVING RUNG FROM 3:15 P.M. ON THURSDAY, FEBRUARY 16, 1984, TO 2: 45 P.M. ON MONDAY; FEBRUARY 27, 1984)

The Tory bell-ringing walk-out, a walk-out, not over any of the principles involved in the language question, but over the right of the legislature to debate and decide, lasted eleven days, a record that has not yet been surpassed anywhere in the parliaments of the world. It ended only when the government capitulated, allowed the entire language initiative to die and the issue to proceed to the nation's highest court and called upon the lieutenant governor to prorogue the assembly.

The Tories later claimed the government had cut and run before its own two-week deadline for bell-ringing. It was disingenuous. The government had run out of money to pay its bills and was caught between a rock and a hard place. The legislature had been so consumed with the language issue that the government had not been able to pass most of its spending estimates. But because the legislature was still technically sitting, the government was blocked from obtaining the lieutenant governor's warrants available to it when the House was in recess. But even as they were accusing the government of cutting and running prematurely, the Conservatives remained coy on whether they had any intention of coming back into the legislature.

The formal words of ancient precedent uttered by Pearl McGonigal at 2:45 p.m. on February 27th had an aura of mocking unreality:

> The work of the second session of the Thirty-Second
> Legislature has now been completed. I wish to commend
> the members for their faithful attention to their duties ... In
> relieving you now of your present duties and declaring the
> Second Session of the Thirty-Second Legislature prorogued,
> I give you my best wishes and pray that under the guidance
> of Divine Providence, our province may continue to provide
> the things which are necessary for the health, the happiness
> and the well-being of our people.

Debates and Proceedings reported that *God Save The Queen* was sung.

The *Free Press* castigated all players in a blistering editorial which said the fiasco in the legislature gave no one cause for pride. The Tories could claim a significant victory, but achieved it "by the simple and brutal tactics of spreading communal fear and suspicion throughout the province and of carrying obstruction in the legislature to the ultimate". The premier gave the Tories their opening because "he could not adequately explain [the language proposals] to the majority of Manitobans". The editorial concluded with a warning that the defeat of the initiative was not the end of the matter.

> Canada's future still depends to a large extent on the ability
> of its two major linguistic communities to live together in a
> spirit of equality, acceptance and understanding. That future
> will be determined in part by the ability of French-speaking
> Manitobans to have their language protected and respected
> by the English-speaking majority. The job of providing that
> protection has been bungled by Manitoba's legislature. It
> now returns to the Supreme Court ... Some of the remedies

open to it have the potential of creating problems for Manitoba without providing useful solutions for Franco-Manitobans. The people of Manitoba must hope that the judges in Ottawa are wiser than their own elected politicians. [34]

Nationally, the actions of the Manitoba Conservatives were almost universally condemned in editorials in a dozen major newspapers and dominated both news and commentary in Québec. Midway through the bell-ringing, *Le Devoir* published a comment piece written by a fourth-generation Manitoban, Gordon K. MacIvor, which traced the province's bitter history and, in so doing, demonstrated how Manitoba had changed the course of Canadian history. He talked of the bilingual-bicultural dream of Canada's founding fathers and its destruction in a continent where, "in the final analysis, ignorance dominates". It ran under the haunting headline "Not far from Deschambault Street", recalling Manitoba's pre-eminent international author, Gabrielle Roy:

My ancestors came to Winnipeg at the beginning of the nineteenth century, during the period when it was known as Fort Garry. They discovered a little settlement where the wolves roamed in the night outside the houses. They were Scottish: they named their dwelling Stornoway House in remembrance of their native city and one of its most famous sons, the explorer Alexander MacKenzie.

Fort Garry grew in importance; the expansion of Canada towards the West attracted colonists and businessmen who dreamed of a new existence under prairie skies. From Lower Canada came families with names like Ledoux, Levanc, Montigny, Casgrain, Pelletier and Lemieux and many more like them. They settled from the north of Alberta to the south of Manitoba, staying together to preserve their language and culture.

Stornoway House, located not far from the French hamlet known as St. Boniface, found itself receiving francophone visitors. In this part of Manitoba, francophones and anglophones lived side by side with little problem except for a certain mistrust due to the irreconcilable differences of language and religion. The guests of Stornoway accepted these differences as they would accept those with the Ukrainians and the Poles much later. Unfortunately, the atmosphere in Stornoway House was that of an enclave protected from the storms of the outside world. When, in 1890, a law passed by the Legislative Assembly of Manitoba made English the sole official language of the province, it was the beginning of the end of the dream of the founding fathers: a country where English and French were to be used everywhere throughout the country.

When I look at the old, brown photographs of Stornoway House, I often ask myself if my ancestors were aware of the fate of the francophone minority outside Québec. Did they know that Manitoba would be the place where the great federalist dream would be put on trial? ... After two centuries, it is draining to hear oneself called "Frenchy" and to know that is the majority public opinion of a race that is put up with, denigrated and detested.

What is happening today in Manitoba is fully in the tradition of our great dream of national destruction. Those opposed to francophone rights pretend that the entire affair is nothing but a federal plot. The premier of Manitoba faces a bitter opposition. Aware that his province will, once again, serve as the executioner of our great national myth, he tried to negotiate secretly with La Société franco-manitobaine. Meanwhile, francophones themselves, shattered by the hatred displayed towards them by those citizens who cannot comprehend why a minority should have special rights, hide and keep silent.

At its origin, Canada rested on the principle of two founding peoples, each having the possibility to live in their language and transmit it to their children ... Stornoway House has disappeared ... But I know that my ancestors would not be astonished at the events in Winnipeg. They already knew, living as they did not far from Deschambault Street so well described by a young St. Boniface woman, Gabrielle Roy, that the national dream of bilingualism and biculturalism would easily transform itself into a nightmare under the pressure of an immense continent where, in the final analysis, ignorance dominates. [35]

On February 25th, the day after the legislature prorogued, *Le Devoir's* publisher, Jean-Louis Roy, devoted the paper's entire editorial column to a lengthy article entitled "Failure. Hypocrisy. Indifference". The political and parliamentary crisis stirred up by the Pawley government's proposal was complete and total, he said. The issue would now have to proceed to the Supreme Court.

> Only the sinister bell reminds us that this empty enclosure is the home of legislators in a democratic society, as well as of their refusal to respect the rights of a minority as justice and the constitution require …

> Regrettably, all hope for a political resolution is now gone. The agreement negotiated between the government in Winnipeg, the SFM and Ottawa would have been far superior to any decision from the Supreme Court. It would have gone further in the provision of language services. Most of all, it would have expressed a new consensus in the province of Manitoba, a consensus with incredible significance and meaning for the country as a whole. It would have been a sign that attitudes had changed, that the idea of duality had matured. This political agreement is a long-awaited, mutually-agreed-upon, mutually-consented concept of a country; a concept required for the very survival of this country. This agreement did not happen …

Even after the government watered down the package, the opposition wasn't prepared to give up, Roy continued. On the contrary, it merely intensified its struggle and blocked the funtioning of the province's institutions by frankly "terrorist" methods. The Conservative party is celebrating its total victory. Its error is also total, he warned. Recourse to the Supreme Court doesn't close off the political debate. On the contrary, a favourable decision for the minority could have political impacts beside which the government proposal would pale.

Roy went on to note that the outcome shouldn't surprise anyone familiar with Manitoba. In 1964, André Laurendeau, co-chair of the Royal Commission on Bilingualism and Biculturalism, said that the language question in the province was "foreign" even to opinion leaders. Fifteen years later, the Pépin-Robarts Royal Commission on Canadian Unity was rudely shaken by its reception in Winnipeg. "Insults, injuries, verbal violence, reached their peak. For the last six months, the same scenario has rallied the majority," Roy continued. "This imposes a renewed duty of vigilance and solidarity. In this country, francophones should never take anything for granted."

Ottawa's position before the courts was extremely misleading, Roy said. Lawyers for the federal justice minister had taken an ambiguous position about the interpretation of Section 23 of the Manitoba Act, specifically, that it didn't create a strict obligation on the City of Winnipeg.

"And what of the position of the Québec government?" he asked. "In all logic, the Québec government should give its support to the Manitoba Conservatives. The practical Péquiste has little interest in the fate of francophones outside Québec" except for the "dubious notion" of reciprocity in the treatment of minorities.

> One of the minorities is gambling its own future and is
> a historical victim of a heinous campaign with the most
> vicious prejudices. To be outraged is not very useful ...
> neither is the predictable comment about Trudeau's failure.*
> [Trudeau] will pack his bags one day. The Franco-
> Manitobans will never do so ...

After that ringing affirmation of the courage and fortitude of Franco-Manitobans, the editor of Québec's most prestigious – albeit separatist – newspaper concluded by lamenting that Franco-Manitobans were, indeed, isolated; wounded at home, treated with hypocrisy in Ottawa and indifference in Québec. "It is bad enough that the minority is wounded ... without

---

*Québec separatists always celebrated any defeat of Trudeau's plan for pan-Canadian official bilingualism because they saw it as a dagger to the heart of their own "national project" for the "homeland" of French Canadians.

its misfortune being increased by the hypocrisy of one and the indifference of the other."

La Presse gave the Pawley government's decision to bow to the bells and prorogue the legislature its Page One banner headline on February 24th: "The rights of the Francophones of Manitoba – Pawley abandons the struggle". The next day, the editor of Québec's leading federalist daily wrote that Manitoba's crisis inevitably is Canada's crisis. The Manitoba premier, Michel Roy said, was a politician of good will who honestly wished to re-establish the rights illegally and unilaterally taken away from Franco-Manitobans in 1890. Unfortunately, Pawley had underestimated the fierce resistance in the province to the notion of duality, to the idea of two founding peoples, to the concept of official bilingualism. He hadn't understood that prairie Canadians of many diverse ethnic origins who had come West decades ago would only recognize one official language, a sentiment the Conservatives of Manitoba expressed.

Meanwhile, Roy continued, the opposition was creating chaos in the legislature, turning the rules of parliament into a derisory parody, refusing to vote and engaging in interminable and absurd debate. Unwilling to allow parliamentary anarchy to continue for long, the premier had chosen capitulation. He lost a decisive battle. But, Roy said, he still believed that, with courage, Franco-Manitobans will be victorious in the end. "For the moment, the legislators of Manitoba are evading their constitutional obligation which is nonetheless imposed upon them by a judgement of the Supreme Court."

Franco-Manitobans, who constitute six per cent of the Manitoba population, have two choices, the La Presse editor continued. They can pursue their own case to the Supreme Court through Roger Bilodeau's speeding ticket to obtain the practical consequences of the original 1979 judgement. Or they can appeal to the federal government to itself intervene before the highest court with a reference case asking it to specify the exact obligations of the Manitoba government to its French minority. But, Roy warned, even if it delivers another victory to a declining minority, the court won't provide a real solution to the problem. "All authentic and democratic solutions must be the fruit of political will that expresses popular consensus. Politicians on all sides must strive to achieve it." [36]

Québec Intergovernmental Affairs Minister Jacques-Yvan Morin told law students at l'Université Laval that it would have been counterproductive for the Parti Québécois government to go to bat for Franco-Manitobans. "The result would have been the opposite to what we want. We were extremely wary of creating a situation worse than it was for the Franco-Manitobans. It would have been perceived as some kind of support for French power and for Trudeau, which would have provoked more backlash." The best way to protect Franco-Manitobans would be for Québec to increase its own powers within Confederation so that the rest of the country would have to pay attention, Morin said. [37]

Premier René Lévesque said what happened in Manitoba proved that Canada was "basically unilingual". Speaking in mirror image, Liberal Robert Bourassa, described the outcome as "a tough blow for national unity". [38]

In an article published in the *Free Press*, respected Québec anglophone journalist Frank Walker said the imbroglio inflicted a great deal of damage on Manitoba "as a civilized and decent province" and also on national unity.

> For the French of this province it is further evidence that
> English Canada has not changed, that French rights outside
> this province are no more secure than they were … When
> all is over, however it is resolved, all that will be remem-
> bered will be nasty words and nasty attitudes. Somehow we
> should be able, in this age of easy travel and the miracles of
> communication, to do better. Just as in Québec, reality is
> reflected in the decent attitudes of millions of people, so we
> should be able to see in the Manitoba situation, at this dis-
> tance, something more than a libel on a whole people. [39]

The Montréal *Gazette* said that "in bitterness and betrayal the legislature of Manitoba has washed its hands of its responsibility to that province's French-speaking citizens.

> The rednecks and those who cynically exploit fears born of
> ignorance have won this battle. They have not won the war.
> Franco-Manitobans have shown incredible patience, dignity
> and tenacity in the face of a century of denial of their rights.

The fact their provincial government could not keep its promise to enshrine their rights in the Constitution, that it could be shouted down by opposition so clearly based on bigotry is a national shame.

"Deplorable," was the operative word in the *Ottawa Citizen's* editorial: "The Tories deliberately chose to polarize the province over the issue in the

The Canadian Crucible

hope of riding the redneck vote back to power. Their tactics are deplorable." The *Globe and Mail* said the "political extortion" used by the Conservatives to resist French language rights in Manitoba achieved its desired result, but warned the issue will not go away. "It is too fundamental to the structure of the country to be swept aside by an intolerant minority who, in the absence of rational argument, turned to obstruction." The *Kitchener-Waterloo Record* said the death of the Manitoba language initiative "is a victory for bigotry over the concept of Canada as a coast-to-coast home for two founding nations".

The *Edmonton Journal* voiced a measure of support for the Opposition: "Manitoba francophones are in a distinctly favourable position compared with seven other anglophone provinces ... The decision to extend language rights so shortly after the Supreme Court ordered Manitoba to start recognizing existing rights ... was a provocation upsetting the delicate balance in a strongly multicultural province." Oppositions have the right to voice dissenting views and attempt to convince governments to change their course, said the *Regina Leader Post*. But they do not have the right to paralyze a legislative majority's ability to act.

> A majority of Manitobans may be opposed to the NDP's language policy and its handling of the issue but that does not give an opposition party a carte blanche to subvert the legislative process. A minority's right to recognition and recognition of the majority's right to govern have both been set back by events in Manitoba.

The *Red Deer Advocate* said "bells tolling for the death of Manitoba's French language legislation also ring for the death of common sense and political fairness". The Tory minority had stalled and obstructed and paralysed the legislature, substituting blackmail for debate. "Democracy requires majority rule, with consideration for the rights of all. If the minority ... persists in making its own rules – that is anarchy." [40]

Manitoba's own French language weekly, *La Liberté*, said the actions of the provincial Conservatives were an invitation to civil disobedience and chaos.

> But there must be a limit to the patience of Franco-Manitobans. By their astonishing rejection of Canada's parliamentary and judicial systems, the Tories have thrown

the province into chaos. For Manitobans, the actions of the Conservatives are an invitation to civil disobedience. At this hour, it seems that anybody in this province can break any law and have no fear of legal consequences. [41]

On March 5th, the *Free Press* published six astounding letters written by the major actors that charted the final climactic end to the legislature bell-ringing drama. The letters were exchanged among the premier, the leader of the opposition and the speaker between February 21st and 24th.

The exchange began with a letter from Filmon to Pawley on February 21st, after 104 hours and sixteen minutes of bell-ringing. In it, the opposition leader appeared to take over the premier's role as the leader of the government:

> The constitutional resolution dealing with the French lan-guage issue has been before the legislature and the public for many months, in various forms. The proposals under debate have caused unprecedented frustration, anger and divisiveness among the people of our province. In fact, it is apparent that the overwhelming majority of Manitobans oppose your proposal which may entrench an extension of French language rights in our constitution.

> The Official Opposition, therefore, requests your support for the sub-amendment to the constitutional resolution … Your support for this sub-amendment would, of course, confirm the validity of our statutes and limit the obligation on the part of the province to translate many old statutes into French – two concerns which have been raised consis-tently in debate by your government.

> More importantly, your support of this sub-amendment would allow the constitutional resolution to proceed to the Parliament of Canada with the support of both parties in the Manitoba legislature. To forward a resolution of this importance to Ottawa without such support cannot be in the long-term interest of the people of Manitoba who we were elected to serve.

I would appreciate having your written response to this request at your earliest convenience.

Pawley penned his reply the very same day:

Further to your letter of this date, I find it extremely peculiar for a leader of the Opposition to debate and question by courier service rather than debate and question in the legislative assembly, especially when you have no new position to suggest. A vote on your suggested sub-amendment can be held today, if your caucus enters the house to participate in the votes on the important question of house privilege [the two-hour limit on bell-ringing] now before us. Your letter makes it more clear than ever that both parties want the legislature to develop a made-in-Manitoba solution rather than have the decision imposed on Manitoba by the Supreme Court in Ottawa. The legislative assembly is now the place for a discussion of the made-in-Manitoba solution that will avoid the Supreme Court decision. Continued obstruction of the legislature both prevents a made-in-Manitoba solution and attacks the basis of parliamentary democracy in Manitoba. I urge you to return to the House today. Members of the government caucus intend to be in the chamber at two p.m. for these votes.

The same day, the premier also sent a letter to Speaker Walding:

On February 8, 1984, you stated in your ruling on repeated bell ringing that "the house should not be prevented from deciding whether this [bell-ringing] constitutes a breach of privilege."

You had ruled that on the face of the evidence, obstruction by repeated bell-ringing was an abuse of the rules, a contempt of the house and therefore a breach of its privileges. Your ruling was supported by a vote of the house.

Now, the Official Opposition are using prolonged bell-ringing to prevent a decision by the legislative assembly to deal with the breach of privilege by providing a two-hour limit to bell ringing.

This is an extraordinary and unprecedented situation. There can be no more serious attack upon the house than a deliberate decision to prevent the members from protecting their right and privilege to duly execute the powers of the legislative assembly. This defiance of the rights of the assembly also attacks the constitutional principle of responsible government. A fundamental right of the house is that a majority of members may form a government and assure it of support. The operation of this constitutional principle ensures that the choice of the electorate, expressed at a general election, will be respected.

The opposition has had an unusually full opportunity to question and debate the matter of privilege. The rights of the minority in the house have thus been respected. It is unacceptable for the rights of the house and the principle of responsible government to be defied any longer. With all due respect, and in view of the continuing obstruction, I request that you act now to notify both whips of a specific time when the two votes will be conducted to decide the question of privilege before the house. Members of the government caucus intend to be in the chamber at 2 p.m. today for these votes …

Walding, the frustrated cabinet aspirant whose wife was active in the anti-bilingual Grassroots Manitoba movement, responded immediately to the premier, sending copies to Filmon and to the two party whips:

Thank you for your letter of February 21st containing your request that I intervene and set a definite time for the division now in progress.

The rules and procedures of the legislature are well-known and well-established. They constitute a clear set of procedures which the house expects to be enforced by its speaker with fairness and impartiality.

It has been made clear to you and your colleagues that the rules of the house would be observed and that any change in those rules would come from the house itself.

Since the house is close to effecting a change in its rules, I am surprised that you would request that I contravene the existing rules and procedures at this time. Any unilateral action on my part could only be a betrayal of the impartiality of the chair and would seriously undermine the integrity of the speakership. In view of the foregoing, I cannot accede to your request to contravene our rules and procedures.

The next letter was written two days later after the bells had rung for a total of 152 hours and sixteen minutes. It was from the speaker to government house leader Andrue Anstett with a copy to Tory house leader Harry Enns:

The present impasse whereby the division bells have been sounding continuously to call members in to vote has now entered its second week. I am most anxious to see this impasse resolved so that the house may again address the public business.

To this end I would like to meet with you and with the Opposition house leader at a mutually convenient time which can be arranged.

The purpose of the suggested meeting would be two-fold. First, so that I may be brought up to date on the status of ongoing negotiations. Second, so that I may offer my assistance with a view to satisfactorily resolving this situation.

Only Enns wrote back to the speaker. His letter, written February 24th after the bells had rung continuously for 176 hours and sixteen minutes, constituted an attempted coup d'etat:

I acknowledge receipt of your letter of February 23rd. I am authorized by my leader and caucus to meet with you and the government house leader pursuant to your view of your role as stated to the premier in your letter of February 21, 1984. I understand that 11 a.m. Friday, February 24 is convenient to you and the government house leader. I wish to be accompanied by the Opposition whip, Bob Banman and, of course, have no objection if the government house leader wishes to bring a colleague with him.

You mention that you wish to be brought up to date on the status of negotiations between the government and the opposition. In my opinion, the only negotiation of importance have [sic] been the letters from the leader of the Opposition to the premier and the latter's response, copies of which are enclosed for your perusal.

I am therefore prepared to meet with you and the government house leader to discuss the matter raised in the letter from the leader of the Opposition to the premier, or alternatively, the dropping of the government's language proposal, prorogation or dissolution.

Faced with this audacious grab for power by an opposition buoyed by a wave of populist bigotry and anger, aided and abetted by a hostile speaker, the government took the only course available to it short of resignation. The second session of Manitoba's 32nd legislature prorogued at three p.m. February 27, 1984. The language initiative, the subject of two major debates in the House of Commons of Canada, died. The bells had rung for 263 hours and thirty minutes. [42]

The Bells and the Legislature

Could the eleven days of bell-ringing happen again in Manitoba? The answer is no. In June, 1984, the legislature adopted a rule restricting bell-ringing to fifteen minutes. In August, 1986, the time was extended to two hours. As well, the legislature no longer has a "speed up" rule allowing it to sit mornings, afternoons and evenings; that is, from 10 a.m. to 10 p.m. with lunch and supper breaks. Today, the House sits from 1:30 p.m. to 6 p.m. Monday to Thursday and from 10 a.m. to 12:30 Friday.

Why were the 1983-84 bells stopped some days and not others? As noted in the text, the bells were rung when the opposition demanded a recorded vote, usually on an adjournment motion, and then refused to re-enter the House. Once the normal adjournment hour was reached, the bells were turned off. However, the speaker decided that the bells could not be turned off if the call for a recorded vote and the refusal to re-enter the chamber arose from a substantive issue, such as closure, a rule change or a bill. The twelve days of bell-ringing were set off by a government motion to restrict the length of time the bells could ring to two weeks – a rule change. Thus the speaker determined the bells had to keep ringing until members re-entered the chamber. The bells were finally silenced when the lieutenant governor entered the chamber to prorogue the House at 2:45 p.m., February 27, 1984.

– With thanks to Beverley Bosiak, deputy clerk of the Legislative Assembly of Manitoba and Justice Minister Gordon Mackintosh, former clerk assistant of the Legislative Assembly of Manitoba.

The Canadian Crucible

11

The Court

Speaker James Walding had been true to his word. Every bell throughout the building save the one nearest the government caucus office on the legislature's second floor had been turned off later in the afternoon of February 16, 1984. It was mercifully padded with wadding to muffle its unholy klaxon to a barely audible rattle. Day and night, the bell rang – and rang – and rang.

It rang day and night, all through the next weekend when the NDP held its annual convention in Brandon. There, delegates cheered their leadership and any fleeting reference to the language proposal at every opportunity. But the government was by now so intimidated and so fearful of even a single voice of dissent within its own membership that it refused to permit a resolution supporting the language initiative to be moved from the floor. Had it been put, it likely would have passed unanimously. As one delegate said privately to a reporter: "Look, I'm not thrilled at the way it has been handled, but I'm in favour of French language rights and I'm a New Democrat." [1] The language issue did come before delegates indirectly. Herb Schulz used his right to appeal his dismissal from the party to launch a blistering attack on the government and its language policy. His tasteless remark that French Canadian Olympic gold medallist Gaetan Boucher wouldn't have skated any better "if he had done it in French" was met with boos and his announcement that he no longer wanted to belong to the NDP was greeted with sustained applause.

The bell rang day and night, all through February 24th when the Canadian House of Commons, in what was to be the last major act of Prime Minister Pierre Trudeau's political life, set aside routine business for a second time to unanimously, but futilely, call upon Manitoba to respect its constitutional obligations to its official minority.

On February 22nd , the provincial Conservatives issued an ultimatum, which some observers characterized as a *coup d'etat*, an extra-legal attempt to seize power. They demanded the government either accept their sub-amendment gutting the constitutional initiative or the bells would ring indefinitely. House leader Harry Enns said that was their "bottom line". The Tory sub-amendment eliminated the clause declaring Manitoba officially bilingual and all other references to official language throughout. It left intact only the sections validating the province's unilingual statutes. Government House leader Andy Anstett characterized this as "blackmail" and said the government would prorogue the House rather than submit to dictation by the minority party. "That clearly prompted us to say, 'Look, if it's a question of blackmail or the bells ringing … well, we will not be blackmailed'," he said. [2]

The developments in Manitoba galvanized the prime minister, who publicly expressed his concern the Manitoba constitutional initiative would die. On February 24th, *Le Devoir* headlined his alarm. "Trudeau interviendra pour 'sauver le pays' – (Trudeau will intervene to 'save the country'). In a scrum outside the House of Commons the prime minister said he would be speaking to Official Opposition leader Brian Mulroney and NDP leader Ed Broadbent. He continued:

> It's a question of saving the country. If one moves towards a
> Canada where there are only anglophones outside Québec
> and francophones in Québec, that is not the conception of
> the country for which one fights, and that is what is neces-
> sary to try to make Manitobans understand. [3]

On February 23rd Liberal House leader Yvon Pinard told reporters there would be another parliamentary resolution on the Manitoba question similar to the one debated and unanimously passed on October 6th. "The

Manitoba government is looking for encouragement. They'll get it from the federal government," Pinard said. (4)

Manitoba Tory leader Gary Filmon reacted angrily, saying even if the federal Conservatives supported the prime minister, his party would not back down. "It's obviously a very transparent political ploy to try to interfere with an area of provincial jurisdiction," he said. "Language rights are the responsibility of the provincial government." (5) But Filmon was wrong. Official language rights are beyond the purview of any government. They are part of the Canadian constitution and therefore belong to the people.

The initial resolution proposed by Trudeau stated in part:

> The House urges the government of Manitoba to persist
> in its efforts to fulfill the constitutional obligations of the
> province and protect effectively the rights of the French-
> speaking minority in a spirit of tolerance and civility, amity
> and generosity.

> The House urges the legislative assembly of Manitoba to
> bring to a vote without further delay the constitutional
> resolution introduced by the government of the province to
> amend the Manitoba Act 1870 and thereby the Constitution
> of Canada. (6)

Mulroney said he was willing to show support again for "the noble and hon-ourable" principles contained in the October 6th resolution, but was uncom-fortable with the phrase asking the legislature to vote "without further delay". The federal Tory leader said he was not just concerned about giving instruc-tions to Manitoba but to "any sovereign legislature in the country". (7) After an eighty-minute meeting the morning of February 24th, the three federal leaders emerged with an agreement on the resolution to be introduced, debated and passed that afternoon.

This time, the Liberals and New Democrats put forward, not their party leaders, but one of their Manitoba MPs. However, as testimony to the tension the issue was creating within Tory ranks, Mulroney, again, spoke for his party. The resolution was introduced by Manitoba's representative in the federal cabinet, Transport Minister Lloyd Axworthy. It read:

> WHEREAS the House, in a resolution adopted on October
> 6, 1983 with unanimous support from all parties, invited

the Government and Legislative Assembly of Manitoba to take action as expeditiously as possible to fulfil their constitutional obligations and to protect effectively the rights of the French-speaking minority of that province;

WHEREAS the House also endorsed on that occasion the essence of the agreement reached to that end of May 16, 1983 by the Government of Canada and the Government of Manitoba with the participation of the Société Franco-Manitobaine;

WHEREAS the Government of Manitoba introduced in the Legislative Assembly of the province on July 4, 1983 a constitutional resolution providing for the amendment of the Manitoba Act 1870 and subsequently, amdendments thereto as well as a bill respecting public services which, together, are consistent with the essence of the agreement reached on May 16, 1983 by the Government of Canada and the Government of Manitoba;

WHEREAS the Legislative Assembly of Manitoba after several months of debate is being prevented from bringing the constitutional resolution to a vote, and therefore from ful-filling its constitutional obligations;

(1) the House urges the Government of Manitoba to persist in its efforts to fulfil the constitutional obligations of the province and protect effectively the rights of its French-speaking minority in a spirit of tolerance and civility, amity and generosity;

(2) the House urges the Legislative Assembly of Manitoba to consider such resolution and legislation in an urgent manner so as to ensure their timely passage. [8]

Axworthy said he believed all Manitoba's members of parliament, regardless of party, "ache with what we see in our home territory ... All too often, news reports coming from Manitoba are full of stories of paralysis, stalemate, rancor, indignation and frustration."

The deadlock gripping the Manitoba legislature underlined the

importance of the House of Commons speaking unanimously once more
to "reassert and reconfirm its commitment to the Constitution of Canada."
Axworthy said those who believed Parliament had no role in the issue were
"dead wrong".

> This is not a matter that can be confined or limited
> simply to the boundaries of Manitoba; it is an issue for
> all Canadians. We are going to the very heart of what this
> country is all about, to the very basic fundamentals of our
> Constitution...

> Whether it be linguistic, sexual or moral treatment, every-
> one must be treated equal ... Language rights are a fact
> of life in Canada and an essential part of our Federation.
> Therefore, we must accept official recognition of French
> in Manitoba.

The transport minister set out the danger that the behaviour of the provincial
Tory opposition posed to parliamentary government everywhere.

> What future can there be for parliamentary government in
> Canada if in every legislature certain groups try to halt the
> process when their arguments fail? How can legislatures
> remain the central focus of legitimacy and authority in our
> society? How can they remain the central decision-making
> body if a government has to prorogue because some ...
> members prevent the taking of a vote – perhaps the funda-
> mental right of any democracy, the right finally to decide?

He expressed the hope that the resolution would encourage
Manitoba's political leaders to find a "common sense solution" and "extinguish the fumes and vapours of extremism that are beginning to seep over
that territory and have the possibility of spreading even further". He warned
the Manitoba Conservatives that their sub-amendment stripping away all references to official languages was "not acceptable to the House of Commons".
And he concluded by telling MPs that they were "debating the future of our
country". (9)

Mulroney desperately tried to square Canada's bedevilled circle and
reconcile east and west, French and English. Again and again, he sought to

bridge the chasm between his own feelings and those of his political brethren in Manitoba and Western Canada, between his own deeply-held convictions and the political exigency of the moment, between political principle and electoral expediency. It was a masterful performance by a man who, within seven months, would win one of the most massive majorities in Canadian history.

Saying "we are all creatures of our environment", the Tory leader acknowledged the different historical realities of Eastern and Western Canada.

> In Eastern Canada from the very beginning, the French-English alliance, uneasy though it has been, became a daily reality ... Millions of French Canadians could not be ignored, nor could their rights be set aside ... I acknowledge, Mr. Speaker, that the view in some areas of Western Canada is different. It is neither pernicious nor benighted. It is simply different. It is different because the evolution of Western Canada did not in some very important respects parallel the evolution in the east ... That precious and fragile dimension of linguistic duality which Macdonald and Cartier saw as an indispensable characteristic of nationhood was submerged by growing demographic realities of the new west.

The "vast waves of courageous immigrants" from the Ukraine, Central Europe and elsewhere and the growing dominance of the English language were "the silent and inexorable toll of history".

> But what of the small group of Franco-Manitobans who were there at the beginning as one of the founding partners of the dual linguistic dimension of Canada? They were there with rights and obligations, establishing the unique beachhead for Canada ... (T)he linguistic rights of Franco-Manitobans were not submerged. They were removed. They were removed by a wilful act of the legislature in violation of a historic understanding. Today, Mr. Speaker, we ask simply that these rights be returned.

The Tory leader cast Franco-Manitobans as heroes, preserving through decades of anguish "the unique and priceless vision of our founding fathers".

He credited them with demonstrating that French Canadians do not have to be locked into an enclave in one province and even with making it "possible for Canada and millions of French Canadians to reject the ultimate siren call of separation based on language".

Franco-Manitobans were those "courageous few" deserving the "gratitude and not the harrassment of their fellow citizens" for keeping the French language and culture alive in Manitoba. But he also thought of "other Manitobans" whose vision of Canada was "formed and shaped in different circumstances" and whose motivations stem from "a different historical perspective and not ... a sense of malice". Still, Mulroney ultimately came down on the side of his own passion.

> There could be no doubt where I stand. There can be no question as to where the obligation of a national political party lies. It lies today, as it shall tomorrow, in ensuring that our minorities in Canada are treated at all times with dignity and with justice. [10]

Rod Murphy (NDP, Churchill) sought to redeem his province's reputation. The vast majority of Manitobans, he said, were neither bigots nor racists, but tolerant of difference and welcoming to immigrants from around the world . What the nation was seeing on television every night was the "antics" of those who have "disgraced Manitoba and shamed me personally".

> We in this nation are anything but monolithic. But if the majority of our nation ever decides that it is going to use its power as some in the Province of Manitoba are presently trying to do ... then, Mr. Speaker, no Canadian is safe; no religious minority is safe, no linguistic minority is safe, no individual or group of individuals with different beliefs from the majority is safe in this country. [11]

The motion was deemed to have been adopted by prior agreement of all parties.

Le Devoir's publisher, Jean-Louis Roy, ridiculed the Parliamentary effort. "This symbolic gesture didn't 'save the country,'" he said. "It hadn't changed a thing."

According to a formula which prevented the usual individual

expression of their individual convictions, the MPs reaffirmed their apparent common will on the constitutional rights
of the Franco-Manitoban minority. All well and good. But
the impact of the gesture could hardly be more slight. [12]

Four days later, Prime Minister Pierre Trudeau took a walk in an
evening snowstorm and on February 29, 1984, Leap Year Day, announced
his retirement from politics.

The parliamentary debate opened an ominous breach in federal Tory
unity. None of Manitoba's five Tory MPs were present in the House to hear
their leader. Charles Mayer (Portage-Marquette) made the split official. He
told reporters he didn't agree with his leader's decision to back the provincial
government's language resolution. MPs, he said, should "keep their nose out
of it until it's dealt with at the provincial level". It made him "uncomfortable"
to have a federal leader opposing the position taken by his provincial counterparts. "It's most despicable on the part of the prime minister that he uses
language as a divisive rather than a unifying issue," Mayer continued. [13]
Filmon accused Mulroney of being "manipulated" by the prime minister.

Axworthy told reporters the federal government was considering
ratcheting up the pressure on the provincial Tories by proceeding with
its own constitutional resolution endorsing official recognition of French
language rights in Manitoba. But he added Ottawa would only do so if it
believed the action would help the situation in Manitoba.

On February 27th, the *Free Press* reported that SFM president Léo
Robert had moved his family from their St. Vital home to an undisclosed
location after numerous death threats. The most alarming was his photograph
wrapped around a .22-calibre bullet.

The prorogation of the legislature and the death of the language
proposals ended nine months of agony for all involved. It was a serious blow
to two issues fundamental to Canadian democracy: linguistic duality and the
institution of parliament. Health Minister Laurent Desjardins, the MLA for St.
Boniface, warned the outcome had placed democracy in peril. "I'm disgusted
with the members of the Opposition. I think democracy is in danger when
… the Opposition can determine what can be done and what can't be done. I
think we're sending a message to all Canadians … It's a sad day for Canada.
It's a sad day for democracy as well." Neil McDonald, a spokesman for
Manitoba 23, the coalition of ethnic organizations that had come together

to support the language initiative, called the outcome a tragedy and a black day for parliamentary democracy. "I never in my wildest dreams thought that any legitimate political party would do this (stall the legislature). I am just appalled … If the French language is not safe, other minorities are not safe …" (14)

Premier Howard Pawley accused the Conservatives of hijacking the political system. "It's disgusting behaviour." But Filmon, understandably, saw things differently. It's rare indeed for an opposition party to force a majority government to capitulate. "It certainly was a victory for the public of Manitoba," he said. "The proposals would have been too divisive for Manitoba." Maverick New Democrat Russ Doern who, more than anyone, turned the language initiative into a veritable firestorm of populist hysteria and rage, agreed. "It's a victory for the public." Grant Russell, leader of the anti-bilingual Grassroots Manitoba movement, said he was pleased but tired. He said he was now frightened at what Ottawa might do. (15)

In an interview two weeks later, Conservative House Leader Harry Enns mocked the government. He said he wouldn't have tolerated bell-ringing had he been in Anstett's shoes. "Those bells would have rung for twelve hours and that's it. A determined government, a government with will, can exercise its will. I would not have tolerated the bell-ringing." (16)

Enns' braggadoccio had an element of truth to it and underlined the government's constant defensiveness. Pawley was simply unable to frame the issue in the kind of evocative and compelling language it called for, the noble phrases associated with the finest impulses of civilized societies – human rights and dignity, the righting of historic wrongs, the completion of the task of nation-building, the unity of Canada. This elevated language had been heard twice in the House of Commons. It had several times been heard in the Manitoba House too, from ministers like Roland Penner, Andy Anstett and Gérard Lécuyer. But it was never heard from the premier. In the words of one commentator, Pawley always left his white charger in the barn when he rode to the defence of his government's course. His arguments were bloodless, always framed in the language of means rather than ends. He preferred a "solution" that was "made-in-Manitoba" rather than "judge-made" or "Ottawa-imposed". And he always added the rider that it would "save money". It was about as inspiring – and appealing – as being told by your dentist that a root canal was preferable to a tooth extraction.

One of the great unanswered questions of this dark period in

Manitoba history will always be whether an impassioned instead of cheese-paring government could have prevented the anti-bilingual populist tidal wave from smashing on the beach, perhaps even from gathering in the first place. The hysteria reached almost comic proportions. One farmer in Anstett's Springfield constitutency expressed fear that if the government package went ahead, he would have to "farm in French". [17] It prompted this column by Christopher Dafoe, grandson of the legendary *Winnipeg Free Press* editor, John W. Dafoe:

> The grosteque but dismal outcome of the Manitoba lan-
> guage debate serves to prove, once again, that once some
> people have made up their minds that the world is flat there
> is simply no talking them out of the notion … When storms
> threaten, cows have been observed to assemble in a tight
> group at the edge of a field, usually near a fence. Something

similar seems to happen when some Manitobans hear the word "French".

Somehow the notion persists that if anything is done to give some sort of status to the French language the entire population of Manitoba – man, woman, child and parrot – will be required to abandon the version of English they are accustomed to and adopt, under threat of penalty, the language of Molière, de Gaulle and René Lévesque ... Recognition, to a modest degree, of the "official" status of the French language in Manitoba would, in the end, have been largely symbolic. There are, after all, not that many francophones left in the old province. Not enough, certainly, to form anything resembling a Fifth Column for Trudeau. Nevertheless, we have witnessed the grotesque absurdity of a near panic on the part of a large number of English-speakers, a phenomenon that could be compared to the frantic stampede of a herd of bison by the arrival on the scene of a couple of gophers. ([18])

If the Manitoba government and legislature had executed a humiliating and disorderly retreat from the official language battlefield, the federal government clearly had not and would not. In mid-March, Justice Minister Mark MacGuigan announced Ottawa was framing a broad language reference to proceed to the Supreme Court in concert with Roger Bilodeau's speeding ticket and its threat to Manitoba's unilingual laws. The federal government wanted the issue of Manitoba's constitutional obligations to its official language minority settled in all its various ramifications and at once, rather than through an endless procession of individual court cases, each likely to be fought to the finish by an equally endless procession of bloody-minded, recalcitrant and mean-spirited provincial governments.

The reaction in the still-fevered atmosphere of the province was sadly predictable. The premier, now relieved of the intolerable burden of his own failed compromise, tried to edge towards the wildly-popular territory of his anti-bilingual opponents. The thought of a second bout with Sterling Lyon and Grassroots Manitoba clearly terrified him.

Dear knows what we will end up with. I have always

expressed doubt that the Supreme Court would end this matter ... I have always foreseen the possibility we would have to return to the legislature after the Supreme Court decision. I hope I am pleasantly surprised. I don't think we need this matter again on our platter in the legislature. [19]

If the language issue was a Gordian knot to Ottawa and a terrifying spectre haunting the dreams of the Manitoba premier, it was a veritable migraine to the federal Conservatives and their new leader. Mulroney had won his party's leadership in large part due to his promise to end the long Tory trek in the wilderness, thanks to the Liberal Party's stranglehold on Canada's 110 predominantly francophone federal seats. But it would be self-defeating for the party to win francophone ridings only at the steep price of watching its crucial base in Western Canada evaporate.

Shortly after the second Commons debate, word spread that western Tories were tearing up their party memberships. Then, Manitoba Tory leader Gary Filmon took Mulroney on directly and publicly. The provincial opposition leader said party members were increasingly disenchanted with the way the federal leader was handling the issue. Unless matters healed, there would be problems getting ready for the federal election expected after Trudeau's successor was picked in June. Mulroney's repudiation of outspoken anti-French Winnipeg Assiniboine MP Dan McKenzie, his speech in the Commons and what Filmon characterized as his "my way or the doorway" ultimatum to his caucus to support official language rights or else were hurting the party, he continued. "I think there's an obligation on his part to become involved in Manitoba and understand peoples' views here," the Tory leader said. "I would like to see him come to Manitoba." [20]

On March 29th, Mulroney did just that. A large ballroom on the second floor of the downtown Holiday Inn in Winnipeg was rented for the occasion. A big, sullen and predominantly elderly crowd surged into the ornate setting, many faces familiar from the equally big, sullen and elderly crowds that seemed to materialize out of nowhere at a moment's notice to bolster Grassroots Manitoba's winning campaign against the language initiative.

Mulroney was to speak from a small, low platform only a few feet away and almost at eye level with those in the front row. Accompanied by his wife, Mila, he mounted the stage. The nervousness of both was clearly visible in the way he grabbed and squeezed her hand – and she hung onto his and

gripped his arm with her other hand – as they waited for the formalities and introductions to be completed.

"I want to talk to you tonight about Canada, about Manitoba, about you and me," he began. "I have heard that some people here feel I do not understand their position; that Brian Mulroney is just another easterner who wants to impose his vision of the country on the province and on all Western Canada."

He told the audience he had first come to the west twenty-two years earlier as private secretary to Alvin Hamilton, John Diefenbaker's agriculture minister. "I had never before seen a wind blown wheat field or the tranquil glory of a prairie sky." Of that experience, he said he remembered most the uncommon sense of sacrifice and commitment of ordinary people across the prairies, their pride in family, sense of community, respect for tradition and attachment to region. "These are the simple qualities of which great nations are built." Because he cared deeply for the west, "I was as offended as you" to hear Manitobans called reactionaries and racists.

That is why I said in the House of Commons 'I acknowledge that the view in some areas of Western Canada is different from mine. It is neither pernicious nor benighted. It is simply different. It is different because the evolution of Western Canada did not in some very important respects parallel the evolution in the east.'

The Tory leader then tried to deflect the issue away from language to the much broader panoply of longstanding western grievances – freight rates, the domination of Bay Street, the National Energy Program, the heavy-handedness of metrification and "resentment about the way bilingualism has been implemented" and above all, resentment against the "imperial" Liberal government that ruled with neither representation from nor consultation with the west.

Next came a frank political pitch. He pledged to form a government with the largest number of western Canadian MPs since John Diefenbaker's sweeping 1958 majority; to bring Western Canada back to the cabinet table and to treat the west as an equal partner in Confederation. However, he continued, Manitoba's historic grievances against Ottawa "must not be allowed to cloud our judgement on the question of minority language rights.

> Language is a gift meant to bring people together. The sad
> irony of bilingualism as it has been implemented by the
> Liberal government, is that language has been used to keep
> English and French-speaking Canadians apart … Instead
> of uniting Canadians in a golden national purpose, they
> have used language to divide the country into unbecoming
> regional factions.

He wanted to start a new dialogue among Canadians, to reconcile the two very different views of history – one which sees Canada as a French-English compact, a duality; and the other which regards Canada as a cultural mosaic, a land of diversity.

> I know there is a strongly held view that all those who
> found and settled the west – including our native Indians
> and Métis – are founding peoples of today's Canada. I
> appreciate that, to many Canadians, it was not only the
> English and the French, but the Germans, Ukrainians, Poles,

The Canadian Crucible

Jews, Icelanders, Indians, Métis and many others who built Manitoba; who first broke the soil, built the churches and schools, and made the province what it is today.

The Canadian challenge, he continued, is to allay the fear that acceptance of linguistic duality means the rejection of cultural diversity. He was in Winnipeg, he continued, not to meddle in Manitoba's affairs or to lay down any laws within the Conservative party. He was in Winnipeg as the national party leader "to explain our party's position on the issue of minority language rights.

> Our caucus considered this issue for many, many hours. The debate was vigorous, emotional and honest. The Manitoba members participated in every aspect of the debate and conveyed the Manitoba sentiment movingly and well. In the end, caucus decided – as all democratic parties must – and I articulated that decision in the house.

He remained steadfast to his vision of Canada. "Real national unity will never be achieved until French-speaking Canadians living outside Québec enjoy no less rights than English-speaking Canadians in my native province." He recognized many in the audience disagreed with him. But they would have no respect for him if he had tried to come down on both sides at once. The goal of language guarantees was not to make all Canadians bilingual – to force people to become something they were not. The purpose of language guarantees was to ensure that English and French-speaking Canadians could be themselves, that they could live their lives, communicate with their governments and with each other in one or the other of Canada's two official languages. "Surely this is a small price to pay for national harmony." He was not going to tell Manitobans what to do, but he was going to ask them to reflect carefully "on the consequences of their decisions … as they touch upon the future of our national life." [21]

Mulroney got a rough ride from the 2,000-strong audience. He was interrupted several times by hecklers and his one attempt to say something in French was cut off mid-sentence by loud booing. Afterwards, Jerry Webb of Swan River gave this assessment of the Tory leader's speech: "I'm afraid Trudeau has dragged him into it to make him look bad so he would lose support in the West." Rebel NDP MLA Russ Doern dismissed the effort in three sharp words. "He blew it." [22]

The *Free Press* delivered a stern lecture to the provincial Conservatives in an editorial the next day.

> Manitoba Conservatives got their noses rubbed in a little bit of Canadian reality last night. They were not all happy with the experience ... Manitoba's Conservatives cannot, like their provincial leader, Gary Filmon, simply leave behind the mess they have made and go off to play elsewhere. They, like the rest of Manitobans, will have to come to terms with the reality described by Brian Mulroney. [23]

For all the opprobrium Mulroney heaped on the Liberals, that speech as well as the two he had delivered in the Commons made it obvious that the new Conservative leader was Pierre Trudeau's natural successor, the man to whom the retiring prime minister could safely pass the torch, the inheritor of his central political passion of reconciling Québec to Canada and reviving Sir George-Étienne Cartier's dream of a bilingual, binational Canada from sea to sea. There were some commentators who even speculated that Mulroney's performance emboldened Trudeau to depart at the same time the failure in Manitoba warned him he had probably become the single biggest obstacle to the achievement of his life's goal.

Former finance minister and Liberal prince-in-exile John Turner's reappearance on the national stage as the frontrunner in the race to succeed Trudeau bolstered that analysis. In one of his first pronouncements of the leadership campaign, he scandalized his party by declaring that language rights, whether in Québec or Manitoba, were primarily a provincial matter. In March, he said French-language rights in Manitoba were "a provincial initiative, and that solution will have to be provincial". He tried to calm the ensuing furore both inside the party and in the country by issuing a statement to clarify the "confusion" and to go on record as supporting federal involvement in language disputes. Then in April, referring to Québec's Bill 101, he said that "in principle" the province had "the right to protect language within its borders. That is a constitutional right. In attempting to achieve it, I believe they went constitutionally too far. That's a legalistic view. In human terms, I know they went too far."[24]

These gaffes involving the Liberal Party's ark of the covenant – the French-English compact – weren't enough to deny him the Liberal leadership.

The Canadian Crucible

But they demonstrated that the world had changed since he had left politics to become a Bay Street lawyer and he hadn't changed with it. He was rusty; his political touch and instincts had dulled. Turner's stumbles and blunders continued through the summer election campaign and fuelled one of the greatest electoral routs in Canadian history. On September 3, 1984 Mulroney romped to victory with fifty per cent of the vote and 211 of the 265 Commons seats. The Turner Liberals were reduced to a humiliated rump of just forty MPs. Not long thereafter, Jean Chrétien, "le petit gars de Shawinigan", the justice minister who had shepherded the Charter of Rights and Freedoms through Parliament, the man described by Liberal party president Iona Campagnolo as "first in our hearts" the night Turner captured the Liberal crown, went into exile to lie in wait to pick up Turner's pieces six years later.

Meanwhile, on April 5, 1984, the Minister of Justice and Attorney General of Canada posed four questions to the Supreme Court of Canada in what was to be called the Manitoba language reference although it carried equal weight for the federal government and the Province of Québec. Federal justice minister Mark MacGuigan told a news conference that "the government of Canada, because of the political paralysis in Manitoba, has had no option but to try to save the legal order of Manitoba through this reference". [25] Both Ottawa and Manitoba were worried that the Bilodeau case was too narrow to proceed alone, opening the possibility that the court would leave a number of vital questions unresolved.

Ottawa's four questions went to the very heart of Canada's national purpose and existence, probing the fundamental tensions between majority rule and minority rights, between popular democracy and the rule of law.

WHEREAS the Minister of Justice reports:

(1) That it is important to resolve as expeditiously as possible legal issues relating to certain language rights under section 23 of the Manitoba Act, 1870 and section 133 of the Constitution Act 1867.

(2) That in order that such legal issues be addressed without delay, it is considered necessary that the opinion of the Supreme Court of Canada be obtained in relation to the following questions, namely:

Question #1

Are the requirements of section 133 of the Constitution Act 1867 and of section 23 of the Manitoba Act 1870 respecting the use of both the French and English languages in

a. the Records and Journals of the Houses of the Parliament of Canada and of the Legislatures of Québec and Manitoba, and

b. the Acts of the Parliament of Canada and of the Legislatures of Québec and Manitoba mandatory?

Question #2

Are those statutes and regulations of the Province of Manitoba that were not printed and published in both the English and the French languages invalid by reason of section 23 of the Manitoba Act, 1870?

Question #3

If the answer to question 2 is affirmative, do those enactments that were not printed and published in English and French have any legal force and effect, and if so, to what extent and under what conditions?

Question #4

Are any of the provisions of An Act Respecting the Operation of section 23 of the Manitoba Act in Regard to Statutes, enacted by S.M. 1980, Ch. 3, inconsistent with the provisions of section 23 of the Manitoba Act, 1870, and if so are such provisions, to the extent of such inconsistency, invalid and of no legal force and effect?

Therefore, His Excellency the Governor General in Council, on the recommendation of the Minister of Justice, pursuant to section 55 of the Supreme Court Act, is pleased hereby to refer the questions immediately above set forth to the Supreme Court of Canada for hearing and consideration. [26]

The Supreme Court heard arguments on the federal reference June 11th, 12th and 13th, 1984. In all, nine parties were granted standing: Canada, Manitoba, Québec, Roger Bilodeau, La Société franco-manitobaine, Alliance

Québec, La Fédération des Francophones hors Québec, Freedom of Choice (an anglophone rights group from Québec) and six members of Grassroots Manitoba including James Richardson, Russ Doern, Herb Schulz and Pat Maltman.

The federal government was represented by Pierre Genest, Edward R. Sojonky and Peter W. Hogg. Its brief was tough-minded and strongly-worded. It dismissed the Manitoba Court of Appeal ruling that Section 23's bilingual obligations were discretionary and not mandatory. And it declared Sterling Lyon's 1980 law "reinstating" Section 23 unconstitutional – as unconstitutional as the original 1890 act that had sought to repeal the official status of the French language.

Noting the wording of Section 23, Ottawa's lawyers stated "the word 'shall' is prima facie imperative and admits of no discretion ... [27]

> It is accordingly submitted that the requirements of bilingual acts and bilingual records and journals in 133 and s 23 are imperative as opposed to permissive. Thus, no option is given to the Parliament of Canada or the Québec legislature or the Manitoba legislature as to whether each body will comply with the requirements.

> The difference between a mandatory and a discretionary requirement is that the breach of a mandatory requirement results in invalidity, whereas a breach of a directory does not. [28]

The federal lawyers then drew their bead on Manitoba's appeal court.

> It is submitted that the majority of the Court of Appeal erred in holding that the requirement of bilingual enactment was directory only. It is submitted that the requirement is a mandatory one because the whole purpose of section 23 is to protect language rights ...

> If the commands of section 133 and section 23 to use both languages were held to be directory, the whole object of these entrenched constitutional provisions would be defeated...

> The reason for entrenching language rights and the public

duties necessary to secure them is to give an enduring substance to those rights so that constitutional change alone may remove or restrict them. If rights such as those of minorities are to have reality and substance, the duties imposed by the constitution on the legislators must be seen as substantive also, and not merely as technicalities that may be passed over with impunity. (29)

Having smote the Manitoba government and the Manitoba Court of Appeal hip and thigh, the federal government was finally prepared to give it quarter by invoking the doctrine of necessity to preserve the province's body of unilingual English laws "but only for a sufficient time to enable Manitoba to bring it laws into compliance with s 23". [30] As far as Ottawa was concerned, two years was all the time the province should have. Anything more might encourage backsliding and, likely, non-performance once again. The federal lawyers noted that the unprecedented situation of ninety-four years of invalidity left Manitoba with hardly a shred of legal substance.

The situation of the various institutions of provincial government would be as follows: The courts, administrative tribunals, public officials, municipal corporations, and all other public bodies, to the extent that they purport to exercise powers conferred by Manitoba laws enacted since 1890 in English only, would be acting without legal authority. The situation of the Manitoba legislature would be that it was not a valid legislature at all … If this were so, the vacuum of law in Manitoba could not be corrected. Past laws could not be validly re-enacted in both languages. Future laws could not be enacted, even in both languages. [31]

The federal factum cited some instances to illustrate the severity of Manitoba's illegality. Not only was the legislature invalid, but so also was the franchise of its citizens, since acts passed since 1890 in English only had extended the vote to women, lowered the voting age from twenty-one to eighteen years and increased the number of MLAs from twenty-four to fifty-seven. There would thus be a "period of legal chaos and disorder" the consequences of which were "grave and unusual".

While acknowledging the need to save the province, the federal lawyers turned again to Manitoba's less-than-exemplary conduct.

> The period of time (for the province to repair itself) should be fixed on the basis that the repair of Manitoba's constitutional default is a matter of the utmost urgency and of the highest priority, requiring the commitment of whatever resources are necessary to accomplish the task in the shortest possible time...

> In Manitoba, the vacuum of law requires the application of the doctrine of necessity to preserve temporarily Manitoba's legal system. But it should not be overlooked that the situation has been created by the deliberate disregard of constitutional obligations designed for the protection of Manitoba's French-speaking citizens. It is submitted that the doctrine of necessity should preserve Manitoba's unilingual laws only for the time required to recify the default, in order that the French-speaking citizens of that province may enjoy their constitutionally-recognized rights at the earliest possible date. The time required to rectify the default should be fixed on the basis that the rectification of the default is not a matter to be accomplished at a leisurely or even a convenient pace. (32)

Ottawa noted wryly that the speed of Manitoba's compliance "is simply a function of the resources devoted to the task. Plainly, sixty translators will accomplish more than six translators." Manitoba, it suggested, could offer to pay more. And it could look outside its boundaries. "In these circumstances, the Attorney General of Canada submits that Manitoba could comply with any time limit fixed by this court that does not entail practical impossibility." (33)

Then the federal lawyers turned their attention to the constitutionality of Lyon's much-touted 1980 act. It failed the constitutional test on not one but every ground: it permitted the continued enactment of laws in English only for translation later into French, allowed the continued use of English alone in the records and journals of the House, and accorded primacy to the English versions of all acts.

"The overall effect of the 1980 Act is that Bills need not be in French when they are debated and passed by the Legislature; and, when a French version is later supplied and deposited, the French version is accorded an inferior status to the original English version." All this violates "the evident purpose of s. 23 to make the laws of Manitoba equally accessible to both French speaking and English speaking citizens. [34]

So, in answer to the four questions, Ottawa was emphatic that official bilingualism in the Manitoba legislature was mandatory; that Manitoba's English-only laws were invalid; that they should be saved for a period of two years only while the legislature remedied the situation and that the main operative sections of the 1980 law were "invalid and of no legal force and effect". [35]

Not surprisingly, the factum filed by the Attorney General of Manitoba took a very different position on the four questions. Official bilingualism was directory, not mandatory – for Canada and Québec as well as Manitoba.

Manitoba's lead counsel, once again, was A. Kerr Twaddle. He was assisted by William S. Gange. In the province's opinion, Manitoba's unilingual English laws were valid. "At worst, those statutes and regulations not printed and published in both the English and French languages are voidable but should not in the circumstances be set aside. In the further alternative … the statutes and regulations … are valid of necessity".

But the province seemed to know what was coming and to be preparing itself for the worst. As to the final two questions, whether laws not printed and published in both official languges could still have legal force and effect and if the 1980 remedial legislation was constitutional, Manitoba conceded that if the court found unilingual legislative procedure to be invalid, then "those enactments not printed and published in English and French have no legal force or effect"and the 1980 statute, too, "is of no legal force and effect". It went further, acknowledging that the two-step process laid down in the 1980 law would not be valid for new statutes. But if the court found unilingual legislative process valid on the basis the constitutional requirement was directory only, then the 1980 law would survive "to the extent that it creates a remedial mechanism for giving force to French language versions of acts passed improperly in English only". [36]

The province's forty-five-page brief devoted itself almost entirely to arguing that Manitoba's bilingual obligations were directory and that "not every failure to comply with a statutory requirement results in invalidity of the irregular act". [37] It argued that Section 23 of the Manitoba Act was not central to the province's constitutional authority to enact laws nor did the section give citizens the right to obtain laws printed and published in the minority language.

> The requirement that statutes be enacted bilingually is sepa-
> rate and apart from the provisions empowering the provin-
> cial legislature to make laws ... the obligation to enact
> statutes bilingually is a public duty imposed upon the mem-
> bers of the Legislative Assembly ... no private rights are
> involved. [38]

The factum agreed that the right of French-speaking Manitobans to laws in their own language must be respected, but it said the court should be content with the attorney-general's assurances that translations were proceeding. It raised again the frightful spectre of invalidity.

> Manitoba would be virtually a lawless state; serious general
> inconvenience and injustice would result...It is inconceiv-
> able that the Parliament of the United Kingdom or the
> Parliament of Canada in enacting the Constitution Act 1867
> and the Manitoba Act 1870 respectively intended that the
> consequence of non-compliance with the bilingual require-
> ment in the enactment of laws should be disorder and legal
> chaos which is the very opposite of the object of each enact-
> ment. [39]

The legislators of the day, Manitoba continued, could not have intended unilingually-enacted laws "through inadvertence or by reason of emergency" would be invalid. "Legislators would not have intended the serious public inconvenience which would result. The language requirement does not qualify the power to enact laws, but is a distinct right enforceable by another section." [40]

The province then marshalled a little-known but powerful argument dug out of Manitoba's provincial archives. No less a person than Canada's first prime minister, Sir John A. Macdonald, had been telegraphed by Lieutenant-Governor John Christian Schultz and asked whether he should withhold Royal Assent to the 1890 law repealing the status of the French language. The prime minister telegraphed back in code instructing him not to. "You had better consent to all bills", Macdonald said. [41] Earlier, Macdonald had told Schulz that he thought "it safer to assent to all bills, leaving them to be dealt with here afterwards." [42].

The province also put forward the legal opinion the provincial lieutenant-governor had received from federal justice minister John Thompson on March 21, 1890 in which Thompson advised him to let the law stand and allow it to be tested in court. (As noted in Chapter Four, the Macdonald cabinet feared disallowance would give Premier Greenway an excuse to call an election on the language issue and win an enormous victory, forcing the divisive issues of language and religion again to the top of the national agenda. For the sake of national unity as well as for political reasons, both Macdonald and Thompson preferred the court route. Thompson himself stated he believed the legislation was of doubtful legality.)

The Manitoba factum went on to state that "historically witholding of assent or reservation of a bill was not only constitutionally possible, but was done," pointing out that Manitoba Lieutenant-Governor Joseph Cauchon reserved Premier John Norquay's 1879 law restricting the printing of public documents in French. Ottawa had always had the means to "preserve the integrity of the constitution" but in Manitoba's case in 1890 chose not to. The province's brief argued this proved Ottawa did not believe unilingual enactment caused laws to be invalid. And it added

> (Leaving the matter to litigation) may well have been a pru-
> dent decision as the validity of the act was a contentious
> issue, but only if acts passed in English only in the mean-
> time would be valid. Clearly those responsible for leaving
> the act to its operation were of the view that the intent of
> the Canadian Parliament had not been that acts passed in
> contravention of section 23 would be invalid. [43]

Falling back on the argument of cost, the province argued against "artificial deadlines" for translation. It proposed that the province be given until the next general revision of statutes to provide its full body of French laws. In 1984, that task could have been as much as a decade later.

> Whilst the right of French-speaking citizens of Manitoba to
> have statutes in the French language must be respected, the
> wrongs of our forefathers should not result in the present

day citizens of Manitoba having to pay excessive costs for the translation of 90 years of laws due to a time limit for translation being imposed. [44]

And it told the court that if it found the province's laws invalid, it had to save them by using the docrtine of necessity.

If the law is to treat the statutes of Manitoba enacted in English only as void ... the resulting legal chaos would, from the point of view of the public at large, including the francophone population Section 23 of the Manitoba Act was intended to protect, be far worse than the absence of statutes enacted in French which the finding of invalidity would be intended to cure. [45]

The Province of Québec, represented by Jean Samson and André Binette, asked the nine justices to find Manitoba's obligation to enact laws in both languages "imperative" and argued further that Manitoba's entire body of English-only laws should be declared void. It suggested no remedy. [46]

La Société franco-manitobaine's case was put forward by Université d'Ottawa constitutional lawyer Joseph Magnet. Magnet's brief noted that Manitoba's politicians had encouraged the province's citizens to believe the court wouldn't do anything to "impeach Manitoba's admittedly unconstitutional actions...

The legal order is predicated on the existence of effective and consistently applied sanctions. The rule of law cannot survive widespread perception that courts will not dare to condemn illegal conduct if the illegality is sufficiently huge, blatant, political and intimidating. [47]

The brief quoted Filmon, Lyon and Enns to the effect that the province needn't worry about the challenge to its laws and warned the court of the danger of failing to confront such defiance.

Perceptions such as these cripple the capacity of litigants to settle their own problems and dwarf the rule of law as the basis of Canadian political culture.

On the view that this court will not condemn English only

publication of legislative records, journals and acts, the government and legislature of Manitoba blithely continue publishing English-only records, journals and regulations and have made little serious effort to publish French statutes. This behaviour continues notwithstanding the judgement of four courts since 1892 and notwithstanding the unanimous judgement of this court almost five years ago which left fully potent the rigorous command of Section 23 ... The belief that this court would not invalidate illegal Manitoba legislation destroyed the ability of willing federal and Manitoba governments to find a political solution to the problems caused by longstanding constitutional defiance. [48]

The SFM brief quoted numerous judgements to demonstrate that public officials in dereliction of their duty can be and have been prosecuted. "If officers of the government or the legislature could refuse to carry out their constitutional duties, and act according to their own arbitrary priorities, the rule of law would be at an end." [49]

The factum proposed an ingenious pressure tactic as a solution to the question of invalidity. It suggested the court find the current legislature valid and all rights, contracts, penalties and actions flowing from Manitoba laws binding until the day of the court judgement. After that, the legislature would exist but the laws would be inoperative until the legislature corrected them, either by adopting the constitutional amendment that failed February 27, 1984, or by immediately passing all its laws in French as Québec did to translate all its unilingual laws into English the night and early morning of December 13-14, 1979.

The SFM's sister minority language lobby group, Alliance Québec, also had a respected constitutional law professor as its lawyer, McGill University's Dr. Stephen Scott. He had sent a telegram to Governor General Edward Schreyer on December 13, 1979 to warn of the perils of legal invalidity and chaos facing Manitoba as a result of the first Supreme Court decision on Georges Forest's parking ticket reinstating Manitoba's official bilingualism.

In his brief to the Supreme Court on the federal reference, Scott gave no quarter to the recalcitrant province. Echoing some of Magnet's phrases, Scott's brief stated:

The Canadian Crucible

> To shrink from the sanctions of invalidity ... would indirectly weaken all constitutional guarantees, all law-making processes – the entire constitutional system. For it would suggest to the political authorities that constitutional processes can be violated with impunity ... that in large-scale confrontation, the courts must retreat. This rewards and even encourages massive violation of constitutional processes – the more massive, the better. By contrast, a judicial demonstration that constitutional processes will be enforced regardless of consequences would be a clear and salutary lesson to all political authorities in Canada, would immensely strengthen the rule of law and would represent a major triumph for the constitutional system. Striking down nearly one hundred years of statutes for violation of a constitutional guarantee would be a monument of constitutionalism. It might never have to be repeated. [50]

Also like Magnet, Scott sought to give the nine justices some flavour of the atmosphere and drama of the events in Manitoba the previous fall and winter.

> Throughout the period of pendency of the proposed (constitutional amendment) resolution before the assembly, certain members ... notably Mr. Russell Doern and Honourable Mr. Sterling Lyon, leader of the Opposition for most of the period—waged an intransigent campaign, within and outside the assembly, against passage of the resolution, founded ... on their assertion that this court could or would never declare invalid the laws of Manitoba ... and indeed that any such decision by this court would be irresponsible and even insane ... From the time of the announcement of the May 1983 agreement, the proposed resolution became the chief subject of public controversy in the province, and feelings of hatred and hostility to the linguistic minority and those sympathetic to their rights, addressed indeed to the undersigned, became widespread ... [51]

Scott proposed the most radical solution of all intervenors – either an immediate provincial election held under pre-1890 electoral law, which could then pass the NDP's aborted constitutional amendment, or a specific court ruling sustaining the current government and legislature solely for the purpose of passing the amendment. He dismissed the federal solution of invoking the doctrine of necessity to save Manitoba's laws, noting it was an extreme measure only used at times of revolution and terming it "a Kafkaesque circle".

> First, public opinion having been inflamed, the legislative assembly of Manitoba is dissuaded, or more accurately obstructed, from passing a curative constitutional amendment on the pretext that this court would never strike down unilingual Manitoba legislation ...

> Second, this court is now pressed to sustain the unilingual legislation as valid through necessity: the necessity arising purely because the assembly has not yet passed and may be unwilling to pass, the curative constitutional amendment. This, surely, might be called "Catch 23". The constitutional amendment need not be passed because the laws will not be struck down; but the laws cannot be struck down because the amendment will not be passed. [52]

Scott told the justices that the legal system had a very large interest in showing it can cure historic injustice by restoring those who have suffered it to the position they should have had. Excusing a wrong merely because of its large scale and long continuance has exactly the opposite effect, he continued. "The enforcement of the constitution cannot be made to depend on public opinion, or even seem in the slightest degree to depend on it. This is fatal to all constitutional government." [53]

Winnipeg lawyer Vaughan Baird's brief on behalf of Roger Bilodeau, the man whose speeding ticket had launched the federal reference, sounded the same themes of the other intervenors. Both the Canadian constitution and the rule of law in Canada were at stake, the factum said, but beyond that, so was the very survival of the country.

> Manitoba, described as the keystone province of Confederation, could become the lynch pin of the destruction of our confederation ... If you knock out the "keystone", what is known as the "Canadian dream", could be destroyed. If Manitoba does not have to conform to the law

The Canadian Crucible

and protect the French language within its borders then
Québec has every right to be unilingual and not protect the
English language. [54]

Bilodeau's factum provided the court with a brief run-down of the
number of bilingual bills presented to the Manitoba legislature since the
Forest ruling in 1979 to show that Franco-Manitobans "were losing ground
even with this court's decision". In 1982, eighteen of fifty-eight bills were
bilingual but in 1984, only forty-five of 103 were. [55]

The Grassroots Manitoba group was represented by Winnipeg
lawyers D.C.H. McCaffrey, Colin Gillespie and J.F. Reeh Taylor. Its factum took
the extreme opposite position to the other intervenors. While accepting that
Manitoba's obligation to enact laws in both official languages was mandatory,
Grassroots argued that the obligation was "no more than the obligation to
enact in the second language within a reasonable period of time after enactment in the first." [56] And it also argued that Manitoba's unilingual laws were
not invalid.

It postulated a difficult conundrum for the justices. If the court were
to find Manitoba's body of statutes invalid, then any and all routes available
to fix the invalidity were also all invalid. For instance, the attorney general
of Manitoba could not argue the case before the court and the legislature
would be powerless to effect a remedy. The factum also pointed out that
the Parliament of Canada did not enact the Manitoba Act in both official
languages in 1870. Instead, it produced a later translation.

It went on to make the potent observation that it was improper for
the federal government to now be demanding the court declare all Manitoba's
laws illegal since, for the entire period between 1890 and 1984, no federal
government had instructed the provincial lieutenant governor to withhold
royal assent to unilingual legislation. And it gave a new and very different
twist to Scott's concept of a Catch-23. Since invalidity would create chaos and
since chaos was the opposite intention of a constitution like the Manitoba
Act, the court had no choice but to find Manitoba's ninety years of English-
only laws valid.

What was done in 1890 by the Manitoba Legislature, in
the belief that it was constitutionally proper, was wrong. It
has led to further wrongs. The need is for the wrongs to be
rectified, not compounded…

The manifest object of the Manitoba Act 1870 was to establish and provide for representative government of the province of Manitoba…An intention that the representative government should be swept away and that fundamental reconstruction should be required upon failure to comply with Section 23 is inconsistent with this object … It is submitted that the present (federal) reference has unfathomable potential for embarrassing the administration of justice… The laws which the Attorney General of Canada asks the court to declare invalid, have been relied upon and used by all citizens of Manitoba to govern their affairs for almost a century … The submission of the Attorney General of Canada is that this court should now … create a legal

LE DEVOIR / JUNE 14, 1985

The Supreme Court requires Manitoba to henceforth pass its laws in the two languages

The Canadian Crucible

vacuum, deem this to constitute a condition of necessity,
and of this necessity, act to fill the legal vacuum…

These intervenors submit that there is no precedent for such
immoderate measures; nor should precedent be created, for
the measures suggested by the Attorney General of Canada
are inconsistent with the role of this Court as guardian of
the constitution …[57]

The court took exactly a year to hand down its ruling. When it
came in the morning of June 13, 1985, it was both breathtaking – and moderate. Breathtaking because of the powerful language the unanimous decision
used to uphold the rule of law and defend the rights of minorities; moderate
because it hewed a middle course between the warring sides and threw the
province a liferaft. The seven judges who heard the case were Chief Justice
Brian Dickson, Justice Jean Beetz, Justice Willard Estey, Justice William
McIntyre, Justice Antonio Lamer, Justice Bertha Wilson and Justice Gérard
Le Dain.

Manitoba's ninety years of unilingual laws were declared invalid
but were given temporary force for the minimum time necessary for their
translation, re-enactment, printing and publishing in English and French.
The obligations of Section 23 were ruled mandatory.

The history and language of Section 133 of the Constitution Act,
1867 and Section 23 of the Manitoba Act, 1870 demonstrate that their
entrenched guarantee must be obeyed, the justices ruled. Manitoba's legislative process had to operate fully in both official languages at all times. The
Tories' much-vaunted 1980 law giving English paramountcy over French in
the legislative process – the law the Tories had always insisted was sufficient
to meet the province's constitutional obligations to Franco-Manitobans – was
judged "invalid and of no force and effect in its entirety" [58] The justices went
so far as to declare the province "in a state of emergency" because of its persistent violation of its constitution. However, they did not set a time limit
on their temporary stay of legal chaos, inviting the province to draw up a
timetable for statute translation and submit it to the court for approval.

The Court must declare the unilingual acts of the legislature
of Manitoba to be invalid and of no force and effect. This
declaration, however, without more, would create a legal

vacuum with consequent legal chaos … [59] Law and order
are indispensable elements of civilized life. This Court
must recognize both the unconstitutionality of Manitoba's
unilingual laws and the Legislature's duty to comply with
the supreme law of this country, while avoiding a legal
vacuum in Manitoba and ensuring the continuity of the
Rule of Law …[60]

The court, however, was not prepared to extend validity to any
future unilingual acts. "From the date of judgement, laws not enacted, printed
and published in both languages will be invalid and of no force or effect ab
initio." [61] The following gives some sense of the evocative power of the
court's language:

> Section 23 of the Manitoba Act, 1870 is a specific manifes-
> tation of the general right of Franco-Manitobans to use their
> own languge. The importance of language rights is ground-
> ed in the essential role that language plays in human exis-
> tence, development and dignity. It is through language that
> we are able to form concepts; to structure and order the
> world around us. Language bridges the gap between isola-
> tion and community, allowing humans to delineate the
> rights and duties they hold in respect of one another and
> thus to live in society … The judiciary is the institution
> charged with the duty of ensuring that the government
> complies with the Constitution. We must protect those
> whose constitutional rights have been violated, whomever
> they may be, and whatever the reasons for the violation.
> The Constitution of a country is a statement of the will of
> the people to be governed in accordance with certain prin-
> ciples held as fundamental and certain prescriptions restric-
> tive of the powers of the legislature and government. It is,
> as Section 52 of the Constitution Act, 1982 declares, the
> "supreme law" of the nation, unalterable by the normal
> legislative process, and unsuffering of laws inconsistent
> with it. The duty of the judiciary is to interpret and apply
> the laws of Canada and each of the provinces and it is thus
> our duty to ensure that the constitutional law prevails …

The Canadian Crucible

The difficulty with the fact that the unilingual acts of the legislature of Manitoba must be declared invalid and of no force and effect is that, without going further, a legal vacuum will be created with consequent legal chaos in the province of Manitoba. The Manitoba legislature has, since 1890, enacted nearly all of its laws in English only. Thus, to find that the unilingual laws of Manitoba are invalid ... would mean that only laws enacted in both French and English before 1890 would continue to be valid ...

The situation of the various institutions of provincial government would be as follows: the courts, administrative tribunals, public officials, municipal corporations, school boards, professional governing bodies and all other bodies created by law, to the extent that they derive their existence from or purport to exercise powers conferred by Manitoba laws enacted since 1890 in English only would be acting without legal authority.

Questions as to the validity of the Manitoba Legislature might also be raised...

The Province of Manitoba would be faced with chaos and anarchy if the legal rights, obligations and other effects which have been relied upon by the people of Manitoba since 1890 were suddenly open to challenge. The constitutional guarantee of the Rule of Law will not tolerate such chaos and anarchy... Because of the Manitoba Legislature's persistent violation of the constitutional dictates of the Manitoba Act, 1870, the province of Manitoba is in a state of emergency ...[62]

The judgement canvassed the suggestions of the intervenors and found fault with them all. It was particularly critical of the proposals by Québec, the SFM and Alliance Québec on the one hand and Manitoba and the Grassroots group on the other. The court's chosen remedy came closest to that proposed by the federal government.

Québec, the SFM and Alliance Québec had argued the court should declare Manitoba's laws invalid and go no further, relying on the legislature to work out a constitutional amendment. The justices made it clear that this was not only unsatisfactory, but that they were not prepared to trust the province.

> This approach, because it would rely on a future and uncertain event, would be inappropriate. A declaration that the laws of Manitoba are invalid and of no legal force or effect would deprive Manitoba of its legal order and cause a transgression of the rule of law. For the court to allow such a situation to arise and fail to resolve it would be an abdication of its responsibility as protector and preserver of the constitution. [63]

Manitoba's argument that the linguistic rights of Franco-Manitobans should be left to the lieutenant-governor to protect through reservation or federal disallowance was also rejected by the court. "The fundamental difficulty with the Attorney General of Manitoba's suggestion is that it would make the executive branch of the federal government, rather than the courts, the guarantor of constitutionally entrenched rights."

Once again, the justices demonstrated their unwillingness to trust the province. Noting that a decision to withhold assent or reserve is not reviewable by the courts, the justices said Manitoba's proposal would "insulate the legislature's failure to comply with Section 23 from judicial review. Such a result would be entirely inconsistent with the judiciary's duty to uphold the Constitution." For the same reasons, the court rebuffed the Grassroots group's argument that the federal power of disallowance be used as an alternative to judicial invalidation.

The court accepted Ottawa's proposal to invoke the doctrine of necessity – a doctrine it noted was normally only required with revolutionary or insurrectionary governments – to preserve Manitoba's laws. But it refused Ottawa's suggestion to set an arbitrary limit of two years, saying it had no factual basis for knowing how long it would take Manitoba to comply.

> As presently equipped the court is incapable of determining the period of time during which it would not be possible for the Manitoba legislature to comply with its constitutional duty. The court will, however, at the request of either the attorney general of Canada or the attorney general of Manitoba, made within one hundred and twenty days of

the date of this judgement, make such a determination …
Following such a request, a special hearing will be set and
submissions will be accepted from the attorney general of
Canada and the attorney general of Manitoba and the other
intervenors. [64]

Overall, the judgement was a stunning rebuke, not just to the
opponents of the 1983 constitutional initiative, but to the conduct of the
province for all but twenty years of its history. Over and over again, the
eighty-eight-page judgement was punctuated with phrases like this: "It is
this court which must take steps to avoid the deleterious consequences of
the Manitoba Legislature's persistent failure to observe the Constitution." [65]

Just how accurate the court was in its jaundiced view of Manitoba
and its distrust of the province's willingness finally to cease its constitutional
defiance demonstrated itself once again the very day of the judgement. The
court's refusal to save any unilingual legislation before the legislature at the
time of the judgement – 9:30 a.m. June 13th – meant that no less than twenty-
six of the fifty-five bills on the Manitoba legislature order paper immediately
died. One bill that failed was dear to the NDP's heart. It was an amendment
to the Manitoba Health Insurance Corporation Act banning extra-billing.

The house was still following the policy adopted by the previous
Tory government to amend unilingual English legislation with unilingual
English bills and only use bilingual enactment for new statutes. This meant
that Manitoba's core and most important laws were still being kept up to date
in English only while they awaited their turn in the translation queue. Asked
why, a red-faced government House leader, Andy Anstett, explained: "No
one anticipated the house procedure would be affected by the ruling." [66]

In a clarifying judgement handed down on November 4, 1985, the
court set a time limit of five years for the province to complete its mammoth
translation task and endowed its English-only laws with temporary validity
until the deadline. Manitoba was spared the time-consuming process of re-
enactment of all laws. Instead, the approach to translation agreed to by the
SFM and made part of the failed constitutional amendment was adopted. All
new laws and amendments to unilingual laws had to be bilingual. The existing English-only laws were left to be translated as part of the province's continuing statute revision. Manitoba's laws became fully bilingual on December
31, 1990. The cost was $7 million. But, as we shall see, that was not quite the

end of the translation controversy.

The saga of Manitoba's statutes had a further interesting footnote. Midway through the language crisis, a vital part of the province's history - its body of pre-1890 bilingual laws, journals and votes and proceedings, all bound in red with gold lettering – was moved from the open shelves in the Legislative Building's second floor reading room to the closed rare book room in the main Legislative Library. The rare book room can only be accessed by a librarian and is climate controlled. However, when one librarian confirmed the move had been taken for safe-keeping, it was obvious the concern went beyond temperature and humidity. Volumes from the same set in the law courts' Law Library had already disappeared.

12

Coming to Terms

THE SUPREME COURT JUDGEMENT on the Manitoba language reference was pointed, frank, at times almost brutal. So too, were the questions the justices had directed at the various intervenors in the three-day hearing a year earlier.

"How do entrenched language rights get protection?" Supreme Court Chief Justice Brian Dickson asked Manitoba's counsel, A. Kerr Twaddle. Twaddle conceded that the guarantee of statutes in both official languages was "mandatory in the sense that it must be done. But it is not mandatory in the sense that invalidity flows from a failure to comply."

Demanded the chief justice: "Well, Mr. Twaddle, what does flow then?"

Pierre Genest, counsel for Canada, asked the court to find Manitoba's laws invalid but to use the doctrine of necessity – employed never before in Canada and elsewhere only in the case of revolutionary governments – to validate the laws for two years to give the province opportunity to translate them and avoid legal chaos.

Asked the Supreme Court chief justice: "At the end of the two years, you might be back in the chaotic position you came from. Has this court ever done this vis-à-vis a provincial legislature before?"

Mr. Justice Jean Beetz asked Genest why he thought Manitoba would be any more willing to listen to the Supreme Court in 1984 than it was to its own courts in 1892 and 1909. The government of the day simply ignored rulings declaring the 1890 English-only law invalid. When Genest replied that the court should not assume any Canadian legislature would disregard its ruling, Mr. Justice Willard Estey was quick with this stinging retort: "The record of the last 90 years is against you."

While it was clear the justices had little or no patience with Manitoba, it was equally clear they were not about to make the citizens of Manitoba bear the brunt of the province's ninety-year constitutional defiance. Justice Beetz wondered if La Société franco-manitobaine lawyer Joseph Magnet's idea of a legislature stripped naked of its laws would not create a legal vacuum, no matter how swiftly the legislature acted. "I feel there is a legal vacuum here that the legislature would not be able to fill. There is no obligation (on the legislature) to pass a constitutional amendment (to save itself and its laws.)"

The justices attempted to find out how much time Manitoba would need to comply with its constitutional obligations. "Assuming there is a finding of invalidity, what would be the position of authority in Manitoba?" Chief Justice Dickson asked Twaddle. "The position would be to seek a constitutional amendment," Manitoba's lawyer replied. But, reflecting on the unprecedented 263 hours of bell ringing, Twaddle acknowleged that "the question would be whether the legislature could be persuaded to pass it. The government can't dictate that the resolution pass. A constitutional amendment, therefore, is the only route, but I can't say it would be taken."

Alarmed, the chief justice probed further. "What could the court do to prevent lawlessness?" Replied Twaddle: "Find the laws valid." Pursued the chief justice: "Assuming otherwise?" Twaddle played his final card. "There would be nothing the court, Parliament or Manitoba could do. You would create a lawless state, a province that would be outside the constitution."

Going on the basis that about half of Manitoba's 4,500 unilingual laws were either ready for passage in French or nearly ready, Justice Estey inquired of the Manitoba counsel: "How chaotic would missing the rest be? How quick could Manitoba get back on side?" Twaddle answered that he didn't know. When Estey asked what the province would be prepared to give as a *quid pro quo* to its French minority if the court gave the province ten years, Twaddle ducked. Any recompense or *quid pro quo* was political and not a matter for a court.

The language was often tough. Genest called on the justices to take note that Twaddle had "leaped like a trout" for the ten-year grace period, but called anything for the Francophone population political. "Well, the extension of time for translation was political, too," Genest continued. "The federal government only agreed to the extension of time in exchange for (French language) services."

Justice Estey asked SFM lawyer Magnet if "any portion of your argument depends on proving animus (by the legislature towards its obligation)". Replied Magnet: "This court is being asked by some of the parties to accept assurances about the provincial attorney general's compliance and co-operation ... Manitoba has remained unmoved, inflexible and mulish ... It has engaged in consistent and deliberate constitutional defiance."

If nothing else, these exchanges made clear just how high the stakes were in the Manitoba language reference. Chaos can hardly be the instrument to uphold the rule of law. But defiance of the rule of law is in itself chaos. The conundrum of the court was a sobering reminder to Manitobans that the issues at stake went far beyond passing political pressures and personalities as well as bilingualism. Manitoba's longstanding constitutional breach posed a serious threat, not just to the country's soul and meaning, but to its legal foundations.

The questions the federal justice minister had posed to the high court brought into stark conflict the two pillars of the Canadian legal system: Canada's written constitution with its codified protections for minorities and the British common law tradition of parliamentary supremacy and the right of democratic majorities to continously remake their societies in their evolving images without pain of punishment for discarding outdated obligations.

Canada's counsel sought to allay some of the justices' fears of legal and constitutional chaos in his final rebuttal to Manitoba's arguments. The court shouldn't be frightened of using the doctrine of necessity even though it had never before had to be resorted to in Canada. "This case is unprecedented in this country and all others, as far as we know," Genest said. " It is unlikely ever to rise again. Using necessity does not undermine either the legal order or the constitution. It is not meant to thwart the constitution but rather to facilitate compliance with it. Canada is founded on the principle of the rule of law. The submission of the attorney general of

Canada upholds the rule of law."

Reflecting on the course of the arguments outside the Supreme Court chamber in June 1984, Alliance Quebec president Eric Maldoff said the Manitoba reference case went to the "absolute essence" of the Canadian constitution. [1]

When the court's strong, balanced ruling came down a year later, both sides in Manitoba attempted to claim victory. Speaking in the legislature, Premier Howard Pawley tried to throw it back in the teeth of those who had preferred the court route to the government's chosen path of a negotiated settlement.

> No one should be surprised by today's decision, for all
> Manitobans were aware of the uncertainty in having the
> Supreme Court in Ottawa provide a solution for us ...
> As premier, I believe it is a tough decision with which
> Manitoba can live if the court provides the province with
> sufficient time. The decision may disappoint some and may
> strike others as imposing a too stringent obligation on the
> province ... [2]

But it was the Conservatives who felt most vindicated and, because of that, continued to give no quarter, either to the government or to Franco-Manitobans. Opposition Leader Gary Filmon persisted, at least publicly, in treating the issue solely as the need to translate laws. His party had saved Manitoba from dreaded official bilingualism, a claim the actions his own government subsequently took would belie.

> One of the fundamental responsibilities of governments is
> to maintain peace, order and social comity ... What the
> Supreme Court decision has done is demonstrate that the
> current administration in Manitoba has failed absymally
> to meet this challenge ... (It) is evident from the Supreme
> Court decision today that this NDP administration has
> unnecessarily caused a great deal of trauma, confrontation
> and deep social division amongst the people of Manitoba
> as a result of its ill-conceived and unwarranted proposals.
>
> To entrench an amendment to fully bilingualize our
> province and to enact legislation mandating French-

language services in all government departments, that needless trauma, that convulsion to the people of our province,
will take a good deal of time to overcome…Because, Mr,.
Speaker, it was not necessary for the government to proceed
in the manner in which it did.

Filmon insisted that the government's package took the province "a
quantum leap" beyond what was required by the constitution and imposed
a status on Manitoba that was "historically, socially and practically not
warranted or, for that matter, not supported by the vast majority of our
citizens …

Some observers have said that this judgement …
confirms that we are fully bilingual. Section 23 makes
us bilingual to the extent that Section 133 of the federal
constitution makes Canada bilingual in the courts, in
the legislature and in the printing and publishing of
our laws.

But I remind members that it was not Section 133 of
the federal constitution that made Canada fully bilingual.
It took an act of parliament passed by the Trudeau government in 1968 (sic) to do that. Only by further constitutional amendment or legislative action could the additional obligations be placed on Manitoba such as were
being proposed by those ill-conceived plans of this NDP
administration, a proposal that Manitobans rejected." (3)

In the subsequent question period, Filmon asked the premier if the government was planning any further constitutional amendments with respect
to bilingualism in Manitoba. The premier's reply was, not surprisingly, an
emphatic no.

In the House of Commons, the tone was far more high-minded
than in the Manitoba legislature. Senior Manitoba MP Lloyd Axworthy called
June 13, 1985 "a very historic day in the establishment of a more civil tolerant and equitable society in Canada. The opinion rendered by the Supreme
Court on the establishment of minority rights is a very clear verdict and a
very clear signal which, considering the past judgements of this house, I am
sure we all endorse." (4)

The new prime minister was absent from the House that day, but the next, Mulroney signed on.

> There has been a decision by the Supreme Court which, of course, the Government of Canada will respect fully. We will work closely with the parties to ensure its full implementation ... The government of Canada is supportive not only of the decision but of any initiative (that) the government of Manitoba would bring forward. [5]

The *Globe and Mail* castigated the Manitoba Conservatives in an editorial June 14, 1985:

> In 1890, the Manitoba Legislature declared English the only language of use in Manitoba's Legislature and Courts. On at least three occasions since, Manitoba Courts have ruled that law to be unconstitutional (in 1892, 1906 and 1976). But a defiant Manitoba Legislature ignored its courts and pressed on in English only. Manitoba pressed on in English, for the most part, even after the Supreme Court of Canada unanimously supported the Manitoba court in 1979 ... A clear constitutional outlaw for ninety years, an unenthusiastic inmate for five, the Manitoba Legislature cannot feel pride in this important aspect of its history – our history ...

> At the height of the Manitoba schools question in the 1890s, historian Alexander Begg wrote, "Unfortunately for Manitoba, and unfortunately for Canada, any question that involves a conflict between race or creed is eagerly seized upon by unscrupulous politicians to stir up the spirit of bigotry that unhappily underlies the surface of our social and political fabric." ... (A)s the Supreme Court said yesterday, the Manitoba language case "combines legal and constitutional questions of the utmost subtlety and complexity with political questions of great sensitivity." Manitoba's political leaders owe their province and country an appreciation of that fact.

La Presse's Michel Roy weighed in with an editorial headlined "Unachieved victory for a minority". Even a full century later, he wrote, it was moving to

hear the highest court in the land confirm that Manitoba francophones have
been unjustly treated.

> A triumph of right over injustice, the Supreme Court judge-
> ment nevertheless poses another danger – stagnation,
> indeed, retreat, by this little French Canadian collectivity,
> already so vulnerable. The constitutional victory of the
> Franco-Manitobans will be derisory if it isn't accompanied
> by language services, the only means to assure the protec-
> tion of a minority scoffed at for the decline that menaces
> them … One can only hope that English-speaking
> Manitobans who rejected the Pawley government's compro-
> mise in favour of the francophones, will resign themselves
> to accepting what has been imposed by the Supreme Court.
> Henceforth, in fact as well as law, Manitoba could gradually
> become a bilingual province and the francophone collectiv-
> ity, instead of weakening, could prosper, especially if it was
> to receive considerable help from Québec. [6]

Jean-Louis Roy, publisher of *Le Devoir*, saw the Supreme Court
decision as seminal in Canadian affairs. He dismissed the popular assumption
that the people of Québec no longer cared about the fate of francophone
minorities elsewhere in Canada, attributing it to "less than honourable political manoeuvring" by the Parti Québécois and English Canadian hostility. A
"solid majority" of Québécois "shares the conviction that protecting and guaranteeing the language rights of all Francophone minorities is fundamental to
the very definition of Canadian federalism", he wrote in the September 1985
special issue of *Language and Society*, the publication of the Official Language
Commissioner for Canada. It was entitled *Manitoba and the Language Question:
a Story of Conflict*.

His article, *Cousins in Law*, pointed out that Manitoba's founding
legislation never left any doubt about its obligations to the French language
and to a constitutionally-recognized linguistic minority, identical as it was
to Section 133 of the British North America Act. Continued Roy:

> The difference is that Québec kept its promise. Manitoba
> did not. On this point, history cannot be denied: its effects
> are so visible, the injustice perpetrated against Franco-

Manitobans so glaring and permanent. To forget the 1890 injustice would be to betray generations of victims, both Franco-Manitobans and Québécois, whose respective struggles and mutual support have combined to produce a single, century-old movement ....

The other provinces and Canadians of every origin must understand the true meaning of la francophonie canadienne ... The redress provided in the Supreme Court's decision on language rights in Manitoba ... is irreversible and, to some, excessive. The latter have forgotten the scope of the century-old injustice suffered by Franco-Manitobans. But the Supreme Court judgement is mandatory...

Unless the Government of Manitoba and the Francophone minority forge a new agreement for amending the Constitution along the lines of the one a racist and violent opposition aborted less than two years ago, Manitoba will have to translate every one of its "invalid and inoperative" laws.

A century has been lost, the limits of endurance long ago exhausted. But if the Franco-Manitoban minority has been decimated by the majority's policy of cultural and linguistic hegemony and "things appear hopeless", the determination of Québécers and others "to make them otherwise" once again appears to be the firm will of the majority.

Roy concluded by saying the fate of Québec is intimately linked with that of francophone minorities. "It knows that their failure could well spell the beginning of (Québec's) own demise and a slow decline into insignificance."

Howard Pawley's New Democrats were re-elected in 1986 with a one-seat majority. In a post-election news conference, Tory MLA and former attorney general Gerry Mercier declared all-out political war on the NDP. The opposition, he said, was determined to bring down the government at its very first opportunity. The Tories commenced a full frontal assault on every aspect of NDP policy, including, of course, any sign of movement on the language file. In early 1987, Conservative MLA Charlotte Oleson spied a cave-in to pressure from La Société franco-manitobaine as well as a plot to force bilingualism on Manitobans from the government's decision to follow the federal practice of printing both languages side by side in the statutes. She wanted separate texts. She complained the dual language statutes made the statute books "cumbersome", wasted "reams" of paper and "litres" of ink and increased printing costs. Not mentioned but obviously paramount to her objection was the "French on the cereal box" factor. Dual language statutes meant English-speaking Manitobans would be forced to see French every time they had to look at their laws.

The 1986 election witnessed the defeat of Andy Anstett, the municipal affairs minister and government House leader who knew he was doomed electorally after he repeatedly had to face down his furious Springfield constituents while serving as the spirited and passionate point man on the language file. Jim Walding, the speaker who had presided over the 263 hours of bell-ringing, was re-elected in his St. Vital riding. This time, however, he was left on the backbench, where he became even more embittered. He finally took his revenge in early 1988. With numerous wives of Tory MLAs watching from the gallery – a hint that the opposition knew what he was about to do – he toppled the government by voting with the Conservatives against the provincial budget. The NDP was then at a nadir in popularity due to stiff tax increases and a big jump in automobile insurance premiums. In the subsequent election, it was reduced to third-party status while the Liberals under Sharon Carstairs, the "lady in red", soared from just one to twenty-two seats. She became Manitoba's first female leader of the Official Opposition.

Filmon's Conservatives won a minority government in April 1988. Throughout their eleven years in office, the Tories presented a "good cop, bad cop" image to the province on the language issue. There were only two Dr. Jekylls (the premier and later, French Language Services Minister Darren Praznik), while all the rest of the cabinet and caucus were Mr. Hydes. The issue's progress was, not surprisingly, marked by startling steps forward alternated with discouraging slides backward.

At first, the Hydes seemed firmly in the saddle. Two major cabinet orders-in-council, one by the NDP just before it left office setting up the Aboriginal Justice Inquiry and another by the Conservatives authorizing a $13 billion hydro sale to Ontario (later cancelled), were issued in English only. The first had been invalidated by Manitoba's Court of Appeal and the second faced a similar court challenge. Characteristically, the Tories opted to fight rather than translate. Responded the *Free Press*:

Manitoba is back before the Supreme Court of Canada asking the judges to write public policy for the province. The judges should have none of it. They should tell the Manitoba government to grow up and start being a government ...

The courts are not there to be the policy-maker of last resort when a government is too timorous, witless or spineless to decide its policy and serve its people. Cabinet orders should be made in the languages of Manitoba's public administration, which are French and English. The Conservative Party fought a long battle in 1983 and 1984 to keep the present Manitoba language requirements in the constitution. It should be happy to respect them. [7]

The Supreme Court did hear Manitoba's case and on January 23, 1992, it ruled just as the SFM believed it would. Cabinet orders of a legislative nature, referring to codes of conduct or an indeterminate number of people – in other words, virtually all cabinet orders – had to be in both official languages.

This court fight turned out to be the next-to-last stand of the Conservatives' overt anti-bilingual perosna. Beginning in 1989 with an address to the SFM annual meeting, Gary Filmon opened the door to a regimen of French language services within the government at least as broad, if not broader, than that envisaged in the aborted constitutional amendment his party had so vehemently opposed.

As observers had suspected, the young opposition leader had indeed been riding a tiger when he succeeded Lyon in those dark, super-charged days in the early winter of 1984. His discomfort and embarrassment during that time were visible to all who watched him up close. He was caving in to political necessity. His hold on his leadership was tentative; the party's strong rural caucus predisposed to distrust and even plot to overthrow him. He went along with their extreme tactics to survive and also, of course, because he was a politician and those tactics, however distasteful he found them, seemed to be inflicting a mortal wound on his political opponents.

Roger Turenne, the first director of the province's French Language Services Secretariat, believes Filmon used the language issue to gain control over his party and caucus. Following the June 1985 Supreme Court decision, Turenne had returned from a leave of absence to continue work on the government's overall plan to implement French language services. The court ruling had not dealt with French language services, so he was instructed to carry on as if nothing had happened. His proposal was approved at the last meeting of the outgoing Pawley cabinet in May 1988. Turenne presented its broad outlines to the incoming cabinet as " a Progressive Conservative policy on French language services", bound in a Tory blue cover. Filmon showed himself to be more open than Turenne could have possibly dreamed.

While the Tory caucus was decidedly unsympathetic, the premier's office was staffed with moderate Conservatives like cabinet secretary Don Leitch. Eight months after taking office, Filmon took Turenne's policy to cabinet. "He got a lot of flack," Turenne said in one of two lengthy interviews in the late fall of 2002. [8]. The implementation was delayed.

Then, in early November 1989, Turenne arranged for the premier to speak to the SFM annual meeting. Cloaking his initiatives in the non-threatening language of "common sense" while avoiding the dreaded phrases of "constitutional entrenchment" and "official bilingualism", Filmon moved the linguistic goalposts astonishingly far down the field. Not only would French language services be expanded to all provincial Crown corporations and a broad range of government services, including hospitals and social services where numbers warranted, but highway signs would be bilingual in parts of the province with a significant francophone population and Manitobans would have the right to appear before quasi-judicial tribunals in the official language of their choice. The province, he continued, had identified 130 government offices and services where both languages would be offered, including vital statistics, driver testing, community social services, the human rights commission, Legal Aid Manitoba and landlord and tenant affairs. The premier also promised to improve the delivery of French language services in the City of Winnipeg.

Just as important as the actual announcement itself was his open and conciliatory language. "The Franco-Manitoban community is a vibrant and active part of our province," he said. They are not a protected creature of government. Franco-Manitobans exist today despite the actions of past governments. "They are one of the fundamental characteristics of Manitoba and help define it as a province." He also held out the possibility of establishing French school boards. "We will deal with this question in the same spirit of fairness and common sense which has guided our approach on other minority language issues." Even though outgoing SFM president Denis Clement said the initiatives stopped short of official bilingualism, they were a step in the right direction. Filmon was rewarded with a standing ovation from SFM delegates. [9]

The next day, the premier, without comment, tabled in the House Sessional Paper Number 99 – "French Language Services in Manitoba". The policy had eleven points, the first of which stated unequivocally:

> The French Language Services Policy of the Government of Manitoba is hereby established in recognition of the fact that the French-speaking population of Manitoba is a constituent part of one of the fundamental characteristics of Canada. Its purpose is to allow this community and the institutions which serve it to access comparable government services in the language of the laws of Manitoba.

Among other commitments, the government undertook to provide all correspondence with individuals and groups in the "official language" – yes, here was a Conservative government using the freighted phrase "official language" – preferred by the recipient and to issue all forms, identity documents and certificates and informational documents intended for the general public in a bilingual format. It also pledged to use both official languages on signs and public notices in designated francophone areas and to ensure that designated health care and social services institutions in francophone areas of the province were able to function in French. The policy applied not just to the government but to its four Crown corporations and agencies like the ombudsman, Elections Manitoba and the Manitoba Human Rights Commission.

Contacted by the *Free Press*, anti-bilingualism crusader and Grassroots Manitoba head Grant Russell, who had just been appointed by the Tories to the province's Inter-Cultural Council, attempted to downplay the initiative. "I have no more objection to seeing French signs in Lorette than I do to Chinese signs in Chinatown and Ukrainian signs in Dauphin," he said. Bilingual Manitoba Hydro bills rank with bilingual driver's licences as mere symbolic gestures, he continued. It all added up to little beyond what had already been happening. But *Free Press* columnist Fred Cleverley, a long and ardent foe of bilingualism, wasn't prepared to be dismissive. He had a blunt warning to the premier. His openness to French would be politically costly.

The Canadian Crucible

… Gary Filmon's conversion to a policy approaching
bilingualism is difficult to understand. He may put up
bilingual highway signs in Manitoba, only to have them
irritate ninety-four out of every 100 drivers who pass
them. Perhaps what we are seeing is only evidence of a
well-known political disease …

When in opposition, every politician clearly understands
that he needs only the support of a majority to gain power.
Once in power, most politicians are seized by a desire to be
loved not just by the majority, but by every single voter. [10]

Turenne regards Filmon's SFM appearance and its immediate aftermath as the high point of his career. The following day, Filmon convened a
meeting of all deputy ministers and heads of the major Crown corporations
to tell them that the French language services policy had the full support of
his government, that he expected them to take personal responsibility for its
implementation, that is, they were not allowed to delegate, and that they
should refer all matters of interpretation to Turenne who spoke on the premier's behalf on these questions. After one cabinet minister attempted to side-
step a provision of his department's French language services plan, Filmon
intervened personally.

"The only appeal from me was to the premier, and I was never over-
ruled," Turenne recalls. "I remember someone in his office said: 'We're not
going to be facing the likes of us in the legislature. All the bigots are on our
side and we're going to sit on them.'" The premier also kept in place the previous government's practice of having one civil servant per department placed
in charge of coordinating minority language services. That civil servant
would be answerable to Turenne, and to his deputy minister, bypassing normal reporting channels.

Turenne cites one exchange between the premier and a recalcitrant
cabinet minister that he thinks may illustrate how Filmon stickhandled the
contentious language issue past his members. Two positions in the provincial
government services centre in the minister's hometown were to be designated
bilingual because the centre served a wide area which included French-
speaking communities. The minister objected on the grounds that the town
where the office was located was almost exclusively English-speaking. The
premier replied that if that was a problem for the minister, then he would be

happy to move the office down the road to a town with a Francophone majority. The minister backed down. The same minister was alarmed that a bilingual highway sign was to be posted right at his farm. Filmon postponed putting up the sign until after the upcoming election. "When he (the premier) was questioned or challenged, he always had a ready answer," Turenne says. While the Tory premier may not have convinced his colleagues, he deftly silenced them. [11] Filmon's job of fending off his cabinet and caucus critics became much easier once he won a majority government in the summer of 1990.

It was also under Filmon's leadership that the equally ancient and vexed question of public aid to private schools as well as the matter of French education rights were resolved. The separate schools matter provided an ironic twist to recent history. To avoid yet another court challenge, the Conservatives negotiated a constitutional settlement on private and parochial schools with an umbrella group of denominational and private school advocates including the province's Roman Catholic community, both English and French. The settlement gradually raised provincial funding to eighty per cent of that provided the public school system. In 1993, the Supreme Court of Canada confirmed that Section 23 of the Canadian Charter of Rights and Freedoms gave Franco-Manitobans total governance of their schools. In 1994, the provincial government created la Division Scolaire Franco-Manitobaine, the province-wide French language school division the premier promised in that 1989 speech.

The DSFM means the Franco-Manitoban community now not only has a network of twenty-three schools across the province using French as the language of instruction, but school governance – complete control over staffing appointments, cultural programs, buses, special needs, speech therapy, in other words, a full program of educational services. Not surprisingly, local French-English tensions and controversy, particularly in rural areas, centred on issues of busing and whose community obtains the local school, are ongoing. While they are not unlike the tensions that exist within the English language school system itself over the same issues, the DSFM faces some problems peculiar to all new entities, particularly in the supercharged area of language. As Franco-Manitoban journalist and author Jacqueline Blay puts it:

> The DSFM was not welcomed by every school board. Only the Seine River School Division shared its surplus with it.

Other school boards that were losing their Français schools, staff and resources sometimes had a difficult time. Making room for an unusual first of a kind school board required adjustments and dialogue. One community in particular suffered greatly from the lack of understanding of what the DSFM was all about. Students from Laurier School (École Jour de Plaine) had to be housed for two years in a bingo hall without access to the services provided to English pupils because Turtle Mountain School Division trustees were not in agreement with the concept of school governance "en français". The Filmon government refused to intervene in the matter. But there were success stories in other parts of the province and had it not been for internal strife at the political level, the DSFM would have been a shining example of a political structure imposed by the courts with the intent of restoring rights that were denied more than a hundred years before. [12]

Things seemed so rosy by 1991 that Manitoba received the equivalent of a gold star in the annual report of the federal Official Languages Commissioner. In his seventh and final report to Parliament, D'Iberville Fortier stated: "Manitoba distinguished itself as one of this year's leaders in the West with continued tangible progress" in the improvement of French language services. "It is a success story which long appeared to be an impossible dream." Filmon took pride in this, and was gracious to share the credit. In a speech in the House upon Turenne's retirement after ten years on the linguistic hotseat he said much of Fortier's praise was due to Turenne's hard work. "Roger has left a lasting contribution to Manitoba and deserves our thanks and commendation. [13]

While it may have seemed that Manitoba had finally exorcised its linguistic ghosts and closed Pandora's Box, those passions will never be completely damped. The beast of linguistic and ethnic hostility and bigotry only sleeps, it never dies. And no matter how good a language services plan is on paper, its true test is in practice, in accessibility to real people. Finally, the personal commitment, even of a premier, can't make it happen virtually alone in a political climate of fear, resistance and reluctance. Fortier's gold star was soon revealed to have been a bit premature.

In the fall of 1996, Manitoba introduced new licence plates for the first time since the 1985 Supreme Court decision. The green, gold, blue and white plates, displaying a river winding through a prairie landscape framed by a forest, bore the provincial bison logo and "Friendly" Manitoba motto.

When the design was unveiled, the SFM was outraged, noting that it didn't comply with the province's official languages policy. Initially, Highways Minister Glen Findlay said he would be willing to meet with the SFM and "respond as best we can" about its concerns. But he obdurately insisted that an English-only licence plate was "completely consistent" with the province's language policy because licence plates were not a designated French service.

The SFM offered its own plate design, merely adding the word "Bienvenue" in the same script as "Friendly" to the bottom of the plate. The SFM also consulted its lawyer, Roger Bilodeau, who gave his opinion that the licence plate was a constitutional, not a services, matter. And Vaughan Baird, the lawyer who had fought Bilodeau's case up to the Supreme Court a decade earlier, was appalled at such governmental cowardice and hair-splitting. "This isn't a matter of discretionary French language services, this is a constitutional obligation," he told the *Free Press*. "The Highway Traffic Act is a bilingual act and the licence plate is part of that act. We have bilingual drivers' licences and bilingual Autopac registrations. How can a licence be a service? It is not. It is a constitutional obligation, just like the statutes."

Noting that the province's tourism department had launched an aggressive advertising campaign touting Manitoba's bilingual character, Mr. Baird said the government's decision was incomprehensible. "Why would you not make your licence plates bilingual? What better way to show that we are bilingual?" [14] Eventually, the province forged a compromise that, according to Rénauld Rémillard, director of l'Institut-Joseph Dubuc, might now be interpreted as unconstitutional. In 1999, the Supreme Court of Canada asserted a new principle in a judgement involving the right of a British Columbia francophone to a trial in his own language. Language rights meant not only the right to services and education in an official language, but also the promotion of minority language communities. Said the court: "Language rights must in all cases be interpreted purposively, in a manner consistent with the preservation and development of official language communities in Canada." [15]

Rémillard, the former director of the Language Rights Section of the Court Challenges Program of Canada said in a 2003 interview that "in light of this decision, the argument can now be made that even though the Manitoba

Act of 1870 talks only about bilingual courts and the legislature, implicit in that Act is the right to bilingual services." [16] The case was a watershed, Rémillard continued, because it reversed the court's highly restrictive and narrow approach to language rights embedded in a series of decisions often called "The Trilogy" handed down in 1986 and 1987. In them, the court enunciated the idea that language rights were inferior to other rights in the Charter because they were political compromises and so should not be given broad interpretation. But the 1999 decision, Regina v. Beaulac, turned the 1987 one on its head. Essentially, Rémillard says, Beaulac means that "all language rights, non-constitutional as well as constitutional, (are) part of the Canadian fabric and must be interpreted in a broad and liberal manner, including all language rights in Manitoba."

The licence plate compromise meant that once again, Franco-Manitobans were made into just one of the province's many ethnic minorities, all of whom, the government said, were free to fashion licence plate stickers saying whatever they wanted in their languages. The SFM decided against another court battle after a public intervention by Roger Turenne. Now the former director of the province's French Language Services Secretariat, he strenuously opposed a return to court, fearing a loss could halt the incremental steps forward the government was taking on its own. Turenne's fear was based on the fact that despite the high court's bold words in the federal reference case, it nevertheless obliged Bilodeau to pay his speeding ticket which it said was not covered by the bilingual requirement.

Instead, the SFM printed off "Bienvenue" stickers by the thousands and they became a popular fund-raiser. Most of the stickers – in all languages – succumbed to Manitoba's rigorous weather within one or two years. Turenne believes the licence plate imbroglio was a matter of oversight, not conscious planning, followed by an obdurate refusal to admit error. However, it demonstrated that there remained gray and confused areas in the government's conduct of its official languages policy. As compensation to the SFM and to clarify issues as much as possible, the Filmon government established a review of its decade-old strategy to meet the needs of its official language minority, choosing Provincial Court Judge Richard Chartier as its commissioner. His report, *Above All, Common Sense – Avant Toute Chose, Le Bon Sens*, was released in May 1998.

His report was brilliant, both conceptually and strategically, and is being studied by Ottawa as a possible blueprint for its own language policy.

The report has two key features – territorial, or community, bilingualism and "active offer" linguistic services. Chartier grounded his report firmly within Manitoba's history and traditions, dwelling extensively on Manitoba's historical and constitutional past, even to the point of reproducing Louis Riel's 1869 Provisional Government invitation and 1870 List of Rights as well as early maps of Fort Garry.

The concept of territorial bilingualism – bilingualism based on population numbers – Chartier felt, arose naturally from Manitoba's history. As a colony leading up to Confederation, Fort Garry had equal numbers of French and English-speaking parishes. Territorial bilingualism is the practice in European countries like Switzerland with more than one language. Territorial bilingualism was proposed by the Royal Commission on Bilingualism and Biculturalism in 1964 and was also the original intent of Ottawa's 1969 Official Languages Act, an intent that died due to political cowardice in the face of bitter anglophone resistance to the law, particularly in Western Canada. And finally, a form of territorial bilingualism, "where numbers warrant", undergirded Manitoba's approach to education as well as the initial languge services policy drafted by Turenne.

The idea of "active offer" language service stemmed from a speech given by Filmon in November 1991 in which the premier said:

> This concept encompasses all communications in the official language of the client's choice, either by phone, in person or in writing. The Active Offer concept means that the service providers will publicize the availability of services in both languages and will ensure that people feel equally comfortable in dealing with the designated offices in the language of their choice. The offer of French Language Services must be evident. Members of the general public should be convinced from the outset that using the official language of their choice will not result in a diminished quality of service … [17]

Chartier's watchword in drafting the report was his belief that four elements are essential for a non-dominant language to survive. The language must be used at home, be taught in the schools, be used in the mass media and be used at work.

Prior to his appointment, the government's French Language

Services Secretariat had asked a mystery client named Mrs. Diane Dubé to test out language availability in a cross-section of government departments and agencies. Her findings were sobering in comparison to the premier's 1989 and 1991 undertakings. Stated the report: "Only in fifteen per cent of the cases did the client receive service comparable to that enjoyed by the major-ity of Manitobans." It defined comparable service as being greeted and served in French. "Almost forty per cent of the time, she received no service in French at all." [18]

Chartier relied heavily on population data from Statistics Canada to come up with his plans for territorial bilingualism. He uncovered some inter-esting facts about Canada as well as Manitoba. For example, according to the 1991 Census, Canadians of French descent were the largest single origin group, at 6,146,600, followed by Canadians of English origin, including Irish, Scottish and Welsh, at 5,611,050. The next most numerous ethnic group was German at 911,560. Yet in the same Census, French was the mother tongue of one out of four Canadians, or 6,642,643 while English was the mother tongue of fully sixty-two per cent of the population. Italian, Chinese and German followed with two per cent each. In Manitoba, the largest ethnic group, English, represented only seventeen per cent of the population, yet fully seventy-eight per cent of Manitobans claimed English as their mother tongue. Germans formed the second largest ethnicity at nine per cent. Aboriginal and Ukrainian claimed seven per cent each, while French was five per cent. The multitudinous other nationalities or mixtures of nationali-ties comprising Manitoba's famous ethnic mosaic thus made up the majority – fifty-three per cent – of the province's citizens.

Significantly, while Manitoba had 52,465 citizens who cited French as their mother tongue in 1991, almost double that number – 100,700 or nine per cent of the population – reported that they spoke French. The diff-erence of close to 50,000 souls Chartier attributed to three factors: graduates of immersion schools, children of anglophone-francophone mixed marriages and anglophone adults who had become bilingual. Stated the report:

> In this report, the term "clientele" is used to refer to all French-speaking Manitobans, including the Métis, French-Canadians, French-speaking Europeans (Belgians, French, Swiss), French-speaking Africans and Asians and the children of francophone-anglophone parents …

Statistics Canada considers these adults to be assimilated. This is completely false. They are proud of their identity as bilingual Canadians and their mixed background has much in common with the Franco-Manitoban culture, based in large part on the melding of the French, Scottish and Native cultures ...[19]

To establish which areas of Manitoba should be designated bilingual, Chartier drew up a scale of linguistic vitality in which he assigned points for certain characteristics, including the presence of a French elementary or high school or both. The Franco-Manitoban "reality", as he called it, was found to be present in eighteen rural municipalities in their entirety and part of six others. Taken together, the total population of the rural designated areas was about 46,000, or four per cent of the Manitoba population. The eighteen designated municipalities were Taché, Ste. Anne, La Broquerie, Piney, Ritchot, DeSalaberry, Montcalm, Lorne, Grey, St. Laurent, Cartier, St. François Xavier, Ellice, Ste. Rose and Alexander. The six partial municipalities were MacDonald, Morris, South Norfolk, Dufferin, Portage la Prairie and Woodlands.

With eleven per cent of its citizens able to speak French and English, Winnipeg was Canada's fourth largest bilingual city. Canada's most bilingual city was Montréal (forty-eight per cent), followed by Ottawa-Hull (forty-three per cent) and Québec City (twenty-eight per cent). Winnipeg also had a designated bilingual area, its south-east corner including St. Boniface, St. Vital, Radisson, St. Norbert and Transcona. These five communities together accounted for all but one per cent of the city's francophone population.

To properly serve citizens in these designated communities, Chartier proposed a network of six multi-tasked government community service centres that would offer programs from the departments of education and training, family services, health and to the extent possible, justice, agriculture and others. All employees in these centres would have to be bilingual. "I don't care if your name is Myshkowski, Smith or Chartier, as long as you're bilingual," Chartier said in an interview in late 2002. [20] Most importantly, their language of work would be French. To the extent possible, the CSCs would be located in towns or villages with a high or very high degree of French vitality. One CSC would be dedicated to service the province's Métis community in the White Horse Plain area including the villages of St. Laurent,

St. Ambroise and St. Eustache. The report said that it was important for the CSC in that area to have a distinct Métis character.

The CSC concept was designed to address a two-pronged problem. While few designated government offices were located in the designated bilingual areas, the bilingual civil service positions that did exist were almost all to be found in anglophone towns or villages. Thus, the government was simultaneously failing to provide services to its official minority while needlessly irritating the linguistic majority. "These communities have trouble understanding why a number of government jobs in their town are designated as requiring bilingualism." [21]

The report was tabled in the Legislature on June 2, 1998 by Darren Praznik, Minister responsible for French Language Services. Praznik spoke in English and then in French. It was endorsed – entirely in French – by NDP MLA Dave Chomiak, who would go on to become health minister in the NDP government of Gary Doer elected on September 21, 1999. French Language Services is currently the responsibility of the province's finance minister, Greg Selinger, the MLA for St. Boniface.

As of 2003, three of the six CSCs had been established – in St. Boniface, St, Pierre Jolys and Notre Dame des Lourdes. The St. Boniface CSC has become a tri-government facility, dispensing government services from Ottawa, Manitoba and Winnipeg. This trial is being closely watched by the federal government for use in other provinces.

In the interview in his Law Courts office in mid-December 2002, Chartier pronounced himself "very happy" with the progress on his report to date. All twenty-nine recommendations are either implemented or in the process of being implemented, he said. He recalled being most worried about getting cabinet acceptance of the idea of French as the working language of the CSCs. "That's the only thing that's different, that's radical," he said. He found an instant and powerful ally in the premier. "One of the comments Filmon made at cabinet when it came to the language of work was that his kids went to French immersion school and they didn't want to graduate and not have the opportunity to practice the language. Since French wasn't spoken at his home, he thought it so much the better that there would be places in Manitoba where they could use it."

Australia was the inspiration for his CSCs, Chartier said. The unique concept was developed to deliver government services to that nation's remote, geographically vast and sparsely-populated Outback.

The idea was for a one-stop shop, for multi-tasked general-
ists rather than individual employees for each department.
The Australian Outback was considered too small to justify
that, so they created these centres with generalist employees, one who could work for four different departments at
once ... If I had a wish, it would be that the federal government would adopt the territorial zones. It would be a
smarter use of public funds (than individual employees
scattered everywhere). It's something that would ensure
there is a French-speaking population outside Québec
and an English-speaking one inside Québec.

The lesson of the combined Pawley-Filmon experience seems to be
this: So long as it is kept *sotto voce*, half-hidden, seen but not really noticed,
the French language issue will not ignite. Thus, Manitoba's extensive and
generous program of French language services was consciously crafted and
implemented as a policy, by cabinet order, not legislation. Legislation would
have been too public and therefore too dangerous, especially for a party
whose core vote depended so heavily on those who had provided the muscle
for Grassroots Manitoba—rural middle-aged to older white Anglo-Saxon
Protestants and German Mennonites.

Franco-Manitobans themselves disagree on whether a cataclysm
like 1983–84 could ever be brought forth in Manitoba again. Roger Turenne
thinks it could not, believing that 1983-84 saw a unique combination of personalities and circumstances unlikely ever to be repeated. He describes it as
"the last gasp of that old divisive, anti-French character of Manitoba". [21]
But Chartier isn't so sure. He remembers his mother, a schoolteacher, being
insistent that her children learn to speak English without a trace of a French
accent. "I hate to say this, but she used to tell us to learn the language of the
enemy. She'd say 'You can't trust the English. You can't trust the Protestants.'"
He paused for a long moment when asked if he thought the bigotry could
again burst out. "I would hope not," he finally answered. "I like to think it
all comes down to the fact the two groups haven't mingled enough; they
don't know each other."[23]

Both Turenne and Chartier agree that at some point Manitoba should
put its language provisions into law. While there is no practical difference
between policy and statute, Manitoba's reluctance to put on its statute books

what is accomplished fact throughout the province keeps Manitoba hostage to its bitter past.

The 2001 Census dealt a blow to the efforts of the last twenty years to make amends for Manitoba's infamous "ninety years of injustice". Manitoba experienced the largest decline among the provinces in terms of francophone population. In 1991, Franco-Manitobans (defined as the population with French as the mother tongue) numbered 50,730 or 4.7 per cent. By 1996, that had shrunk to 49,110 or 4.5 per cent. In 2001, it had fallen again to just 45,920 or 4.2 per cent. This represents an overall 3.3 per cent drop between 1991 and 2001 but, ominously, a much steeper 6.5 per cent decline between 1996 and 2001.

Statistics Canada says that the decrease was due to a shrinkage in the number of francophone children aged four and under and, as a result of the ageing of the population, an increase in the number of deaths. The proportion of francophone seniors aged sixty-five and over rose from eighteen per cent in 1996 to 19.8 per cent in 2001. Nor can francophiles take solace from an increasing number of bilingual non-francophones. The 2001 Census found Manitoba's bilingualism rate had declined too, albeit slightly, from 9.4 per cent in 1996 to 9.3 per cent. Manitoba is now in sixth place among the provinces in terms of bilingual capacity. Nova Scotia edged it out, rising from 9.3 per cent in 1996 to 10.1 per cent. The other provinces ahead of Manitoba, with their 1996 numbers in brackets, are Québec (37.8) 40.8; New Brunswick (32.6) 34.2; Prince Edward Island (11) 12, and Ontario (11.6) 11.7. The Yukon also bests Manitoba, (10.5) and 10.1.

To Chartier, the Census was further confirmation of the importance of his four conditions for linguistic and cultural preservation – and the damage the loss of precious time and opportunity has wreaked in Manitoba.

If we had had these (bilingual districts) put in place in 1969–70, we wouldn't be in the place we are now. I am fearful; I really am. I tend to be an eternal optimist, but when I look at those statistics … hearing that Manitoba was the only place where the French-speaking population went down, that's disconcerting because you still need a base of French-speaking first language, if not, the language is not as solid, you don't have the right expressions. [24]

****

The other vivid strand in Manitoba history, that of Louis Riel and the Métis, is also constantly changing and evolving. An instensely personal but dramatic vignette that pierces right to its heart, an interview with Jean Teillet, Louis Riel's great grand-neice, was published in the Winter 2003 issue of the *University of Toronto Magazine*. The Manitoba-born dancer, artist and finally, law graduate of the university is devoting her career to fighting for Métis rights across Canada. Her great grand-uncle is obviously her inspiration – and her model. As a nine-year-old schoolchild in St. Vital, she once heard her teacher call Riel a traitor to his country. She exploded, she recalled. "My teacher said that Riel was some kind of madman, and she presented a version of history that was absolutely disgusting. I have never been shy and I don't know what I said to her but it probably wasn't very nice," she laughed.

Teillet also recalled her childhood spent within a large, extended family whose lifeblood was political discussion and action. "I think it was just part of my breathing. I grew up thinking that you were Catholic, Métis and Liberal. I didn't know you had choices in these things."

Torn between dance and law, she chose the former, dancing professionally in Toronto and eventually combining performing with writing, teaching, choreography, directing and visual art. Reaching forty, she decided to turn to her other love – and family legacy – law. Since graduating from the University of Toronto's Faculty of Law in 1994, she has worked tirelessly on behalf of the Métis people's constitutionally entrenched Aboriginal rights. In the spring of 2002, she received the Law Society of Upper Canada's first Lincoln Alexander Award for her legal achievements and her contributions to the Aboriginal community as a mentor and teacher. She helped establish the Métis Nation of Ontario and, at the time of the interview, was preparing to fight an important hunting rights case before the Supreme Court of Canada on behalf of two Métis men from Sault Ste. Marie, Ontario.

"I think most people think that the Métis died in 1885 when Riel was hanged ... Somehow, a whole people died on the gallows with one man," she continued. She is convinced that her great grand-uncle surrendered to shift the struggle from the battlefield to the courtroom to gain a legitimate forum to argue his case on behalf of his people. His execution cut off the dialogue, leaving the fate of Canada's "forgotten people" unresolved. "That's what Riel left undone," she told the magazine. And that's what she hopes to finish.

****

Although the Franco-Manitoban contribution to this province's character, history and definition is too large ever to be erased or forgotten, a question mark hangs over the future of the French language here. Have the measures of the last twenty years come too late to stem the assimilationist tide? Certainly, there is now a consensus that Franco-Manitobans should have fought for their language rights, not their school rights, in 1890. The choice of schools as their battleground dealt them a triple defeat: they lost on point; they lost their constitutional visibility for almost a century, and most important of all, they lost, for the same crucial time frame, their historic official status as one of the founding peoples of Canada and Manitoba. It was a monumental error with incalculable consequences for them and for all Canadians.

In a letter to the *Free Press* published December 31, 2002, historian and author Michel Gaudette appealed to English Canadians to appreciate the relentless erosion of their language and culture experienced by French Canadians outside Québec and to understand that is the reason many Québécois favour sovereignty. He wrote:

> From their beginning, each Census has shown the decline of francophones inside Canada … More than two-thirds of French Canadians outside Québec have been assimilated, from two million to 600,000. In Ontario, the 2001 Census shows that forty per cent of francophones don't speak French at home.
> English Canadians should realize how disastrous the French Canadian experience has been, disastrous in this land since Wolfe defeated Montcalm in 1769 …

****

Try to imagine a very different Canada, a Canada where English and French are in common use throughout Manitoba, Saskatchewan, Alberta and perhaps also British Columbia, as well as New Brunswick and parts of Ontario. Try to imagine how that might have blunted Québec nationalism and Western alienation. Would separatism and alienation never have emerged? Would our national party system never have fractured?

More importantly, try to imagine how that would have changed the balance of power in North America by arming Canadians with a potent defence against the pressures of American Manifest Destiny. Canadians would see themselves, yes, as a nation of immigrants, but one that has not one, but two, national narratives; a nation that has as its defining character linguistic and cultural difference and is united in its respect, celebration and institutionalization of it. Would not such a Canada be stronger, sturdier and less inclined to self-doubt, introspection and fear for its survival?

This book is an exploration of one reason – a very major reason – why this Canada never happened. As Jacqueline Blay says in the Prologue, we must keep asking ourselves the fundamental questions. Do you remember when? Do you remember why? What if? These questions illuminate our understanding of who we are and how we got here. They help us to address and heal, as well as to cherish and advance, our national story.

To remind ourselves once more, more than 400,000 French Canadians left the province of Québec during the period 1870 to 1890. Had even one third or one quarter come West, instead of the few thousand who finally succumbed to the entreaties of Bishop Alexandre-Antonin Taché and Joseph Dubuc's colonization society, the original bilingual character of Manitoba would have gelled sufficiently to accommodate subsequent non-francophone migration without being overwhelmed.

It is undeniable that the cumulative effect of the events of 1869-70, the subsequent anti-French bigotry in Ontario and the tragic fate of Louis Riel played a major role in discouraging all but a relatively few francophones from venturing across what appeared to be an ever more hostile, foreign country to claim French Canada's birthright to an equal place in the North West, a birthright made clear by Sir George-Étienne Cartier, Adams Archibald and tacitly, even by Sir John A. Macdonald in the Manitoba Act debates of 1870.

As Brian Mulroney said in the House of Commons in October 1983, Manitoba's ninety years of constitutional defiance helped to feed a deep sense of communal injustice within French Canada. That injustice contributes to this day to the periodic rise of Québec nationalism and, more recently, political parties advocating separation at both the provincial and federal level.

Manitoba's status as the "first in" of the provinces carved out of the vast lands of the Hudson's Bay Company meant that it defined the character of those that followed. As Manitoba went, so went the rest of the West. By

1890, Manitoba had become unilingual English. Through constitutional defiance beginning in 1890, that unilingual Englishness triumphed, erecting an almost-impenetrable barrier to western francophone migration. French Canadians could only feel secure in Québec. Sequestered within that linguistic and cultural redoubt, their alienation from the rest of Canada and their ancient fears of linguistic and cultural extinction were confirmed and intensified.

A nation founded on linguistic dualism then became burdened with another duality constructed as a deliberate refutation of the other. It propounded Canada as a second United States of America, a nation of individuals not cultural communities, a nation of one language, not two, of many ethnic minorities within an Anglo-Saxon hegemonic culture, not a nation of two founding languages and cultures. This United States-style Canada became known as the "New" Canada as opposed to the "Old" Canada of linguistic duality.

In the years following the Second World War, political power began to flow from Ottawa to the provinces. The rise in importance of natural resources fuelled the forces of decentralism. Provincial premiers became significant players on the national stage and those from the big, wealthy provinces began to wield almost co-equal power with the federal prime minister. Federal-provincial conferences became a new level of government. The resource-rich New West of Saskatchewan, Alberta and British Columbia, often led by the highly-Americanized province of Alberta, challenged virtually all the traditional tenets of Canadian federalism. The tensions between Old and New Canada, between the two duelling dualities, increased to the point the national party system ruptured.

Brian Mulroney won another majority government in 1988 on a platform of free trade with the United States, a perilous "leap of faith" that was particularly popular in the two provinces that formed the foundation of the Mulroney coalition – Alberta and Québec. But two failed attempts to bring Québec into the 1982 constitution with, in Mulroney's phrase, "honour and enthusiasm", a major economic recession, a string of sordid scandals and a prime ministerial style that struck many Canadians as unctuous and hyperbolic plunged the Conservative Party to the lowest popularity ratings ever measured in Canada. His unstable and essentially mutually antithetical coalition of Québec's soft nationalists and western decentralists fractured and two regional and intensely antagonistic parties arose from the debris, the Bloc

Québécois and the Reform Party. The former pursued the sovereignist agenda in Ottawa while the latter, under the leadership of Preston Manning, became, in the words of American historian Seymour Martin Lipset, "Canada's American Party". It and its successor, the Canadian Alliance, seek greater Americanization of Canadian life and emulation of American political forms and institutions. As such, the Reform Party became the instant home for many of those westerners most offended by the "Old" Canada, specifically, by French Canada, Québec, bilingualism and the idea of bi-nationalism structured on language and culture.

Reform and its successor, the Canadian Alliance, see language as a purely provincial matter in clear disregard of the Canadian constitution. Shortly after his election in March 2002, new leader Stephen Harper launched a broadside against official bilingualism. Mr. Harper described it as a religion that cost too much to be practical and was now causing direct harm to the cause of national unity. Mr. Harper's comments earned him a stern rebuke from one of his own party organizers in Québec as well as from La Fédération des communautés francophones et acadiennes du Canada. The Alliance leader's views, FCFAC said, recalled the Canada of fifty years ago and confirmed the party's status as a regional entity only. [24]

Given Ontario's reluctance to embrace a political party that has no appeal in Québec, Reform/Alliance appears virtually unelectable east of the Ontario/Manitoba border. Significantly, within Manitoba itself, it is confined to the province's rural south and has yet to make a breakthrough in Winnipeg, the city with over half Manitoba's population.

Canada always was an act of conscious political will, a courageous east-west rebuke to North America's natural north-south forces of geographic and economic determinism. Today it faces two daunting threats. Externally, eighty-six per cent of its trade now is with the United States, making its dependence on the American market nearly total and economic and perhaps defence and security integration of some form almost inevitable. Internally, potent political and cultural centrifugal forces compel regions and provinces to seek their individual destinies with scant regard for the nation as a whole. Canadians must struggle harder than ever before in their history to keep their country's flame alight. As the province where the founding dream of Canada died, Manitoba has ensured that struggle is not only more difficult, but far less sure of success.

Epilogue

My GREAT-GRANDFATHER JOSEPH TURENNE came to Manitoba in 1870 to help strengthen the French presence in this province. He became a county clerk and, among other things, was the mayor of St. Boniface in 1904. At that time, Provencher Boulevard in St. Boniface and Broadway in Winnipeg were one long continuous street joined by the Broadway bridge over the Red River. Joseph Turenne led a delegation of St. Boniface citizens over the bridge to protest the planned cutting off of Broadway to build a railway station. This would have the effect of severing the direct and symbolic link to Winnipeg, and reroute St. Boniface traffic through an industrial area. The St. Boniface citizens did not prevail, however, and for the better part of the next century English Winnipeg turned its back on French St. Boniface in the form of railway yards and industrial buildings. Francophones were henceforth to enter the city through the back door.

The preceding pages conclude that Manitoba is where the founding dream of Canada died. That dream died in 1885, 1890 and 1916. The more recent events were an attempt to revive that dream, and that attempt failed. Or did it? On the morning of February 26, 1984, when the hijackers of the Manitoba Legislature triumphed and the government finally capitulated to the forces of intolerance, the future looked very bleak indeed. Yet the night is often darkest just before the dawn. Who could have foreseen that twenty years later virtually all the services envisaged in the government's legislative and constitutional package would be in place, that the provision of French language government services and the support of francophone institutions would enjoy nonpartisan support from all political parties in Manitoba, and that the greatest impetus for their establishment would have come from some of the very people who had created such havoc in the early '80s. How could this come about? Could it mean that the dream is still alive?

While there are many interesting parallels between the events of 1890 and 1916 and those of 1983-84, there is one important difference. In the earlier period, it was governments, with the support of the elites, that were trying to culturally eradicate the French minority. In the more recent period, it was a government, with the support of the elites, that was trying to make amends and support the official language minority. That government would have finally prevailed, in spite of all its blundering, but for one embittered man who used his position as speaker to prevent a vote from being held.

After the events of 1916, the Franco-Manitoban community turned inward, becoming defensive and insular, convinced that cultural salvation could only come from within their community, with no help from the hostile society around them. The events of 1983-84 however, had the opposite effect. They gave that community a sense of cohesion and pride and self-confidence unlike anything it had experienced in at least a half-century. Georges Forest notwithstanding, francophones rallied behind their community leaders as they never had. Never before or since have they gathered in their thousands as they did on that chilly September evening in 1983 in Ste. Anne, to proclaim loudly and clearly and proudly that they were there to stay and that the rest of society had better get used to it. A large part of the explanation lies in the fact that they were not isolated or alone, and that they gained strength and pride from the support of others. In Ste. Anne, they were there to support a government that was trying to help them, not, as in the earlier period, defending themselves against a government trying to crush them. They were energized by the support they were getting from the mainstream media (on the editorial pages, it must be noted, not in the letters to the editor), from church leaders of all denominations, and from the leadership of virtually all of Manitoba's multicultural groups. They also felt the solidarity of the rest of the country as expressed through the two House of Commons resolutions. And in the end, they felt fully vindicated by the judgment of the Supreme Court of Canada.

Franco-Manitobans were, of course, greatly saddened by the hostility of the majority towards the government's constitutional package. They were also aware, however, of the fact that, with some exceptions, this hostility was not directed against themselves as individuals, but against a grossly distorted and misunderstood legislative proposal. They knew their enemy was more ignorance than bigotry, notwithstanding the fact that ignorance is a necessary component of bigotry. After the defeat of the attempt to entrench the right to French language services in the Constitution, the francophone leadership did not retreat to nurse its wounds. Instead, it proceeded with renewed vigor to lobby for the provision of such services in every way they could, refusing to accept defeat, refusing to see themselves as the persecuted minority, continuing to see themselves as full partners in Manitoba's socio-political landscape. Franco-Manitobans did not accept that the founding dream of Canada had died. They only acknowledged that the road to its rebirth had encountered a major speed bump.

The Franco-Manitoban community could not have ultimately prevailed in its political objectives if the climate of hostility witnessed in 1983-84 had been an accurate reflection of the mindset of the majority of Manitoba society. The francophone leadership perceived, accurately in my view, that the anti-French agitation of that period was akin to a storm on the surface of the ocean that belies the direction of the broad current underneath.

How much of a freak storm was it and could it recur? Prior to the 1980s, the last major language crisis in Manitoba had taken place in 1916. The subsequent decision of the Franco-Manitoban community to withdraw into itself and avoid public confrontation was generally successful in its objectives of preserving the cultural integrity of that community, especially schools where French was the language of instruction. By remaining out of sight and out of mind of the broader community, it allowed passions to cool over several generations to the point where in the 1960s and 1970s the Duff Roblin and Ed Schreyer governments could make major strides in reintegrating French into the public school system without creating a major upheaval. Under Schreyer, Franco-Manitoban politicians took a more prominent position in cabinet than at any time in the previous eight decades, without raising a fuss. It is in this context that government of Howard Pawley thought it could safely ride that current and adopt its constitutional proposals, also without raising a fuss.

But, however necessary it might have been for other reasons, making the Franco-Manitoban community invisible to the general public for so many decades had one unintended and unfortunate consequence. It basically led the entire province to believe that francophones were satisfied with their status and that they accepted the broad consensus that had developed after 1916: that of a multiethnic society unified by the common use of the English language and where the use of other languages was a private matter that should not involve the state. In the minds of many, perhaps most, Manitobans, the Pawley government's constitutional package was an attempt to fix something they did not believe was broken, a first gust of wind on the surface waters.

There were other gusts blowing in from outside the province. The federal Official Languages Act, a manifestation of the "Old Canada" politics of French-English duality, also appeared to Manitobans and other Westerners as a solution to a problem they did not believe they had. By the time a home-grown language issue arose within Manitoba, many Manitobans had already worked themselves into a state of agitation over language issues generated from within Québec. Both the Official Languages Act and the Pawley government's constitutional package represented a new concept to a generation of Manitobans raised in profound ignorance and denial of their history: that of legislative support for a minority group. This offended their sense of egalitarianism, a feeling that was further exacerbated by a separatist government in Québec apparently beating up on its own language minority, creating a sense of unfairness in the eyes of many Manitobans.

In such a context, only strong and adroit leadership could have successfully adopted legislative change without creating major controversy. Unfortunately, strong leadership was missing in action on the government side. It was the opposition that possessed the leadership skills and sense of strategy that, combined with an absence of scruples and naked ambition, caused the storm to develop with such fury. Below the surface however, other significant factors gave reasons for hope.

It is significant that, throughout the maelstrom of 1983-84, the NDP Caucus, with the sole exception of Russ Doern, held firm in its resolve to push through its language proposals. Once Doern was out of the caucus, there were no serious divisions with regard to the objectives the government was pursuing, only disagreements as to tactics. To the very end, the government was not prepared to ditch the Franco-Manitoban minority, even to save its own skin. When it finally did cave in after eleven consecutive days of bell ringing, it did so only after a secret meeting with the SFM in which the SFM itself told the government to throw in the towel. By that time, the Franco-Manitoban leadership had come to believe that the atmosphere had been so poisoned that passage of the government's weakened proposals would not lead to the kind of peace it sought with the Manitoba majority. It preferred to take its chances with the Supreme Court. (That is not to say, however, that the government was not hugely relieved to be let off the hook.)

It is significant that the government's electoral downfall did not come when expected. To the surprise of many, the NDP managed to eke out a bare majority in the 1986 election. The Manitoba electorate, it seems, did not consider support for French language rights to be a hanging offense. This so raised the level of confidence within the government that the French Language Services Secretariat was given the green light to move vigorously forward with the implementation of French language services. Prior to the 1986 election, its instructions had been to "low bridge it". When defeat did come two years later, it was not at the hands of a strengthened Conservative party, but as a result of a huge surge in the Liberal vote at the expense of the NDP, which allowed the Tories to form a minority government with one seat less than they had in opposition. Language was not a factor in that election. The Liberal leader, Sharon Carstairs, was an unabashed supporter of "Trudeau bilingualism", a fact no one bothered to mention. As opposition leader, she gave Premier Gary Filmon tacit support in his moves to expand bilingualism.

It is significant that the anti-bilingualism Reform/Alliance Party never made any meaningful inroads into Winnipeg where the majority of Manitobans live. To the extent that Reform candidates made their anti-bilingualism views known, it did not help them. To the extent that other parties were associated with support for bilingualism, it did not hurt them. This is indicative of the fact that language rights have largely become a political non-issue.

It is equally significant that, even in the superheated atmosphere of 1983-84, a government poll reported that the majority of Manitobans supported French language services while at the same time they opposed the government's constitutional package. This is not a symptom of a bigoted province, only of a very confused one, thanks to the egregious distortions successfully disseminated by opponents of the proposed legislation. While there were certainly a goodly number of anti-French bigots among the eighty percent of Manitobans who voted against the proposals where referenda were held, there were a great many more who simply felt that they were being put upon, misled, had the status of their province changed without their consent, and who just did not see why they should rush into major changes to solve a problem they did not believe they had.

Most significant of all perhaps, is that it took less than seven years for the Conservative Party to change from being legislative hijackers to becoming a government fully implementing the very substance of what was contained in the legislation they had so vigorously opposed. The Tories had always claimed, of course, that they had never been opposed to French language services per se, but rather to their entrenchment in legislation. This "cover" allowed them, under the strong leadership of Gary Filmon, to rejoin the main underlying current in Manitoba of middle-of-the-road pragmatic accommodation, even in the linguistic area. This was also an implicit recognition, on the part of the perpetrators of the 1983-84 fiasco, that they had gone too far and did not want to go there again. Another place they did not want to go again was bell ringing. In the immediate aftermath of their bell ringing tactical victory, the Conservatives publicly expressed no regret at what they had done. But within two years, an all-party legislative committee unanimously approved a new set of rules that put a one-hour cap on bell ringing.

In the early '80s, fear of the unknown was a potent force. Opponents of the legislation could paint a picture of all sorts of horrible things that would happen if the legislation was adopted. Today, even though they only have the status of cabinet orders, these horrible things are all in place. The bilingual positions required to implement French language services have all been identified in the civil service, and mostly filled. The sky has not fallen and careers have not been ruined.

It could even be argued that the defeat of the French Language Services Act was not at all harmful to the actual implementation of the intended services. Had such an act been in force, the entire government apparatus would have proceeded in such a way as to do only the minimum required by the wording of the legislation. Such is the way of bureaucracy. In 1983, the implementation of French language services in the Manitoba government had barely begun. We were still feeling our way. With the government's French language services policy having the status of an administrative directive that could be modified at will by cabinet, this allowed full scope for flexibility and creativity when unexpected problems arose in the course of implementation. In that context, legislation could have been as much a limiting factor as an enabling one. For example, would implementation of the Chartier report have run into trouble because it was outside the framework of the French language services bill?

With two decades of experience in the provision of French language services, however, and with the Chartier report well on the way to full implementation, a provincial law guaranteeing the services could be drafted fairly easily and realistically. It would give greater legitimacy and permanency to the bilingual face of government, and provide the francophone community with the necessary leverage to ensure compliance. Given Manitoba's history however, any government proposing to introduce such legislation should do so only after having been assured of multiparty support.

With the infrastructure of official bilingualism now largely in place at the federal, provincial and even municipal levels (Winnipeg is the only major city in Canada with a legislated requirement to provide services in the official minority language), does this mean that the dream of Canada has been resurrected in Manitoba? Or have the trappings of the dream come too late to be of use to those they were intended to protect?

One of the perennial themes of Franco-Manitoban life over the last fifty years has been whether the community's numbers constituted a critical mass to survive as a distinct society into the future. Every five years, new Census figures come out pointing to a relative decline in the number of francophones, and the anxiety-ridden debate starts all over again, complete with the usual predictions that French will be gone in a generation. At some point of course the numbers will indeed become too small. I don't believe that point has yet been reached, because the Franco-Manitoban community has strengths that the numbers do not reveal. One of those strengths is its relative geographic concentration, which allows some degree of community life to take place in French, an advantage that French-speaking communities in Saskatchewan and Alberta do not have. The communities in those two provinces, as well as in British Columbia, suffered just as much from the nineteenth-century linguistic storms in Manitoba as their Franco-Manitoban brethren did, by having been denied an influx of reinforcing French-speaking immigration. Their future is much more precarious.

The Franco-Manitoban community has another advantage in its very strong institutional base. The SFM's annual guide to French language services in Manitoba – a 300-page publication – lists seventy-two different French-speaking groups and organizations of various sorts, from the Boy Scouts to women's groups to economic development corporations. Most of these receive government funding in one form or another. There is a strong French-language media presence in Winnipeg, including one television station, two radio stations, one newspaper, and two publishing houses. The Franco-Manitoban cultural centre is a provincial Crown corporation mandated to promote the French language and culture. The francophone school division administers twenty-three Français schools throughout the province. Graduates can then go on to community college or seek a university degree at the Collège universitaire de Saint-Boniface, entirely in French.

In spite of these advantages, there is no question that the francophone minority today is struggling. Its enemies are no longer hostile majorities and their hostile governments. They are the community's own weak demographics, MTV, Wal-Mart, the Internet, and globalization. Low numbers mean that the odds of young people finding a mate within their own culture become poorer with each passing year. Already, more than half of young francophones marry unilingual anglophones. In most cases, their children will be raised in English. It is indeed a cruel irony of history that at the very moment when French language institutions in Manitoba reach their full development, their clientele may not be there to benefit from them.

Today I stand on the banks of the Red River in St. Boniface watching the construction of an impressive new pedestrian bridge linking old St. Boniface to The Forks, at exactly the same place where the old Broadway Bridge once stood, and where my great-grandfather once marched. The railway yards are gone now, replaced by the wonderful meeting place of The Forks. Soon, there will be an official inauguration with ribbon-cutting and speeches. Winnipeg's first ever bilingual mayor, an acknowledged francophile, will no doubt make part of his speech in French. (This is no doubt an improvement over the situation of twenty years ago, when Winnipeg's mayor cast his tie-breaking city council vote to allow a referendum on French language rights, thereby making his city, for a time, the intolerance capital of Canada.) Manitoba's minister of finance, the MLA for St. Boniface and another bilingual anglophone with strong connections to the Franco-Manitoban community, will no doubt say appropriate things in French as well. The signage and plaques on and around the bridge will all be in both official languages. The people of St. Boniface will enter through the front door again.

But fifty years from now, what language will be spoken in the shadow of the bridge's stunning center mast and soaring cables? Knowing the fierce determination of Manitoba's francophone community, now supported by strong institutions, I would wager French will still be heard, and the dream of Canada will not yet be extinguished.

Roger Turenne, September 2003

End Notes

Notes to Introduction

1. Michael Adams with Amy Langstaff and David Jamieson, *Fire and Ice: The United States, Canada and the Myth of Converging Values* (Toronto: Penguin Canada, 2003), p.5.

2. C.J. Jaenen, "The History of French in Manitoba: local initiative or external imposition," in *Language and Society*, Ottawa, Commissioner of Official Languages, no. 13 (spring, 1984), p.6.

3. Gerald Friesen, *The Canadian Prairies: A History* (Toronto: University of Toronto Press, 1987), p.202.

4. Robert Painchaud, "The Catholic Church and the Movement of Francophones to the Canadian Prairie 1870–1915" (PhD dissertation, University of Ottawa, July 1976), p. 96; and Bruno Ramirez, *On the Move: French Candian and Italian Migrants in the North American Economy, 1860-1914* (Toronto: McClelland & Stewart, 1991), p. 126

Notes to Chapter One

1. Manitoba, Legislative Assembly, *Debates and Proceedings*, 32nd Legislature, 2nd Session, 1982-84, p. 2977.

2. The author [column], *Winnipeg Free Press*, May 30, 1997.

3. Supreme Court of Canada, reference by the Governor in Council concerning certain language rights under Section 23 of the *Manitoba Act, 1870*, and Section 133 of the *Constitution Act, 1867* and set out in Order -2 in -4. Council P.C. 1984-1136 dated the 5th day of April, 1984, [Media text], June 13, 1985, p. 27.

4. J.E. Rea, "The Roots of Prairie Society," in *Prairie Perspectives: Papers of the Western Canadian Studies Conference, 1969*, (Toronto/Montreal: Holt, Rinehart and Winston of Canada, 1970), p. 46 [prepared by the Department of History, University of Calgary].

5. Rea, "Roots of Prairie Society," p. 47.

6. The author [column], *Winnipeg Free Press*, April 18, 1992

7. C.J. Jaenen, "The History of French in Manitoba: local initiative or external imposition," in *Language and Society*, Ottawa, Commissioner of Official Languages, no. 13 (spring, 1984), p. 3.

8. Jaenen, "History of French," p. 4.

9. Jaenen, "History of French," p. 5.

10. Jaenen, "History of French," p. 5.

11. Lionel Dorge, "The Métis and Canadien Councillors of Assiniboia, Part One," in *The Beaver* (Outfit 305.1, summer, 1974), p. 16.

12. Dorge, "The Métis and Canadien Councillors,"

Part Three," *The Beaver* (winter, 1974), p. 58.

13. Dorge, "The Métis and Canadien Councillors," Part Three," *The Beaver* (winter, 1974), p. 58.

14. Jaenen, "History of French," p. 5.

15. Jaenen, "History of French," p. 5.

16. Gerald Friesen, *The Canadian Prairies: A History* (Toronto: University of Toronto Press, 1987), p. 57.

17. Friesen, *Canadian Prairies*, p. 68.

18. Maggie Siggins, *Riel: A Life of Revolution* (Toronto: HarperCollins Publishers, 1994), p. 7.

19. Barbara Huck, *Exploring the Fur Trade Routes of North America* 1st ed., (Winnipeg: Heartland Associates, 2000), p. 243.

20. Nancy Vincent, "Margaret Taylor Hogue, 1819-1885: 'Country Wife' of the Governor of Rupert's Land" in *Extraordinary Ordinary Women* (Winnipeg: Manitoba Clubs of the Canadian Federation of University Women, 2000), p.3.

21. Arthur S. Morton, *Sir George Simpson: Overseas Governor of the Hudson's Bay Company: A Pen Picture of a Man of Action* (Toronto/Vancouver: J.M. Dent & Sons [Canada], 1944), p. 165.

22. A.S. Morton, *Sir George Simpson*, p. 167.

23. Internal correspondence, Papers of Moose Factory, HBCA, B135/c.2, as quoted in A.S. Morton, *Sir George Simpson*, pp. 167–168.

24. Dorge, *The Beaver*, (summer 1974), p.14.

25. Denise Fuchs, "Embattled Notions: Constructions of Rupert's Land Native Sons, 1760–1860," in *Manitoba History Magazine* (autumn/winter 2002/2003), p. 13.

26. Frits Pannekoek, *Snug Little Flock: The Social Origins of the Riel Resistance of 1869-1870* (Winnipeg: Watson & Dwyer Publishing, 1991), pp. 61-62.

27. Pannekoek, *Snug Little Flock*, p. 59.

28. Siggins, *Riel: A Life*, pp. 41-42.

29. Pannekoek, *Snug Little Flock*, p. 62.

30. Irene Spry, "The Mixed-Bloods and Métis of Rupert's Land before 1870", in *New Peoples: Being and Becoming Métis in North America*, Jacqueline Peterson and Jennifer Brown, eds. (Winnipeg: University of Manitoba Press, 1985), p. 97.

31. Spry, "Mixed Bloods and Métis," p. 113.

32. Pannekoek, *Snug Little Flock*, p. 70.

33. G.F. Stanley, *Louis Riel* (Toronto: The Ryerson Press, 1963), p. 9.

34. W.L. Morton, *Manitoba: A History* (Toronto: University of Toronto Press, 1957), p. 54.

35. James A. Jackson, *A Centennial History of Manitoba*, under the auspices of the Manitoba Historical Society (Toronto: McClelland & Stewart, 1970), p. 67.

36. W.L. Morton, *Manitoba: A History*, pp. 78-79.

37. W.L. Morton, *Manitoba: A History*, p. 79.

38. W.L. Morton, *Manitoba: A History*, p. 80-81.

39. Siggins, *Riel: A Life*, p. 40.

Notes to Chapter Two

1. N.E. Allan Ronaghan, "The Archibald Administration in Manitoba, 1870-72", PhD dissertation, University of Manitoba, 1987), abstract and xxxv.

2. George F.G. Stanley, *Louis Riel*, (Toronto: The Ryerson Press, 1963) p. 117.

3. Ronaghan, "Archibald Administration," xi.

4. Ronaghan, "Archibald Administration," xvi.

5. Ronaghan, "Archibald Administration," p. 911.

6. *L'Union des Cantons de l'Est,* November 14, 1885; *Le Nouveau Monde,* September 21, 1885 and November 14, 1885 ; and *Le Canadien*, November 12, 1885, all as quoted in Arthur Silver, *The French Canadian View of Confederation, 1865-1900,* (Toronto: University of Toronto Press, 1982), p. 160.

7. Hartwell Bowsfield, *Louis Riel: The Rebel and The Hero*, (Toronto: Oxford University Press,1971), p. 28.

8. Maggie Siggins, *Riel: A Life of Revolution*, (Toronto: HarperCollins Publishers, 1994), p. 45.

9. Riel to Taché, July 24, 1885, Riel Papers, Public Archives of Manitoba, as quoted in Stanley, *Riel*, p.19.

10. Bowsfield, *Louis Riel: The Rebel*, p. 17.

11. Stanley, *Louis Riel*, p. 12.

12. Lenoir to Taché, August 26, 1865, Archives de l'archevêché de St. Boniface, as quoted in Stanley, *Louis Riel*, p. 30.

13. Riel to Cartier, February 24, 1865, Public Archives of Québec, as quoted in Stanley, *Louis Riel*, p. 33.

14. Stanley, *Louis Riel*, p. 34.

15. J.B. Brebner, *North Atlantic Triangle, the Interplay of Canada, the United States and Great Britain,* (New Haven and Toronto, 1945), as quoted in Stanley, *Louis Riel*, p. 40.

16. Roderick Campbell, as quoted in W.L. Morton, *Manitoba: A History*, (Toronto: University of Toronto Press, 1957), p. 110.

17. *Nor'Wester*, March 21, 1864, as quoted in Stanley, *Louis Riel*, p. 46.

18. Lewis Thomas, "Louis Riel" in *Dictionary of Canadian Biography* (herafter cited as *DCB*), Francess G. Halpenny and Jean Hamelin, eds., (Toronto: University of Toronto Press and Québec City: Les Presses de l'université de Laval, 1982), vol. xi, p. 737.

19. Siggins, *Riel: A Life*, p. 85.

20. Siggins, *Riel: A Life*, p. 86-87.

21. Siggins, *Riel: A Life*, p. 87.

22. Siggins, *Riel: A Life*, p. 88.

23. Siggins, *Riel: A Life*, p. 89.

24. Siggins, *Riel: A Life*, p. 90.

25. Thomas, "Louis Riel", in *DCB*, p. 738.

26. Bowsfield, *Riel: The Rebel*, p. 30.

27. Bowsfield, *Riel: The Rebel*, p. 35.

28. Bowsfield, *Riel: The Rebel*, p. 36.

29. Siggins, *Riel: A Life*, p. 107.

30. Stanley, *Louis Riel*, p. 66.

31. Alexander Begg, *The Creation of Manitoba, or a History of the Red River Troubles,* (Toronto, 1871), p. 49-50; and *Canada Sessional Papers*, 1870, v. no. 12, as quoted in Stanley, *Louis Riel*, p. 68.

32. Alexander Begg, *Alexander Begg's Red River Journal & Other Papers Relative to the Red River Resistance of 1869-70,* (Toronto: The Champlain Society, 1956), as quoted in Stanley, *Louis Riel*, p. 69.

33. Masson, Masson Papers, Riel's notes of the Fort Garry Convention enclosed in Riel to Masson, April 4, 1872, Public Achives of Manitoba, as quoted in Stanley, *Louis Riel*, p. 69.

34. Joseph Kinsey Howard, *Strange Empire: The Story of Louis Riel*, (St. Paul: Minnesota Historical Society Press, 1994), p. 143.

35. Riel's notes of the Fort Garry Convention as quoted in Stanley, *Louis Riel*, p. 73.

36. Riel's notes, as quoted in Stanley, *Louis Riel*, p. 74.

37. Young to Granville, November 26, 1869, Public Record Office, Cabinet Order 42/677 (hereafter cited as PRO, CO), as quoted in Stanley, *Louis Riel*, p. 76.

38. Macdonald to McDougall, November 27, 1869, PRO, CO 42/678, as quoted in Stanley, *Louis Riel*, p. 76.

39. Macdonald to McDougall, December 8, 1869, as quoted in Donald Creighton, *Sir John A. Macdonald: The Old Statesman* (Toronto: The Macmillan Company of Canada, 1955), p. 44.

40. Joseph Howe to Donald Smith, *December 10, 1869, Canada Sessional Papers*, as quoted in Stanley, *Louis Riel*, p. 83.

41. Smith to Howe, April 12, 1870, PCO, CO 42/685 as quoted in Stanley, *Louis Riel*, p. 87.

42. New Nation, January 21, 1870, as quoted in Stanley, *Louis Riel*, p. 90.

43. New Nation, January 21, 1870, as quoted in Stanley, *Louis Riel*, p. 90.

44. Hartwell Bowsfield, ed., *The James Wickes Taylor Correspondence, 1859-1870*, as quoted in Alastair Sweeney, *George-Étienne Cartier: a biography*, (Toronto: McClelland & Stewart, 1976), p. 205.

The Canadian Crucible

45. Thomas, *"Louis Riel"*, in DCB, p. 740.

46. Stanley, *Louis Riel*, p. 112.

47. Siggins, *Riel: A Life*, p. 160.

48. Ronaghan, "Archibald Administration", p. 233.

49. Henry Waddington, "Diary of a Prisoner in the Red River Rebellion," in *Niagara Historical Society*, vol. 25 (1913), p. 51.

50. Irene M. Spry, "The 'Memories' of George William Sanderson 1846-1936," in *Canadian Ethnic Studies*, vol. 17, no. 2, (n.d.) pp. 129-30, as quoted in Siggins, *Riel: A Life*, p. 161.

51. Auguste Henri de Trémaudan, "The Execution of Thomas Scott," in *Canadian Historical Review*, vol. 6, no. 3, (1925), p. 23 ln, as quoted in Siggins, *Riel: A Life*, p. 161.

52. Ronaghan, "Archibald Administration,", p. 240.

53. Stanley, *Louis Riel*, p. 112.

54. *Le Nouveau Monde*, February, 1874; *Le Métis*, February 28, 1874.

55. Begg, *Red River Journal*, as quoted in Siggins, p. 163n.

56. Ronaghan, "Archibald Administration," pp.241-242.

57. Stanley, *Louis Riel*, pp. 116-117.

58. Thomas, "Louis Riel," in *DCB*, p. 741.

59. W.L. Morton, ed., *Manitoba: The Birth of a Province* (Altona, Manitoba Record Society, 1965), xviii.

60. Siggins, *Riel: A Life*, p. 164.

61. Ronaghan, "Archibald Administration," p. 465.

62. Ronaghan, "Archibald Administration," p. 465.

63. Stanley, *Louis Riel*, pp. 137-138.

64. Stanley, *Louis Riel*, p. 142.

65. Stanley, *Louis Riel*, pp. 142-143.

66. Canada, Parliament, House of Commons, Dominion *Debates*, 1870, vol. 1, 1287-1320.

67. *Debates*, 1870, vol. 1, 1287-1320.

68. *Debates*, 1870, vol. 1, 1287-1320.

69. *Debates*. 1870, vol. 1, 1287-1320.

70. *Debates*, 1870, vol. 1, 1287-1320.

71. W.L. Morton, *Birth of a Province*, xxvii.

72. *Debates*, 1870, vol. 1, 1424-1431.

73. *Debates*, 1870, vol. 1, 1424-1431.

74. *Debates*, 1870, vol. 1, 1424-1431.

75. *Debates*, 1870, vol. 1, 1499-1504.

76. John Boyd, *Sir George Étienne Cartier, bart., his life and times: a political history of Canada from 1814 to 1873* (Toronto: The Macmillan Company of Canada, 1914), p. 303.

77. *Debates*, 1870, vol. 1, 1499-1504.

78. Boyd, *Cartier*, p. 304.

79. W.L. Morton, *Birth of a Province*, xxix

80. Alastair Sweeney, *George-Étienne Cartier: a biography*, (Toronto: McClelland & Stewart, 1976), p. 211.

81. Siggins, *Riel: A Life*, p. 182.

82. Siggins, *Riel: A Life*, p. 182.

83. Siggins, *Riel: A Life*, p. 183.

84. Sweeny, *Cartier*, p. 211.

85. Siggins, *Riel: A Life*, p. 183.

86. Sweeny, *Cartier*, p. 213.

87. Stanley, *Louis Riel*, p. 155.

88. Taché deposition, *Report of the Select Committee, 1874*, Canada, Parliament, House of Commons.

89. Stanley, *Louis Riel*, p.156.

91. F.M. Viscount Wolseley, *The Story of a Soldier's Life*, (Westminster, 1903), as quoted in Stanley, *Louis Riel*, p. 155.

89. Stanley, *Louis Riel*, p. 157.

Notes to Chapter Three

1. Northcote to Disraeli, Rideau Hall, Ottawa, April 28, 1870, Iddesleigh Papers, Add. MSS.50, British Museum, as quoted in W.L. Morton, ed., *Manitoba: The Birth of a Province*, (Altona, Manitoba Record Society, 1965), xxi-xxii.

2. N.E. Allen Ronaghan, "The Archibald Administration in Manitoba, 1870-1872," PhD dissertation, University of Manitoba, 1987), pp. 904-905.

3. Archibald Memorandum on the Fenian Invasion of Manitoba in October, 1871, Report of the Select Committee, 1874, Canada, Parliament, House of Commons, as quoted in George F.G. Stanley, *Louis Riel* (Toronto: The Ryerson Press, 1963), p. 160.

4. Stanley, *Louis Riel*, p. 177.

5. K.G. Pryke, "Adams Archibald" in the *Dictionary of Canadian Biography* (hereafter cited as DCB), Francess G. Halpenny and Jean Hamelin, eds., (Toronto: University of Toronto Press and Québec City: Les Presses de l'université de Laval, 1990), vol. xii, p. 36.

6. *Globe* [Toronto], February 3 and 13, 1871, as quoted in Stanley, Louis Riel, p. 177.

7. J.W. Bengough [cartoon] in *Grip*, October 25, 1873, as quoted in Stanley, *Louis Riel*, p. 182.

8. Riel to Masson, April 24, 1872, Masson Papers, Public Archives of Manitoba, as quoted in Stanley, *Louis Riel*, p. 183.

9. Riel to Taché, May 19, 1872, Archiepiscopal Archives, St. Boniface, as quoted in Stanley, *Louis Riel*, p. 183.

10. Macdonald to Archibald, September 4, 1872, Report of the Select Committee, 1874, Canada, Parliament, House of Commons, as quoted in Stanley, *Louis Riel*, p.186.

11. Taché deposition, Select Committee, 1872, Canada, Parliament, House of Commons, as quoted in Stanley, *Louis Riel*, p.186.

12. Jean Friesen,"Alexander Morris," *DCB*, vol. xi,p.610.

13. Jean Friesen, "Alexander Morris," p. 611.

14. *Canada Sessional Papers,* 1874, p.151.

15. Morris to Macdonald, September 20, 1873, Morris Papers, Public Archives of Manitoba, as quoted in Stanley, *Louis Riel*, p.193.

16. Dorion to Morris, January 2, 1874, Report of the Select Committee, 1874, Canada, Parliament, House of Commons, as quoted in Stanley, *Louis Riel*, p.199.

17. Taché to Dorion, January 3, 1874, Select Committee, as quoted in Stanley, *Louis Riel*, p. 200.

18. E.A. Collard, Canadian Yesterdays, (Toronto: n.p., 1955) p. 43; and James Young, *Men and Public Life in Canada* (Toronto: n.p., 1912), II, pp. 187-189, as quoted in Stanley, Louis Riel, p. 202.

19. Joseph Schull, *Laurier: The First Canadian*, (Toronto: Macmillan of Canada, 1965), p. 96.

20. Stanley, *Louis Riel*, p. 204.

21. Rumilly I, p. 301, as quoted in Stanley, *Louis Riel*, p. 206.

22. Maggie Siggins, *Riel: A Life of Revolution*, (Toronto: HarperCollins Publishers, 1994), p. 233.

23. Stanley, *Louis Riel*, p. 209.

24. Stanley, *Louis Riel*, p. 211.

25. Dufferin to Carnarvon, December 10, 1874, *Canada Sessional Papers*, 1875 VII, No. 11.

26. C.W. Kiewiet and F.H. Underhill, *Dufferin-Carnarvon Correspondence*, 1874-1878 (Toronto: n.p., 1955) as quoted in Stanley, *Louis Riel*, p. 212.

27. *Canada Sessional Papers*, 1875, as quoted in Stanley, Louis Riel, p. 212.

28. Canada, Parliament, House of Commons, *Debates*, 1875, February 11, 1875, 50, as quoted in Stanley, *Louis Riel,* p. 213.

29. Stanley, *Louis Riel*, p. 213.

30. *Le Travailleur*, Worcester, Massachusetts, December 24, 1874, as quoted in Stanley, Louis Riel, p. 218.

31. Riel to Tachereau, January 20, 1875, Archives de l'Archevêché, Québec, as quoted in Stanley, *Louis Riel*, p. 342.

32. Stanley, *Louis Riel*, p. 242.

33. Keith Wilson, *Hugh John Macdonald,* (Winnipeg: Peguis Publishing, 1980), p. 26.

34. Tom Flanagan, *Riel and the Rebellion: 1885 Reconsidered*, 2nd ed., (Toronto: University of Toronto Press, 2000), pp. 158-160.

35. Flanagan, *1885 Reconsidered*, p. 164.

36. Flanagan, *1885 Reconsidered*, p. 162.

37. G.R. Parkin, *Sir John A. Macdonald*, November 9, 1885, as quoted in Stanley, Louis Riel, p. 367.

38. Parkin, as quoted in Stanley, *Louis Riel*, p. 371.

39. Chapleau to Lynch, November 21, 1885, Chapleau Papers, Public Archives of Canada, as quoted in Arthur Silver, *The French-Canadian View of Confederation, 1864-1900*, (Toronto: University of Toronto Press, 1982), p. 162.

40. Chapleau to Lynch, November 16, 17 and 18, 1885, as quoted in Silver, *French-Canadian View*, p. 163.

41. Canada, Parliament, House of Commons, *Debates*, July 7, 1885, p. 3119.

42. Schull, *Laurier*, p. 178.

43. Schull, *Laurier*, p. 178.

44. Canada, Parliament, House of Commons *Debates*, March 16, 1886.

45. Louis Riel to Henriette Riel-Poitras, October 26, 1885, St. Boniface Historical Society.

46. *Collected Writings of Louis Riel*, as quoted in Siggins, Riel: A Life, p. 101.

47. Siggins, *Riel: A Life*, xviii.

48. Gerhard Ens, "Dispossession or Adaptation? Migration and Persistence of the Red River Métis, 1835-1890," in *The Canadian Historical Association Historical Papers, Windsor, 1988* (Ottawa: Bonanza Press, n.d.), pp. 137, 144.

49. Ronaghan, "Archibald Administration,",. p. 899.

50. Chapleau as quoted in Silver, *French-Canadian View*, p. 71.

51. Chapleau as quoted in Silver, *French-Canadian View*, p. 71.

52. John Boyd, *Sir George Étienne Cartier, bart. his life and times: a political history of Canada from 1814 to 1873*, (Toronto: The MacMillan Company of Canada, 1914), p. 302.

53. Boyd, *Cartier*, p. 302.

54. Boyd, Cartier, p. 302.

55. *L'Union des Cantons de l'Est,* April 14, 1870. Also *Le Courrier du Canada*, April 8, 1870; *Le Pionnier de Sherbrooke*, April 15, 1870; *Le Pays*, April 8, 1870; *L'Ordre*, April 14, 1870; *Le Nouveau Monde*, April 14, 1870; *Le Courrier de St. Hyacinthe*, April 16,19 and 21, 1870; *L'Opinion Publique*, April 23, 1870; *Le Journal de Québec*, April 5 and 9, 1870, as quoted in Silver, *French-Canadian View*, p. 81.

56. *Le Journal des Trois-Rivières*, April 18, 1870, as quoted in Silver, *French-Canadian View*, p. 81.

57. *L'Opinion Publique*, October 13, 1870, as quoted in Silver, *French-Canadian View*, p. 85.

58. Silver, *French-Canadian View*, p. 101.

59. *Le National,* October 1, 1873, as quoted in Silver, *French-Canadian View*, p. 97.

60. *Le Courrier de St-Hyacinthe*, November 14, 1874, as quoted in Silver, *French-Canadian View*, p. 96.

61. *Le Canadien*, February 3, 1875, as quoted in Silver, *French-Canadian View*, p. 100.

62. Silver, *French-Canadian View*, p. 103

63. *Le Nouveau Monde*, June 1, 1874, as quoted in Silver, French-Canadian View, p. 103.

64. In order: *Le Minerve*, January 29, 1875; *Le Journal des Trois Riviéres*, April 23, 1874; and *Le Pionieer de Sherbrooke*, January 29, 1875, as quoted in Silver, *French-Canadian View*, p. 105.

65. Silver, *French-Canadian View*, p. 61.

66. Gerald Friesen, *The Canadian Prairies: A History*, (Toronto: University of Toronto Press, 1987), p. 202.

67. Bruno Ramirez, *On The Move: French Canadian and Italian Migrants in the North Atlantic Economy*, (Toronto: McClelland & Stewart,1999), pp. 17,126.

68. Robert Painchaud, "French Canadian Historiography and Franco-Catholic Settlement in Western Canada, 1870-1915," in *Canadian Historical Review*, (hereafter cited as *CHR*), Robert Bothwell, David Bercuson, eds., (Toronto: University of Toronto Press, December, 1978), vol. lix, no. 4, pp. 448-449.

69. Jean Bruchési, *Histoire du Canada pour tous, II: le régime anglais,* (Montréal 1935), as quoted in Painchaud, *CHR* p. 449.

70. Bruchési, *Histoire*, p. 267, as quoted in Painchaud, *CHR*, p. 449.

71. Albert Tessier, *Québec-Canada: Histoire du Canada. II: 1763-1958*, (Québec 1959). P. 182, as quoted in Painchaud, *CHR*, p. 449.

72. Robert Rumilly, *Le probléme national des Canadiens français*, (Montréal 1961) p. 19, as quoted in Painchaud, *CHR*, p. 449.

73. Michel Brunet, *Québec-Canada anglais: deux itinéraires – un affrontement*, (Montréal 1969), p. 214, as quoted in Painchaud, *CHR*, p. 449.

74. Bruchési, *Histoire*, p. 305, as quoted in Painchaud, *CHR*, p. 450.

75. Tessier, *Québec-Canada: Histoire*, p. 247, as quoted in Painchaud, *CHR*, p. 450-451.

76. Phillipe Garigue, *L'option politique du Canada français*, (Montréal 1963), p. 61, as quoted in Painchaud, *CHR*, p.451.

77. Garigue, *L'option politique*, p. 61, as quoted in Painchaud, *CHR*, p. 451.

78. La Minerve, April 8, 1876, as quoted in Painchaud, CHR, p. 451.

79. Robert Painchaud, "The Catholic Church and the Movement of Francophones to the Canadian Prairies, 1870-1915," (PhD dissertation, University of Ottawa, July 1976), p. 438.

80. Painchaud, "Catholic Church," p. 96.

81. Ramirez, *On The Move*, p. 126.

82. *Joseph Dubuc*, Historic Resources Branch, Manitoba Department of Cultural Affairs and Historic Resources, 1981, p. 1.

83. Painchaud, "Catholic Church," p. 436.

84. C.J. Jaenen, "The History of French in Manitoba; local initiative or external imposition," in *Language and Society*, Ottawa, Commissioner of Official Languages, no. 13 (spring, 1984), p. 9.

85. Jacqueline Blay, interviews by author, 2001-2003

86. Painchaud, "Catholic Church," p. 199.

Notes to Chapter Four

1. A.I. Silver, *The French-Canadian View of Confederation 1864-1900*, (Toronto: University of Toronto Press, 1982), p. 171.

2. Tom Flanagan, Riel and The Rebellion: 1885 Reconsidered, 2nd. Ed., (Toronto: University of Toronto Press, 2000), p. 4.

3. Ernest Tremblay, "Riel, Réponse à Monsieur J.A. Chapleau, [St. Hyacinthe: L'Union 1885], as quoted in Silver, *French-Canadian View*, p. 176.

4. T.A. Bernier, "Le Manitoba, champ d'immigra tion," pp. 21, 29, as quoted in Silver, *French-Canadian View*, p. 176.

5. La Vérité, April 24, May 15 and July 3, 1886, as quoted in Silver, *French-Canadian View*, p. 177.

6. Silver, *French-Canadian View*, p. 179.

7. Gerald Friesen, *River Road: Essays on Prairie and Manitoba History*, (Winnipeg: University of Manitoba Press, 1996), pp. 24-25.

8. N.E. Allen Ronaghan, "The Archibald Administration in Manitoba, 1870-1872," (Ph.D. dissertation, University of Manitoba, 1987), p. 894.

9. Ronaghan, "Archibald Administration," p. 896.

10. Lovell Clark, *The Manitoba School Question: Majority Rule or Minority Rights*, (Toronto: The Copp Clark Publishing Company, 1968), p. 3.

11. Ruth Swan, "Robert Atkinson Davis," in *Dictionary of Canadian Biography*, (herafter cited as DCB), Ramsay Cook and Jean Hamelin, eds. (Toronto: University of Toronto Press and Québec: Les Presses de l'université Laval, 1994), vol. xiii, p. 254.

12. Swan, "Davis," in *DCB*, p. 254.

13. G.O. Rothney, "Marc-Amable Girard," in *DCB*, p. 370.

14. Swan, "Davis,", in *DCB*, p. 254.

15. Gerald Friesen, personal communication with author, June, 2002.

16. *Manitoba Weekly Free Press*, January 29, 1876.

17. Gerald Friesen, "John Norquay", in *DCB*, vol. xi, p. 644.

18. Friesen, "Norquay", in *DCB*, p. 644.

19. C.J. Jaenen, "The History of French in Manitoba: local initiative or external imposition," in *Language and Society*, Ottawa: Commissioner of Official Languages, no. 13, (spring, 1984), p. 10.

20. Jaenen, "History of French", p. 10.

21. Friesen, "Norquay", in *DCB*, p. 644.

22. Attorney General of Manitoba, Factum, In the Supreme Court of Canada, Appendix B, 1984.

23. Jaenen, "History of French", p. 11.

24. Jaenen, "History of French", p. 11

25. Manitoba: Legislative Assembly, *Journals*, 3rd Parliament, 1st Session, 1879, pp. 62-63.

26. *Journals*, p. 65.

27. *Journals*, p. 65-66.

28. *Manitoba Free Press* (herafter cited as MFP), June 30, 1879.

29. *MFP*, June 30, 1879.

30. *MFP*, June 30, 1879.

31. *Le Nouveau Monde*, June 5, 1879, as quoted in Silver, *French-Canadian View*, p. 145.

32. *Le Courrier de St. Hyacinthe*, June 7, 1879, as quoted in Silver, *French-Canadian View*, p. 145.

33. *La Minerve*, June 17, 1879, as quoted in Silver, *French-Canadian View*, p. 146.

34. *Le Nouveau Monde*, June 9, 1879, as quoted in Silver, *French-Canadian View*, p. 147.

35. W.L. Morton, *Manitoba: A History*, (Toronto: University of Toronto Press, 1957), p. 199.

36. W.L. Morton, *Manitoba*, p. 229.

37. W.L. Morton, *Manitoba*, p. 230.

38. W.L. Morton, *Manitoba*, p. 232.

39. W.L. Morton, *Manitoba*, p. 233.

40. Clark, *Manitoba Schools Question*, p. 3

41. Joseph Hilts, "The Political Career of Thomas Greenway", (PhD dissertation, University of Manitoba, 1974), p. 221.

42. *MFP*, as quoted in Hilts, p. 217.

43. Morton, *Manitoba*, p. 241.

44. Donald Creighton, *Canada's First Century*, (Toronto: Macmillan Company of Canada, 1970), p. 72.

45. Creighton, *First Century*, p. 73.

46. Canada, Parliament, House of Commons, *Debates*, February 7, 1890, as quoted in Clark, *Manitoba Schools Question*, p. 9.

47. Creighton, *First Century*, p. 73.

48. Morton, *Manitoba*, p. 242.

49. Paul Crunican, *Priests and Politicians: Manitoba schools and the election of 1896*, (Toronto: University of Toronto Press, 1974), p. 10.

50. *Winnipeg Sun*, August 1 and November 28, 1889.

51. Keith Wilson, *Thomas Greenway: Manitobans in Profile*, Winnipeg, Faculty of Education, University of Manitoba, (1985), pp. 29-30.

52. Morton, *Manitoba*, p. 244.

53. Manitoba, Legislative Assembly, *Debates* [*MFP*] February 6, 1890.

54. *MFP*, as quoted in Clark, *Manitoba Schools Question*, p. 9.

55. *Winnipeg Tribune*, as quoted in Clark, *Manitoba Schools Question*, p. 11.

56. *Le Manitoba*, August 29, 1889 and September 5, 1889

57. *Le Manitoba*, December 12, 1889.

58. Archbishop Alexandre-Antonin Taché, as quoted in Clark, *Manitoba Schools Question*, pp. 74-75.

59. La Fléche to Chapleau, letter to *Le Canadien*, March 14, 1889, as quoted in Silver, *French-Canadian View*, p. 144.

60. Canada, Parliament, *Sessional Papers*, No, 63. 1891, as quoted in Clark, *Manitoba Schools Question*, pp. 122-123.

61. *MFP*, February 12, 1890.

62. *MFP*, February 12, 1890.

63. *MFP*, February 12, 1890.

64. *MFP*, February 12, 1890.

65. *MFP*, February 12, 1890.

66. *MFP*, February 12, 1890.

67. W.L. Morton, *Manitoba*, pp. 247-248

68. *MFP*, February 12, 1890.

69. *MFP*, February 12, 1890.

70. *MFP*, February 12, 1890.

71. Manitoba, Legislative Assembly, *Sessional Papers*, vol. xxii, 159-162.

72. W.L. Morton, *Manitoba*, pp. 247-248.

73. Lovell Clark, "Sir John Christian Schultz," in *DCB*, vol. xii, p. 953.

74. Clark, "Schultz,", in *DCB*, p. 953.

75. Public Archives of Canada, *Macdonald Papers*, as quoted in Hilts, "Thomas Greenway,", p. 223.

76. Provincial Archives of Manitoba, 1841 and 1844, MG12E1.

77. Hilts, "Thomas Greenway," p. 223.

78. Hilts, "Thomas Greenway," p. 221.

79. *Le Manitoba*, June 25, 1891.

80. François Ricard, *Gabrielle Roy: A Life*, Patricia Claxton, trans. (Toronto: McClelland & Stewart, 1999), pp. 12-13.

81. Friesen, *River Road*, p. 26.

82. Roger Turenne, "The Minority and the Ballot Box: A Study of the Voting Behaviour of the French Canadians of Manitoba", (masters thesis, University of Manitoba, 1969), pp. 25-26.

83. Friesen, *River Road*, p. 26.

84. Crunican, *Priests and Politicians*, p. 300.

85. W.L. Morton, *Manitoba*, p. 271.

86. C.J. Jaenen, "The Manitoba School Question: An Ethnic Interpretation", in *Ethnic Canadians, Culture*

The Canadian Crucible

and Education, Martin L. Kovacs, ed. No. 8 of Canadian Plains Studies, Canadian Plains Research Centre, University of Regina (1978), p. 323.

87. Ricard, *Gabrielle Roy*, pp. 66-67

88. *Laurier à la tribune*, as quoted in Silver, *French-Canadian View,* p. 186.

89. *La Patrie*, January 27, 1890, as quoted in Silver, French-Canadian View, p. 187.

90. All as quoted in Silver, *French-Canadian View*, p. 184-193.

91. Silver, *French-Canadian View*, p. 222.

Notes to Chapter Five

1. *Winnipeg Tribune,* February 24, 1916.

2. *Manitoba Free Press* (hereafter cited as *MFP*) March 27, 1914.

3. W.L.Morton, *Manitoba: A History* (Toronto: University of Toronto Press, 1957), p. 351.

4. Murray Donnelly, *Dafoe of the Free Press*, (Toronto, Macmillan of Canada, 1968), pp. 13-14.

5. Donnelly, *Dafoe*, p. 29.

6. Donnelly, *Dafoe*, p. 29.

7. Donnelly, *Dafoe*, p. 58.

8. Donnelly, *Dafoe*, p. 58.

9. W.L. Morton, *Manitoba*, p. 351.

10. *MFP*, March 1, 1916.

11. *MFP*, January 13, 1916.

12. *MFP*, January 18, 1916.

13. *MFP*, January 18, 1916.

14. *MFP*, January 18, 1916.

15. *La Liberté*, February 29, 1916.

16. *La Liberté*, Febrary 29, 1916.

17. *La Liberté*, February 29, 1916.

18. *MFP,* February 24, 1916.

19. *MFP*, February 25, 1916.

20. *MFP*, February 26, 1916.

21. *MFP*, March 1, 1916.

22. *MFP*, February 25, 1916.

23. C.J. Jaenen, "The History of French in Manitoba: local initiative or external imposition," in *Language and Society*, Ottawa, Commissioner of Official Languages, no. 13 (spring, 1984.)

24. Paul Ruest, "Les etttentes educatives de la population Franco-Manitobaine", (PhD dissertation, University of Manitoba 1987).

25. Donald Creighton, *John A. Macdonald – The Old C Chieftain,* (Toronto: Macmillan Company of Canada, 1955), p. 534.

26. Donald Creighton, *Canada's First Century*, (Toronto: Macmillan Company of Canada, 1970), p. 73.

27. Origins of the population of Manitoba, source, Statistics Canada, reproduced in Jaenen, "History of French", pp.10-11.

28. *La Liberté,* February 29, 1916.

29. Jacqueline Blay, *L'Article 23, les péripéties législatives et juridiques de fait français au Manitoba 1870-1986*, (St. Boniface: Les Editions du Blé, 1987), p. 64.

30. François Ricard, *Gabrielle Roy: A Life*, Patricia Claxton, trans., (Toronto: McClelland & Stewart, 1999), p. 12.

31. Ricard, *Roy: A Life*, p. 12-13.

32. Ricard, *Roy: A Life*, p. 15.

33. Gabrielle Roy, "Souvenirs of Manitoba", in *Mémoires de la Société royal du Canada*, 3rd series, vol. 48, (June, 1954), pp. 1-3.

34. Ricard, *Roy: A Life*, p. 67-68.

35. Jaenen, "History of French," p. 14.

36. The author [article], *Globe and Mail*, December 16, 1970.

37. Roy, "Souvenirs of Manitoba", p. 5.

38. Gabrielle Roy, *Enchantment and Sorrow*, Patricia Claxton, trans., (Toronto: Lester & Orpen Dennys, 1987),[originally published in French under title *La Détresse et l'enchantment* by Les Editions du Boréal Express, 1984], p. 3-4.

39. Roy, *Enchantment and Sorrow*, p. 6.

40. Ricard, *Roy: A Life*, p. 108.

41. *Canadian Encyclopedia*, Year 2000 Edition (Toronto: McClelland & Stewart, 1999), p. 2042.

42. Le Soleil, July 29, 1967, p. 3; and Le Devoir, July 31, 1967, p. 3, as quoted in Ricard, *Roy: A Life*, p. 410.

43. Roy, *Enchantment and Sorrow*, p. 111.

44. Ricard, *Roy: A Life*, p. 468.

45. Cornelius Jaenen, interview by author, June, 2003.

46. Jacqueline Blay, interviews by the author, 2001-2003.

47. Raymond Hébert, *Manitoba's French Language Crisis*, Chapter 1 (draft), p. 24 (forthcoming).

48. *Le Manitoba*, March 8, 1892, as quoted in Blay, *L'Article 23*, p. 34.

49. *Le Manitoba*, March 8, 1892, as quoted in Blay, *L'Article 23*, p. 34.

50. Re: Forest and Registrar of Court of Appeal of Manitoba, June 22, 1977, *Dominion Law Reports* (Third Series), vol. 77, pp. 459-462.

51. *La Liberté*, June 21, 1916, as quoted in Blay, p. 48.

52. Jacqueline Blay, interviews with author, 2001-2003

53. Roger Turenne, "The Minority and the Ballot Box: A Study of the Voting Behaviour of the French Canadians of Manitoba", (masters thesis, University of Manitoba).

54. Turenne, "Ballot Box", p. 61.

55. Turenne, "Ballot Box", p. 47-48.

56. Turenne, "Ballot Box", p. 65.

57. Turenne, "Ballot Box", p. 166.

58. Jaenen, "History of French", p. 15.
59. Hébert, *Manitoba's Crisis*, p. 33.
60. The author [article], *Winnipeg Tribune*, January 14, 1964.
61. The author [article], *Winnipeg Tribune*, May 16, 1965.
62. Turenne, "Ballot Box," p. 160.
63. Manitoba, Legislative Assembly, Debates and Proceedings, 28th Legislature, 1st Session, 1966-67, p. 1821.
64. *Debates and Proceedings*, p. 2545.
65. *Debates and Proceedings*, p. 2545.
66. Blay, *L'Article 23*, p. 71.
67. *Winnipeg Free Press* (hereafter cited as WFP), January 12, 1967.
68. *WFP*, January 12, 1967.
69. *WFP*, January 14, 1967.
70. Cornelius Jaenen, interview by author, June, 2003.
71. Turenne, "Ballot Box", p. 168.
72. Turenne, "Ballot Box", p. 155.
73. Turenne, "Ballot Box", p. 155.
74. Turenne, "Ballot Box", p. 157.
75. *WFP*, November 24, 1962.
76. Turenne, "Ballot Box," p. 159.
77. Hébert, *French Language Crisis*, p. 35.
78. Manitoba, Legislative Assembly, *Debates and Proceedings*, 29th Legislature, 2nd Session, p. 3370.
79. Hébert, *French Language Crisis*, p. 36.
80. Hébert, *French Language Crisis*, p. 36.
81. Manitoba, Legislative Assembly, *Debates and Proceedings*, 29th Legislature, 2nd Session, p. 3163,
82. The author [article], *Globe and Mail*, December 16, 1970.
83. The author [article], *Globe and Mail*, February 19, 1971.
84. Hébert, *French Language Crisis*, p. 39.
85. Raymond Hébert, interview by author, July 3, 2003.
86. Jacqueline Blay, interviews by author, 2001-2003.

Notes to Chapter Six

1. *Winnipeg Free Press* (hereafter cited as WFP), June 6, 1978.
2. *Winnipeg Tribune* (hereafter cited as WT), July 21, 1979.
3. WT, July 21, 1979.
4. WT, July 21, 1979.
5. WT, July 21, 1979
6. WFP, June 6, 1978.
7. WT, July 21, 1979.
8. WFP, June 6, 1978.
9. WT, July 21, 1979.
10. *WT*, July 21, 1979.
11. *City of Winnipeg Act*, Section 80 (3).
12. Jacqueline Blay, *L'article 23, les péripéties législatives et juridiques du fait français au Manitoba 1870–1986* (St. Boniface: Les Éditions du Blé, 1987), p. 93.
13. Raymond Hébert, *Manitoba's French-language Crisis, 1983–84* (forthcoming), chapter 1 (draft), p. 40.
14. *WT*, July 21, 1979.
15. *University of Toronto Law Journal*, vol. VIII, no. 2, p. 205.
16. Forest v. the Queen, Manitoba County Court Reports 1976, 17.
17. Forest v. the Queen, Manitoba County Court Reports 1976, 28.
18. Forest v. the Queen, Manitoba County Court Reports 1976, 29
19. *WT*, March 3, 1977.
20. *WT*, July 21, 1979.
21. *WT*, July 23, 1979.
22. Frank Muldoon, QC [letter to editor], July 23, 1979.
23. *WFP*, June 6, 1978.
24. *WFP*, July 23, 1979.
25. Jacqueline Blay, interviews by the author, 2001-2003
26. Hébert, *French-language Crisis*, p. 43.
27. Hébert, *French-language Crisis*, p. 42.
28. *WT*, July 23, 1979.
29. *WFP*, June 6, 1978.
30. Hébert, *French-language Crisis*, p. 43.
31. WFP, January 20, 1977.
32. Hébert, *French-language Crisis*, p. 44.
33. Hébert, *French-language Crisis*, p. 45.
34. Hébert, *French-language Crisis*, p. 45.
35. Hébert, *French-language Crisis*, p. 46.
36. *Re: Forest and Registrar of the Court of Appeal of Manitoba*, June 22, 1977, *Dominion Law Reports*, (Third Series), Vol. 77, 458–467.
37. Forest and Registrar, 453.
38. *WFP*, December 9, 1977.
39. WFP, February 21, 1978.
40. *WFP*, June 1, 1978.
41. *WFP*, June 2, 1978.
42. *Forest v. Attorney General of Manitoba*, Attorney General of Canada, Intervenor, July 18, 2978, *Dominion Law Reports* (Third Series), Vol. 90, 234.
43. *Forest v. Attorney General*, 234–235.
44. *Forest v. Attorney General*, 235–238.
45. *WFP*, August 24, 1978.
46. *Forest v. Attorney General of Manitoba*, Attorney General of Canada, Intervenor, July 18, 2978, *Dominion Law Reports* (Third Series), Vol. 98, 408.

47. *Forest v. Attorney General*, 413.

48. *Forest v. Attorney General*, 414.

49. *Forest v. Attorney General*, 418-419.

50. *Forest v. Attorney General*, 421.

51. *Forest v. Attorney General*, 423.

52. *Forest v. Attorney General*, 423-424.

53. Globe and Mail, May 7, 1979.

54. *WT*, July 23, 1979.

55. *La Liberté*, as quoted in WT, July 23, 1979

56. *La Presse,* June 23, 1979.

57. *Le Devoir*, June 23, 1979.

58. *Globe and Mail*, June 13, 1979.

59. Société franco-manitobaine, recommendations of the ad-hoc committee studying the possible judgements flowing from the Forest Affair, Société franco-manitobaine (translation) December 1979, p.2.

60. La Société franco-manitobaine, recommendations, (translation) p. 2.

61. *Attorney General of Manitoba v. Forest, Dominion Law Reports* (Third Series), Vol. 101, 386.

Notes to Chapter Seven

1. Jacqueline Blay, L'article 23, *les péripéties législatives et juridiques du fait français au Manitoba 1870–1986* (St. Boniface: Les Éditions du Blé, 1987), p. 52.

2. Russell Doern, *The Battle over Bilingualism: The Manitoba Language Question 1983-85* (Winnipeg: Cambridge Publishers, 1985), p. 5.

3. *Winnipeg Free Press* (hereafter cited as WFP), December 13, 1979.

4. Winnipeg Tribune (hereafter cited as WT), December 4, 1979.

5. Globe and Mail, December 14, 1979.

6. La Presse, December 14, 1979.

7. La Presse, December 14, 1979.

8. La Presse, December 14, 1979.

9. WT, December 14, 1979

10. La Presse, December 15, 1979.

11. Le Devoir, December 15, 1979.

12. WT, December 14, 1979.

13. WFP, December 14, 1979.

14. WFP, December 14, 1979.

15. WT, December 13, 1979.

16. WFP, January 25, 1980.

17. WT, January 25, 1980.

18. *Canadian Press* in *Globe and Mail*, March 24, 1980.

19. Blay, L'article 23, p. 52.

20. WT, December 14, 1979.

21. Manitoba, Legislative Assembly, *Debates and Proceedings*, 31st Legislature, 5th Session, 1980, pp. 2003–2003.

22. *Debates*, 1980, pp. 2004-2005.

23. *Debates*, 1980, pp. 2005-2009.

24. *Debates*, 1980, pp. 2332-2333.

25. *Debates*, 1980, p. 2334.

26. *Debates* 1980, pp. 2573-2577.

27. *Debates*, 1980, p. 2843.

28. *Debates*, 1980, p. 5406.

29. WT, May 22, 1980.

30. WFP, May 25, 1980.

31. WFP, May 25, 1980.

32. Jules Dechénes, "Jewers, Co. Crt. J," in *Ainsi parlèrent les tribunaux, conflits linguistiques au Canada 1968–1980*, Montréal, n.p.,1980, p. 432.

33. WFP, August 15, 1980.

34. WT, August 15, 1980.

35. WFP/WT, August 15, 1980.

36. WFP/WT, August 20, 1980.

37. WFP/WT, August 20, 1980.

38. WFP/WT, November 22, 1980.

39. WFP/WT, November 28, 1980.

40. WFP/WT, February 24, 1980.

41. WFP/WT, February 24, 1980.

42. WFP/WT, February 25, 1980.

43. WFP/WT, February 25, 1980.

44. WFP, April 7, 1981.

45. *Winnipeg Sun*, (hereafter cited as WS), April 16, 1981.

46. Manitoba, Office of the Premier. To: All ministers, deputy ministers and heads of agencies. From: Sterling Lyon, Q.C. Subject: French Language Services. March 21, 1981.

47. WFP, May 12, 1981.

48. WFP, July 4, 1981.

49. WFP, September 4, 1981.

50. WFP, July 11,1981.

51. WFP, November 24, 1981.

52. *Bilodeau v. Attorney General of Manitoba*, Manitoba Court of Appeal, *Western Weekly Reports*, vol. 5, 1981, 401.

53. *Bilodeau v. Attorney General*, 406-408.

54. *Bilodeau v. Attorney General*, 410.

55. *Bilodeau v. Attorney General*, 414.

56. *Globe and Mail*, November 4, 1981.

57. *Globe and Mail*, September 16, 1981.

58. WFP, March 6, 1982.

59. Roger Turenne, Manitoba, Office of the Premier. To: The Honourable Roland Penner, Q.C., Attorney-General From: Roger Turenne, Senior Advisor, French Language Services Secretariat. Subject: The political implications of the Bilodeau case. January 15, 1982, p. 1.

60. Roger Turenne, interviews by the author, October -November, 2002.

61. Turenne, Memo to Penner, Janury 15, 1982, p.2.

62. Turenne, Memo to Penner, January 15, 1982, p. 3.

63. Roger Turenne, Manitoba, Office of the Premier. To: The Honourable Roland Penner, Q.C., Attorney -General.From: Roger Turenne, Senior Advisor, French Language Services Secretariat. Subject: The political implications of the Bilodeau case. February 5, 1982.

64. Roger Turenne, interviews by the author, October-November, 2002.

65. WFP, March 11, 1982.

66. Statistics Canada, Census, 1971

67. *United Press International in the Winnipeg Sun*, March 22, 1982.

68. WFP, March 25, 1982.

69. WFP, August 5, 1982.

70. WS, July 6, 1982.

71. WFP, August 27, 1982.

Notes to Chapter Eight

1. *Winnipeg Free Press*, (hereafter cited as WFP), July 29, 1982.

2. *Winnipeg Sun,* (hereafter cited as WS) August 4, 1982.

3. WFP, August 5, 1982.

4. The author [column], WFP, July 19, 1974.

5. The author [column], WFP, June 20, July 5, 1974

6. *Globe and Mail*, February 9, 1983.

7. WS, February 9, 1983.

8. WS, February 9, 1983.

9. Roger Turenne, interviews by author, October-November, 2002.

10. Manitoba, Legislative Assembly, *Debates and Proceedings*, 32nd Legislature, 2nd Session, 1982-84. p. 2909.

11. Jacqueline Blay, interviews by author, 2001-2003.

12. *WFP, WS*, March 3, 1983.

13. *Globe and Mail*, (hereafter cited as G&M), March 24, 1983.

14. WFP, April 8, 1983.

15. WFP, April 8, 1983.

16. *La Presse*, May 21, 1983.

17. Manitoba, Legislative Assembly, *Debates and Proceedings*, 32nd Legislature, 2nd Session, 1982-84.p. 2878-79.

18. Roger Turenne, interviews by author, October-November, 2002.

19. Roger Turenne, interviews by author, October-November, 2002.

20. Manitoba, Legislative Assembly, *Debates and Proceedings*, 32nd Legislature, 2nd Session, 1982-84. p. 2974-78.

21. WFP, May 25, 1983.

22. WS, May 19, 1983.

23. WFP, May 25, 1983.

24. Jacqueline Blay, interviews by author, 2001-2003.

25. G&M, May 26, 1983.

26. WFP, June 10, 1983.

27. WFP, June 16, 1983.

28. WFP, June 18, 1983.

29. WS, June 23, 1983.

30. WS, July 22, 1983.

31. Manitoba, Legislative Assembly, *Debates and Proceedings*, 32nd Legislature, 2nd Session, 1982-84. p. 4285.

32. WFP, June 24, 1983.

33. WFP, June 22, 1983.

34. The author [column], WFP, June 25, 1983.

35. WS, June 29, 1983.

36. WFP, June 30, 1983.

37. WFP/G&M, July 8, 1983.

38. WFP, July 9, 1983.

39. WFP, July 13, 1983.

40. G&M, July 27, 1983.

41. Manitoba, Legislative Assembly, *Debates and Proceedings*, 32nd Legislature, 2nd Session, 1982-84. pp. 4057-4063.

42. Manitoba, Legislative Assembly, *Debates and Proceedings*, 32nd Legislature, 2nd Session, 1982-84, p. 4065.

43. Manitoba, Legislative Assembly, *Debates and Proceedings*, 32nd Legislature, 2nd Session, 1982-84. p. 4066.

44. Manitoba, Legislative Assembly, *Debates and Proceedings*, 32nd Legislature, 2nd Session, 1982-84. pp. 4267-4293.

45. WS, June 29 and July 11, 1983.

46. Roger Turenne, interviews by author, October-November, 2002.

47. Manitoba, Legislative Assembly, *Debates and Proceedings*, 32nd Legislature, 2nd Session, 1982-84. p. 4351-4354.

48. WFP, July 23, 1983.

49. WS, July 20, 1983.

Notes to Chapter Nine

1. *Globe and Mail* (hereafter cited as G&M), September 16, 1983.

2. *Le Devoir*, August 23, 1984.

3. *Winnipeg Free Press* (hereafter cited as WFP), September 16, 1983.

4. WFP, July 28, 1983.

5. G&M, September 17, 1983.

6. WFP, September 7, 1983.

7. *WFP*, September 9, 1983.

8. *WFP*, September 10, 1983.

9. *WFP*, September 10, 1983.

10. *WFP*, September 14, 1983.

11. *WFP*, September 15, 1983.

12. *G&M*, September 21, 1983.

13. *G&M*, September 21, 1983.

14. *G&M*, September 21, 1983.

15. *G&M*, September 22, 1983.

16. *WFP*, September 13 and 15, 1983.

17. *WFP*, September 17, 1983.

18. *WFP*, September 23, 1983.

19. *WFP*, September 27, 1983.

20. *WFP*, September 28, 1983.

21. Winnipeg Sun (hereafter cited as WS), September 29, 1983.

22. *WFP*, September 29, 1983.

23. *WFP/WS*, September 29, 1983.

24. *WFP*, September 30, 1983.

25. *WFP*, October 1, 1983.

26. *Le Devoir*, September 16, 1983.

27. *WFP*, September 30–October 5; and Russell Doern, *The Battle over Bilingualism: The Manitoba Language Question 1983–85* (Winnipeg: Cambridge Publishers, 1985), pp. 108, 112.

28. *WFP*, October 15, 1983.

29. The author, [column], *WFP*, October 19, 1983.

30. *WFP*, October 5, 1983.

31. *WS*, October 6, 1983.

32. *La Liberté*, October 7, 1983.

33. *WFP*, September 17, 1983; and G&M, September 22, 1983.

34. *WFP/WS*, September 22, 1983.

35. *WFP*, September 20 1983.

36. *WFP*, September 30, 1983.

37. *WFP*, September 22, 1983.

38. *WFP*, September 14, 1983.

39. *WFP*, September 15, 1983.

40. *WFP*, September 19, 1983.

41. *WFP*, September 29, 1983.

42. *La Presse*, October 5, 1983.

43. *G&M*, October 6, 1983.

44. Canada, Parliament, House of Commons, Debates, 1st Session, 32nd Parliament, Thursday, October 6, 1983, 27817.

45. *Debates*, October 6, 1983, 27816-27818.

46. *Debates*, October 6, 1983, 27818-27820.

47. *Debates*, October 6, 1983, 27820-27821.

48. *WFP*, October 7, 1983.

49. *WFP*, October 7 and 8, 1983.

50. *G&M*, October 5, 1983.

51. *WS*, October 19, 1983.

52. *WFP*, October 15, 1983.

53. *G&M*, October 26, 1983.

54. *WFP*, October 21, 1983.

55. *WFP*, October 22, 1983.

56. *WFP*, October 27, 1983.

57. *WFP*, October 27, 1983.

58. *WS*, October 27, 1983.

59. The author [column], *WFP*, October 29, 1983.

60. *WFP*, October 28, 1983.

61. Roger Turenne, interviews with author, October-November, 2002.

62. *WFP*, October 29, 1983.

63. *WFP*, October 29, 1983.

64. *La Presse*, October 26, 1983.

Notes to Chapter Ten

1. *Winnipeg Free Press/Winnipeg Sun,* (hereafter cited as WFP and WS), October 31, 1983.

2. *Globe and Mail,* (hereafter cited as G&M), October 27, 1983.

3. *WS*, November 23, 1983.

4. *WFP*, December 10, 1983

5. *WFP*, December 15, 1983

6. *WFP*, December 16, 1983

7. *WFP*, December 16, 1983.

8. *WS,* January 4, 1984.

9. *WFP*, January 5, 1984.

10. *WFP/WS* January 9&10, 1984.

11. *WFP*, January 9, 1984.

12. *WFP*, January 19, 1984.

13. *WFP*, January 24&26, 1984.

14. Manitoba. Legislative Assembly. *Debates and Proceedings*, 32nd Legislature, 2nd Session. 1982-84. 5599.

15. *WFP*, January 27, 1984.

16. *WFP*, January 27, 1984.

17. *WFP*, February 1, 1984.

18. *WFP*, January 28, 1984.

19. *WFP*, January 30, 1984.

20. The author, [column] *WFP,* January 28, 1984.

21. *WFP/WS*, January 28, 29 & 31, 1984.

22. *WFP*, February 3, 1984.

23. *WFP*, February 4, 1984.

24. *WFP/WS*, February 5, 1984.

25. *WFP*, February 8, 1984.

26. *WFP*, February 9, 1984.

27. *Le Devoir*, February 6, 1984.

28. *WFP*, February 6, 1984.

29. The author [column], *WFP*, February 8, 1984.

30. *WFP*, February 8, 1984.

31. The author [column], *WFP*, February 11, 1984.

32. *WFP*, February 14, 1984.

33. Manitoba, Legislative Assembly, *Debates and Proceedings*, 32nd Legislature, 2nd Session, 1982-84. 6097.

34. *WFP*, February 28, 1984

35. *Le Devoir*, February 21, 1984

36. *La Presse*, February 25, 1984

37. *Canadian Press*, (hereafter cited as *CP*), *WFP/WS*, February 29, 1984.

38. *CP/WFP/WS*, February 29, 1984.

39. WFP, March 1, 1984.

40. *CP/WFP*, February 29, 1984.

41. *La Liberté*, March 9, 1984.

42. The author, [article] *WFP*, March 5, 1984.

Notes to Chapter Eleven

1. *Winnipeg Free Press*, (hereafter cited as *WFP*, February 22, 1984.

2. *WFP*, February 24, 1984.

3. *Le Devoir*, February 24, 1984.

4. *Winnipeg Sun*, (hereafter cited as *WS*), February 24, 1984.

5. *WFP*, February 24, 1984.

6. *WFP*, February 24, 1984.

7. *WFP*, February 24, 1984.

8. Canada, Parliament, House of Commons, Debates, 32nd Parliament, 2nd Session, vol. 127, no. 41. p. 1710.

9. Canada, Parliament, House of Commons, Debates, 32nd Parliament, 2nd Session, vol. 127, no. 41, 1710-1711.

10. Canada, Parliament, House of Commons, Debates, 32nd Parliament, 2nd Session, vol. 127, no. 41, 1711-1713.

11. Canada, Parliament, House of Commons, Debates, 32nd Parliament, 2nd Session, vol. 127, no, 41, 1713-1714.

12. *Le Devoir*, February 25, 1984.

13. *WFP*, February 25, 1984.

14. *WFP*, February 28, 1984.

15. *WS*, February 28, 1984.

16. *WFP*, March 14, 1984.

17. The author [personal source].

18. *WFP*, March 3, 1984.

19. *WFP*, March 14, 1984.

20. *WFP*, March 15, 1984.

21. All references, Brian Mulroney, MP, Leader of the Opposition, notes for an address to the public meeting, Hotel Holiday Inn, Ballroom, Winnipeg, Manitoba, March 29, 1984 [Media text].

22. *WFP*, March 30, 1984.

23. *WFP*, March 30, 1984.

24. *Globe and Mail*, April 13, 1984.

25. WS, April 6, 1984.

26. Attorney General of Canada, (hereafter cited as AGC), factum, in the Supreme Court of Canada, reference by the Governor in Council concerning certain language rights under Section 23 of the *Manitoba Act*, 1870, and Section 133 of the *Constitution Act*, 1867 and set out in Order-in-Council P.C. 1984-1136 dated the 5th day of April, 1984, [Media Text], 10-20.

27. AGC Factum, 22.

28. AGC Factum, 27-28.

29. AGC Factum, 30, 40 and 41.

30. ACG Factum, 58.

31. AGC Factum, 61-62.

32. AGC Factum, 67 and 83.

33. AGC Factum, 84.

34. AGC Factum, 102.

35. AGC Factum, 107.

36. Attorney General of Manitoba, (hereafter cited as AGM), factum, in the Supreme Court of Canada, reference by the Governor in Council concerning certain language rights under Section 23 of the *Manitoba Act*, 1870, and Section 133 of the *Constitution Act*, 1867 and set out in Order-in-Council P.C. 1984 [Media text], 3.

37. AGM Factum, 5.

38. AGM Factum, 10.

39. AGM Factum, 10-14.

40. AGM Factum, 15.

41. AGM Factum, Appendix C, Macdonald to Schultz, March 29, 1890, [CPR telegram], Provincial Archives of Manitoba, (hereafter cited as PAM), 1427 – MG1 2E1.

42. AGM Factum, Appendix C , Macdonald to Schultz, [n.d. communication] 1391 – MG12E1 and [n.d. communication] PAM 1402 – MG12E1.

43. AGM Factum, 19.

44. AGM Factum, 42.

45. AGM Factum, 30.

46. The author [article], WFP, June 8, 1984.

47. La Société franco-manitobaine, factum, in the Supreme Court of Canada etc.1984, [Media text], 20.

48. SFM Factum, 21.

49. SFM Factum, 5.

50. Alliance Québec, (hereafter cited as AQ), factum, in the Supreme Court of Canada, etc. 1984, [Media text], 41.

51. AQ Factum, 14.

52. AQ Factum, 56.

53. AQ Factum, 44.

54. Roger Joseph Albert Bilodeau, factum, in the Supreme Court of Canada, etc., 1984, [Media text], 47-48.

55. Bilodeau Factum, 33

56. Campbell, Richardson, et al., intervenors, factum, in the Supreme Court of Canada, etc.1984.[Media text], 81

57. Intervenors' Factum, 19, 37, 46, 74 and 75

58. Supreme Court of Canada, (hereafter cited as SCC), reference by the Governor in Council concerning certain language rights under Section 23 of the Manitoba Act, 1870, and Section 133 of the Constitution Act, 1867 and set out in Order-in- Council P.C. 1984-1136 dated the 5th day of April, 1984, [Media text], June 13, 1985, pgh. 3

59. SCC, June 13, 1985, pgh. 5

60. SCC, June 13, 1985, pgh. 6

61. SCC, June 13, 1985, pgh. 8

62. SCC, June 13, 1985, pghs. 27, 28, 31, 32, 49 and 63

63. SCC, June 13. 1985, pgh. 41

64. SCC, June 13, 1985, pghs. 67-68

65. SCC, June 13, 1985, pgh. 58

66. WFP, June 14, 1985

Notes to Chapter Twelve

1. All above, the author, [columns] *Winnipeg Free Press*, (hereafter cited as WFP), June 13 & 15, 1984.

2. Manitoba, Legislative Assembly, *Debates and Proceedings*, 32nd Legislature, 3rd Session, p. 2920.

3. Manitoba, Legislative Assembly, *Debates and Proceedings*, 32nd Legislature, 3rd Session, p. 2921.

4. Canada, Parliament, House of Commons, Debates, 33rd Parliament, 1st Session, vol. 128, no. 124, p. 5724.

5. Canada, Parliament, House of Commons, Debates, 33rd Parliament, 1st Session, vol 128, no. 124, p. 5775.

6. *La Presse*, June 15, 1985.

7. *WFP*, July 21, 1990.

8. Roger Turenne, interviews by author, October-November, 2002.

9. *WFP*, November 5, 1989.

10. *WFP*, November 15, 1989.

11. Roger Turenne, interviews with author, October-November 2002.

12. Jacqueline Blay, interviews by author, 2001-2003.

13. Manitoba, Legislative Assembly, *Debates and Proceedings*, 35th Legislature, 1st Session, April 29, 1991.

14. The author, [column] *WFP*, October 7, 1996.

15. *Globe and Mail*, August 23, 2000.

16. Rénauld Rémillard, interview by author, April 14, 2003.

17. Judge Richard Chartier, Commissioner, *Above All, Common Sense – Avant Toute Chose, Le Bons Sens*, (Manitoba: Report and Recommendations on French Language Services within the Government of Manitoba, May, 1988). pp. 4-5.

18. Chartier, *Above All-Avant Toute Chose*, vi.

19. Chartier, *Above All-Avant Toute Chose*, pp. 9 and 28.

20. Judge Richard Chartier, interview by author, December 16, 2002.

21. Chartier, *Above All-Avant Toute Chose*, p. 54

22. Roger Turenne, interviews by author, October-November 2002.

23. Judge Richard Chartier, interview by author, December 16, 2002.

24. Judge Richard Chartier, interview by author, December 16, 2002.

25. *La Presse*, March 14, 2002

Index

A

Above All, Common Sense-Avant Toute Chose, Le Bon Sens (Chartier), 505–510

Act Respecting Public Printing, An, 151, 153, 155

Adam, A. R. "Pete," 267, 278–279

Adam, Marcel, 389–390

Advisory Committee on Bilingualism and Biculturism, 215

Alliance Québec, 338; brief to Supreme Court, 478–480, 485-486, 492

amendment, constitutional (see also Conservative Opposition to amendment; Pawley government): background to, 299–302; compromises on, 350, 352–353, 361, 409–410, 430–431; content of, 318–319; defeat of, and reaction, 439–448, 452; House debate, 323–325, 326–329, 335, 341–346, 347–349, 435; launched, 313, 326–327; Lyon speeches, 327–328, 343–346, 410–411, 419–420; Parliament's role, 356, 379–380, 383–388; plebiscite results and reaction, 394–402, 403–405; praise for, 320–323, 340–341, 374, 375; public hearings, 361–373, 375, 406, 424; public protest, 333, 335, 337, 338–340, 361, 403–404, 418–420, 422–423, 429–430; referenda/plebiscites on, 352, 355–356, 359–360, 388, 391–394; view of, outside Manitoba, 376–378, 381–383, 400–401, 434; worry over unilingual jobs, 350, 359, 372, 392

Andrews, J. V. "Jock," 243

Anstett, Andrue "Andy," 361, 364, 369, 406, 451, 487, 497; bell ringing speech, 437–438; as leader of amendment, 407, 408, 409, 417, 418, 435, 454; violence towards, 419, 422–423, 429

Archambault, Gérard, 240

Archibald, Adams: correspondence with Macdonald, 100–101, 102, 105; as Lt. Gov., 93, 96, 97, 102; Manitoba bill speech, 90–91

Archibald government, 101; Dominion Lands Act, 145, 146; first elections, 97–98

Armstrong, George, 194

Arpin, Maurice, 218, 219, 220

Assiniboia. see Red River Colony

Association d'Éducation des Canadiens-Français du Manitoba, (AECFM), 197–198, 201, 205, 214. see also Société franco–manitobaine

Association des Pro-Canadiens du Manitoba, L', 426

Association Saint-Jean-Baptiste de Manitoba, L', 148. see also Société St. Jean–Baptiste

Aubin, Claude, 292

Aubry, Jean-Paul, 202, 227

Axworthy, Lloyd, 358, 432–433, 455, 456–457, 460, 493

B

Badoux, Maurice, 216

Bailey, Donald, 363, 411–412

Baird, Vaughan, 293, 306, 504; as Bilodeau's lawyer, 283, 284–285, 287, 295–296, 480–481

Ballenden, John, 49

Ballenden, Sarah, 43

Banman, Bob, 452

Bannatyne, Annie, 62–63

Barbeau, François, 321

Barker, Joan, 303, 304

Barrett, John Kelly, 177

Barrett Decision, 179

Baryluk, Mike, 292

Beetz, Jean, 490

Begg, Alexander, 494

Beliveau, Arthur, 201

Bénard, Aimé, 191–192

Bend, Bobby, 394, 425

Benoit, Francis, 335

Bernard, Phillipe, 263

Bernier, Joseph, 189, 214

Bertrand vs. Dussault and Lavoie, 210–211

Big Bear, Chief, 116

bilingual government service (see also translation of gov't proceedings): attacks on, 307–312, 317, 330, 333, 335, 403–404, 496–497; in Chartier report, 506, 508–510; in courts, 291–292, 293; Filmon gov't policy, 499–500; Pawley gov't policy, 304, 305, 346–347, 481, 487, 496–497; Winnipeg, 280, 292

Bilingual Today, French Tomorrow (Andrews), 243

Bill 2, 272–279, 473–474, 483

Bill 25, 151–152, 153–155

Bill 32, 153–155

Bill 59, 217–218

Bill 113, 225–229

Bilodeau, Roger, 283, 504; amendment negotiations, 314, 316; Manitoba language brief, 480–481

Bilodeau case: in Court of Appeal, 287–288, 293–296; implications for gov't, 313–314; in Provincial Court, 283, 284–285

Bird-Bannatyne compromise, 69, 70

Bissonette, Lise, 254, 266, 397; on amendment, 353–354, 357, 373, 430–432

Black, John, 76, 87

Blaikie, Peter, 257

Blake, Edward, 52, 85, 103

Blay, Jacqueline: on amendment, 316–317, 329; on Franco-Manitoban schools, 212, 502–503; on SFM, 240–241

Bocquel, Bernard, 340

Bolster, Charles, 236, 239

Boucher, François, 46

Boulton, Charles Arkoll, 76–77

The Canadian Crucible

Société franco-manitobaine (SFM): attacked,
311–312, 409; brief to Supreme Court, 477–478,
485–486; on Filmon gov't policy, 504, 505; Filmon's
speech to, 499–500; Forest case, 236, 240–241, 255;
Magnet advises, 431, 433–434; on minority rights,
285–286; plebiscite, 392–393, 393–394, 398–399,
404–405; reaction to Supreme Court case, 258–259,
280–281; role in amendment, 313–317, 324, 329,
345, 350, 361, 374, 375; role in Pawley gov't policy,
306, 312, 496; supports 'yes' in referendum, 279–280;
view of Pawley gov't policy, 299, 407, 409–410

Société St. Jean-Baptiste, La, 394, 400

Sojonky, R., 471

Spence, Thomas, 100

Spivak, Mira, 375

Spivak, Sidney, 375

Spolsky, Myron, 399–400, 435–436

Spry, Irene, 42–43

St. Boniface: Franco-Manitoban experience in,
199–201; protest against amalgamation, 233–234;
school question, 303, 304–305

Stanley, F. G., 55, 82; Riel's reelection, 112–113

Stewart, Ron, 436

Stuart, James, 39

Supreme Court of Canada: 1979 ruling and
reaction, 260–272; 1981 ruling on translation,
288–290; 1985 Manitoba language ruling, 28;
1990's Manitoba rulings, 498, 502; 1999 BC
decision, 504–505; Manitoba language reference,
469–470, 483–487, 489–492; Quebec-Manitoba
case, 257–260; translation limits case, 286–287

survivance, la, 132, 133, 213, 220–221

Sutherland, Hugh, 77

Swan, T. H., 436

T

Taché, Alexandre-Antonin, 34, 64, 105, 138, 158;
accuses Macdonald of lying, 111–112; as educator, 57,
58; negotiation with federal gov't, 82, 94, 95, 96; as
Riel's emissary, 96, 103, 109; school question,
167–168, 178

Talbot, P. A., 187, 191

Tallin, Rae, 284, 302

Taschereau, Elzéar Alexandre, 115

Tassé, Roger, 318

Taylor, J. F. Reeh, 481

Taylor, James Wickes, 75

Taylor, Margaret, 38, 39

Teffaine, Rhéal, 235

Teillet, Jean, 512

Thom, Adam, 33, 40, 43

Thompson, John, 176, 476

Thornton, R.S., 189–190

Thornton Act, 182; implications of, 194, 195–197;
passed, 187–194

Toronto Daily Telegraph, 85

Toronto Star, 401

Toupin, René, 244

translation of government proceedings (see also
bilingual government service): 1979 Supreme Court
ruling, 260, 268; 1981 Supreme Court ruling,
288–290; Bill 2, 272–279; Conservative proposal,
416, 417; Filmon gov't policy, 497–498; Lyon gov't
policy, 267, 268–269, 285, 286, 287–288; Pawley
gov't policy, 298–299, 304, 305–306, 409, 487

Trudeau, Pierre Elliott, 242, 298; Morin's view of,
396–397; resigns, 460, 468; role in amendment, 320,
357, 378, 379–380, 384–386, 454; seen as force
behind amendment, 344, 345, 346, 351, 377, 382,
388, 394

Trudeau government: Forest case, 247–248, 250;
Manitoba language reference, 469–470, 471–474,
486–487; patriation of constitution, 296–298; role
in amendment, 313, 381, 463

Trudel, Robert, 291, 405

Tsai, Yantai, 341

Tupper, Sir Charles, 179

Turenne, Bernard, 405

Turenne, Roger: advises Penner, 299–302; as
Filmon advisor, 498–499, 501–502, 503; on Franco-
Manitoban attitudes, 179, 213, 220–221, 223; as gov't
French minder, 290, 346–347; role in amendment,
318, 324, 510; as SFM advisor, 505

Turner, John, 468–469

Twaddle, Kerr: Forest case, 248, 250; Manitoba
language reference, 474, 489, 490–491; as Pawley
gov't advisor, 302, 313; translation limits case, 286,
287, 289

U

Ukrainian reaction to amendment, 369–370

U.S. government, 66

V

Valade, F. X., 117, 118

Valpy, Michael, 358

Vancouver Sun, 401

W

Walding, Jim, 417, 427–429; letters to gov't,
450–451; sides with Opposition, 439, 497

Walding, Valerie, 428

Waldman, Dany, 340

Walker, Frank, 446

Walker, J. S., 235–236

Weir, Walter, 224–225

Westbury, June, 279

Willcock, Elizabeth, 375